MASTERPLOTS II

POETRY SERIES

MASTERPLOTS II

POETRY
SERIES
SUPPLEMENT

7

A-Fou

Editors

JOHN WILSON **PHILIP K. JASON**

Project Editor
MCCREA ADAMS

SALEM PRESS

Pasadena, California   Hackensack, New Jersey

Editor in Chief: Dawn P. Dawson
Managing Editor: Christina J. Moose
Project Editor: McCrea Adams   *Production Editor:* Yasmine A. Cordoba
Acquisitions Editor: Mark Rehn   *Manuscript Editor:* Douglas Long
Research Supervisor: Jeffry Jensen   *Research Assistant:* Jun Ohnuki

∞ The paper used in these volumes conforms to the American
National Standard for Permanence of Paper for Printed Library
Materials, Z39.48-1992.

Library of Congress Cataloging-in-Publication Data
Masterplots II. Poetry series. Supplement / edited by John Wilson
and Philip K. Jason.
    p.   cm.
    Includes bibliographical references and indexes.
        1. Poetry—Themes, motives. I. Wilson, John, 1948-   .
    II. Jason, Philip K., 1941-   .
PN1110.5.M37   1992
809.1—dc20   91-44341
Supplement   CIP
ISBN 0-89356-625-X (set)
ISBN 0-89356-626-8 (volume 7)

First Printing

PRINTED IN THE UNITED STATES OF AMERICA

PUBLISHER'S NOTE

Masterplots II: Poetry Series Supplement contains discussions of 376 poems from the eighth to the late twentieth century. Works of 263 poets, writing in a plethora of languages, genres, and styles, are included. The supplement's three volumes complement the original six-volume *Masterplots II: Poetry Series* (1992), continuing its pagination and volume-number sequence.

The supplement is intended to expand the original series in two primary ways: first, to include discussions of well-known poems that were not in the original series, and second, to extend coverage to more twentieth century poetry—thereby allowing more discussions of work by African American, Hispanic, Asian American, and American Indian writers. Consequently, the focus of this set, although it does include poems from around the world, is primarily on English-language poetry. In compiling the contents for the supplement, particular consideration was given to poems that have been collected in many of the fine anthologies—some general, some with a particular thematic, ethnic, or gender focus—that have appeared in recent years. Because teachers and readers of poetry all discover their own favorite gems, we have attempted to collect articles on poems written in a wide range of poetic voices and styles.

Of the 263 poets with works discussed in this supplement, 128 did not appear in the original *Masterplots II: Poetry Series*. Among them are Nobel Prize-winner Wisława Szymborska, American Book Award winner Lisel Mueller, and Henry Taylor, whose title poem from his Pulitzer Prize-winning volume *The Flying Change* is included. Among the other poets appearing for the first time in the supplement are such notables as Sir Walter Ralegh, Jonathan Swift, John Greenleaf Whittier, Louis MacNeice, Stephen Spender, Amy Lowell, Kenneth Koch, John Hollander, and Henry Reed. Attention was given to including recent works; more than thirty of the poems in the supplement were first published in the 1990's, from Derek Walcott's long poem *Omeros*, published in 1990 and central to Walcott's being awarded the Nobel Prize in 1992, to Alan Shapiro's "Girlfriend" and Amy Gerstler's "Montage of Disasters," published in 1996 and 1997 respectively.

Among the well-known poems included are Henry Reed's heavily anthologized "Naming of Parts," Lord Byron's "She Walks in Beauty," E. E. Cummings's "in Just-," Thomas Hardy's "The Darkling Thrush," W. H. Auden's "As I Walked Out One Evening," Amy Lowell's "Patterns," John Milton's "On Shakespeare," Emily Dickinson's "I bring an unaccustomed wine," Edna St. Vincent Millay's "Renascence," Robert Browning's "Meeting at Night," Wallace Stevens's *Notes Toward a Supreme Fiction*, Archibald MacLeish's "Ars Poetica," and Robert Frost's "Home Burial." Many other great poets covered in the original series have additional works included here; among them are William Shakespeare, John Donne, William Wordsworth, Percy Bysshe Shelley, William Butler Yeats, Walt Whitman, Hart Crane, Allen Ginsberg, Seamus Heaney, Sylvia Plath, Ezra Pound, Adrienne Rich, and William Carlos Williams. Among the foreign-language poets are writers from France, Russia, Mexico, Chile, Germany, Italy, Poland, China, Spain, and Sweden. Included are examinations of poems by Charles Baudelaire, Federico García Lorca, Friedrich Hölderlin, Osip Mandelstam, Czesław Miłosz, Pablo Neruda, Octavio Paz, Rainer Maria Rilke, Arthur Rimbaud, and Tu Fu (Du Fu). All told, more than thirty foreign-language poets are featured.

African American poetry covered ranges from Paul Laurence Dunbar's nineteenth century collection *Lyric of Lowly Life* to Rita Dove's sequence "Persephone in Hell," first published in 1995. Also among the nineteen African American poets included are Gwendolyn Brooks, Charles Wright, Wanda Coleman, Robert Hayden, Langston Hughes, Audre Lorde, Etheridge Knight, Claude McKay, Ishmael Reed, and Yusef Komunyakaa. Asian American works include poems by Garrett Kaoru Hongo, Li-Young Lee, Wing Tek Lum, Pat Mora, and Cathy Song. Among the Hispanic poets are Julia Alvarez, Sandra Cisneros, Judith Ortiz Cofer, Simon J. Ortiz, and Gary Soto. American Indian writers include Louise Erdrich and Linda Hogan.

Masterplots II: Poetry Series Supplement is arranged alphabetically by poem title. Poems in translation are listed according to the title by which they are best known to English-speaking readers. Each essay is divided into four sections. The first section, ready-reference top matter, provides information at a glance, first giving the author's name and birth and death dates, then noting the type of poem being discussed (such as lyric, dramatic monologue, narrative, or elegy). Next, the year of the poem's first publication (in either a periodical or a book) is given. Additional information is also provided on this line. For English-language poems that initially appeared in a periodical, the first book in which the poem was collected is listed. For poetry in translation, the original foreign-language title of the poem is given, followed by the title and date of an accessible English-language collection in which the poem may be found.

The essay's text is divided into three sections. "The Poem" presents an overview of the work. It takes the reader through the poem's content, noting events, situations, objects, and places the poem describes. "Forms and Devices" looks closely at the poetic devices the poet uses, such as imagery, metaphor, rhyme, and meter. "Themes and Meanings" examines the underlying concerns that are expressed in the work.

Four useful reference features appear at the end of volume 9. A Glossary of Poetical Terms defines 103 crucial aspects of poetry, such as irony, metaphor, meter, narrator or speaker, and rhyme. The three indexes that follow—Title Index, Author Index, and Type of Poem Index—are cumulative, including the original six *Masterplots II: Poetry Series* volumes as well as the supplement. The Title Index, in addition to listing all titles in the series and noting their authors, includes the first lines of poems otherwise referred to by a number (such as "Sonnet 35"), occasional alternate titles, and cross-references for the foreign titles of poems in translation. The Author Index provides poets' names, followed by a list of their poems in the set and the page numbers on which they appear. The Type of Poem Index groups poems by genre—such as lyric, narrative, epic, elegy, and ode—thus allowing easily accessible comparisons of works within a genre.

PUBLISHER'S NOTE

Salem Press wishes to thank the coeditors of this supplement, Philip K. Jason, of the United States Naval Academy, and John Wilson, for their diligent work and expertise. We also acknowledge the contributions of the many academicians and other writers who contributed articles; a list of their names and affiliations may be found in the front matter to volume 7.

CONTRIBUTING REVIEWERS

Opal Palmer Adisa
California College of Arts

Betty Alldredge
Angelo State University

Diane M. Almeida
University of Massachusetts, Boston

Daniel Altamiranda
Universidad de Buenos Aires

David J. Amante
University of North Carolina at Charlotte

Christopher Ames
Agnes Scott College

Phillip B. Anderson
University of Central Arkansas

Candace E. Andrews
San Joaquin Delta College

Andrew J. Angyal
Elon College

Stanley Archer
Texas A&M University

Bryan Aubrey
Independent Scholar

Edmund August
Jefferson Community College

James J. Balakier
University of South Dakota

Linda Kearns Bannister
Loyola Marymount University

Jack V. Barbera
University of Mississippi

Henry J. Baron
Calvin College

David Barratt
Independent Scholar

Kathleen M. Bartlett
University of Central Florida

Cynthia S. Becerra
Humphreys College

Carol F. Bender
Alma College

Alma Bennett
Clemson University

Gaymon Bennett
Northwest Nazarene College

Richard P. Benton
Trinity College

James J. Berg
Independent Scholar

Dorothy M. Betz
Georgetown University

Cynthia A. Bily
Adrian College

Margaret Boe Birns
New York University

Nicholas Birns
The New School for Social Research

Richard Bizot
University of North Florida

Pegge Bochynski
Independent Scholar

Bernadette Lynn Bosky
Independent Scholar

Douglas Branch
Rust College

Wesley Britton
Grayson County Community College

Mary Hanford Bruce
Monmouth College

Paul James Buczkowski
University of Michigan, Dearborn

Susan Butterworth
Independent Scholar

Edmund J. Campion
University of Tennessee

Linda M. Carter
Morgan State University

C. L. Chua
California State University, Fresno

Steven Clotzman
Independent Scholar

Judith Collins
University of Kentucky

Sandra Cookson
Canisius College

David Conde
Metropolitan State College of Denver

Bill Coyle
Salem State College

Marsha Daigle-Williamson
Spring Arbor College

Koos Daley
Adams State College

Jo Culbertson Davis
Williams Baptist College

Todd Davis
Goshen College

William V. Davis
Baylor University

Bill Delaney
Independent Scholar

Francine Dempsey
College of Saint Rose

Carolyn F. Dickinson
Columbia College

Shoshanah Dietz
La Sierra University

Susan Dominguez
Independent Scholar

Gene Doty
University of Missouri, Rolla

William R. Drennan
University of Wisconsin, Baraboo

Gloria Duarte-Valverde
Angelo State University

Stefan Dziemianowicz
Independent Scholar

K Edgington
Towson State University

Eduardo F. Elías
University of Utah

Robert P. Ellis
Independent Scholar

Carrie Etter
University of California, Irvine

Beth Ann Fennelly
University of Arkansas

John W. Fiero
University of Southwestern Louisiana

T. A. Fishman
Purdue University

Thomas C. Foster
University of Michigan, Flint

June M. Frazer
Western Illinois University

Joe B. Fulton
Dalton College

Robert L. Gale
University of Pittsburgh

Jeffery Galle
Northeast Louisiana University

Jo K. Galle
Northeast Louisiana University

Ann D. Garbett
Averett College

Joshua Alden Gaylord
New York University

Michelle Gibson
University of Cincinnati

Jill B. Gidmark
University of Minnesota

Carla Graham
University of Wisconsin, La Crosse

Jeffrey Greer
Western Michigan University

Louise Grieco
Independent Scholar

Gary Grieve-Carlson
Lebanon Valley College

H. George Hahn
Towson State University

Robert Haight
Kalamazoo Valley Community College

Jay L. Halio
University of Delaware

CONTRIBUTING REVIEWERS

William T. Hamilton
Metropolitan State College of Denver

Katherine Hanley
St. Bernard's Institute

Betsy P. Harfst
Kishwaukee College

Susan Tetlow Harrington
University of Maryland Eastern Shore

Sandra Hanby Harris
Tidewater Community College

Betty L. Hart
University of Southern Indiana

Nelson Hathcock
Saint Xavier University

Greig Henderson
University of Toronto

Diane Andrews Henningfeld
Adrian College

Andrew C. Higgins
American University

Paula Hilton
University of New Orleans

Joseph W. Hinton
Independent Scholar

Mary Ann Hocgberg
Independent Scholar

W. Kenneth Holditch
University of New Orleans

Sandra J. Holstein
Southern Oregon University

Gregory D. Horn
Southwest Virginia Community College

Kenneth L. Houghton
Independent Scholar

Patricia J. Huhn
Trinidad State Junior College

Maura Ives
Texas A&M University

Helen Jaskoski
California State University, Fullerton

Jeffry Jensen
Independent Scholar

Christopher D. Johnson
Francis Marion University

Sheila Golburgh Johnson
Independent Scholar

Leela Kapai
Prince George's Community College

Daven M. Kari
California Baptist College

Steven G. Kellman
University of Texas, San Antonio

W. P. Kenney
Manhattan College

Claire J. Keyes
Salem State College

Mabel Khawaja
Hampton University

Kimberley H. Kidd
East Tennessee State University

Judith Kitchen
State University of New York, Brockport

Dave Kuhne
Texas Christian University

Kathryn Kulpa
Independent Scholar

Eugene Larson
Pierce College

William T. Lawlor
University of Wisconsin, Stevens Point

Jacqueline Lawson
University of Michigan, Dearborn

Linda Ledford-Miller
University of Scranton

L. L. Lee
Western Washington University

Steven Lehman
John Abbott College

Bruce H. Leland
Western Illinois University

Elisabeth Anne Leonard
Kent State University

Holli G. Levitsky
Loyola Marymount University

Leon Lewis
Appalachian State University

Thomas Lisk
North Carolina State University

Elizabeth Losh
University of California, Irvine

Bernadette Flynn Low
Dundalk Community College

Loretta McBride
State Technical Institute, Memphis

Janet McCann
Bethel College

Joanne McCarthy
Tacoma Community College

Andrew Macdonald
Loyola University

Gina Macdonald
Loyola University

Ron McFarland
University of Idaho

Edythe M. McGovern
West Los Angeles College

S. Thomas Mack
University of South Carolina, Aiken

Joseph McLaren
Hofstra University

A. L. McLeod
Rider University

Mary E. Mahony
Wayne County Community College

Lois A. Marchino
University of Texas, El Paso

Tony A. Markham
State University of New York, Delhi

Paula M. Martin
University of New Orleans

Wayne Martindale
Wheaton College

H. A. Maxson
North Carolina Wesleyan College

Kenneth W. Meadwell
University of Winnipeg

Patrick Meanor
State University of New York, Oneonta

Julia M. Meyers
Duquesne University

Michael R. Meyers
North Carolina State University

Vasa D. Mihailovich
University of North Carolina

Jane Ann Miller
Dartmouth College

Timothy C. Miller
Millersville University

Judith N. Mitchell
Rhode Island College

Christian H. Moe
Southern Illinois University, Carbondale

Scott Moncrieff
Andrews University

Robert A. Morace
Daemen College

Bernard E. Morris
Independent Scholar

Roark Mulligan
Christopher Newport University

D. Gosselin Nakeeb
Pace University

Joseph M. Nassar
Rochester Institute of Technology

Arthur A. Natella, Jr.
Independent Scholar

William Nelles
University of Massachusetts, Dartmouth

Robert Niemi
St. Michael's College

Edward F. Palm
Glenville State College

Janet Taylor Palmer
Caldwell Community College

Jay Paul
Christopher Newport University

David Peck
California State University, Long Beach

CONTRIBUTING REVIEWERS

Ted Pelton
Lakeland College

Thomas Amherst Perry
Texas A&M University, Commerce

Marion Boyle Petrillo
Bloomsburg University

Rhonda Pettit
Northern Kentucky University

John R. Pfeiffer
Central Michigan University

Norman Prinsky
Augusta State University

Charles Pullen
Queen's University

Gregory J. Racz
Parsons School of Design

Robin Anne Reid
Texas A&M University, Commerce

Rosemary M. Canfield Reisman
Charleston Southern University

Mark Rich
Independent Scholar

Janine Rider
Mesa State College

Larry Rochelle
Johnson County Community College

Carl Rollyson
Baruch College, City University of New York

Paul Rosefeldt
Delgado Community College

Lynn Sager
Alverno College

Scott Samuelson
Ricks College

Mark Sanders
College of the Mainland

Alexa L. Sandmann
University of Toledo

Karin Schestokat
Oklahoma State University

Peter A. Schneider
College of Saint Elizabeth

Beverly Schneller
Millersville University

Daniel M. Scott III
Rhode Island College

James Scruton
Bethel College

Rita M. Scully
Chestnut Hill College

Lisa A. Seale
*University of Wisconsin Center, Marathon
County*

Paul Serralheiro
Dawson College

Helen Shanley
Independent Scholar

Chenliang Sheng
Northern Kentucky University

Julie Sherrick
St. Bonaventure University

Agnes A. Shields
Chestnut Hill College

R. Baird Shuman
University of Illinois, Urbana-Champaign

Anne W. Sienkewicz
Independent Scholar

Charles L. P. Silet
Iowa State University

Marjorie Smelstor
University of Wisconsin, Eau Claire

David P. Smith
Naval War College

Jean M. Snook
Memorial University of Newfoundland

Valerie C. Snyder
Independent Scholar

George Soule
Carleton College

Anca Mitroi Sprenger
Brigham Young University

Scott M. Sprenger
Brigham Young University

Brian Stableford
Independent Scholar

Isabel B. Stanley
East Tennessee State University

Stefan Stoenescu
Cornell University

Sue Storm
Independent Scholar

Gerald H. Strauss
Bloomsburg University

Michael Stuprich
Ithaca College

Thomas F. Suggs
University of Kentucky

James Sullivan
California State University, Los Angeles

Charlene E. Suscavage
University of Southern Maine

Roy Arthur Swanson
University of Wisconsin, Milwaukee

James Tackach
Roger Williams University

James T. F. Tanner
University of North Texas

Lorenzo Thomas
University of Houston, Downtown

Tony Trigilio
Northeastern University

Veta Smith Tucker
Grand Valley State University

Richard Tuerk
Texas A&M University, Commerce

Linda Turzynski
Rutgers University

Scott D. Vander Ploeg
Madisonville Community College

J. K. Van Dover
Lincoln University

Dennis Vannatta
University of Arkansas, Little Rock

Martha Modena Vertreace
Kennedy-King College

Mark Vogel
Appalachian State University

Albert Wachtel
Pitzer College

Steven C. Walker
Brigham Young University

Sue B. Walker
University of South Alabama

Jaquelyn W. Walsh
McNeese State University

Qun Wang
California State University, Monterey Bay

Gladys J. Washington
Texas Southern University

Dennis L. Weeks
University of Great Falls

Tiffany Werth
Portland State University

Albert E. Wilhelm
Tennessee Technological University

Thomas Willard
University of Arizona

Judith Barton Williamson
Sauk Valley Community College

Raymond Wilson
Fort Hays State University

Sharon K. Wilson
Fort Hays State University

Michael Witkoski
Independent Scholar

Qingyun Wu
California State University, Los Angeles

Jennifer L. Wyatt
Civic Memorial High School

Joanna Yin
University of Hawaii

John Young
Independent Scholar

LIST OF TITLES IN VOLUME 7

	page
Ache of Marriage, The — *Denise Levertov*	2525
Affliction (I) — *George Herbert*	2528
After a Stranger Calls to Tell Me My Mother's Been Hit By a Car in Front of the Buddhist Church — *James Masao Mitsui*	2531
After Our War — *John Balaban*	2534
Afterword — *Joseph Brodsky*	2537
Against Confidences — *Donald Davie*	2540
Against the Evidence — *David Ignatow*	2543
Airy Tomb, The — *R. S. Thomas*	2546
All Souls' Night — *William Butler Yeats*	2549
American Change — *Allen Ginsberg*	2552
Angel of History, The — *Carolyn Forché*	2555
Anti-Lazarus, The — *Nicanor Parra*	2559
Apology of Genius — *Mina Loy*	2562
Appraisal — *Sara Teasdale*	2565
April Inventory — *W. D. Snodgrass*	2568
Ariosto — *Osip Mandelstam*	2571
Arms and the Boy — *Wilfred Owen*	2574
Ars Poetica — *Archibald MacLeish*	2577
As I walked out one evening — *W. H. Auden*	2580
As We Forgive Those — *Eric Pankey*	2583
At Grass — *Philip Larkin*	2586
At Luca Signorelli's Resurrection of the Body — *Jorie Graham*	2589
At the Executed Murderer's Grave — *James Wright*	2592
Atlas of the Difficult World, An — *Adrienne Rich*	2595
Atomic Pantoum — *Peter Meinke*	2599
Autobiography — *Dan Pagis*	2602
Available Light — *Marge Piercy*	2605
Awakening — *Lucien Stryk*	2608
Bait, The — *John Donne*	2611
Balcony, The — *Charles Baudelaire*	2614
Ballad of an Old Cypress — *Tu Fu*	2617
Ballad of Birmingham — *Dudley Randall*	2620
Ballad of Rudolph Reed, The — *Gwendolyn Brooks*	2623
Ballad of the Landlord — *Langston Hughes*	2626
Battle-Pieces and Aspects of the War — *Herman Melville*	2629

page

Before an Old Painting of the Crucifixion — *N. Scott Momaday* 2634
Before I Knocked — *Dylan Thomas* 2637
Bermudas — *Andrew Marvell* 2640
Between the Wars — *Robert Hass* 2643
beware: do not read this poem — *Ishmael Reed* 2646
Bight, The — *Elizabeth Bishop* 2649
Black Riders, The — *Stephen Crane* 2652
Black Walnut Tree, The — *Mary Oliver* 2657
Blindman, The — *May Swenson* 2660
Blue Dress, The — *Sandra Cisneros* 2663
Blue Wine — *John Hollander* 2666
Bogland — *Seamus Heaney* 2670
Bomb — *Gregory Corso* 2673
Born of Woman — *Wisława Szymborska* 2676
Brass Furnace Going Out — *Diane di Prima* 2679
Bread Without Sugar — *Gerald Stern* 2682
Break of Day in the Trenches — *Isaac Rosenberg* 2685
Briggflatts — *Basil Bunting* 2688
Buffalo Bill 's — *E. E. Cummings* 2693
Bushed — *Earle Birney* 2696

Cambridge ladies who live in furnished souls, the — *E. E. Cummings* 2699
Canto 4 — *Ezra Pound* 2702
Canto 29 — *Ezra Pound* 2706
Canto 81 — *Ezra Pound* 2709
Canto 116 — *Ezra Pound* 2712
Captivity — *Louise Erdrich* 2715
Cargoes — *John Masefield* 2719
Cello Entry — *Paul Celan* 2722
Chambered Nautilus, The — *Oliver Wendell Holmes* 2725
Cherrylog Road — *James Dickey* 2728
Chicago *Defender* Sends a Man to Little Rock, The —
　　Gwendolyn Brooks 2731
Childe-hood — *Henry Vaughan* 2734
Childhood — *Rainer Maria Rilke* 2737
Children in Exile — *James Fenton* 2740
Children of the Night, The — *Edwin Arlington Robinson* 2743
Chimes of Neverwhere, The — *Les A. Murray* 2748
Churchill's Funeral — *Geoffrey Hill* 2751
Circulations of the Song — *Robert Duncan* 2754
Circumstance, The — *Hart Crane* 2757
City Without a Name — *Czesław Miłosz* 2760

page

Clearances — *Seamus Heaney* 2763
Cloud, The — *Percy Bysshe Shelley* 2766
Concord Hymn — *Ralph Waldo Emerson* 2769
Conversation Overheard — *Quincy Troupe* 2773
Coole Park, 1929 — *William Butler Yeats* 2777
Country of Marriage, The — *Wendell Berry* 2780
Craftsmanship and Emptiness — *Jalal al-Din Rumi* 2783
Credences of Summer — *Wallace Stevens* 2786
Cumberland Station — *Dave Smith* 2789
Cut Flower, A — *Karl Shapiro* 2792

Dance Script with Electric Ballerina — *Alice Fulton* 2795
Danny Deever — *Rudyard Kipling* 2798
Dark Harbor — *Mark Strand* 2801
Darkling Thrush, The — *Thomas Hardy* 2806
Day Zimmer Lost Religion, The — *Paul Zimmer* 2809
Day's Chores: A List, The — *Patricia Hampl* 2812
Dead Soldiers — *James Fenton* 2815
Dear Aunt Chofi — *Daisy Zamora* 2818
Death & Co. — *Sylvia Plath* 2821
Depression Days — *Pat Mora* 2824
Description of a City Shower, A — *Jonathan Swift* 2827
Description of the Morning, A — *Jonathan Swift* 2830
Desert Music, The — *William Carlos Williams* 2833
Design — *Robert Frost* 2836
Dien Cai Dau — *Yusef Komunyakaa* 2839
Difficult Times — *Bertolt Brecht* 2844
Disappointment, The — *Aphra Behn* 2847
Display of Mackerel, A — *Mark Doty* 2850
Distances, The — *Charles Olson* 2854
Do not weep, maiden, for war is kind — *Stephen Crane* 2857
Dover Bitch: A Criticism of Life, The — *Anthony Hecht* 2860
Dream of a Brother, A — *Robert Bly* 2863
Dream of Governors, A — *Louis Simpson* 2866
Dream of the Unified Field, The — *Jorie Graham* 2869
Dreaming in Daylight — *Robert Penn Warren* 2872

Each and All — *Ralph Waldo Emerson* 2875
Easter 1984 — *Les A. Murray* 2878
Effort at Speech Between Two People — *Muriel Rukeyser* . . . 2881
Elegy for Jane — *Theodore Roethke* 2884
Elegy for John Donne — *Joseph Brodsky* 2887

page

Eleven Addresses to the Lord — *John Berryman* 2890
Emmett Till — *Wanda Coleman* 2894
Ethics — *Linda Pastan* 2897
Exequy, The — *Henry King* 2900
Exile — *Julia Alvarez* 2903
Explosion, The — *Philip Larkin* 2906
Exposure — *Wilfred Owen* 2909

Face in the Mirror, The — *Robert Graves* 2912
Farmer's Bride, The — *Charlotte Mew* 2915
Feelings, The — *Sharon Olds* 2918
Flesh and Blood — *C. K. Williams* 2921
Flying Change, The — *Henry Taylor* 2926
Formal Elegy — *John Berryman* 2929
Four Good Things — *James McMichael* 2932

MASTERPLOTS II

POETRY SERIES

THE ACHE OF MARRIAGE

Author: Denise Levertov (1923-1997)
Type of poem: Lyric
First published: 1962; collected in *O Taste and See*, 1964

The Poem

"The Ache of Marriage" is part of a Denise Levertov collection entitled *O Taste and See*. In the title poem and others in the collection, Levertov moves outward from the sensual and immediate to the wider implications of actions or concepts. The poems are filled with rich physical detail, which the poet uses in this particular poem to present the essential qualities of a marriage. Levertov had written about marriage in earlier poems such as "The Marriage, I" and "The Marriage, II" (in her 1958 and 1960 collections), but those love poems are somewhat more conventional and romantic than her work in *O Taste and See*. In this collection she achieves a new sense of immediacy, coupling personal experience with myth. These qualities are evident in such poems as "Abel's Bride" and "Divorcing" as well as in "The Ache of Marriage." In *O Taste and See* Levertov seems to have found her personal poetic voice.

"The Ache of Marriage" is a short poem in free verse, its thirteen lines divided into irregular stanzas of one, three, three, three, and two lines. The title, which is repeated as the first line, establishes the essential conflict and dilemma of the poem: the yearning for a total communion within marriage that is probably not attainable. The poem uses the first-person-plural point of view, suggesting that both the man and the woman are searching for joy but are finding that joy tempered with sadness. As is true in most lyric poetry, there is no noticeable distinction made between the author and the speaker (part of the "we").

The poem employs a series of sensual images to convey both joy and pain: thigh, tongue, throbbing teeth, the belly of the leviathan, and the ark. The images progress from the highly personal to the archetypal and biblical—moving from the familiar and sensual to the universal. The speakers (the partners in the marriage) are expressing the aching quality of a marriage through the senses rather than through spoken words of love.

The last image of the poem is the ark, with the two marriage partners aboard—safe and removed from the outside world yet not happy. The phrase "The ache of it" echoes the first line and concludes the poem, leaving both the speakers and the reader unsatisfied with the knowledge that marriage continues to embody both joy and pain and probably does not allow total communion.

Forms and Devices

Born and reared in England, Levertov moved to the United States after World War II as the bride of an American soldier. Her work was much influenced by American poets, especially William Carlos Williams, Robert Creeley, and Robert Duncan.

Added to her traditional British poetic experience, the American influence encouraged Levertov to adopt innovative forms.

The poetic devices most important to the poem in achieving both immediacy and voice are the seemingly unstructured free-verse form, the heavy use of sensual imagery, and the use of biblical myth. Levertov used what could be called organic form in "The Ache of Marriage." As she has indicated in interviews and writing, she lets the content or subject matter of a poem determine its form. Free verse, with its irregular meter and irregular line and stanza lengths, gives her the freedom of prose combined with the intensity of poetry. The term "projective verse" could also be applied to her work in this poem. Projective verse regards meter and form as artificial constraints and seeks to "project" a voice through the content and the pauses for breath that determine the line. The result in this case is a poem of fragmented prose poetry that expresses, through its lack of strict form, the quality of a marriage as being both a yearning for and an inability to communicate fully. Both partners are reaching out but are almost clumsily unable to reach each other.

Since the poem is composed primarily of a series of images linked by abstract concepts, the reader can perhaps best understand the poem by looking at the images separately. The first group of images includes thigh, tongue, and teeth—the last one seeming incongruous until it is examined in context. Thigh and tongue are clearly sensual, suggesting lovemaking by the marital partners. The use of the words "beloved" and "throbs" also contributes to this sense of physical love. However, the "throbs" goes on to include "in the teeth." One clearly sees an added image here—a toothache.

These images are followed by a stanza of abstract statement expressing the couple's yearning for commitment. Then the following stanza uses one major image—the leviathan and "we in its belly." Adding "belly" to the image clarifies the fact that this is a biblical allusion, referring to the story of Jonah, who was swallowed by a sea monster, or leviathan (whale). In this image the couple is depicted as having been swallowed by something they welcome yet cannot escape. They are still searching for some kind of "joy, some joy not to be known outside of it."

The final image in the cluster is the ark, again a biblical allusion, suggesting qualities similar to the belly of the whale: The ark is a safe haven for the couple ("two by two"), yet no escape is in sight. The cluster of images Levertov uses in this poem work together to form a progression from the personal to the universal. By incorporating the biblical images, the poet moves the concerns of marriage into the mystical and spiritual realm. The biblical images also add a quality of timelessness. Myth in literature makes concrete and particular a perception of human beings or human institutions. In this case, the "ache" of the institution of marriage is made concrete.

Themes and Meanings

The poem's two primary themes are expressed immediately: the simultaneous longing for total communication and the knowledge that such communication is probably not possible. Love and marriage have been subjects for poets throughout the centuries, so Levertov is certainly not tackling a new subject. Yet she breaks from tradition by presenting her themes from both a twentieth century and a timeless perspective.

Levertov is often discussed as a feminist poet, but her reflections on love, marriage, and even divorce are never occasions for "male bashing." Rather, she suggests that both men and women have difficulty in functioning wholly either within or outside marriage. In "Divorcing" she writes, "We were Siamese twins,/ Our blood's not sure/ it can circulate,/ now we are cut apart." In the poems in *O Taste and See* she presents a realistic rather than a romantic picture of love and marriage. Twentieth century works (with the exception of romance novels) do not romanticize love and marriage with a "happily ever after" conclusion. They are honest in their sometimes puzzling conclusions. Levertov, like other modern poets, leaves the reader feeling both hope and despair.

Betty Alldredge

AFFLICTION (I)

Author: George Herbert (1593-1633)
Type of poem: Meditation
First published: 1633, in *The Temple*

The Poem

"Affliction (I)" is a lyric poem of eleven six-line stanzas. The rhyme scheme is *ababcc*. Lines 1,3,5, and 6 are generally iambic pentameter, with lines 2 and 4 using iambic trimeter. The poem is part of a collection entitled *The Temple*. George Herbert, a priest in a country parsonage, is said to have given the manuscript to a friend as he (Herbert) lay near death. The message accompanying the manuscript called the work "a picture of the many spiritual conflicts that have past betwixt God and my Soul, before I could subject mine to the will of Jesus my Master, in whose service I have now found perfect freedom." Whether Herbert did indeed speak these words or they were put into his mouth by a devoted biographer, they well describe the movement in the collection of poems and effectively introduce the reader to "Affliction." Called "Affliction (I)" because there are four other poems in *The Temple* with the same title, the poem relates the speaker's personal journey in the spiritual life. The speaker tells readers that, captivated early by the beauty of serving God, he responded with great eagerness and dedication. The first three stanzas are exuberant, unrealistic. The speaker finds joy in God's service and a certain payback in the satisfaction he derives from his efforts to live in a holy manner. Serving God, "the King," is sufficient. His spirituality is sincere but superficial and self-seeking.

The fourth stanza introduces a shift: "But with my yeares sorrow did twist and grow." Suddenly the spiritual life, formerly a source of deep peace, becomes painful and difficult to bear. The speaker experiences even physical discomfort: "My flesh began unto my soul in pain." The poem does not indicate the cause of the depression but suggests that God simply removes himself from the speaker's consciousness.

The letdown is predictable. The poem continues its description of the spiritual and physical pain in which the speaker lives, without hope or joy. Searching for some meaning in life, he turns to the life of the mind and becomes an academic, studying at a university. Here, "academick praise" sustains him for a time and gives him the joy he sought. Knowing on some level that this respite is also temporary, he nevertheless pursues this course until illness again overtakes him. The last two stanzas show the speaker in distress, in sadness, in "affliction," but turned toward God, patient in his distress and willing to endure God's will for him, however difficult that might be. He cries to God: "Now I am here, what thou wilt do with me/ None of my books will show." As the poem finishes he displays an act of faith and love: "Ah my deare God! Though I am clean forgot,/ Let me not love thee, if I love thee not."

Although it is possible that this poem reflects an actual struggle experienced by Herbert regarding his priesthood, it is more probable that the poem describes a general inner struggle to be faithful to God's designs and plans. The speaker is more concerned with the *why* of his actions—his motives—than with the *what*, or the literal decisions.

Forms and Devices

"Affliction (I)" is a fine example of Herbert's writing. As do most of his poems, it uses the first person throughout, giving a reader the sense that the spiritual experience is actually taking place. The poem reads like a cross between a journal entry and a biblical psalm, reviewing the speaker's spiritual life and coming to a conclusion that accepts God's actions in his life.

The affliction of the title works on several levels. The speaker early sees God as afflicting him with suffering and discouragement. He eventually realizes, however, that the real afflictions are those of the world: self-seeking, vanity, and earthly pleasure.

Herbert is considered a writer of the Metaphysical school, of which his contemporary John Donne was the originator and remains its most famous example. Like Donne, Herbert uses ordinary language, the rhythms of conversation, explosive outbursts, a deeply personal approach to God, and daring figures of speech. Describing his first religious fervor, he says, "There was no month but May." He also exaggerates for effect: "consuming agues dwell in ev'ry vein,/ And tune my breath to grones." Herbert's vocabulary, though some of it may seem stilted to the modern reader, is in fact conversational, even colloquial at times. "Affliction" is not a formal prayer so much as a dialogue with God.

Like Donne, Herbert uses a formal structure, keeping to his iambic rhythms and firm rhyme scheme. The intense struggles of the spiritual life are played against this careful structure so that the reader perceives both order and chaos simultaneously. Similarly, the speaker is both disordered in his efforts to run away from God and supported by God's care for him.

Schooled in classical rhetoric, Herbert combines a conversational tone with elegant figures. The last line of the poem, "Let me not love thee if I love thee not," is a chiasmas. This term means "cross," and the placement of "love," "thee," "thee," and "love" makes an *x*, or cross, when the poem is diagrammed. A key influence on Herbert was the Psalms, with their frequent cries to God for mercy, deliverance, and salvation. Like many of the Psalms, "Affliction" uses past tense to review the speaker's actions up to the present moment, moving then to the present tense as the speaker describes his current spiritual state.

Themes and Meanings

"Affliction (I)" relates a classic part of the traditional spiritual journey. Descriptions of such journeys were particularly common in poetry of Herbert's period, but they recur in almost every century. A good nineteenth century example is Francis Thompson's "The Hound of Heaven." Herbert's religious training for his ordination as a priest had given him a great sensitivity to God's actions in his life. The poem may be autobiographical, but it also mirrors the experience of countless others who aspire to a life of holiness.

The early stanzas show the stage of a spiritual life common to beginners, those in an early fervor in which everything is joyful, grace-filled, even easy. It is a traditional spiritual high point, and it is followed, not surprisingly, by a massive letdown in which the speaker finds the spiritual life not only difficult but also meaningless and distasteful. This state is also traditional, even predictable, in the spiritual life. The movement is from consolation to desolation, from first fervor to letdown. Countless believers have experienced this passage, each believing that he or she is the only one encountering these difficulties.

When the speaker seeks solace or refuge in the academic life, he follows a common path: He substitutes another good for the difficult and often unrewarding good of serving God. Here he falls prey to inappropriate motives, sustained by praise and the easy recognition of the university. Though the intellectual life is a good one, the temptation to intellectual pride is too great. Once again sickness overtakes him.

The end of the poem shows the speaker in another classic state: experiencing the "dark night of the soul." Herbert does not use this phrase, but the great mystic John of the Cross, who coined the term, described it as helplessness, lack of consolation, and feelings of uselessness, joined with a conviction that God is somehow involved in the entire process. This helpless waiting is the first step toward true conversion of heart. The speaker confronts his self-seeking, even in good endeavors, and opens his life to God's activity and power. (Some later writers have noted the similarity of this state to the first of the "twelve steps" of Alcoholics Anonymous and similar programs.) Having handed over his power to God, the speaker can now grow in the spiritual life. This is not a one-time conversion of heart but a central part of the journey.

It should be noted that the speaker's description of his turning from God's service does not imply turning to a life of sin. Like most spiritual poems, "Affliction" shows a good person turning toward a deeper life. The speaker is not struggling with affirming the existence of God; rather, he is a devout believer who freely engages in conversation with God. The poem is written *after* the most intense struggle, not during it. The speaker is firm in his conviction that God does indeed care for him, however remote God may seem at times.

Another term for the stage that the poem depicts is the Purgative Way, the way of conversion and formation. It is followed by the Illuminative Way, in which God instructs the soul in the ways of holiness, and the Unitive Way, in which God and the soul are united in holiness.

Reading George Herbert requires an appreciation of both his theology and his seventeenth century approach to the spiritual life. It is not always an easy task for the modern reader, but the effort can be richly repaid as Herbert's poems unfold. "Affliction" and many other poems in *The Temple* will stand with other literature of Herbert's period as a rich record of struggle, sorrow, and surrender in the journey toward spiritual peace. The later poems in the volume depict the soul progressing in the spiritual life toward deep contemplation and joy in the presence of God.

Katherine Hanley

AFTER A STRANGER CALLS TO TELL ME MY MOTHER'S BEEN HIT BY A CAR IN FRONT OF THE BUDDHIST CHURCH

Author: James Masao Mitsui (1940-   )
Type of poem: Lyric
First published: 1986; collected in *From a Three-Cornered World: New and Selected Poems*, 1997

The Poem

"After a Stranger Calls to Tell Me My Mother's Been Hit By a Car in Front of the Buddhist Church" is written from the first-person point of view. It consists of forty lines divided into four stanzas: a six-line introductory stanza, followed by a twenty-two-line stanza and two concluding stanzas of six lines each. The title notes the event and subject that inspired the poem and prepares the reader for the tone and voice of the narrator, who is easily assumed to be the poet, James Mitsui.

The poem begins dramatically in the present tense with the narrator entering a hospital setting. Mitsui's images in the initial stanza plunge the reader *in medias res* into the experience. Flashes of color combine with the image of gurneys being pushed "through swinging doors" to re-create the sense of panic one feels when rushing into the hospital upon hearing of an injured loved one.

After this dramatic entry, the poem takes a more retrospective turn with a stanza-long flashback in past tense. Written as if it were a film or theater script, it creates the impression that the mother is a character who is being forced to play a set role. This "script" has directed her through four significant and difficult moves in her life, the most traumatic being the hasty move to Tule Lake, a World War II relocation camp for Japanese Americans. This move is described with vivid details and highlights the fact that the narrator's mother was constantly compelled to reinvent her life and identity to fit unforeseen and undesired circumstances.

After revealing the mother's past, the poet returns to the present in the last two stanzas. He depicts her as being more assertive than in his previous description. By this time in her life, she has learned to swear and complain in broken English. Although the physical trauma of the automobile accident is limited to a small bruise, the incident serves as a metaphor for many events in her past. Mitsui writes: "There are no answers./ No cause./ No driver saying he's sorry." As the title implies, she was leaving church, a place of tranquillity and spirituality, and was run down by a stranger who showed no remorse. The final image of the poem portrays a woman who has suffered many indignities in her life, not the least among them being American society's view of her as little more than a cipher written on vinyl.

Forms and Devices

Readers familiar with classical East Asian poetry will recognize that Mitsui's long-winded title signals a particular kind of lyric, the occasional poem. (One such poem is Chinese poet Han Yü's "Demoted I Arrive at Lan-T'ien Pass and Show This Poem to My Brother's Grandson Han Hsiang," from the ninth century.) Their seemingly cumbersome titles are actually licenses for immediacy; they free their authors from providing prosaic background introductions, allowing them direct entry into the essential action or meaning they wish to communicate. Often the occasions of such poems then become points of departure or objective correlatives for observations about life.

This poem's title also appears to encode an allusive irony, a device used repeatedly throughout the poem. It is ironic that the mother is struck by a callous hit-and-run *vehicle* in front of a Buddhist church. Readers acquainted with Buddhism will recall that its two major denominations (analogous to Christianity's Catholicism and Protestantism) are the Hinayana and Mahayana, Sanskrit for "Lesser Vehicle" and "Greater Vehicle." All Buddhists seek nirvana (salvation), but Hinayana Buddhists believe in achieving a personal salvation, whereas Mahayana Buddhists believe in seeking a common salvation (for the self and others). Hence Mahayana Buddhists revere bodhisattvas, who (like some saints) are qualified to enter nirvana but compassionately stay to help their more benighted fellows. The hit-and-run driver, out to save himself or herself, must have been in a much lesser vehicle—no bodhisattva he (or she).

Mitsui also chooses words carefully for their symbolic value. For instance, when the mother was released from her relocation camp, she settled in a region of the United States "surrounded by cheatgrass and rattlesnakes"—words that contain connotations of treachery and danger and that quietly characterize the environment into which America's dominant majority has historically situated its ethnic minorities.

Situational irony occurs in Mitsui's description of the mother's hospital setting. The care the mother receives in the hospital conjures up her memories of the degradation and dehumanization of the relocation camp. Thus her bed curtains remind her of the blankets used in the camp barracks to designate families' quarters. The nurses' ministrations remind her of the camp's dearth of privacy, with its doorless privies and partitionless showers. Finally, the hospital's "vinyl I.D. bracelet" on her wrist forms an ironic image contrasting the preciousness ("bracelet") of her identity with cheapness ("vinyl"), symbolizing the low regard society has of it.

The second stanza's shift from present action to past memory is entirely natural. When one loses or is about to lose a close friend or relative, that person's character and significance pass in review before the mind's eye. Thus the flashback in the second stanza serves to evoke the hard life and indomitable character of the mother. Her life is described as a "script," a course determined by family and society. She performs her scripted role as if following the inevitabilities of her karma, spelling out the characteristics of her ordained dharma as victim (of family circumstance), wife, cook, victim (of a racist society), homemaker, and again victim (of an automobile accident). Through it all, her integrity, undaunted courage, and fierce will to survive shine steadfast. The hard knocks life dealt her would have broken a brittler spirit, but hers is resilient and adamant—in the end, she has merely sustained "a bruise on her wrist."

Themes and Meanings

Many occasional poems not only convey a vivid impression of the fleeting event but also make an observation about the larger human experience—hence Ben Jonson's "Inviting a Friend to Supper" (1616) is not only a dinner invitation but also a model of Elizabethan taste and civility. In Mitsui's poem, the shock and anxiety occasioned by the mother's automobile accident become also a poetic vehicle to appraise the woman's character and thereby apprise the reader of the historical experience of her ethnic group in twentieth century America: The individual woman becomes an exemplar of her ethnic genus, the Japanese Americans.

The heart of Mitsui's poem, the lengthy flashback of the second stanza remembering the mother's "script"-like life, contains two highlighted events: immigration and incarceration. Both reveal the quality of the woman's character and strike key themes of Japanese American history. She emigrated to the United States not by individual choice but because her family decided to make a marriage of convenience between her and a previous Japanese American immigrant, the widower of her elder sister. (One may gather from another of Mitsui's poems, "Katori Maru, October 1920," that this occurred to Mitsui's own mother in 1920.) Somewhat like the so-called picture brides of that era who came from Japan and Korea to marry immigrant men known to them only through photographs, the mother emigrated to the United States to replace her sister in a female variant of a leviratic marriage. In her patriarchal Asian society, her preferences were not consulted. She confronted her destiny with a stoic, can-do determination and a denial of self-gratification. In this spirit she created a home and a family for a new generation of Americans.

Wrongful incarceration was also writ large into the script of this mother's life, as it was into the lives of the nearly 120,000 Japanese Americans who were rudely relocated from their homes and put into "concentration camps" (President Franklin Roosevelt's term) during World War II. Mitsui's family was actually relocated in 1942 from their home in Washington State to the exceptionally harsh Tule Lake camp named in the poem. However, like the Japanese Americans of her generation, the mother in Mitsui's poem survived this indignity and injustice perpetrated by her government and her society, but she could not forget. Hence, being hospitalized after her accident, removed from home, deprived of privacy—with only a curtain demarcating her personal space and with her identity reduced to a vinyl band cuffing her wrist—all these circumstances provoke a flood of frightening associations with her experience of the wartime camp. This brave woman thus cries out to be free, to go home. The reader may well see this frail-bodied but tough-spirited woman laid low by a callous and conscienceless driver as emblematic of her ethnic coevals whose human freedoms were trampled by the political machinery of racism and xenophobia in the land of the free.

C. L. Chua and Keisha Blakely

AFTER OUR WAR

Author: John Balaban (1943-   )
Type of poem: Lyric
First published: 1974; collected in *Blue Mountain*, 1982

The Poem

"After Our War" is a twenty-five-line poem in free verse. John Balaban uses the first-person plural point of view, thereby including and implicating the reader in the horror of the Vietnam War. Although the poem appears to be one stanza, internal divisions marked by structure, sense, and tense divide the poem into three eight-line sections, followed by a one-line concluding question. The first and last lines begin with the phrase "After our war." This phrase therefore frames the poem, returning the reader at the end of the poem to its beginning. This device reminds the reader that the implications of the war continue long after the soldiers returned home.

The poem opens with a horrific, surreal listing of the "dismembered bits" of those killed and wounded in the Vietnam War. Balaban credits the body parts with movement of their own; they "came squinting, wobbling, jabbering back." This series of verbs gives ghastly movement to the poem, as does the image of "genitals . . ./inching along roads like glowworms and slugs."

The second eight-line section turns to a description of the "ghosts" of the war, the "abandoned souls" of those who died. It seems likely that these ghosts are Vietnamese dead, because they appear "in the city streets,/ on the evening altars, and on the doorsills of cratered homes," all images of Vietnam. The ephemeral ghosts stand in contrast to the physical fragments of the first eight lines. Thus there is a marked shift from physical disembodiment in the opening lines to the spiritual disembodiment in the second section. Lines 14-16 return to the dismembered body parts, depicting their arrival in the United States. The first sixteen lines are unified by the poet's use of the past tense, letting the reader understand that he speaks of events "after our war" but before the present.

In line 17, Balaban shifts into the present tense, telling the reader how fragments of the war have lodged themselves in the present in the United States as an "extra pair of lips glued and yammering" on the cheek of a "famous man" or as a "hard keloidal scar" on "your daughter's breast." The shift to present tense signals the poet's conviction that the remnants of the war continue to blight the present. In line 22 the poet once again shifts tenses, moving toward an uncertain future. The uncertainty is underscored by Balaban's use of three questions that close the poem.

The movement of the poem, then, is from past to future, from grotesque specificity to abstract reflection. This movement reminds the reader that the war, which happened in the past, continues into the present, and it raises questions about the possibility of meaning in the future.

Forms and Devices

Balaban's use of imagery in this poem is both startling and complex. Visual images abound; genitals look like "glowworms and slugs," ghosts appear like "swamp fog," homes are "cratered." There is also the image of *not* looking. The fragments that attach themselves to friends and famous men make it difficult to shake hands, make it "better, sometimes, not to look another in the eye."

Imagery is not limited to visual descriptions, however; Balaban also uses auditory images, kinesthetic images that create a sense of movement, and tactile images. Lip fragments are "jabbering" and "yammering," for example, making meaningless noise, unable to make sense of their current situation. Kinesthetic images such as genitals "inching along roads" and body parts "squinting" and "wobbling" create a particular sense of movement in the poem. Although these "snags and tatters" might be better left in Vietnam, they make their jerky, uneven movement home, arriving in the United States.

Finally, the reader's sense of touch is addressed early in the poem by such images as "pierced eyes," "jaw splinters," and "gouged lips." The graphic adjectives, derived from verbs, evoke physical pain. Balaban turns again to tactile imagery toward the end of the poem with the handshake, a symbol of friendship and accord. Now, after the war, handshakes are "unpleasant." With the phrase "at your daughter's breast thickens a hard keloidal scar," Balaban uses a tactile image to push the images of the Vietnam War into the next generation.

A second device that Balaban uses skillfully is literary allusion, a figure of speech that makes brief reference to some earlier literary figure or work. In lines 22 and 23 Balaban writes, "After the war, with such Cheshire cats grinning in our trees,/ will the ancient tales still tell us new truths?" The Cheshire cat is an obvious allusion to Lewis Carroll's *Alice's Adventures in Wonderland*, a nineteenth century children's book. Here, however, Wonderland is invoked not for its appeal to children but rather for the violent, irrational, upside-down world that Alice finds when she slips down the rabbit hole. In Wonderland, meanings are topsy-turvy, truths change with the moment, and the Cheshire cat fades in and out of view as Alice tries unsuccessfully to make sense of a world in which she finds herself. Likewise, Balaban suggests, after the Vietnam War, people must try to make sense of a world that seems to have lost rationality and meaning.

A second, less obvious allusion is to Balaban's own earlier poem "Carcanet: After Our War," the title poem of his first major collection of poetry, published in 1974. Balaban used the phrase again in his 1991 autobiographical account of his time as a conscientious objector in Vietnam, *Remembering Heaven's Face: A Moral Witness in Vietnam* (as both section and chapter titles). That Balaban continues to return to this phrase suggests his concern with finding meaning in a changed world.

Themes and Meanings

"After Our War" is about the possibility of meaning in the world, about a generation of people who question whether either meaning or love is possible after the Vietnam

War. Balaban's use of lips in lines 3 and 18 suggests that speech or words are inadequate for expressing the experience of the war. The closing four lines of the poem raise questions about this inadequacy:

> After the war, with such Cheshire cats grinning in our trees,
> will the ancient tales still tell us new truths?
> Will the myriad world surrender new metaphor?
> After our war, how will love speak?

Balaban questions whether "ancient tales" can hold adequate answers for the world after the war. Although he looks for new truths, it seems unlikely that the texts and language that spoke so eloquently in the past will have anything to say in this new world. In this questioning, Balaban seems to connect himself to World War I poet Wilfred Owen, who rejected the "old lie," that it is fitting and sweet to die for one's country, in his poem "Dulce et Decorum Est." In line 24 Balaban introduces the notion of "metaphor," which is a figure of speech. Again, he questions whether the world, in all its variety, will offer language capable of describing life and capable of imparting meaning after our war.

Finally, in the last question, Balaban wonders whether love will find language to express itself. By its placement in the poem, this line signals Balaban's most important concern and his conviction that meaning in the world is a product of love. Further, the introduction of love at this last possible moment requires the reader to look again at the entire poem. Love "speaks," metaphorically and physically, through the birth of a child. Yet when one returns to the opening lines of the poem, one reads not only of lips and tibias but also of disembodied, destroyed genitals—a reminder that many men came home from the war impotent from either physical or emotional wounds.

Still others came home from Vietnam unknowingly made sterile through their exposure to the defoliant Agent Orange (a topic Balaban addresses in other poems). Both Vietnamese and Americans exposed to Agent Orange also had genetic damage that was passed on to their surviving offspring in the form of devastating deformities. (Balaban reveals in *Heaven's Face* that his wife Lonnie suffered a miscarriage while they were in Vietnam in 1971; they were unable to conceive again for sixteen years.) The "extra pair of lips" and the "hard keloidal scar" take on terrible significance in this context. Thus, the literal and metaphorical toxicity of the war makes even procreation, birth, and rebirth questionable. Love, Balaban seems to be saying, is what repopulates and regenerates the world, but the offspring of war are dismemberment, death, sterility, scars, and deformity.

Diane Andrews Henningfeld

AFTERWORD

Author: Joseph Brodsky (1940-1996)
Type of poem: Lyric
First published: 1987, as "Posleslovie," in *Uraniia*; English translation collected in
    To Urania, 1988

The Poem
    "Afterword" is a poem of forty lines divided into five numbered sections of eight
lines each (two quatrains, in the English translation). As the title suggests, it is a look
backward, but, in this case, over a life still in progress rather than a finished work. It
is written in the first person. The speaker, at first, seems to be talking to himself or to
no one in particular. By the end, he seems to be talking to a single interlocutor, but the
"you" could be the distant reader just as easily as the person across the table. This
move from singular experience to common fate is at the heart of much lyric poetry,
but here the change takes on material form: The self, with time and age, becomes not
merely something else, but everything else.
    The first section begins with the most general of lyrical-elegiac observations: "The
years are passing." The speaker observes their passage around him almost as if he is
sitting at a café table. A palace facade is cracking and the Holy Family, whether on a
relief, a painting, or a calendar, moves ever-so-slightly closer to Egypt. The world is
crowded with the living, the city is full of lights, and the astronomer counts up his
"sparkling tips."
    The next section shifts from the general to the particular. The pronoun "I" appears
for the first time and notes rather dispassionately, seemingly without complaint, that
it can no longer remember exactly when or where events took place. The speaker also
observes that the events themselves cannot remember anything, so that whoever was
involved ("saved or fled") is away and clear.
    The next step is both logical and crucial to the poem. The speaker defines what all
this means—he, the individual, is, with time, becoming part of the whole. Life, in
general, is a "rustling . . . fabric," and now his individual skin is taking on the look of
what enwraps it. His profile could be a wrinkle, a patch, or a leaf, all visible things
that could be wholes or parts in themselves. Whether whole or part, however, they
have always been something apart from him, and anything outside of himself can be
"ignored, coveted, stood in fear of."
    If the previous stanzas are addressed to the reader—or someone—in general, the
next two stanzas narrow the focus. "Touch me—and you'll touch dry burdock stems"
might be figuratively addressed to the reader in general but, by virtue of that imperative, sounds more immediate. By touching the speaker, one also touches whatever and
whomever one has seen or known.
    The final section moves from sight to sound, or rather speech. "I am speaking to
you, and it's not my fault/ if you don't hear." However, the listener is not at fault either.
Rather, like the cracked wall or the gaunt Holy Family, the vocal cords wear out. The

voice is muffled and hard to distinguish from other sounds around it. The speaker, however, does not complain about losing his voice on top of all the other losses; that loss makes it easier for the listener to hear those other sounds, which are part of life's rhythm—the rooster's crow, the ticking sound made by a needle on a record. The poem ends with a twist on the story of Red Riding Hood: "The better to hear you with, my dear," says the wolf when the girl tells him what big ears he has. Here, the line is, "the better for you not to notice when my talk stops," and it is anyone's guess who is the wolf and who is not.

Forms and Devices

For Joseph Brodsky, poetry was always a process of thought more than an exploration of emotion or music. That is not to say that he ignored the latter two, but "Afterword" is a good example of poetic logic at work.

The translation follows the original Russian's rhyme scheme (*abab cdde*, with some variations) and rhythm without observing a strict metrical pattern. There is also a good deal of internal rhyme and alliteration, while the end rhymes used in the translation themselves are often near, rather than full, rhymes. Still, for the English-speaking reader, what ties the poem together is image and metaphor rather than sound.

Each section represents a shift in focus and direction: The first three are linked by imagery of accumulation and profusion. The first abounds in visual images: the passage of time expressed in space, the palace facade cracking, the eyeless seamstress finally threading her needle, the Holy Family inching its way toward Egypt. Important, too, is what occupies the space. The emphasis is on "the visible world" and its multitudes, its numbers upon numbers of living beings, its bright and "extraneous" light, its quantity of "sparkling tips" that strain the astronomer's eyes. When the speaker begins questioning his own memory of events, there follows a list of possible times and places, and, after that, a list of almost generic events, "an explosion, or say, a flood,/ the lights of the Kuzbas derricks or some betrayal." The transition from section 2 to section 3 introduces the paradox that drives the poem: Events themselves cannot remember, so, when those who "were saved or fled" lose track, that means their tracks are covered. Therefore, loss, in some way, equals survival.

The answer section 3 offers is not an answer to individual questions of what, where, or who, much less how or why. Rather, it is a statement of what all this, taken together, now undifferentiated, means. The poet, too, can no longer be set apart from the surrounding shapes and objects, the "fractions or wholes," or their more abstract effects or the feelings they evoke. This section contains another list, this time combining physical objects, actions, and emotions.

Touch dominates section 4—the first stanza contains images of dryness and dampness, while in the second stanza returns to a list that ends with the word "loss." In the final stanza, sense of hearing replaces sense of touch, with the addition of time ("The sum of days") again equated with subtraction of sound ("when my talk stops").

Themes and Meanings

Pure elegies, or elegiac lyrics on the transience of life, may start out with someone else's life and death but, more often than not, work their way around to the poet's own—something Brodsky himself pointed out in "Footnote to a Poem," his essay on Marina Tsvetaeva's elegy for German poet Rainer Maria Rilke. Mourning oneself through others is a time-honored tradition in lyric poetry, with the tone of the lament ranging from defiant (Dylan Thomas's "Do Not Go Gentle into That Good Night") to nobly hopeful of immortality in some other form. The poet may be losing hair and teeth, but the consolation is a permanent place in art and memory.

The standard elegiac themes of time passing, age, and loss run through "Afterword"; what makes the poem interesting is not so much their presence but their relationship. Brodsky has often written about exile and loss, and the themes have often taken the form of meditations on separation forced either by history or geography—in other words, by time or space. In Brodsky's poetry, those are not abstract notions but things that can be smelled, touched, seen, felt, and heard.

Here, Brodsky's speaker is not so much mourning as he is musing over an observable, tangible process. The tone is both philosophical and wry. Mortality itself is a process, not an event: In his singular version of the law of preservation of matter, life reclaims its own in segments, increments, and fractions. That includes speech, because words, like the body, have their own mass and gravity. The moment at which the body is dispersed or reclaimed, when the sound of someone muttering can no longer be heard, is also called death—a word that is nowhere in this poem. It is also, mercifully, hard for the listener to pinpoint.

An afterword is meant to comment on what has come before, to present conclusions, to sum it all up. The controlling irony here is that the sum is actually a remainder: The more miles a car has on it, the more rust it accumulates, the more it becomes "a heap," the less it is a car. So it goes with the body and its voice. Still, the transformation of one kind of matter into another somehow clears the way for another form of being, one that is truly eternal. How much comfort that provides is another question.

Jane Ann Miller

AGAINST CONFIDENCES

Author: Donald Davie (1922-1995)
Type of poem: Meditation
First published: 1958; collected in *New and Selected Poems*, 1961

The Poem

Formally, "Against Confidences" consists of eight quatrains, with very short lines of between three and five syllables and an exact alternating rhyme scheme of *abab*. The poem argues against the modern popularity of pouring forth intimate details, whether in tell-all books, confessional poetry, psychoanalysis, or personal relationships. In a humorous and satiric tone, the poem explains how "Candour," one of the poem's series of personified abstractions reminiscent of the British neoclassical verse that Donald Davie esteemed, has changed in its relationship to "loose lips" (stanza 1) or "mouths that now/ Divulge, divulge" (stanza 8).

In the present time—the present being emphasized by the repetition of the word "now" in the opening and closing stanzas—loose lips or divulging mouths describe Candour, in Davie's British spelling, as "friend." This situation suggests that would-be confidants, whether in writing or in personal relationships, confuse the indiscriminate spilling of confidential details with frankness and truth.

Moving from a third-person objective point of view to the first-person plural, the poem's speaker asserts that the genuine revelation of (or quest for) truth signified by Candour cannot exist in the apparently heedless flow of expression in an environment created or distorted by "our compulsive/ Needs" on "couches" where "we sleep, confess,/ Couple." The word "couches" may signify the bed as the site of an individual's dreaming or a couple's lovemaking as well as the psychiatrist's couch. All these are spheres in which self-interest undermines the ultimate truthfulness of what appears to be candid outpouring.

Returning to the third-person point of view, the speaker defines the main facets of Candour as "reticence" or restraint, the subjection of all talk and feeling to actual test and intellectual examination, and toleration of a degree of privacy, hazy belief, or half-illuminated conviction but discouragement of self-indulgent and deceptive effusiveness.

Forms and Devices

The poem's notable compression in its grammar and in its short lines reflects as well as expresses the idea of truth and meaning inherent in "reticence" rather than its opposite. Likewise, multiple meanings are compacted into several puns and wordplays. The confidences of the title may refer to intimate details; to the state of feeling confident, which would be misplaced in dreaming, lovers' talk, confessional writing, or psychoanalysis; and to the duplicity of a confidence game, since the apparent candor of flowing expression may not be what it seems.

In contrast, reticence is Candour's "practise"—a word whose primary meaning is habitual operation but whose secondary meaning of intrigue contrasts Candour's honesty with the deceptiveness of "loose lips." This deceptiveness is conveyed by the oxymoron of the "pleased distress" (stanza 3) that people experience on their various "couches." The distress in turn suggests a discrepancy between the surface of the dream, confessional writing or talk, lovers' intimate conversations, and the true meanings or feelings that underlie them. Thus, in the midst of an anguished confessional poem, a sense may be conveyed of the poet's pleasure in his or her pain, in the act of complaining about the causes of the pain, or in the accomplishment of a literary work about the subject.

Several features of neoclassical verse also contribute to the poem's warning against effusiveness. Its precise and straightforward rhymes and rhyme scheme suggest the poem's emphasis on exactitude and forthrightness. Also, the several balanced antitheses in grammar signaled by the repeated "Not . . . , But . . ." constructions convey the speaker's thoughtful weighing, comparing, and defining of aspects of candor and effusiveness. That is, the poem is patterned to show that Candour does not reside in particular values or activities but does reside in other values and activities. The synecdoches for effusiveness, "loose lips" and "mouths" that "divulge," help suggest the absence of intellect, as if the anatomy of the effusive person were working by itself, without the brain. In contrast, the synecdoche characterizing Candour's disapproval of "loose lips" and "mouths" that "divulge," Candour's "brow" that is clear (stanza 1) or clouded (stanza 8), conveys not only a facial expression but also the anatomical location of intelligence and thought. Finally, use is made of the proverbial metaphor of the light of reason and truth contrasting with the darkness or shade of irrationality and error. This metaphor is subtly linked to the etymology of the word *candor*, from the Latin words meaning "white" and "shine." Like the circular form of the poem, whose first and last stanzas repeat, the recurrent imagery of light and dark suggests the inevitability of the poem's truths about its subject.

The "shade" of the couches of sleep, confession, and coupling (stanzas 2-3), and of "shy belief/ Too bleakly lit" (stanza 7), in which Candour cannot "live," is a metaphor not only of the darkness of weakened rationality and truth but also of the comfort provided by avoiding the harsh glare of both Candour and intelligence, particularly the latter. Candour will "respect/ Conviction's plight" in "Intellect's/ Hard equal light" (stanzas 5-6). Candour is thus humane and makes some allowances for emotional and spiritual truths, whereas the intellect is harsher. Likewise, in the concluding two stanzas, Candour's brow is not "clouded" by permitting "To shy belief/ Too bleakly lit,/ The shade's relief"; rather, what clouds Candour's brow is "to indulge/ These mouths that now/ Divulge, divulge."

Themes and Meanings

"Against Confidences" focuses on two main areas: the development of personal relationships and the modern popularity of effusiveness in print, speech, psychiatric treatment, and some social relationships. The repeated word "now" may apply to the development of personal (especially romantic) relationships, in which the participants may wrongly believe that a complete, uncritical outpouring of the self is mandated. Such an outpouring, the poem implies, will probably be warped by the romantic partners' deep-seated fears of injury to their self-esteem or by concerns about damage to the relationship.

The repeated word "now" may also point to modern times. Against the modern popularity of self-indulgently telling all, Davie's speaker counterposes the precise, vaguely archaic literary word for despising or scorning, "contemned" (stanza 1). In the 1950's and early 1960's, when "Against Confidences" was published, highly autobiographical, confessional poetry was gathering momentum in American and British literature. Confessional poetry is perhaps best exemplified by the work of a group of talented American poets that includes Robert Lowell, W. D. Snodgrass, Anne Sexton, Sylvia Plath, Allen Ginsberg, Adrienne Rich, Theodore Roethke, and John Berryman. This strand of modern poetry, which extends back to the poetry of Walt Whitman and William Wordsworth, continues to the present.

Davie's "Against Confidences," far from the vividly specific word choice and autobiographical imagery of confessional poetry, employs austerely general and abstract word choices and imagery as well as figurative language reminiscent of classical sculpture and neoclassical verse. Davie's poem remains a polished refutation of confessional poetry, as do perceptive remarks in his books of literary criticism *Purity of Diction in English Verse* (1952), *Articulate Energy: An Enquiry into the Syntax of English Poetry* (1955), and *Under Briggflatts: A History of Poetry in Great Britain, 1960-1988* (1989). The purity of diction and word choice in "Against Confidences" provides a fitting parallel to the title of Davie's first important book of literary criticism, which, like the poem, continues to be a touchstone of English literature.

Norman Prinsky

AGAINST THE EVIDENCE

Author: David Ignatow (1914-1997)
Type of poem: Lyric
First published: 1968, in *Rescue the Dead*

The Poem

"Against the Evidence," a thirty-three-line meditative poem, is characteristic of the autobiographical nature of much of David Ignatow's poetry. In free verse, it presents the contrast between the "estrangement among the human race" and the narrator's determination to live.

The poem opens with a seven-line stanza in which the narrator attempts to "close each book/ lying open on my desk" but is attacked by the books themselves as they "leap up to snap" at his fingers, causing pain. The action suggests a mutiny of the books against the speaker, although they have obviously been a significant part of his life.

The conflict is heightened when, in the second, longer stanza, the poet reflects on his heretofore harmonious relationship with books. He has "held books in my hands/ like children, carefully turning/ their pages." This harmony has resulted in a close identification of the poet with what he reads: "I often think their thoughts for them." Following this benign reflection, a jarring shift occurs as the narrator plunges into the dark message of his musing: "I am so much alone in the world." The books, which have been such a dominant part of his world are not, after all, human beings. Their mutiny at the beginning of the poem seems to suggest that the speaker is becoming estranged even from them. The poet mourns the loneliness of his preoccupation with inanimate elements such as stars or steps. He then links humans with these cold, unfeeling objects: "I can look at another human being/ and get a smile, knowing/ it is for the sake of politeness."

He has finally arrived at the core of his sadness and disillusionment, "estrangement/ among the human race," about which "Nothing must be said." In fact, "nothing is said at all" because to speak about estrangement might begin to break it down. The evidence has been building throughout the poem. It seems as though the poet has taken refuge in inanimate objects such as his books. Despite all this evidence, however, and despite his troubles, the poet asserts: "Against the evidence, I live by choice."

Forms and Devices

David Ignatow's language is deceptively simple, his images spare, and his metaphors often obscure. Like William Carlos Williams, he uses few typically poetic devices. Rather, his language carries his message. Initially in this poem Ignatow personifies his books. As he attempts to close them, they "leap up to snap" at his fingers. As realization explodes upon him, he is weakened and must sit down.

The uprising of his books seems to jar his whole existence. He reflects on the prior harmony he felt with his books, which might almost be considered symbiotic: "All my life/ I've held books in my hands/ like children." One wonders whether this means that he holds them as he holds children or as children hold books. In either case, he implies a nurturing relationship. However, the books betray him, unable to fulfill his need for community.

Juxtaposed with his comfortable perception of the books in his life is the alienation that breaks into verse 2: "I am so much alone." He reinforces his aloneness with a series of sterile images: "the stars," "the breeze," and the "steps/ on a stair" that he can count as he climbs and descends them. When he speaks of other human beings, they are no more communicative, for he feels that their smiles are only "for the sake of politeness." He pinpoints his apparent despair in the word "estrangement."

The feelings of alienation, separation, and estrangement are further expressed in the unresponsive images of familiar objects around him: "I stroke my desk,/ its wood so smooth, so patient and still." Despite all this "evidence" of his isolation and lack of community, the poet finishes with a note of affirmation that belies the note of despair in the poem: "I live by choice."

In addition to metaphor and imagery, the poet uses the arrangement of lines and stanzas to reinforce his consciousness of estrangement. The mutiny portrayed in the first seven lines of the poem in a single stanza shatters the comfortable life that many people experience with books and catches the poet in the knowledge of his own isolation. The beginning of stanza 2 lulls the reader into that former life. However, in line 15, a jarring change occurs. The suddenness of this change heightens the mood of separation, although no separation in format occurs in the stanza arrangement.

Themes and Meanings

David Ignatow has been called the "most autobiographical of writers" by the *Dictionary of American Biography*. "Against the Evidence" bears this out, as do many of his other poems. Rather than create a persona as narrator, Ignatow himself is obviously the speaker, confronting life and the human condition. In another poem, "Communion," he sees little in human experience to inspire communion.

> Then let us be friends, said Walt, and the graves
> were opened and coffins laid on top
> of one another for lack of space
> It was then the gravediggers slit
> their throats being alone in the world
> Not a friend to bury.

In "Communion" he creates an ironic contrast between himself and nineteenth century American poet Walt Whitman, who greatly influenced him. However, Ignatow considers Whitman optimistic and his own view of life realistic. Although he regards language as paramount in his writing, he also regards his work as a vehicle for moral leadership in that it points out—in his own words—"the terrible deficiencies in man. Whitman spent his life boosting the good side. My life will be spent pointing out the bad." "Against the Evidence" reflects on the harsh realities of life, yet it reiterates the poet's choice of life over death or defeat. Ignatow has said, "My avocation is to stay alive. My vocation is to write about it."

The spare, direct images of William Carlos Williams also exerted a strong influence over Ignatow. Ignatow has noted that what he appreciates most in Williams's work is the "language of hard living." In "Against the Evidence," the evidence to which the poet refers consists of elements of hard living, especially "estrangement." His alienation is represented by the direct, though unresponsive, images of his books, the stars, the breeze, the steps, and the polite smile on the face of a fellow human. He also develops this theme in the poem "Wading Inside," in which he bemoans the dearth of human interaction: "Guilty, my oppressor/ and I go separate ways/ though we could relieve each other/ by going together as Whitman wrote/ With our arms around each other."

While much of Ignatow's poetry carries a message similar to that of "Against the Evidence," it often does so in a darker, angrier manner. In "Epitaph" he speaks of his father: "There were not hidden motives to his life,/ he is remembered for his meanness." He contrasts love and life in "Rescue the Dead," picturing love as a kind of madness: "To love is to be led away/ into a forest where the secret grave/ is dug, singing, praising darkness/ under the trees." Life itself, on the other hand, is sanity: "To live is to sign your name,/ is to ignore the dead,/ is to carry a wallet/ and shake hands."

"Against the Evidence" is, at first glance, relatively mild. When one considers elements of nature such as the stars and the breeze one is lulled into a placid, almost peaceful mood. Only when one thinks of these images as sterile and uncommunicative, when they are joined with the "polite" but uncaring smile, does one experience the stark isolation that the poet confronts in the rest of the poem. The poem is a model of understatement; however, this very understatement underscores the aloneness of the narrator and the despair that grips all humanity at different times. Although he experiences this loneliness, he struggles to take action:

> I stroke my desk,
> its wood so smooth, so patient and still.
> I set a typewriter on its surface
> and begin to type
> to tell myself my troubles.
> Against the evidence, I live by choice.

Patricia J. Huhn

THE AIRY TOMB

Author: R. S. Thomas (1913-
Type of poem: Narrative
First published: 1946, in *The Stones of the Field*

The Poem

"The Airy Tomb" begins with the phrase "Twm was a dunce at school" and describes in the first stanza what Twm cared for instead of school: the noise and motion of birds and the land around him. Though the first stanza contains the word "I," thus establishing the presence of a speaker who is narrating the poem, the speaker remains largely absent from the poem, occasionally asking the reader for a judgment but for the most part describing what Twm did and what his world was like. The language is simple, consisting of phrases with nouns and strong verbs rather than extensive descriptive adjectives or metaphor.

The poem's second stanza describes Twm's work on a farm among the hills once he leaves school; he is more comfortable among the animals and the harsh working conditions than he was in the classroom. The third stanza tells of his father's death, and the fourth of his mother's. In the fifth stanza the poem shifts slightly from the narrative of what has happened and asks the reader to participate; the first lines are, "Can you picture Tomos now, in the house alone,/ The room silent, and the last mourner gone/ Down the hill pathway?" This question is followed by two others asking what Twm did, a device that allows the reader to imagine Twm's feelings and options rather than being told by the speaker what they are. The stanza then moves back into a narrative of Twm's life, alone on the farm.

The sixth stanza continues the description of his life, but it emphasizes how alone he is after his parents' death; one of the stanza's final images links the "Hearts and arrows" that symbolize love to his "school fractions"; Twm remains separated from other people. The poem's tone becomes somewhat fiercer and grimmer. In the last two and a half lines, "the one language he knew/ Was the shrill scream in the dark, the shadow within the shadow,/ The glimmer of flesh, deadly as mistletoe," the sense conveyed is one of the harshness of life and Twm's closeness to the tough lives of animals.

The final stanza states that Twm was desired by some of the girls around him but that he did not respond. His separation from other people leads to his becoming almost a local legend. The narrator again speaks to the reader, saying, "you, hypocrite reader, . . . are you not also weary/ Of this odd tale, preferring the usual climax?" The speaker goes on to suggest that surely there was someone whom Twm loved, but then steps back to say that there was not. The title's meaning is revealed in the final lines, with a description of Twm's body decomposing in the open air before he is finally found.

Forms and Devices

R. S. Thomas's use of rhyme and rhythm is not consistent throughout the poem, but he does use both. In the first stanza, for example, the first line does not rhyme with anything, but the second line rhymes with the third, the fourth with the fifth, and the sixth with the eleventh. While the lines tend to be about the same length, they are not always. Most of Thomas's words are one or two syllables, with the stresses falling rather unevenly, giving the poem the rhythm of someone speaking instead of an obviously metrical beat. Thomas makes use of iambic rhythms, as in the lines, "And then at fourteen term ended and the lad was free," and "And coax the mare that dragged the discordant plough," but the lines do not contain an equal number of feet and do contain additional syllables that break up the rhythm. Thomas also uses the device of enjambment; his sentences and clauses are as likely to end in the middle of the line as at the end.

In terms of imagery, Thomas relies largely on nouns and verbs; even his metaphors are free of adjectives. When he describes a dead hawk whose "weedy entrails" are "Laced with bright water," his language achieves its power through the unusual juxtaposition of two ordinary things: weeds and entrails, lace and water. The images are startling because unexpected, but the words themselves are quite ordinary. This adds a conversational tone to the poem; it also provides very specific and vivid descriptions for the reader, thus focusing the reader's attention on the scene.

Thomas's addresses to the reader are perhaps the most interesting formal aspects of the poem. By asking the reader to imagine Twm's circumstances, and later by accusing the reader of being complicit with those of Twm's neighbors who mock him, Thomas compels the reader to think about his or her expectations for both a poem and a person. He summons the socially comfortable ideas of romance and conformity, only to replace them with the image of a man who is very much alone and who wants to be so. He pushes readers to make a judgment and then to reconsider that judgment, a device that asks readers both to see the poem without the assumptions they might have brought to it and to reexamine their own attitudes toward other people. "Hypocrite reader" is a phrase used by the French poet Charles Baudelaire in his 1857 book *Les Fleurs du Mal* (*Flowers of Evil*, 1931), and one taken up in the French by T. S. Eliot in *The Waste Land* (1922); it therefore resounds with literary associations in the midst of a poem that is otherwise simple and grounded in unliterary language. By using it, Thomas calls further attention to the readers' position as readers and to their difference from Twm, the dunce at school.

Themes and Meanings

The title "The Airy Tomb" is almost an oxymoron; one expects a tomb to be closed and stuffy, rather than airy. The poem continues to overturn expectations and surprise the reader. One can initially read it as idealizing the working man or the peasant, as much Romantic poetry did, but Thomas is careful to keep the poem from becoming a soft pastoral. He describes the harshness of the Welsh farmer's life, using images such as rotting sheep or "Deadly as leprosy." In the last stanza, he writes, "you must face the fact/ Of his long life alone in that crumbling house," lines that do not allow the reader to see Twm's life as anything but desolate without human company.

The poem is about place; Twm belongs on the farm, not in school or town. When people attempt to force him out of himself in his early years at school, the attempt does not work. The only poems he can read, the only language he can understand, is that of animals. "The Airy Tomb" is also about being alone. When Twm's father dies, his mother does not live through the next winter. He is left therefore to keep the farm in much the way his father did, making a place for himself with the land. Other of Thomas's poems speak of the relationship between the Welsh peasant and the land; the farmer is often portrayed as part of the landscape, but the landscape itself is bleak and unyielding. Thomas is aware of the poverty and the difficulty of farming on the rocky and cold mountains of Wales. One cannot make a living under those harsh conditions if one does not give oneself entirely to the work. Twm's relationship with the land and the animals is what causes his solitude, but it is also necessary for his survival.

This is also a poem about mortality. Thomas represents humans as having moved away from the cycle of life and death in which the animals and the rest of the natural world participate. Animals die under the sky, but humans are buried in confining coffins that separate them from the earth. Twm, however, is able to become part of the rhythm to which the animals belong; his grief for his parents subsides into his work and into the coming of spring; life goes on. Unlike other people, he dies with the sheep under the sky. In his solitude and separation from other people, he is able to enter the natural cycle of life and death as other humans cannot. "The Airy Tomb" does not romanticize nature as something beautiful and sweetly pleasant, but it does suggest that a closer connection to the natural world and the solitude that such a connection entails can enable one to have a better death.

Elisabeth Anne Leonard

ALL SOULS' NIGHT

Author: William Butler Yeats (1865-1939)
Type of poem: Meditation
First published: 1921; collected in *The Tower*, 1928

The Poem

"All Souls' Night" is the last poem in William Butler Yeats's most important collection of poetry, *The Tower* (1928). Organized into ten stanzas of ten lines each, it is a meditation, during All Souls' Night, on several friends who have died. A subtitle indicates that the poem is an epilogue to Yeats's book *A Vision* (1925), which is the codification of his theories of magic and history that were given to him by "Unknown Instructors" in the form of automatic writing transcribed by his wife Georgia. As such, the poem is meant to comment on and to celebrate this achievement. The first stanza is primarily descriptive as it sets the scene for the rest of the poem. It is midnight and the "great Christ Church bell" of Oxford University and other lesser bells "sound through the room." In this special and sacred time, a "ghost may come" to drink of the fumes of the wine that the poem's speaker has placed there. The ghost is so refined by death that he can only drink the "wine-breath."

In the next stanza, the speaker explains that he needs a mind that is armed against the "cannon sound" and other intrusions of the world, a mind that "can stay/ Wound in mind's pondering,/ As mummies in the mummy-cloth are wound." The description of souls being wound in the "mummy-cloth" comes from another of Yeats's important poems, "Byzantium." He needs this special mind or soul because he has "a marvellous thing to say/ a certain marvellous thing/ None but the living mock." That "marvellous thing" is contained in his book *A Vision*.

In the third and fourth stanzas, the speaker calls on the spirit of William Thomas Horton, a mystical painter and illustrator who was a casual friend of Yeats a number of years before the poem was written. What he discovers in Horton's life is a refusal to accept loss and tragedy as something mortals must bear. This refusal to accept such losses is crucial to *A Vision*, in which Yeats claims to have discovered a system that could explain the mysteries of life and death. Horton refuses to accept the death of his "lady," and nothing can console him: "Nothing could bring him, when his lady died,/ Anodyne for his love." The only hope remaining to him is that the "inclemency/ Of that or the next winter would be death." In the fourth stanza, Yeats amusingly describes how Horton's thought is "so mixed up" that he cannot tell "Whether of her or God he thought the most." When Horton turns his mind's eye upward, it falls "on one sole image," a vision that makes him "Wild with divinity" and illuminates heaven, "the whole/ Immense miraculous house/ The Bible promised us." Horton's vision thus achieves one of the central aims of *A Vision*: to unite the two disparate worlds of heaven and hell.

The next ghost that Yeats calls up is Florence Farr Emery, an actress of great beauty who, when she grew old and was about to lose that beauty, went to "teach a school" in Africa so those who had known and loved her would not see her decay. She had discovered "the soul's journey" from a "learned Indian," in which the soul would find a place where it could be "free and yet fast,/ Being both Chance and Choice." As Horton had unified heaven and hell, Emery had discovered the final unity that the soul would achieve.

The last ghost called up is a lesser and more controversial one, McGregor Mathers. Yeats describes him as "half a lunatic, half knave." Although he did not discover any occult knowledge, his "meditations on unknown thought" made "human intercourse grow less and less." So he, like the others, removed himself from the world to seek occult knowledge. The last part of the poem is Yeats's celebration of his own achievement in *A Vision*. He has "mummy truths to tell," and, wound within these truths, he needs "no other thing." They stand before the assault of the world and of both heaven and hell.

Forms and Devices

The ten-line stanza is one of the most important formal devices in the poem. The rhyme scheme is *abcabcdeed*, and the middle lines are iambic trimeter while the first and last lines are iambic pentameter. Yeats maintains this difficult pattern through each stanza and still manages to make the verse appear conversational and casual. Its complex arrangement mirrors that of *A Vision* to which it is connected. There are a number of sound images in the poem, including "the great Christ Church Bell" and the many "lesser" bells that "sound through the room" in the first stanza. These insistent sound images define the hostile outside world of the living who mock Yeats's vision; the sounds are contrasted to the quiet of Yeats's meditation upon the familiar ghosts who, through their quests for occult knowledge, managed to escape the world.

Although "All Souls' Night" is sparing in its use of the traditional devices of poetry, there are several important metaphors in the poem, the most significant being the comparison of the "mind's pondering" with being wound "As mummies in the mummy-cloth are wound." This suggests that the speaker has knowledge possessed by no one else but the dead. Another metaphor is the "soul's journey" in the Florence Emery section. She has discovered how the soul whirls around the moon (the cycles of the moon are central to *A Vision*) and then plunges "into the sun" where it can "sink into its own delight at last." These metaphors are ways of describing the spiritual truths that these seekers have discovered.

Yeats's verse portraits of his friends in the middle sections of the poem act as structural parallels and counterpoints to his own visionary achievement. The use of his dead friends in such a manner is a staple that also appears in such poems as "In Memory of Major Robert Gregory" and "The Municipal Gallery Revisited." "All Souls' Night," then, acts as a meditation on those friends who helped Yeats's spiritual search in his early life and provided an example of dedication to the occult. However, Yeats outdid those efforts of his friends to discover the system explained in *A Vision*.

Themes and Meanings

"All Souls' Night" functions as an epilogue to and something of a defense of *A Vision*. The book uses the phases of the moon and other mystical symbols to organize human character into cycles. Furthermore, it places these cycles into historical cones. It is therefore clear why Yeats insists in "All Souls' Night" that he has marvelous things to say. The ghosts that Yeats calls up in the poem are symbolic of the ability of Yeats's system to connect the living and the dead. The ghosts provide an example the poet's success, and they join him in celebrating his creation of a system that provides all the answers about time, humanity, and history.

One important theme is the claim that Yeats has united heaven and hell, a concept that he learned from English poet William Blake. At the end of the poem, Yeats speaks of how his meditation can both defy the world and penetrate "To where the damned have howled away their hearts,/ And where the blessed dance." His vision is capable of encompassing both parts of the afterlife and reconciling these opposites. Yeats's vision also involves a rejection of the world, which remains outside the ceremony of calling up the ghosts. However, he describes Horton as achieving a reunion with his lost beloved. The reunion must, of course, be in the afterlife. This brings to mind Yeats's assertions of a union with Maud Gonne, a woman who spurned him and his proposals of marriage, in the other world if not this world. The reconciliation of "Chance and Choice" is another important theme in Yeats's work. The reconciliation that is claimed in "All Souls' Night" is a symbol for "Unity of Being," a state that Yeats sought all his life. In a note to his play *Calvary* (1921), Yeats said that the union of "Chance and Choice" was only to be found in God. In "All Souls' Night," it is a discovery made by Emery and is comparable to the reconciliation of opposites that Yeats achieves in both the poem and *A Vision*.

James Sullivan

AMERICAN CHANGE

Author: Allen Ginsberg (1926-1997)
Type of poem: Lyric
First published: 1961; collected in *Reality Sandwiches*, 1963

The Poem

"American Change" is Allen Ginsberg's meditation on the figurative and literal meanings and values of money. Written in 1958, as Ginsberg was returning to the United States from a stint in the merchant marine, the narrative of the poem traces the speaker's changing attitudes toward his country as he reflects on the American coins in his pockets. Without their value as American currency, these coins were only souvenirs when the speaker was at sea, but as the poem plots his return to New York, he removes the change from his pocket and re-values it.

The poem is structured in a free-verse form in the breath-unit line structure that Ginsberg popularized. In such a structure, each line represents what Ginsberg once termed "one-speech-breath thought," fusing each line with equal emphasis on body, speech, and mind, a poetic concern Ginsberg borrowed from his Buddhist practice. "American Change" is divided into five stanzas, each organized according to the particular piece of money the speaker takes as his subject matter. Stanza 1 is devoted to the speaker's meditation on an Indian-head nickel; in stanza 2 the speaker explores the cultural meanings of a dime; stanza 3 is occasioned by a quarter. The poet takes a five-dollar bill as his subject matter in the fourth stanza, and the last stanza is devoted to a meditation and description of the cultural significance of a one-dollar bill.

The speaker immediately contrasts the symbolic money of his country with the sacred potential of the land. The movement from materialism to idealism is appropriate, given that two of Ginsberg's greatest influences, Walt Whitman and William Blake, perceived the United States as an idealistic answer to the threats to liberty inherent in monarchical systems of government. Ginsberg's speaker, however, sees the Native American on the front of the nickel as a "vanished man" and the buffalo on the back of the nickel as a prophetic "vanishing beast of Time." Ginsberg commonly synthesizes several religious traditions in his poetry, and "American Change" is no exception. The Native American is a "Rabbi Indian" whose "visionary gleam" has been swallowed by modern consumer capitalism. This "candy-store nostalgia of the redskin" is "dead on silver coin," and the sacredness of his culture is "gone into the great slot machine of Kansas City, Reno—." Ginsberg cuts off the line at "Reno," suggesting that a continued list of empty, consumerist cities would only be redundant.

"American Change" is framed by this contrast between the sacred and the material. With every new coin or bill, the speaker finds that the visionary origins of the United States have been swallowed by a "Vision of Money." This monetary vision is portrayed as a dead end; this path produces failure at both the figurative and literal registers of the poem. Figuratively, the money produces a "sexless," impotent erasure of vision, leaving the speaker with nothing but a "poor pile of coins." At the literal level, too, the poem dramatizes the "Vision of Money" as a futile one. The speaker reminds himself that the same money he took with him when he left the United States will buy much less now upon his return. Even when he attempts to be materialistic, the speaker despairs: "Money, money, reminder, I might as well write poems to you." He "might as well" do so because he is returning to an America that has transformed the visionary into the material, and in doing so has left the imagination as a reminder of loss, incapable of originality.

Forms and Devices

As with two other poems of the same period in his career, "America" (*Howl and Other Poems*, 1956) and "Death to Van Gogh's Ear!" (*Reality Sandwiches,* 1963), Ginsberg builds "American Change" on a shifting foundation of despairing and ironic statements. In the first stanza, the speaker opens with nostalgic articulations of home; yet as he meditates upon his return, he sadly realizes that the home he yearns for never existed. He longs for an ideal, and the tiny nickel in his hand contains within it all the deadness that prevents this ideal from coming into being. The next stanza introduces a dime, with its "sexless cold & chill." The George Washington quarter in the following stanza is "snub-nosed" and reflects the wishes of a designer who idealized Washington as a "sexless Father."

The speaker becomes miserable in the next stanza, emphasizing in the five-dollar bill "Lincoln's sour black head moled and wrinkled." The poem shifts to an ironic tone in this stanza. The speaker addresses his American change as the "dear American money" he clutches at his arrival at the Statue of Liberty. He accedes that he might as well dedicate his poetry to money—as if he, too, has been consumed by American materialism. Irony links this stanza to the final stanza, which begins with mock joy. His return to the United States is reflected in his return in the poem to George Washington—this time Washington on the face of a dollar bill: "Ahhh! Washington again, on the Dollar, same poetic black print, dark words, The United States of America, innumerable numbers." The speaker reminds himself that the words "Legal Tender" actually signify the opposite of tenderness in a consumer capitalist culture and that the sacrifice of American idealism to American economics is as absurd as his own characterization of the country's wealth as a collection of "innumerable numbers."

Irony and despair combine in the poet's final rumination on the dollar. He reflects on its unitary value—its currency as the singular dollar—by closing the poem with one word: "ONE." Ironically, the unity of his country depends upon the suppression of difference and the extinguishing of passion. The speaker remarks that the back of the bill is dominated by the "Great Seal of our Passion," a seal which indeed seals (contains) passion from further growth. The Treasury Department's attempt to prevent counterfeit bills symbolizes how cultural practices outside the norm—outside the "ONE"—cannot achieve cultural currency in the country to which he returns. What remains, for the speaker, are empty symbols of mysticism robbed of their visionary claims: the American eagle and "halo of stars," and the masonic and Swedenborgian influences that early American leaders saw fit to adapt as images on their currency.

Irony and despair combine in this final statement of "ONE" in "American Change," suggesting ultimately that, for the speaker, America has changed from a visionary land to a culture that contains and restricts dynamic American "change."

Themes and Meanings

For Ginsberg, the privilege granted to economics in American culture robs the imagination of cultural currency as it emphasizes the importance of actual hard currency itself. In "American Change," as in much of Ginsberg's work, American economic and imperial expansionism devalue the individual spirit as they increase national wealth. Discourses of history and culture are complicit in this movement away from individual freedom. The fate of the individual is much like that of the buffalo in the first stanza of "American Change": A pluralist convergence of individual identities is reduced to a "hoar body rubbed clean of wrinkles and shining like polished stone." The gleam is deceptive, just as it is when the speaker reveals that the nearly baroque illuminations on the dollar bill are merely safeguards against counterfeit currency rather than artistic renderings of the creative imagination.

The literal value of money, too, is reduced in "American Change." From *Howl* onward, Ginsberg's poetry concerned itself with both the materialist and the visionary consequences of contemporary social injustice. Thus, as the visionary potential of the country fades in the poem, so does material value. In the midst of the third stanza, the speaker counts the coins he has thus far described—a nickel, dime, and quarter—and states: "Quarter, remembered quarter, 40¢ in all—What'll you buy me when I land—one icecream soda?" He is more explicit in the next stanza, where he argues that the "immense promise" of what can be bought with five dollars shrinks with each new day.

Ginsberg's conception of visionary and creative imagination is predicated upon divine images that are fully desired and desiring. Therefore, the emptied passion of the cultural figures in the poem symbolizes the deadening of spirit in the America that occasions the poem. Much of this movement from passion to coldness is fueled by Ginsberg's attention to the potential for multiple meanings in poetic language. The "fathers" of the country—from Washington to Dwight D. Eisenhower (president at the time of the poem's writing)—no longer father (produce) anything of the imagination. They are figures of "sexless" discipline who debase the idealistic, sacred moment of the country's founding. Ginsberg reflects this debasing in language that invokes, then parodies, the power of religious language and syntax: "O Eisenhower & Washington—O Fathers—No movie star dark beauty—O thou Bignoses—." The speaker reminds the reader that Washington's image on the quarter is "naked down to his neck." However, the naked spirit of Washington is contained by the stiffness rendered on the quarter. This stiff image of Washington emphasizes only "falsetooth ideas." Thus, despite the speaker's attempt to coin a visionary body from this meditation, all that remains for him is the threat of "foul counterfeit" and the reality of diminished desire.

Tony Trigilio

THE ANGEL OF HISTORY

Author: Carolyn Forché (1950-
Type of poem: Meditation
First published: 1988; revised and collected in *The Angel of History*, 1994

The Poem

Many of the eighteen sections of "The Angel of History" recount recollections of World War II, particularly horrors of persecution, dislocation, and loss. The memories belong primarily to a war victim named Ellie, a deported Jew whom the speaker befriended and has known for a number of years. Ellie is the poem's magnetic center, attracting a variety of associations, some of which are clarified in notes. While the poem does not proceed chronologically, images and repeated phrases link the sections, some analytical, others narrative.

Indeed, the mental and emotional work of comprehending shapes the poem. The first section portrays the shock of knowledge upon the speaker, and the next three sections elaborate. When children are destroyed in concentration camps, windows seem blank, games become ominous, sleep is impossible, and "the silence of God is God." The speaker's descent into the poem takes the form of disconnected fragments, but images of sea, light, vigilance, sleeplessness, fire, and memory create a matrix of emotion.

The next seven sections develop Ellie's experience—the loss of sons, her husband's death from cholera, her affliction with St. Anthony's Fire, the memory of her wedding dress, prompted by news of a plane crash. The events range from the war to her confinement much later in a French sanatorium. Her suffering and hatred of France have made her bitterly defiant. Homeless, sure that no country is safe, she believes that God is "insane," and she wants "to leave *life*." The speaker devotes herself to caring for Ellie, missing events of her own son's childhood. She laments that Ellie's predicament "is worse than memory, the open country of death."

Whereas many poems move toward resolution, the last seven sections of "The Angel of History" emphasize disturbance. The speaker is haunted by an undefinable presence ("as if someone not alive were watching"). An unidentified voice in section 12 recounts a nightmare of nonexistence, in the process referring to sites of atrocities in El Salvador. The process of empathizing, recounted in the thirteenth section, affects the speaker to the extent that it seems "As if it were possible to go on living for someone else." The next two sections depict her disorientation. A letter from Ellie describes changes over eight years, but in the speaker's memory, Ellie does not change: "Here you live in an atelier."

The sixteenth section opens with a bitter definition—"Surely all art is the result of one's having been in danger, of having gone through an experience all the way to the end"—and recounts the terrifying evacuation of Beirut, Lebanon, where the women first meet and the speaker first tried to comfort Ellie. The repeated phrase "And it went on" suggests not only the rigors of the evacuation but also their lasting impact upon the speaker. Just as her recollection of Ellie seems more vital than the more recent events Ellie describes in her letter, the speaker's mind has associated (her word is "confuse") Ellie and the entirety of wartime horror. Logic and language both falter, as difficulties in translation illustrate. Initially a polite inquiry, Ellie's "Est-ce que je vous dérange?" ("Am I disturbing you?") sounds here and in the final section like a bell tolling and assumes ironic resonance. The final section serves as a musical coda, reiterating emptiness and irreparability. The poem ends not with any final pronouncement but with the voice of Ellie, or perhaps a nameless victim, inquiring of the reader what the speaker has said.

One understands that the poem, while cohesive, cannot resolve. The horrors that Ellie (and countless others) have endured radically alter the world and the way one speaks of it. Like writers who endured the horrors of Naziism—Nobel Laureate Elie Wiesel, critic George Steiner, and poet Paul Celan, to name a few—the speaker becomes a witness even as she questions the adequacy of language to carry out her task.

Forms and Devices

"The Angel of History" looks unconventional. Its lines are sentences—one or more. Never enjambed, they cross the page like prose. Often the sections have divisions, but they have more to do with content than with stanza structure. On the other hand, "The Angel of History" *sounds* like a poem. The lines are lyrical and emotional, the limpid images a consistent synthesis of the beautiful and the ruined. Repeated phrases (repetends) create powerful rhythms, and a sense of recurring dream.

That the subject is distant, even exotic, contributes to the mystique. That the poem is not continuous or linear may also contribute, at least at first. Forché is employing montage—the technique of combining disparate elements into a unified whole. In Forché's hands, montage means composing without violating essential qualities of the vision she describes in her notes on the poem as "polyphonic, broken, haunted, and in ruins, with no possibility of restoration." Individual images may not be surreal, but the world about which she writes and her discontinuous presentation of it may seem to be. Thus, montage permits one to share in comprehending and feeling.

Themes and Meanings

Few American poets of the last hundred years have dedicated themselves to witnessing great human rights catastrophes. From Forché's early interest in people's vibrancy and suffering has grown a poetry that applies a persuasive lyricism to some of the worst horrors of our age. In portraying what she observes (and what she feels while observing), Forché imparts immediacy and emotional intensity to vignettes of political significance. After observing the grisly prelude to El Salvador's civil war in the 1970's, she vowed, "I will live/ and living cry out until my voice is gone/ to its hollow of earth." The power and desperation of this declaration must be understood against the background of two realizations that Forché made at that time. First, language lacked the means to describe horrors she was seeing; in fact, the shock might well render one speechless. Second, among the societies and nations of the world, Americans were anomalous—protected yet confined in relative calm "like netted fish." Witnessing events in various parts of the world severed Forché from the complacency of her country and from hope of comfort and rest.

The travel—geographical and spiritual—that led to "The Angel of History" might be seen as fulfilling the legacy of Anna, the Slovak grandmother Forché mentions throughout her poetry, who had firsthand experience of World War II and became, in "What It Cost," the first other voice to speak an entire Forché poem. Forché's program, explicit by the end of the 1970's, has included intensive study of languages, translations of poets such as Salvadoran Claribel Alegría, and the production of the 1993 anthology *Against Forgetting: Twentieth-Century Poetry of Witness*. Thirteen years separate the publication of her second and third books of poems, a period that she calls "the muffling and silence of a decade." When the "wound" of her accumulated experiences opened, "The Angel of History" took her beyond the limits of the "first-person, free-verse, lyric-narrative of my earlier years."

Another valuable context for appreciating the poem is its epigraph, the German Jewish Marxist philosopher and critic Walter Benjamin's description of the angel of history's helplessness amid ruin. To the angel, history is "one single catastrophe which keeps piling wreckage." He would like to "make whole what has been smashed," but he is propelled "irresistibly . . . into the future." The storm blows from Paradise, indicating both the origin of the angel and the standard against which he views history. Moreover, the storm, carrying him backward, blows so hard that the angel cannot close his wings. That such a figure, longing to repair the infinite ruins, cannot free himself from the catastrophe suggests the immensity against which Forché's characters struggle.

When the Modernist poet T. S. Eliot wrote of the horrors and disillusionment of World War I in his famous poem *The Waste Land* (1922), he chose urban European settings and pitted imagery of illness and dissipation against the vulnerable beauty of the month of April. Seven decades later, when Carolyn Forché wrote of the horrors of World War II in "The Angel of History," April was the time that "The tubercular man offers his cigarette and the snow falls, patiently, across the spring flowers." Eliot is notorious for having composed, from fragments of the world's cultures, allusions to traditions that he and many of his contemporaries believed had been destroyed by World War I. Forché, too, composes from fragments, but "The Angel of History" consists of individuals' memories. Her main character has survived the horrors of persecution, grief, dislocation, and continuing trauma, while the speaker herself has lived through the evacuation of Beirut.

The speaker's carrying and giving birth to her boy emphasize one of the great causes of Ellie's suffering—the loss of two sons. Forché also makes gestation and birth her metaphor for the immense importance of "The Angel of History" and the other poems published with it, referring to it as "a work which has desired its own bodying forth." In the language of the poem's opening, the speaker's time of "intimacy and sleep" has given way to a "vigilance" of the irreparable damages that the rest of the poem—as well as the book it initiates—reveals.

Jay Paul

THE ANTI-LAZARUS

Author: Nicanor Parra (1914-
Type of poem: Lyric
First published: 1982, as "El anti-Lázaro"; collected in *Poemas Inéditos*, 1984;
  English translation collected in *Antipoems: New and Selected*, 1985

The Poem

"The Anti-Lazarus" is an "antipoem" composed of forty-seven free-verse lines divided nonsystematically into eleven stanzas. Its title is a compound word that encloses references both to the Western cultural heritage and to Nicanor Parra's own innovative artistic ideals. It points, on the one hand, to the biblical figure of Lazarus, the brother of Mary and Martha who was raised from the dead at Jesus's command (John 11:1-44). In this sense, it refers to the miracle of resurrection, one of the most important miracles within the Christian tradition. On the other hand, the use of the prefix "anti" refers to the concept of the antipoem, implying a conscious attempt at breaking with traditional lyric forms and constituting Parra's most significant contribution to contemporary poetics.

The speaker of the poem is addressing an absent interlocutor. Under the guise of an impossible and thwarting telephone call, the poetic voice speaks to an anonymous deceased poet, trying to dissuade him from rising from the dead. The poet reminds his addressee of the many negative aspects of earthly life—the daily routine, human needs and anxieties, the increasing loss of tolerance when facing setbacks, and the vacuity of literature. As a counterweight to all of these, he notes the many positive aspects that the dead man's present condition has to offer: the happiness of being a corpse, which assures absolute independence and peace, and the perfect communion of the body and the land in which it was buried.

The topic of resurrection occupies the center of the first stanza. In it, anecdotal information is reduced to a minimum, so the reader seems to witness a lyrical monologue in which one human being addresses another in order to impart his wisdom: To resuscitate oneself would be a real deed, but instead of leading to a glorious future, it would evolve into unvarying routine. The next two stanzas enumerate and unfold different aspects of that routine, both at the level of direct vital experience and at the level of philosophical concerns. Three other stanzas retrieve personal recollections from the dead poet's past, and it is in the last stanza of this group that he is characterized as a poet. In this sense, the seventh stanza becomes a central point in the poem, since it defines poetry, emblematized by Dante Alighieri's *Inferno*, as a mirage—more than an ostentatious amusement but inadequate to the task of making sense out of the effort of living.

A change of perspective is shown in the last four stanzas of the poem. Rather than continuing and advancing the skeptical depiction of life, the poetic voice discusses the beneficial elements of being dead, particularly the fact that, unlike life, death is eternal. With all of these, the name "Lazarus" acquires a new significance, and the concept of resurrection, losing its liberating potential as a tool for providing hope beyond the natural limits of human life, is reduced to a senseless effort.

Forms and Devices

The first example of Parra's innovative approach to poetry may be found in his book *Poemas y antipoemas* (1954; *Poems and Antipoems*, 1967), which gained international recognition for the author. Although "The Anti-Lazarus" does not belong to this early collection, it marks a continuation of all the formal and thematic characteristics of the antipoem. Essentially, an antipoem aims to surpass the traditional language of poetry through the recovery of the language and topics of everyday life. The search for this voice implies a new treatment of linguistic resources and the inclusion of colloquialism.

"The Anti-Lazarus" challenges and subverts literary conventions in various ways. Reviving some of the innovations introduced in modern poetry by avant-garde and post-avant-garde writers, Parra puts aside the norms of punctuation and uses only occasional quotation and exclamation marks. He also abandons the principles of regular capitalization and mixes numerals and letters. In addition, the use of formulas typical of a telephone conversation ("hello-hello"), of colloquial and affectionate expressions commonly used to attract someone's attention, and of the grammatical second person as well as several clichés taken from oral language ("my foot") contributes to the creation of an atmosphere of informality.

Another characteristic that helps to strengthen the sensation of colloquial communication is the absence of stylized imagery, of conventionally poetic vocabulary and tropes. This does not mean that the poem lacks metaphorical elements—in fact, Parra uses some metaphors from everyday speech ("you used to explode/ in insults right and left")—or other dominantly poetic devices such as chaotic enumeration ("pride blood greed"). The poet is looking for a way of generating a communication in which rhetorical and literary resources do not interfere in the fluency of the act of reading. The goal of all these expressive searches is to revive language, restoring to it a lost effectiveness.

As Naín Nómez remarks in *Poesía chilena contemporánea* (1992; contemporary Chilean poetry), "the antipoem is an inverted image of a poem, but it is not governed by the total principle of symmetry. Instead, it is governed by a particularly intense asymmetric force." This distorting force, essential to the antipoem, is satire, conceived as the center of many literary resources such as duplication, inversion, and deformation. In "The Anti-Lazarus," the satirical impulse intends to destroy the distinctive aureole that tradition has assigned to the poetic word through the ages.

Themes and Meanings

Together with love, death has been one of the major themes throughout literary history. Its presence in poetry has been a constant from the beginnings of humankind, and death has prompted various poetic forms, from elegies to epitaphs and funeral chanting. Parra believes that poets have lost their capacity for redemption if they are concerned either with the recovery of an original harmony or with access to the absolute. Since Parra's attitude as a poet is intentionally antiromantic and antisacral-izing, his concept of the "antipoem" is a reaction against the metaphysical function of language.

"The Anti-Lazarus" is a perfect example of this stance. In the poem, Parra inverts the semantic values ordinarily associated with the idea of death. He is interested neither in the pain it provokes among the survivors nor in the possibilities of life after death. On the contrary, the poet understands death as a natural phenomenon, deprived of any sacred connotation. Death is simply a state of being that is superior to all others insofar as it frees human beings from suffering while giving them endless perma-nence. Because of this conceptual shift, death is not completely emptied of meaning but is reconfigured with a new and unusual semantic value.

A second aspect present in the poem, through the characterization of the dead person being addressed as a poet, is the questioning of literature's effectiveness. Parra chooses the first section of *The Divine Comedy* as a quintessential example of literary tradition. In the *Inferno*, Dante descends through nine internal circles of Hell in a purifying journey that will finally lead him to Heaven. There he will meet Beatrice, his true love, in celestial form. Contrary to this idea of the spiritual quest, Parra seems to suggest that the real Inferno is earthly life and that, in spite of all hardships and sufferings, life is not the doorway to a better and more fulfilling state of being. Thus, the poet rejects any metaphysical way out and implies, further, that the many efforts, both religious and poetic, to sacralize death are useless.

Adopting literary historian Harold Bloom's terminology, it may be said that Parra developed his notion of antipoetry as a reaction to the modern imperative to become a strong poet. In fact, three Chileans poets figure prominently in twentieth century Latin American literature: promoter of the avant-garde Vicente Huidobro and two Nobel Prize winners, Gabriela Mistral and Pablo Neruda. In an interview with the writer Mario Benedetti, published in the Uruguayan journal *Marcha* in 1969, Parra defined his poetic project as "an anti-Neruda poetry, also anti-Vallejo, anti-Mistral, a poetry against everything, but at the same time . . . a poetry where all those echoes still resound." Ultimately, in "The Anti-Lazarus," Parra states that literary processes and the creative forces behind them are incapable of renovating the meaning of death beyond its natural condition as an everyday phenomenon. Nevertheless, Parra's negation is only partial: He does not affirm the complete fruitlessness of literary communication. Through his poetry, he expresses his faith in poetic experimentation as a way of permanent renovation.

Daniel Altamiranda

APOLOGY OF GENIUS

Author: Mina Loy (1882-1966)
Type of poem: Lyric
First published: 1922; collected in *Lunar Baedeker*, 1923

The Poem

The title "Apology of Genius" invokes the classical meaning of "apology" as *apologia*: a vigorous explanation and defense of the subject. In the poem the speaker will defend "genius," or inborn talents and capacities beyond the normal or ordinary. In particular, the poem refers to an artistic avant-garde that creates new kinds of beauty unrecognized by the philistine masses. The voice in the poem speaks for this group, explaining that "we are with God" and "we come among you." "We" appears to be those infused with genius, who are radically different from the audience being addressed. The audience within the poem is an indeterminate "you" representing those who are ignorant, insensitive, unreceptive, or otherwise incapable of comprehending the innovators and their productions.

At the outset the speaker, on behalf of all who embody genius, describes these artistic souls as superior and alienated: "Ostracized as we are with God." The sentence is truncated, as the speaker abruptly turns to the guardians of convention, "watchers of the civilized wastes," who "reverse their signals" in attempts to thwart the forward movement of the avant-garde. The theme of alienation recurs in the second stanza, when the geniuses are further characterized as "lepers" and "magically diseased." The geniuses are unaware of how deeply they disturb the masses until suddenly they confront the "smooth fools' faces" of a mocking, ignorant audience.

The next two stanzas emphasize again the separateness of geniuses from ordinary people: Geniuses are a special priesthood, "sacerdotal clowns" who can "feed on" the beauty of nature although they are materially poor. They are essentially different from ordinary people, for their inner life is structured by "curious disciplines" that are "beyond your laws," not subject to commonplace rules of art or society.

The speaker then goes on to explain that, although geniuses may be related by birth or marriage to ordinary people, they are not bound by the same rules. The avant-garde acts without reference to the constraints of convention. In another fragmentary aside the speaker characterizes genius as an armor of the soul that "still shines" in spite of ignorant people who try to suppress such inspiration. The speaker then returns to the relationship of the inspired individual with a conformist family, stating that the geniuses simply pay no attention to the attempted possessiveness of relatives (or anyone understood under the general "you").

The poem's last two stanzas describe the artistic avant-garde as creative workers set apart from everyday people and at work in mysterious hidden places hammering out beautiful objects from the raw materials of indifferent matter. Although geniuses exert monumental labor in creating great and stunning works of art, their works are misunderstood and attacked by the ignorant. The speaker again castigates the "you" who do not see the beauty being created but who regard the birth of new, original art as a crime that must be controlled or even killed by censorship.

Forms and Devices

In keeping with its subject, the defense of avant-garde art, "Apology of Genius" employs unconventional grammatical and poetic features. The only punctuation is four dashes; capital letters signal initial words of sentences as well as terms set off as abstract universals, and they mark other terms as ironic. Stanza divisions do not correspond with sentence endings, and indented lines occur in unexpected places. The first line is extended beyond the left margin, suggesting that the entire poem hinges on the initial statement of alienation and superiority. The metrical structure is thirty-eight short lines of "free verse" with a basic pattern of two-stressed lines.

"Apology of Genius" contains virtually no rhyme, with the possible exception of reverse rhymes on "wills" and "laws" in the fifth stanza and "eyes" and "scythe" in the last. However, subtle effects of vowel assonance recur, as in "moon" and "among" in the first stanza, "passion" and "man" in the second, and "corrosion with possession" in the seventh; the echoing of "Beautiful" and "immortelles" at the end is another hint of rhyme. In contrast to the absence of rhyme, the poem's rhythm is heavily marked by alliteration, with reinforcement from consonantal echoes. The second line introduces alliteration as a device with the repetition of *w* in "watchers of the civilized wastes." In the second stanza the alliterative repetition is suspended from "Lepers" at the beginning of the sentence to "luminous" five lines later, but the liquid sound pattern is sustained in "all" and "magically" and continues into the following stanza (still within the same sentence) in "lights," "until," and "fool's." Within the alliteration on the liquid *l* in the first stanza the poet introduces a nasal pattern on *m* and *n* with "moon" and "magically," echoed in "among," "innocent," and "luminous" and continuing with "unknowing," "passion," "Man," "until," "turn" and "smooth." The delicate intricacy of these patterns contrasts with the harsh plosives that abruptly end the sentence by characterizing the poem's audience as having "fools' faces" resembling "buttocks bared." The voiced plosive *b* then continues three lines down with unvoiced plosives in "pulverous pastures of poverty," bringing the alliterative emphasis almost to the point of parody. Alliteration in the last three stanzas turns on the hard *c* of "cuirass" repeated in "confuse," "corrosion," "caverns" and "Chaos".

Metaphor is the predominant figure of speech. An implicit metaphor introduces the notion of the avant-garde: "Avant-garde" is a military term denoting soldiers who lead a charge into battle and was adopted by the modernists to describe artistic innovators. The speaker of "Apology of Genius" states that guardians of conformity "reverse their signals on our track," suggesting an attempt to derail the forward progress of a group whom the poem goes on to characterize as innovative artists. The speaker returns to the metaphorical domain of the military in referring to an armor of the soul. Other metaphors are drawn from the realm of medicine and disease, as artists are called "Lepers" with "luminous sores," and from religion in references to "spirit" and the "passion of Man," to geniuses as "sacerdotal clowns" and to works of art as "mystic."

In the last stanzas the speaker suggests a mythological allusion in a vision of artists as blacksmiths or jewelers working in "raw caverns" to "forge" a kind of "imperious jewelry." Finally, the speaker asserts that ignorant people construe new art in an organic metaphor as a "delicate crop" of "immortelles," flowers preserved by drying.

Themes and Meanings

In "Apology of Genius" Mina Loy draws on the romantic vision of the artist as a uniquely gifted and inspired individual set apart from and incomprehensible to ordinary people. In Western culture the idea is as old as Plato, who regarded poets as visited by a kind of divine madness and therefore unsuitable citizens of a totally rational society. "Apology of Genius" emphasizes the ostracism of the innovative or avant-garde artist through metaphors and images calculated to shock anyone who subscribes to the philistine values that the poem deplores. The initial characterization of artistic genius as a "disease" and artists as "lepers" initiates the series of outré images, but the most startling is the poem's single simile, which likens the uncomprehending gaze of the ignorant audience's "fools' faces" to "buttocks bared" in primitive rituals of mockery. A yoking together of disparate concepts, as in the figure of "sacerdotal clowns," linking buffoon performers and priests in a single image, may call to mind the extreme conceits of seventeenth century metaphysical poems. However, Mina Loy was more immediately inspired by the Italian futurist poets who were her friends, mentors, and lovers during the years when her poetic style was being formed. Violent joining together of images drawn from the most diverse and contradictory sources is an explicit strategy of futurists, according to the manifestos of Italian futurist F. T. Marinetti. Another fusion of contrary images occurs in the final image of a field of "criminal mystic immortelles," which links the themes of antisocialism and marginalization (criminal), religious ecstasy (mystic), and organic beauty (immortelles) in a metaphor for works of art.

"Apology of Genius" also belongs to the tradition of writing that defends art and artists; examples go back to Ovid and Sir Philip Sidney. Unlike earlier writers, however, who offered arguments intended to persuade their audiences of the beauty and virtue of poetry, Loy frames this strong, even savage harangue attacking ignorance and misunderstanding as a sermonlike speech that purports to affront the ignorant reader. The poem can evoke highly charged, emotional responses, depending on whether the reader identifies with the poem's internal audience (the "you" that the speaker castigates) or with the "we" for whom the persona speaks. The choice of "cuirass" is indicative of the highly charged emotional tone of the poem; the image refers to armor protecting the soul of the genius from the casual damages of the ignorant, but a cuirass is specifically armor for the torso, suggesting that protection of the heart and other internal organs, traditional seats of the emotions, is paramount.

Helen Jaskoski

APPRAISAL

Author: Sara Teasdale (1884-1933)
Type of poem: Lyric
First published: 1926, in *Dark of the Moon*

The Poem

Sara Teasdale's "Appraisal," a metrical lyric poem, displays remarkable complexity despite the surface clarity of its nineteen lines. The poem falls within the tradition of love lyrics that celebrate rather than critique, probe, or explore. As a consequence, it creates poetic dissonance from its first line: "Never think she loves him wholly." Simultaneously the reader learns that the loved one of the poem, a man, is under critical scrutiny and that the lover, a woman, is the scrutinizer. The reader also immediately understands that the poet is distancing herself from her subjects: She presents her third-person lovers as if under a bright light, without coyness or deception. Even though the literary vehicle is a lyric poem, her intent to make a statement is clear. "Appraisal," the poet seems to say, will not be another simple evocation of a notoriously elusive emotional state. The worldly and possibly cynical connotations of the title itself reinforce this.

The blanket statements of the first two lines, "Never think she loves him wholly,/ Never believe her love is blind," could stand as universal declarations. The "she" could be any woman and the "him" any man. From these generalizations, which suggest the existence of shortcomings in the loved one, the poem moves swiftly to particulars. The shortcomings are defined and placed in context: "All his faults are locked securely/ In a closet of her mind," the poet says first. She then specifies two such faults: indecisiveness and cautiousness. She couches them in familiar terms. The indecisions appear "folded/ Like old flags that time has faded,/ Limp and streaked with rain." Similarly, the poet characterizes cautiousness as being like old clothes, "frayed and thin, with many a stain."

The middle line of the poem provides a pivot point on which the poem's focus turns. "Let them be, oh let them be," the poet says, less to the woman in the loving relationship than to the reader. The poet then makes her central statement: "There is treasure to outweigh them." The reader thus learns how the poem will circle back into the proper realm of the love lyric. The faults of the loved one may be serious, they may be of consequence, yet the man has strengths, too. From this second general statement, the poet proceeds to particulars, first by identifying a trait conventionally masculine, "proud will," followed by virtues that are more domestic: gentleness, humor, and tenderness.

Forms and Devices

Teasdale achieves part of her effect by playing against expectations, beginning with her choice of the anacreontic for a lyric form. Conventionally, anacreontics speak of the pleasures of wine, women, and song. In tone, the lyrics rarely move beyond the celebratory and joyous to the critical or even realistic. While Teasdale does address the matter of love, she chooses realism as her mode. Moreover, she delays any sense of celebration until the latter half of the poem. Anacreontics are usually in trochaic tetrameter, which refers to the poem having lines of four two-syllable feet with stresses falling on the first syllables. In "Appraisal," the poet uses this meter, although not rigidly. Teasdale, one of the most consciously musical of twentieth century poets, employs several devices to achieve rhythmic variety, including the measured substitution of iambs for trochees. Many of the lines are varied by catalexis (the dropping of the final, unaccented syllable). Strikingly, the seventh line, "Limp and streaked with rain," has only three feet, perhaps as a means of underlining the inadequacy or insufficiency being discussed.

Teasdale supports the two halves of the poem with different sets of imagery. In the first listing of shortcomings, she uses metaphors that are anything but romantic: She speaks of faded cloth and old clothing and of a closet that conceals the unwanted. The subsequent list of strengths then adopts terms of the natural world, reclaiming the romantic territory of the love poem. The shift in types of imagery provides a means of creating movement within the lyric, which otherwise lacks narrative flow. Teasdale similarly shifts poetic gears in the lyric "Those Who Love." The short poem's first stanza states its contention that "Those who love the most,/ Do not talk of their love" and supports it with such elevated examples from myth and literature as Iseult, Heloise, and Guinevere. The second stanza, in contrast, descends to the everyday, referring to "a woman I used to know." Teasdale's poem "Wisdom" similarly uses a shift of imagery to create a sense of progression. The word "spring" occurs in a literal sense, or nearly so, in the first two stanzas, then recurs in the third in a new and figurative sense, symbolizing love that was never realized.

Like these two poems, the shifting imagery in "Appraisal" includes a change from the tangible or accessible to the intangible and unreachable. "Those Who Love" turns its focus to one of those "who love the most," whose love was never requited. Similarly in "Wisdom," the "spring" that never arrived seems now forever out of reach. The shift of imagery in "Appraisal" moves the poem from the controlled realm of the domestic world to the uncontrollable realm of nature. The loved one's will is compared to the ocean's tide. He exhibits gentleness not to people but "to beast and bird." In the most beautiful evocation of his elusiveness, the poet describes him as possessing "Humor flickering hushed and wide/ As the moon on moving water." Even his tenderness escapes the lover's grasp, for it is "too deep/ To be gathered in a word." Ironically, these strengths are typically considered domestic virtues.

Also like "Those Who Love" and "Wisdom," "Appraisal" strikes a tonal balance characteristic of Teasdale's mature works. In this balance, the romantic and practical coexist. Romance never becomes sentimental just as the poet's sense of practical limits never becomes too coldly conclusive. The title "Appraisal" is thus entirely appropriate. The poem describes a judgment of value, a weighing of pluses and minuses. In the end, the balance weighs toward the heart. Teasdale stretches but does not break the anacreontic form.

Themes and Meanings

Outwardly, "Appraisal" appears to be a mature variation on a theme introduced in one of Teasdale's earliest poems. "Faults" begins with the line "They came to tell your faults to me" and ends with these lines: "Oh, they were blind, too blind to see/ Your faults had made me love you more." "Appraisal" seems to reflect the similar but more mature viewpoint of long-married lovers who have grown to know each other's weaknesses without losing sight of their strengths.

While none of Teasdale's poems depends on knowledge of her life for their understanding, such knowledge gives added dimension to many. "Appraisal" ranks among these. In her youth, Teasdale had the habit of speaking about herself in the third person. While it is common enough for poets to write of themselves from behind the guise of the third person, with Teasdale the practice was apparently a commonplace. Readers acquainted with this fact might tend to read her line in "Those Who Love" about "a woman I used to know," for instance, as referring to herself. One might approach "Appraisal" in much the same way.

The poem itself appeared in Teasdale's 1926 collection *Dark of the Moon* in a section entitled "Portraits." Alongside "Appraisal" are "Those Who Love," which portrays an unrequited but intensely felt love, and "The Wise Woman," which paints a similar picture of a woman contemplating an affair that never occurred. In "The Wise Woman," the poet wonders about a woman "who can forego/ An hour so jewelled with delight." She suggests that "She must have treasuries of joy/ That she can draw on day and night." The poem concludes with rational reconciliation: "Or is it only that she feels/ How much more safe it is to lack/ A thing that time so often steals." The collection also includes the poem "Wisdom," which speaks most pointedly and poignantly of a mutually felt love that has existed for years without physical realization. It also expresses the lover's reconciliation with the state of affairs: "It was as spring that never came,/ But we have lived enough to know/ What we have never had, remains;/ It is the things we have that go."

According to biographer Margaret Haley Carpenter, many of Teasdale's poems, especially later works, were written with poet John Hall Wheelock in mind. Among others, she points to "Appraisal" as being written specifically about Wheelock. Seen in this light, the imagery of the poem takes on a new aspect. The shift from domestic imagery to images drawn from uncontrollable nature in itself becomes part of the portrait: The man under discussion, who was never a part of Teasdale's domestic life, was as elusive to her as "the moon on moving water."

Mark Rich

APRIL INVENTORY

Author: W. D. Snodgrass (1926-   )
Type of poem: Lyric
First published: 1959, in *Heart's Needle*

The Poem

The sixty lines of "April Inventory" comprise ten stanzas of six lines each. The stanzas consist of a quatrain followed by a couplet, rhyming *ababcc*. Though W. D. Snodgrass varies the metric foot in many of his lines, the basic structure is iambic tetrameter. Many of the structural features create an interplay between fluidity and disconnection, between pause and flow. All the stanzas are closed, for example, and within all but two of them the concluding couplet is set off from the quatrain by punctuation. These minor divisions create distinct units of thought, while other features—such as the repetition of words, enjambment, and rhyme—sustain the poem's continuity.

The focus of the speaker's subjectivity is established from the beginning. The blooming of the trees reminds him of his own failure to blossom, both academically and personally. They will lose their flowers and leaves, and he will lose his teeth and hair, not to be replenished by another spring as the flowers and leaves will be. In the fourth stanza, as the speaker turns from the spring blossoms and their symbolic meaning to the academic world, the natural and the human elements merge. The girls he teaches have the pinkness of the cherry blossom, and they "Bloom gradually out of reach," as the cherry tree does. His attention broadens to include his friends, parents, and psychoanalyst—all those who expect him to flower—as he reviews his failure in academic pursuits: He has not read "one book about a book," memorized a plot, remembered the one date he learned, or found a mind he did not doubt. As a consequence, his colleagues, and not he, have advanced.

Midway through his inventory, his introspection takes another turn, and the mood shifts from the negative to the positive—from his academic failures to the modest successes in his private life. If he has fallen short in the world of books, he can name some accomplishments in personal relationships. Implicit in his assessment is that human contact and love offer more promise to him than academic competition and career obligations. He taught his classes "Whitehead's notions," taught a young woman "a song of Mahler's," and taught a child "the colors of/ A luna moth and how to love." He has learned to be tender, nurturing, caring. What he has, and has not, learned has brought important understanding and the ability to see better how he still can grow. He has not learned the old lie, that love "shall be blonder, slimmer, younger"; that he loves by his "body's hunger"; or "that the lovely world is real." Yet he has achieved a better perspective on himself and his academic shortcomings: As scholars develop ulcers and the seasons pass, he is left with the knowledge of his own worth. His inventory has brought him self-understanding and self-assurance, and the poem ends on triumphant acceptance of his own limitations and eventual decline, for he now knows that he has the strength to endure, as well as gentleness. He now can see beyond the narrow world of academics, can see that in the world at large "a loveliness exists,/ Preserves us." Ironically, he has had to fail in one respect to succeed in another, more important one, and in the expression of this ultimate insight he includes his readers.

Forms and Devices

Despite the freshness of its highly personal voice, the poem is grounded in tradition. By using the same stanzaic structure William Wordsworth used in his famous lyric, "I Wandered Lonely as a Cloud," Snodgrass gives notice that the ancestry of his poem is Romantic. This tradition is evident also in the speaker's affinity for natural objects and in his seeing his own condition mirrored in seasonal changes in the landscape, particularly the trees. The fact that the speaker is introspective, solitary, contemplative, even melancholy, is reminiscent of the Romantic spirit.

The use of conventional devices is a constant reminder throughout the poem that the speaker is a scholar struggling to come to terms with his academic obligations. Convention offers the advantages of structure, organization, and direction; at the same time, it limits the speaker to pursuits that are unsuitable to his intellectual and emotional interests and gifts. The poem's structural features and language reflect the speaker's dual loyalties. The poem's vocabulary, for example, is for the most part modern, but it includes echoes of Snodgrass's literary forebears. In the first stanza, "The blossoms snow down in my hair," recalls the well-known line in the poem "Song" by Metaphysical poet John Donne, "Till age snow white haires on thee." In the third stanza, "they smile and mind me how" recalls a similar usage by Walt Whitman in "Song of Myself": "I mind how once we lay."

These elements, together with the use of rhyme, meter, simile, and stanzaic structure, play off the poem's departure from convention as the poet conducts his self-examination in a mode that is thoroughly modern. Readers see him, as it were, on the analyst's couch confessing his innermost feelings and very private concerns, including self-doubt, a sense of failure, and moral errancy, evident in his "equivocating eye" that loves only by his "body's hunger." He is conscious of his falling teeth and hair; the "dandruff on a tabletop" is probably his own; he cannot remember plots, names, dates. The six iambic tetrameter lines set within closed stanzaic units offer a secure framework well suited to the confessor's self-doubts, vocal rhythms, and need for guidance as he takes stock of his life. The revelations are delivered in measured units of thought that can be seen as distinct stages in the speaker's growing awareness of his own worth.

Themes and Meanings

Snodgrass surveys the landscape of his life with the same equipoise and solitary grace with which Wordsworth regards the golden daffodils in his poem. There the resemblance ends, however, for Snodgrass's subject is pointedly himself—his failures and modest accomplishments. The catalpa tree, green with white blossoms, symbolizes the speaker's fundamental ambivalence toward himself. The April of the title represents early spring, when the natural landscape is festooned with blossoms. Yet April also reminds one of T. S. Eliot's pronouncement in *The Waste Land* (1922) that "April is the cruellest month, breeding Lilacs out of the dead land." This sentiment underlies what the poet says of his own landscape: Though it is spring and the natural world is blossoming, and his colleagues in the academic world are prospering, his own efforts have not borne fruit; moreover, he is all too aware of his own physical decline. This April inventory is a cruel revelation that he has fallen far short of his early promise and that his time is short.

Despite the speaker's emphasis on his own failings, he conducts his inventory with a detachment that keeps the poem from slipping into maudlin self-pity and self-abasement. One of the ways he maintains control is to keep the reader's attention on the manner of his speaking and on the poetic conventions he is employing. While being deeply sincere and personal, he is also showing wit and dexterity in the use of rhyme, meter, and language. "I taught myself to name my name," for example, momentarily diverts one's attention from the speaker's feelings to his skill with language, and the couplets concluding every stanza reiterate the fact that the speaker is practicing poetic skill as much as he is confessing. He confesses to having made "a little list" for the tenth time of all that he ought to know, and he has told others he would be "substantial, presently." That final qualifier, "presently," has the wry irony of one who knows the futility of promising what is not in his heart to do. He is sincere enough to admit that in some ways he is not entirely sincere.

The antithesis of the speaker's personal vision is the narrowness of scholarship, which blinds one to the loveliness of the world beyond academic ambition and isolates one from the gentleness and nurturing aspect of personal relationships. The "authority" of the scornful scholars in their "starchy collars" causes ulcers and, presumably, speaks in the rhythms of conventional rhyme and meter. This authority is offset by the speaker's "equivocating eye," which in academic circles is a deficit but in "the lovely world" can see the human worth beneath appearances. Throughout the poem, the academic world is seen to be at odds with the human. The mind that lapses from the strict discipline of scholarship and falls short of its demands cannot prosper in that world, but, ironically, it is through doubt, equivocation, and human imperfection that the speaker has acquired knowledge of his real worth and the "lovely world" outside. Discovery of what is in the heart is at the heart of this poem. In the end, the poem reaches beyond the personal to include all of humanity in its plea to discover where the loveliness lies, to get in touch with the worth beneath the outer trappings of life, and to feel the gentleness.

Bernard E. Morris

ARIOSTO

Author: Osip Mandelstam (1891-1938)
Type of poem: Lyric
First published: 1964, as "Ariost," in *Sobranie sochinenii*; English translation collected in *Selected Poems*, 1974

The Poem

"Ariosto" is one of many poems by Osip Mandelstam published posthumously. Written on May 4-6, 1933, during a difficult time for the poet (he was arrested only one year later by the Soviet authorities for writing a poem criticizing Joseph Stalin's cruelty), the poem expresses Mandelstam's long-standing interest in, and infatuation with, the Italian culture. The poem was written while Mandelstam was in the Crimea, in the south of Russia, where he also wrote an essay about another Italian poet, "Conversation with Dante." There are two variants of "Ariosto," but the one discussed here is considered to be more authentic. According to Nadezhda Mandelstam, his widow, his poems were confiscated upon his arrest, and he wrote the second version during his house confinement in Voronezh in 1934; the original version was found later.

Mandelstam opens the poem with the name of Ludovico Ariosto (1474-1533), thus establishing at the outset the focal point of the poem. Mandelstam considers Ariosto to be one of Italy's most delightful and wisest poets, but lately Ariosto "has a frog in his throat" and "amuses himself with the names of fish," spilling "nonsense into the seas." This mixture of profound respect and lighthearted familiarity is typical of Mandelstam's treatment of great poets he admired. In his poetry, Ariosto is playing like a musician "with ten cymbals," lost somewhat in "the maze of chivalric scandals"—a reference to the problems he faced as a diplomat at the Italian courts of his time.

In the third stanza, Mandelstam likens Ariosto to the greatest Russian poet, Alexander Pushkin, calling him "a Pushkin in the language of cicadas," who combines "Mediterranean haughtiness" with the Russian's melancholy. Ariosto plays wanton tricks with his hero Orlando in *Orlando furioso* (1516, 1521, 1532; English translation, 1591), undergoing his own metamorphosis in the process. His playfulness is further exemplified by his command to the sea, "roar but don't think!" and to the maiden on the rock, "lie there without bedclothes!" which are taken directly from the tenth song of *Orlando furioso* and indirectly from Pushkin. Indeed, Mandelstam claims, humankind has not had enough of such powerful voices, who can tell wonderful stories again and again that make one's blood run quicker and cause one's ears to roar—an allusion to an artist's power to inspire and make life more vibrant. Mandelstam calls Ariosto's native city, Ferrara, a "lizard city with a crust for a heart, and no soul," voicing his disdain for the intrigues, cloak-and-dagger atmosphere, and disregard for the well-being of the common person. He calls on Ferrara to produce more men like Ariosto and fewer men like the ruthless rulers and courtiers with whom Ariosto had to contend.

In the next stanza, Mandelstam turns to the present, saying that it is cold in Europe and dark in Italy. Both adjectives, cold and dark, are the opposites of what the south and Italy, indeed all Europe, should stand for. He bemoans the fact that raw power has taken over in the 1930's. Despite all of this, Ariosto continues to improve on his act, looking blissfully on the "lamb on the hill" (peasant in the field), at a "monk on his donkey" (Ariosto himself had a desire at one time to become a monk), and at "Duke's men-at-arms" carrying out the silly orders of their masters, drunk and bloated with drink and food, while the common people are living in blight (a baby "dozing under a net of flies"). Mandelstam continues to admire Ariosto in the eighth stanza. He loves "his desperate leisure,/ his babble, the salt and sugar of his words,/ the sounds happily conspiring in twos and threes." Ariosto's works are beautiful as they are and should be accepted as such rather than be subjected to detailed analysis. By asking, "Why should I want to split the pearl?" Mandelstam leaves well enough alone, as if afraid to succumb to the lure of Italian loquaciousness and thereby betray his own language.

In the last stanza, Mandelstam wishes to unite Ariosto's azure sea and the Black Sea "into one wide fraternal blue." He assures Ariosto that this difficult age will eventually pass. The line "We too know it well" resembles a formulaic phrase from a Russian fairy tale as well as from Pushkin's *Ruslan i Lyudmila* (1820; English translation, 1936). By using the pronoun "we," Mandelstam acknowledges that the Russians have feasted on the poetry of their Italian colleagues, assuring the great Italian poet of their fraternal bond because they have drunk wine from the same source—the shores of the Mediterranean.

Forms and Devices

"Ariosto" consists of nine quatrains of twelve-syllabic lines regularly rhymed *abba*. It is replete with images and metaphors. Speaking of Ariosto's poetry, the poet mentions the frog in Ariosto's throat, his preoccupation with the names of the fish, and his raining of nonsense into the seas as a sign of diminution of his poetic power, despite calling him a "musician with ten cymbals." While averring that his greatest love in Italian culture is Dante, while Ariosto and Torquato Tasso, for example, are not without reproach, Mandelstam cannot deny the mellifluousness of Ariosto's language as being "the language of cicadas." He points out again the musicality of Ariosto's language, referring to it as "the salt and sugar of his words" and to its sounds as "happily conspiring in twos and threes," clearly having in mind the highly rhythmical and uncomplicated interchange of vowels and consonants that lend the Italian language its sonorous quality.

Mandelstam reserves his harshest criticism for the circumstances of Ariosto's surrounding, calling Ferrara a "lizard city" teeming with crawling, slimy creatures, its collective heart encrusted and cold, without a soul. With the image "swallowing a barber's hand," however, Mandelstam refers to Ferrara, Peter the Great (who was in the habit of shaving beards, pulling teeth, and chopping heads off of his incalcitrant subjects), and, in a roundabout way, Joseph Stalin. These references are contrasted by peaceful and charming figures, a lamb on the hill and a monk on a donkey, from Ariosto's artistic milieu.

Other striking images are "the maze of chivalric scandals," which underscores the underground atmosphere of the authorities in Ariosto's surroundings; "the maiden on the rock," which is borrowed from both Ariosto and Pushkin's poem "Storm," thus binding the two poets; the cold of Europe and darkness of Italy as befitting the climate in Europe of the 1930's; and the soldiers of Ariosto's rulers, "silly with wine and the plague and garlic," as creatures unworthy of a high artist such as Ariosto.

Themes and Meanings

The basic theme of the poem is encapsulated in Mandelstam's repeated declaration, through the invocation of Ariosto, of his physical and spiritual longing for Italy and Europe. He visited Italy only twice in his life, but he always manifested a kinship with this country and its culture. However, it is not so much the love for Italy's beauty and pleasant climate, although that too is often acknowledged, as it is the love for its spirit as a focal point of an entire culture to which Mandelstam subscribes. The fact that Italy lies in the south of Europe enhances Mandelstam's admiration for it, for he always had a soft spot in his heart for southern regions, be it in Russia or in Europe. Mandelstam goes a step further and declares his love for the entire Mediterranean, calling it a "holy land" and thinking of it as the cradle of Western civilization.

That Mandelstam thought highly of this civilization at its peak can best be seen when he contrasts it with the "cold" and "darkness" of the present, in both Italy and the poet's own land. Yet, noblesse of the spirit and art will survive and triumph over the brute force of evil and darkness, as he assures Ariosto at the end of the poem. At the same time, Mandelstam declares a fraternity of poets ("we've drunk mead on its [Mediterranean] shores") by uniting Ariosto's "azure and our Black Sea together" as a manifestation of a universal brotherhood of spirit and art.

Another theme, appearing in many of Mandelstam's poems in the last decade of his life, is the spirit of the time and a poet's role and fate within it. He finds a parallel between Ariosto's Ferrara and his own Russia in that they are both in the throes of tyranny. In his troubles with the Soviet regime, Mandelstam finds kinship with Ariosto and his time. Even when he is critical of Ariosto's disregard for the plight of his fellow citizens and his avoidance of the wrath of the powers-that-be, Mandelstam only wishes he himself could do the same. By blaming the dictatorial conditions in Ferrara for the diminution of Ariosto's art, Mandelstam alludes to similar phenomena in his own land. Ariosto was frequently at loggerheads with the authorities but managed to survive and even to flourish—something Mandelstam wished to do but of which he was incapable. By extolling the achievements of Ariosto under such circumstances, he is expressing his faith in the survival of poets and the arts.

Vasa D. Mihailovich

ARMS AND THE BOY

Author: Wilfred Owen (1893-1918)
Type of poem: Lyric
First published: 1920, in *Poems by Wilfred Owen*

The Poem

The poetry of Wilfred Owen must be discussed in its historical context. Owen was one of a generation of British poets of World War I, an educated class of soldier-poets whose poetry can be divided into two distinct periods. The first period is roughly from 1914 to the Battle of the Somme in 1916. In this period, the poetic voice of the generation was generally patriotic and heroic. However, as the war dragged on, the carnage and suffering seemed ceaseless and pointless, since the front lines changed by only a few miles from year to year. The second period of British war poetry is the period to which Owen's important work belongs.

While the officer-poets were becoming deeply disillusioned by the war, a gap was growing between the men fighting and the civilians at home in Britain: Soldiers home on leave found it impossible for their families to understand the realities of trench warfare. Owen wrote, in a preface to a volume of poems planned but not published in his lifetime, "My subject is War, and the pity of War. The Poetry is in the pity." Owen's purpose in "Arms and the Boy" is to communicate some of his view of the "pity of War" to British civilians.

"Arms and the Boy" is a twelve-line meditation on the unnaturalness of weapons. In the first two stanzas, the poet presents a method of training a young boy to know, use, and appreciate a bayonet blade, bullets, and a cartridge. The instructions are heavy with irony. The poem begins: "Let the boy try along this bayonet-blade/ How cold steel is." The first four lines describe, in harsh detail, the "madman's flash" of that blade, "Blue with all malice."

The second four lines speak of the "blind, blunt bullet-heads" and the sharp "cartridges of fine zinc teeth." It is clear that the boy is not familiar with these weapons; this is a first acquaintance with the implements of death. While the first stanza emphasizes the cold malice of the blade, the second stanza moves on to the "sharpness of grief and death."

In the final four lines, the poet makes his point. This child's teeth "seem for laughing round an apple." He hides no claws, nor talons, nor antlers for fighting. God has not made this boy for war, but he will be carefully taught and groomed in the implements of death by the elder generation that Owen condemns as responsible for the war.

In this poem Owen has written of a general situation rather than a specific war. He creates a picture that any English citizen at home can imagine, of boys playing soldier. This is Owen's voice in 1918, saying that war is cruel and that its greatest cruelty is in the destruction of youth and beauty. In the context of 1918 and a generation of young men killed in the trenches, this innocent youth is doomed. The universality of the statement does not weaken its bitterness, for the boy and the "blind, blunt" bullets are not mere generalities after all.

Forms and Devices

Owen was not merely a poet of protest. He was also a poet of technical accomplishment, originality, and assurance. He was greatly influenced by classical models, particularly the nineteenth century British poets John Keats and Alfred, Lord Tennyson. He was accomplished in the art and beauty of the form and language of poetry.

The title of the poem is literary, calling to mind Bernard Shaw's *Arms and the Man* (1894), as well as the opening of Vergil's *Aeneid* (30-19 B.C.): "Of arms I sing, and of the man." Such is Owen's control of his material, that by the simple contrast of the heroic man of Vergil's Greek epic with the British schoolboy of his poem, he manages to set a tone of ironic contrast at once.

"Arms and the Boy" is similar in feeling to an elegy, a meditative poem of lamentation for the dead. By the use of this classic form, he is able to indicate a complex progression of feeling, from protest against the futile carnage of the war, to anger at the waste of young life, to a turning inward toward sadness and grief. He mourns an entire generation of innocent youth.

Throughout the poem, Owen uses sensuous, beautiful language and the languid *l* sounds in "Let," "Lend," and "blind, blunt bullet-heads" to heighten the contrast with his harsh message, the cold ugliness of his subject: guns, bullets, implements of carnage, suffering, and death. Thus the rich, musical language of the poem is carefully chosen for its dissonance. The sensuous *l* contrasts with the alliteration of the cold, hard *c* and *k* of the "cold steel," which is "keen with hunger or blood," and the "cartridges of fine zinc." Owen's skill as a poet is evident not only in this use of alliteration but also in his rhyme scheme. He uses inexact or slant rhymes: blade/blood, flash/flesh, heads/lads, teeth/death, apple/supple, heels/curls.

Owen makes no attempt to conceal his homosexual orientation. The homoerotic elements in the poem reflect an intermingling of feelings. Owen presents the relationship of war to the young soldier in the terms of sexual experimentation: "long to nuzzle" and "try" and "stroke" and "famishing for flesh." His imagery is strongly physical, with emphasis on parts of the body: teeth, fingers, heels, and hair. This language reflects the deep feelings that developed between the fighting men and the young officers in the heightened atmosphere of imminent death found in the trenches.

The camaraderie of the trenches is intensified into a love that is, in Owen's case, homosexual but also expresses his deep sorrow at the waste of tender young lives. Even in the works of heterosexual poets of 1918, the image of a beautiful young man dying in the arms of fellow soldiers aroused feelings of love. This homoerotic motif in Great War writings is an expression of a very literary war, reflecting the classical education of the generation, raised on the Greek and Latin of the *Iliad* and the *Aeneid*, and the love of heroes like Achilles and Patroclus.

Themes and Meanings

"Arms and the Boy" is a poem written for a specific purpose: to convey a message about the horror of World War I, from the experience of a soldier who has witnessed the catastrophe of trench warfare to a public composed of patriotic civilians at home in Britain. The poem is an expression of the alienation between the separate worlds. The poet sees the life at home as make-believe, like boys playing soldier, while the world of bombardment and slaughter, the world of malice and madmen, is the real world for the duration of the war. The reality for an entire generation of young men was that they were not likely to survive the horror of the "blind, blunt bullet-heads."

Owen was strongly moved by the waste of young life, of children whose laughter and play would be cut off by bullets which would "nuzzle in the hearts of lads." His poem is a protest against the exploitation of the younger generation for a political purpose that he sees as increasingly futile. By deliberately using images of childhood and the school yard, of "the boy" and "lads" playing at soldiers, he conveys the theme that war and weapons must be taught, that they are not natural to the innocent young of the species but are a tool of the older generation of government and military decision makers. This is one of the meanings Owen seeks to reveal to the civilian population.

There is, however, a sense of the inevitableness of death for these boys in the poem. They are no match for the bullets and cartridges, and the final end is sure to be "grief and death." There is a sense of endurance, an acceptance that there is no fate but violent death, a state that Owen reached only after a period of inward contemplation during his own convalescence in the hospital. He would go back to join the boys at the front, in a war that civilians could never understand and poets could never explain. Owen died in action only a few days before the armistice. He could not save the innocent child, the boy with supple fingers and thick curls. He could not save himself. All that the true war poet could do was warn the next generation.

"Arms and the Boy," for all its graphic description of malicious weaponry, has a musing quality. While Owen's aim is to communicate the horror, futility, and unnatural state of war to civilians and future generations, the poem is his personal meditation on the "pity of War." He reveals his own political protest, his homosexual love for the beauty of young men, and his mastery of classical poetic devices.

Susan Butterworth

ARS POETICA

Author: Archibald MacLeish (1892-1982)
Type of poem: Lyric
First published: 1926, in *Streets in the Moon*

The Poem

"Ars Poetica" is a short poem in free verse, its twenty-four lines divided into three stanzas of four couplets each. The Latin title may be translated as "art of poetry," "art of poetics," or "poetic art." Using the poetic form, the author attempts to portray his concept of the "art of poetry." For this reason, "Ars Poetica" is often used as an example of what (and how) a poem "should be."

The poem uses loosely rhymed couplets to project the author's powerful images. A dash follows every third couplet, emphasizing the importance of the fourth couplet in summing up the stanza. In the beginning, MacLeish draws the reader in with three couplets that compare a poem to various physical objects and which seem perfect in both word and cadence. These similes appear to illustrate the author's belief that a poem must be silent in its clarity, transcending words themselves. In the final couplet of the first stanza, he repeats the phrase "A poem should be." While the first six lines describe objects in repose, the last couplet both ties together and climaxes the building images by sending the reader upward in the rush of birds taking to the sky.

In the second stanza, the poem becomes more specific, using the stark image of branches silhouetted against a moon to denote the eternal quality of a poem. MacLeish repeats the first couplet in the last two lines: "A poem should be motionless in time/ As the moon climbs." Though the juxtaposition of a climbing moon with the assertion of motionlessness seems contradictory, the middle two couplets explain his thinking. The second couplet likens the hypothetical poem to the twigs that, once impressed on the mind in their vision of black "night-entangled trees" against the bright moon, remain fixed there as the moon moves. In the third couplet MacLeish becomes even more specific, asking the reader to recall the memories brought to mind by such an image and to compare them to a poem that is as firmly anchored in time as those memories.

The poem's third stanza departs from the previous two in its tone as MacLeish becomes bolder in his assertion of what a poem "should be." In the middle two couplets, he takes the reader on a journey through all of humankind's strife and love with only a few strokes of his metaphorical pen. Yet in his first and last couplets, he abandons image and states precisely his feelings about the art of poetry. The final two lines, "A poem should not mean/ But be," are brief and to the point, having an almost Zenlike quality to them. The words bring the reader to a place of simple rest after an emotive passage through the more esoteric images of the poem. These last two lines of "Ars Poetica" are famous and are often quoted in books on poetry.

Forms and Devices

In a sense, "Ars Poetica" must be in its entirety a metaphor for poetry itself; when it is pulled apart piece by piece, one can see the clever construction that pushes the reader along to an inevitable conclusion. As MacLeish wrote in his *Poetry and Experience* (1960), "If the fragments of experience are in truth parts of a whole, and if the relation of the parts to each other and thus to the whole can in truth be *seen, sensed, felt* in the fragments themselves, then there is meaning in that seeing, in that sensing, in that feeling—extraordinary meaning."

The best poetry needs only a few words to engage readers' imaginations and to make them participants in the poem's creation. In "Ars Poetica" MacLeish employs similes to evoke the reader's senses. The couplet "A poem should be palpable and mute/ As a globed fruit" allows the reader to imagine the fruit—perhaps an apple lying on a bench in the late afternoon sun. It is beautiful yet silent. The next two lines employ the sense of touch. It is easy to conjure up the feeling of rubbing a metal medallion, noting its worn ridges and wondering about its history. Again, in the third couplet, the reader relates to the person suggested by "the sleeve-worn stone." Someone (or perhaps generations of people) has leaned for long hours on the window ledge, waiting, perhaps hoping for a lover or watching anxiously for a child. With similes such as this, the reader is able to fill in the spaces, to embroider the words with his or her own experiences, thus creating a poem unique with each reading.

Note, too, the careful placing of words to make rolling, alliterative sounds: palpable, mute, globed, fruit. In the second couplet, the words dumb, old, medallions, and thumb carry the reader along, as do the phrases in the third couplet. In the second stanza, the similes employ repetitive sounds. The first and last couplets seem almost to murmur with their preponderance of soft words using the letter *m*. In the second couplet, the line "Twig by twig the night-entangled trees" uses the harsher *t* sound to portray a certain amount of conflict.

In the last stanza metaphor takes center stage. An empty doorway and a maple leaf symbolize "all the history of grief." More obscure, perhaps, is the line "The leaning grasses and two lights above the sea," denoting love. Again, the reader must fill in his or her own experience. As Robert Frost said, "Poetry begins in metaphor, in trivial metaphors, and goes on to the profoundest thinking that we have."

Themes and Meanings

Although MacLeish was originally strongly influenced by Ezra Pound and T. S. Eliot, he later came to believe their scholastic poetry was not relevant to society. He turned to the poets of the past, such as Geoffrey Chaucer, William Shakespeare, and John Milton, as examples of how modern poets should make it their duty to participate in the social and political issues of the day.

"Ars Poetica," however, seems more clearly influenced by MacLeish's reverence for Chinese poetry. In *Poetry and Experience*, he quotes extensively from the third century Chinese poet Lu Chi and his famous poem, the *Wên Fu* (*Essay on Literature*). He asserts that "Far more than either Aristotle or Horace, Lu Chi speaks to our condition as contemporary men." In Chinese poetry, relationship is left to be inferred from the context, from the logic of the situation. MacLeish believed that the skill of the Chinese as imagemakers in paint, ink, or words has never been equaled.

In "Ars Poetica" he tries to capture an uncomplicated and direct path to the heart. Each of the couplets can almost be seen as a separate Chinese painting, drawn quickly and masterfully with the sparest of strokes. In particular, the quirky fourth couplet stands out. Its arrhythmic, atonal lines ("A poem should be wordless/ As the flight of birds") not only shows MacLeish's belief that a poem transcends the words of which it is composed but also includes the image of birds in flight, one that is seen repeatedly in Chinese art and poetry. It is a strong archetypal symbol for freedom, including freedom from the common words and meanings that bind all of humankind. The fourth couplet's break in rhythm from the previous three seems to echo this freedom.

In every word of this poem, MacLeish strives for such simplicity and passion, almost as if he were creating an extended haiku. Lu Chi writes "We poets struggle with Non-being to force it to yield Being;/ We knock upon silence for an answering music." MacLeish elaborates on this in the following passage: "The poet's labor is to struggle with the meaningless and silence of the world until he can force it to mean: until he can make the silence answer and the non-Being BE. It is a labor which undertakes to 'know' the world not by exegesis or demonstration or proofs but directly, as a man knows apple in the mouth."

It is futile to spend too much time attempting to extract meaning from a poem which has as its basic tenet the idea that a poem does *not* mean, but simply exists. MacLeish maintains that the art of poetry is a magic one and that the poet is a magician who extracts substance from nonsubstance. He cites often Lu Chi's belief that the poet is one who "traps Heaven and Earth in the cage of form."

Sue Storm

AS I WALKED OUT ONE EVENING

Author: W. H. Auden (1907-1973)
Type of poem: Narrative
First published: 1940, in *Another Time*

The Poem

"As I walked out one evening" contains fifteen four-line stanzas rhyming *abcb*. The rhymes are masculine; the meter is a flexible iambic trimeter with all the unrhymed lines ending with an additional unstressed syllable. The language of this poem, which has no title but is usually designated by its first line, is relatively simple, but the poem presents three voices, one of which conveys a relatively short but beautiful love lyric, embedded in a more elaborate structure that complicates the reader's response.

The first voice, not that of a lover but of an observer who is walking on an urban street toward a river, occupies the first stanza and three lines of the second. The walker is in a mood to characterize the passing crowds of people as "fields of harvest wheat." Nearing the "brimming river," this person hears a voice brimming with the rapture of love.

The lovers are embracing under a railroad bridge. One of them, the poem's second voice, is first heard in the last line of the second stanza, "Love has no ending," an assertion that may serve as a title of the song that follows and certainly expressive of its theme. In the next three stanzas the lover pledges undying love in a series of extravagant assertions reminiscent of Robert Burns's "A Red, Red Rose" (1796), in which the speaker vows to love his lady "till a' the seas gang dry." In this poem the couple's love will continue "till the ocean/ Is folded and hung up to dry."

Whereas with Burns the love lyric is the whole poem, however, here there is not only the human observer but also, beginning in the sixth stanza, "all the clocks in the city." The third voice, which proceeds from the mention of the clocks, occupies thirty-four of the poem's sixty lines and ominously contradicts the lover's vow in a series of stark images which have the effect of darkly telescoping the lovers' real, finite time—a time that "leaks away" to its inevitable end. Auden encloses these lines within single quotation marks. The images pile up: snow, glaciers, deserts, tears, and agonized looks in mirrors, as well as perverse variations of nursery rhymes in which, for instance, Jill does not simply tumble down a hill after Jack but, in a context that suggests sexual violence, "goes down on her back." This voice does not deny love, but insists, in the poem's penultimate stanza, that human love is not only finite but "crooked."

The observer's voice returns in the last stanza. The hour is now late, the lovers are no longer there, the clocks are no longer chiming, and the river continues to flow.

Forms and Devices

"As I walked out one evening" reflects Auden's interest in the ballad, a form which he often practiced in the late 1930's, when this poem was composed. The stanza is a slight variation of the ballad stanza of alternate tetrameter and trimeter lines, while the rhyme scheme is typical of the ballad. Several characteristics of the venerable English and Scottish folk ballad tradition are found here: plain diction, carefully calculated repetitions of words and phrases, a tendency toward dialogue, abrupt transitions, and a pervasive sense of irony.

Only four words in the poem have more than two syllables, and a number of lines are entirely monosyllabic. The repetitions include the lover's "I'll love you"; the third voice's iteration of imperative verbs such as "plunge," "look," and "stand"; and the adjectival repetition at the beginning of the last stanza: "It was late, late in the evening." The simplicity of the language heightens the emotional complexity of the poem. The lover's vows are packed with images of vitality, but the stark imagery that follows suggests a world whose corruption threatens to infect lovers no matter how sincere their intentions.

The irony exists on two levels. It is of course ironic that the lovers can hardly imagine the difficulties involved in maintaining their devotion through the ordinary vicissitudes of life. This poem, however, envelops not only the characters but also its audience in the irony. The faithless, nightmarish world depicted beginning in the sixth stanza has the effect of defying the common hopes and aspirations not only of young lovers but of all who believe in the effectuality of human love.

The voices of the poem do not engage in dialogue in the ordinary sense. Only one of the lovers is heard; the reader can only wonder about the reaction of the other. However, the third voice of the poem, representing time, is in effect "talking back" to the lover, although it seems unlikely that the latter is listening. The voice of time dismisses the lover's promises bluntly but ambiguously: "Life remains a blessing/ Although you cannot bless." Love exists in the world, but the young lover, busy with his own affirmations, has no inkling of its obstacles and contrarieties.

The first transition is the abrupt interposition of the voice of time in the sixth stanza, which is not the voice of author or observer-narrator, neither of whom offers any overt comment on its ominous message. The transition from that message to "late, late in the evening" in the last stanza renders interpretation problematic. The lovers have gone away, whether together or individually the reader does not know. The fact that the clocks are no longer chiming but that the "deep river" flows on might be read as a repudiation of a society given to technological measurement of time and a reaffirmation of the natural order of which young love is a universal component—but the river is its own symbol of the passing time that bids to challenge the lover's vows.

Themes and Meanings

An almost obsessive concentration on time—particularly its clash with the aspirations of young love—dominates the poem. It is not, however, a *carpe diem* ("seize the day") poem of the type that became popular in the seventeenth century and has found many echoes in the twentieth. In the *carpe diem* tradition the lover's intent is often seductive, or can be easily so interpreted. Typically he reminds his beloved that her youthful beauty will soon fade, that she cannot long expect such appreciation as he is now bestowing on her. If he has a certain measure of tact, he may even concede that he too is subject to the ravages of time, but in any event he urges consummation of their love.

"As I walked out one evening," like Burns's "A Red, Red Rose," works quite otherwise. Here is a speaker whose evident sincerity—and naïveté—leads to exaggerated pledges which any observer but a thoroughgoing cynic might applaud. It seems fitting, after all, that true love should generate such vows. A failure to utter them would be somehow disappointing.

The love lyric of Auden's poem, however, is framed not only by the observer, who may well approve, but by the stern and uncompromising voice associated with the city clocks. A future the lover can scarcely imagine will test him with a succession of buffets while life "leaks away." Do the lovers under the railroad bridge sense this truth in the chiming of the town's clocks? Auden's poem does not answer such a question, but surely if the two do not hear the message now, they will soon enough.

This voice which occupies the major portion of the poem strikes a tone that suggests not only time, however, but a particularly harsh and forbidding time. "As I walked out one evening" deviates from the usual ballad in its tendency toward interpretative comment in this third voice, not so much the voice of *time* as the voice of *the times*. Auden composed the poem in 1937, when forces were gathering for a world war, the second of the poet's lifetime. While no explicit references to the era mark this poem, its insistence on the "crookedness" of humans in the face of cataclysmic disorders and vague horrors represents a challenge to the lovers beyond the ordinary power of time considered as an agent of the natural order.

Nature, however, reasserts itself in the consciousness of the observer in the last stanza. Although the clocks will strike again, they are quiet at least for now. The lovers are gone but will presumably meet again and confirm their love in these most difficult of times. The final image of the river, which flows on as time does in the most tumultuous epochs, may signify time according to nature. If so, the last line of the poem affirms an order in which human love has a chance to prevail—an order that persists through the most disorderly of times.

Robert P. Ellis

AS WE FORGIVE THOSE

Author: Eric Pankey (1959-
Type of poem: Lyric
First published: 1987; collected in *Heartwood*, 1988

The Poem

"As We Forgive Those," a relatively short poem in free verse, is divided into four stanzas of unequal length and makes use of a natural, almost colloquial, tone to examine rather weighty theological issues. The poem's title is drawn from the Lord's Prayer, widely used in Protestant Christianity, and suggests the struggle of the poet to reconcile his understanding of that prayer, especially its admonitions concerning forgiveness, with his own family experience.

The bulk of Pankey's verse—collected in *For the New Year* (1984), *Heartwood* (1988), *Apocrypha* (1991), and *The Late Romances* (1997)—suggests both a deep fascination with and strong commitment to Christianity, as well as an uneasiness concerning its many permutations and manifestations. While Pankey's discomfort with Christian dogmatism and facile fundamentalism is evident, it is equally clear that such discomfort leads him to examine carefully his own faith and its relationship to his childhood growing up in the United States during the 1960's and early 1970's.

In various poems, particularly those collected in *Heartwood* (where "As We Forgive Those" appears), no clear line exists between the speaker's voice in the poem and that of the poet. While such conflation is common in contemporary poetry, in Pankey's case it is used to dramatic effect to speak about religious experience. Like the poet Andrew Hudgins in his *The Glass Hammer* (1994), Pankey explores his family's history, demonstrating how it shapes his way of seeing the world and his understanding of God's ways in that world.

"As We Forgive Those" begins with the most ordinary of domestic rituals: a father excusing his son from the dinner table. This ritual, however, resonates in the poem because it clearly helps determine the speaker's notion of forgiveness. By demonstrating the power of his father who "excuses" him from the dinner table, a most desirable pardon for any young boy, Pankey intimates that his earthly existence offers him his only clues for coming to terms with his faith.

Although the speaker in the poem says that "All my life I was a child," the poem itself presents the action as part of the past. Thus, Pankey writes from an adult perspective about the innocence of childhood faith and the youthful tendency toward a literal understanding of the language of faith. Instead of a child's thoughts, the poem displays a grown man mulling over his boyhood memories, an activity through which he gains insights that are distinctly mature. Moreover, the poem hinges upon the speaker's explication or close reading of the Lord's Prayer—an intellectual activity that demands reflective distance and allows the poet to understand better how his boyhood activities shaped his use of the prayer—while suggesting the universal power of both earthly and heavenly forgiveness.

Forms and Devices

"As We Forgive Those" finds much of its power in Pankey's use of juxtaposition and allusion. A kind of prayer itself, the poem's clear reference to the Lord's Prayer establishes a pattern of comparison for the poet that allows him to move back and forth between philosophical meditation and the remembered actions of his past.

Derived from the Latin, the word "allusion" literally means "to play with or touch upon," and it remains one of the most effective means of compression in poetry. Merely by mentioning certain names, places, events, or, in this case, specific lines from a spiritual text, the poet creates powerful associations for the reader. Clearly the historic significance of the Lord's Prayer in Christianity and the profound effect of this religion upon the Western world determines the power and resonance of this particular allusion. However, at several points in the poem, Pankey's use of allusion shifts from a universal human history, as reflected in Christendom, to the individual history of Pankey's own American boyhood—a pattern that keeps the poem from becoming mired in theological conundrums of interpretation that ultimately cannot be resolved.

Thus, in the poem's first stanza, Pankey establishes, through juxtaposition, that his own boyhood experience will serve as a metaphor for forgiveness. He remembers that as a boy he learned "to forgive from those who forgave." This is a slight alteration of the Lord's Prayer, which entreats God to "forgive us our trespasses as we forgive those who trespass against us." Yet not all Christian churches translate the word "trespass" in the same manner, and the mature Pankey struggles to remember whether he "was supposed/ to forgive those who trespassed, or my debtors."

Therefore, Pankey not only uses juxtaposition as a tool for organizing the poem's shifts from boyhood experience to theological meditation but also uses it to contrast the significant differences between the words "trespass" and "debt." These levels of juxtaposition, skillfully connected so that they cannot be completely separated, suggest the complexity of forgiveness and its direct relationship to one's own cultural context.

As the poem reveals, because Pankey's family "always owed someone or someone owed" them, he cannot remember a time when they used the word "debtor" while praying the Lord's Prayer. Instead, the poet says they concentrated on the lines, "Give us this day," a prayerful request that seemed odd to the young Pankey because he believed the day already was theirs. His parents, nevertheless, fashion the young boy's understanding of the prayer and, ultimately, his understanding of forgiveness, so that as he grows he too will pray for "this day." The poet also recalls that as a boy, when his parents argued, yelling at each other, he was told not to worry, that such fights did not concern him. From this example, he came to think of forgiveness as a condition in which one was excused from the unknown.

As the poem concludes, the poet juxtaposes the ignorance of his youth against his growing desire for knowledge. This final comparison leads Pankey closer to the mature insight toward which the poem struggles: Forgiveness demands knowledge. Fittingly, the poem culminates with the image of a shadow sweeping across all that the family owns, all for which they are in debt, and it is at this moment that the poet finally comes to a true knowledge of his condition and his need for forgiveness.

Themes and Meanings

In much of his writing, Pankey grapples with the idea of redemption in the contemporary world, a condition that, for him, is intimately linked to the Christian concept of forgiveness. The word "grapples" is appropriately used in this context because of the intellectual honesty that characterizes his struggle with faith. Pankey demands that faith be described as that which is unknown, yet believed. He contests the notion that the knowledge one finds in faith is somehow rational and provable.

In the poem "If You Can," which follows "As We Forgive Those" in *Heartwood* and may be considered a companion piece, Pankey addresses his daughter, describing his own mystical understanding of forgiveness and redemption to her. While he is perplexed by this encounter, he does indeed believe that he has been "saved." However, it is nothing he fully understands. He says, somewhat bewildered, "But saved by whom or for what/ I don't know." "If You Can" turns on a father's loving appeal to his daughter: "If you can, please, believe," the poet says, but he makes no promise that with such belief the world will miraculously become an easier place in which to live. Rather, he tells her that the rocks that will bruise her heel will be no less hard; belief will merely give her the knowledge of forgiveness and show others "where the pain is."

This faith and the hope that faithfulness may touch others seem to hover near the center of "As We Forgive Those," linked to "the maple that ruled/ [Pankey's] house half the day in sunlight, half in shade," an image that the poet uses to great effect to conclude his meditation on forgiveness. In the poem's final lines, Pankey tells of the day he walked out beneath the formidable maple and finally understood the weight of its shadow, how it "swept every inch of what we owned." He realizes that such immature pranks as his trespassing for apples, his stealing of green tomatoes to drop from trees on unsuspecting pedestrians, and his hiding behind juniper bushes to spy upon others were insignificant compared to the knowledge of his family's and his own precarious position in the world.

While the poet tells us that during that year he learned the word "omniscient" in school, as a boy his knowledge of what the word meant was woefully inadequate. Only after his prayer for knowledge is answered does he come to know that to be forgiven is to be covered in the darkness of this world while seeing to the light that lies beyond, or, as Pankey explains while looking backward, "When it covered me I knew I was forgiven."

Todd Davis

AT GRASS

Author: Philip Larkin (1922-1985)
Type of poem: Lyric
First published: 1951, in *XX Poems*

The Poem

This lyric poem, written in formal verse, presents a meditation that is triggered by a pastoral scene of two horses "at grass." The speaker first observes the horses as an unspecified "them" whose identity must be pieced together, since they are hardly noticeable against the landscape of "cold shade" in which they are comfortably at grass. They "shelter" in it and are noticeable only when the wind brushes across their tails and manes. They are not outstanding but anonymous, simple horses pasturing peacefully.

So far the speaker has only pointed out what an uninformed passerby might notice, but he knows something more about these horses: They have had their moments of fame. The reader learns that fifteen years ago they were at the center of attention at the races, surrounded by excited concern, trophies, crowds, and the colors of the "silk" worn by the jockeys. There was much at stake, as evidenced by "numbers," "distances," and "stop-press columns on the street."

This recollection leads the speaker to wonder (in a phrase with echoes from William Shakespeare), "Do memories plague their ears like flies?" That is, do memories of busier, more glorious and exciting days nag at them and stir regret? The speaker recognizes in the simple shaking of the horses' heads that regret and nostalgia are human experiences and that, on the contrary, the horses seem content to be where they are. The fact that their glory days are gone goes hand-in-hand with their aging, and they are now surrounded by shadows at dusk rather than the sunny-day "parasols" and bright silks. "Summer by summer all stole away," the speaker reflects, musing in a melancholy tone on the passage of time and the inevitable evening of life. On the other hand, the meadows are "unmolesting," in contrast with their demanding days of distinction.

These horses' names are "almanacked" and will be remembered for some time to come. However, the fact that they have "slipped" their names implies that their fame was restricting, like halters, bridles, bits, and all the other paraphernalia of racing. They "stand at ease," and the speaker notices joy and well-being in their present state. They are not measured by "fieldglass" or "stop-watch," and the only ones who see them home are their caretakers, the groom and his boy at evening, in a touching domestic relationship that is lacking in sparkle and acclaim but is caring and durable.

Forms and Devices

A scene that at first seems insignificant yields a story and an understanding of these simple horses and, by extension, given the poet's musings, of human life. The speaker reconstructs the scene of the pasturing horses and the sport of horseracing—a competitive, lucrative undertaking—in a way that can be easily understood as a metaphor for human activity. What starts off as a seemingly simple descriptive lyric raises issues that make the reader reflect more deeply.

Using sport as a metaphor for life is not a novel idea, but seldom is this metaphor presented in calmly, evenly paced metrical language. Formally this poem is quite traditional, with an involved rhyme scheme (*abcabc*) in stanzas of six metered lines that consist of four fairly regular iambic feet; with few exceptions, there are eight syllables per line. Remarkably, these conventional features are not constricting; the poet manages flexibility in his phrasing and works with rhymes whose subtle musicality provides one of the age-old pleasures of poetry. Larkin often complained that modern verse, with its formal experiments and semantic subversions, leaves out the reader. Here Larkin involves the reader not only by means of the comforting, recognizable rhythms and look of the verse but also by presenting an absorbing scene that leads the reader to ponder the issues the poet raises.

In his accurate yet colloquial phrasing, the poet evokes details of the races ("Cups and Stakes and Handicaps," "Silks," "Numbers and parasols," "fieldglass," and "stop-watch"). The crowded excitement of glory days is suggested in words and phrases such as "heat," "littered grass," "the long cry/ Hanging unhushed," words that also connote discomfort and strain. They provide a semantic echo of the opening scene, in which the wind is said to "distress tail and mane." Saying that the horses have "slipped their names," while literally referring to the fact that the horses have outlived their celebrity, also points to the freedom of quiet anonymity.

Finally, "dusk," "shadows," and "evening" alert the reader to the symbolic suggestiveness underlying the whole poem. In his diction Larkin subtly raises metaphysical issues that are dealt with in an accessible manner. The ideas come from a particular situation. They are not superimposed, nor is the scene manufactured merely to illustrate an idea. The reality takes center stage.

Themes and Meanings

Larkin sees in these horses an enviable equilibrium; they finally "stand at ease." With evening comes a world of darkness, but the horses are in the "unmolesting meadows" where only the wind "distresses" them now. One cannot help but conclude that anonymity is something Larkin treasures; the spectacle of competition and risk—vital affairs of the world though these may be—is merely momentary glitter and show. Most living occurs in the quiet and nameless moments when stability and true caring flourish. The groom and his son care for the horses, whereas the "stop-watch" crowds at "starting gates" are interested in the vagaries of worldly fortune. The racetrack and other such arenas may have their appealing features, but once these are stripped away, a more stable reality emerges. As critic Alan Brownjohn noted in his book *Philip Larkin* (1975), "Life, for Larkin and, implicitly, for all of us, is something lived mundanely, with a gradually accumulating certainty that its golden prizes are sheer illusion." Brownjohn also remarks that in Larkin's poetry "the recognized rewards and goals in life are deceptions."

Larkin sees something relieving, even joyful in the anonymous decline of the horses. Furthermore, there is something undignified about the past's "starting-gates, the crowds and cries," in contrast to the present's "unmolesting meadows." Measuring life in terms of performance violates the dignity of the spirit. Perhaps, like racehorses who are valued for three or four years of their prime, human lives are also measured and valued for a brief time but continue for some time after. "At Grass" subtly poses a number of questions. Is public acclaim the only measure of value? Can one live anonymously and be happy? Does acclaim bring happiness? Horses, unlike humans, do not invest in worldly activities; it is all the same to them whether their names are "artificed" or "faded." That seems to be Larkin's view as well.

One might wonder why the poem ends with "the groom's boy" as well as with the groom himself. The poem posits no grand reward of life as "Dusk brims the shadows." The ease that comes at evening is apparently its own reward. The way that the horses at grass fit into the overall pattern of life is that there will always be another generation of horses. Human continuity and involvement are suggested by the inclusion of the groom and his boy. The fact that Larkin mentions the boy suggests that the groom shares in the horses' fate and their rising and "faded" glory. A. E. Houseman, in his 1896 poem "To an Athlete Dying Young," celebrated the early death of a record-breaking athlete because it served to assure his lasting glory. Larkin's poem, by contrast, suggests that the fading of the glory brings fulfillment of a larger life plan. Everyone must fade and be sheltered in the "cold shade" and will be met at evening by caretakers, be they nurses and orderlies or, ultimately, the undertaker with the "bridles" of his trade.

Paul Serralheiro

AT LUCA SIGNORELLI'S RESURRECTION OF THE BODY

Author: Jorie Graham (1951-
Type of poem: Meditation
First published: 1983, in *Erosion*

The Poem

"At Luca Signorelli's Resurrection of the Body" is a long, free-verse poem of 106 lines divided into eighteen stanzas; the first seventeen stanzas have six lines and the final stanza contains four lines. The lines of this poem are mostly short and vary from two to six syllables per line, although some lines have as many as eight or nine syllables. The title immediately locates the poem's speaker in front of a fresco by Luca Signorelli, an Umbrian painter known for depicting muscular bodies in violent action, capturing them in a wide variety of poses and foreshortenings. *Resurrection of the Body* is in the San Brizo Chapel in Orvieto Cathedral, where, between 1499 and 1502, Signorelli painted a series of scenes depicting the end of the world.

Jorie Graham's persona speaks in the first person in a voice that is likely analogous to, if not wholly imitative of, the voice of the poet. With the speaker's voice so similar to Graham's, one is encouraged to read the tone of this poem as serious and philosophical. It appears that Graham will attempt to pose an answer to the introductory question, "Is it better, flesh/ that they/ should hurry so?" The poem is organized into three unannounced sections that show the speaker's meditation progressing from one subject to another. The first section comprises the first thirty-three lines, in which Graham gazes at the details of the fresco. She notices the violence of the bodies and points out how the subjects of the painting "hurry/ to enter/ their bodies." There is a bombastic and cacophonous quality to these images. Angels "blare down/ trumpets and light." Graham questions whether the spirits entering these bodies truly desire perfection because the precision of Signorelli's work, evident in the detailed muscles of the subjects in the painting, suggests that only the painter desires such perfection.

In the second section, Graham looks outside the cathedral. When she states that "Outside/ it is 1500," she brings together the time of the fresco's composition with the lyric moment of the poem. This suggests that Signorelli's frescoes have powerfully altered her perceptions of the world. Graham also juxtaposes thoughts about the figures on the wall, which remain ignorant of their experience, with a recognition that she, as a viewer of this fresco, is unable to tell them that there will be no fulfillment of their dreams of "wanting names,/ wanting/ happiness." In the third movement of the poem, Graham's thoughts lead her away from the fresco and the cathedral to a narrative about how Signorelli dissected the body of his young son who died in an accident. Graham portrays this action as a loving search for truth, emphasizing words such as "beauty," "care," and "caress." In order to understand his grief and loss, Signorelli, a master of depicting the muscles of the body, must explore what is unknown to him: the inside of his son's body.

Forms and Devices

The experience of standing in front of a painting and contemplating its meaning is an experience that is likely familiar to most readers. Poems written about this type of experience are part of a genre called ekphrastic poetry. Ekphrastic poems often show a speaker attempting to find meaning or feeling by looking intently and deeply at a painting, sculpture, or photograph. The images of the art object often become a part of the imagery of the poem. Two familiar examples of ekphrastic poetry are John Keats's "Ode on a Grecian Urn" and William Carlos Williams's "Pictures from Brueghel." There are several other ekphrastic poems in Graham's *Erosion* collection. Paintings by Signorelli, Piero della Francesca, Masaccio, Francisco de Goya, and Gustav Klimt allow Graham to interact with visual art in a way that makes art objects part of a living, breathing tradition of attempting to make philosophical sense of the world. Signorelli's painting is as real and as vivid as any image in twentieth century poetry. Just as Williams's "The Red Wheelbarrow" is about the visual importance of a commonplace object because of the mental connections that it can stimulate in one who sees it, Graham's poem focuses upon the value of art's ability to focus her thought. Art allows Graham to understand how one can make sense of the relationship between body and mind. This specific fresco is not only valuable for its intellectual and historical importance, but it is also of value because of the thoughts and responses that it continues to trigger in its viewers.

One of the most obvious aspects of this poem's form is Graham's use of a short line that approximates Williams's trimeter line. These lines, barely long enough to contain more than three or four words, require the reader to move down the page quickly. Instead of reading each line as a freestanding unit of thought or imagery, Graham's short line encourages the reader to recognize the dependence of each line upon the lines that precede and follow it. In the first stanza, an associative logic becomes apparent as Graham's thinking leads her from her command to notice the fresco to a questioning of whether such action is good and back to a recognition of the image of the angels in the fresco.

While there is a sequential, orderly logic that leads Graham from a contemplation in front of the painting into a meditation about the relationship between the body and mind, this logic may not be obvious to the reader. Graham's poem does not proceed line by line as much as it proceeds step by step. There is a movement between discursive commentary and imagistic detail that organizes the poem thought by thought. These thoughts are then broken down into lines that reflect the complications of tonal change that occur. Graham's philosophical poem does not offer a coherent argument with thesis, proof, and conclusion; it is more analogous to a private moment that the reader has been privileged to overhear, a moment in which an engaged and intelligent speaker attempts to sort something out.

Themes and Meanings

"At Luca Signorelli's Resurrection of the Body" is a poem that contemplates the relationship between body and mind. At what point, the poem asks of its readers, subject, and speaker, can the work of the mind transcend the body, or is the mind permanently fixed to the body? There is a paradox in this relationship in Graham's poem. Signorelli, who painted bodies of exquisite precision and beauty, who understood the physical nature of the body as well as anyone of his time, found himself plagued by doubt upon the death of his son and could not understand his son's death until he explored every cavern of his corpse.

Graham's attempt to understand how Signorelli graduates from the "symbolic/ to the beautiful" causes her to ask, "How far is true?" Her poem does not answer this question definitively. For Signorelli, truth was found by an exploration deep inside the body. For Graham, truth is less easily defined. The present-tense lyric moment of this poem is permanently altered by the experience of viewing the frescoes when she looks out and finds Orvieto of 1500. After this experience, Graham is unable to recognize Orvieto in the present; she can only understand it through the artifice of the past. As for the question of truth, there is no definitive truth, only a multiplicity of particulars that swirl around in the poet's mind like leaves rising in the wind. The beauty of such experience is unlike the confident assertion at the end of Keats's "Ode on a Grecian Urn": "Beauty is truth, truth beauty,—that is all/ ye know on earth, and all ye need to know." Unlike Keats's assurance that truth is beauty, Graham is unable to offer a definitive answer. Graham's truth is unstable and mutable; it is difficult to understand because it is constantly shaped by experience.

In an interview, Graham speaks of her poems as "exploded instants," moments in which sequential and lyrical moments in time move the poem along. This method allows her to capture the immediacy and timing of sequential instants in a way that mirrors the processes of thought. Instead of using narrative progression, Graham's poems are organized more impressionistically. They are composed of haikulike moments that accumulate musically instead of logically. This strategy allows Graham to incorporate moments of doubt, questioning, and uncertainty into her work. These moments, because they allow readers to understand the processes of thought in their full complexity, are the distinct achievement of Graham's poetry.

Jeffrey Greer

AT THE EXECUTED MURDERER'S GRAVE

Author: James Wright (1927-1980)
Type of poem: Meditation
First published: 1958, revised and collected in *Saint Judas*, 1959

The Poem

"At the Executed Murderer's Grave" is composed of seventy-seven lines of freely rhymed iambic pentameter. The title expresses the subject. The poet is meditating on the grave of the convicted murderer George Doty, a taxi driver from Belaire, Ohio. Doty drove a girl out of town, made a pass at her, and, when she resisted, killed her. In an interview with Dave Smith (in *The Pure Clear Word: Essays on the Poetry of James Wright*, 1982, edited by Smith), Wright explains, "Many people in that community thought [Doty] was terribly wicked, but he did not seem to be wicked. He was just a dumb guy who was suddenly thrust into the middle of the problem of evil." Doty was executed in the electric chair.

Like many of Wright's poems, this one is about the outcast. Part of his concern is the incapacity of some members of society to understand other members. The severing of communications between the living and the dead becomes, for him, the ultimate barrier to human connectedness. Kindness and vengeance, pity and loathing, empathy and fear are important contrasts in the poem.

The poem begins by showing Wright's position to the killer: "I was born/ Twenty-five miles from this infected grave." He says that his father "tried to teach me kindness," that he once went to the grave ("I made my loud display"), that he is "Now sick of lies," and that he will "add my easy grievance to the rest."

It is no easy grievance, however, as the rest of the poem will show. In fact, Wright identifies himself with the insane, "Pleased to be playing guilty." In an early version of the poem, he wrote, "I killed this man,/ This man who killed another," for "Man's wild blood has no heart to overcome/ Vengeance." In the final version, he says truly, though still ironically, "I croon my tears at fifty cents per line."

In stanza 3, after a list of Doty's crimes, the poet's disgust is expressed in the image of Doty as a dog, "Fitter for vomit than a kind man's grief." He also confesses no love for "the crying/ Drunks of Belaire," brutalized by the police. "I do not pity the dead," he says, "I pity the dying," of which he is one.

In stanza 4, Wright focuses on three key issues: "If Belmont County killed him, what of me?/ His victims never loved him. Why should we?/ And yet, nobody had to kill him either." In answer: "I kick the clods away."

Stanza 5 is a key section. According to John 8:7, Jesus told the one among the accusers "without sin to throw the stone first." Here the poet acknowledges "My sneaking crimes" and believes "the earth/ And its dead" shall be judged by "the princes of the sea." In the short stanza that follows, he concludes that none will "mark my face/ From any murderer's," since "We are nothing but a man."

In stanza 7, the final one, Wright realizes that "God knows, not I," when "suicides will stop." Doty "Sleeps in a ditch of fire," like one of Dante's souls, and Wright feels "fear, not grief." He bids the ground to open, knowing Doty, "Dirt of my flesh," is "defeated, underground."

Forms and Devices

Despite iambic pentameter and end rhyme, the lines are not always dulcet, unlike many of Wright's earlier efforts. The poet and his commentators, including Smith and poet and critic Donald Hall, see "At the Executed Murderer's Grave" as a "watershed poem," dividing his earlier style from his more mature work.

Wright's first book, *The Green Wall* (1957), contains "A Poem About George Doty in the Death House." This precursor poem has six stanzas in trimeter verse with regular rhyme scheme and unobtrusive diction. Though scorned by community members for caring more about Doty than the murdered girl ("I mourn no soul but his"), his language is passionless, guarded, and devoid of commitment. The later poem, with its harsh colloquial language and candid utterance, is another case entirely.

What changed? Hall, in his introduction to *Above the River* (1990), quotes Wright describing himself as "a literary operator (and one of the slickest, cleverest, most 'charming' concoctors of the do-it-yourself . . . verse)." Hall says Wright was thinking of quitting poetry altogether because it was not real to him anymore. Then he began this poem.

Though still producing a metric line, Wright's use of diction creates a different kind of poetry. For one thing, proper nouns appear in abundance. By using his and Doty's names and the place-names of his region, the poet acquires a direct voice. As a consequence, he stops using persona (speaking as though he were someone else, as in "Sappho," for example, where he speaks as a barren woman). What is more, frank admissions ("To hell with them") and strong language ("giggling muckers") present a sharper, more nonliterary surface.

At times, the iambic pentameter is roughened up. The aforementioned last line of stanza 3 has an extra foot, and two lines of stanza 6 have an extra syllable. The eleventh line of stanza 7 requires an elision ("th' Ohio grass"), setting off the imagery of sea and stars with near rhyme, "a tide of gray disastrousness." In themselves, these are only mild aberrations. In stanza 7 alone, however, eleven of fifteen lines begin with a noniambic foot and the tenth line (the only line in the poem using parentheses and exclamation marks) begins in trochaic measure, to stark effect.

The greatest deviation from iambic pentameter occurs in stanza 5, the only part of the poem that speaks of the future otherworld. These ten lines are a study in metrical contrast and meaning. They contain two sentences, one very short and one very long. More interestingly, the perfect iambic pentameter sixth line ("To lay away their robes, to judge the earth") is embedded in four irregular lines; and these, in turn, along with the sixth, are embedded in regular lines. The effect is to highlight the imagery of Judgment Day against "bodies" in Ohio—Wright's, his father's, Doty's—which "Ridiculously kneel" under "God's unpitying stars."

Themes and Meanings

The first two versions of the poem appeared in *Botteghe Oscure* (a quote from which appeared above) and *Poetry*, respectively. Wright was unsatisfied with both versions and asked James Dickey (the J. L. D. to whom the final version is dedicated), the poet who would later write "The Fiend" and other psychological poems, for help. While aboard a train, without a copy of the earlier versions and with only the memory of Dickey's verbal comments, Wright wrote the final version.

Topical poems such as this are difficult. No matter which insights the poet brings to bear, opinions precede him. With controversial subjects like capital punishment and sympathy for criminals, he knew he could not avoid treading on zealously held beliefs of the 1950's. As a result, he and the poem were vulnerable to attack. Commendably, Wright allowed his beliefs and feelings to shine forth, and the subsequent development of not only his own poems but also of modern poetry in general is better for this painstaking exhibition.

The epigraph of the poem is from Sigmund Freud's *Das Unbehagen in der Kultur* (1930; *Civilization and Its Discontents*, 1961), a work that shows that civilization is possible only by the individual's renunciation of deep-seated pleasures and aggressions. The puzzling quote is about the biblical admonition "Love thy neighbor as thyself," a topic that leads Freud to declare subsequently, "[Civilization] hopes to prevent the crudest excesses of brutal violence by itself assuming the right to use violence against criminals."

A poet who was to grow with each of his books, Wright's first poems glittered with promise. This is true because he possessed a fine ear for meter and rhyme early in his career. Later, when he abandoned these devices, his ear held fast to near-perfect rhythms and economies of emotive phrase. His ability to turn personal experience into poetry was his finest asset.

"To a Fugitive" and "American Twilights, 1957" are also about slain prisoners. The latter is about Caryl Chessman, the Red-Light Bandit, who smuggled his writings out of death row before being executed in California for murder and rape. "The Fugitive" is a sonnet advising a man in flight from the law to "break the last law" and "race between the stars." The title poem, "Saint Judas," is a sonnet about one who knew "The kiss that ate my flesh." Ostensibly from the Gospel, this poem reveals the betrayal of man by man.

The theme of the grave occurs throughout Wright's writings. "A Dream of Burial," in *The Branch Will Not Break* (1963), is a vision about his own decomposition. The poem preceding "At the Executed Murderer's Grave," entitled "Devotions," tells how "I must find/ A grave to prod my wrath/ Back to its just devotions." Wrath seems a doubtful quality to turn into devotion, yet Wright is able to assume the "dual role" (as Edward Butscher says in Smith's book) "of outcast and savior." This spiritual stance, not unlike that of poet Sylvia Plath, produces an "inward voice" capable of turning death into art. Even so, Wright is one who affirmed the goodness of life.

John Young

AN ATLAS OF THE DIFFICULT WORLD

Author: Adrienne Rich (1929-
Type of poem: Poetic sequence
First published: 1991, in *An Atlas of the Difficult World: Poems 1988-1991*

The Poem

"An Atlas of the Difficult World" is a long poem divided into thirteen sections or short poems that relate experiences and observations. The sections are of varying length and are identified only by roman numerals, except for the seventh and the final ones, parenthetically titled "(The Dream-Site)" and "(Dedications)," respectively. Although in the poem the persona, or poetic voice, is often an assumed identity, Adrienne Rich's poetic journey is enriched by personal images and observations. In this, her thirteenth volume of poetry, Rich provides readers with a mural that does not begin or end with this poem but connects with previous works dating back to 1951, when her first collection, *A Change of World*, was published.

As denoted by the term "atlas," the series of poems describes a collection of American scenes that are bound together. Starting in California's Salinas Valley, "THE SALAD BOWL OF THE WORLD," Rich characterizes the place not only by location but also by the people who live and work in the "agribusiness empires."

Throughout the poem, the people she describes are not famous but are always recognizable. They are, in a sense, the landscape of the American journey, which, as the title implies, is part of a difficult world. In the second section Rich addresses the central focus of the poem, looking at "our country" as a whole and alluding to social and economic conditions in the United States. The section ends with an imagined dialogue with a reader: "I promised to show you a map you say but this is a mural." Rich responds to the hypothetical comment by replying that such distinctions are not important: "where do we see it from is the question."

In section III Rich relates experiences and memories in the East as she sits "at this table in Vermont." She describes past summers with her husband and children, which then connect with her own childhood. The image of her father, a Jew whose motto was "Without labor, no sweetness," illustrates the continuity of existence that the poet conveys in every section of the poem; it also allows Rich to comment that she now knows that "not all labor ends in sweetness." Next, in section IV, she mentions the girasole plant (a type of sunflower), which "laces the roadsides from Vermont to California," the implied cross-country trip providing a desperate view of a countryside in decay, in need of repair. In California (section V) she takes the reader to San Francisco and its contrasting images of splendor and human waste—from views of the Palace of Fine Arts to San Quentin, Alcatraz, and "places where life is cheap poor quick unmonumented." From the start she is the reader's tour guide, deciding the itinerary and providing the background needed to appreciate the scenes. In section VI, set in nineteenth century Ireland and America, poetry becomes the necessary tool for expressing the nature of the human condition: "poetry of cursing and silence," "of

I.R.A.-talk, kitchen-talk, dream-talk." Section VII, "(The Dream-Site)," is about New York City, where Rich once lived, and it conveys a sense of why she had to leave the East.

Sections IX and X depict scenes of loneliness and isolation. Citing the Mohave Desert and the Grand Canyon, the poems describe human loneliness as immense and infertile. In section X she includes excerpts from a book entitled *Soledad Brother: The Prison Letters of George Jackson* (1970). Soledad, a California prison located near Monterey, is an artificial structure, unlike the Mohave Desert and Grand Canyon, but it still signifies through its cavelike structure the loneliness that the poet sees carved into the human landscape of the country.

In section XI the people of Monterey have gone through several natural disasters, including earthquakes and a devastating drought. Analogous to these natural holocausts is war. Rich meditates on what it means to love one's country, to be a citizen, to be a patriot. Some march for peace, some contemplate "the shapes of/ powerlessness and power." The poet attempts to define the word "patriot"—an emotionally charged word that has been used on all sides of the political spectrum—and comes to a series of conclusions, including the concepts that a patriot "wrestles for the soul of her country" and is "a citizen trying to wake/ from the burnt-out dream of innocence."

In section XII Rich as tour guide takes the reader to New Mexico, with its "Indian distance, Indian presence." She had driven through it with her companion a month ago, she writes; at the time she did not speak of her companion's beauty, her spirit's gaze, or her hands but, she says, "I speak of them now." Section XIII, "(Dedication)," captures the connection between reader and poet. Like Walt Whitman, she reaches out to the reader with empathy and simple yet universal images. Repeatedly beginning lines with "I know you are reading this poem," Rich presents descriptions of her imagined readers. They range from an office worker on her way home to an elderly reader with "failing sight" to a young mother warming milk for a crying child. Each figure, despite difficulties, is reading the poem, "listening for something, torn between bitterness and hope."

Forms and Devices

"An Atlas of the Difficult World" is a mural of the American landscape—emotional, economic, social, political—painted through imagery and metaphor. Images of ordinary people, especially women, are highlighted in each of the thirteen segments. The scenes, although specific and detailed, represent the universality of women's experiences. Rich's metaphoric language adds richness to the vignettes, and she appeals to the senses with such phrases as "strawberry blood on the wrist." However, it is her use of the atlas as the extended metaphor that synthesizes the discrete scenes, unifying them into a comprehensive whole.

In section V each image describes "your country's moment"; each is a significantly historical event that has left devastation, from the Battle of Wounded Knee to the last airlift from Saigon to a more recent event: Rich records a heinous attack on two lesbians who were camping along the Appalachian Trail in 1988. One was killed, and the other managed to drag herself back to town to notify the authorities. The attacker, in defending himself, states that they had "teased his loathing." The image of death, literal and powerful, sparks a universal connection as Rich realizes, "A crosshair against the pupil of an eye/ could blow my life from hers."

Reaching out to those who are disfranchised from the politics of the American landscape, Rich cites excerpts from *Soledad Brother* in section X. Soledad Prison is aptly named; Rich introduces the section with the dictionary meanings of the Spanish word *soledad*: "Solitude, loneliness, homesickness; lonely retreat." The passages from the prison letters not only provide a glimpse into prison life but also allow the reader to comprehend the impact that imprisonment has on a human being: "a man's thoughts/ become completely disorganized." The desperate man understands that this "college of force," as Rich calls it, has made him bitter, angry, and full of self-hatred. All these feelings are comprehended by women, Rich implies, because they also are oppressed. In the poem's final section, the images of women are patterned after imagined readers, struggling in various situations to read the poem. They read it because "there is nothing else left to read."

In Rich's poetry, metaphors involve thriving, ongoing processes that are linked together by memories or imagination. For example, in section VI, the potato exploding in the oven alludes to the potato famine that brought many Irish immigrants to the United States at the turn of the twentieth century. The famine and immigration are linked metaphorically to the poetry that is not taken seriously as such, the colloquialisms of workers and common people: "Poetry/ in the workhouse," "poetry of cursing and silence." In section XI, natural disasters become metaphors for both internal and universal devastation: "Earthquake and drought followed by freezing followed by war." Every person, Rich contends, is in crisis. Extending the metaphor, the poet focuses on the poet as patriot: "A patriot is one who wrestles for the soul of her country/ as she wrestles for her own being." Rich guides the reader to a redefinition of "patriot" as one remembering "her true country."

Rich's atlas, her collection of maps, becomes a human mural that stretches from coast to coast. Like Dante's Vergil in the *Inferno*, Rich as a guide possesses the vision and the wisdom needed to make the poetic journey. With the ultimate goal of reconstructing society, Rich must represent contemporary failings and atrocities to the reader. The tone is urgent as Rich escorts the reader across the American landscape, commingling past and present, personal and universal events. She provides a view of a "familiar globe," as she described it in a 1984 essay entitled "Notes Toward a Politics of Location" (collected in *Blood, Bread, and Poetry*, 1986). Continuing, she states that only by repairing the "toxic rivers, the cancerous wells, the strangled valleys" can humankind move to a better place.

Themes and Meanings

"An Atlas of the Difficult World" is a poetic pilgrimage to a place where change is possible. As Adrienne Rich states in "Notes Toward a Politics of Location," "*I am the woman who asks the questions*." Advocating social and political change is not new for

Rich, who since the 1960's has been prominent in the women's and the feminist-lesbian movements. The theme of inclusion rather than separatism permeates this poem as it identifies and reaffirms the poet's connection with the common woman and even the common man. Unlike *The Dream of a Common Language* (1978), written for and about women, this poetic sequence embraces all who are disfranchised, disenchanted, and conscious of the oppression and decay of Western society. Rich sees hope resting in her readers, notably her female readers, as envisioned in the final section. The questions she reiterates in two earlier sections (V and XI) resonate with her purpose:

> Where are we moored?
> What are the bindings?
> What behooves us?

Both challenging and embracing the reader by using the pronoun "we," she bridges the gap between herself, a self-described white, Jewish, middle-class woman, and others who are very different. This tone of inclusiveness provides a sense of community in the struggle and dramatizes the poet's recognition that she is not alone, that there are others "torn between bitterness and hope."

Ultimately, the text of feminism is too confining to construct the foundation necessary to build a better world. Therefore, the philosophical framework for her vision of the transformation of women, depicted in earlier works including *Diving into the Wreck* (1973) and *The Dream of a Common Language*, must be expanded. It must include both men and women in order to create the changes necessary for emerging from "the death-freeze of the century." Rich calls to those who have marched before and are homesick for their "true country" and to those who have the moral courage to ask difficult questions.

A formidable poet, Rich is unwilling to let her poetic voice for change be silenced because of political expediency or immobilizing apathy. As she explained in *On Lies, Secrets, and Silence* (1979), a collection of prose written between 1966 and 1978, she feels compelled to speak for those who "are less conscious of what they are living through." In "An Atlas of the Difficult World" she is not only speaking for other women but also describing them and internalizing their lives in an attempt to enlist them in the struggle for change. They, she believes, are the hope for the future. As she states in "Final Notations," the last poem of the collection *An Atlas of the Difficult World*, the struggle "will take all your heart, it will take all your breath."

Cynthia S. Becerra

ATOMIC PANTOUM

Author: Peter Meinke (1932-
Type of poem: Meditation
First published: 1987, in *Night Watch on the Chesapeake*

The Poem

"Atomic Pantoum" angrily reflects on the human fascination with destruction, specifically the terrible power of nuclear weapons. The first two stanzas describe the chain reaction that generates the energy for such a weapon: The force of individual neutrons splitting splits the centers of others, releasing energy to split still more in a rapidly enlarging progression impossible to stop. By the third and fourth stanzas, the factual, even colloquial, language ("start this all over") of the opening turns strongly emotional. Let the process continue, Peter Meinke warns, and destruction will expand as wildly as the splitting of the atoms. Churches will collapse and people and creatures of the sea will incinerate in the terrific, irresistible inferno. Meinke thus extends the term "chain reaction" to the uncontrollably expanding effects of the colossal weapon.

The fifth and sixth stanzas involve and implicate human beings. Whereas in the first two stanzas Meinke limits his description to a physical process, he now reminds readers that humanity is responsible for this process. The model of the sun's energy, also generated by nuclear fission, has imprinted itself in people's minds, he suggests. By using the word "blazed," he implies that the imprinting is a sort of blinding. The sixth stanza clarifies the connection: The sun has provided the model for the "plutonium trigger," a small initial explosion that supplies the energy to detonate the main weapon. Humans have learned to create nuclear weapons from the sun's model, and, he adds, punning grimly, "we are dying to use it." That is, humans are both eager to exert their immense power and destined to be the victims.

The next two stanzas complete the meaning implicit throughout the poem. Humans control the trigger. Describing the trigger as "curled and tightened" may be intended to evoke the more familiar image of the trigger finger (an analogy that would be visually misleading). The word "torching" in the seventh stanza reveals the sheer sadistic delight of striking out in hatred. The phrase "blind to the end" in the eighth stanza makes explicit the irrationality of such hatred, and this is followed by a heartbreaking self-delusion—the human inclination to dedicate even warfare to the greatness of a god. The ninth and final stanza adds no new lines but makes the central analogy of the poem explicit. The concept of a "chain reaction" characterizes both the process by which nuclear weapons generate force and the situation in which humans find themselves, having devised ways to use nuclear fission in weapons. Blinded by a fascination with the potential to destroy their enemies, humans are "split up like nuclei," and even their worship is part of—and consumed in—the chain reaction.

Forms and Devices

The repetition of lines is perhaps the poem's most important device. When repeated, a phrase may accrue additional meanings or assume entirely new ones.

Repetition is a type of rhythm, and it also establishes predictability or a sense of expectancy. Because the final stanza includes two lines from the first stanza, the poem seems rounded off or circular. The form Meinke employs is the pantoum, in which the second and fourth lines of each four-line stanza (or quatrain), moving as a pair, become the first and third lines of the next stanza. These repeated lines are sometimes called repetons. In the final stanza, the first and third lines of the opening stanza appear, in inverted order, as the second and fourth lines; thus, the poem opens and closes with the same line. Conventionally, the quatrains rhyme *abab*.

Meinke employs all these devices except the rhyming. After becoming familiar with the sense of the poem, one should linger over individual stanzas to appreciate the effects. In the second stanza, the repeton "blow open some others" states the effect of the released neutrons during the chain reaction. However, in the third stanza, Meinke turns "blow" into an imperative as the chain of cause and effect becomes destructive. Similarly, in the third stanza the phrase "with eyes burned to ashes" pertains to humanity, but when the line recurs it refers to the destroyed fish. Finally, "curled and tightened," which appears first in the seventh stanza, applies to the plutonium trigger, the small explosion that starts the chain reaction. Repeated, however, the phrase describes the human psyche in its irrationality. The return of the poem's first and third lines to shape the final stanza imparts finality and completeness. Like previous repetons, the reused lines are themselves affected. In fact, Meinke alters "split other nuclei" to read "split up like nuclei" as he likens humanity to—and implicates it in—the process of chain reaction. In regard to the final line, "in a chain reaction," it is worth noting that its earlier recurrence—in stanzas 4 and 5, where it helpfully reminds readers of the poem's focus—is not obligatory and may in fact diminish the line's impact at the end of the poem.

Another device is the lack of punctuation. Far from unique in modern poetry, this device nonetheless contributes an appropriate sense of inconstancy or randomness. One is tempted to entertain alternative ways to connect the parts of a sentence. For example, the phrase "eyes burned to ashes" in the third stanza may characterize victims of nuclear holocaust or suggest the fallibility of the perpetrators of the destruction, or both.

Themes and Meanings

"Atomic Pantoum" does not try to conceal its meaning. It might be possible to imagine Meinke, teeth clenched in anger, stabbing his words into paper with the point of his pen. However, meaning and significance accumulate from many contexts, connections that radiate outward from the poem like rings on water or, more appropriately, shock waves from an explosion.

The effects of the pantoum form become meaningful as they conspire with the subject. Like a chain reaction, repetition, as described earlier, is generative. Some pantoums emphasize circularity, but "Atomic Pantoum" gains complexity as it extends the meanings of the chain reaction. The first stanzas state the theme, while later iterations vary the theme, always focusing on it, until the poem ends in the slamming together of meanings that have been implicit in the images all along. Like the chain reaction itself, the form lets details split and release more energy and meaning. Also, the form establishes a kind of inevitability, the lines necessarily repeating and obligating the poet to devise applications for them, a process that continues as long as the poem requires. By writing a poem about the fission of nuclear weapons, Meinke has kept the pantoum alive, redefined it in relation to this subject, and shown that it can apply to what might seem to be a very unpoetic facet of the contemporary world.

The imagery of "Atomic Pantoum" draws on the poetry of others. The word "choirs," for instance, recalls William Shakespeare's "bare ruined choirs" in his famous sonnet (73) about aging and mortality. The phrase "fish catch on fire" might remind one of Gerard Manley Hopkins's famous sonnet that starts with the line "As kingfishers catch fire," a poem about the immanence of Christ in all things. Meinke has declared an interest in the "formal problems of sounding contemporary in traditional forms," and *Night Watch on the Chesapeake* contains many poems with some or all of the features of several traditional forms, particularly sonnets. Therefore, "Atomic Pantoum" might be regarded as part of a conversation between poets, centuries old, on subjects essential to the human experience; moreover, this poem seems to subsume some famous predecessors.

Finally, one can consider "Atomic Pantoum" in relation to Meinke's other work, particularly selections grouped under the heading "Night Watch" in *Night Watch on the Chesapeake*. When one considers the horrible effects of nuclear weapons, devices that can quickly exceed human capacity to control them, one begins to understand the moral agenda behind "Atomic Pantoum." Like the poem "Hermann Ludwig Ferdinand von Helmholtz," "Atomic Pantoum" is concerned with the fact that, for the poet and the scientist, "there is always another layer/ above, beyond, below/ the last answer." As Meinke says in "Rage," another poem from this part of the book, "rage, too, will never go away, never." Some of the "Night Watch" poems, which tend to be darker than others in the book, refer to sites notorious for violence and atrocities. There is a sinister quality in his work as he deals, from an adult perspective, with matters such as the need for alertness and responsibility.

Meinke, however, is not a poet of despair. He does not dismiss humanity as hopeless. A single one of his poems can contain both delight and doom. "Atomic Pantoum" is an unusually outraged poem for Meinke, but one should not miss the inspired playfulness in his use of the pantoum form. As one reads more of his work, one may appreciate the pervasiveness not only of humor but also of a great and unwavering passion for people and for life. Rage, then, is part of something bigger and more diverse, something with moral legitimacy, part of the moral imperatives by which one tries to fashion a life.

Jay Paul

AUTOBIOGRAPHY

Author: Dan Pagis (1930-1986)
Type of poem: Lyric
First published: 1975, as "'Ōtōbiyōgrafyah," in *Moah*; English translation collected
  in *Points of Departure*, 1981

The Poem
  "Autobiography," a poem of twenty-six lines divided into six stanzas of four or five
lines apiece, requires some knowledge of Dan Pagis's biography. Pagis, a leading
Israeli poet of his generation, was born in Radautz, in Romanian Bukovina (now
Russia). A Jew, he was incarcerated for three years of his early adolescence in a Nazi
concentration camp. At the age of sixteen, in 1946, Pagis, like many Jewish survivors
of the Holocaust, emigrated to Palestine. (The nation of Israel was officially established by the United Nations as a homeland for Jews in 1948.) His native tongue was
German, and he learned Hebrew in order to assimilate into Israeli society. He began
writing poetry in Hebrew in about four years; it is remarkable that he later became a
preeminent poet—not to mention a respected scholar of the literature—in a language
not native to him.
  The first line of the poem establishes that the speaker is dead. Clearly, the poem
cannot be an "autobiography" in a literal sense. When the reader considers the
author's biography, it begins to seem possible that the "I" who "died with the first
blow" is collective rather than individual. The "I" in this poem symbolizes Jews
murdered by the Third Reich's diabolical "final solution" or perhaps, in a larger sense,
all Jewish people who have endured persecution. The identification of the "I" with
victimized Jews becomes stronger in the next stanza, in which the speaker reveals that
he was murdered by a brother who "invented murder." This brother is Cain, the slain
speaker Abel, and the parents who "invented grief" Adam and Eve. The story of the
first murder, from Genesis 4, here represents the brutal persecution of Jews, especially
those murdered during the Holocaust.
  If Abel is the world's first murder victim, many others followed. The third stanza
seems to make a leap forward in history to the twentieth century, when "the well-
known events took place" and "our inventions"—presumably the elaborate death
machinery systematically and efficiently employed by the Nazis—"were perfected."
  Abel continues reflecting on his death in the final three stanzas. He declines, in
stanza 4, to "mention names," the names of generations murdered after him; such
"details," he says, horrifying at first, are finally "a bore." The suggestion is that human
beings, the poem's readers included, have a limited capacity for details of horror.
Stanza 5 develops this idea further: "you can die once, twice, even seven times,/ but
you can't die a thousand times." The narrator, however, does claim the power to die a
thousand deaths, and his "underground cells reach everywhere."
  Neither of the brothers is mentioned by name until the sixth stanza, in which Cain's
name appears in the first line. Cain, the murderer, has multiplied "on the face of the

earth," while Abel, his victim, "began to multiply in the belly of the earth." Victimiz-
ers proliferate and live; their victims' bodies pile up in graves. Nevertheless, the
speaker claims that his strength "has long been greater than" Cain's. The poem
concludes with an explanation and emotional assessment of why this is and how it
feels: "His legions desert him and go over to me,/ and even this is only half a revenge."

Forms and Devices

Pagis uses allusions to Old Testament myth in much of his work and alludes to the
story of Cain and Abel, archetypes in the Judeo-Christian tradition for the victimizer
and victim, in at least two of his best-known poems, "Brothers" and "Written in Pencil
in the Sealed Railway Car." Clearly, Pagis is using imagery from this archetypal
murder metaphorically, and the most immediate comparison is to the Nazis' murder
of millions of Jews during the Holocaust.

The reader may well ask just how this is so clear. No details in the poem refer
specifically to the Holocaust, or even World War II. Lines from stanza 3, "Our
inventions were perfected. One thing led to another,/ orders were given," contain the
most direct references in the poem, and even these are oblique. Again, knowing the
poet's personal history is helpful, as is a passing familiarity with Pagis's other work,
in which the Holocaust is a persistent, although hardly omnipresent concern.

The very fact that Pagis refers to the Holocaust only indirectly—there are no
swastikas, no images of crematoria—is in itself of interest. Pagis is a master of
understatement, which is a form of irony; and irony is perhaps the dominant mode for
serious literature written after the horrors of World War II. It is almost as if mere
language were incapable of rising to the occasion of describing or paying appropriate
homage to human suffering on a scale as vast as the Holocaust deserved. The German
philosopher and critic Theodor Adorno wrote, "After Auschwitz, to write poetry is
barbaric." Pagis wrote poetry, but the mask he wears as a poet is of one unable or
possibly unwilling to give full voice to the incomprehensible suffering of millions.

This poem was originally written in Hebrew, a language richer than English in
sound devices such as assonance and consonance. Although it would not have been
possible for Stephen Mitchell's translations of Pagis's poetry to approximate the
poet's sense of sound play, Mitchell's translations have been praised for their "re-
sourcefulness and sensitivity," and readers of Hebrew have admired how Mitchell
captures Pagis's sparse, elusive qualities in English.

One of Pagis's poetic devices which Mitchell is able to incorporate is repetition.
Lines such as "My brother invented murder,/ my parents invented grief,/ I invented
silence" and "There were those who murdered in their own way,/ grieved in their own
way" use repetition and, in the first example, parallel structure to give the poem an
Old Testament flavor. If the Old Testament is the principal book of myth for Jews, this
poem, alluding to the Old Testament both in its use of metaphor and through stylistic
devices like repetition and parallel structure, serves as a fragment in the Jewish
people's continuing, modern saga—a story with the Holocaust persistently looming
in the background.

Themes and Meanings

Perhaps the first question the reader confronts is why Pagis uses Cain's murder of Abel as a metaphor for the Nazi persecution of the Jews. It may seem a startling choice: Cain murdered his brother out of jealousy because God delighted in the sacrifices of Abel but was displeased with those of Cain. Enraged, Cain killed Abel. As punishment for the first murder, God placed a mark on Cain and made him forever, in the language of the King James Old Testament, a "fugitive and vagabond."

Pagis's choice of metaphor becomes especially interesting when the reader considers Cain and Abel as brothers. If Cain represents the Nazis and Abel the Jews, the implication is that the Nazis and the Jews are also, at least on a metaphorical level, brothers. What Cain is not, from Abel's point of view, is an animal, a monster, one completely alien or "other." It is easy, perhaps, for readers to think of Nazis as inhuman, completely incomprehensible, not true human beings at all. Abel, as the speaker of this poem, does not seem to share that perspective.

It is tempting to think of the categories Jew and victim, and Nazi and victimizer, as falling at opposite ends of the spectrum of human experience; one surprise in this poem is that Pagis, himself having suffered at the hands of the Nazis, resists that impulse. The notion of a thread of commonality between the Jew and the Nazi is strengthened when the reader considers that it is Cain, in the Old Testament story, whom God makes the eternal wanderer. The Jews have historically been a people who wandered, always searching for a place where they might be free from persecution. In this sense, Pagis adds another layer of irony to his poem.

Nazi and European Jew share a European heritage and, more specifically, in Pagis's case, the German language. German was Pagis's native tongue, and he was raised in a family without an especially strong connection to Jewish traditions or the Hebrew language. Although genocide is horrific in any circumstance, it may at least be comprehensible when it is carried out against a people very foreign, very different from the perpetrators. The attempt to eradicate a group of people whose differences from the perpetrators are minimal, however, is so absurd as to be nearly beyond comprehension.

The reader should not conclude, however, that this sense of shared identity between victimizer and victim means that neither the poet nor the speaker feels anger. The last stanza, the concluding lines in particular, makes clear that Cain desires and to an extent has achieved a certain revenge: "His [Cain's] legions desert him and go over to me/ and this is only half a revenge." These enigmatic lines suggest a continuing and perhaps eternal conflict between the brutal and the brutalized—a conflict only partially relieved by the fact that death, that great common denominator, comes eventually to even the cruelest person.

Douglas Branch

AVAILABLE LIGHT

Author: Marge Piercy (1936-
Type of poem: Meditation
First published: 1988, in *Available Light*

The Poem

"Available Light" is an autobiographical meditation in free verse. It consists of eleven six-line stanzas. Each of the first five of these stanzas has a definitive ending. However, the last six stanzas are paired: In each case, the first stanza ends in mid-sentence, unpunctuated, and the thought moves without a pause into the second. The final stanza ends with two lines that sum up all that has gone before. Though the title is a term taken from photography, it is meant to be a play on words: It is not visualized reality but the development of her own inner vision that Marge Piercy will be describing. A mature woman, she is looking back over her life in order to understand the person she has become.

"Available Light" begins in the present. In middle age, the poet asserts, sexual appetites are both "rampant" and "allowed," and she is as filled with desire as nature itself. In the second stanza, the poet moves to another favorite activity, her four-mile morning walks. However, in this stanza she also introduces the theme of self-knowledge: "I know myself," she begins the stanza, but she later modifies this statement by explaining that she also knows that her knowledge is imperfect. The poem, then, will shed some light on her past and on herself, but only the light that is "available."

In the third stanza, Piercy moves into the past, recalling scenes from four different times in her life, the last when she was twenty-four. As she points out in the fourth stanza, there seems to be no logical connection between these memories. The past is a medium in which, like a person under water, she has difficulty breathing. She is assaulted with details; she is confused as she keeps finding "new beings" in herself, unlike the friends mentioned in the fifth stanza, each of whom is committed to a single cause or faith. For someone who is Jewish, she explains, it is not so easy. Her God expects believers to remake themselves continually, while at the same time God refuses to intervene between cause and effect.

The two-stanza segment that follows begins with this problem of "consequences." Though the poet yearns to see "the larger picture," she knows that she cannot change nature, with its "million deaths" per inch, or, brought down to more comprehensible terms, its grounded "pilot whales," which human beings are struggling so desperately but perhaps so hopelessly to save. Appropriately, the next two-stanza segment is set in winter, the darkest time of year. The fifty-year-old poet's effort to learn Hebrew is somehow connected with the need to forgive her parents, who she now realizes, like the poet herself, were hampered by having only "scanty light." Finally, the poet once more ventures out into the night. Tranquil at last, she can now see even the distant stars, and she can also see all the creatures around her. Though this is called the "dead of winter," she concludes, it contains more life than she can ever "live to name and speak." Thus, surrounded by the profusion of nature, she seems to accept the limitations of her own understanding and of her own life.

Forms and Devices

In a generally enthusiastic review of the book *Available Light* for the *Women's Review of Books*, Diane Wakoski raised questions about the book title, pointing out that Piercy's poetry depends much less on visual perception than on the other senses. It may be relevant that by the time this collection appeared, Piercy had developed such serious problems with her eyes that she had difficulty reading and even traveling. A decade later, despite eighteen operations, she had only one eye that was of much use. Given this personal history, the title *Available Light* seems more than appropriate. However, there is not necessarily any connection between Piercy's physical problems and her imagery; it may be that she is simply more attuned than other writers to input from the other four senses.

Images are certainly of major importance in the title poem of the collection, and it is true that they are perceived in various ways. Many are visual: The poet sees the sky, the airplanes, the tracks in the snow, the skunk, and the weasel. Naturally, before the use of television became common, she would hear about the president on the radio instead of viewing him. However, she also mentions a "p.a. system" and the hooting of the owl, while she imagines smelling "Leviathan" (a whale). As for touch or feeling, the poet describes the frozen ground beneath her feet, the cold air against her skin, sexual experiences, the sensation of trying to breathe under water, and even the imagined penetration of the blood by "glowing isotopes." By depending on so many different modes of perception for her imagery, Piercy creates a texture that is strikingly vivid and rich. However, she also utilizes patterns of imagery as a device for suggesting her own conflicts and her abiding concerns. Piercy's images fall naturally into such dichotomies as light and darkness, sky and earth, indoors and outdoors, past and present, and life and death. As "Available Light" progresses, specific images appear and disappear, but these conflicting elements are evident throughout. For example, the poem begins with the "solstice moon" and the dark places of the female genitalia, proceeds to a winter day when "the light is red and short," and ends with a starlit night. In the third stanza, the procreative impulse is followed immediately by a friend's death, and, in the final lines, the "dead" time of the year is more alive than the poet "can ever live to name and speak." It is these contrasting images that dramatize Piercy's stated theme.

Themes and Meanings

The dichotomies in imagery are so important in "Available Light" because the real subject of the poem is the search for a harmonious life. At fifty, Piercy is learning how to accept the past, the present, the future, and her own limitations. Admittedly, much of what she remembers from the past is a jumble of impressions such as the clipper ship and the radio broadcast. However, there are also old conflicts that Piercy now has the courage and the wisdom to resolve. Since she now knows that she will never know or understand everything, she can forgive her dead parents for living by "their own squinty light," much as she realizes she must do.

Piercy has suggested to interviewers that one of her parents' omissions actually worked to her benefit. Probably because only her mother was Jewish, as a child Piercy was exposed to Judaism just enough to capture her interest but not enough to make her rebellious. The fact that she is learning Hebrew of her own volition indicates the degree to which the poet has accepted her Jewish heritage. Judaism also saved Piercy from building her expectations of life on a simplistic faith such as those that her friends have chosen. As a person who feels strongly about right and wrong, Piercy could have become committed to an easy answer with which she would have become disillusioned in time. Fortunately, she has a God who, rather than promising miracles, promises only that life is hard and that morality, though expected, will go unrewarded.

If learning about life, like learning Hebrew, demands great patience, it can also bring unexpected joy, such as the fact that sex is just as pleasurable in one's mature years as it is when one is young. Piercy has also found new fulfillment in living close to nature. She often speaks of the difference between her early years in New York, which, along with her excessive smoking, almost killed her, and her present contentment in a pleasant little town on Cape Cod in Massachusetts. Like Judaism, nature has taught Piercy acceptance of that which cannot be changed, cold, darkness, old age, even death. However, nature has also taught her to look for beauty everywhere: in those long morning walks in the winter, for instance, or when, venturing out into the winter night, Piercy realizes that almost total darkness makes it possible for one to see the distant stars.

The dichotomies in "Available Light," then, must not be perceived in terms of good or evil. The years have brought to Piercy a deeper knowledge of herself and of the world around her so that now she sees such opposites as past and present, life and death as more apparent than real. Now she understands that though the past cannot be changed, it can be newly understood in the present and thus, in a sense, redeemed. Similarly, the very fact that she will not "live to name and speak" all that she sees around her makes her own poem, produced in the "dead of winter," just that much more a celebration of life.

Rosemary M. Canfield Reisman

AWAKENING

Author: Lucien Stryk (1924-
Type of poem: Meditation
First published: 1973, in *Awakening*

The Poem

"Awakening" is an unrhymed poem in numbered sections that run I through VII. The title suggests an epiphany, referred to in Zen as *satori*. The dedication reads, *Homage to Hakuin, Zen Master, 1685-1768.*

In section I Shoichi, a sixteenth century Japanese painter and calligrapher, has drawn a black circle. Above the circle he has composed a poem, a haiku. Having been penned in the traditional Japanese fashion, with the lines and individual symbols running up and down the page, the poem and circle take on the appearance of budding flowers growing from a bowl. Shoichi tells the reader that the bowl has, "Since the moment of my/ pointing," held "nothing but the dawn."

In section II Lucien Stryk presents a winter scene, frost on a window that looks like "laced ice flowers" and a meadow covered with ice and frost that looks as if it drifted off the side of a glacier. The scene reminds the poet of a description by Hakuin in which Hakuin was alone, "Freezing in an icefield," so cold he "could not move." The poet realizes that, even though his legs have cramped and he cannot see beyond the frost, his mind is still "pointing/ like a torch." He does not move. In section III it is spring. The poet examines a stone as he holds it in the palm of his hand and turns it "full circle/ slowly, in the late sun." He feels a sting in his hand, like the pressure of a "troubled head." The stone falls from his hand, and "A small dust rises."

In section IV the poet describes the air that moves westward, "Beyond the sycamore," as something nameless and dark, like smoke or a cloud. He traces "a simple word" in the condensation that his breath has left on a window. In section V the poet presents a scene in which he and his daughter are on a beach where the poet, thirty years before this time, had played with shells. His daughter gathers shells and directs him in making a model of the universe. They watch the "planets whirling in the sand" till sundown.

In section VI the poet presents the reader with a series of elusive though generic sensations, mostly of touch, and abstractions such as "Time. Place. Thing." In section VII Stryk presents a setting that is very much like a mirror image of section I. Instead of an ancient artist drawing and composing a poem in the light of dawn, the poet is writing a poem himself and using a watercolor image to describe what the fading light of evening is doing to the trees. He ends the poem by saying that dusk is the time of day that always makes him happy and ready for death if it should come.

Forms and Devices

The first device this poem uses is a dedication. Presenting the poem as homage to a great (perhaps the greatest) Zen master, Stryk prepares the reader for what most

Western writers try to lay before their readers whenever they write about Zen— paradox.

Stryk uses a set of framing elements that give the poem a sense of unity and a feeling of formality. Whenever a poem is presented to the reader in numbered units it is natural for the reader to expect that each unit will have both an independent sense of its own and a modular function within the larger framework of the poem. In classic Zen fashion, the author opens the poem at dawn and closes with dusk. Along with reinforcing the unity of the poem and all its elements, this adds a sense of completeness. Typical of Zen thinking, the five sections between I (dawn) and VII (dusk) do not have to carry a sense of having equal importance or of occurring at specific or evenly spaced points within the progression. It is sufficient that they all occur between dawn and dusk.

By dividing most of the poem (all but the first section) into tercets, the poet creates a visual resonance with a large body of Japanese poetry. This is especially true of haiku—and of the work of Hakuin in particular because of his fame not only as a composer of haiku but also as an artist who enhanced his paintings with haiku. Beginning the poem with a reference to another classic Japanese artist who enhanced his paintings with haiku, and ending the poem with a modern poet who describes the world from the perspective of a painter is another framing device that further unifies all elements of the poem.

Metaphor is important to almost all Western poetry and plays a large role in Asian poetry as well; however, the role of metaphor within cultures heavily influenced by Zen can be very confusing to people of Judeo-Christian-Islamic cultures. Although Zen poetry is full of objects found in nature, these objects will rarely be metaphors for individual aspects; however, any physical object found in nature can represent the nature and workings of all existence. With Zen it is all or nothing.

Stryk has used the most basic of Zen symbols. Dawn symbolizes beginning and ending, and dusk ending and beginning. The circle, much like the figure-eight symbol for infinity, represents the endless cycle of life.

Themes and Meanings

One of the prominent themes of the poem, perhaps the most prominent, concerns Zen, the form of Buddhism that holds meditation as the primary key to all knowledge, and how Zen compares to Western philosophies, especially those that rely on more analytical approaches to understanding the universe. The circle that Shoichi paints in the first section of the poem is a mystic circle, a Zen symbol for a personal awakening—a sudden awareness or epiphany that bypasses the rational part of the human mind. Such epiphanies often come after meditation.

In section II the poet's meditation on the "laced ice flowers" leads to a vision, a sudden transformation to a meadow, born from the side of a glacier, and the near-death experience of Hakuin "Freezing in an icefield." These associations lead to an identification with Hakuin that is so strong that the poet vicariously experiences leg cramps and such an overpowering feeling of cold that he cannot move. He has been transformed into a state of understanding that is unattainable through simple logic.

In section III the poet presents another conflict between Zen and Western patterns of thought, especially in regard to the physical world. At first the poet tries to make too much of the stone. As he turns it in his hand he searches the stone for metaphorical meanings, perhaps something relating to the sun and the changing of the seasons. To the practitioner of Zen, the stone is itself, a stone, a part of the whole of existence that needs no further justification. Its true nature and purpose are found when the poet drops it. "It falls. A small dust rises." What seems so paradoxical to Westerners is that, although an object is not used as a metaphor for some other object, the object can be representative of the whole of existence, the entire universe, physically, mentally, spiritually. The stone cannot hold just the seasons or just the sun; it holds everything at once, and everything holds the stone.

Section IV, one of the more elusive sections, deals with naming and with uncertainty, a principle that makes most Westerners uncomfortable. Westerners depend heavily on analytical thinking and on attributing names to things so that they can pin them down or compartmentalize them. When one's understanding of things expands them beyond one's expectations, one often finds the names inadequate. In Zen the name simply expands and contracts with the object named. The poet has, through his meditations, learned from the objects about the nature of the world.

In section V the poet's daughter amazes the poet with her sudden desire to understand the shape and nature of the entire universe and by her intuitive knowledge that the only devices she needs are pieces of the universe, each of which carries within it the nature of the whole. There is at least an implication here that Zen or Zenlike understanding is sometimes possible without the tutelage of a mentor or master. It may even be possible for the uninitiated to function as mentor. Children may be more receptive to Zen because their experiences have not yet encouraged them to prioritize and categorize.

In section VI the poet provides the reader with a taste of the universe and its total lack of discrimination. It is "Softness everywhere,/ snow a smear,/ air a gray sack." The final section of the poem is like a summary of everything presented in the six preceding sections. The meditations of the poet have brought the poet full circle. By understanding the inevitability and the beauty of his beginning, he is now prepared for the necessity and the beauty of his death.

Edmund August

THE BAIT

Author: John Donne (1572-1631)
Type of poem: Lyric
First published: 1633, in *Poems, by J. D.: With Elegies on the Author's Death*

The Poem

"The Bait," a seven-stanza, twenty-eight-line invitatory, reveals its indebtedness to Christopher Marlowe in its first line, which imitates the opening of Marlowe's "Passionate shepherd to his love." Moreover, the general construction of John Donne's poem—four lines of two pairs of rhymed couplets, or quatrains, with the exception of an added stanza—is not, at first glance, unlike that of the earlier poem, in which a would-be lover entices his beloved by calling up scenes of exquisite bliss. Before and after Donne, this type of poem found a wide audience. Before Donne, there was a unity between purpose and technique, and the voice of the importunate lover combined flattery with pleading. Donne, however, broke with this pattern; one has only to listen to "The Bait" (a title whose meaning deliberately contains ominous overtones) to hear a lover's voice by turns wily, suggestive, flattering, almost threatening, and ultimately rueful. Further, the abrupt changes in mood and tone coalesce to impart a characteristically rough sense of urgency found in much of Donne's work.

The poem begins conventionally enough, with pretty images and compliments. The sands, brooks, river, and sun, the lovely eyes of the beloved, are familiar territory. The mood shift in the third quatrain catches the reader unprepared; the beautiful beloved is now (apparently unclothed) swimming in "live" water, sought eagerly, even passionately, by the hitherto quiescent fish. Should this intimacy intimidate the lover, she is reminded that her own brilliance outshines both sun and moon and that thus neither gives its light to the proceedings. Significantly, the lover is at home in the darkness. In the fourth and fifth stanzas, the lover ostensibly establishes the superiority of his own type of "fishing" to the methods of his colleagues or competition, whose techniques vary from brute force, "the bedded fish in banks out-wrest," to the false and fatal promises held out by the "sleavesilk flies." This introduction of the specters of violence and treachery is only partially dissipated by the return to amorousness in the concluding verse, in which the speaker acknowledges that, ironically, it is he who has surrendered to the attractions of his purported prey.

The reader is challenged to discern who is fish, who is fishing, and who catches whom, all of which is bound to cause some confusion. Furthermore, the manifold sudden changes of emotional gear, all the more startling for being so economically presented, form an integral part of Donne's technique and account for, at least in part, the fascination with which he is regarded by readers more than 350 years after his death.

Forms and Devices

The Marlowe poem consisted of six quatrains; by adding a seventh, Donne brings the line total to twenty-eight, or twice fourteen (the length of a sonnet). Donne, in the interests of parodying Marlowe, chooses not to utilize sonnet form, but he has demonstrated to his contemporaries that the choice is his, and in choosing he has established a distinction between speaker and poet. The speaker is the captive of his desires; the poet weighs every word and leaves a bread-crumb trail through the poem so that the discerning reader might appreciate the subtleties of technique.

The element that most stands out in Donne's poetry is his intelligence—not even his passion or his wit can equal it. His dazzling manipulations of syntax, his juxtapositions of unlikely images, are as calculated as they are effective. Tracing Donne's intent in his poetry is a bit like watching a hunting cheetah spin and seemingly reverse direction. It takes some concentration to pursue "Begging themselves [the fish] they may betray" to achieve Donne's meaning, that the fish seek to be caught. The reader's deepening involvement with the text is further challenged by the pivotal third quatrain, which couples the languor of the bath with the eroticism of underwater pursuit and capture. Soon Donne moves from flattery to a hint of indirect but threatening force. Images such as "cut legs," "coarse bold hands," "slimy nest," and "curious traitors" would be jangling and discordant in a conventional love poem, but they work well here to establish Donne's emotional detachment from and, to some degree, cynicism about the process in which he is engaged. Even when the body is most needy and the passions most persuasive, the speaker wants his audience to admire his intellectual sophistication and his innovative mastery of form.

A reader in Donne's own times would have marked the many "conceits" that operate in the poem. These images and manifestations of design would conspire to create a bond between poet and reader. This becomes clear as one recalls the lack of complexity in Marlowe's poem; by loading his poem with ironic ambiguities, Donne assumes the willingness of his reader to be challenged and stimulated. The reader who correctly decodes Donne is intrigued and flattered, ready to draw inferences from every departure from the norm.

Donne certainly did not invent the love lyric; in this poem, for example, Donne assumes that the reader is familiar with Marlowe's earlier work. Donne's genius lies in his ability to take what was current and transcend it, changing its form while he ostensibly conforms to it. One can trace this pattern in his satires, his sermons, and his invocations to lovers.

In fact, the speaker never uses the word "love." If the hearer, or for that matter, the reader, thinks that the poem is about love, the speaker-and the poet-are not to be held accountable, even when the last stanza ruefully, even reluctantly, returns to the conventional image of the enthralled suitor. Very few poets have been as able as Donne to calibrate the differences between love and lust; here he and his speaker are as one. Both know perfectly well that the driving force in "The Bait" has to do with a hoped for physical union in which the absence of spiritual commitment is clear and not without meaning.

Themes and Meanings

Very few of Donne's poems were published in his lifetime, although hand-written copies enjoyed a wide readership. What appealed to his contemporaries was his open treatment of seduction, expressed typically through the voice of a would-be seducer. One can conjecture at length, and many critics have, as to how much his poetry mirrors Donne's direct experience and how much of it is an exaggeration of both his prowess and his stamina. Donne studied the ways of the court, the intricacies of the law, the controversies of religious disputation, and he uses and refers to them all in his poetry. Yet it would be a mistake to try to infer specifics about his self from the poetry; readers can see the connections that Donne allows them to see.

"The Bait," like the well-known "The Flea," is directed toward one end, the capitulation of a woman listener. She is the one who is to be overcome "with silken lines, and silver hooks." She is bombarded with language, and if she should have modest, if perhaps unlikely, second thoughts, she is assured that the lover who sees her surrender has already testified to the strength of his feelings, such as they are, for her. She is played, like a fish; dangling before her are all the protestations of the speaker, in which the reader may choose to place limited faith.

The speaker, in the last stanza, claims that it is he who has been unable to resist the pull of her allure; she is fisher, he fish. This may express Donne's considered opinion on the sport—that one should not engage in it if one is not willing to be caught. On the other hand, the reader may well dismiss this as another of the speaker's gambits; the speaker is certainly clever enough to manipulate his lover's feelings by appealing to her pity. The end result in either case, however, is a constant: She is to yield, he to triumph.

That this is the work of a man who later became known for his sermons as well as for his poetry, and that his poetry itself later underwent a radical reconfiguration of theme, seems unlikely if not preposterous as one reads "The Bait." Both the frank sensuality and the tour de force technique catch and hold the attention of the reader. To admirers of Donne's religious poetry and prose, "The Bait" may seem like a prodigal wasting of talent—but Donne, as his later life proved, always knew about prodigals.

Judith N. Mitchell

THE BALCONY

Author: Charles Baudelaire (1821-1867)
Type of poem: Lyric
First published: 1857, as "Le Balcon," in *Les Fleurs du mal*; English translation collected in *The Flowers of Evil*, 1993

The Poem

"The Balcony" first appeared as number 34 in the "Spleen and Ideal" section of the first, banned edition of *Les Fleurs du Mal* (*Flowers of Evil*, first translated in 1931) and as poem number 36 in the second, definitive edition (1861). The poem consists of six five-line stanzas in the "enveloped strophe" form—that is, the first line of each stanza reappears as its last line. The first, third, and fifth line of each stanza rhyme, as do the second and fourth.

In "The Balcony" a first-person voice, closely associated with the poet himself, speaks to a beloved woman using the familiar form of address, reserved in nineteenth century French for the most intimate relationships. The first stanza apostrophizes the beloved as "Mother of memories, Mistress of mistresses" and invites her to remember an earlier period of shared love. These memories are located in the home, or hearth; their time is evening, and the tone of the stanza, as of the poem in general, is elegiac and directs the reader's attention to a lost past of beauty, caresses, sweetness, and charm.

The second stanza is written in the imperfect tense, indicating habitual action in the past. The scene is set in early evening, either by the glow of a coal fire or of sunset on the balcony of the title. In an atmosphere of warmth and enclosure, the breast and heart of the beloved are offered to the poet; they say "imperishable" things.

The third stanza opens in the present tense; it evokes the eternal beauty of evening skies, the depth of space, and the power of the heart. The beloved is addressed as a queen. The poet remembers physical closeness so intense that he used to breathe the scent of her blood. This stanza is remarkable in its simultaneous evocation of light, warmth, and scent.

The fourth stanza, in the imperfect tense, moves from sunset to nightfall, when darkness deepens to form a wall about the balcony. The poet divines, rather than sees, the eyes of the beloved. Within this wall of darkness, intimacy is absolute. The poet "drinks" the breath of the beloved, which is both sweet and poisonous, and holds her slumbering feet in "brotherly" hands. The fifth stanza returns to the present tense and declares the poet's power to evoke past happiness; he relives the past paradise in the present embrace of the beloved. It is her "languorous beauties" which defined the past and provide the key to recalling it.

In stanzas 1 through 5, each first line is repeated word-for-word in the fifth line. In the sixth stanza, the first and fifth lines, although similar in their wording, are not identical. The first line refers to "These vows, these sweet perfumes, these kisses" as objects, the fifth line apostrophizes them. This strophe turns wistfully to the future and asks if past delights can be born again as setting suns are reborn.

Forms and Devices

Baudelaire chose the enveloped strophe form for several poems in *Les Fleurs du mal*. In "Reversibility" (number 44), a beloved woman is addressed as an angel and implored for her prayers. The repeated formulas shape the poem as an incantation, a way of controlling the powers of beauty, joy, and health attributed to the angelic woman. In "Moesta et errabunda" (Latin for "sorrowful and wandering woman"), number 62, the poet invites the beloved to escape with him from the monstrous city to the purity of the ocean, a return to the innocent "green paradise" of childhood.

In these poems, and particularly in "The Balcony," the repetitive stanza structure establishes a powerful echo, musically evocative and strongly nostalgic. Each stanza looks backward and forward simultaneously. The returning note of the last line changes subtly by progression through the rest of the strophe. In "The Balcony," where the central theme of the poem is a wish to re-create a happy past, coupled with the image of rebirth in the setting sun, this formal feature is especially important.

Within the polished, formal universe of the poem, the dominant images are the glowing hearth and the setting sun. The hearth, necessarily, is enclosed within walls, but the balcony also is defined as an enclosed space, since first the "pink veils" of sunset light, then the wall of descending night cut it off from the world, the profound space which lies outside the circle of warmth. The body of the beloved is an intimate part of this circle. "Mother of memories," she is breast, heart, blood, eyes, breath, feet, knees, the "dear body" to which the poet must have recourse to relive these happy moments.

The setting sun offers a final redemptive image in "The Balcony." As the ultimate source of light and warmth, descending each evening into the sea, it is a universal symbol of age and death. However, each day it returns "rejuvenated" to repeat its cycle of life. The past is a "gulf we cannot sound," deep as space beyond the walls of the balcony, deep as the seas, yet the daily return of the sun in its rising and setting allows the rebirth of hope.

Themes and Meanings

Baudelaire's poetry returns often to the moment of sunset, the poignant melting of light into darkness, and the evocation of erotic pleasures in the half light. However, this sunset moment is also a little death; it brings a heightened consciousness of mortality and the passage of time. Love is the most delicious at that moment when it most resembles death.

Many of Baudelaire's love lyrics, including the notorious "A Carcass" (number 29), identify the loved woman with suffering in some way. Sometimes she is threatened with injury, sometimes accused of injuring the poet or reminded of impending death. His idealized goddess of Beauty is "a stone-fashioned dream" whose essence is paralysis, a mineral fascination in which all movement ceases (number 17, "Beauty"). "The Balcony" offers no overt violence to the beloved woman. Indeed it seems exceptionally gentle in its evocation of sweet memories.

The beloved woman is presented immediately as a powerful figure, the mother of memory in a poem devoted to memory, the "mistress of mistresses" in a poem devoted to love. These incantations are introduced and echoed in the repetition of the first stanza. Her physical presence is felt through all the senses; sight that persists through darkness, the voice that speaks "imperishable things," touch of her breast and hand, scent of her blood, taste of her breath. She is, indeed, the human hearth, the glowing sun, source of warmth and light.

Yet the reader must remember that all these charms and all this happiness are expressed in the past tense. The beloved must recall them as memories and must lend her body to the poet for him to relive them. Although she is still physically present and available to his caress, the paradise of the balcony is gone. In every way that the beloved is physically real, warm and living, thus capable of inspiring and rewarding love, she is also mortal, aging, and herself moving into darkness. In the recollection of their moments of greatest intimacy, the poet evokes the scent of her blood in the darkness, the taste of her breath, both delight and poison. Her breath is poisonous because it is not only proof of physical life but also a measure of mortality.

When the fifth stanza proclaims knowledge of an "art" as a means of reliving happiness, the poet is not speaking of his verse. Rather, this "art" consists of burying himself in the knees of the beloved, returning to her physical presence, which paradoxically must eventually fail him. The exceptional changes in the repeating fifth line of the stanza subtly acknowledge the futility of the poet's attempt to return to past experience. The profound gulf of past time is too deep to sound, and the beloved, in whose physical beauty the past happiness is personified, will not transcend time to rise "rejuvenated" like the sun.

The poem itself, however, remains as incantation and invocation. Without the physical presence of the beloved—indeed, long after the death of both poet and loved woman—"The Balcony" continues to present the polished form, the glowing warmth of memory. The true art of the poet, his true evocation, lies in the verse he created to preserve the magic of happy memory.

Anne W. Sienkewicz

BALLAD OF AN OLD CYPRESS

Author: Tu Fu (Du Fu, 712-770)
Type of poem: Ballad
First published: Written after 766; collected as "Gǔ bó xíng," in *Jiu-jia ji-zhu Du shi*,
1181; English translation collected in *A Little Primer of Tu Fu*, 1967

The Poem

"Ballad of an Old Cypress" is a short poem written by a talented Confucian scholar
in his old age, who had tried repeatedly but failed, in the end, to realize his dream of
serving a noble ruler in order to build a just and harmonious society. The poem
addresses scholars who have "grand aims" as well as men who "live hidden away." It
explores the issue of how to cope with the ironic situation that great talents often lack
the opportunity to meet rulers eager for their services. The advice it offers to its
readers is that they should accept the irony without a "sigh."

The poem can be divided into three eight-line sections. In the first section, the
poet first depicts an aging cypress planted in Kuizhou in front of the shrine of Zhuge
Liang (A.D. 181-234), a scholar, statesman, military strategist, and tactician who was
fortunate to meet Liu Bei, the ruler of Shu, who anxiously sought Zhuge Liang's
advice. The depiction is characterized by realistic details about the tree's boughs
and bark fused with romantic hyperbole about its height of two thousand feet. The
poet then reflects on the significance of the tree in history, saying that it is a treasured
reminder of the meeting between a talented scholar and an ideal ruler. Finally, Tu Fu
assesses its effect on the meteorological condition of the Three Gorges and the
Mountains of Snow.

In the second section, the poet first carries his audience, through his memory, to the
Brocade Pavilion in Chengdu, the site of the adjacent shrines dedicated respectively
to Zhuge Liang and his lord (in most English translations of the poem, the two are said
to share one shrine). There were cypresses looming "high there,/ ancient upon the
meadows"; however, the poet felt a sense of loss when he caught sight of "paintings
dark and hidden away/ through the empty doors and windows." Tu Fu had reasons for
his sense of loss: Zhuge Liang died in a military campaign before he had time to carry
out his political program, and the story of Zhuge Liang was considered to be a very
rare instance in history of a gifted scholar serving a high-minded ruler. The poet then
refers to the tree in Kuizhou, saying that, unlike the trees in Chengdu that cluster
together, it stands "firm," "high and alone in the black of sky" in defiance of "many
violent storms." These qualities of the tree, according to the poet, are attributed to the
creative power of nature itself.

The last section opens with the poet's reflection on the troubled political condition
of his time and similar situations in the past. He compares the Tang Dynasty to "some
great mansion" about to collapse and compares talented scholars to the giant cypress
in Kuizhou, which can serve as the "beams and rafters" needed to save the mansion.
Unfortunately, there is no way to move the tree to the mansion; even ten thousand oxen

would not be able to accomplish the mission. The implication is that a ruler with Liu Bei's temperament is what is really needed, but there is simply no such ruler in sight. Tu Fu ends his poem by urging his fellow scholars not to lament over their own fate, for "it has always been true that the greatest timber/ is hardest to put to use."

Forms and Devices

"Ballad of an Old Cypress" is written in *qigu* (*chiku*), an old poetic form in which each line consists of seven words. This form was an effective vehicle for Tu Fu's impassioned poem on the issue concerning great talents. As an ancient, popular ballad form, it allowed him to convey his own views and emotions directly to his audience—aspiring Confucian scholars or disappointed talents in seclusion.

Among the most important technical aspects of the poem that have survived the translation into English is Tu Fu's skillfully orchestrated presentation of the cypress as the central image in the poem. He presents the tree from various perspectives and distances. A close-up of its "frosted bark" is accompanied by a distant shot of it standing on the northern bank of the Yangtze River with the Snow Mountains looming in the distance. A vertical view of the tree of "forty armspans" is followed by an angle shot of it reaching the sky "two thousand feet" above the ground. A mystic vision of the tree "vapor-linking" to the Wu Gorge is placed beside a heroic image of it standing "high and alone" braving "many violent storms." Finally, a current view of the tree against the background of a tottering "great mansion" is complemented by a historical survey of it in light of the tumultuous years of the Three Kingdoms.

The poet's artistic manipulation of the central image in the poem endows the tree with metaphorical, symbolic, and allegorical meanings. The cypress stands for Zhuge Liang as well as other gifted scholars, including the poet himself; it embodies their "upright straightness" and their aloofness; it manifests their potential to shape the destiny of their country; and it reflects their aspirations and frustrations. The cypress also stands as a symbol of the ideal that Confucian scholars pursue, that of bringing their talents and skills into full play in the service of a noble ruler. However, as the meeting of Zhuge Liang and Liu Bei is considered to be a rare event in history, the lone cypress also points to the tremendous odds against a "man of grand aims."

Stylistic diversity is another important aspect that remains somewhat visible in the English translation of the poem. Objective depictions of the cypress in Kuizhou are juxtaposed with extravagant statements about its mystic role on the grand landscape. As shown at the very beginning of the poem, use of prose coexists with indulgence in poetic elevation, as indicated in lines depicting the "vapors" of the tree touching "the full length of Wu Gorge" and its "chill" reaching "the white of the Mountains of Snow." Finally, an optimistic voice calling for persistent participation in politics is intermingled with a somewhat pessimistic voice endorsing resignation. Hence, one finds incorporated into the poem such diverse elements as authentic details and romantic visions, prosaic narrative and euphoric exaltation, the language of confucian political activism and the rhetoric of taoist passivism.

Themes and Meanings

"Ballad of an Old Cypress" is, among other things, Tu Fu's reflection on a paradox with which he and his fellow Confucian scholars have to cope, namely, that their great talents are "hard to put to use." It ends with the poet urging his audience not to "sigh." Since Tu Fu's audience consists of aspiring scholars and disappointed talents in seclusion, his appeal has different implications for them. It encourages the former to strive for active participation in politics but, at the same time, warns them of the difficulty ahead. It consoles the latter in their Taoist seclusion but reminds them of the possibility of a return to active service. This thematic multiplicity is informed and reinforced by many of the devices in the poem. Among these devices are the historical allusion to Zhuge Liang and Liu Bei and the poet's symbolic depiction of the cypresses.

A genius in political and military affairs, Zhuge Liang chose to live under a thatched roof in a remote place called Longzhong; however, he closely watched the political development in the Three Kingdoms that divided China, and he cherished a secret desire to help achieve the reunification of his country. Liu Bei, ruler of Kingdom of Shu, visited him three times in order to seek his advice on effective strategies against the other two kingdoms. It was Liu Bei's visits that "sent" the "cypress" or the "timber" to the "great mansion." Zhuge Liang was named prime minister and devoted himself to the cause of ending the wars among the Three Kingdoms.

Tu Fu's reference to Zhuge Liang provides his audience with a shared context. Regardless of their own situations, the two groups of scholars will see the meeting of Zhuge Liang and Liu Bei as a Confucian scholar's dream come true. To the men of "grand aims" among the audience, the historical event is encouraging: There was a high-minded ruler in the past, and what happened in the past may very well repeat itself in the future. To the disappointed scholars in seclusion, the event is comforting. It at least makes them wonder whether it is possible that some day a royal visitor will come to knock at the door of a thatched hut again. However, the story of Zhuge Liang is also a story of dreams unfulfilled. The prime minister was completely exhausted by the very mission that he worked arduously to accomplish. Like the cypress with "its bitter core" unable to "keep out/ intrusions of termites," he fell seriously ill during a prolonged military campaign. He died in Wuzhangyuan at the age of fifty-three before he was able to complete his magnificent political and social programs.

Chenliang Sheng

BALLAD OF BIRMINGHAM

Author: Dudley Randall (1914-   )
Type of poem: Ballad
First published: 1965, as a broadside; collected in *The Black Poets*, 1971

The Poem

September 15, 1963, was not a typical Sunday in Birmingham, Alabama; it was a day of devastation. Sunday school had just ended at the Seventeenth Street Baptist Church when nineteen sticks of dynamite, stashed under a stairwell, exploded. Twenty-two of the black congregation's adults and children, although injured, survived the bombing. Four little girls, Addie Mae Collins, Denise McNair, Carole Robertson, and Cynthia Wesley, did not. The bombing was a horrific reminder of the dangers of the Civil Rights movement of the 1960's as well as of the even greater danger and murderous power of unchecked racism. Americans were shocked as they watched televised accounts of the explosion. It was unfathomable that four little girls would be murdered in church.

Dudley Randall's poem about the event, "Ballad of Birmingham," was set to music and recorded prior to its 1965 publication as a broadside. The poem of thirty-two lines is divided into eight four-line stanzas; in each stanza, the second and fourth lines rhyme. In the first stanza, Randall begins a dialogue between a daughter and her other and presents the child's unusual request to forsake play in order to participate in one of the civil rights demonstrations that were prevalent in the South during the 1950's and 1960's. In the second stanza, the mother denies her daughter's request because she fears for her daughter's safety amid the clubs, police dogs, firehoses, and guns; she also worries that her child could be jailed. Hearing her mother's fears, the daughter appears unafraid and determined to participate in the freedom demonstration. The child responds in stanza 3 that she will not be alone because "Other children will go with me,/ and march the streets of Birmingham/ to make our country free." In the fourth stanza, the mother, worrying about gunfire, continues to tell her young daughter no. The mother then gives her permission to go to church instead and "sing in the children's choir," and the dialogue between child and mother ends.

Randall writes the remainder of "Ballad of Birmingham" in the third person. In the fifth stanza, the girl's preparations for church are described: combing and brushing her hair, bathing, and putting on white gloves and white shoes. In stanza 6 the mother, no longer fearful for her child's safety, smiles because her daughter is in church, "the sacred place"; then, in stanza 7, she hears the explosion. Her peace of mind is abruptly shattered, and with eyes "wet and wild" she runs toward the church "calling for her child." The mother arrives at the church, the site of the bombing, in the final stanza. Amid the "bits of glass and brick," she finds a shoe. "Ballad of Birmingham"ends with the distraught mother's extremely brief monologue: "O, here's the shoe my baby wore,/ but, baby, where are you?" The little girl does not respond. Never again can the daughter and mother engage in conversation. The child who eagerly wanted to raise her small voice in protest of social injustice has been silenced.

Forms and Devices

Typical of a ballad, Randall's poem presents a brief narrative that includes a dramatic event—the bombing of the church and the loss of lives. Imagery is an important device in "Ballad of Birmingham." Imagery is the use of a word or a group of words to elicit various sensory experiences. From the first to the last stanzas, readers of "Ballad of Birmingham" encounter multiple images that are primarily visual and associated with the dialogue, the girl's preparation for church, and the explosion. Randall invites readers to visualize and hear a mother-daughter conversation in stanzas 1 through 4. Their dialogue evokes visual images of the many civil rights demonstrators marching through the streets of Birmingham and elsewhere. In stanza 2 are the dogs, clubs, firehoses, guns, and jails used to control the primarily black protesters; in stanza 3 are children marching the Birmingham streets; in stanza 4 are "guns [that] will fire." The mother sends the child to church "to sing in the children's choir," and auditory images of young voices singing are called forth.

The next group of images is centered on the little girl's preparations for church in stanza 5; readers see her combing and brushing "her nightdark hair," bathing "rose petal sweet" (which also evokes a fragrant image), and putting "white gloves on her small brown hands" and "white shoes on her feet." The last group of images focuses on the explosion in stanza 7. Readers visualize and hear the explosion, see the mother's wet, wild eyes, see her frantically racing through the streets of Birmingham, and hear her calling for her daughter in vain. Then, in stanza 8, readers visualize the mother clawing through "bits of glass and brick" and ultimately lifting her daughter's shoe from the bombing debris.

A second major device is irony. The central irony in the poem involves the fact that the mother, in trying to keep her daughter safe, wishes her to go to church rather than to a demonstration, and the girl is killed in church. Subsumed within this irony are lesser ironies: The daughter's preparations for church become her preparations for death; knowing that her child is "safe" in church causes the mother to smile before the explosion occurs; a church is expected to be a sanctuary, not a place of death.

Themes and Meanings

"Ballad of Birmingham" is a tribute to Addie Mae Collins, Denise McNair, Carole Robertson, and Cynthia Wesley, the bombing's four fatalities, as well as their mothers. Randall's presentation of a nameless daughter and mother is significant. Although he focuses on one daughter, he honors all four deceased girls. His omission of names also allows him to represent and remember the anonymous multitude of victims of racism and the civil rights struggle and to remember the families left behind to mourn their dead. Thus "Ballad of Birmingham" is their tribute as well.

Randall's nameless daughter and mother also represent the bonds that exist between daughters and mothers everywhere. An important message of the poem is that a mother's love cannot protect her offspring from racism; nothing can. The most powerful aspect of this message is that as recently as 1963 in the United States there was no place safe from the destructive power of racism. The church is sacred ground, yet it proves to be no sanctuary.

"Ballad of Birmingham" concisely interprets a tragic event in American history and recalls the intense racial tensions and strong emotions of the civil rights era. Although there were many other important civil rights events, including the freedom rides, sit-ins, school desegregation attempts, bombings, fires, and racially motivated murders, the September 15, 1963, bombing of the Seventeenth Street Baptist Church remains among the most poignant moments in black Americans' collective quest for equality, liberty, and identity. Dudley Randall's "Ballad of Birmingham" is one of the most dramatic and memorable of the many works of literature that document the African American struggle for equality.

In 1977, fourteen years after the bombing, Robert Chambliss, a member of the Ku Klux Klan, was finally convicted of first-degree murder and sentenced to life in prison. Federal authorities, continuing to believe that Chambliss had accomplices, reopened the case in 1980, 1988, and 1997—the last also being the year that filmmaker Spike Lee's documentary film on the bombing, *4 Little Girls*, debuted.

Linda M. Carter

THE BALLAD OF RUDOLPH REED

Author: Gwendolyn Brooks (1917-
Type of poem: Ballad
First published: 1950; collected in *The Bean Eaters*, 1960

The Poem

"The Ballad of Rudolph Reed" employs a traditional verse form to tell a heroic and finally tragic story of human struggle against the contemporary forces of discrimination and hate. Gwendolyn Brooks's poem is powerful and unrelenting in its cry for social justice, and it holds only a small hope for redemption for its characters. The story is told in sixteen ballad stanzas of regular structure, broken roughly into three sections. The first five stanzas describe the players in the drama and their dreams. In the first stanza, readers are introduced to the central character, Rudolph Reed, and his wife, two daughters, and son. The only thing Rudolph wants, readers learn in the second stanza, is a house, a house, stanzas 3 and 4 continue, that is not in a slum where "a man in bed" may "hear the roaches" but rather one that is "full of room." Rudolph warns readers in stanza 5 that he will "fight" for such a house when he finds it.

In stanzas 6 through 10, Rudolph finds his dream dwelling and moves in "With his dark little wife,/ And his dark little children three." The house is on a "street of bitter white" residents, but the Reeds are "too joyous to notice" the reactions ("a yawning eye/ That squeezed into a slit") of their bigoted neighbors. In the final six stanzas, the tragedy waiting to befall the Reeds is acted out. Rocks are thrown through their windows, presumably by their white neighbors trying to force them to move, but Rudolph does not act until his daughter Mabel's blood is "staining her gaze so pure":

> Then up did rise our Rudolph Reed
> And pressed the hand of his wife,
> And went to the door with a thirty-four
> And a beastly butcher knife.

The conclusion is tragically predictable: Rudolph kills four white men before he himself is killed. The gathered neighbors kick "his corpse" and call him "Nigger." The final stanza leaves readers without poetic resolution or catharsis:

> Small Mabel whimpered all night long,
> For calling herself the cause.
> Her oak-eyed mother did no thing
> But change the bloody gauze.

Rudolph's revenge has only resulted in his own death; his surviving family exists in a tableau of guilt and blood. There is no redemption here for any of the characters—and yet the "oak-eyed" mother gives readers at least a small hope that the violence is finished and the Reeds will be able to stay in the house they have now earned with their own blood.

Forms and Devices

There are a number of important poetic devices in this poem. Most noteworthy is the ballad form itself, which Brooks has taken from an ancient and popular tradition and which she uses in a fairly traditional way. The rhyme scheme in every stanza (*abcb*) is that of the ballad form, and the meter is also fairly regular; while line length varies, there are either three or four accented syllables to each line, usually in the typical ballad stanza of four beats to the first and third lines and three beats to the second and fourth lines. Variations on this pattern (as in the first line of stanza 1) are made for emphasis. In stanza 7, the irregularly accented third line captures the natural rhythms of the real estate agent's voice, but the regularity of the surrounding three lines contains that variation to its one line:

> The agent's steep and steady stare
> Corroded to a grin
> *Why, you black old, tough old hell of a man,*
> *Move your family in!*

Echoes of the older ballad form are also found in the archaic syntax or word arrangement ("her gaze so pure," "Then up did rise"). Brooks occasionally uses alliteration ("steep and steady stare," "beastly butcher knife") to help hold the various poetic elements together.

If the ballad form is fairly traditional, however, Brooks's poetic diction is contemporary. While her language is quite simple and accessible—which is true to the narrative tradition of the ballad form, which often exhibits an almost childlike or fairy-tale quality—Brooks allows herself a number of figurative phrases ("yawning eye," "silvery ring," "fat rain," "oak-eyed mother"). The most interesting metaphorical figure in the poem is the use of "oak" as a descriptive word. Rudolph, readers learn in the very first line, "was oaken./ His wife was oaken too./ And his two good girls and his good little man./ Oakened as they grew." Several other times in the poem Brooks reminds readers that Rudolph is "oaken"; he is, in fact, as line 23 tells readers, "oakener/ Than others in the nation." The word conveys not only a sense of color but also a feeling of strength and toughness, and Rudolph lives out that figurative description. Whatever hope readers have at the end of the poem comes from the fact that, in the penultimate line, Rudolph's wife is now the "oak-eyed mother," which implies that she has the strength to live through this tragedy. If Rudolph was "oakener" than others, perhaps his family has inherited that strength as part of his legacy to them.

Themes and Meanings

The meaning of "The Ballad of Rudolph Reed" is as accessible as its language. Brooks's poem dramatizes the blatant discrimination, especially in housing, that characterized American society until the Civil Rights movement of the late 1950's and the 1960's. In this sense, Brooks's poem was ahead of its time, but a number of African American writers dramatized the problem of discrimination in this country shortly after World War II; for example, Lorraine Hansberry's powerful and popular play *A*

Raisin in the Sun (1959) dealt with the same issue of housing discrimination in Chicago. Brooks had experienced that discrimination personally when she was unable to find adequate housing in Chicago for her family as city officials continued to confine black residents to restricted areas at the same time that the population was rapidly increasing (particularly because of northward migration from rural Southern regions of the country).

As in most ballads, Brooks's poem traces the heroic struggles of a set of characters as they act out their tragedy. They have a home of their own, the dream of many American families; their own blindness and the implicit greed of their real estate agent combine to make them "block-busters"—the first family of color to move into an all-white neighborhood—and the tragedy spirals out of control after this move. The Reeds even ignore the first signs of trouble; it is only when Mabel's blood is spilled that Rudolph acts. In the heroic language of the inherited ballad form, Brooks tells readers "Then up did rise our Rudolph Reed." His instinctual protection of his family turns into revenge upon the white neighbors who are trying to drive the Reeds from their home. Even in his death, the hatred continues as the neighbors kick and insult his corpse.

Brooks leaves the issue hanging in the last stanza: The family survives, but will they have the strength to carry on Rudolph's fight? Will they continue to be "oaken"? Will they move or will they stay? In certain ways, "The Ballad of Rudolph Reed" has the feel of classical Greek drama, with characters playing out their fated and tragic roles. The main difference is that in Brooks's poem there is no *deus ex machina* at the end to resolve the conflicts, no sense of resolution to provide catharsis for the audience. Readers, Brooks insists, must provide that for themselves. The civil rights struggles of the 1950's and 1960's were composed of hundreds, perhaps thousands, of tragic battles and sacrifices such as this one. Brooks's Pulitzer Prize in poetry in 1950, like her many awards since then, was in part a tribute to her poetic efforts to point out and eradicate some of the worst inequities in her society.

David Peck

BALLAD OF THE LANDLORD

Author: Langston Hughes (1902-1967)
Type of poem: Ballad
First published: 1940; collected in *Montage of a Dream Deferred*, 1951

The Poem

In "Ballad of the Landlord," Langston Hughes appropriates the traditional ballad form but uses it in a contemporary urban setting to relate a current and crushing social problem. This conjunction of traditional form and contemporary content lends further power to the poem's cry for social justice. The poem contains nine ballad stanzas (although the strict stanzaic structure is abandoned in the last three) that, in traditional use of the form, would narrate a tale of a dramatic or romantic adventure. The story here, however, tells of protest and jail. In the opening five stanzas, the first-person narrator/tenant is talking to and complaining about a landlord who has not done the repairs that would justify paying the rent on his house. In the remaining four stanzas, readers are told of the terrible consequences of the narrator's protest.

In the first stanza, the persona of the poem complains to the landlord (in direct address) about the leak in the roof that he first mentioned to him "Way last week." The complaint in the second stanza is about the stairs that have not been fixed; the narrator is surprised that the landlord (who has apparently come by the narrator's house to collect the rent) has not injured himself: "It's a wonder you don't fall down." In the third stanza, the tenant refuses to pay the ten dollars the landlord is demanding until the landlord fixes "this house up new." In the fourth stanza, the tenant repeats the multiple threats of the landlord—to get an eviction notice, to cut off the heat, and to throw the tenant's furniture into the street—and, in the fifth stanza, the tenant replies by threatening to "land [his] fist" on the landlord.

The remaining four stanzas undergo a radical shift in point of view and tone and move further and further away from the tenant's perspective and pleas. The sixth stanza is italicized in order to convey the hysterical and exaggerated words of the landlord: "*Police! Police!/ Come and get this man!/ He's trying to ruin the government/ And overturn the land!*" The last three stanzas, in machine-gun fashion, contain society's responses to those unfair charges: The police arrest the tenant (stanza 7) and throw him in jail (stanza 8); the newspaper headlines proclaim "MAN THREATENS LANDLORD/ TENANT HELD NO BAIL/ JUDGE GIVES NEGRO 90 DAYS IN COUNTY JAIL" (stanza 9).

The poem, therefore, breaks into two uneven parts. In the first five stanzas, the tenant gives his story to a landlord who ignores the cries for adequate housing and fair treatment. In the last four stanzas, the point of view shifts to the landlord, then to the society as a whole, and finally to the newspaper headlines about the incident in the final stanza. It is significant that the word "Negro" is only used in the last stanza when the point of view shifts and the society that now has control wants to identify those it labels as criminals. The social justice the tenant demands in the first two-thirds of the poem becomes the jail this society imposes on its victims in the final third.

Forms and Devices

The most important device in "Ballad of the Landlord" is the ballad form itself. Meant to recount a story, the popular ballad form often includes dialogue (as here) and employs a simple four-line stanza rhyming *abcb*. Readers must wonder why Hughes would use such a traditional form for such an untraditional topic and employ it for only two-thirds of the poem. Actually, the ballad form has been used for centuries, as it is here, as a vehicle of social protest, and it is significant that a number of other twentieth century African American poets have employed the form in a similar way: Gwendolyn Brooks, for example, in "The Ballad of Rudolph Reed" (1960), Robert Hayden in "A Ballad of Remembrance" (1966), and Dudley Randall in "Ballad of Birmingham" (1966). African American poets, in short, have often utilized the ballad form as a convenient way to convey their multiple messages of social protest.

Again, however, Hughes only uses the form for two-thirds of the poem and then violates it with two three-line stanzas of a harsh, fragmentary third-person description of what happens to the protesting tenant followed by the concluding three lines of newspaper headlines. (Notice that a continuing rhyme helps to tie these three short, final stanzas together: bell/cell, bail/jail.) The simple ballad form of the first six stanzas, which conveys the struggles of the tenant against his landlord, gives way to the staccato response of the tenant's society: eviction, arrest, and, finally, jail. Hughes has used the ballad form to build a poetic structure of contrasts that works well to his purposes.

Beyond the ballad form, the poem uses several other devices that define Hughes as among the most prominent African American poets of the middle decades of the twentieth century. The poetic diction of the tenant's narration, like the meter, is conversational and colloquial ("Don't you 'member . . . ?" and "You gonna cut off my heat?") and works well in contrast to the more objective vocabulary of the concluding stanzas (like the staccato rhythm), especially the supposedly "neutral" language of the newspaper headlines ("MAN THREATENS LANDLORD"). The language of Hughes's poetry, In "Ballad of the Landlord" and elsewhere, helps make it perfectly accessible in both form and content and is meant to convey an obvious, if ironic, message. Hughes, like many of his fellow African American poets in the 1920's and 1930's, wanted nothing to do with the difficulty and obfuscation that characterized so much of the high modernist verse of those decades.

Themes and Meanings

The themes of "Ballad of the Landlord" come out of a vital American literary tradition: The poem taps the energy and meaning of much of the social protest literature of the 1930's. Poems, stories, and essays about tenant evictions, rent protests, and similar activities were common fare in the social realist American literature of the 1930's. In that tradition, Hughes represents the unfair advantage of society in this struggle: The landlord has only to call the tenant a communist (*"He's trying to ruin the government/ And overturn the land!"*) for the police to throw the tenant in jail. Another example of the influence of radical 1930's literary roots is the abrupt form of the last three stanzas and, particularly, the capitalized words of the last stanza, which may remind readers of the "newsreels" in John Dos Passos's trilogy of novels, *U.S.A.* (1930-1936), in which he creates montages of newspaper headlines to construct a realistic background for his fictional narratives. Nowhere was this 1930's social realism stronger than in the African American literary tradition, which goes back to the Harlem Renaissance (1920-1929), a literary, musical, and artistic movement that included Hughes as one of its major practitioners: His first collection of poetry, *The Weary Blues* (1926), is one of the landmarks of the movement.

What makes "Ballad of the Landlord" unique is Hughes's own special treatment of this incident. In the early stanzas, he establishes the justice of the tenant's claims against his landlord but closes realistically with American society's typical response to protests similar to the tenant's, especially in the 1930's: eviction and jail. There is no justice in this society, Hughes complains, particularly for African Americans. The landlord has all the weight of the police and the judicial system on his side; the tenant has only truth and moral rightness. Like many traditional ballads about folk heroes fighting for justice (Robin Hood, for example), Hughes's "Ballad of the Landlord" honors the struggle of the poor and disenfranchised. However, the title of the poem ultimately and ironically tells readers who the hero of the poem in this society really is and who will finally win this struggle.

David Peck

BATTLE-PIECES AND ASPECTS OF THE WAR

Author: Herman Melville (1819-1891)
Type of work: Book of poems
First published: 1866

The Poems

Battle-Pieces and Aspects of the War is a collection of seventy-two poems that depict key episodes and individuals of the Civil War as well as the temperament of the American people during the great conflict. Herman Melville arranges the poems in a chronological order so that the collection becomes an impressionistic history of the war delivered in verses rather than in prose. The first poem of the volume, "The Portent," depicts the hanging of John Brown, the abolitionist who, in 1859, failed in his attempt to start a slave rebellion by capturing the United States military arsenal at Harpers Ferry, Virginia, and arming the slaves on nearby plantations. Brown's Harpers Ferry raid is often cited as the first skirmish of the Civil War, and the poem refers to Brown as "The meteor of the war." *Battle-Pieces* concludes with "A Meditation," a poem in which the speaker speculates on whether the United States will be able to heal its war wounds and reunite itself after a four-year conflict that bitterly divided the nation and took the lives of more than 600,000 Americans.

Individual poems in *Battle-Pieces* re-create many of the key engagements and incidents of the war—the battles of Manassas, Fort Donelson, Shiloh, Antietam, Stones River, Gettysburg, Lookout Mountain, Wilderness, Cedar Creek; the fall of Richmond; the assassination of President Abraham Lincoln; General Robert E. Lee's surrender at Appomattox court house—and provide portraits of many of the war's important individuals, among them General Stonewall Jackson, General Philip Sheridan, and Colonel John Mosby. Several poems in *Battle-Pieces* depict war waged from sailing vessels. Melville, who spent much time at sea as a young man, had previously used an ocean setting in many of his best-known fictional works, including *Moby-Dick* (1851), generally considered Melville's masterwork.

The poems vary in type and length. *Battle-Pieces* contains narrative poems, ballads, hymns, elegies, meditations, and epitaphs. The shortest poem, "On the Grave," an inscription for the gravestone of a cavalry officer killed on a battlefield in Virginia, comprises only five lines; the longest, "The Scout Toward Aldie," which depicts the guerrilla tactics of Confederate colonel John Mosby, runs 798 lines.

The collection's title comes from the world of art. Paintings and sketches depicting war were generally called battle pieces. Melville had developed an interest in such art works even before the Civil War began; after the war, when he commenced writing poems that captured the conflict, Melville attempted to render in verse what he had seen artists create on canvas and paper. Indeed, a few of the poems in *Battle-Pieces* are named specifically for famous paintings. In the poem "'The Coming Storm,'" for example, Melville draws an analogy between the wilderness landscape at the start of a storm, depicted in the 1865 painting by Sandford Robinson Gifford, and the situation in the United States as the Civil War approached. In " 'Formerly a Slave,' " Melville also re-creates in verse the woman who is the subject of an 1865 painting by Elihu Vedder.

The poems of Battle-Pieces clearly reveal Melville's position on the great conflict. Melville dedicates the volume "to the memory of the three hundred thousand who in the war for the maintenance of the union fell devotedly under the flag of their fathers"; the dedication makes no mention of the three hundred thousand Confederate dead. In "The Fortitude of the North," Melville asserts that the Union soldiers "fight for the Right." In "Dupont's Round Fight," a poem depicting a Union naval victory engineered by Commander Samuel Francis DuPont, Melville states that the Union fleet "Warred for Right,/ And, warring so, prevailed." The South, according to Melville, fought in defense of slavery, described in "Misgivings" as "man's foulest crime." In an essay appended to the collection, Melville condemns the South for supporting a war "whose implied end was the erecting in our advanced century of an Anglo-American empire based upon the systematic degradation of man." Hence, a poem that recognizes the battlefield prowess of Stonewall Jackson also identifies the great Confederate general as a man "who stoutly stood for Wrong."

Nonetheless, Melville shows much sympathy for the defeated South. For example, in a poem titled "Rebel Color-Bearers at Shiloh," and subtitled "A plea against the vindictive cry raised by civilians shortly after the surrender at Appomattox," Melville paints an admirable portrait of Confederate color bearers; he advises readers, "Perish their Cause! but mark the men." In "A Grave near Petersburg, Virginia," Melville describes a Rebel soldier's grave and declares, "May his grave be green, though he/ Was a rebel of iron mould." Melville praises President Lincoln in "The Martyr" for his conciliatory postwar policy, and in "Meditation," the volume's concluding poem, he urges Americans to set aside wartime animosities and engage in the act of reconciliation.

Melville never saw the war first hand. He did not join the Union army; he spent the war years in Pittsfield, Massachusetts, and New York. He did visit a cousin at the front in Virginia in 1864 and heard the war stories of battle-tested troopers. He also read about the war in newspapers, in magazines such as *Harper's Weekly*, and in a postwar publication titled *The Rebellion Record*. Moreover, after the war, while Melville was working on *Battle-Pieces*, he spoke with many veterans of the conflict who supplied him with the details that he used in the poems.

Forms and Devices

No two poems in *Battle-Pieces* look or read alike. Besides varying in length and type, the poems also differ according to rhyme scheme and meter. In some poems Melville employs traditional rhyme schemes, while others read like prose poems. In "A Dirge for McPherson," for example, the four-line stanzas adhere to a traditional *abab* rhyme pattern. "The House-top," on the other hand, reads more like a descriptive paragraph than a poem and is virtually without rhyme.

Weather imagery dominates *Battle-Pieces*. For Melville, the Civil War was a storm that threw the nation into disorder and chaos. For example, "Misgivings," the second poem of the collection, opens with these lines:

> When ocean-clouds over inland hills
>   Sweep storming in late autumn brown,
> And horror the sodden valley fills,
>   And the spire falls crashing in the town,
> I muse upon my country's ills—
> The tempest bursting from the waste of Time
> On the world's fairest hope linked with man's foulest crime.

Likewise, "Apathy and Enthusiasm," another poem set early in the collection, compares the mood of the nation on the eve of war to a "clammy, cold November" day with "the sky a sheet of lead." The events precipitating the war "came resounding/ With the cry that *All was lost,*/ Like the thundercracks of massy ice/ In intensity of frost—/ Bursting one upon another/ Through the horror of the calm."

Melville also sometimes compares the fury of battle to the raging power of a storm. In "Gettysburg," for example, the speaker describes Confederate general George Pickett's fatal charge into the center of the Union line on the third day of the battle as a storm at sea: "Before our lines it seemed a beach/ Which wild September gales have strown/ With havoc on wreck, and dashed therewith/ Pale crews unknown—/ Men, arms, and steeds." In "The College Colonel," Melville describes a regiment of battle-weary soldiers as "castaway sailors . . . stunned/ By the surf's loud roar."

Melville frequently juxtaposes images and moods within individual poems. "Shiloh," for example, features a sharp contrast between the peaceful setting and the fury of the battle that recently took place. In the Old Testament, Shiloh is a place of peace, and the poem opens with swallows flying gently over the "forest-field of Shiloh," where one of the bloodiest battles of the Civil War has just concluded. Rain is falling, but instead of producing new life, it merely provides solace to "the parched ones stretched in pain"—the dying soldiers still lying untreated on the field. The violent battle has taken place on a Sunday, the traditional Christian day of peace, near a church, a place of sanctuary and peace. The noise of battle is now replaced by quiet, as the swallows skim over the dead and dying soldiers, "And all is hushed at Shiloh."

In "The College Colonel," Melville juxtaposes the public celebration of a war hero returning to his hometown with the veteran's private thoughts. As the wounded colonel marches through the streets of his hometown, "There are welcoming shouts, and flags;/ Old men off hat to the Boy,/ Wreaths from gay balconies fall at his feet." However, the colonel's private thoughts are of his terrifying war experiences—frightening episodes during the battles of Seven Days, Wilderness, Petersburg, and his captivity at Libby prison:

> But all through the Seven Days' Fight,
>   And deep in the Wilderness grim,
> And in the field-hospital tent,

And Petersburg crater, and dim
Lean brooding in Libby, there came—
Ah heaven!—what *truth* to him.

Throughout *Battle-Pieces* Melville makes frequent allusions to the Bible and to *Paradise Lost* (1667), the epic poem by John Milton that recounts the war between God's heavenly angels and the legions of Lucifer. Like many Northerners, Melville viewed the Civil War as an epic struggle between the forces of good and evil. In several poems he personifies the South as Satan waging a war of disunion against the North, whose troops are identified with God's angels, led by Michael the archangel. In "The Fall of Richmond" Melville equates the capture of the Confederate capital with the fall of Babylon and says that the Northern armies have deterred "the helmed dilated Lucifer." During the conflict, "Hell made loud hurrah," but now, with Richmond in Northern hands, "God is in Heaven, and Grant in the Town." In his novels, Melville makes frequent allusions to the Fall of Man, the sin of Adam and Eve in the Garden of Eden, as recorded in the book of Genesis. In *Battle-Pieces* he depicts the United States as a second Eden, corrupted by the sin of slavery,

Themes and Meanings

The overall thematic movement of *Battle-Pieces* is from the chaos of war to the order of peace and reconciliation, a movement also evident in *Drum-Taps* (1865), Walt Whitman's collection of Civil War poems. Melville's volume's early poems depict a nation torn asunder by a violent storm, but the war's end and the North's victory reestablish order in the American universe. For example, "Aurora-Borealis," a poem commemorating the end of the war, opens with the question, "What power disbands the Northern Lights/ After their steely play?" The northern lights, which appeared vividly in the evening sky after the devastating Union defeat at Fredericksburg, symbolize both the Confederate victory in that battle and the triumph of the forces of night, the forces of disorder and chaos. Yet at the war's end, "The phantom-host has faded quite,/ Splendor and Terror gone," giving way to "pale, meek Dawn." In "Lee in the Capitol," a poem depicting a postwar visit to the Capitol by Robert E. Lee, Melville describes a nation at peace: "Trees and green terraces sleep below" the Capitol building.

A frequent theme in individual poems of *Battle-Pieces* is the loss of innocence, a common theme in the literature of the Civil War. Melville, like other Civil War-era writers, viewed the war as the violent initiation experience that ended American innocence. Melville expresses that theme in "The March into Virginia," a poem marking the Battle of First Manassas (called the Battle of Bull Run by the North), the first major engagement of the Civil War. Melville declares that "All wars are boyish, and are fought by boys," and the young Yankee soldiers depicted in the poem march off to battle as if they were going on a picnic. The youthful troops anticipate the war as an exciting adventure, but many "who this blithe mood present,/ . . . Shall die experienced ere three days are spent."

The same theme is present in "Ball's Bluff." The speaker observes a regiment of soldiers marching past his home on their way to an engagement at Ball's Bluff:

> One noonday, at my window in the town,
>   I saw a sight—saddest that eyes can see—
> Young soldiers marching lustily
>   Unto the wars,
> With fifes, and flags in mottoed pageantry;
>   While all the porches, walks, and doors
> Were rich with ladies cheering royally.

The young men marching off to battle have hearts "fresh as clover in its prime." The speaker, however, sensing the horrors that lie ahead, asks, "How should they dream that Death in a rosy clime/ Would come to thin their shining throng?" Melville articulates a similar lament in "On the Slain Collegians," a poem commemorating the many regiments of college students who took sabbaticals from their studies to join in the war effort:

> Each bloomed and died an unabated Boy;
> Nor dreamed what death was—thought it mere
> Sliding into some vernal sphere.
> They knew the joy, but leaped the grief,
> Like plants that flower ere comes the leaf—
> Which storms lay low in kindly doom,
> And kill them in their flush of bloom.

Another persistent theme is Battle-Pieces is the endurance of nature in the face of the affairs of humankind. This theme is evident in "Shiloh" in Melville's description of the swallows swooping over the battlefield to reclaim it after the terrible battle has ended. Melville expresses a similar idea in "Malvern Hill," a poem depicting an engagement during the Seven Days' Battle. The speaker addresses the elm trees that stand on Malvern Hill, asking if they recall the great conflict that took place there. The speaker recounts the bloody battle that occurred, describing "rigid comrades" who lay dead in the forest and soldiers fighting with "haggard beards of blood." The elms respond that they "Remember every thing;/ But sap the twig will fill:/ Wag the world how it will,/ Leaves must be green in Spring." Regardless of the violent battle, regardless of the heroic stand made by the Union soldiers who fought at Malvern Hill, the elms must simply conduct nature's business, filling twigs with saps so that the trees will sprout leaves again.

The themes articulated in *Battle-Pieces* are also present in many of Melville's fictional works. Melville earned his place in American literary history as a fiction writer and is not generally appreciated as a great poet. Nonetheless, *Battle-Pieces* represents an ambitious effort by Melville, an attempt to compose an American *Iliad*, a history of the Civil War in verse.

James Tackach

BEFORE AN OLD PAINTING OF THE CRUCIFIXION

Author: N. Scott Momaday (1934-
Type of poem: Lyric
First published: 1965; collected in *Angle of Geese and Other Poems*, 1974

The Poem

"Before an Old Painting of the Crucifixion" by N. Scott Momaday is a poem divided into six stanzas, each with six verses. As a lyric poem, it is a variation of the Italian or Petrarchan sonnet usually defined as fourteen lines of iambic pentameter. Although differing in the number of stanzas and verses, "Before an Old Painting of the Crucifixion" retains the traditional iambic pentameter rhythm of the Italian sonnet and follows the most frequently used rhyme scheme of its second stanza, *abcabc*.

The title informs the reader of the subject of the poem, an old painting of Jesus Christ's Crucifixion. The title's opening word, "before," serves to position the reader with the poet, facing the painting. The subtitle or heading, "The Mission Carmel," defines the setting. Overlooking California's Monterey Bay, the Mission Carmel's landscape enhances the reader's appreciation of the poem.

The poem opens in the first person: "I ponder how He died, despairing once." By using the proper pronoun "He," the poet assumes familiarity with the narrative of Jesus Christ. Christ's despair is the focus of the first stanza. Momaday suggests that the stillness following Christ's anguish offers no comfort.

The second stanza continues the pondering of Christ's Crucifixion and death, using as its subject the "calm" introduced in the first stanza. This quiet following Christ's cry of despair is one where "no peace inheres but solitude." Momaday closes this stanza implying that not only the poet but also the artist(s) of the mural are incapable of comprehending Christ's agony. He writes, "Inscrutably itself, nor misconstrued,/ Nor metaphrased in art or pseudonym."

Momaday has now shifted the focus away from the actual Crucifixion and death to the painting itself, which becomes the subject of stanza 3. Momaday ends the first half of the poem by declaring, "The mural but implies eternity."

The remaining stanzas respond to the first three in a manner not unlike the Petrarchan sonnet (where the second stanza responds to the first). Returning to death in the fourth stanza, the poet joins the reader as he connects Christ's agony and despair with "our sorrow." Stanza 4 closes with Momaday's first criticism of the painting as he writes, "There shines too much a sterile loveliness." He is referring to the brightness of the blue sky in the mural as well as at the mission.

As evening shadows approach the mural in stanza 5, the visual "Passion" (or Crucifixion story) becomes less apparent. Both the approaching darkness and the centuries that have passed since the mural was painted are "of little consequence." In response to stanza 3, the poem closes with a comment on the "eternity" of the mural and the message it has held for centuries.

Forms and Devices

Landscape imagery and storytelling perform important functions within American Indian literature. Although Momaday refers to himself not as an Indian writer but as an Indian and a writer, his poetry is decidedly informed by the importance of landscape and by oral tradition. The subject of "Before an Old Painting of the Crucifixion," while not Indian in nature, is thoroughly informed by landscapes and stories.

Momaday's use of both landscape imagery and storytelling derives from within the mural itself (Christ and the Judean hills) and his immediate surroundings (the mission at Monterey Bay). The reader not only sees the mural but also hears its silence. This is also true of the reader's placement with the author at the Mission Carmel as the reader sees and hears the sea.

In "Before an Old Painting of the Crucifixion," Momaday relies on the reader's knowledge of biblical crucifixion stories that have been handed down for centuries. For instance, the "cry" in stanza 1 is translated in the New Testament Gospels of Matthew (27:26) and Mark (15:34) as, "My God, My God, why hast thou forsaken me?" In his interpretation of the scene depicted in the mural, Momaday contrasts Christ's cry of "despair" to the "calm" following it. Many of Momaday's images combine with others, such as the "calm" of the sea in stanza 2 and the "silence after death" in the Judean hills (stanza 4). Both the mural and the sea are "mute in constancy!" (stanza 3).

The author's use of nautical imagery throughout the poem is both visual and aural. For instance, "calm" can mean lack of sound and lack of movement. In stanza 3, Momaday moves the reader's vision from the old, fading mural to the "fainter sea" that lies beyond the mission. In stanza 5, he applies the imagery of waves swelling and waning in his description of time passing and its effect on the importance of the Passion. The last nautical image lies in the final verse of the poem. The reader can see and hear the surf while reading of "flecks of foam borne landward and destroyed." The eroding surf represents the time that has passed since the Crucifixion. Here Momaday uses imagery from outside the mural (the surf) in response to the internal message of the painting (the Crucifixion).

Just as Momaday's nautical imagery is both visual and aural, the landscape imagery, both inside and outside the mural, has a dual nature as well. For example, the "vacant skies" behind Christ on the cross (stanza 1) are not only silent, as the poem informs readers, but also cloudless, while the background of the actual mural to which Momaday refers in the poem is a sunlit blue. Stanza 4 contains another example of duality in the poem's imagery: The "farther groves and arbors seasonless" of the Judean hills are similar to the area below the mission. Both landscapes have mild climates with year-round vegetation and fruit-bearing trees.

Themes and Meanings

"Before an Old Painting of the Crucifixion" is a poem that goes deep into the meaning of the Crucifixion and explores Christ's despair. The poem questions whether anyone, artist or writer, is capable of comprehending, much less conveying, the purpose of Christ's Passion. Centuries lie between the painting of the mural and the writing of this poem, and yet there seems to be "no peace," only "solitude." Christ is still hanging on the cross in the quiet following his despair: "The mural but implies eternity." The closing verse in stanza 3 emphasizes the major theme of the poem, that of time and timelessness. Again, as with Momaday's imagery, duality is represented in the theme of time. Time stands still within the mural even though it fades. However, it is only the colors that begin to pale, not the agony and despair it depicts.

As evening approaches at the mission and shadows fall upon the mural, "time is stayed" even though it swells like a wave on the sea (stanza 5). Momaday releases the authoritative voice of author at the end of stanza 5 by telling the reader, "time and timelessness confuse, I'm told." It becomes apparent that while this section of the poem is in response to the opening stanzas, Momaday is not offering any definitive answers to his initial pondering. How did He die? Was it for the timelessness of His message?

While never really declaring the actual message of the Crucifixion, Momaday does offer examples of how time and timelessness affect it. "Change" that can occur only in time is "silence after death" (stanza 4). The centuries that have passed since the Crucifixion and the painting of the mural are insignificant. Humanity's attempt to record, in stone, "the void" or feeling of emptiness and loss caused by His death is, according to Momaday, "outrageous" and in "vain" (stanza 6).

The lyricalness of the poem reflects Momaday's love for language and his sense of artistry. He vividly describes not only what the mural looks like but also the feelings it evokes. This poem is as much about art and writing as it is about its subject, an old painting of the Crucifixion. The main message concerns the timelessness of Christ's agony. Final interpretation of His death is left to the individual, as it was at the beginning of the poem. Interpretation is different for the painter, the author, and the reader. It is what ones sees, hears, and feels it to be. Although the message disappears like the "flecks of foam" on the surf, the waves will continue to swell and move forward to the shore.

Susan Dominguez

BEFORE I KNOCKED

Author: Dylan Thomas (1914-1953)
Type of poem: Lyric
First published: 1934, as poem number 4 in *18 Poems*; as "Before I Knocked" in *Collected Poems, 1934-1952*, 1952

The Poem

"Before I Knocked" is a monologue consisting of seven six-line stanzas and a concluding stanza of four lines. The speaker throughout is Christ, who describes his consciousness of his own existence, and the conditions under which that consciousness functions, from the prenatal state to his incarnation in human form.

In the first stanza the speaker describes his essence, before he became a fertilized egg in the womb, as liquid, shapeless as water. This essence might also be understood as the seminal fluid. Christ already possesses, before his growth in the womb, a relationship to the world: He was a brother to "Mnetha's daughter" and sister to the "fathering worm." Mnetha is a character in "Tiriel," a poem by William Blake, whose daughter's brother is named Har. Har is usually seen by commentators as old and senile, which links the unborn Christ in the poem to the tragic world of human process, an interpretation that is supported by the image of the worm, a symbol of death.

Stanza 2 reveals that the unformed, unborn Christ was unaware of the passages of the seasons and had no knowledge, at least by name, of sun and moon. Yet even when the "flesh's armour," his human body, was still in "molten form," he could feel, and he had an awareness of the sexual act that created him in time.

The speaker's relationship to the physical world is the subject of stanza 3. He knew winter, with its hail, snow, and wind, and he knew night and day. The images are largely negative, which prepare the way for stanza 4, which clearly reveals that the speaker is Christ, who describes his capacity to experience suffering, even in the womb, in terms that strongly suggest the crucifixion: "gallow crosses," for example, and "brambles in the wringing brains," which suggest the crown of thorns that was placed on the head of Christ.

The emphasis on suffering continues in the next stanza. Like Christ on the cross, the Christ of the poem knew thirst, but he knew it even before his mouth and throat were formed. He also knew love and hunger and was aware of decay and death and the world of natural process ("I smelt the maggot in my stool").

Christ's birth is described in contradictory terms in stanza 6. In the first two lines he resembles a helpless, passive infant with no control over his destiny. The situation shifts in mid-stanza with the more positive connotations of "salt adventure," and the "tides that never touch the shores" suggest an infinite dimension to Christ's experience. By the end of the stanza, the incarnation has become, for the only time in the poem, a wholly positive event. Already rich in eternity, Christ was made richer by partaking in the temporal world.

The paradoxes of Christ's life, already hinted at, are approached again in stanza 7.

He was born of flesh and of spirit ("ghost"), but it is the mortal side that is emphasized here. This emphasis can be seen especially in the lower-case "christ" of the final line, which humanizes him. Stanza 8 is addressed directly to the Christian worshipper. Again it is the mortal figure that speaks (the lower-case "me"), asking the worshipper to pity God ("Him"), who "doublecrossed" his mother's womb by promising a savior but delivering only a man.

Forms and Devices

Each stanza has three feminine (unstressed) endings that all end with the *r* sound. These occur in lines 1, 3, and 5. In stanza 1, for example, the feminine endings are "enter," "water," and "daughter." In stanza 2 they are "summer," "armour," and "hammer," and so on throughout the poem. Masculine (stressed) endings occur in lines 2, 4, and 6 of each stanza. Stanza 1, for example, produces "womb," "home," and "worm." The masculine endings are always monosyllabic and usually have one consonant in common: *m* in the first and second stanzas; *s* in stanzas 4, 6, and 7; *l* in stanza 5.

One of Thomas's most frequent poetic devices is partial rhyme. He employs it extensively in one of his most famous poems, "The Force That Through the Green Fuse Drives the Flower," which was written within a few weeks of "Before I Knocked." Partial rhyme is a noticeable feature of the latter poem, occurring with both vowels and consonants. Examples include enter-water, womb-home, womb-worm (stanza 1); name-dome, winter-suitor, snow-dew, dew-day (stanza 3); suffer-cipher-liver; bones-lines-brains (stanza 4); structure-mixture (stanza 5) creature-adventure (stanza 6); neither-feather (stanza 7).

The language is less dense and more lucid than is usual in Thomas's early style, and the predominant imagery establishes an interplay of the cosmic with the individual and the infinite with the finite; the physical universe is found within the human physiology. In stanza 1, for example, the formless liquid that will become the fetus is compared in a simile to the River Jordan; the "rainy hammer" suggests at once rain in the natural world, the mythological hammer of Vulcan the blacksmith at his forge, and, in anatomical terms, the phallus of the father. The cosmic image of "leaden stars" also suggests—because of its link to "molten form" in the previous line—the drops of the seminal fluid as seen by the as yet unformed fetus. This is an imaginative leap typical of this period of Thomas's work. In stanza 3, the wind that leaps in the still unborn Christ is also, perhaps, the oxygen that reaches him in the womb. His veins flow not with blood but with the "Eastern weather."

Thomas himself commented almost apologetically on the "almost totally anatomi-cal" imagery of a group of five poems that included "Before I Knocked." Yet he continued, "[I]t is impossible for me to raise myself to the altitude of the stars, and . . . I am forced, therefore, to bring down the stars to my own level and to incorporate them in my own physical universe." In this characteristic practice of incorporating the entire universe in the human form, Thomas was following his mentor, Blake.

Themes and Meanings

"Before I Knocked" is a poem about Christ, but what sort of Christ does it portray? In orthodox Christian thought, Christ was both fully man and fully God; he combined two natures within one person. He suffered and died to save fallen man, and he rose from the dead.

It is obvious that "Before I Knocked" is not a pious poem in the traditional sense. Christ is not exalted as God; his death is emphasized without implication that anyone is saved as a result of it, and there is not even a hint of the resurrection. It is by no means clear that Thomas means to impute any divine status to Christ at all. While it is true that his Christ possesses a consciousness prior to his incarnation, there is little about it that could properly be said to be divine. Moreover, it is not uncommon in Thomas's poetry for a fetus, or simply an unborn spirit, to be the speaker, so the fact that in this poem Christ has life, feelings, and thought prior to his birth does not mean that any special status is attributed to him.

From an orthodox point of view, then, "Before I Knocked" might be seen as heretical. It emphasizes the human dimension of Christ while slighting the divine. Even the two lines in which an exalted status is suggested ("I who was rich was made the richer/ By sipping at the vine of days") subverts orthodox thought, in which Christ, even before his incarnation, was fully God and therefore could not be made richer by entering the temporal world. Indeed, traditionally, the incarnation is referred to as an emptying, not an augmentation. It was humanity, not Christ, who was enriched by it.

The Christ of this poem is therefore not transcendent but human, and in that respect he is simply a representative of humanity: We are all Christ. Once again Thomas may have been inspired by Blake, who wrote in "The Everlasting Gospel," "Thou art a Man, God is no more/ Thy own humanity learn to adore."

The bringing down of Christ to human level and the debunking of orthodoxy is implied also in the powerful last line of the poem, with its reference to "double-crossed." Attempts have been made to interpret this in an orthodox sense: The Holy Spirit first crossed the womb to make Christ's mother pregnant, then crossed it again in the form of the Son of God, whom she bore. The implication of betrayal in "doublecrossed" seems too strong to ignore, however, and might be seen in the context of the annunciation scene in the Gospel of Luke, in which the angel announces that Mary is to give birth to the Son of God who would rule without end over the house of Jacob. Instead, Thomas's Christ is "struck down by death's feather" and asks only that God himself should be pitied.

Bryan Aubrey

BERMUDAS

Author: Andrew Marvell (1621-1678)
Type of poem: Lyric
First published: 1681, in *Miscellaneous Poems*

The Poem

"Bermudas" is a short poem of eight-syllable (octosyllabic) lines arranged in iambic tetrameter couplets. The poem begins with a four-line exordium, or introduction, by a narrator. The next thirty-two lines consist of a song of thanksgiving being sung by people in a boat as they row. The poem then ends with a peroration, or conclusion, of four lines by the narrator, who identifies the people as English.

In the first section, an omniscient narrator—a mysterious persona who is so objective that he seems to be absent from the scene—immediately situates the action of the poem in the Bermudas (a group of more than two hundred islands, also simply called Bermuda). His description of the islands as "remote" and "unespy'd" creates the image of a distant, hidden, and private place. Since there are no human observers to the scene, only "The listning Winds" hear the song of the people in the boat.

The song, which is a hymn of praise and gratitude to God, has four parts. In the first part (lines 5-12), the boatmen praise God for having brought them safely across the Atlantic Ocean ("the watry Maze") to the Bermudas. Although these waters had begun to be charted since the discovery of the New World, ocean voyages were still risky undertakings in Marvell's day. (The islands had been discovered by Europeans only in 1515 and settled in 1609 by Sir George Somers.) The reference to this "Isle" as "far kinder than our own" has at least two levels of meaning. First, the weather in this tropical area is much kinder than the harsh weather, especially winter, in England. Second, these islands, like much of the New World, represent a place of religious freedom, in contrast to their own land where religious persecution ("Prelat's rage") was occurring. (In the 1630's, William Laud, the archbishop of Canterbury during the reign of Charles I, was persecuting and imprisoning Puritans; many religious refugees fled to the New World at this time, and one of those groups landed on Bermuda.)

The next part of the poem (lines 13-28) describes the islands. The "eternal Spring" weather produces colors everywhere (it "enamells every thing") all year long. Every day God sends fowl through the air as food for the people. There is an abundance of exotic fruit: oranges, pomegranates, figs, melons, and pineapples ("Apples"). The shore is full of ambergris, an expensive waxy substance from sperm whales used in making perfume. Continuous verdancy, abundant food, and costly ambergris all point to the rich bounty of these islands and to an effortless existence for the inhabitants.

The third part of the song (lines 29-32) focuses on the spiritual significance of the islands as a temple for worship. When the sailors sing, "He cast . . ./ The Gospels Pearl upon our Coast," they imply that the Bermudas are a manifestation of the Kingdom of God and also that the gospel message has been brought here by them.

The fourth part (lines 33-36) is a prayer that the gospel will reach beyond these islands. As their praise reaches heaven, they hope that it will rebound off "Heavens Vault" and produce an echo of praise past the Gulf of Mexico (*"Mexique Bay"*), reaching other parts of the New World. After the song, the narrator provides a descriptive commentary on the cheerful boatmen whose song is dictating the rhythm of the oars, implying that prayer and praise set the pace for their life and work.

Forms and Devices

The sailors' narrative points to God, or Divine Providence, as the main protagonist in the poem. The narrator is unidentified and impersonal; the nameless, faceless boatmen are only indirectly identified through the phrase "the *English* boat." Almost all the action verbs in the song have God as the subject: He is the prime agent, and the boatmen are the passive receivers of God's actions. God is credited with having protected them from the dangerous waters and from persecution; he is the one who has given these refugees this new home. He is the one who "sends" the fowls, "hangs" the oranges in the trees, and "throws the Melons" at their feet. The boatmen's description reflects their belief in the daily action and care of God in all the details of their lives.

Marvell conveys the significance of this island-paradise through a confluence of several archetypes. First, there are parallels with the biblical Garden of Eden. Just as God planted a garden and brought Adam to it, so too he has prepared this new "garden" and brought these people to it. In this place where all is provided—where God "makes the Figs our mouths to meet"—there is no labor, no sweat, no toil.

Second, there are specific reminiscences of the Garden of Hesperides. This classical paradise lay far to the west of known civilization, across a vast body of water, just as the Bermudas do. The oranges in the Bermudas, that are hung "Like golden Lamps in a green Night," function as a parallel image to the famous golden apples of the Hesperides.

Third, these islands bear some similarities to the New Jerusalem in the book of Revelation. That whole city, like the Bermudas in this poem, is the Temple of God and is full of his presence. There is no need for sun and moon, since God is the light of that city (Revelation 21:23); on these islands, there is no darkness or night—only bright colors and the "green Night" of the orange trees whose fruits are like golden lamps. In the heavenly Jerusalem, God will feed his chosen at a banquet that he has prepared (Revelation 19:7-9); on this island, God supplies food for the people. Each of the twelve gates of the New Jerusalem is a huge pearl; the coast, or "gate," to the Bermudas is the place upon which God has "cast . . ./ The Gospels Pearl." For his description of the Bermudas, Marvell draws from classical and biblical archetypes, weaving together details from various paradisiacal garden models in Western tradition, to create a powerful depiction of a land of beauty, abundance and blessedness.

Themes and Meanings

One of the central elements of the boatmen's song is their description of life in an earthly paradise. Ancient classical writers shared a tradition about a "Golden Age," an idyllic pastoral existence of peace, whose biblical counterpart is Eden. Every civilization and culture has had its dream of paradise, although there are variations in the details. The human dream of a paradisiacal life can represent a memory of the distant past (human beginnings), can function as an ideal for the future, or can take the shape of a fictive utopia occurring any time.

Marvell's depiction of this age-old dream has a number of distinctive characteristics. As a synthesis of classical, Old Testament, and New Testament elements, it transcends specific nations or cultures and thus has a universal quality. Unlike mythological garden-paradises and utopias whose locations are vague or unknown, Marvell's garden-paradise has a real geographical and historical existence. Finally, Marvell's "Eden" is neither in the distant past nor in the distant future, but in the present, and it functions as a fulfillment of humankind's dream.

However, Marvell's primary theme is not the proclamation that humankind's idyllic dream has finally come to pass. Rather, the paradise theme is subordinated to, and helps support, the chief emphasis of the poem, which is a celebration of a new Exodus, a new deliverance of God's people to a new Promised Land. Marvell establishes the similarity between the boatmen and the Israelites primarily through a situational parallel. Just as the chosen people were led out of Egypt during a period of persecution by the pharaoh, the boatmen were led from their land during their persecution. Just as the Israelites crossed the Red Sea to arrive at the Promised Land, the boatmen crossed a new sea to arrive at a new Promised Land. Just as the Israelites were protected and guided throughout their journey, the boatmen were protected and guided to this new destination.

Marvell strengthens this metaphoric identification of the two groups through structural elements and story details. The poem has forty lines, recalling the forty years it took the Israelites to reach the Promised Land. The boatmen's song is a poetical prayer, sung in unison by the people, recalling Old Testament psalms of thanksgiving for deliverance. The fowls sent through the air by God recall the quail sent to the Israelites during their journey. The cedars of Lebanon, "chosen by his [God's] hand" and transplanted in Bermuda, were the trees used in building Solomon's Temple in the Promised Land.

Marvell, well known for his defense of independence and his championing of civil and religious liberties during the reign of Charles I and under the subsequent rule of Oliver Cromwell, uses the biblical Exodus as a paradigm, a prototype, to make his metaphoric statement about the Puritan refugees of pre-Cromwellian England. Although Marvell never visited the Bermudas himself, the islands presented him with the chance to render poetically an image of a garden paradise while making a political and religious statement concerning an actual historical event.

Marsha Daigle-Williamson

BETWEEN THE WARS

Author: Robert Hass (1941-
Type of poem: Lyric
First published: 1989, in *Human Wishes*

The Poem

"Between the Wars" is a lyrical meditation of fifty-one lines. The opening lines place the poet in his setting and report on his activities: He runs in late afternoons, in the midsummer heat and humidity of upstate New York. He is writing, and at the same time reading Polish history; he is also thinking of a woman. He addresses the woman, speaking to her of his desire in the voice of Poland, in the *"'era of the dawn of freedom,' nineteen twenty-two."* The title, "Between the Wars," and this line inform the reader that he refers to the time between the two world wars, actually between 1918 and 1939. Why he refers to Poland specifically in 1922 is not stated. Poland gained its independence in 1918, but its independent existence was precarious and short-lived, for Adolf Hitler invaded it in 1939. As a country overrun for most of its history by more powerful neighbors, Poland's people have suffered the worst indignities and persecutions of war. Knowing Poland's history in the twentieth century, the reader realizes that the optimism expressed in the phrase "dawn of freedom" will prove naïve.

The poem is not divided into stanzas and may be thought of as consisting of long sentences rather than lines demarcated by end-breaks, as in most shorter lyric or rhymed poems. Though it has no spatial divisions on the page, the opening sentence, "When I ran, it rained," repeats at line 15, introducing a deepening of the poet's preoccupation with the late-afternoon light of this region, which he terms a version of the "American sublime." Late afternoon turns to a fiery sunset, then to night. "Out of nothing/ it boils up," he writes, tracking the setting sun through the color spectrum toward night: "pink flame,/ red flame, vermilion, purple, deeper purple, dark."

At this point, the focus shifts to a personification of night as a god disguised as a beggar and offers two folk legends as cautionary tales that function as the poem's moral center. The first tells what will happen to the populace that turns away the beggar from their door. The second offers a parable of why the leaves of the aspen quiver: "it failed to hide the Virgin and the Child/ when Herod's hunters were abroad." These folk tales call forth a strong peasant tradition, as in a country such as Poland; together with the mention of the children of the "eastern marches," they connect this section of the poem to its opening and to the title.

In the final section of the poem, the poet returns to his tale of night as "the god/ dressed as the beggar drinking the sweet milk." He extends the description of the beggar, comparing him to an alternately suckling and crying infant. Here Hass associates himself with the beggar, saying that he too would like to suckle at that breast, the one which has mysteriously appeared as his tale evolved out of the darkness of night into an image of nurture and desire ("The pink nubbin/ of the nipple glistens"). The reader will be reminded of his desire for the woman expressed in the first section of the poem.

The mysterious glistening breast is also connected to the fiery colors of sunset: "the muttering illumination/ of the fields before the sun goes down," before the American relief train came to Poland from Prussia bringing medicine and canned goods (this would have to be at the end of World War I, before Prussia ceased to exist). The concluding lines, presumably also drawn from Hass's reading of Polish history, proclaim the end of the war and catalog his ambiguous feelings about this "era of the dawn of freedom"—on the positive side, there is a new day with "skylarks singing," but on the negative side, there are unburied dead and "starved children begging chocolate on the tracks."

Forms and Devices

The reader will quickly notice that imagery of light and dark dominates the first half of the poem. Within a landscape darkened by rain, then lighted by an incendiary sunset, and finally settling into darkness, Hass depicts a world alive in its sensual particularities. Hass is a careful namer of plants and animals, a barometer of the slightest changes in the weather, a recorder of the sounds of birds, insects, and odors rising from the land. With great care he specifies the redwings in the cattails, the blackbirds in the reeds, the blossoms of the wild carrot, the sour odor of the sumac, the sweetness of the fescue, the loud insistence of cicadas, the colors of the sunset.

All of this teeming life—what he terms "the moody, humid/ American sublime"—is organized into a metaphor of encroaching night as death, and presented in quasireligious terms in the first half of the poem. The redwings and the "massed clouds" perform a "requiem," a Mass for the dead. Possibly the red stripe on the wings of the otherwise black birds is what Hass means when he refers to them as "death's idea of twilight."

The American sublime suggests a nineteenth century view of nature that elevated it to quasi-religious status, assigning it transcendental powers. The description of "the levitating, Congregational, meadow-light-at-twilight/ light" continues the religious connotations by associating the quality of the light with religious experience. The Congregational church is an American denomination of Protestantism founded in colonial New England. Working against the temptation to sacralize nature, however, is the imagery of impending darkness, the heavy air, the sour smells, the "impure" sunset, "maniacal cicadas"—earth itself seems violent, capable of evil.

Hass employs two modes of discourse in the poem. The first is colloquial, as in the opening line, "When I ran, it rained." This is his hook; it is catchy (it almost rhymes), and it invites the reader's commiseration with a familiar situation. This line is also a structural device, since it is repeated midway through the first half of the poem, the point at which Hass wishes to draw attention to the darkening afternoon. He also tends to address the reader directly, informally ("You could wring the sourness of the sumac from the air"; "Think: night is the god dressed as the beggar").

Set against this familiar, colloquial style is Hass's second mode of discourse, the self-consciously poetic, in which he employs several traditional poetic devices. The first, italicized, as if to call attention to it, is the apostrophe to the *"Lady of eyelashes,"* presumably the woman he has been thinking about a few lines earlier. Apostrophe is the love poet's time-honored way of expressing his desire for his lady. This passage eroticizes the already sensual descriptions of "the moody, humid" afternoon by connecting them to the poet's desire.

Readers will also note the personification of night as the god disguised as a beggar, and the development of this personification into an extended metaphor. The rather revolting beggar in his extreme old age turns back into an infant as he sucks the nurturing milk from the breast. Thus his symbolic value becomes apparent. Moreover, this figure appears to serve multiple symbolic functions. Hass makes him represent night turning into day, war giving way to peace, Poland in its new era of independence, as well as the ages of man, or Everyman, an ancient allegorical figure.

Themes and Meanings

If one takes the title, "Between the Wars," as an announcement of the poem's main concerns and considers the ambiguous images of the concluding lines, wherein the "era of the dawn of freedom" brings both the end of war and the specter of starving children and unburied dead, then the poem's theme is the precariousness of peace in this world. Peace is difficult to maintain because people are governed by desire. In this poem, Hass is governed by his desire for a woman, by his running, his reading and writing—the urges and impulses that make up an individual human life. As a poet, he is governed by his desire to praise the world and its multiple beauties even though the evidence of war's horrors haunts his descriptions of fields and sunset from the outset. It is noteworthy that the voice of unqualified praise goes to the newly independent Poland, cast (appropriately) in the role of passionate and hopeful lover.

Thus the poem is divided between the poet's impulse to praise and his moral imperative to warn and caution. People who turn away the beggar and refuse to shelter the innocent will be punished for their selfishness. War is the ultimate failure of love. If the evidence of his century will not permit him to write the sensual poem of praise that arises out of desire for the world, he will write a parable, a poem of moral instruction. This impulse nearly wins out in the second half of the poem. In the end, however, desire for the beautiful world is the breast that "glistens" with promise, and the poet appears to find its temptation irresistible. Nevertheless, his acceptance of the world is qualified by the closing lines, drawing the reader back to images of war and its aftermath. Optimistic statements about a new "dawn of freedom" can only be read as tragically ironic in the light of history.

Sandra Cookson

BEWARE: DO NOT READ THIS POEM

Author: Ishmael Reed (1938-
Type of poem: Satire
First published: 1970; collected in *Conjure: Selected Poems, 1963-1970,* 1972

The Poem

"Beware: do not read this poem" is written in free verse, divided into six unequal stanzas. There are no capital letters, and the poem has many spelling irregularities and abbreviations, with apparently random spacing in many lines. There are very few punctuation marks except for an occasional comma or slash, usually in an odd place. However, a single voice speaks the whole poem, and, although there are no neat markers to indicate divisions, the poem can be divided into three distinct parts. Moreover, despite its appearance on the page, the "grammar" of the poem is straight-forward and clear.

A story is told in the first three stanzas. This story, a kind of modern folktale, is related by the speaker as he synopsizes the plot of a television show he has just watched ("tonite, *thriller*"). The episode concerned an old woman who was so vain that she filled her house with mirrors, becoming finally so wrapped up in the mirrors that they became her life and she locked herself indoors. Eventually "the villagers" broke into her house, but she escaped by disappearing into a mirror. Thereafter, she seemed to haunt the house. Everyone who lived there "lost a loved one to/ the ol woman in the mirror."

In the fourth stanza the poem changes; instead of narrative fantasy, the poem becomes more discursive, and the speech pattern becomes more concrete. Now the voice speaks of the poem itself as though it were the mirrors or the old woman, warning the reader that "the hunger of this poem is legendary" and telling the reader to "back off," for the poem swallows people. Thus the poem itself becomes a kind of devourer, not merely a mirror that reflect the external world. There is a significant difference, though, between the poem and the mirrors: The poem is alive—and this is a major point of the poem. The voice goes on to say that "you," the reader, are being swallowed by the poem. The reader is advised to "go w/ this poem," to "relax." Finally, with the reader no longer being directly addressed as "you," poem and reader become one.

Now, disconcertingly, the language changes again. In the last short section there is a flat, bureaucratic statement about the great numbers of people who disappeared without a trace in 1968. Yet at the end the flatness is transformed into a short, abrupt cry of feeling, almost a protest, about the loss felt by the friends of those who have disappeared.

Forms and Devices

The poem is not realistic narrative or even a typical fantasy story. It is, rather, about language and how language makes culture. Three types of language usage appear in the poem. In the first section, although the voice seems to be African American, there is an underlying European speech and a European subject. It is written with run-on sentences, the sense going from line to line. The run-on sentences have a different rhythm from the second section, suggesting a cultural difference. The second section is much more rhythmic, more African American. The last section is almost dry, until the final quietly sad statement about there being a "space" in the lives of those left behind.

The sounds in the poem are essential to its meaning. Most European American poetry is umbilically connected to the written word. Even the oral poetry of poets such as Allen Ginsberg is very "literary"; its roots are in the letter. Reed's poem, on the other hand, uses the rhythms and short lines of actual speech—at bottom African American speech—although there are some careful exceptions to the accurate representation of speech. The deliberate misspellings, the lack of standard punctuation, the contractions, are speech, speech with rhythm, reflecting the community that is their base. The poem is, despite or even because of its appearance on the page, the result of a living oral tradition—yet, paradoxically, it uses "literature" as a foil.

In the first part, the run-on sentences do indeed tell the story, which emphasizes time, past, present, and, especially, future, an emphasis that is European American. The second part of the poem, however, is composed of lines that are complete sentences in themselves, even with the expected punctuation left out. There are no run-on lines until the final couplet, where the speaker asserts flatly that "this poem is the reader & the/ reader this poem." This couplet, solidly closing the section, is also a summation of the series of statements above it. However, it also speaks of time as a now, something to be lived in, emphasizing life—a more African American approach.

Reed also rejects the standard grammatical forms and poetic formulas of the past, but he uses those forms for contrast. Like the American poet Ezra Pound, Reed is saying, "Make it new," but to make it new one must show what one is rejecting. Reed himself has pointed out that his earliest poetry was influenced by poets such as William Butler Yeats; by implication, he is both using and refusing such influence here.

Themes and Meanings

Thematically, "beware: do not read this poem" is a complex case. It is about language, about art, about people, and about politics. Language and art are intimately bound to one another, and they are central aspects of culture. Culture, at least in part, makes people. The poem is therefore about how people are made by, and lost to (other), cultures. It is a protest against cultural dominance, and it works by concrete demonstration.

In the immediate sense, the poem's theme is about how the poem itself affects, even creates its reader by involving the reader in the world created by the poem. That concept is an exhibition of the power of poetry, for poetry is an act of speech, showing that language, how one uses language, is vital to one's existence. The poem also shows how a culture can swallow one up, denying one's real existence. It rejects the idea of art as a simple mirror reflecting life; art is, rather, a living experience.

There are some generic conventions in the poem that may seem at first to be merely decorative or entertaining, but they actually represent essential elements of the theme. In the first section, the convention of the European folktale is, of course, derived from a literary, European tradition. This folktale is presented as the product of modern technology—a television plot—which makes it very European American, mechanical and hypnotizing in a negative way. Too, the tale, with its "ol woman," essentially a witch, in the house which is attacked by "villagers" uses words and images that are not American ("villagers" is not a term commonly used in the United States). Yet, as has been already noted, the poem's basic language is the language of African America, and there is a deliberate tension between the convention and the language. Indeed, here the language is a protest against the culture implied in the folktale.

The second section is an assertion that the poem, made of language, creates a culture. Although the "ol woman" and her house seem to become the poem, this section really rejects the European American culture of the first part. For the moment, all is African American. Instead of being swallowed by mirrors and disappearing, one is swallowed by the rhythms of the language and is made more alive.

Yet the larger world encompasses, surrounds, this positive one, so the poem must return to the European American world. In the first line of the last section, the speaker speaks of the "us bureau of missing persons," the "us" obviously standing for United States. However, it is also the pronoun "us," and the bald statistic presented is a reference to us. We are involved in this world of loss, where words do and do not quite make connections between us. Moreover, there is a contrast between the state, the national apparatus, and the individuals, the "us" of the United States. When the poem turns to the dry official language of this section, the language of the dominant culture that the poem is rejecting, the reader again is shown how that culture has swallowed people. The poem must therefore end with its note of regret, for those who have lost people to that culture have a "space" in their lives.

L. L. Lee

THE BIGHT

Author: Elizabeth Bishop (1911-1979)
Type of poem: Lyric
First published: 1949; collected in *Poems: North & South—A Cold Spring*, 1955

The Poem

"The Bight" is a lyric of thirty-six lines that provides a veritable showcase of Elizabeth Bishop's aesthetic of observation and her metaphoric impulse. The bracketed subtitle—"On my birthday"—suggests both an occasion and, perhaps, a gift. Such an occasion usually implies the assessment that people are prone to on their birthdays, but, in this case, the poet seems to be tallying up the contents of a localized landscape.

A bight is a small bay between two points of land, and here the topography in question is Garrison Bight in Key West, Florida, where Bishop lived during the winter of 1948-1949. The poem draws heavily from a letter Bishop wrote to poet and close friend Robert Lowell in January, 1948. The details of her description of Key West appear in the poem's opening lines, and she tells him that the untidy bay resembles her desk.

One of the problems Bishop faces in this poem is how to infuse what seems like a purely descriptive exercise with some of the impetus of narrative. The poem consists of an apparently random survey of activity, both natural and human, and the detritus left behind by it all. Each focused detail, however, is an invitation to concentrate and see clearly not just what is but also what can be. The speaker seems separate from the scene, distanced, but her imaginative capacity closes the gap. The water, the birds, the "frowsy sponge boats," the ramshackle scenery are eventually taken in by the speaker/observer, a gift on her birthday, one might say, to herself and to the reader. In the following passage, the movement from distance to interiority, from disparate object to meaningful symbol, reflects the overall movement of the poem:

> Some of the little white boats are still piled up
> against each other, or lie on their sides, stove in,
> and not yet salvaged, if they ever will be, from the last bad storm,
> like torn-open, unanswered letters.
> The bight is littered with old correspondences.

Like her early mentor, poet Marianne Moore, Bishop finds a more compelling reality in the imagined scene, the individualized, personalized world. "The Bight" depicts that reality as it comes into being.

Forms and Devices

One of Bishop's aesthetic standards as a poet was accuracy; poet-critic Randall Jarrell noted in one of his reviews that "all her poems have written underneath, *I have seen it.*" Yet accuracy for Bishop means something more than objective, literal transcription. She must allow her reader not only to see the object before her but also to experience the whole meditative, discursive act of perception. To re-create this experience, she brings to bear a range of poetic devices, tactics that give her language the expansiveness and elasticity of a mind freed by engagement with the world around her. Thus, the envisioned objects can take on symbolic significance.

The mention of the great French poet Charles Baudelaire seems justified by his own proclivity for searching the material world for analogies to the human soul, as when he writes: "Imagination is an almost divine faculty which perceives immediately and without philosophical methods the inner and secret relations of things, the correspondences and analogies." In her allusion, however, Bishop treats this idea ironically, noting that "if one were Baudelaire/ one could probably hear" the evaporating water in the bay "turning to marimba music." The qualifications in this passage ("*if* one were . . . / one could *probably* . . . ") suggest that Bishop herself draws back from such fanciful and elaborate flights of invention. Later she confirms a less exalted, more modest intention than Baudelaire: "The bight is littered with old correspondences."

In keeping with this urge for a down-to-earth clarity, Bishop's tropes are designed to link whatever is seen with something that is at least as common or more so. Pelicans crash into the water "like pickaxes"; man-of-war birds open their tails "like scissors" or tense them "like wishbones"; shark tails are hung on a fence, "glinting like little plowshares." All such similes envelop the reader in Bishop's own conception of the interconnectedness of things. We are meant to delight in their sheer appropriateness.

The poet's presence is also registered in the masterful but subtle control she exerts over the form of the poem. She constructs sentences that sprawl over the course of several lines, seemingly casual but pulling the reader from phrase to phrase by means of their accumulated detail and sporadic enjambment. Note the momentum in the following passage and the way in which Bishop herself slips into the description, less to qualify it than to endorse it:

> The birds are outsize. Pelicans crash
> into this peculiar gas unnecessarily hard,
> it seems to me, like pickaxes,
> rarely coming up with anything to show for it,
> and going off with humorous elbowings.

Bishop also links the various images of the poem by her use of sound, employing feminine rhymes ("jawful"/"awful") and assonance ("plays"/"claves"; "jawful of marl"). In the passage cited first, near the end of the poem, she quietly puns on Baudelaire's "correspondences," aligning them with "torn-open, unanswered letters." As "untidy" as the poem itself might appear, she reminds the reader, it has been carefully arranged, and such rhymes and word-play are there as inconspicuous evidence. However, it is just such allusion and figurative language that establishes Bishop's claim upon the scene.

Themes and Meanings

The theme of poetic intervention and invention is fairly clear. Early in the poem, Bishop alludes to another poet and gently mocks his kind of intervention in the observed world; she then sets about producing her own. A few characteristics of that vision are important to note since they contribute to whatever meaning might be drawn.

First, there is a suggestion of violence about the scene—the remnants of previous upheaval and the potential for some explosive instant to come. The water is "the color of the gas flame turned as low as possible" and is turning to gas, while the pilings are "dry as matches." Pelicans "crash" into the surface of the bay, while above them soar "man-of-war birds." Sharks have been harvested along with the sponges, and their tails hang on a fence, drying, *memento mori* from the sea beyond. The dredge itself brings up a "dripping jawful of marl," personifying the mechanism with the traits of some carnivorous beast. The little boats have been piled up or stove in by the last hurricane. This impression of violence is countered with the simultaneous, ongoing actions of exposure. The water absorbs, but low tide has left much of the content of the bight revealed, and the work of the dredge is the "untidy activity" of bringing to light what is yet beneath the surface. Even the pelicans and the "frowsy sponge boats" are engaged in bringing something up. What is one to make of these impressions when one considers as well the work of the poet in presenting them to us, and her pronouncement upon the whole scene as "awful but cheerful"? Should one of these adjectives be stressed more than the other?

The reader must keep in mind that Bishop's "accuracy" is not a matter of photojournalism, of absolute fidelity to fact. Instead, she recognizes that the poetic vision—even of a negligible panorama like Garrison Bight—involves a certain wrenching on her part. (The word *trope*, in its Greek origin, means "to turn or twist.") Poetry wreaks a kind of violence on the real world in order to reveal the imaginative potential of what lies before one. On one hand, this poem reveals some anxiety on Bishop's part about this; on the other hand, one can see that she is committed to it nonetheless. She knows that this activity is paramount to possess the world more fully and dispel whatever isolation she may feel as a human being.

Bishop's resistance to Baudelaire's exotic analogies, her rootedness in the physicality of the witnessed scene, her embrace of the whole range of activity—"awful but cheerful"—all suggest an allegiance to the world of objects. "The Bight" insists not on grand design and poetry as statement but upon the power of the ordinary to inspire a kind of loving attention. The bight itself, that grab-bag of a body of water, becomes a symbol of the poet's mind. Through the creative labor of dredging, what is least promising, what is nondescript to the point of invisibility, what is in fact buried under a shifting load of psychic debris becomes visible, tangible, and fraught with possibility. The poem gives us an artfully staged but privileged glimpse of the poetic imagination in process.

Nelson Hathcock

THE BLACK RIDERS

Author: Stephen Crane (1871-1900)
Type of work: Book of poems
First published: 1895, in *The Black Riders and Other Lines*

The Poems

Stephen Crane was well launched into a career as a fiction writer before he ventured into poetry. As early as 1890, he was writing sketches for a college monthly, and shortly thereafter he began producing columns for the *New York Tribune*. In 1893 Crane published one novel, *Maggie: A Girl of the Streets*, began work on another, *The Red Badge of Courage* (1895), and ventured into poetry. Since at that time he had only seven more years to live, it is hardly surprising that in all Crane produced only 136 poems. Half of these appeared in *The Black Riders*, another thirty-seven in a later volume, *War Is Kind* (1899). Only eight more poems were published during Crane's lifetime; the remainder were collected and printed after his death.

Though Crane's important first collection is usually referred to as *The Black Riders*, it actually appeared under the title *The Black Riders and Other Lines*. His poems deal with serious issues, but they are not based on a systematic theology or philosopy. Instead, they are speculations, born of fleeting thoughts or experiences, that the poet jotted down and then shaped into a coherent form. Like lyrics, each of the poems in *The Black Riders* is clearly tied to a moment, and therefore there are often marked differences between various poems on the same subject. Crane's poems are not intended to express emotion as a lyric does, but to be little essays in poetic form—or, as the author also described them, "pills" to remedy the spiritual and intellectual ills that afflict humanity.

One reason Crane used words such as "lines" or "pills" to describe his poems was that, while he was happy to be classified with fiction writers, he did not want to be considered a poet. For him the term implied effete bohemianism. On the other hand, Crane was proud of his own works in the genre. He even admitted liking *The Black Riders* better than *The Red Badge of Courage*, explaining that the novel was limited in scope, whereas the poetry covered all areas of human existence.

The sixty-eight poems in *The Black Riders* are all written in free verse. They are very short, many of them no more than three to six lines in length. Only four are over twenty lines. Moreover, because most of Crane's lines are themselves so short, sometimes consisting of just a word or two, even the longest of the poems in the collection (number 49) does not seem as lengthy as its forty lines might indicate.

Despite their brevity, however, Crane's poems have internal conflict and move to a conclusion. For example, the first poem in the collection begins with a dramatic description of the "black riders" and ends with a startling explanation: The ride of the mysterious men, readers learn in the last line, is like that of "Sin." By contrast, the drama in the second and third poems involves a contrast in perspective, in one case between the judgments of birds and human beings, and in the other between the persona and a "creature, naked, bestial," who may or may not be human but in any case is acting in a very peculiar fashion, at least as far as the narrator is concerned. Crane introduces his unnamed persona for the first time in number 3; though he does not appear in all of the poems, he does so frequently enough to provide a degree of unity to the collection.

The book does not have the same tight structure as the poems within it or as any of Crane's fiction, however. While a dozen themes or motifs appear, disappear, and reappear as the collection proceeds, no thematic divisions are evident, nor does the work as a whole move toward any conclusion. It has been suggested that *The Black Riders* is meant to represent a journey through life, perhaps that of the persona, whose presence could be imagined even when he does not appear. If so, the journey is circular rather than linear, for though each poem moves toward some discovery, the work as a whole does not move toward any transforming vision or redeeming certainty. Of course, this may be exactly the point Crane is making—that while one may appear to be progressing in life, making one discovery after another on the way to some final understanding, actually one ends where one began, except that one's mind is now crowded with conflicting truths, flooded with metaphors that still refuse to form a coherent pattern.

Forms and Devices

Crane's experiments with poetic form came as a direct result of his exposure to the work of another highly original poet. In the spring of 1893, Crane had been invited to call on the prominent novelist William Dean Howells. During their visit Howells read Crane several of Emily Dickinson's poems, and almost immediately thereafter Crane began writing the poems that would appear in *The Black Riders*. It is not difficult to see why this exposure to Dickinson, along with Howells's obvious admiration for her, so inspired Crane. Like her, he decided to ignore the conventions of the genre, even in so superficial a matter as the way his book would look. For instance, Crane insisted that his poems be given no titles, only numbers, and that they be printed, one to a page, in capital letters throughout. As a result, they looked at least as strange as Dickinson's dash-filled lines.

There was also much in Dickinson's style that appealed to Crane, notably her terseness and her use of epigrams. In number 34, for example, Crane's persona spurns those who are attempting to foist their own images of God upon him: "I can't buy of your patterns of God,/ The little gods you may rightly prefer." In number 62, a final epigram denies the significance of a man's entire life: "Yet when he was dead,/ He saw that he had not lived." One of the antiwar poems, number 5, describes how a well-intentioned suggestion by a single individual led to a bloody and long-lasting conflict. In time, readers are told, the man died, broken-hearted. The poem ends with a memorable epigram: "And those who stayed in bloody scuffle/ Knew not the great simplicity." The shortest poem in the collection, number 56, does not just contain an epigram, but is an epigram in its entirety: "A man feared that he might find an assassin;/ Another that he might find a victim./ One was more wise than the other."

In other ways, however, Crane's poetry is very different from that of Dickinson. Instead of meter and rhyme, he used the looser rhythmic patterns of free verse. Moreover, where Dickinson's references to the natural world—a snake, a bird, a fly—were always exact and particular, Crane's images are general, used primarily for allegorical purposes. The "little birds" in number 2, for example, have no individuality, and, except for his grin, the "fat, stupid ass" in number 55 is as unrealized as the "green place" where he is standing. Often Crane mentions mountains, deserts, gardens, and stars, but he does not describe them. Instead, he uses the words as stimuli which will prompt his readers to sketch appropriate landscapes from their own experience, while he proceeds to indicate the metaphorical implications of his imagery.

In *The Black Riders* Crane uses imagery to reinforce the statement he makes so often in his poems: that the world is, above all, a place of suffering and conflict. Even when his point about the seeming inevitability of human conflict is not made explicitly, as it is in number 27, where an encounter turns into a murder, and in number 5, where killing seems to be humanity's favorite pastime, it is implicit in such images as the "clang of spear and shield" in the title poem and even the "noise of tearing" that threatens the persona in number 40. There is no refuge. If various gods do not attack a man, as in number 19, the mountains will, as in number 22. In number 41, the very landscape, with its rocks and briars, seems malevolent. Frequently the world is described as a hostile desert (number 3, number 42) or a place of "snow, ice, burning sand" (number 21).

Crane's use of color imagery in *Black Riders* is particularly significant. At least a dozen times, the poet refers to red or to such associated images as fire and blood, and about as often, he mentions black or darkness. Thus blackness symbolizes not only sin (number 1) and death (number 68), but also existential fear (number 10) and the unknowable nature of the universe (number 29). This earth is indeed "a place of blackness" (number 23).

Though red is sometimes associated with life and hope, in Crane's poems it symbolizes pain, torment, and, like black, inevitable death. There are specific references to the color red, such as the red demons in number 46, but red is also associated with fire, with the desert heat, with the "crimson clash of war" (number 14), and with blood. In number 30, for example, the "red sword of virtue" means virtual suicide. In the final analysis, it does not much matter whether one dies on a "burning road," on the bloody field of battle or, more quietly, in black despair. In *The Black Riders* the serene, green gardens all lie "at impossible distances" (number 26). Red and black are the colors of this world, and there is no comfort in either of them.

Themes and Meanings

The Black Riders begins with an affirmation of the existence of sin and ends with an affirmation of the existence of God. While the title poem demonstrates the power of sin, it does not offer any hint as to its origin or indicate a possible remedy. One cannot derive any more comfort from the final poem in the collection, for although

God finally strikes down a spirit for denying him, thus proving that he exists, he would not aid the spirit or even admit his presence during the spirit's long and anguished search for him. Thus what seem to be certainties are not certain at all, and what appear to be answers merely direct one toward more questions.

It is not surprising, then, that one of the dominant themes in the collection is that of the search for truth. Crane does not minimize the difficulty of this quest. Too often, he thinks, the overconfident find themselves in the position of the "learned man" in number 20, who confidently leads the persona into the unknown, only to find that he himself is lost. Crane is skeptical of people like the man in number 28, who insists that he has ascended to the "mighty fortress" which is truth and viewed the world from his unassailable position. In Crane's opinion, it is more likely that truth is a "shadow, a phantom" that he may never discover. Nevertheless, Crane knows that something in the human spirit yearns for truth. It may be that one is a fool for seeking it, like the man in number 24, who keeps "pursuing the horizon" even though he is told his quest is utterly "futile." It is interesting to compare this poem with number 7. Here the searcher is pictured not as a fool but as a person of some courage: "Fear not that I should quaver,/ For I dare—I dare./ Then, tell me!" Perhaps the difference between being a fool—one of Crane's favorite terms—and being a brave man is simply the difference between pride and humility. A fool does not know his limitations, either as an individual or as a human being; a brave man acknowledges them but refuses to embrace despair.

Whatever his uncertainties about truth or the possibility of discovering it, Crane did have firm opinions as to what constitutes human error. High on his catalog of sins was pride. Sometimes he points to this epitome of folly by contrasting human beings with animals, as he does in number 2, when the birds mock a man who cannot sing anywhere as well as they can, and in number 55, where anyone can see that the "stupid" ass who is enjoying himself in an earthly paradise is really cleverer than the man working so hard on the "burning road." In number 18 Crane sums up the issue in the form of a parable. Brought before God for judgment, various little blades of grass boast of their achievements. One of them is diffident, confessing that he cannot remember his good deeds, whereupon God praises him as being best of all.

If human beings possessed the humility of the diffident blade of grass, they would not be so certain of their own infallibility. In number 47 an insufferably arrogant man insists that the persona think just as he does, threatening that if he does not, he is "abominably wicked," a despicable "toad." After due deliberation, the persona decides that under those circumstances, he would prefer to be a toad. However, as Crane points out in number 17, it is far easier to be a conformist. Very few people are brave enough to think for themselves. As a result, the poet suggests, they are herded into church (number 32), where they worship other people's gods (number 34), or go willingly to war in order to kill those they have been told are their enemies (number 14).

Even though the poet can see the weaknesses of humanity, he does not himself fall into the trap pride sets for nonconformists. Thus in number 45, he reveals his scorn for tradition, which he says is "milk for babes," not "meat for men," but then he admits quite honestly that "alas, we all are babes."

While Crane seems firm in his ethical principles, he still wonders whether God exists, and if he does, how he relates to his creation. Sometimes the poet inclines toward nihilism (numbers 10, 66, and 67); at other times he taxes either an omnipotent God or some lesser divinity with being unjust (number 12, number 19). In number 6, he compares the world to a ship, marvelously made by divine hands, that slipped away before it could be equipped with a rudder and now drifts aimlessly through space. In this interpretation, God is not evil, just a bit careless and much too busy—it was his need to remedy a wrong that caused him to turn aside just when the world most needed him. Elsewhere, however, Crane is more hopeful. Clearly he would like to believe in a God of compassion (number 33) and of tender, "infinite comprehension" (number 51). Perhaps, the poet muses in number 49, there is a "radiance/ Ineffable, divine" that would give meaning to the universe. Perhaps it is only his own spiritual blindness that causes the vision to elude him. At the end of *The Black Riders* Crane is as uncertain about the existence and the nature of God as he was at the beginning.

Although Crane's fiction has long been admired, his poetry has been largely neglected both by readers and by critics. It deserves better. The poems in *The Black Riders* are worth reading for the surrealistic landscapes alone, but they have other virtues as well, including stylistic originality, profound subject matter, and, above all, uncompromising honesty in their search for truth.

Rosemary M. Canfield Reisman

THE BLACK WALNUT TREE

Author: Mary Oliver (1935-
Type of poem: Lyric
First published: 1978; collected in *Twelve Moons*, 1979

The Poem

"The Black Walnut Tree," written in free verse, is a short poem of thirty-five lines. The title immediately draws the reader's attention toward the natural world and the center of emotional conflict in the poem. Like the large branches of an ancient walnut tree, Oliver's poem is shrouded in the shadow of her family tree. Using the first person, Oliver makes no distinction between the speaker of the poem and herself; in fact, the poet's family history is the source for the events described. In this poem, as in much lyric poetry, the speaker addresses the reader directly about her personal experience, and, by using this poetic form, Oliver makes the reader part of the events she describes, forcing one to consider the poem's dilemma as if it were one's own.

"The Black Walnut Tree" concerns the poet's and her mother's struggle to decide whether they will have a tree on their property cut down. If they decide to have the black walnut tree removed and to sell it for lumber, they will be able to pay off their home's mortgage; however, if they remain faithful to everything the tree represents, they risk a limb falling through the roof of the house in some storm or, worse, foreclosure and the loss of the house itself.

The poem opens with this general dilemma but moves quickly to its inevitable consequence: the two women trying to sort out what is really the best course of action in such a situation. Part of the poem's strength originates in what Oliver, in typically understated fashion, calls a "difficult time." While the responsibilities of home ownership are often thought too mundane to be the subject of poetry, Oliver manages to make a connection with her audience by plumbing the joys and burdens of owning a home or, more precisely, exploring how a home becomes more than a physical property.

In an attempt to convince each other that the only logical and financially responsible action is to cut down the tree, the poet tells her mother that the tree's roots are in the cellar drains, to which the mother replies that she has noticed the leaves growing heavier in the fall, when they must be raked, and the tree's fruit becoming increasingly difficult to gather. Clearly, however, the fruit this tree bears represents strong and essential connections to the past, an issue with far greater consequence than the tree's present inconveniences.

Thus, in the sixteenth line of the poem, there is a shift: The speaker realizes, in the process of her deliberation over the physical problems the tree presents, that "something brighter than money/ moves in our blood." At this point, the problem evolves from merely a physical dilemma to a spiritual one, and Oliver's insight is confirmed that night as she sleeps. Her dreams are populated by her Bohemian fathers—men who worked the "blue fields/ of fresh and generous Ohio"—and she wakes with the knowledge that she can never remove the tree. However, even though the poet is reconciled to the threat of high winds, heavier leaves, and falling fruit, she still hears "the whip-/ crack of the mortgage" as the poem closes.

Forms and Devices

Poet and novelist James Dickey suggests that Oliver's poems are "graceful and self-assured, serene even when they treat the ordinary agonies of life . . . richly complex without throwing complexities in the way of the reader." In "The Black Walnut Tree," Oliver does indeed suggest the complexity of what might be overlooked as merely mundane. She does so, however, without obscuring the events of the poem. As in much of Oliver's poetry, she achieves clarity in this poem by using common language to develop a short poetic line and metaphor that grows naturally out of her subject matter, all couched in a domestic narrative.

In "The Black Walnut Tree," as in much of her work, Oliver makes use of the lyric as plainsong, never allowing traditional verse forms to intrude on her subject. The short line she favors appears to have little to do with phrasing; rather, it establishes white space for contemplation. By placing so few words in each line, Oliver insists that the reader account for each word and the possible connections that the word may offer within the line and then within the poem as a whole. Perhaps this formal consideration culminates most dramatically in the final two lines of the poem, when Oliver hyphenates and splits the word "whip-/ crack," placing the emphasis equally between the two. The split allows the word to take on the physical characteristics of a whip: On one line it is drawn back; on the next it comes forward to lash its subject, the "crack" of the mortgage sounding.

At the same time that this "crack" relates to the mortgage, it also suggests the movement of the walnut tree's limbs. By constructing her metaphors from the very fabric of her narrative, Oliver gracefully and unobtrusively pushes the reader toward a recognition of the many levels at work. Truly, one might best describe Oliver's use of metaphor as organic or holistic, a practice that suits her spiritual perspective nicely. However, because of this practice, upon a first reading of the poem, it is relatively easy to overlook the extended conceit that Oliver carefully constructs.

The conceit grows from the black walnut tree at the center of the poem, taking on three interrelated meanings that function on significantly different levels. First, the black walnut tree exists on the physical plane, creating tangible, concrete problems for the poet and her mother. The tree has grown old, making inroads into the foundation with its roots, its falling fruit is more of a nuisance than a blessing, and its leaves pile higher with each passing autumn, becoming more difficult to dispose of.

Second, the tree exists on a spiritual plane that involves the deeply entwined history of the family. The walnut tree, like any other living organism, has started from a seed, and the poet realizes that "an edge/ sharp and quick as a trowel/ that wants us to dig and sow" moves in her blood. She is beckoned by this tree, in her own and her "fathers' backyard," to remember her fathers who filled the fields of Ohio with "leaves and vines and orchards." Thus, the tree in her yard comes to represent both the spiritual and physical call of her heritage.

Finally, as the poem closes, the tree takes on yet another meaning. The tree, limbs moving in "leaping winds," becomes a symbol of the mortgage that threatens to destroy the poet's own life with her mother, as well as the memory of her fathers. This final move allows the reader to recognize the complex and potentially tragic dimensions of this situation. The metaphor coalesces, encompassing both the physical and the spiritual, both the past and the present, to profound effect.

Themes and Meanings

"The Black Walnut Tree" is a poem about connection. Like her fellow Ohio native James Wright, to whom she dedicated her Pulitzer Prize-winning volume, *American Primitive* (1983), Oliver continually strives to illustrate the ties between people and place, often ending in some transcendent moment or epiphany. As the title of the collection *Twelve Moons*, in which "The Black Walnut Tree" first appeared, suggests, Oliver often discovers the connections between people and place in the primitive, natural order.

Oliver's search for elemental connections, like those associated with the moon, occur in "The Black Walnut Tree" when the poet and her mother are confronted with the demands of the present. However, the true conflict in this poem, which leads more toward insight than epiphany, is the undeniable hold that the past has on the present.

What prevents the poet or her mother from having the tree removed and paying off the mortgage is the knowledge of the tree's connection to a past that includes generations of men and women working the fields of Oliver's Ohio home, where the vines of their lives were woven into the very soil that they lived upon. To remove a visible symbol of this past connection—a living history told in the limbs, leaves, and fruit of this looming tree—would be to ignore and, in a sense, betray the universal truth that we are known and come to know others by recognizing the lines of our history and their intersection in the present, pushing ever on toward an unknowable future. Consequently, with this insight, after dreaming of her fathers working the orchards they had planted, Oliver explains what she and her mother both know, "that we'd crawl with shame/ in the emptiness we'd made," a truly profound insight for what appears to be a rather modest poem.

Todd Davis

THE BLINDMAN

Author: May Swenson (1919–1989)
Type of poem: Lyric
First published: 1965; collected in *Half Sun Half Sleep*, 1967

The Poem

"The Blindman" unfolds in six stanzas consisting of three lines each. Its irregular meter is not without rhyme. The poem consists of rhyming couplets, some of which span the stanza breaks, as the last line of one stanza is completed by the rhyming first line of the next. The title prepares the reader for an experience without sight. As a blind person must rely on other forms to "see," those with sight are shown how color can be more than an abstract concept for someone who has never witnessed rainbow hues.

Those who are born with the ability to see take color for granted. Children learn color at a very early age without much difficulty. This simple lesson is recorded, and for the remainder of one's life the brain recognizes various colors with no need for translation. In May Swenson's "The Blindman," the speaker watches as a blind man uses his other senses to "see" colors. The poem begins with the man tasting the color purple by placing "a tulip on his tongue." In the second stanza, feeling the blades of grass against his cheek, the man construes the color green.

In the third stanza, the blind man's tears are described as "fallen beads of sight." This image leads one to believe that the blind man is not quite satisfied with his limited grasp of color. Nonetheless, he continues to grope for answers and lets the reader know that he is aware of these descriptive words.

The poem shifts from the third person to the first as the blind man speaks for himself, continuing to solve the mysteries of color by using objects for comparison. These clues give the man a basis for imagining what color means. He uses the sense of touch to feel the fibers of a scarf for the color red. His association of red with the warmth of the sun matches his interpretation of orange as he feels this color from the heat of a flame. These bright, vivid colors must be strong, like the intensity of fire.

He realizes that there is a multitude of colors; the "seven fragrances of the rainbow" are interpreted through various scents. In the last stanzas the use of all the senses is complete when the blind man tells how he can hear certain colors through the sound of an instrument. Even the sound made by rubbing the smooth surface of a piece of fruit—"a pomegranate lets me hear crimson's flute"—allows the blind man to conjure up an idea of deep pink. He must use everything around him in his attempt to capture the mysterious phenomenon of light. The second half of the last line, "Only ebony is mute," ironically sums up his concept of color, for black is the only color he truly understands.

Forms and Devices

Poetry is an imaginative expression of consciousness, and in this poem Swenson illustrates an acute awareness of something that is taken for granted by those fortunate enough to see. The poet and the blind man are similar in being able to reach beyond what is directly in front of them. In the words of Dylan Thomas, poetry is "the movement from an overclothed blindness to a naked vision." In "Blindman," rather than lifting the cloth to see more clearly, Swenson shields the eyes for a better look. The poem magnifies the colors as they take on a new dimension.

Just as art dates back to the beginning of humankind, imagery and metaphors have been used for centuries to describe a vision. Poetry has been a part of human expression since antiquity. The Greek lyric poet Simonides of Ceos defined poetry as "painting with the gift of speech." A painting is said to be "worth a thousand words," and in poetry only a few words are needed to tell an entire story. Swenson once noted that a "poem must be rich and evocative, but at the same time compact and exact."

Her imagery in "The Blindman" provides a masterful peek into the blind man's world. Seeing an image is difficult enough without looking at it. Seeing color without sight is impossible, but the blind man compensates for his missing sense of sight by fully using the remaining four. He tastes and feels the ocean: "In water to his lips,/ he named the sea blue and white." Stimulated further by sound, he notes that his sightless world is embellished by music: "Trumpets tell me yellow." Again, the crimson flute of the pomegranate may come from the squeaky sound heard from the hard shell of that fruit when he rubs the skin and listens with his ear. The colors that the blind man sees are imaginary, but the poet tries to expand his world with different ways of imagining. It is typical of Swenson to draw upon nature for her imagery, and the nature imagery is especially appealing in this poem.

Themes and Meanings

While the blind man discovers ways to see color in this poem, the sighted person experiences something that is equally unimaginable: how one can *not* know what color is. In the only way he knows how, the blind man must taste, touch, smell, and hear the different colors of the spectrum, knowing that there is a vast array from which to choose. He holds and runs his fingers all over an object to know its shape and texture so that he will recognize it the next time. He will know the scent of a rose after the first time he smells the sweet fragrance of that flower, likewise he will know the sound of the piano. Color is used extensively in language, but it can be neither touched nor heard. Whatever he is told about the color green, the blind man can know only what an object feels or tastes like. He has been told that grass is green, so he feels that color by rubbing the smooth blade across his cheek.

Human curiosity forces the man to try in every way he can to seize some kind of understanding. He creates his own interpretations, but he realizes their limitations. The poet includes the blind man's tears of defeat in the only line of the poem that expresses any kind of emotion. The blind man desperately longs to see the colorful world that he hears so much about. In the last line of the poem, "Only ebony is mute," he tells the reader what he actually knows—blackness, darkness.

Swenson has written other poems about color that are strictly visionary. In "Colors Without Objects," for example, her "painting" has no shape, but it becomes a kaleidoscope of colorful images that blend from one scene into the next. In "The Blindman" color has an entirely different meaning. What is implicitly known by a sighted person is totally perplexing to the blind man, yet he refuses to allow his blindness to shut him out from the brilliant world.

The sighted person has never had a reason to question what color is, but this poem urges readers to think how blind they may have been in not considering the experience of the person they see walking with a cane or seeing-eye dog. He is not only someone who is disabled but also someone with an awareness that goes beyond the obvious. If one looks a little deeper than usual, the world can be even more colorful than it appears.

Mary Ann Hoegberg

THE BLUE DRESS

Author: Sandra Cisneros (1954-
Type of poem: Meditation
First published: 1980, in *Bad Boys*

The Poem

"The Blue Dress" consists of six short stanzas of brief lines in free verse. In spite of its brevity and informality, the poem successfully conveys a multitude of feelings. Cisneros looks at a young man's breakup with a his girlfriend, the events precipitating it, and his consequent anxiety and pain. The poet narrates the details of two final visits between the former lovers, suggesting metaphorically the distance and the lack of commonality the young man feels at separating from the woman for whom he had once felt a close bond but who now goes her way alone to wait out the final days of a pregnancy. The speaker of the poem is an observer uninvolved in the actions of the couple, so she identifies with both, understands the dynamics of their relationship, and urges the reader to meditate on the situation. By describing little more about the woman than the blueness of her dress, Cisneros makes her fuse with the horizon. Inherent in this fusion is a sadness about how the events of life have turned.

In the first stanza the focus on the "curve of the belly" is the first clue to the details of the pregnancy that will be alluded to repeatedly. The emphasis is on external details, on objects: the bulging dress, the farewell and the bouquet, all of which fuse and fade into the background. Nothing is stated directly about facial expressions, about feelings.The inexpensive (and possibly artificial) flowers from the "Five & Ten" (stores such as Woolworth, known for stocking myriad domestic products and clothing at inexpensive prices), point to the overall paucity or meagerness of the scene at all levels. The "you" referred to in the second stanza is the young man, who is living out the final details of his obligation to the young pregnant girl. His ambivalent emotions are made clear: "You . . .// Want to tell her that you love her/ You do not love her."

In the next two stanzas one sees that each person lives in different settings and worlds. They meet for a few hours on Sunday, each commuting to a common meeting place, going through the motions of socializing. Each offers a topic for conversation, but they no longer know the same places or the same people. The only moment of sharing occurs when she eats the food he cannot swallow because of his discomfort.

The last two stanzas seem to describe the final visit and parting. The woman has summoned him by letter, requesting that they meet at a museum, away from the residence for females, operated by nuns, where she is staying. The image of the whale exhibit in the museum parallels the gravid and sluggish image of the young woman's final stages of pregnancy (the "curve" of her stomach has become a "swell") as she arrives dressed again in the blue dress. Once again, the reader only perceives the appearance of the dress rather than a person with specific characteristics.

This rhetorical device of using the part to represent the whole (her blue eyes, her white skin), helps more to depict the situation than to portray characters and their sentiments, as would be more common in a lyric text. The poem describes the man as dressed formally, according to societal norms, wearing "your best suit/ and the tie your mother gave you," signifying that this formal meeting is also only a polite rit- ual—more form than substance. No conversation, no details of sharing. The farewell and rupture become more definitive, as he purchases the airline ticket that will put even greater distance between the two. The speaker of the poem need say no more. This chapter is now closed.

Forms and Devices

Sandra Cisneros began her writing career as a poet and continued to write poetry as she progressed into the writing of short stories. (In a later book of short prose, *The House on Mango Street*, 1983, one finds pithy stories in a prose so full of sound and visual images that they are akin to poems.) The reader senses that every word, every turn of phrase, is carefully chosen for sound, for metaphorical capacity, and for the image it can convey. "The Blue Dress" is among her earliest published work, written during her years in graduate school. It is the only poem in a brief chapbook entitled *Bad Boys* that does not reveal specific details of Cisneros's Mexican-American roots.

In this particular poem, the color blue of the dress is the dominant image. The color and garment evoke the image of the young woman. She is only a vague, fading image that fuses with the color of the surroundings, particularly the air ("blue wind") and the horizon. The weight of the burden both people carry (their separation, single parent- hood, guilt, imposed obligations, and the ruptured relationship) is in contrast to the poem's brief, fragmentary lines, which are like brush strokes that barely suggest the essentials of the story. Cisneros's style has been aptly described as minimalist.

The constant understatement of details serves to emphasize the impossibility of communication, reunion, or a positive outcome. The speaker takes the position of the young man as actor and observer. There is paucity at every moment, whether in the meagerness of the flowers, the lack of dialogue, the man's lack of clear vision as he watches the approaching figure of the woman, or his oversight of surrounding details ("Someone offers his seat/ You never noticed").

The tension mounts as the couple attempt to eat; the man does not know what to say, and when he speaks, he blurts out a statement about himself (his upcoming birthday). Both people seem to act as if directed by the norms and constraints of proper societal behavior. He wears the suit and tie given to him by his parents, the prescribed clothing for formal encounters. She, in turn, has only a few hours away from the rules of the institution and the nuns who house her. This portrait is dominated by the cool blue color of detachment, vagueness, and sadness. The blue and painful feelings of the protagonists and the situation are well represented by the repetition of the color.

Themes and Meanings

"The Blue Dress" is concerned with the pathos of broken relationships and prom- ises. By representing a couple who meet occasionally, constricted by a variety of rules (transportation schedules, house rules, codes of dress and behavior), and who convey no joy during their brief encounters, Cisneros makes the reader sense and empathize with their discomfort and anxiety. The events and situations that lead to the birth of an infant are usually associated with excitement, anticipation, and joy. None of that is suggested in the poem. The reader must conclude that the young woman will become a single parent or that her new baby will be given to the nuns for adoption.

Both protagonists were involved in this event initially, but at the time and place in which they are represented in this text, their ties are strained and untenable. While the young woman is left in the background in a swath of blue, she demonstrates more tranquillity in her situation than he, by eating heartily and by stating in the last stanza, "I am fine." The young man, however, is burdened, ambivalent, and anxious at each meeting and departure. Finally, he buys the airline ticket which will take him far from these duties.

Eduardo F. Elías

BLUE WINE

Author: John Hollander (1929-
Type of poem: Meditation
First published: 1979, in *Blue Wine and Other Poems*

The Poem

"Blue Wine" comprises eleven numbered sections. They vary in length from the three-line seventh section to the twenty-nine lines of the eighth section. Each line in the poem is fourteen syllables long. One key to the poem is its dedication: "for Saul Steinberg." The inspiration for the poem was a visit by John Hollander to Steinberg's home, where Steinberg (an artist, humorist, and cartoonist) had done a drawing of several bottles of "blue wine." The whimsical names Steinberg gave the bottles in that initial drawing are given in the poem's eleventh section. From there, Hollander "thought about blue wine, and what it might mean." He was also thinking about Steinberg's art, specifically the 1979 second edition of The Passport, to which Hollander contributed the introduction. *The Passport*, a melange of real and false immigration documentation, is similar in tenor to Hollander's *Reflections on Espionage*; both acknowledge by undertone that authority is always authority, but it is not always correct.

As "Blue Wine" opens, a winemaker "worries over his casks," but the wine has its own consciousness. Red wine or white wine "broods on its own sleep." One cannot learn anything about blue wine, however, by looking in the barrels; "a look inside . . . would show/ Nothing." The difficulty of understanding blue wine is established.

The next four sections delineate methods of apprehending the wine. These result in mutually exclusive conclusions and arrays of half-truths. The second section presents intellectual approaches ranging from the scientific to the contemplative, while the third evokes the sensual, emotional reactions of the wine itself, such as "a blush of consciousness/ (Not shame)." By the final two lines of the third section, neither emotional nor intellectual interpretations are seen as more than convenient representations, unable to fully comprehend "immensities like blue wine."

The fourth and fifth sections show modes of "high" and "low" culture, respectively. The scholar translating Plutarch stands in sharp contrast to Hollander's rearranging of the "bluing for extra whiteness" of a television advertisement. Again, neither is in itself sufficient. In the sixth section, the names tell the tale: The name of the wine may translate as "The Blue Heart," but the wine comes from a nobleman whose title translates as the "marquis of silliness." What follows is a preposterous description of personal revelation. By the end of this section, the reader will trust in no one's authority on the matter of blue wine.

Sections 7 through 9, like section 6, are tales of personal encounters. They are, respectively, apocryphal, epic ("Homeric"), and naturalistic. The eighth section, with its blatant evocation of Homer's *The Odyssey*, anchors the poem solidly in the poetic tradition. The ninth both returns the reader to the contemporary world and links the arts to the world around them.

Section 10 is the only part of the poem to present the first-person experience of the author with "blue wine," which he remembers as only occasionally (with "domestic reticence") being poured at family meals. The last section ties the various perspectives together, and the poem's final four lines concurrently reject and affirm their own incomplete nature. The last words, "to see what he will see," refers to drawing one's own conclusions and having one's own encounters. The final line's evocation of Ralph Waldo Emerson's essay "Nature" brings the poem to a close.

Forms and Devices

Connections and evocations abound in Hollander's poetry. Nowhere is this shown more clearly than in the linkages (the following examples are by no means all-inclusive) between sections 3 and 8 of the poem. The concluding word of the eleventh line of section 3, "surmise," while appropriate in and of itself, also evokes the similarly phonemed "sunrise" as an element of the wine itself. This schemata of structural linguistics would not be so effective had not Hollander set it up by invoking "the dark moon of the cork" and "the bottom over which" the wine has come: The reader is subtly led to expect the sun beginning to broach the horizon. Hollander makes further connections. He has described poetry as an ongoing dialogue with poets previous, and the phrase "mild surmise" evokes the "wild surmise" in the penultimate line of John Keats's "On First Looking into Chapman's Homer." The explicitly "Homeric" eighth section is thus linked to this section.

Once the first link is noticed, the appearance of others comes as no surprise. One is especially delightful: The wine's "blush of consciousness/ (Not shame)" in section 3 invokes Adam and Eve in the Garden. Hollander uses this reference obliquely to reinforce the fourth and fifth lines of section 8. Even as the "gnashing rocks to leeward" evoke the Scylla and "the dark vortex" Charybdis from *The Odyssey* (book 12), so that which Charybdis "display[s] in its whorls/ . . . what it could never have/ Swallowed down from above" is a fig tree—the type of tree whose leaves Adam and Eve used to cover themselves after their first "blush of consciousness."

In Hollander's reconception of *The Odyssey's* book 12, Odysseus's crew, instead of eating Helios's cattle, drinks blue wine. As with Hollander's more complex poem "Spectral Emanations," the blue is evoked through the colors leading to it. The spectrum is described, from "Brightness of flame" to "flavescent gold," with both all colors (white, "blinding bleakness") and the absence of color ("the shining black of obsidian") limned. What remains on the island is the "constant fraction" of blue that abided "even after every sky/ Had been drenched in its color." The final phrase of section 8, the joyous "the sea-bright wine," is an inversion of "the wine-dark sea" of *The Odyssey.*

Themes and Meanings

The theme of the poem has been identified by many people as how people react to art. This conceptualization is a rather broad stroke, yet it is arguably incomplete, as it disregards Hollander's omnipresent consciousness that the line between art and life is a chimera.

Hollander's development as a poet follows a predictable arc. An ardent admirer of W. H. Auden in his early days, Hollander's first book, *A Crackling of Thorns* (1958), was published under Auden's aegis as a volume in the Yale Younger Poets series. As Hollander developed, Auden's influence ebbed, while Hollander's admiration for Wallace Stevens grew, leading to the explicit "Old W. H., get off my back!" in "Upon Apthrop House" from his collection *Spectral Emanations: New and Selected Poems* (1978), immediately previous to *Blue Wine and Other Poems*. Possibly even more telling is the Auden-like poet Myndal from Hollander's *The Quest of the Gole* (1966), a bard who values his powers so much that he rewrites that which needed no changes solely because he can. It is not Myndal who succeeds in the quest, but rather his younger brother who saves the kingdom through his heart, his good will, and attention to the world around him. The transition from the verse of Auden to the work of Stevens is a movement from art for its own sake to art as part of the world around it.

The contemplative sections of "Blue Wine," notably sections 2 and 5, emphasize the reactions that people filter through their senses—taste ("vinosities"), sight, and smell are considered at length, with contradictory conclusions. It is not that the senses are inadequate; rather, people use them in preconceived ways, thereby failing to realize the wine's essence. Similarly, the personal narratives (especially 6, 7, and 9) minimize the sensory for the sake of the experience, leaving conclusions that are ultimately unsatisfying because of their uniqueness ("reality is so Californian").

The key sections are those that show art (as exemplified by blue wine) and life as coincident, most notably sections 4 and 10. The "heavy leaves of the rhododendrons" are complemented by the "quickening leaves" of the scholar's translation, while the father's "abashed/ Smile" and the narrator's having "hid [his] gaze" emphasize interactions and influences, each making the other seem more real.

The final meaning that should be considered is the explicitly and implicitly Jewish nature of the poem. Critic Harold Bloom observed that Hollander "has no way back to Judaism, but is ruggedly and constantly aware of his almost-lost tradition." Knowing that the Zohar compares the Torah explicitly to wine, it is not a great leap to the realization that "Blue Wine" is, in many ways, an exploration of the Jewish experience in America.

Section 10 is the most explicit in this regard, evoking as it does the holiday of Passover, a celebration of the Jews attaining freedom from oppression. Hollander expresses his own position in lines 3-5: He honors the tradition even though he abjures some of the halachal laws ("commandments"). When the final stanza lists wine bottles with German, French, and even Romanian ("*Vin Albastru*") names, the reader may think of those who have left Europe for this continent, leaving behind their laws but not their traditions.

Written during the period of Hollander's works that most explicitly deal with the role of the Jewish poet ("Spectral Emanations" being the other most noteworthy),

"Blue Wine" is a poem to make Saul Steinberg, himself a Jewish immigrant from Europe, proud of the path that he and Hollander have chosen, in making their experiences with the world into art—and making both the world and the art the better for it.

Kenneth L. Houghton

BOGLAND

Author: Seamus Heaney (1939-
Type of poem: Meditation
First published: 1969, in *Door into the Dark*

The Poem

"Bogland," a short poem of seven four-line stanzas (quatrains), is the final work in Seamus Heaney's second collection of poetry, *Door into the Dark*. Heaney was born in the small town of Mossbaum, in County Derry, and is considered one of the most accomplished of the "Ulster poets," or writers from Northern Ireland. As is much of his early poetry, "Bogland" is heavily influenced by the writer's rural upbringing and reflects his close ties to the Irish landscape. The title originates from Ireland's often swampy countryside and from Heaney's childhood memory of the local interest generated by the discovery of an elk's skeletal remains in a bog near his hometown. The event was significant because, as he writes, "I began to get an idea of bog as the memory of the landscape, or as a landscape that remembered everything that happened in and to it." The poem's link to issues concerning the Irish countryside is further emphasized by its dedication to Thomas P. Flanagan, who authored several novels that reflected the political turmoil and class struggles in rural Ireland during the late nineteenth and early twentieth centuries; he also wrote influential critical texts on Irish prose. Flanagan taught at the University of California at Berkeley when Heaney was a guest lecturer there from 1970 to 1971.

"Bogland" opens with the poet comparing the landscape of the American West to that of Ireland and contrasting the vastness of the prairie to the close horizon of the Irish countryside, which seems to "encroach" upon the poet. Unlike American history, which in its westward expansion seemed to explore limitless horizons, Irish history turned inward, toward the center. The poem's perspective moves inward from the horizon to a nearby "tarn," or mountain lake, and the poet imagines that all of Ireland is reflected in the pool and its swampy surroundings, as if it were the eye of the Cyclops, a mythical, one-eyed giant.

The poet's attention focuses more closely on the marshy land around the lake and its "crusting" surface that appears firm but is in reality unstable. Continuing to turn inward, the third stanza moves the poet's imagination back to the time when the elk's carcass was discovered in the bog. Readers are led to the edge of, and then into, the bog itself. For Heaney, the elk raises the question of what other articles are suspended in the bog's "black butter." He remembers childhood stories of people storing food in the peat for long periods of time; the bog therefore becomes a repository, not only of archaeological artifacts, but of Irish culture, history, and identity. Ireland's mythic past, suggested by the Cyclops reference, is joined in the bog with its physical, organic past. The swampy landscape, soft and unstable, swallows anything laid to rest on it yet preserves and combines these objects into an amalgamation of personal and cultural histories.

The poet is led deeper into the peat, as if he were sinking in quicksand, and sees objects suspended in the bog. The poem concludes with Heaney attempting to strip away all the layers of soil and history that have accumulated over thousands of years. He discovers that there is no bottom, as if the swampy hole were so deep that the Atlantic Ocean itself had seeped up through the Irish landscape. If he should go farther down, he would ultimately go below the island itself and straight through the earth, never reaching the bottom.

Forms and Devices

Written in free verse, the poem's progression depends largely on the lines' enjambment, which pulls readers down the page as the poet is drawn deeper into the landscape. For example, stanza 1 concludes with the image of the poet's eye surveying the "Encroaching horizon," which is completed in the opening lines of the second stanza as his eye is "wooed into the cyclops' eye/ Of a tarn." Similarly, the last line of stanza 4, "The ground itself is kind, black butter," is continued in the first line of the fifth stanza, which echoes the theme of the bog's "Melting and opening underfoot." Just as stanzas 4 and 5 are linked syntactically by "butter/ Melting," so the grammatical distinctions between stanzas and sentences become blurred.

"Bogland" presents the poet as historical, cultural, and artistic archaeologist. Heaney had been influenced by P. V. Glob's *The Bog People* (1966), an account of a Danish excavation of a first century settlement in Windeby, Germany. The marshy German terrain had nearly perfectly preserved several bodies and artifacts, and Heaney recognized the swamp's potential to serve as a metaphor for human experience. Instead of civilization progressing linearly along a time line, cultures were built upon each other like the layers of sediment in the bog. This treatment of history is reminiscent of T. S. Eliot's description in part 5 of *The Waste Land* (1922) of how civilization is built upon the ruins of previous cultures. Heaney observes that "Every layer they strip/ Seems camped on before." For Heaney, the layers are not easily distinguishable because, unlike the layers of solid ground, the bog is continually "melting and opening underfoot." What was long past mingles with what has recently found its way into the marsh, and distinctions between time periods become unclear.

As the poet-archaeologist of "Bogland" digs deeper into the peat, he travels back not only through historical time but also into the collective human consciousness. The artifacts uncovered in the upper layers give way to increasingly primitive objects: the butter, the "waterlogged trunks" of ancient trees, and finally a primordial sea deep below the surface where the "wet centre is bottomless." Leaving the historical, physical world, the poet enters the realm of myth and the supernatural. Here he seeks to reveal the foundations of culture and the roots of identity by literally penetrating below the surface and identifying previously obscured social and artistic origins. In the end, though, the poet is unable to reach a solid beginning, having found instead a vast ocean of experience that is beyond humanity's knowledge and power of understanding.

Themes and Meanings

In part, "Bogland" illustrates the poet's quest to break free from artistic conventions and traditions. Historically, poets have struggled with the need to create their own identities as artists, and this struggle has been difficult for twentieth century Irish poets living in the shadow of influential writers such as William Butler Yeats (1865-1939). Searching for his own artistic roots, Heaney followed the advice of fellow Irish poet Patrick Kavanagh (1905-1967), who believed that the local, or parochial, could transcend its mundane, or provincial, limitations to represent universal themes. The close scrutiny of the landscape in "Bogland" provides the poet with a metaphor for exploring larger cultural themes.

One of the most omnipresent themes in Irish literature is the search for a national identity. Having lived in Northern Ireland during the "Troubles" (the political and religious conflicts between unionists and separatists with origins that trace back hundreds of years), Heaney is keenly aware of the difficulties associated with establishing a national identity. The poet avoids the problems of essentializing his definition of Irish culture by presenting culture as a landscape in a perpetual state of metamorphosis. Ireland and the Irish are not a single, simply identifiable entity determined solely by political or religious affiliations. Rather, they are the accumulation of thousands of years of history, which becomes jumbled and confused in multiple layers of collective cultural consciousness. The bog serves as the landscape's archetypal memory, preserving everything that has occurred. It contains an organic record of each generation that has lived on it. Therefore, Ireland's identity is constantly re-defining itself as successive generations add to the bog and are made part of the whole.

For Heaney then, the bog functions as a metaphor for the search for significant patterns, a means of unifying a fractured, postcolonial society. Establishing what it means to be "Irish" is possible, but only as an accumulation of meanings that reverberate back and forth from present to past to present again. While Heaney's search terminates in the vast, bottomless center of the world, the poem's conclusion is neither pessimistic nor nihilistic. As he digs deeper, the poet uncovers increasingly ancient levels of culture and consciousness until he verges on the mysterious origins of history itself. Here, in the dark roots of Ireland, the poet can explore his origins free from the political, religious, and artistic limitations that confine him on the surface.

Thomas F. Suggs

BOMB

Author: Gregory Corso (1930-
Type of poem: Dramatic monologue
First published: 1958; collected in *The Happy Birthday of Death,* 1960

The Poem

"Bomb" is an extended dramatic monologue presented as shaped verse in the form of the mushroom cloud of an atomic blast. The title refers to the object addressed in the poem. The speaker talks to the silent atomic bomb, comparing it with the other works and practices of humankind, declaring the bomb worthy of laughter, admiration, and love.

"Bomb" opens as the speaker begins the address, exclaiming, "You Bomb/ Toy of Universe   Grandest of all snatched-sky   I cannot hate you." How, the speaker wonders, can he hate the bomb in particular when no similar hate is felt for the thunderbolt, the caveman's club, Leonardo Da Vinci's catapult, or Cochise's tomahawk? Indeed, the speaker asks, "[H]ath not St. Michael a burning sword   St. George a lance   David a sling[?]" The bomb is, after all, "no crueller than cancer."

To all others, death in any other form, whether "car-crash   lightning   drowning/ Falling off a roof   electric-chair   heart attack" or "old age   old age," is better than death by the bomb, but to the speaker, the bomb is "Death's jubilee/ Gem of Death's supremest blue." The speaker imagines the effect of the atomic blast on pedestrians and subway riders in Manhattan but quickly lets imagination soar, envisioning "Turtles exploding over Istanbul" and "The top of the Empire State/ arrowed in a broccoli field in Sicily." With the atomic blast, the ruins of antiquity, the structures of the present, and the possibilities of the future shall all be at an end, and the bomb can "tee-hee finger-in-the-mouth hop/ over its long long dead Nor." Even God will be gone: "A thunderless God   A dead God/ O Bomb   thy BOOM His tomb."

The speaker justifies the unusual perception of the bomb, announcing, "I am able to laugh at all things," adding, "I say I am a poet and therefore love all man." As a poet, the speaker does not need to be "all-smart about bombs," for if "bombs were caterpillars" the speaker would "doubt not they'd become butterflies."

The poem continues with a comic vision of "a hell for bombs," where they remain after being blown to bits, singing German and American songs, longing for songs in Russian and Chinese. There is also comic sympathy for the "little Bomb that'll never be," the Eskimo bomb, with whom the speaker longs to frolic in play. The comic effect reaches a peak when the speaker becomes the bomb's suitor, arriving at its doorstep with flowers in hand, pleading to be allowed to enter, saying, "O Bomb I love you/ I want to kiss your clank   eat your boom."

The poem climaxes with a crescendo of sound:

> BOOM   BOO M   BOOM   BOOM   B OOM
> BOOM ye skies and BOOM ye suns

> BOOM BOOM ye moons   ye stars BOOM
> nights ye BOOM   ye days ye BOOM
> BOOM BOOM ye winds   ye clouds ye rains,
> go BANG ye lakes   ye oceans BING
> Barracuda BOOM and cougar BOOM
> Ubangi BANG   orangoutang
> BING BANG BONG BOOM   bee bear baboon
> ye BANG ye BONG ye BING

This orchestration of words signals the thunderous arrival of the bomb, but the poem's last lines take a serious and prophetic turn. Simply to say that the bomb will explode and all the world will yield to its force is insufficient. "Know that the earth will madonna the Bomb," the speaker declares, and "in the hearts of men to come more bombs will be born/ magisterial bombs wrapped in ermine   all beautiful/ and they'll sit plunk on earth's grumpy empires."

Forms and Devices

The most obvious device in "Bomb" is the shaping of the poem to give it the pictorial impression of a nuclear mushroom cloud. The top section of the poem is round like the top of an atomic blast, while the portion beneath is tapered like the stem of the cloud rising from the earth. In using shaped verse, Corso makes the design of his poem conform to the object of the poem's focus. If the poem is read as part of *The Happy Birthday of Death* (1960), the illustration of the atomic blast on the volume's cover provides additional emphasis on the appearance of the detonated bomb. Furthermore, the title of the volume suggests that "Bomb" is about the birthday of the bomb, or "Death's jubilee," the anniversary of the explosion of the nuclear weapon over Japan in August, 1945, and that this birthday, at least in the surprisingly playful mind of the speaker, is a happy occasion. However, if the poem is read in *Mindfield: New and Selected Poems* (1989), the visual impression of the original broadside or the subsequent foldout are lost.

A second feature of "Bomb" is the dramatic situation, in which Corso exploits the apostrophe, making the speaker address an object that cannot literally answer. With the apostrophe, the poem becomes a dramatic monologue well suited for a live reading, especially by Corso himself, whose talents as a reader lend themselves well to comedy based on the improbable personification of a nuclear weapon.

A third feature of the poem is Corso's juxtaposition of antiquity with modernity. The speaker refers to St. Michael, St. George, David, Hesperus, Homer, and Zeus, but also mixes in Rathbone, Dillinger, Bogart, Boris Karloff, and Harpo Marx. He pits Hermes, the mythic messenger with winged shoes, against Jesse Owens, the track star of the 1936 Berlin Olympics. The interruptive, conversational lines often marked by the informality of contractions are juxtaposed with archaic words such as "hath," "thy," "false-talc'd," and "ye." There is a "final amphitheater/ with a hymnody feeling of all Troys," but for the "Ritz Brothers from the Bronx caught in the A train/ The smiling Schenley poster will always smile." This juxtaposing of the old and new is characteristic of many of Corso's poems, including "Marriage," his most famous work. Corso's experience as an abandoned child, an imprisoned thief, and a streetwise young man give him dominion over contemporary idiom, but he is also proud that he devoted much of his time in jail to studies of the classics and antiquity. He enjoys demonstrating his erudition.

The subtlest feature of "Bomb" is its ironic confounding of standard expectations. One might expect a poem about atomic weaponry to denounce the bomb and its power to destroy humanity; instead, the speaker loves and celebrates the bomb. He is protective and sympathetic; he even tries to woo the bomb. One might expect images of horror and death, but Corso mutes the horror with comic effects, such as the "top of the Empire State/ arrowed in a broccoli field in Sicily." One might expect the onomatopoeia of the climactic outburst of sound to underscore the thunder of the bomb, but the selections of sound include "Barracuda," "cougar," "Ubangi," "orangoutang," and "bee bear baboon," steering the poem toward humor. One might expect the bomb to be associated with the work of the devil, but the poem concludes with a reference to the Madonna and the birth of the savior. This last twist deflates the previous comic antics, giving special impact to the closing prophecy that not only the speaker, but all others as well, contribute to the birth of the ultimate blast.

Themes and Meanings

"Bomb" asks the reader to reconsider his or her understanding of nuclear weaponry. Is the bomb the most terrible thing that humankind has ever developed, or is it the natural progression of destruction signaled by all previous human behavior, and will the progression continue until the ultimate bomb arrives? Corso is prophetic, but he is also cautionary, warning all readers and listeners that the ultimate bomb will be all-powerful and even capable of dispatching God. If Corso were to deliver this warning in a straight and serious tone, he might not hold the reader's attention. However, Corso uses the surprise of the speaker's declaration, "O Bomb I love you," the comic effect of juxtapositions of the ancient and the modern, and a tumult of sound to seize the reader's attention and make him or her think in new ways. The final turn in the poem, however, demands reflection. Is all humankind, despite the lip service people give to peace, actually courting the bomb? By adopting the lifestyle that suppresses fear, even awareness, of the pending apocalypse, do people tacitly revere the bomb?

The poem also reflects strongly on poetry and the role of the poet: Does a poem have to be printed on a standard page in a book with its lines aligned at the left margin, or can it work on the scale of an illustrative poster with its lines arranged to depict its subject? Does the poet have to strive for consistency in tone and reference, or can the poet blend ancient culture and language with contemporary references and informal idiom? Does the topic of the end of the world and the entombing of God require absolute solemnity, or can humor and playfulness successfully serve to issue an urgent warning?

William T. Lawlor

BORN OF WOMAN

Author: Wisława Szymborska (1923-
Type of poem: Lyric
First published: 1967, as "Urodzony," in *Sto pociech*; collected in *Sounds, Feelings,*
   Thoughts Seventy Poems by Wisława Szymborska, 1981

The Poem

   "Born of Woman" is a poem in free verse, containing forty-five lines divided into sixteen stanzas of varying length. The ending on the Polish word that comprises the original title, "Urodzony," makes it clear at the outset that the subject is a man; the poem represents the musings of his wife or lover, who has just caught her first glimpse of his mother. Her words are directed inward; she is talking to herself.

   The first stanza begins abruptly, as if the speaker were somewhat surprised or bemused: "So that is his mother." What follows is barely a description, for the only physical details offered are that she is gray-eyed and small. Small she may be, but she is the cause, the "perpetrator" of the man's existence. From "perpetrator" Wisława Szymborska moves into one of her controlling metaphors. The mother is the boat in which he floated to shore and out of which he struggled into this temporary world. The fourth stanza finally defines the relationship between the speaker and the man— between the "I" and the "he" of the poem—but does so in the barest of terms. The mother is "the bearer of the man/ with whom I walk through fire."

   The next four stanzas focus on the mother, who, unlike the wife, did not choose him but rather created him. She seems to be complete in herself, the ultimate beginning, the "alpha" who molded him into the form and shape that the wife now sees. She gave him the gray eyes that in turn looked at the woman who would be his wife. This section ends with a question that might be plaintive, annoyed, or simply rhetorical: "Why did he show her to me."

   The next section shifts the focus to "him" and to the speaker's discovery that he is like everyone else, and most of all like the speaker herself. He was born and must die. Here Szymborska returns to her metaphor of the journey and describes the man as a newcomer to this world, a traveler on his way to his omega, his end. As a newcomer he is confused by the world and moves through it dodging, bobbing, and weaving, hoping to avoid the inevitable. While he may not yet understand the inevitable, the speaker does. She knows that he has passed the halfway mark on the road to omega. Returning to the beginning, she reminds the reader and herself that he himself never said so. All he said was, "This is my mother."

Forms and Devices

   The poem's short, sometimes incomplete sentences, short lines, and short stanzas create the impression of a woman talking to herself, trying to cope with what seems to be an unpleasant surprise. However, the tone is more reflective, wry, and controlled than it is overtly emotional, and the thought process does not seem fragmented or disjointed. Szymborska uses both repetition and metaphor to connect the thoughts, moving the poem coherently from beginning to end.

Stanzas often begin with parallel constructions. "So that is . . ." introduces three stanzas describing the mother and is used one last time midstanza when the speaker comes to the crux of the problem: "So he too was born." The same construction may link the opening lines of two successive stanzas; for example, stanza 13 begins with "And his head," and stanza 14 begins with "And his movements." Although there is no rhyme or fixed meter, there is rhythm.

Single words, too, are repeated, most strikingly in Szymborska's use of pronouns—or more accurately, in her repeated avoidance of specific nouns. The speaker names no one; the poem is dominated by "his," "she," "her," "I," "my." (This effect is even more exaggerated in the English translation, because Polish verbs indicate gender in the past tense. So "he floated" in Polish can leave out the actual "he," with the verb ending making it clear whether the subject of the verb is male or female.) The nouns used to refer to the personages are among the most basic, such as man, woman, mother, son, or parts of the body, such as eyes, skin, bones. The rest is metaphor.

The overarching metaphor of the poem is of life as a journey. The mother is the boat that has carried the man to this shore, "from body's depths." He begins by struggling out of that boat, and ever afterward the journey is a difficult one. A newcomer to this world, he walks, wanders, dodges, and bangs his head against a metaphorical wall. Regardless of whether he accepts or understands the fact, he is already more than halfway down the road. On a more abstract level, his mother is "his alpha"—the beginning not of life, but of "non-eternity," and if there is a beginning, then there must be an end. He is "a wanderer to omega" whether he likes it or not.

The speaker certainly does not like it, and Szymborska brings in a smaller metaphor (smaller in the sense that it is less developed), that of a trial. The first noun used to describe the mother is "perpetrator." Toward the end of the poem it is not the mother, but the son, to whom an inevitable "universal verdict" applies.

Themes and Meanings

"Man that is born of a woman is of few days, and full of trouble. He cometh forth like a flower, and is cut down. He fleeth also as a shadow, and continueth not." So says the Bible's Job, and the Western lyric tradition has been saying so ever since. The fleeting nature of human life has preoccupied poets for centuries, sometimes expressing itself in calls to "gather ye rosebuds while ye may," other times expressing itself in somber contemplation of the dust of kings.

Szymborska's theme, then, is not a new one, and neither is her metaphor of life as a journey. The notion that, side trips and accidental detours notwithstanding, everyone is heading toward the same destination is as old as the story of Gilgamesh and as new as the latest "road movie." What makes Szymborska's treatment interesting is her choice of emotional framework. She places these meditations on "non-eternity" within a set of ordinary human relationships that, like the theme itself, are as ancient as they are troublesome.

Szymborska's speaker takes her own ordinariness for granted. She is like everyone else; she was born and she will die. Yet so far she has managed to avoid the idea that the man she loves is subject to the same eternal law as ordinary people. She does not idolize him; her problem has more to do with the human tendency to take loved ones for granted.

The first line, "So that is his mother," might set the stage for either a tragedy or a comedy; in either case two women have claims on one man. So on one hand the speaker is coolly sizing the mother up, taking the measure of a rival. She has a certain advantage, because the encounter is one-sided. The reader has no idea whether the mother sees the speaker, let alone what she might think of her. On the other hand, the measure is an intimidating one, because the mother is not only the means by which the man came to exist but also the very reason for his existence. She not only brought the man to this shore, she created him. Having "bound him to the bones hidden from me," the mother knows things that the speaker does not. Not only that, his gray eyes are his mother's eyes as well. She has knowledge, and therefore power, that the speaker lacks.

The tension between wife and mother-in-law is implied in the words used to describe the latter. "Gray-eyed perpetrator" is an accusation. Many a wife or lover has leveled accusations at her husband's mother, but this poem contains what might be the ultimate one, which could be paraphrased as, "He is mortal, he is going to die, and it is all your fault." At the same time, as Szymborska knows perfectly well, mortality is no one's fault; it is simply a fact of existence.

Jane Ann Miller

BRASS FURNACE GOING OUT

Author: Diane di Prima (1934-
Type of poem: Ode
First published: 1975; collected in *Selected Poems 1956-1975*, 1975

The Poem

"Brass Furnace Going Out," subtitled "Song, After an Abortion," is a direct address by the poet to the spirit of an aborted baby who functions as a comforting, though haunting, presence throughout the work. It consists of twelve irregular sections written in variants of open verse ranging from three to forty-three lines. In categorizing it as a "Song," Diane di Prima is using the term in the classical sense of an ode—a song composed for performance at a public occasion. Her intention is to take a private struggle and make it accessible to a large audience. The prevailing mood of the song is elegiac as it laments the death of the baby as well as the lost possibilities of life, but there are radical shifts in mood as the poet works through stages of grief and guilt, richocheting from section to section in a pattern of abrupt emotional reversals. The first section finds the poet already part of a world both absurd and horrible:

> and what of the three year old girl who poisoned her mother?
> that happens, it isn't just us, as you can see—
> what you took with you when you left
> remains to be seen.

This question introduces a pattern of reversal by juxtaposing the horror of an abortion with an equally chilling alternative: the child killing her mother. The poet acknowledges her place in the drama but does not yet know what the impact of her actions will be. The second section provides one possibility, a lurch to emotional extremity as the poet expresses resentment toward both the father (now absent) and the baby, accusing the child of "quitting/ at the first harsh treatment." This vindictive bitterness is countered by the motherly tone of the third section, as she imagines a letter to the child, who seems to be merely away at school or on a trip. "I want to/ keep in touch" she writes, "I want to know how you/ are, to send you cookies." This comforting dream is interrupted by a nightmare in section IV in which the poet is consumed, not by anger as in section II, but by guilt. She has a vision of a rotting fetus in a river surrounded by animals who reject the baby just as the poet has. This is the longest section of the poem, a surrealistic picture of a return to origins as the abortion itself is revisited in terms of the natural world absorbing the life-spirit of both the mother and the child.

The harrowing scene in section IV leads to a defensive burst of anger in the next part as the poet attempts to find someone or something to share the blame and then begins a kind of preparation for burial as if ordering the baby out of her mind. There is some sort of release in this action, as the end of the section introduces a feeling of partial acceptance for the first time, the baby relinquished to be reborn in another setting but carrying a message to the new mother warning her away from shared communication.

Section VI reinforces the emotional see-saw pattern by destroying any attempt to come to terms with the baby's absence. Horrific images of the baby's rotting corpse ("your goddamned belly rotten, a home for flies/ blown out & stinking, the maggots curling your hair") actually reflect the poet's disgust with herself. The depth of her feeling is emphasized by the suggestion that a child grown to be a criminal, or one doomed to be starved or shot, would still "have been frolic and triumph compared to this." The agony implicit in her declaration represents the degree to which she has been wracked by the entire process.

Section VIII is pivotal and only three lines long. Here the poet asks for forgiveness from the child, an initial step toward some semblance of recovery. Taking on the responsibility she formerly rejected, the poet's feelings turn in a new direction. Her realization that she may be exiled from the cosmos of reason if she cannot be absolved of the burden of guilt leads her to beg, "forgive, forgive/ that the cosmic waters do not turn from me/ that I should not die of thirst."

Part of this absolution comes in section IX, where a mystic ritual takes place, bringing about the release and transference of the baby's soul. This ritual permits the poet to imagine what could have been. Returning to the motherly stance of section III, the poet revels in the imagined baby's happy infancy in a fantasy projection balancing the awful images of decay with a tender, touching portrayal of domesticity. Inevitably, another reversal occurs, but this time it is overridden by a vision of her young child living a happy, normal life. Section XII concludes with an invitation to the child to come to her again and promises to make the child comfortable, offering her body now ready to nurture again: "my breasts prepare/ to feed you: they do what they can."

Forms and Devices

The poem's title is a symbolic representation of its subject. It suggests the extinguishing of the life of the fetus and eventually of the poet's guilt as well, setting the course which the poem follows. The "Brass Furnace" is a controlling image for the physical and emotional being of the speaker. As a heated enclosure, it objectifies the womb, warming and generating the fetus. When the abortion removes the developing baby, the "Going Out" refers to the extinguishing of its life's fire as well as the literal departure of the fetus from the mother. It also represents the direction of the poet's emotional journey. As a furnace shuts down, it cools over time. The poem chronicles the cooling process that the poet goes through. She is very hot at first—her wrath ignited by her pain. As she works through her feelings, occasional sparks leap up to rekindle her passion before the body image of a fiery forge is replaced by one of a liquid carrying the promise of regeneration.

While the striking image of the brass furnace controls the progress of the poem, the range and variety of the images di Prima uses sustain the high emotional pitch at which it operates and makes each switch in mood convincing. In section II, when di Prima blames the baby for "quitting// as if the whole thing were a rent party/ &

somebody stepped on your feet," the reduction to the colloquial grounds the action in the familiar and tempers the pain with bizarre humor. The vision in section IX, on the other hand, is written as a version of a transformative rite, the images of "orange & jade at the shrine" symbolizing the necessities of the reproductive process as di Prima utilizes sacred objects (the orange suggesting fruitfulness, the jade an emblem of celestial semen) from a hidden feminine subculture.

Throughout the poem, liquid images counter the fire of the furnace, continuing the pattern of reversal, first as manifestations of a polluted river, then as a healing balm, then as the water associated with birth. Similarly, animal imagery which often directly mirrors the poet's feelings is the central motif of many sections. For instance, the dogs playing trumpets in section I reflect the distortion of reality that is part of the poet's confusion; the giraffes "mourning cry" in section IV echoes the poem's tone of lamentation, and the fish in section XI resemble the aquatic state of the baby prior to birth. In addition, the animal imagery enables di Prima to explore her own animal nature as a being whose physicality is always a prime concern.

Themes and Meanings

Although men such as Jack Kerouac, Allen Ginsberg, and William Burroughs have dominated the public's attention in studies of Beat writers, Diane di Prima's close association with them brought her minimal acclaim. She is not only the premier woman poet of this group but also a writer whose prototypical feminist thought introduced an underground feminist mythology to American literary culture. "Brass Furnace Going Out" is a highly personalized poem depicting a shattering experience that transformed the consciousness of the poet as the experiences reflected in "Howl" did for Ginsberg. Both works are intense renderings of emotional responses that explore dimensions of a subject not previously considered appropriate for literary discourse.

Like many of her contemporaries, di Prima was quite familiar with conventional literary forms but recognized that it was necessary to create a distinctly singular voice to capture the full range of her subject. Her inventive employment of the rhythms of speech and thought, combined with an artful insertion of items from an arcane mythological base, not only made her exploration especially vivid but also created new ways of seeing. Her avoidance of easy judgment, her disinclination to preach or moralize, has kept the poem relevant, whereas propaganda for either pro-choice or pro-life positions on abortion can easily become strident and stale.

As Ann Charters observed, di Prima has been "dismayed that her eloquent meditation on her early abortion... has been read by antiabortion groups as supporting their cause." Beyond the compelling nature of a charged subject, di Prima's poem is about loss and acceptance in both a specifically personal and a universal sense. Di Prima has not understated the particularly feminine aspects of the experience in tracing the process of grief that follows a traumatizing event, but the poem is not bound by any definitions of gender.

Amy R. Walter and Leon Lewis

BREAD WITHOUT SUGAR

Author: Gerald Stern (1925-
Type of poem: Elegy
First published: 1989; collected in *Bread Without Sugar*, 1992

The Poem

"Bread Without Sugar" is a long fifteen-page poem in eight unnumbered parts that function not so much as stanzas as discrete sections (each approximately thirty to sixty lines in length). To further complicate the picture, the poem is written in memory of the poet's father, contains an epigraph from Grace Paley ("This is what makes justice in the world—to bring these lives into the light"), and, at its conclusion, is dedicated to the writer and editor Ted Solotaroff. It is necessary to keep these three aspects in mind as the poem unfolds.

The setting for "Bread Without Sugar"—and there usually is an external setting for a Gerald Stern poem—is his father's gravesite in Miami, and it is his father's life that Stern wants to "bring to light." Kneeling in wet December sand to see the headstone, the speaker travels through memory to the day of his father's funeral; he sees the cantor, the boring rabbi, the Jewish businessmen from Newark and Flatbush who, like his father—a retired tailor and buyer—had come to Miami. He then goes back through a cross-section of his father's life ("born in Kiev, died in Miami"), to a cross-section of his own life (memories of Pittsburgh, the "bread without sugar" he had eaten as a boy, his eventual travels), to a day in "1940 or 1941" when the family had first visited Florida. Simultaneously, the governing sensibility of the poem travels outward, embracing the whole of Jewish history, the scattered past that in the end can bring such different people together in the same place.

As the poet contemplates his somewhat strained relationship with his deceased father, what he calls an "odd vexation," he also recounts his interaction with his aging mother and begins to wonder where he himself will be buried. He considers a variety of his favorite places, going from "country/ to country in search of a plot." These imaginative gestures move him into what might be termed "speculative time." Thus Stern is able not only to select several possible burial sites but also to create his death scene (hit by a taxi in Poland). His expansive imagination embraces the future: "I want/ to live with the Spanish forever. I love/ their food and I love their music; I am/ not even dead and I am speaking/ their language already; I hope their poets/ remember me." There is a complicated mix of tenses so that chronological time becomes meaningless. In this way Stern allows himself, at least figuratively, more than one life.

Further, the poet is able to move quickly from remembered time (the family in the Charles Hotel) to his projected old age in the same hotel; he envisions himself drawing his pension, cooking on a hot plate, losing his glasses on the sand, not being able to find his towel. The poem ends with incantation, an individual prayer for the self, fully realized because of its all-inclusive, all-embracing journey through concomitant histories: "May the turtles escape/ the nets: May I find my ocean! May/ the salt preserve me! May the black clouds instruct me!"

Forms and Devices

Over the years Gerald Stern has developed an idiosyncratic voice—one that readers can recognize instantly as belonging to him alone. It is not simply conversational; it is a voice which seems to come from the most visceral center of the man: personal, engaging, spontaneous, often breaking free in impromptu associations. To read Stern is to accompany him on a sort of spiritual autobiography. This voice is not that of a confessional persona pretending to "tell all"—it does not invite or even seem to need the reader. Readers participate fully, but as bystanders. Each poem embodies a thought process—a scattering of real moments and personal connections, a twist of particular synapses, then new observation, new wiring, odd pairings that lead to more memories, more connections.

"Bread Without Sugar" proceeds on just such a circuitous associative route. The sentences seem to spill into one another, a jumble of questions and observations, punctuated by dashes and semicolons, commas linking one fleeting thought to another, one memory to its outlandish extrapolation. A good example is the section in which the speaker is thinking about the people buried near his father:

> The sky
> is streaked tonight; I love the tropics,
> the orange underneath the blue; green parrots
> are flying out of the sun, voices
> are rising out of the ground, it must be
> Yaglom and Sosna, those are his neighbors,
> And Felder and Katz; some are New Yorkers,
> one is from Cincinnati, one
> was born in Africa, one is from Turkey—
> he would know grapefruit. When they sing
> they do it as in the movies or they
> do it as if they were sitting down there
> in Lummus Park, on Wednesday afternoon.
> Schmaltz was our downfall, schmaltz was our horror,
> we wept on the streets or walked to the swimming pool
> weeping, we drove to the bakery weeping.
> What was it for? What did we long for
> so much, what had we lost?

The reader is inside the speaker's head. The poem functions more like a meditative lyric than a narrative, yet its length allows it room to range through the father's history, the poet's own story, and even the ongoing saga of Jews in the Diaspora, regaining Spanish, "remembering words/ they hadn't thought of for five hundred years." The interest is as much in what the poet is thinking and feeling as in any "story" he might tell.

An interesting aspect of "Bread Without Sugar" is the use of the sense of smell.

Each section contains some reference to a memory of a stench—seemingly brought
on by a garbage dump near the cemetery in Miami. The poet's associations are held
together by smell; it crops up as a memory of a rat-strewn bakery where he had to
cover his mouth as a boy, the heavy syrup of his parents' fruit salad sundaes, the
"disgusting smell" of the clinkers in the yellow cloud of air at Union Station in
Pittsburgh, the burning city, pigs "rolling in shit" in Mexico, the angel who "stank
from the sun," each image just a bit more exaggerated than the last.

Themes and Meanings

Many of Gerald Stern's poems are about loss. They hinge on a before and after—his
love poems often have an elegiac note at their inception. "Bread Without Sugar,"
however, contains two simultaneous presents—the one of the immediate, felt world
and the one of his active imagining. Yet the poem is not so much about the present as
it is about the past and the future that are opened by present circumstances. Just as the
poet is able to reflect on several distinct pasts, he confidently projects a variety of
futures.

Because there are fleeting moments of direct address, as though the poem were
intermittently spoken to Ted Solotaroff, it implies a shared history. It documents the
experience of the wandering Jew, but it is also about the simple sustenance—the bread
without sugar—of family, neighborhood, country. In the end the poem pays homage
to America and its immigrant experience. In celebrating his own family's history,
Stern speaks for all the forgotten, for those who died in the Holocaust, producing a
kind of "justice."

"Bread Without Sugar" begins with the speaker standing "between two continents"
and ends with him fixed (in his imagination) on the sandy beach of his past. The poem
is concerned with balance—one version of life versus another, one impulse set against
its opposite, a veritable scale on which justice will be weighed. In every instance,
thought itself is at stake, presenting as it does alternative ways of approaching any
subject. Stern's tentative, self-interrogating voice inevitably complicates the issue.
Thought turns on itself, finally isolating the poet. By questioning itself, this voice
accepts all of human nature, so "Bread Without Sugar" is able to range through
personal and cultural history in order to lay Stern's father to rest. Only through the
written word can they finally be "at peace with each other."

Stern's previous work has fashioned a special relationship between his readers and
the personal (and sometimes very intimate) details he shares with them. The self
presented in "Bread Without Sugar" is created almost exclusively by his poetic voice:
its passions, its peculiar energy, its exuberance and humor. Contrary to what seems a
pervasive critical response to his work, Stern is not a contemporary version of Walt
Whitman. His voice is lonelier, more independent, closer to the bone. It sweeps readers
along in its self-questioning, and fundamental, urgency. It manages to speak movingly
for something larger than itself without pretending to speak for everyone's lives.

Judith Kitchen

BREAK OF DAY IN THE TRENCHES

Author: Isaac Rosenberg (1890-1918)
Type of poem: Lyric
First published: 1916; collected in *Poems*, 1922

The Poem

As its title suggests, Isaac Rosenberg's "Break of Day in the Trenches" is a poem in which time juxtaposes with setting to create a new poetic perception of life and death. It is a short free-verse poem of twenty-six lines, capturing the bemusement of an ordinary infantryman confronting the harshness of existence in the trenches during World War I. It is also a reverie on life and the persistence of life in the midst of war.

Almost every line contains some reference to violent death, sometimes death on a grand scale. Yet even in the midst of mass warfare, Rosenberg notes, there is life of a sort. For instance, the poetic speaker's casual act of plucking a poppy—an act of killing—is juxtaposed with his observations on a living creature, a rat, that approaches close enough to touch the speaker's hand.

With sardonic humor, the speaker compares the rat's situation with that of ordinary soldiers, observing that the "Droll" animal is able to survive in the fields of battle. He observes that the trenches and the other demarcations of war that separate the English soldiers from their "enemies" matter little to the rat, which will perhaps cross no-man's-land to continue its feast on German corpses.

It is this free act of crossing a few miles of open space that figures in the next section of poem. The speaker marvels at the rat's ability to survive, while "haughty athletes" with "Strong eyes, fine limbs" are so easily slaughtered. If the dominant fauna of this environment is the rats that feed on the corpses, the common flora is "Poppies whose roots are in man's veins," flowers of blood from wounded soldiers.

This reduction of humans to mere objects is reinforced later in the poem when the movement of the rat is contrasted with the prostration of soldiers, who are "Sprawled in the bowels of the earth." From the description, the soldiers could be either living or dead; perhaps it does not matter much to the speaker. At least the speaker knows that he himself is still alive, although the slight dust on the poppy he has put behind his ear prefigures the dust of the grave that always stands waiting.

Forms and Devices

Much in "Break of Day in the Trenches" is characteristic of English World War I poetry. For instance, while many English poets wrote in the traditional poetic genres—in this case, the pastoral—they enriched the genres and played on the expectations of their readers by introducing wartime experience as new subject matter. Further, some poets used unconventional meter and rhythm to approximate the broken rhythms of life during war. While "Break of Day in the Trenches" draws on both conventions of war poetry, its visual imagery is its most important aspect.

As a young man, Rosenberg showed considerable natural talent for drawing. Later he studied art at Birkbeck College and the Slade School of Art in London. Although he ultimately gave up the visual arts for poetry, the pictorial quality of some of his poems is particularly notable. In "Louse Hunting" (1917), for instance, Rosenberg first presents his readers with an image of naked soldiers, "Yelling in lurid glee," who have stripped off their clothes to kill the vermin infesting them. This initial image is strongly rendered, dominated by the "Grinning faces/ And raging limbs" that "Whirl over the floor one fire."

Similarly, two strong visual images dominate "Break of Day in the Trenches": the grinning rat and the poppy. In the first place, the rat imagery encompasses both the animal and the speaker who notices it. The line "A queer sardonic rat" refers to the animal, but it also indicates the speaker's tone and situation: He, too, is a sardonic rat. Although the rat imagery is important in establishing connections between these two unwilling victims of the war, the considerably more dense poppy imagery universalizes the situation of this individual soldier. The poppy is both image and metaphor. The plucked poppy serves as an example of the casual killing that accompanies life in the trenches. The poppy is also a well-chosen way to indicate this death, since the flower was normally planted alongside graves.

Metaphorically, the poppy indicates ways of dying. The speaker's placement of the red flower behind his ear points to a considerable more brutal image, the "flowering" of blood from a head wound. That Rosenberg had this subtlety in mind is suggested by his repetition of the poppy imagery a few lines later, where one reads that the poppies grow from "roots [that] are in man's veins." Blood is both flower and fertilizer in this vivid wordplay.

In his early twenties, Rosenberg had felt forced to choose between writing and painting, remarking that art requires "blood and tears." He chose poetry, as Jon Stallworthy points out in *Lost Voices of World War I* (1987). Thereafter, Rosenberg strove to write "Simple *poetry*,—that is where an interesting complexity of thought is kept in tone and right value to the dominating idea so that it is understandable and still ungraspable." While Rosenberg achieved this balance in his greatest poems, it is also true that the concentration on evocative pictorial images renders "Break of Day in the Trenches" as inscrutable and immediate as visual art.

Themes and Meanings

The themes of "Break of Day in the Trenches" emerge from Rosenberg's inversion of the traditions of the pastoral poem. Generally, pastorals take place in stylized, idyllic rural settings, often early in the morning; their central figures are usually innocent shepherds, whose comments on life are intended also as pointed criticisms of larger social issues. Although the speaker of the poem does not share the rural background of shepherds, he—presumably, like Rosenberg, an urban poet from the East End of London—unselfconsciously emphasizes three main themes: the horrors of war, the artificiality of political barriers, and the necessity of maintaining human values, especially humor, to endure trench warfare.

In "Break of Day in the Trenches," the speaker clearly thinks of the war as mass slaughter, hardly a situation where one man's life—or one man's effort—amounts to much. The inversion of pastoral conventions indicates this. In the second line, daybreak is called the "old druid Time," a time of human sacrifice—that is, something to be endured, not welcomed. To the soldiers, day is a time to be dreaded; the horrible reality of war is once again visible when darkness starts "crumbling." This pastoral is not concerned with idyllic moments, but with "shrieking iron and flame/ Hurled through still heavens." Finally, the rat's closeness to the speaker is another buried hint of the conditions that prevail, implying that the living speaker has been mistaken for a corpse, the animal's food supply. This would suggest that the central animal of the pastoral—the sheep—has been replaced in this poem by a rat. This setting is stylized, but hardly idyllic.

Further, while it is a part of the horrors surrounding the war, the literary rat also marks a second theme: the artificiality of human barriers. The speaker describes the rat as "cosmopolitan," implying that it is free of the political barriers that, like trench lines, scar the human landscape. While the English and Germans are physically separated as enemies, they are joined by their subjection to the rat and by their victimization in the war.

Finally, Rosenberg explores a third theme in "Break of Day in the Trenches" growing out of his inverted pastoral: the necessity of humor in the midst of horrors. Rosenberg's contemporary, the English poet Wilfrid Owen, also used pastorals to throw the horrors of war into high relief. Although his poems are compassionate, Owen's tone is almost uniformly bitter. Rosenberg, for his part, makes use of a lighter tone, although his social criticism is as severe and often as biting. The speaker refers to the grim humor of the trenches several times in the poem: the rat is "sardonic" and "Droll," and it "inwardly grin[s]" as it crosses no-man's-land. Juxtaposed against this grim humor, the charnel images have all the more power. For instance, the speaker asks questions of the rat that no one, certainly not the soldier himself, can answer: "What do you see in our eyes/ . . . What quaver—what heart aghast?" In the face of these unanswerable questions, it is easy to believe that the soldiers are the butt of some hideous cosmic joke. Only the speaker's humor and his relief at a temporary moment of safety enable him to pose these questions.

Michael R. Meyers

BRIGGFLATTS

Author: Basil Bunting (1900-1985)
Type of poem: Poetic sequence
First published: 1966

The Poem

Briggflatts is a five-part poem of nearly seven hundred lines combining a celebration of the Northumbrian landscape of England with the poet's meditations on history, aesthetic reality, language, and his own participation in the events and incidents that give the poem its substance and emotional qualities. The title recalls the Quaker meeting house where Basil Bunting, as a young man, first experienced the illuminative insights that he came to believe were at the core of poetic possibility. The five-part structure of the poem is based on the sonata form of exposition/development and recapitulation that Bunting employs in each section and as an overarching frame for the entire work. Using sequences of action drawn imaginatively from personal experience and various mythologies, Bunting has composed a kind of "autobiography of feeling" that attempts to reconcile the poet's instinctive desire for adventurous mobility with his reflective recognition that some kind of home base is necessary to ground and organize the multiple images of a life's course.

The poem begins as an echo of the traditional epic invocation to the gods or Muses, commanding (in this case) the spirit of the West Yorkshire fields, a "sweet tenor bull," to "Brag"—that is, to boast, or announce—the exuberant arrival of the spring season with its promise of passion and fertility. "Descant on Rawthey's madrigal," the poet continues, directing the song of the bull as a counterpoint to the melody of the river Rawthey and as a discourse upon the features of the land itself. This is the place where the poem begins and where the life of the poet who speaks—the narrative consciousness revealing itself as the poem progresses—begins to come into focus. As Herbert Read, a trenchant advocate for unconventional poetry, has pointed out, the poem operates as a series of impressions "recovered and evaluated," and the first section introduces the poet as a young man with a maid, a reprise of figures from classical ballads reaching into Anglo-Saxon antiquity who resonate with the sensual music of the earth coming into bloom.

One of the ordering devices for the entire poem is an ongoing interchange between "then" and "now" as the poet's reflective intelligence shifts from a re-creation or recollection of action to a meditation on its ramifications through time. This pattern of transition is established initially in terms of a rock mason—the maid's father—who carves memorial words into stone, thus embedding ephemeral language into a more permanent medium. The mason is an emblem of the poet as craftsman, and his grave task sets up a counterpoint to the timeless present of the youth's intense moment. His work casts an ominous shadow of temporality and degeneration over the sexual union of the young people, and, as the first section concludes, the "sweet tenor" voice of the bull has been transformed into mere flesh ("the bull is beef"), love has been "murdered," and, accurately or not, the poet accepts blame for the loss. He recognizes that there is "No hope of going back" to an initial state of innocence and that a path for the rest of his life's journey has been opened, a journey launched with no destination in sight.

The guilt and even grief that the poet carries infects the wider world he enters as the second section begins. Surrounded by a debased society of "toadies, confidence men, kept boys," where he wanders aimlessly, "jailed, cleaned out by whores," the poet turns to the sea in a time-tested tactic for finding new horizons. There, he is transported not only away from the sordid urban wasteland but also further into a timeless realm that Bunting evokes by describing the ocean with the rhythms of old English alliterative verse: "Who sang, sea takes,/ brawn brine, bone grit./ Keener the kittiwake./ Fells forget him./ Fathoms dull the dale,/ gulfweed voices." Among other ports of call, the poet visits the Italian peninsula, and, in a series of crisp quatrains, Bunting calls forth the qualities of the landscape with a characteristic appeal to the senses: "It tastes good," "It sound right," "It feels soft," and "It looks well" before adding "but never/ well enough." The seafarer has not been able to escape from himself, so the "wind, sun, sea upbraid/ justly an unconvinced deserter." The defect of character that the poet takes with him is explored in a kind of reverie on the violent death of the ninth century Norwegian king Eric Bloodaxe, who ruled Northumbria for a time and died (according to legend) at the battle of Stainmore. The king is offered as an allegorical parallel for the poet, his voyages to the British Isles depicted in terse, skaldic verses ("Scurvy gnaws, steading smell, hearth's crackle"), his downfall, at least partially, a result of his moral failure. Judgment is withheld, however, as the section closes with the poet making further inquiries: "But who will entune a bogged orchard,/ its blossom gone,/ fruit unformed, where hunger and/ damp hush the hive?" His queries are framed in terms of the natural world, recalling the springtime in Northumbria and suggesting that the summer of the second section is held in suspension while additional data is accumulated. This is preparation for the "hell-canto" of section 3, the center of the poem, a "different thing" that Bunting labeled "a nightmare or dream or whatever you fancy." Among other things, it is a version of the archetypal "Dark Night of the Soul" in which the innermost truth of being is (or can be) revealed.

In accordance with his plan to find semiautobiographical analogues for the poet's journey, Bunting uses the story of Alexander the Great's quest for wisdom, which he took from the Persian poet Firdusi's *Shahnamah* (c. 1010), as his model. In ninety-five lines dense with images of a vile and repugnant realm, the explorer climbs toward a mountain vision. Then, in a transformative dream, the nightmare world is replaced by a scene in which, as Bunting biographer Victoria Forde puts it, the poet is "delighted by the beauty and variety of nature which cleanses and renews." The surge of a beneficent life force suggests the possibility of living in harmony with the natural world: "Sycamore seed twirling,/ O, writhe to its measure!/ Dust swirling trims pleasure./ Thorns prance in a gale./ In air snow flickers,/ twigs tap,/ elms drip."

The fourth section, which was listed as "Autumn" in Bunting's original diagram, contains the ripening of this realization. To objectify it, Bunting uses the ancient

Welsh poets Aneurin and Taliesin ("Clear Cymric voices," *cymru* being the Welsh-language name for Wales) as points of departure for a series of tales that encourage an acceptance of the landscape the poet left and to which he now returns. In the center of the section, the poet recalls, with poignant regret, the woman whose love he betrayed. His apostrophe to her ("My love is young but wise. Oak, applewood,/ her fire is banked with ashes till day./ The fells reek of her hearth's scent") is built on earthly images, and its tone of appreciation signals his readiness to reconcile his wanderlust with a fuller understanding of the value in his native ground. Impediments remain, however, as the poet still must overcome some psychic hurdle before he can rest content with his choices.

The fifth section is clearly set in a wintry vista: "Solstice past,/ years end crescendo," it declares, "Winter wrings pigment/ from petal and slough." There is a strong contrast with the verdant spring of the first part, but the winter landscape is alive with beauty since the poet/artist is able to see beyond the somewhat deceptive appeal of sheer sexual youth into a season of more subtle satisfactions. Pioneering British cultural commentator Eric Mottram calls this "a magnificently sustained pleasure in the particularities of music, sea-shore, the fells, and fishing boats on the water at night." The lyrical surge of these lines is Bunting's method for creating an ethos of awe that permits the joining of "Then is Now," his formulation for the fusion of the fading past and the ongoing present. When he states, near the poem's close, "She has been with me fifty years" in a line separated from the preceding and following lines, he is acknowledging his losses, but he is also accepting the inevitability of his wandering ("A strong song tows/ us") as the burden of his poetic insight. As he states in the beginning of section 2, "Poet appointed dare not decline." Now he is prepared to return to his community, the Quaker meeting place Briggflatts, and offer the poem as a summation of his life experiences. As Bunting told American poet and publisher Jonathan Williams, "My autobiography is *Briggflatts*," and the poem is a way of settling his debt to those he may have unwittingly hurt, including himself. The coda that follows the fifth section is appropriately open-ended, affirming the power of poetry to provide consolation for the trials of existence while continuing to question the meaning of all things: "Who,/ swinging his axe/ to fell kings, guesses/ where we go?"

Forms and Devices

Bunting, who wrote music criticism for *Outlook* and the *Musical Times* during the 1920's, regarded sound as the crucial core of all poetic expression. In a characteristic statement, he proclaimed, "Poetry, like music, is to be heard. It deals in sound. . . . Poetry lies dead on the page, until some voice brings it to life." His preparation for *Briggflatts* included not only a structural pattern based on the sonata but also a specific linking with sonatas by Italian composer Domenico Scarlatti. In a record he made of the poem, he placed selected Scarlatti sonatas before and after each part to emphasize the musical mood. Beyond this, Bunting suggested that an ideal reading would be in the voice of an inhabitant of the Northumbrian region of the British Isles so that the precise sound he had in mind would be accurately rendered. The epigraph he used for the entire poem, "The spuggies are fledged" (itself a translation from a thirteenth century life of Alexander the Great), must be spoken with a hard *g* in "spuggies," typical of what poet Donald Davie calls the "exceptionally tender care for its acoustic values" that Bunting brought to every syllable of the poem.

The sonic subtlety of Bunting's writing is a function of language and form. Bunting has fashioned, with intricate detail and exceptional invention, a demonstration of how musical principles can be applied to poetic form. Examples include the balance of the twelve thirteen-line stanzas in part 1; the accumulated pressure of the repetitive quatrains ("It tastes," "It sounds," "It feels," "It looks") in part 2; the ninety-five lines of dense, compressed descriptive detail of Alexander's ascent in part 3; the turn to the immediate and personal narrative ("I hear Aneurin," "I see Aneurin's pectoral muscle," "Where rats go go I") in part 4; and, as an epitome, the melding of word-sound and word-meaning in the evocation of the winter landscape in part 5. When he refers to "Rawthey's madrigal" at the start, he is establishing a musical style that interweaves numerous voices so that *Briggflatts* can contain examples of lyrical love poetry, elegiac recapitulation of heroic figures from antiquity, laments for various losses, caustic satiric dismissals of the ills of the modern world, numerous vividly descriptive passages that bring the locales of the poem to life, and extended narratives in the Bardic tradition that bring compelling tales of historical relevance to the poem's purpose. His success in unifying what are generally regarded as distinct subgenres depends on the extremely elaborate interlinkages of sound ("rich rhyming and chiming" in poet and literary theorist Charles Tomlinson's application of a phrase from nineteenth century English art critic and writer John Ruskin) that assume not only a skilled reader but also a very committed, attentive listener. The elemental coherence of the poem, however, depends not only on Bunting's extremely painstaking arrangement of sound patterns but also on the emerging narrative consciousness of the poet who is speaking. This is the mechanism that joins the poem's form to its essential themes, the evolving melodic strain around which Bunting's variations and inventions are played and into which they eventually coalesce.

Themes and Meanings

Briggflatts is a poem of departure and return, both in the musical sense and in terms of the poem's architecture. It includes more than five decades in the life of the poet and is structured as a journey from home ground into the world and then back to the poet's origins. The wide range of events and locales that it covers is ordered by the development of the distinctive sensibility of the poet. This central "character" is eager for experience, fascinated by phenomena, determined to confront moral conundrums, in love with learning, and deeply affected by his feeling for the countryside of his birth. He takes, as his task, the reconstruction of the crucial incidents of his formation as an artist and, in accordance with this goal, accepts the challenge of assessing the moral dimensions of the choices he made during that process.

To accomplish this, Bunting likens a person's life course to the progression of the seasons—a familiar and resonant comparison—calling spring a time of "Love and betrayal," summer a period in which there is "no rest from ambition," autumn a season for "reflexion," and winter (or "Old age") the time when one "can see at last the loveliness of things overlooked." Throughout, there is an awareness of mortality, and the semiserenity of the poem's close is more a matter of a willingness to accept the ongoing mysteries of existence as a source of wonder and contemplative delight than any kind of answer to cosmic questions. The wild exuberance of the "sweet tenor bull" in the poem's first passages is eventually and gradually modified into the placidity of the "slowworm," Bunting's symbol for both the return of all living things to the soil and the renewal of the life force in the earth. In part 5, the Northumbrian landscape is celebrated as if from within: Close to the earth, as if from the slowworm's furrow,

> The ewes are heavy with lamb.
> Snow lies bright on Hedgehope
> and tacky mud about Till
> where the fells have stepped aside
> and the river praises itself,
>
> .   .   .   .
> Light lifts from the water.
> Frost has put rowan down,
> a russet blotch of bracken
> tousled about the trunk.

The distance from the bull in part 1, dancing on tiptoe, "ridiculous and lovely," chasing "hurdling shadows" but so consumed with its own energy that it cannot see the depth or totality of the land's richness, is a measure of the growth of the poet's mind. The transformation of language from words chiseled in stone that describe the cold sea to the song of harp and flute and the illuminations of starlight at the end of part 5 signifies the emotional fulfillment of the poet's heart. He has earned the right to live in Briggflatts—the special place where the Quaker community can speak to the spirit of God, the Creator of all things.

Leon Lewis

BUFFALO BILL 'S

Author: E. E. Cummings (1894-1962)
Type of poem: Satire
First published: 1920; collected in *Tulips and Chimneys*, 1923

The Poem

The poem announces that Buffalo Bill (William F. Cody, 1846-1917) is "defunct." Cody had made a name for himself in the wild west as a buffalo hunter and Indian fighter. He subsequently became a showman, hiring many of the Indians (among them was Sitting Bull) who had fought the U.S. Army and doing road tours that featured staged battles between cowboys and Indians, sharpshooting exhibitions, and other events associated with frontier America. Cody was more than a national phenomenon; his wild west show toured Europe, and he was received as an example of the vigorous American spirit that had conquered a continent. To say that he is defunct rather than simply dead is to imply that his example is outmoded and irrelevant.

E. E. Cummings does not limit his attention to the historical Buffalo Bill, however. The typography of the first line, "Buffalo Bill 's," with its space between the name and the apostrophe *s*, implies a pluralization. It is as if the poet is dismissing not a man but a symbol and all the copies of that symbol—all the men who think of themselves as Buffalo Bills. To be more precise, by separating the apostrophe *s* from Buffalo Bill, the poet conjures up an image of both the historical figure and his out-of-date followers or emulators, who trail after him leaving a gap (the space) between him and them. The America these wild west heroes thought they possessed no longer exists, and thus Buffalo Bill as America's representative is defunct.

Like many satires which poke at the pretensions of a subject by evoking and dramatizing it, the poem charges ahead like Buffalo Bill himself. The pigeons that Buffalo Bill is breaking "justlikethat" are most likely the clay pigeons used in shooting matches—in this case, in events contrived for the wild west shows. The pigeons break apart when shot. The show is impressive because Buffalo Bill hits his targets rapidly and easily. The show is also a kind of sham, however, because the birds are not real, and the show does not have much to do with the real wild west. That the poem has less than an admiring view of Buffalo Bill—while conceding his romantic appeal—is evident in the last five lines.

On one hand, the speaker pays tribute to Buffalo Bill's handsomeness, evoking what may be the wonder of an onlooker at a wild west show performance. On the other hand, Buffalo Bill, the "blueeyed boy," is subject to mortality, personified in the figure of "Mister Death." Buffalo Bill, the figure of youth, in other words, gives way to a rather grim reminder of the processes of time. Not even this true-blue American hero can defeat death.

Forms and Devices

Cummings is known as a poet who attacks conventional uses of grammar, and he turns capitalization, hyphens, apostrophes, and spaces between words to new uses. He runs words together. He separates words and lines in unique ways. Indeed, he employs no punctuation in places where most writers would favor a comma or period. His highly individualistic style is, by definition, a challenge to the way most people write and think. So it is not surprising that he would take an irreverent view of an American hero like Buffalo Bill.

The poem satirizes Bill as a idolatrous figure who can do miraculous things—like Jesus. His stallion is silver, gleaming no doubt like a precious metal, with the adjective "watersmooth" emphasizing how glossy and glittery Buffalo Bill's performance is. He is a shining symbol of American energy and know-how, and that easy efficiency of manner is combined with a romantic aura. The image of the "blueeyed boy" focuses on Buffalo Bill as a paragon of American innocence—as if showing off is comparable to conquering the world. Buffalo Bill's looks solve nothing, of course, and over time they prove meaningless. He becomes not America's blue-eyed boy—analogous to someone like movie star Mary Pickford, once known as "America's sweetheart"—but Mister Death's victim.

The figure of Mister Death makes what has seemed a light-hearted poem much more sinister. Death often appears in medieval mystery plays as a character who reminds human beings that they will die and that they are subject to the corruption of the earth. In such mystery plays, people must be reminded that they will not live forever and that their gaudy shows and vanity will be overcome by death. In the poem, Mister Death appears to be the ultimate showman—the one who really controls Buffalo Bill's act. In other words, Buffalo Bill has not really been the master of his fate: He has been a tool of Mister Death.

Along with the shocking appearance of Mister Death comes a change of tone in the speaker's voice. In the first half of the poem, the speaker seems jocular—although he clearly foreshadows his darker tone in the poem's third word, "defunct." Nevertheless, the next six lines seem to indulge in a vivid memory of how pleasurable and exciting it was to watch Buffalo Bill. The words run together in line 6 in imitation of his sharpshooting. It is only with the single word in line 7—the mention of Jesus—that the poem slows down to contemplate the consequences of Buffalo Bill's behavior. The speaker concedes the hero's allure and then suddenly subverts that allure in the sobering last three lines, which form a question (the question mark itself is eliminated). Cummings usually omits end punctuation, as if refusing to come to a conclusion about life, which is, his poems imply, ceaseless, constantly reinventing itself and repeating the process of life and death.

Themes and Meanings

In the broadest sense, Cummings is both celebrating and attacking American optimism. The symbol of the wild west has become an essential part of the American identity. It expresses the American's quest to be an individual and the American worship of those who have created a heroic sense of themselves. On one hand, Buffalo

Bill was handsome, energetic, and successful. On the other hand, what does his fame amount to? What did he really accomplish?

Not only Buffalo Bill himself, but his kind of heroism is defunct, the poem announces. Cody died in 1917, so the poem, first published in 1920, is a kind of obituary for this fallen figure. He is remembered fondly by the speaker—almost as if the speaker is remembering his childhood pleasure in watching Buffalo Bill's wild west show. The adult speaker, however, is wondering what Buffalo Bill's legacy really is.

The poem implies that shows such as Buffalo Bill's are distractions from reality, from the knowledge of death. The idea of youth, of freshness and innocence, is worshipped in a kind of religion, and Buffalo Bill becomes a stand-in for Jesus. Ultimately such substitutes fade in importance. The American myth is that the United States is the New World and that Americans can escape from the tyranny of history, from the death and destruction that has struck Europe and other continents. Cummings insinuates that it is a little late in the day for Buffalo Bills—either for nostalgia about Buffalo Bill himself or for others who might try to pretend that they are "blueeyed" boys who can conquer the world. It is fun to remember this simpler past, the poem affirms, but dwelling on Buffalo Bill's exploits leaves one unprepared when death strikes—as it does abruptly in the poem, suddenly taking away the exciting images of the Buffalo Bill show.

This poem has a trajectory that is easily followed if the eye moves from the poem's first words "Buffalo Bill 's" to the single word Jesus on line 7 at the right-hand margin to Mister Death in the left-hand margin at the poem's end. The story of Buffalo Bill—his self-invention and fame—gives way to Jesus and Mister Death. Buffalo Bill cannot hold his own with these two figures; there is no hint of resurrection for him. He is "defunct."

Cummings, also a painter, provides a visual as well as a verbal demonstration of the promise as well as the demise of Buffalo Bill as a suitable American symbol. The tone of braggadocio in the first lines of the poem, which mimic the boisterous selfconfidence of a wild west hero, gives way to a much more complex statement of the poem's theme in the last three lines. The speaker addresses Mister Death directly, acknowledging Buffalo Bill's demise but perhaps also feeling a little aggrieved that this symbol of the American go-getter has been cut down by death. There may be a bit of anger in the question addressed to Mister Death, a lingering lament for a hero and a way of life that had seemed so inspiring.

Carl Rollyson

BUSHED

Author: Earle Birney (1904-1995)
Type of poem: Narrative
First published: 1951; collected in *The Poems of Earle Birney*, 1969

The Poem

"Bushed" is a free-verse poem in lines of irregular length that convey the experience of a man who succumbs to nature's intimidating force. The title's denotations and connotations are all pertinent to the poem's meaning. In the first place, the title indicates location: the "bush," which in Canada refers to those vast areas of wilderness remote from human settlement. Second, to be "bushed" is to be exhausted, to be bereft of strength and therefore incapable of countering force with force or even cunning. In this case, it means also in effect to be swallowed up by the "bush," by the wilderness that, in the man's mind, seems to lie in wait for its prey and at the moment of greatest vulnerability makes its ambush without mercy. The poem is written from the point of view of an observer who tells the story with both emotional intensity and philosophical detachment.

"Bushed" begins with an observation that foreshadows disaster. "He," or humankind, "invented a rainbow" and saw in it divine assurance that nature would not ultimately destroy human life. Then nature's power, through lightning, turned that dream into cold comfort by smashing the rainbow into a mountain lake. At the edge of that lake, far from civilization, a solitary trapper builds himself a shack. He has "learned to roast porcupine belly" and wears the "quills on his hatband." Soon, however, he senses that he has invaded enemy territory whose inhabitants he cannot slay with impunity. That feeling grows in him and gradually unhinges him; he now perceives nature all around him transmogrifying itself into an enemy force. Whether the day dawns in sunshine or fog, the mountain is alive with messages to remind him that he is a puny, unwelcome intruder in the midst of nature. Instead of conqueror, he is its prisoner.

Mountain goats and ospreys guard him in the daytime; in the evening, the night smoke rises "from the boil of the sunset." At night the moon, the owls, and the cedars threaten and mock him with mysterious totems and incantations. The terrible realization penetrates him: While the mountain is asleep, the winds are forging its peak into an arrowhead that will be poised, with him as its single target. Defeated and resigned, the trapper bars himself inside the cabin, his stronghold of civilization, which he now knows is a delusion. All he can do is wait "for the great flint to come singing into his heart."

Forms and Devices

Earle Birney spent his youth in the Banff area, and thus he became intimately familiar with the awesome presence of the Rockies. Much of his poetry reflects a careful observation of the natural world. That observation is often far from dispassionate. As Northrop Frye observed (in "Canada and Its Poetry," *Canadian Forum* 23, 1943,), Birney achieves an "evocation of stark terror" when all the intelligence and cunning of solitary man is pitted against "nature's apparently meaningless power to waste and destroy on a superhuman scale." "Bushed" is such a poem.

Terror is evoked primarily through the imagery. Much of the imagery Birney selects is used in Psalm 104 in praise of a beneficent God who is "clothed with splendor and majesty," who "makes winds his messengers, flames of fire his servants," whose "high mountains belong to the goats," who "touches the mountains and they smoke," who plants "the cedars of Lebanon," who "brings darkness, and all the beasts of the forest prowl." In "Bushed," however, from the first line to the last, it is not the glory and goodness of God's nature but its hostile power that impresses the trapper and inexorably reduces him to a cowed victim.

First, there is the imagery of the heavens. According to the biblical story, God vowed after the flood that floods would never again destroy so much life, and then He chose the rainbow as the eternal reminder and warrant of that promise. Hence the rainbow came to symbolize divine reassurance of human safety and security. Here the fierce lightning of a mountain storm shatters the rainbow and serves notice to the trapper that he has ventured beyond the pale of human and divine protection. Later, the "boil of the sunset" suggests not beauty and peace but a seething cauldron of witches' brew that foreshadows evil to come. In addition, the moon is linked to the sinister work of carving totems, intensifying the trapper's terror. Even when "the mountain slept" at last, the winds of the heavens gathered for the final fatal attack, shaping the mountain's peak to "an arrowhead poised" to attack the victim's heart.

The land imagery is also central. The immensity of the mountain that towers above the man increasingly assumes the personality of an implacable foe with absolute control. It is "so big his mind slowed when he looked at it." Its lap constitutes a lake that swallows the light and the promise of the rainbow. Its messages sweep down "every hot morning," and its proclamations boom out every noon. All nature does its bidding, and the trapper is convinced that all its bidding conspires against him.

Third, there is the imagery of the animal world. The trapper has slain the porcupine and decorated himself with its quills, but not with impunity. A "white guard of goat" now protects the mountain's domain, and the ospreys "fall like valkyries," an ominous allusion to Odin, the all-seeing god of war and magic whose battle maidens (valkyries) chose the heroes to be slain. Here they choose as their victim "the cut-throat," a large trout that, significantly, resembles the rainbow trout. Twice now the rainbow has fallen victim. Besides, the meaning of "cut-throat" as a murderer obviously points to the trapper as the chosen target of the mountain-god's warriors.

Finally, there is the imagery of the spirit world. The moon uses its magical powers to carve "unknown totems out of the lakeshore." These powerful emblems of another, mysterious world terrify the trapper. When, as the element of animism becomes more pervasive, the owl, traditionally linked to the spirit world, derides him, and cedars shape themselves into moose, circle "his swamps," and toss "their antlers up to the stars," the trapper knows he is trapped: The poised "arrowhead" of the mountain-god will be the final mockery of the porcupine "quills on his hatband."

Themes and Meanings

Earle Birney did not follow in the tradition of earlier nature poets such as Bliss Carman (1861-1929) or Archibald Lampman (1861-1899), whose romantic landscape poems celebrated the beauty, peace, and goodness of nature—but then, the rugged Canadian West of Birney's experience hardly resembled the more tranquil scenery of the East that inspired the imagination of his predecessors. The awe-inspiring and fear-inspiring mountain wilderness shaped such poems as "David" (one of his best-known poems, about the fall and death of a young mountain climber) and "Bushed." These poems are as much about the flaws and fears of human nature as they are about the fierce beauty and power of physical nature. As Birney stresses in such poems as "Maritime Faces" and "Climbers," if humans are to survive in a harsh environment that is indifferent to their pretensions and vulnerability, they must come with respect, humility, knowledge, vigilance, and readiness to solve the problems they encounter, both around them and within them.

"Bushed" exposes the folly of a man who fails to take seriously either nature's threat or his own limitations. His journey into the wilderness is a journey into madness and death. At first he presumes that the place he chooses to build his shack is safe and will accommodate his needs and desires. The "quills on his hatband" flaunt his arrogance. It is not so much nature around him that defeats him but his own nature, which is unprepared to take the proper measure of either his external or internal world. The mighty mountain looms high above him, and the confrontation with its shattering force soon seeps into his psyche and begins the unhinging of his mind. Increasingly, his mind mirrors the irrationality of a terror-stricken soul projected onto the vast indifference and impersonal force of his environment. The mountain comes alive, not with glorious splendor but as an ogre-god who wills the intruder's death and marshals all its resources to accomplish its purpose. Thus the lake becomes the god's lap of destruction, the ospreys become valkyries, the goats turn into guards, the lakeshore into totems, the owls into mockers, the cedars into threatening animals. The woods become "beardusky," and the winds become the aerial blacksmiths that forge the fateful arrowhead. The man who came to conquer the bush rather than to seek kinship discovers that he came in ignorance. He retreats to his puny shelter, bars himself in, and waits for the death that his mind has imagined.

Henry J. Baron

THE CAMBRIDGE LADIES WHO LIVE
IN FURNISHED SOULS

Author: E. E. Cummings (1894-1962)
Type of poem: Sonnet
First published: 1923, in *Tulips and Chimneys*

The Poem

E. E. Cummings's sonnet now known as "the Cambridge ladies who live in furnished souls" was originally published without a title in a section of Cummings's first collection of poetry, *Tulips and Chimneys* (1923). That section, labeled "Chimneys," is divided into three sub-sections: "Realities," "Unrealities," and "Actualities." This particular poem, included in the first sub-section, is an example of how Cummings uses a traditional verse form—the fourteen-line lyric known as a sonnet—and remakes it to suit his purpose of startling the reader into a new understanding and into seeing reality in a new way. In this sonnet, Cummings portrays a group of people, "Cambridge ladies," as representations of people who have money and a certain distinguished class in society but who lack the spontaneity and feeling that Cummings believes are the hallmarks of truly human beings. Cummings shows how these people from Cambridge, Massachusetts, the home of such prestigious institutions as Harvard University, are not what they appear to be.

In the first four lines, Cummings describes the ladies whom he is criticizing. They live in "furnished souls"—that is, their souls, as is the case with their lives, are assembled, readymade, and artificially arranged—and their minds are "unbeautiful" and "comfortable." Furthermore, they live with the approval of the society around them, described as "the church's protestant blessings," which is an indication that they are both representative of their culture and held up as model citizens of this culture.

As he proceeds to describe the artificiality of the Cambridge ladies, Cummings notes that they believe in Christ and Longfellow, thus implying that they hold traditional beliefs in Christianity and art: in this instance, the art produced by Henry Wadsworth Longfellow, an American poet who lived from 1807 to 1882 and who was a professor of Romance languages at Harvard. Longfellow's poetry, traditional in form and very American in its subject matter, suggests that these women are careful to read what is noncontroversial and nationalistic, two qualities Cummings abhors. Just as they believe in acceptable religion and art, these women are also involved in acceptable causes, described by Cummings as "knitting for the is it Poles?/ perhaps."

Appearance is not reality, however, as Cummings goes on to demonstrate in the following lines. These Cambridge ladies are described as actually being gossipers who "coyly bandy/ scandal of Mrs. N and Professor D" and, worse, as people who, being caught up in their hypocritical posturing, neglect the beauty of nature around them. In the concluding lines, Cummings describes the moon above them as being "in its box of/ sky lavender and cornerless," rattling "like a fragment of angry candy." The knitting, gossiping ladies, being preoccupied with themselves, do not care to look up to see this natural phenomenon and, as a result, choose for themselves a lifeless, spiritless existence.

Forms and Devices

Innovation is E. E. Cummings's hallmark, and this lyric embodies virtually all of his experimental efforts. Using a traditional verse form, the sonnet, as his structure, Cummings transforms the fourteen-line poem so that it is neither a Shakespearean nor a Petrarchan sonnet (the two types traditionally associated with this verse form). In the former, sometimes called English, three quatrains, each with a rhyme-scheme of its own, are followed by a rhyming couplet. In the latter, sometimes called Italian, the poem is divided into two sections, an octave and a sestet, each with its own particular rhyming pattern. Cummings uses only the basic structure of the traditional sonnet form—its fourteen lines—and discards virtually everything else, most obviously its disciplined rhyme schemes.

Another innovation Cummings introduces into his poetry is a wrenched syntax; that is, a sentence structure that does not follow the expected order of, for example, a subject followed by a verb or an adjective preceding a noun. Thus, the last four lines jumble the expected arrangement of words, forcing the reader to pause and reconstruct the lines to make meaning out of Cummings's experimental arrangement:

> . . . . the Cambridge ladies do not care, above
> Cambridge if sometimes in its box of
> sky lavender and cornerless, the
> moon rattles like a fragment of angry candy

By forcing this labor upon the reader, Cummings accomplishes one of his poetic purposes, which is to help the reader stop, look, and listen: stop a process of sometimes too-rapid reading, look at and listen to the words on the page, and reassemble those words so they reveal a new reality.

The reassembling process is a challenging one, especially since Cummings's use (or lack) of punctuation does not reflect a traditional, grammatically-correct approach to commas and other marks that might help a reader know when to stop and when to move forward in a poem. A series of adjectives is presented with no commas—"daughters, unscented shapeless spirited"—and a sentence might appear to end with a question mark but actually concludes with a period: "at the present writing one still finds/ delighted fingers knitting for is it the Poles?/ perhaps." If the disregard for punctuation is one challenge, the disrespect for capitalization of letters is still another. Sometimes a sentence does not begin with a capital letter, such as the opening line of the poem, and sometimes it does, such as the last sentence of the poem (which does not conclude with a period). This sonnet, like Cummings's other poems, does not allow for reading in the usual way or at the usual pace.

Just as he creates a new syntax and a new method of punctuation, so Cummings experiments with language, creating his own words and including unusual images. The Cambridge ladies are described as "unbeautiful," one of many examples in

Cummings's poems of his use of the "un-" prefix to contrast a world he sees as ugly and artificial with its alternative world of beauty and spontaneity. His images, likewise, reveal these two worlds. The ladies in the poem, described as "unscented shapeless spirited," occupy "furnished souls," while the sky above them—which they never see—is "lavender and cornerless" and home to the moon, which is described with the simile, "like a fragment of angry candy." Not only is this an unusual way to describe the moon, but it is also a startling way to end a sonnet. This is no neat conclusion to a sonnet, as a reader would expect in a traditional Shakespearean or Petrarchan sonnet. On the contrary, it is a typical Cummings conclusion, an assertion that endings are not artificially neat, like the lives of the Cambridge ladies, but are, instead, naturally unpredictable, like the moon rattling above the neglectful women.

Themes and Meanings

Cummings's poem is both satirical and lyrical. It satirizes the hypocrisy and artificiality of people, represented by the Cambridge ladies, who are more concerned with their own images than with the images of nature around them. While appearing to go about their humanitarian tasks with duty and dedication, these ladies actually spread gossip, and they fail to appreciate and become a part of the natural beauty surrounding them (one of the greatest sins of all in Cummings's inventory of sins). In setting his poem in Cambridge and focusing on the ladies who live there, Cummings uses a city he knows well: He was born there, and he was a student at Harvard. His father, a Congregational minister, taught English and, later, social ethics at Harvard. The poet, therefore, is not satirizing an abstract place and set of behaviors but, rather, a specific location that represents his roots and is frequently associated with high culture and the source of what many consider to be true American culture and civilization.

The poem is also lyrical, demonstrating those qualities that typically characterize a lyric poem: imagination, melody, and emotion. Cummings's description of both worlds in this poem—the artificial world of Cambridge and the natural world around the city—do not offer literal, pictorial views. Rather, they provide imaginative perspectives that emphasize the poet's strong emotions: his deep feelings for the beauty of the natural world and his equally deep feelings against the ugliness of the lives embodied by the world created by human beings.

This artificial world, fashioned by the women of Cambridge, is only an appearance. Reality, an important concept to Cummings (this sonnet first appeared in *Tulips and Chimneys* in a section titled "Realities"), is the essence of life. It transcends what a person sees when looking with ordinary eyes at ordinary life. It transforms the ordinary into the extraordinary. It is the "sky lavender and cornerless" that the Cambridge ladies do not know exists above them.

Marjorie Smelstor

CANTO 4

Author: Ezra Pound (1885-1972)
Type of poem: Poetic sequence
First published: 1919; collected in *Poems 1918-1921*, 1921

The Poem

Canto 4 is one of the 117 cantos, or divisions, that make up Ezra Pound's sequence *The Cantos*, one of the major poetic works of the twentieth century. In Canto 4 Ezra Pound introduces the main factors that promote civilizations: urbanization, writing, and religious worship. He describes the ancient city of Troy sacked and destroyed by the victorious Greeks, its palace "in smoky light," the city "a heap of smouldering boundary stones." Then he speaks of Cadmus, the Phoenician trader who founded the city of Thebes. Cadmus gave the Phoenician alphabet to the Greeks; from it they devised the Greek alphabet as it is known today. Pound refers to religious worship by mentioning the *"Chorus nympharum"*—an assembly of bathing nymphs who are worshipers of Pan, the pastoral god who has the legs and feet of a goat.

Once cities, writing, and religion are combined in such a way as to create a civilization, other things can pull civilizations down: The ignoring of tradition by failing, in the words of Matthew Arnold, "to learn and propagate the best that is known and thought in the world." This reverence for tradition also includes the principles of morality, good government, and economics. In addition, self-discipline on the part of rulers and citizens—the ability to curb the meaner passions, greed, selfishness, revenge, desire for power, hatred leading to murder—is necessary if a culture is to survive. It was the coveting of another man's wife by Paris that led to the abduction of Helen and brought about the Trojan War, which destroyed Troy.

The world has darkened for the poet as he contemplates the burning city of Troy, and he seeks relief by recalling moments of light. He recalls the "victory songs" of Pindar and the "nuptial songs" of Catullus, crying out gleefully, "ANAXIFORM-INGES!" ("Lords of the Lyre!") and "Aurunculeia!" (the name of a virgin bride honored by Catullus).

After experiencing some light, the poet returns to the dark side of life by recalling the horrible crimes and violence that were perpetrated by the members of the family of Tereus, the king of Thrace. Tereus had lost control of his sexual passion and raped his wife's sister. Then he had cut out her tongue to ensure her silence. Nevertheless, his wife learned of his crimes. In retaliation she murdered their little son, Itys, and fed his cooked flesh as a meal to the king. When she informed him of what he had eaten, he tried to kill both women, but the gods turned all three into birds.

Then Pound moves ahead in time to medieval Provence, a region and former province of the kingdom of Naples and later of France. Provence was the home of the troubadours, poet-musicians who composed in Provençal and practiced courtly love (*amour courtois*). Courtly love was a contradictory form of love: It was illicit (the love of someone else's wife), yet as "pure love" it was considered passionate, disciplined, and able to elevate the lover morally. The danger was that if it was passionate but without discipline, it could lead to trouble and violence. Now Pound metamorphoses Itys into the troubadour Cabestan (Guillen da Cabestanh), who carried on a love affair with a married woman. Her husband grew jealous and murdered Cabestan, and he prepared a meal of Cabestan's flesh and served it to his wife, whom he considered unfaithful. After his wife had consumed the meal, her husband informed her what she had eaten. She rushed to a second-story window and jumped to her death.

Turning away from this darkness, Pound sees the glittering roof of the Romanesque gothic church in Poitiers, France. This image, emblematic of Catholicism, is followed immediately by recognition of the classical world and the worship of Diana, the goddess of the moon. Then the poet's vision sweeps far away to Japan and then China. In Japan he notes "the pine at Takasago," which refers to the legend of the twin pines of Takasago and Sumiyoshi. They are the homes of a very old married couple who have not only lived very long lives but also remained strictly faithful to each other all their lives; they have become immortal. She lives in the pine at Takasago; he lives in the other pine at Sumiyoshi, and for countless years he has paid nightly visits to his wife; the two converse until the break of day. Thus this immortal couple symbolize longevity and conjugal fidelity. Pound now returns from Japanese culture to classical Roman culture. In the voice of Catullus he again celebrates the marriage of Aurunculeia, hailing Hymen, the god of marriage.

Pound next moves to ancient China, where he considers the political question of the power of the ruler in respect to the common people and in respect to nature. At the same time he introduces the reader to the literary question of the relationship of Chinese poetry in style and subject to the poetry of the West. He discusses the main theme of a poem by the distinguished Sung Yü (in the third century B.C.), who served as a courtier at the court of King Hsiang Yü, ruler of the state of Ch'u. One day the king was taking his ease on the terrace outside his palace when the wind blew. The king remarked to Sung Yü: "What delightful breeze!" Then he added: "And I and the common people may share it together, may we not?" Sung Yü replied: "The wind does not choose between the high and the low, but it belongs to the place where it seeks out."

Pound concludes Canto 4 by returning to the theme of the city and its violent crime. Pound's city here is Ecbaton (or Ecbatana), the capital of ancient Media during its decline under King Acrisius in the early sixth century B.C. According to Herodotus, it was surrounded by seven concentric walls, each of a different color. It was a planned city that contained "plotted streets." It also contained a brazen tower that was the king's treasure house. King Acrisius had been warned by an oracle that he would be slain by a grandson. A coward, he imprisoned his daughter, Danae, in the tower so that no man could love or wed her. Zeus, however, angry that the king should seek to alter a prophecy of the gods, visited Danae in the form of golden rain and made her pregnant. Although Acrisius tried to kill both her and her child, Perseus, he failed. Later Perseus killed Acrisius accidentally.

Then Pound introduces his reader to the city of Sardis (or Sardes), the capital of

Lydia during the reign of King Candaules (c. 700 B.C.). The city contained a temple to Artemis, the goddess of the moon. Sardis is believed to have been the first city to issue gold and silver coins. A story of considerable irony is associated with King Candaules. Much in love with his wife, he never tired of recounting to other men the beauty of her face and figure. He tried to impress his young bodyguard, Gyges, on this matter. The youth listened politely to his master's ravings, but he was unmoved. Thinking that his bodyguard did not believe him, the king insisted that Gyges hide in the queen's bedroom until she came in to retire for the night; the bodyguard was much opposed to this plan. He obeyed his master, however, and saw the queen naked. However, from the corner of her eye she saw him dart out the door. The next morning she sent for the bodyguard. She informed him that he had two choices. He must kill her husband, marry her, and become king or he must forfeit his own life. He chose the first alternative.

Forms and Devices

Canto 4 is only one segment of *The Cantos*, a poetic cultural history of the world that is multicultural and multilingual. Pound's poetry is cryptic and sometimes aphoristic. Reflecting his interest in myth and world history, his verse is peppered with foreign languages and with English translations of foreign languages. The style of *The Cantos* in general is fragmented; one small bit of history or myth bumps against another from a different era and part of the world. To Pound, poetry is a "charged language" that has a definite relation to music and, to a lesser degree, to painting and sculpture. He employs free verse, precise imagery, and the rhythms of common, sometimes slangy, speech. One of Pound's major devices is the so-called ideogrammatic method, which he took from his impression of the structure of Chinese characters: A character is formed from two or more pictographs (or indicators) to suggest a larger idea.

Pound pays strict attention to the consonance of words and music. In every case he tries to find the most appropriate word, not only in meaning but also in emotional resonance. He held that a poet's rhythm and meter reveal the poet's sincerity and commitment.

Pound makes considerable use of mythology—for example, he applies classical myths to the lives of the troubadours—and this practice makes the reader aware of certain types of constant relations, as between the Tereus and Cabestan. Pound uses these myths to present moral problems and create psychic experiences. Myth enables him to record dark passions and crimes and to contrast them with the bright light of the world.

The principal device Pound uses is the *forma* or *virtù*. The *forma* or *virtù* is the pattern (or simply the "something") that lies behind concepts or techniques of artistic, literary, and social phenomena and enables a notable tradition to develop—as with the songs of the thirteenth century troubadours or the strange metaphysics of light of Grosseteste. Canto 4 presents no formal organization; like *The Cantos* as a whole, it represents the personal improvisation of a great poetic sensibility.

Themes and Meanings

The foundation stones of a civilization, according to Pound, are in essence urbanization, writing, and religious consciousness. If a civilization is to survive, the moral law must be respected and observed. There must be self-discipline and control of the meaner passions: Lust, revenge, murder, and greed must be disallowed and foolish wars avoided. In Pound's view history follows organic time and consists of "ideas in action." These ideas in action result from the exercise of human will in conjunction with certain ethical frameworks. The actions occur at certain places and at certain times to produce cultural complexes. Such a complex includes language, knowledge, religious consciousness, myth and legend, morals, government, law, customs, and the arts. Through presenting selected past ideas in action, Pound wishes his reader to learn important truths about the present. To Pound, civilization is the inevitable destiny of a culture that is allowed to develop. He held that civilization follows the laws of the organic world and that cultural processes repeat themselves in cyclic stages.

According to R. W. Dasenbrock, "the pattern or repeat in history that fascinated Pound" was the "close interrelation between cultural achievement and violence." This relationship is the dominant theme of Canto 4. Yet the focus on violence stands in contrast to five kinds of love that are also illustrated in the poem: lustful love (Tereus), courtly love (the troubadours), married love (Manlius and Vinia Aurancules), self-love (King Acrisius), and love of life (the Transcendental Light).

Richard P. Benton

CANTO 29

Author: Ezra Pound (1885-1972)
Type of poem: Poetic sequence
First published: 1930, in *A Draft of XXX Cantos*

The Poem

Pound begins Canto 29 with a reference to a cosmology and a tribute to light (*lux*). This description is consonant with the metaphysics of light proposed by the thirteenth century philosopher Grosseteste, whose thinking was familiar to Pound. According to Grosseteste light is from God and is the basis of matter and form. Any dimming of light in the cosmos indicates a decline and a decadence in matter owing to the privation of light. This view constitutes Pound's notion of *forma*; *forma* is that something which produces "ideas," especially "ideas in action," which is Pound's definition of history.

Then Pound presents his views on the natures of women and love. Because of their biology and their beauty of face and figure, women are natural lures of men; hence they can be agents of enhancement to men or agents of destruction. Pound presents the latter type in Pernella, the concubine of Count Aldobrando Orsini of Verona. Having given birth to two male children, she wishes her second to be the heir to her lover's estate despite the fact that Aldobrando has an heir in his grown son, Niccolò Orsini, Count of Petigliano, a gifted mercenary soldier. Believing that Niccolò's courage will get him killed in battle in the near future, Pernella murders her first child in order to advance the second. Seeing into her ambition, Niccolò kills her second child. Foiled in her scheme, Pernella through false communication starts a war. For her treason Niccolò kills her.

Next Pound introduces the troubadours—those aristocratic poet-musicians whose favorite subjects were courtly love, war, and nature. They are represented here by Sordello di Goito (d. 1270), who loves the noblewoman Cunizza, the wife of Rizzardo di Bonifacio. Sordello runs away with her but soon loses her to a knight named Bonio. The other model is Arnaut Daniel (d. 1210), who loved a noblewoman of Gascony, the wife of Sir Guillem de Bouvilla. Ideally, courtly love was what the troubadours called "pure love": It consisted of the union of the hearts and minds of the lovers without physical possession of the woman, the aim being the ennobling of the lover. In practice, "pure love" held a danger because it involved the fanning of illicit desires. If the couple's spirits were weak, the lovers could lapse into adultery.

Pound now leaves early Renaissance Italy for the early twentieth century in the United States. He presents the allegorical figure of "Lusty Juventus," who represents the spirit of youth as a life force. He confronts an old funeral director in front of the latter's house. This man has daughters whose behavior has caused comment among residents of the town. The undertaker does not know how he feels about his daughters. Apparently these young women have revolted against their Protestant heritage and have become "flappers" of the Jazz Age. "The wail of the phonograph" is that of a "djassban" hammering out sexy music suggestive of a "pornograph" to the father's ear. As the representative of the Protestant conscience, he is confused. He has habitually been opposed to drinking alcohol, smoking cigarettes, playing cards, and, above all, dancing and free love. It may seem that Pound's leap from Renaissance Italy to the 1920's Jazz Age in the United States is a big leap in "clock time." However, in *The Cantos* Pound is not concerned with clock time, placing the emphasis on "organic time." Pound held that cultural complexes as processes repeat themselves in accord with Friedrich Nietzsche's principle of the "eternal return."

Juventus speaks in the voice of Grosseteste on the relation of light to matter and *forma*. The American landscape merges into the European scene and becomes multilingual. The main theme of Canto 29 is now spelled out: "the female/ Is an element, the female/ Is a chaos/ An octopus/ A biological process." At this point the Lord of Light appears in the person of Helios.

Forms and Devices

Canto 29 has a principal theme—the exploration of the power of the female sex and the danger inherent in the practice of courtly love—but it has no formal pattern. Rather, it proceeds in a manner similar to the jazz improvisations of such virtuosos as Bix Beiderbecke on the cornet or Art Tatum on the piano, whose styles were very personalized. Pound considered poetry to be "charged language" closely related to music and to common speech. His main technical devices are the use of a persona and its metamorphosis; he employs changelings and their voices, juxtaposition of facts, events, and quotations (often in foreign languages), and dependence on an ideographic method based on the pattern of a certain class of Chinese characters or ideograms.

Canto 29 is but a section of a whole, *The Cantos*, a modern epic poem that is a cultural history of the world in which the poet seeks to reveal the organic unity of civilizations. Hence it is multicultural and multilingual. Pound intended it to be didactic and personal. He comments on the past in order to shed light on the present from his unique point of view. He might have said of *The Cantos* what Walt Whitman said of his *Leaves of Grass* (1855): "Camerado, this is no book;/ Who touches this touches a man."

Themes and Meanings

The central theme of *The Cantos* as a whole is the poet's search for a philosophy capable of validating an ideal system of ethics, economics, and politics—for a social order that will prove a "city of Light," or an ideal civilization. In line with this search Pound presents examples of social behavior on the part of humanity which not only can prove self-destructive but also can prevent a city of light from emerging or destroy one that is existing. Apart from the theme that beautiful women can prove Circes, possessing enough sexual power to turn men into swine, there is always the danger that a human being can feel irrational desire, whether it be in respect to wealth and power or in respect to irrational attachment to sexual pleasure.

Canto 29 presents an example of both overweening ambition and attachment to sexual pleasure in Pernella, the concubine of Count Orsini of Verona; these weaknesses bring about her destruction. Pound also presents two examples from the Middle Ages respecting the destructive power of lust: the Italian troubadour Sordella di Goito, who loves the noble lady Cunizza, and the French troubadour Arnaut Daniel, who loves the noble lady of Gascony. "Pure love" is bypassed in both cases.

Finally, Canto 29 moves through time and space to the United States of the 1920's. The period between 1919 and 1929 has been called the Flapper Age, the Jazz Age, and the Roaring Twenties. In 1917, while World War I was still raging, the Prohibition amendment, outlawing the sale of alcoholic beverages, had been adopted. With the war over in 1918, the women's suffrage amendment was adopted in 1920. All at once it seemed to older Americans that the younger generation was revolting against all the former Victorian moral standards in fashions and behavior. Young women wore short skirts, bobbed their hair, and applied rouge to their faces. They danced the fox trot and the Charleston. They drank bootleg whiskey, smoked cigarettes, and believed in "free love" and divorce. It was the period of gangsters such as Al Capone and Jack "Legs" Diamond. Corruption and violence reigned. It seemed to many that the United States was rapidly heading for disaster—and with the stock market crash of 1929 and the onset of the Great Depression, disaster did indeed strike.

Richard P. Benton

CANTO 81

Author: Ezra Pound (1885-1972)
Type of poem: Poetic sequence
First published: 1948, in *The Pisan Cantos*

The Poem

Canto 81 is a free-verse poem of 173 lines in Ezra Pound's long epic poem entitled *The Cantos*. "Canto" is an Italian word for song, poem, or chant. Pound worked on *The Cantos* for more than fifty years, from about 1915 until his death. Canto 81 is part of *The Pisan Cantos* (cantos 74-84), which Pound wrote in 1945 while a prisoner of war in the United States Army's Disciplinary Training Center (DTC) near Pisa, Italy. With a naïve and misplaced faith in the economic reforms of Italian fascist dictator Benito Mussolini, Pound had delivered broadcasts over Rome Radio criticizing the United States' actions in World War II. Without visits from family or friends and without his books, Pound wrote the eleven Pisan cantos mostly from memory as he struggled for survival during seven months of solitary confinement before being formally accused of treason.

This poem has two sections. The first ninety-two lines offer a meditation on attempts to find worth in life. Through short narratives and direct quotations, often in colloquial diction, the speaker presents ways of worship as well as rituals of everyday life from ancient to contemporary cultures. The first line grounds the poem in Greek antiquity: "Zeus lies in Ceres' bosom." Zeus is a newer male god resting like a baby or lover on the breast of Ceres, the older female god of corn and nature. The section ends with a journalistic account which states that "my ole man went on hoein' corn." Pound believed in the community-strengthening power of the Eleusinian Mysteries, during which the Greeks celebrated the seasonal plant cycles of "the green world," to which Pound often turns for organic principles of order. The speaker ends images of worship, friendship, hospitality, writing, communal dance, and newspaper reporting in this section, along with a three-line lament on his loneliness in prison.

The poem shifts at line 96, where the second section is labeled "libretto," or words for music. Here the poem becomes more consciously musical. The speaker turns to the supernatural with an image that suggests the goddess of love, Aphrodite, Pound's personal deity: "Yet/ Ere the season died a-cold/ Borne upon a zephyr's shoulder/ I rose through the aureate sky." This god seems to preside over the seventeenth century English lyric community. The speaker considers the ability and inability to see and know until, at line 133, the section shifts into a powerful prayer, probably spoken by Aphrodite, that starts, "What thou lovest well remains,/ the rest is dross." It is an encouraging and comforting message to artists and others passionate enough to "Make it new," Pound's words that served as the motto of the modern era.

Readers must sort through often confusing and apparently esoteric fragments. This process requires interpretation of the poem in order to find its value. The end of the poem can function as Pound's rationale for radio broadcasts intended to improve rather than betray his country, as the goddess may be addressing Pound: "How mean thy hates// Rathe [quick] to destroy, niggard in charity// But to have done instead of not doing/ this is not vanity." In another interpretation, the goddess may be admonishing Pound's critics, so quick to destroy him and so deficient in compassion. It is up to the reader to ponder whether Canto 81 presents a repentant or defiant Pound—or whether it is more important to contemplate love and love contemplation.

Forms and Devices

This poem, like many by Pound and other modern poets such as T. S. Eliot, accumulates images and documents that leap across time and place without explanatory connective material. Pound used an ordering device that he called the ideogramic method. Taking his cue from some Chinese characters called ideograms, he assembles images that present aspects of an idea. For example, he follows an image of nature comforting Zeus with a Spanish priest who helped Pound with research on the troubadour poet Guido Cavalcanti and a Spanish peasant woman who gave Pound bread. Together, these images convey the idea of kindness.

Pound led a transatlantic poetic movement called Imagism, which opposed nineteenth century Romanticism and sentimentality by favoring sharp, clear images, freedom in choice of subject matter, and common speech. Yet Canto 81 and other cantos have images that are not always clear and often seem to dissolve into other images. In this canto images include Greek and Chinese deities, a Portuguese folk dance, a French economic council, John Adams and Thomas Jefferson, the philosopher George Santayana arriving in Boston, and a reporter getting his story. Pound, along with the painter Wyndham Lewis and sculptor Henri Gaudier-Brzeska, extended Imagism to Vorticism, which declared itself free from the need to imitate nature and celebrated energy changed by the artist into form.

Many fragments in the first section are reportorial or documentary in nature. Languages include Spanish, Chaucer's Middle English, classical Greek, and a shift to some Italian in the second section. All these images and documents give Pound's endeavor authority from different times, places, disciplines, and classes. He starts the canto with classical divinity and ends it with biblical diction and rhythm. Clergy, political leaders, and cultural forces help the speaker to present his theme from different perspectives. This Cubist treatment, which modern writers adapted from painters such as Pablo Picasso, deepened and broadened the treatment of a poetic subject, much as Cubist painter Marcel Duchamp presents on one canvas various views of a nude descending a staircase. Pound used multiple perspectives to write "the tale of the tribe"—the human community—and help it to envision a new "Paideuma . . . the gristly roots of ideas that are in action" in the mid-twentieth century.

In addition, Pound uses music as a formal, stylistic, and semantic device. Refrains such as "Pull down thy vanity" and "What thou lov'st well shall not be reft from thee" dramatize what is important. Cadences from authoritative and aesthetic sources such as the Bible, Ben Jonson, and Geoffrey Chaucer modulate within the poem. As a motif in music alters somewhat yet remains recognizable, Pound works with the main motif of worth and uses the related motifs of love and community to sound its importance. Pound loves the metaphor of a community as a musical group in which each person thoughtfully contributes his or her part to a whole energized by diversity. The music of this canto entrances the reader before he or she can understand its meaning.

Themes and Meanings

Canto 81 is a poem about worth. In the larger work, *The Cantos* as a whole, Pound looks across the history of human civilization and contemplates what endures. Pound thought that civilizations fall because of economic reasons. For example, he dearly loved the intellectual and artistic successes of the Italian Renaissance but believed that it disintegrated because of money lust and private banking. He thought that Italy could serve as the locus of a model or experiment that combined honest Confucian government with the celebration of the Eleusian Mysteries. In Canto 81 he demonstrates the process of finding what is worthwhile.

Overall, this poem uses the scientific method. That is, it starts with observations that the speaker believes are important. From his solitary confinement in Pisa, Pound fondly recalls people who helped other people, both individually and through a community. From this evidence, Pound reaches a thesis: "What thou lovest well remains,/ the rest is dross." The next line, the most famous in *The Cantos*, intensifies this image of purification and relates it more immediately to Pound's desperate condition: "What thou lov'st well shall not be reft from thee." Pound uses the authority of the inductive method to test the value of his conclusion that love and anything done with love have enduring value.

As a guiding principle of love Pound uses Aphrodite, known to Romans as Venus and cited in line 3 as "Cythera," a Greek island where the goddess landed. Directly after Pound's profound cry of loss and loneliness as "a leaf in the current" of life and history with "no Althea" to comfort him, a supernatural figure rises like Botticelli's Venus from the sea. With the cadences and rhetoric of God speaking from the whirlwind in the Book of Job and the preacher in Ecclesiastes, she inspires harmonious community by asking of individual artists and craftspeople, "Has he tempered the viol's wood// Has he curved us the bowl of the lute?" Later she states that "it is not man/ Made courage, or made order, or made grace,/ Pull down thy vanity, I say pull down." She asks them to contemplate the source of their creative energies.

Pound sees worth in community. Canto 81 offers a heterogeneous community that includes peasants, political leaders, and gods. Contrary to the elitism that some people see in Pound's poetry, this canto is inclusive. Unlike the more homogeneous world of the Cavalier poetic tradition, Pound's world is global. Love and caring can create a viable new transnational community. As Pound sifts through the pieces of his life, the people of a Europe wrecked by World War II must choose the fragments worthy of creating a new world.

Joanna Yin

CANTO 116

Author: Ezra Pound (1885-1972)
Type of poem: Poetic sequence
First published: 1962; collected in *Drafts and Fragments of Cantos CX-CXVII*, 1968

The Poem

"Canto 116" (or "Canto CXVI," as it was first known) was composed in Italy in 1959. It is a relatively short poem in free verse. Its seventy-four lines vary in length from three to eleven syllables. The figure the poem makes on paper is jagged because of frequent indentation; many of its lines begin in the middle or toward the end of the page.

Upon scrutiny, "Canto 116" reveals a threefold structure: Part 1, so called, extends from Neptunus (Neptune) of line 1 to Justinian, including the next line (line 22), "a tangle of works unfinished." Muss (Mussolini), the "old crank" dead in Virginia, and the vision of the Madonna are stages in this section. Part 2, comprising the next thirty-four lines, begins with the definite emergence of the first-person narrator ("I have brought the great ball of crystal") and ends with a concession in line 56: "even if my notes do not cohere." This median group of lines may be further subdivided into two unequal parts, from line 23 to line 31 and from line 32 to line 56. Finally, part 3 goes from line 57 ("Many errors") to the end of the poem (line 74), "to lead back to splendour." The quest for paradise is brought to a rest here, but it promises a new dawn and a renewed beginning.

The first character to burst upon the scene is Neptune, the god of the seas in Greek mythology, whose mind frolics like leaping dolphins. Then there is talk about cosmos-making in a world of the possible: the political realm of Benito Mussolini, the dictator of Italy from 1922 to 1943, and the poetic sphere of fashioning an epic poem, Ezra Pound's *Cantos* themselves. The "record" (line 8) and the "palimpsest" (line 9) seem to refer back to both. With line 13 Pound himself gets his picture into the text. He will gradually emerge as the protagonist of "Canto 116." Then a picture of the Madonna, the mother of Jesus, is introduced. The next several lines seem to deal with Justinian, the Byzantine emperor from A.D. 527 to 565, famous for his code of laws.

With line 23 the first-person voice proclaims its presence and firmly takes over. Things become clearer, especially for those readers who are familiar with Pound's troubles in old age: his incarceration and trial for treason at the end of World War II, his subsequent thirteen-year-long confinement at St. Elizabeth's (an asylum for the insane in Washington, D.C.), the scandal caused by the first Bollingen Prize being awarded to his *Pisan Cantos* in 1949, and his final release and return to Italy in 1958. In the middle of "Canto 116" the speaking persona of the poet is intent on building an argument regarding his mismanagement of the entire large-scale project of *The Cantos* as an epic poem. In doing so, however, Pound is also keen in pointing out various extenuating circumstances, and even the relative strengths of his whole endeavor.

While hammering out his pseudo-defense, the speaker evokes the strength and encouragement he drew from a range of benefic agencies, including two beautiful and sympathetic creatures "under the elms," "squirrels and bluejays" popping up from Walt Disney's world of animated films, "Ariadne," the famous heroine of Greek mythology who gave Theseus the thread with which he found his way out of the Minotaur's labyrinth, André Spire, the Jewish French poet and humanist, the French symbolist poet Jules Laforgue, Linnaeus, the great Swedish botanist, and "Venere"—the goddess of love and beauty, also known as Venus or Aphrodite. The point is reached that paradise ("paradiso" in the text, most probably in honor of Dante Alighieri) seems still within reach, here on earth: "a nice quiet paradise/ over the shambles" (lines 49-50). The spirit is upbeat. The failure acknowledged in lines 28-29 is mitigated, even reversed, in lines 55-56.

In the concluding section, the speaker's voice ruminates on the balancing act involved: "many errors,/ a little rightness" (lines 57-58) and "To confess wrong without losing rightness" (line 70). To make most of what endures is the lesson in humility that the poet has learned the hard way. At long last, a glimmer of light flickers, showing the way back to splendor. The whole epic cycle comes to rest on this hopeful note.

Forms and Devices

"Canto 116" is part of a large-scale, 800-page epic poem that was forty years in the making, roughly from 1920 to 1960. *The Cantos* (the later poetry of Ezra Pound) bears comparison in scope, complexity, and difficulty with *Ulysses* (1922), the well-known novel by James Joyce, and with the other masterwork that appeared in that same year, T. S. Eliot's poem *The Waste Land*. All three works are representative of English Modernism, the literary trend that dominated the first half of twentieth century Western culture.

As part of a larger whole, "Canto 116" is only a relatively independent piece of writing. However, being practically the last completed unit of the sequence, it represents a vantage point from which the compositional strategies of the *Cantos* can be surveyed and grasped as a whole. In contradistinction to most of the previous cantos—and, for that matter, to any other epic poem—"Canto 116" is written in the first person. Hence it possesses a higher consistency of viewpoint, even though subjective, and greater clarity and accessibility than much of Pound's work.

The engine that drives this canto's unfolding is Pound's usual resort to parataxis: the placing side by side of bits of information, names of important people and places, mythical allusions, and phrases in foreign tongues (sometimes translated, sometimes not)—all in rapid succession, with no grammatical connectives whatsoever between them. Thus words are grouped in rhythmical, self-sufficient units or paragraphs, a fact which renders their meanings more readily available. The lines of varying length yielded by this process are further highlighted by their typographical arrangement down the page in doublets or triplets. The emotional highs and lows that alternate during the unfolding of the canto can be thus followed and plotted. The reader is also urged to spot the instances of hypotaxis, when such syntactical connectors such as "but," "though," or "even if" (see the beginnings of lines 8, 26, 27, 45, 56, and 66) restrict or qualify the significance of the statements. Likewise, inversion of a Miltonic type (a device generally avoided by Pound) powerfully launches the opening line: "Came Neptunus."

Pound's text production, with its reliance on disconnected fragments, arresting images, and recondite allusions, requires considerable critical research. All modernist works demand initiation prior to comfortable enjoyment. Since there is no such thing as an omniscient reader, an industry of modernist exegesis has flourished. The reader who has developed a taste for Pound, Eliot, or Joyce will eventually have to read the findings of Eva Hesse, Walter Baumann, James J. Wilhelm, George Kearns, Christine Froula, and Peter Stoicheff, to name some of the more insightful commentators on "Canto 116." Likewise, periodically interesting and rewarding articles are published in *Paideuma*, the main journal focusing on Pound's work.

Themes and Meanings

"Canto 116" begins with Neptune's divine mind asserting its presence and prompting some summing-up or self-criticism inspired by impending death. Pound's original ambition of structuring the Cantos on a cosmic scale is found wanting. His many errors, such as his involvement with fascism and the scapegoating of the Jews, prevented him from "making things cohere." Acknowledgment of this is the dominant theme of the canto, so a sense of dark despair underlies it. Along these lines, Pound's constant model and source of inspiration, Dante's *Divine Comedy*, provided him with a vision of Paradise that he could not sustain. What he could attain, though, was a kind of private paradise of personal fulfillment and love, a humble experience of purgatorial ascent.

Although Pound resorts to such limiting terms as "palimpsest," "record," and "notes," he seems eager to uphold and defend his work. There is perfection in it ("the crystal ball") or great promise ("an acron of light") or a reassuring permanence (Ariadne's "golden thread"). The whole setting seems to take part in this positive outlook: the luminous gold of Italian geography and art (the golden mosaic at the church on the island of Torcello, the "lane of gold" in the wake of the setting sun across the Bay of Tiguillo), the equally luminous feminine presences, the muses of memory (Sheri Martinelli and Marcella Booth, née Spann) in the arboretum at St. Elizabeth's, the simplicity and elemental alertness of bluejays and squirrels in Disney's films (contrasted with the "metaphysicals"—modern scientists who disregard the radiance and splendor of the created universe). Pound's confidence is shattered only when it comes to the question of the decoding of his message by some future generation.

Beyond that concern, "charity"—the chief Dantescan value—remains one of his genuine experiences, though somewhat frustrated by his own sense of guilt, which does not allow a full rejoicing in it. Finally, "the dim rush of light," symbolizing his love for his infant daughter, lends to his longing for the "splendour" of bygone days with both poignancy and wistful hope.

Stefan Stoenescu

CAPTIVITY

Author: Louise Erdrich (1954-
Type of poem: Narrative
First published: 1984, in *Jacklight*

The Poem

"Captivity" is a medium-length narrative poem in free verse, its fifty-eight lines divided into six stanzas which are, respectively, nine, ten, eleven, eight, ten, and ten lines long. The title refers to the subject of the narrative: It is a woman's story of her capture by a band of American Indians in the seventeenth century. No names are given for the narrator or any of the other characters—the man she identifies as her captor, a woman associated with him, and the narrator's child and husband. An epigraph, a short quote from Mary Rowlandson's 1676 narrative about her own capture and travels with a band of Wampanoag, follows the title of the poem. The quote reads: "He (my captor) gave me a bisquit, which I put in my pocket, and not daring to eat it, buried it under a log, fearing he had put something in it to make me love him."

Although the poem is written in the first-person point of view, the Rowlandson reference makes it clear that Erdrich is creating a narrator whose culture, experiences, and beliefs are different from the poet's own. The speaker of the poem is based on a historical figure. Erdrich is a twentieth century poet of German and Chippewa descent; the narrator of "Captivity" is a woman like Mary Rowlandson.

The poem begins with a description of the group's flight through the woods. The narrator states that she had trouble crossing a stream but that someone, referred to only as "he," saved her. The captive has learned to recognize him as an individual, and she is afraid that she understands "his language, which [is] not human." In her fear, she prays.

The next two stanzas describe events that occurred during her time with her captors. They are chased and have to march. The narrator's child cries because of hunger, but she cannot suckle, so a woman feeds the baby "milk of acorns." The narrator promises herself to starve rather than take food from her captors, but she does not keep the promise. One night "he" kills a pregnant deer and gives her "to eat of the fawn./ It was so tender,/ the bones like the stems of flowers,/ that I followed where he took me." The events that close the stanza are not clearly described. "He" cuts the ropes that bind her, and it is night. The next stanza describes natural events that the narrator interprets as God's wrath. These events include a lightning storm. She sees that her captor neither notices or fears God's wrath.

The last two stanzas describe her life after she has been rescued and returned to her husband. Although she is back with her family, she is neither happy nor content. She says that she sees "no truth in things," and despite having food for her child, she does not feel at home. She says "I lay myself to sleep" and "I lay to sleep," two lines that echo the prayer taught to children. Instead of untroubled sleep or a completed prayer, she has a vision of herself back with her captors. She is "outside their circle," but as her captor leads them in what the narrator first thinks of as noise, she finds herself part of the chant. She strips a branch and joins them, strikes the earth "begging it to open/ to admit me/ as he was/ and feed me honey from the rock."

Forms and Devices

The narrative and language of the poem are based on another group of texts: historical "captivity narratives." Erdrich explicitly directs the readers to consider the existence and meanings of the captivity narratives by quoting Mary Rowlandson's narrative and providing basic information about her situation. Rowlandson was taken prisoner by the Wampanoag "when Lancaster, Massachusetts, was destroyed, in the year 1676." In order to understand the poem's themes fully, some knowledge of the historical circumstances is necessary. Rowlandson's narrative has become one of the most well known of numerous published captivity stories, but it is by no means the only one. Frances Roe Kestler, in *The Indian Captivity Narrative: A Woman's View* (1990), identifies approximately five hundred narratives, published in twelve hundred editions, during the seventeenth, eighteenth, and nineteenth centuries. The narratives were written by men and women who were held captive by various tribes during the centuries of conflict between the European immigrants and the American Indians who lived in the areas where the Europeans settled.

According to Kestler, Rowlandson's was the first narrative known to be composed by a woman. The experiences of and perceptions about women who were held captive differed from those of men because of the different cultural expectations regarding women, especially regarding sexuality. Rowlandson had immigrated to Salem with her father and later married Joseph Rowlandson, a minister. They had four children. The three children who survived infancy were taken captive, along with their mother, in February of 1676. The youngest child died during captivity; the older two escaped or were ransomed. Rowlandson was ransomed in May after three months of captivity.

The unnamed narrator of Erdrich's poem cannot be Mary Rowlandson, who was taken captive with three children, the youngest age six, but Erdrich clearly intends readers to view the poem as a captivity narrative by a woman who had similar experiences and fears, especially regarding the possibility of being forced to "love" her captor through some charm or spell placed on food. The narrator, like Rowlandson, fears her captors as being completely different and "other" than human.

Another important aspect of the poem is the imagery, especially the image clusters relating to religion and food. The religious images and allusions would be natural usage to a Puritan woman, and they primarily are references to natural disasters as representing God's punishment. The narrator is dragged from "the flood," a reference to the biblical flood, which was God's punishment of humanity. She prays after realizing that she is understanding some of "his" language, recalling the Tower of Babel, which led to God causing humans to speak in different languages. After she goes apart with him, she believes that she is being punished by God: Trees fling "down/ their sharpened lashes." God's wrath is made clear in natural manifestations ("blasting fire from half-buried stumps.")

Her belief that God punishes humanity through the earth changes in the last stanza when the narrator imagines herself joining in the chant, "begging" the earth "to open// and feed me honey from the rock." The change from earth as a place of sinning and punishment to earth as a nurturing mother implies a change from the Puritan world-view to a belief common to American Indians.

The final stanza links religious and food imagery, but the food imagery begins in the epigraph which speaks of Rowlandson's determination not to eat any food from the hand of her captor because it might make her love him. When the narrator's child is hungry, a woman provides food. The narrator herself plans to starve but ultimately accepts food "from his hands," the second time that he saves her life. The food is the flesh of an unborn fawn, and it causes her to follow him ("I followed where he took me"). At the end of the poem, the speaker begs the earth, through her chant, to feed her "honey from the rock," a new and different kind of food, linked to her captor. The food imagery being associated with children (her child and the unborn fawn) shows the link between food and sexuality or birth.

Themes and Meanings

"Captivity" is a poem about identity and culture. The history of the relationships between "Americans" (as the indigenous peoples were called by the early immigrants) and "Europeans" is a long and complicated one, and Erdrich is concerned with re-viewing that history. Erdrich, a twentieth century German-Chippewa woman, creates as her speaker a seventeenth century Puritan woman who travels and lives with a group that she would normally see as her family's and culture's enemies. If the narrator shares Mary Rowlandson's views, shaped by the preaching of Puritan ministers, she would also see her captor and the others as allies of Satan, placed in the "New World" to tempt the Puritans from their religion and culture. Any understanding of or intimacy with a man from this group who are "not human" would be seen as endangering her soul. At the beginning of the narrative, the speaker fears learning to understand her captor, fears accepting food from him, because any intimacy with him will bring down God's wrath on her.

By the end of the poem, the narrator has moved beyond her culture's attitudes about the "Other," and the experience changes her irretrievably. She eats the food her captor brings her, and possibly has sexual relations with him. Rescued, she has lost any sense of her own culture's "truth" and longs to join what she formerly rejected. The poem does not explicitly state that physical intimacy occurred, but a woman writing in the seventeenth century (or even the eighteenth and nineteenth) would probably not be able to say so explicitly, at least not in any published work. The intimacy has to be understood through images, through what is not said, and through changes in her. Even if no sexual act occurred, her vision at the end of the poem shows that she wishes to join in the circle, to join with them, in a chant which is probably of a religious nature. Even if she remained physically faithful to her husband, she has been spiritually changed. The poem's theme subverts the expectations and attitudes of an earlier time and asks contemporary readers to think about those attitudes and about what has changed, or not changed, in the centuries following the events of this poem.

Robin Anne Reid

CARGOES

Author: John Masefield (1878-1967)
Type of poem: Lyric
First published: 1903, in *Ballads*

The Poem

"Cargoes" is a short lyric poem consisting of three five-line stanzas. In each, Masefield describes a different kind of ship. The first two lines of each stanza describe the ship moving through water; the last three list the different cargoes the ships are carrying.

The ship in stanza 1 is a quinquireme, a large vessel rowed by groups of five oarsmen. Masefield's ship is being rowed from "distant Ophir," a region in either Arabia or Africa at the southern end of the Red Sea, to the northern end of that sea. (Masefield must have intended the term "Palestine" to apply to the land at the farthest reach of the present Gulf of Aqaba.) The ship's goal is a happy one, for Palestine is a safe "haven" with sunny skies. This boat carries a cargo of animals, birds, exotic woods, and wine.

Masefield found many of his details in the Old Testament. Nineveh, an important Assyrian city, is often mentioned there. Many of the details of this stanza—ivory, apes, peacocks, and cedars—come from 1 Kings 10. That chapter also mentions drinking vessels, though not the wine in them, and "almug trees," which may be the same as sandalwood trees.

In stanza 3, the poem moves ahead about two thousand years to the sixteenth or seventeenth century and changes its focus to the West Indies. A galleon was a large sailing ship often used in trade between Spain and Latin America, a part of the world Masefield himself knew well from his days as a sailor. This "stately" (splendid, dignified, majestic) ship began its journey at the Isthmus of Panama, and it progresses with a vessel's normal up-and-down motion ("dipping") through the verdant and beautiful islands of the Caribbean. Its cargo contains precious stones (emeralds and diamonds), semiprecious stones, spices, and gold coins. (A "moidore" is a Portuguese coin; the word means literally "coin of gold.")

In stanza 3 the British ship is not so pretty as the previous two (it is "dirty") nor so big. A coaster is a small ship designed chiefly to carry goods along a coastline rather than on the high seas. This coaster is propelled by a steam engine (it has a smoke-stack), and it moves through the English Channel with a force and motion that resemble an animal butting with its head. Part of its cargo are things to burn: wood for fireplaces and coal mined near Newcastle-upon-Tyne on the eastern coast of Britain. The rest is metal that has been processed or manufactured, perhaps in the British Midlands not far from Newcastle: metal rails with which to build railroad tracks, lead ingots or "pigs," items of hardware made of iron, and "cheap tin trays."

Forms and Devices

Masefield's poem is formally precise. Each stanza describes a ship in its historical era. Each ship is pictured in motion, and its cargo is then noted. In each stanza the first two and last lines are long, whereas the third and fourth are short; the second and fifth lines rhyme.

The rhythm of each stanza is very similar. Masefield seems to have abandoned usual English syllabic verse for accentual verse, which was being experimented with in his day. This poem is best read with strong accents, giving two beats to each short line and four beats to each long line. An extra half-accent may be given in the second and fifth lines of each stanza to words such as "white," "green," and "tin."

Because "Cargoes" has no clauses, independent or dependent, it makes no statement, provisional or otherwise. Therefore it must depend for its effect on the associations and connotations of the words Masefield has chosen. These effects differ significantly from stanza to stanza. Readers may not know that the details of stanza 1 describe Solomon's lavish court at the time of the visit of the queen of Sheba. Even so, they will sense the exotic and sensual nature of this cargo. Ivory is lovely to touch; it and sandalwood come from far-off regions, even farther away than distant Ophir. Both sandalwood and cedarwood are pleasingly aromatic; white wine is sweet to taste; apes and peacocks may decorate opulent palaces in sun-drenched Palestine.

Even though a quinquireme had sails, Masefield describes only how it is rowed by human power. Other omissions are significant as well. The Bible says that Solomon possessed great quantities of gold and spices, but Masefield does not mention them. In this stanza Masefield distorts geography and history in order to heighten the poetic effect of his lines. Nineveh was a great distance from the Red Sea and flourished long before the era of quinquiremes. It would have been almost impossible for such a large ship to have navigated down the Tigris River from Nineveh. Moreover, quinquiremes were Roman warships, not cargo-carrying vessels. Masefield probably chose the word "Nineveh" mainly for its sound and rhythm and for its aura of importance.

Stanza 2 is almost as exotic as stanza 1 and even more opulent. Masefield may have omitted gold from stanza 1 because he wanted to save it for stanza 2. The emphasis here is on the riches of gold and gems, not on sensual pleasures. Yet these gems, the galleon, and the palm-green shores have a wonderful beauty that may exceed that of the ancient world.

Stanza 3 offers a stark contrast to the first two. The British coaster is in no way beautiful or exotic or wealthy. Instead of the lovely weather of Palestine and the Caribbean, Masefield now provides unpleasant "mad March" days. The seas that cake the smokestack with salt must be butted through with the help of a steam engine. The coaster's cargo is similarly unexotic,—practical fuels and manufactured goods, some of them ugly.

Masefield varies his sound to suit his subject matter. The first two stanzas are euphonious and slow-moving. Stanza 3 is cacophonous and fairly quick to read; its accents are heavier and less subtle, and its consonants are harsh: "salt-caked smokestacks." One reason "Cargoes" has been anthologized so often is that Masefield's control of his language produces so much pleasure.

Themes and Meanings

Throughout his life Masefield delighted in describing ships and the sea, and the most obvious focus of "Cargoes" simply has to do with ships. Though a dirty coaster is not the sort of vessel to which he usually responded, this poem clearly shows the poet's love of various kinds of ships. Masefield imagines these ships at their most attractive: in action, dipping and butting in both smooth and choppy seas. When Masefield contrasts three very different ships from three very different historical eras, he implies that the wonders of ships and the sea, despite some changes, remain constant. Because the poem contains no clauses and hence no statements, it is tempting to say that Masefield has produced a pretty anthology-piece with very little meaning. Yet the contrast of the poem's stanzas yields a simple but effective view of history as well as a perspective on Masefield's own age.

The ancient world is shown as sensual, given to exotic pleasures. Its boats are propelled by human power over modest distances. In contrast, the world of the sixteenth century is magnificent and heroic. Its wind-driven ships traverse vast oceans and bring cargoes that are beautiful and opulent: gems and gold that are worth a great deal. In both stanzas, the ships are bringing their wonderful things back home for the enjoyment of those who live there.

Regardless of whether Masefield literally believed in these readings of history, they serve as a backdrop for his view of contemporary life in stanza 3. Modern life is one of change. The dirty coaster is propelled by a steam engine, a comparatively recent machine that was supplanting time-honored sail power even as Masefield was serving as a sailor. This world is not a pleasant one. The coaster is not a pretty ship, and it is having a difficult time steaming in the choppy seas. Moreover, it is not bringing wonderful things back home to be enjoyed; it is *taking* a cargo of goods, many of them manufactured goods, away for delivery or sale at some unspecified port, perhaps elsewhere in Britain or across the English Channel in France. These goods are not sensual or beautiful but practical, commercial, utilitarian, and sometimes cheap: rails for railroads, hardware, tin trays.

Even so, this modern ship has an energy that Masefield finds admirable. The coaster suggests the side of British life that Masefield wishes to praise: not the elegant refinements of the Victorian aristocracy but the vigor of the common working people.

George Soule

CELLO ENTRY

Author: Paul Celan (Paul Antschel, 1920-1970)
Type of poem: Lyric
First published: 1967, as "Cello-Einsatz," in *Atemwende*; English translation collected
in *Poems of Paul Celan*, 1988

The Poem

"Cello Entry" is one of Paul Celan's later poems. It appears in the fourth of six
cycles of short poems published under the title *Atemwende* (turn of breath). These
eighty poems are best read together because the images of Celan's refined, referential
poems are less cryptic in the context of the collection. The poems describe mind space.
Both of Celan's parents were killed in concentration camps. Paul was their only child
and subsequently suffered increasingly from survivor guilt, a mental state of grief and
self-recrimination. At the beginning of the poem, it seems as if the sound of the cello,
with its deep, resonant tones, may distract him from his pain. The second stanza, with
its references to "arrival runway and drive," indicates that the poet is moved by the
music but is still unsure of where it will transport him.

Any elevation in mood the music may have afforded him is marred in the third
stanza by the surreal shift in metaphor. It is evening, and he finds that branches he has
climbed are not tree branches but lung branches. This mention of lungs, followed in
the fourth stanza by "smoke-clouds of breath," refers almost certainly to the gas
chambers and crematoria of Adolf Hitler's concentration camps in which millions of
people were murdered simply because they, like Celan, were Jewish. His thoughts are
now back on the horrors of the Holocaust. A book gets opened: not just any book, but
the book, the story of his people, opened by the noise in his own head, which seems
to have drowned out the cello music.

Celan begins the fourth stanza with the word "two" set off in a line by itself, a
typographic arrangement indicating that this word is charged with significance. What
is this significance? Are the two smoke-clouds of breath from his own two nostrils?
Are they from his parents? The poetic effect of naming and placing emphasis on an
exact number is to lend specificity while permitting several interpretations. For the
poet himself, the dreamlike images are fraught with meaning. His interpretive response to them is one of recognition and validation: "something grows true." This
main clause, which stands alone as a single verse and stanza just over halfway through
the poem, is like the peak of a musical phrase and may reflect a high point of the cello
performance. Its lack of concrete detail places the emphasis fully on the emotional
valence of the experience.

Stanza 6 describes twelve flashes of insight. Again, the specific number lends
almost magical significance to the events but may also be determined by referents
external to the poem such as twelve-tone music or the twelve tribes of Israel. The poet
focuses finally on a woman and man engaged in a sexual act that cannot produce
offspring. Their intimacy is paradoxical because they are dead, "black-blooded." This

powerful image conveys feelings of futility, depression, and horror, all perfectly understandable in a bereaved survivor of extreme persecution. In the last stanza, the poet has stopped the frightening flow of images and comments rationally on them as if awakening from a bad dream: "all things are less than/ they are." That is not the last word, however. Celan cannot dismiss the promptings of his subconscious. He ends the poem with a characteristic reversal that augments the intensity of his experience: "all are more."

Forms and Devices

The twenty-two lines of "Cello Entry" contain a total of only sixty words in the original German. Celan had studied the development of the German language from medieval times to the present and had seen it debased by Nazi propaganda between 1933 and 1945. It had gone, he explains, "through the thousand darknesses of death bringing speech." Celan is therefore extremely careful in his choice of words and avoids the arbitrary frameworks of end rhyme and metric pattern. The length of his poems is dictated by inner necessity. His attention is focused on the sounds and meanings of individual words, syllables, and even letters.

Four of Celan's distinguishing techniques that occur in "Cello Entry" are his tendency to split words to emphasize their component parts, his construction of neologisms, his repetition of words and phrases with or without variation, and his inclination to let the sound of a word lead him to a similar one. In "Cello Entry," for example, "the black-/ blooded woman" is split at the hyphen over two lines, whereas "the black-blooded man" is written together on one line. The effect of the initial split is to place more weight on the word "black" and its negative connotations and to emphasize the highly unusual first part of the compound word. "Black-blooded" is also one of Celan's neologisms, a shocking departure from the familiar "blue-blooded," "hot-blooded," and "cold-blooded." Other such thought-provoking new combinations in the poem are "counter-heavens," "lung-scrub," and "temple-din." Celan's most famous poem, "Death Fugue," written in 1952, is replete with repetitions and recombinations. This technique comes close to replicating human thought processes. People dwell on anything that bothers them. In "Cello Entry," "black-blooded" can also serve as an example of effective repetition. By applying the unusual adjective to both the woman and the man, Celan stresses that they are both dead, that they represent two separate deaths. The fourth technique, that of letting one word determine the next, is often lost in translation but is apparent in the German even if one does not know the language. For example, the second stanza of "Cello Entry" ends with the line "Einflugschneise und Einfahrt," in which Celan seems to have selected the second capitalized word for its felicitous resemblance to the first on the accented first syllable and following *f*.

The positioning of Celan's periods is a reliable guide to the understanding of his poems. "Cello Entry" has just one period. The entire poem is a single sentence. Celan gently leads the reader in and out, but the bulk of the poem consists of a highly figurative account of a personal moment of truth. Twelve poems later in the cycle, a shorter poem encapsulates the meaning, method, even the music of "Cello Entry": "A RUMBLING: truth/ itself has appeared/ among humankind/ in the very thick of their/ flurrying metaphors."

Themes and Meanings

It is Celan's great accomplishment to be able to transport the reader into a crystalline mind space. Celan refused to interpret any one of his poems, saying that repeated reading should suffice. His most extended commentary on the nature, function, and experience of art is contained in "The Meridian," his 1960 Georg Büchner Prize acceptance speech. Art, he says, is ubiquitous and capable of transformation. This explains the constantly changing imaginative inner landscape of "Cello Entry" as exemplified by the metamorphosis of evening into something that can be climbed like a tree and then into animal matter with lungs. There are no constraints. Celan's remarks about the function of art are particularly apposite. A poem, he says, can signify a turn of breath, a unique short moment. One writes to release something else, and there is no telling how long its effect will last. Turn of breath, or *Atemwende*, is the title of the collection containing "Cello Entry." The turn of breath in this poem is the solitary line that does not further the phantasmagorical visions but rather registers their effect: "something grows true." The space between images, the time between breathing out and breathing in, these are the moments of stasis that allow the mind to move into another dimension.

Celan's poems are designed to communicate with receptive readers, to facilitate a meeting of minds. They are conceived as conversations, albeit often conversations of despair. At the end of his acceptance speech, Celan describes his experience of the creative process: "I find something—like language—immaterial, but earthly, terrestrial, something circular, meeting up with itself again over both the poles and—happily—going through the tropics en route—: I find . . . a *meridian*." Celan finds the meridian when he succeeds in bringing disparate images into line, giving that line the tension of a circle and making it visible to the reader. It is a helpful construct that does not permit any element of the poem to be dropped from the interpretation. "Cello Entry" is an indivisible entity. It is not primarily about a cello or about any of the fantastic images that follow or their derivation. It describes a mind space in which stream-of-consciousness images synthesize with sudden meaning, providing a moment of truth. That truth encompasses the poet's own reality, human history, and alternate universes. It is accessible to all who have pondered their own existence.

Jean M. Snook

THE CHAMBERED NAUTILUS

Author: Oliver Wendell Holmes (1809-1894)
Type of poem: Lyric
First published: 1858, in *The Autocrat of the Breakfast-Table*

The Poem

In the five stanzas of "The Chambered Nautilus," the poet contemplates the broken shell of a nautilus, a small sea animal which the *American Heritage Dictionary* describes as "a mollusk whose spiral shell contains a series of air-filled chambers." In his contemplation, he moves from a metaphorical description of its beauty and lifestyle to the ultimate lesson that it teaches.

The first three stanzas trace the life cycle of the little animal, emphasizing the various stages of its growth and development and its eventual death and destruction. In the beginning, the poet likens the nautilus to a ship which sets out to sea—beautiful in its majesty as its sails unfurl to the "sweet summer wind." He imagines the many wonderful adventures the nautilus has encountered as it challenged the mighty sea, sailing "the unshadowed main." During its lifetime it ventured into enchanted gulfs and heard the siren songs and has seen mermaids sunning "their streaming hair."

In the second stanza the poet laments the death of the nautilus, whose shell now lies broken and abandoned on the seashore like the wreck of a once beautiful ship—a ship that will no more "sail the unbounded main." Like a ship that once teemed with life and now is silent, the nautilus lies lifeless, useless. Just as when a ship is wrecked, the top may be ripped and torn and its interior laid bare for all to see, so the little sea animal is destroyed—its shell broken, its insides exposed, and every "chambered cell revealed." In the third stanza the poet considers the evolution of the nautilus through the various stages of its life. As it grows, its shell continues to expand in order to accommodate that growth, as evidenced by the ever-widening spirals that mark the shell. The nautilus moves into its new home quite tenuously at first, and for a time it misses the familiarity of its old home. In time, however, the new quarters become familiar and more comfortable.

The fourth stanza is addressed directly to the nautilus, thanking it for the lesson that it has brought him. It is a lesson of great importance, and one which strikes the poet with startling clarity—a message as clear, he says, "as ever Triton blew on his wreathèd horn." This message is stated in the final stanza of the poem, beginning, "Build thee more stately mansions." The lesson is that the growth of the human being should parallel that of the nautilus; the individual should continue to grow spiritually throughout his lifetime.

Forms and Devices

The poet employs three major figures of speech, metaphor, personification, and apostrophe, to create the imagery in the poem—images which are at first quite impersonal but which become increasingly more personal as the poem progresses toward its conclusion. This helps prepare the reader for the intensely personal message of the final stanza.

The poet begins with sea imagery, using a sailing vessel as a metaphor for the nautilus. He refers to it as a "ship of pearl," suggesting not only its beauty and grandeur but also its value as both a living organism and a teacher. The poet's use of the term "venturous bark," in reference to the nautilus, evokes images of the majestic sailing ships of bygone days, eager to explore different worlds. His allusions to the songs of the "sirens," the "enchanted gulfs," and the coral reefs where "sea-maids rise to sun their streaming hair," all help to reinforce the images of grand and glorious adventures reminiscent of the mythological voyages of the great classical heroes of the ancient world. In the second stanza, the poet continues with the ship metaphor, likening the "webs of living gauze," by which the nautilus moves, to the sails which move the ship. The beauty and grandeur of this little ship, however, has now been destroyed and will no longer "unfurl" its lovely sails to the wind.

In the third stanza the imagery becomes personal. Here the nautilus is compared to a human being who, when he outgrows one home, abandons it and moves into new quarters that will better accommodate him. This personal imagery is enhanced by the poet's use of terms usually associated with human behavior to describe the activities of the nautilus, He speaks, for example, of the "silent toil" by which the animal built his new "dwelling," and the "soft step" with which he entered his new home. Finally, the nautilus "stretched in his new-found home," expressing its contentment in the same manner as a human being would. The imagery becomes even more personal in the fourth stanza as the poet abandons the use of metaphor altogether and utilizes the apostrophe to address the nautilus directly, thanking it for the lesson it has brought him, even in death. He refers to it as a "child" cast from the "lap" of the sea—thus using personification to establish a mother-child relationship between the animal and the sea, further enhancing the personal tone and preparing the reader for the final message of the poem.

Themes and Meanings

Much of the poetry of Oliver Wendell Holmes is occasional verse, and as such it is light, witty, and often humorous (as in poems such as "The Deacon's Masterpiece," "My Aunt," and "The Boys"). It is said that such poetry can make delightful reading but that its poetic quality is seldom high. Holmes himself once remarked that his poetry was "as the beating of a drum or the tinkling of a triangle to the harmony of a band." "The Chambered Nautilus," often considered one of his best poems, is not in the vein of his occasional verse and has a more pensive tone than that which generally characterizes his poetry. This poem is not preachy (as is a poem such as "Old Ironsides"), and while its theme is not profound, it is certainly provocative. By observing the nautilus and by essentially "dissecting" its physical body, the poet discovers a profound spiritual truth. To him the "silent toil" of the nautilus as it struggles to achieve physical growth is symbolic of the human endeavor necessary to the growth of the soul.

That individuals should continually be engaged in building broader and more comprehensive lives, growing with age and experience, and that they should be continually concerned with the nourishment of the soul throughout their lifetimes, is the message the poet derives from his experience with the nautilus. Such a conclusion is not only a consequence of a different kind of seeing but also a result of the religious background of the poet, who was born the son of a Calvinist minister. Also, his meticulous "dissecting" of the animal in the earlier stanzas of the poem may well be attributable to Holmes' formal training in anatomy and the many years that he spent as professor of anatomy at Dartmouth and at Harvard Universities.

In developing his theme in the final stanza of the poem, then, it is understandable that the poet makes generous use of biblical allusions, His insistence, for example, that the soul build "stately" or magnificent "mansions" seems to be an allusion to the "mansions" of matchless beauty which, according to the bible, have been prepared in heaven for the souls of the righteous. He further insists that these "temples" of the soul be "new" and noble, or, as scripture contends, that the soul should be clean and "undefiled." Finally, the poet alludes to the body as a shell which is discarded after death; in the same manner as the shell of the nautilus, it is cast from the "lap" of the "unresting sea." Implicit in this statement is the notion that only the soul is eternal. Thus, individuals must strive throughout their lifetimes to nourish and develop that which lasts—the soul. Just as the nautilus continues to grow during its lifetime, ever expanding and creating new and "lustrous coils," so should human beings continue growing spiritually throughout their lives, ever moving toward a higher plane of existence, leaving behind all small thoughts, acts, and desires, ever striving to build "new temples"—each one perfect, each one "nobler than the last."

Gladys J. Washington

CHERRYLOG ROAD

Author: James Dickey (1923-1997)
Type of poem: Narrative
First published: 1964; collected in *Poems, 1957-1967*, 1967

The Poem

"Cherrylog Road" is a narrative poem, a memory recounted in the first person. The title identifies the setting of the event that the speaker recalls: Cherrylog Road is the location of a junkyard in which the speaker meets his teenage lover for secret assignations. As the title suggests, the poem pays a lot of attention to setting, even identifying Cherrylog Road, in the first and last stanzas, as a roadway branching off of Highway 106. In spite of this specificity, the poet identifies the location only as an unnamed "southern-state." Details reveal that the setting is the rural South—bootlegging country—and that the time of year is summer.

The speaker arrives at the junkyard first for a prearranged meeting with his lover, Doris Holbrook. Little information is offered about Doris except that she lives nearby and must meet the speaker on the sly for fear of retribution from her father. While waiting for Doris, the speaker explores the junkyard, moving from wrecked car to wrecked car and fantasizing about their owners or picturing himself as a race-car driver. As his anticipation mounts, his imagination turns to Doris, and he speculates about the unpleasant consequences of being caught by her father. By the middle of the poem, the speaker hears the sound of Doris approaching, tapping the wrecked cars with her wrench (she must return with used car parts to explain her absence from home). However, it is not until the fifteenth of eighteen stanzas that the two lovers are united. Three stanzas describe their lovemaking in passionate and metaphorical terms, and then the final stanza chronicles the speaker's elated departure—from Cherrylog Road to Highway 106—on his motorcycle.

The core of the poem is description, and the junkyard setting occupies most of the poet's attention. The description enumerates automobiles and their parts, detailing the fragmented condition of the cars. The rural setting emerges through the natural denizens of the junkyard: snakes, toads, mice, and roaches. However, the poem also seeks to describe youthful passion, and much of its interest lies in how the poet uses the junkyard to evoke the speaker's anticipation and recklessness. The poem mixes realistic description with fantasies played out in the speaker's mind. Thus, "Cherrylog Road" evokes a vividly remembered scene and explores the emotions of the speaker, who recalls the scene in detail. The poet blends those two levels of presentation—description and psychological analysis—seamlessly.

Forms and Devices

"Cherrylog Road" is an easy poem to read, and its accessibility results from James Dickey's use of straightforward diction, conventional syntax, and grammatical sentences. Yet the poem's 108 lines make up only nine sentences, which are spread over eighteen six-line stanzas. Though the stanza structure is regular, the verse is unrhymed and the line length varies from four to ten syllables. Six- and seven-syllable lines with three stresses are the most common, but the metrical variation approaches free verse.

The most notable poetic devices appear in the use of figurative language, which reinforces the poem's emphasis on connecting descriptive detail to the speaker's state of mind. Some of the figurative language seems natural to the junkyard setting, as when the poet uses a simile to compare the speaker's posture in a wrecked car to a driver "in a wild stock-car race" or when a metaphor presents the junked vehicles as "stalled, dreaming traffic." The automobile imagery becomes more blatantly symbolic, however, when the junkyard is called "the parking lot of the dead" or when the sun is personified as "eating the paint in blisters/ From a hundred car tops and hoods." Other examples of figurative language hint at how the speaker's erotic anticipation colors his description. The sun-warmed interiors of the cars are described as possessing "body heat," the center of the junkyard is its "weedy heart," and the torn upholstery of a luxury car is "tender." When the speaker spins a fantasy about being a wealthy old woman directing her chauffeur to an orphanage where she will dispense toys, the car's brand name ("Pierce-Arrow") combines with the metaphor for the reflected sun ("platters of blindness") to suggest the avatars of love, a blind god served by an arrow-wielding cherub.

The weedy and littered garden of the junkyard has a teeming animal life, and Dickey identifies snakes three times: a "kingsnake" in stanza 6 and a "blacksnake" in stanzas 14 and 15. Given the gardenlike setting and the sexually charged occasion, the associations of the snake with Original Sin and with phallic imagery seem deliberate. Indeed, the developing symbolism of the description helps the reader understand how Dickey describes the passionate encounter. Doris's appearance is heralded by a simile comparing her noise to the scraping of a mouse. Along with the phallic connotations of the snake, this association explains the natural description inserted into the midst of the lovers' embrace in stanzas 15 and 16: "So the blacksnake, stiff/ With inaction, curved back/ Into life, and hunted the mouse/ With deadly overexcitement." The curious phrase "deadly overexcitement" brings together the traditional hunt or chase imagery of courtship with the story of Original Sin, in which a snake and a sexual fall bring death into the world.

At the heart of the poem, the lovers come together in language that suggests union and imprisonment: "clung," "glued," "hooks," "springs," and "catch." Given the dangerous nature of their tryst, they part quickly, and the poet describes them leaving "by separate doors," passing through "the changed, other bodies/ Of cars," just as the union of their bodies has changed them. The narrator's youthful exuberance is visited upon the inanimate body of his motorcycle, which is compared by simile to "the soul of the junkyard/ Restored" and through metaphor to "a bicycle fleshed/ With power." The reader knows that it is the speaker, not his motorcycle, that feels restored and powerful, but the transference of animate qualities to the mechanical vehicles of the junkyard is consistent with the imagery and methods of the poem.

Themes and Meanings

That the speaker's recollection of his junkyard meetings with Doris is positive emerges clearly from his memories and exuberant tone, but one must ask why Dickey chooses a junkyard for this encounter. What significance does he place on wrecked automobiles as a ground for the blossoming of love and sexuality? The landscape of wrecks becomes a sort of code to be deciphered, just as the speaker hears the banging of Doris's wrench as "tapping like code." The speaker himself reads the lives of past generations into their wrecked vehicles. This exercise of imagination works two ways: It suggests how the mind erects its palaces or playgrounds anywhere it must, turning a junkyard into a paradise; but it also suggests how youthful passion, like all things, becomes subject to age and deterioration. The junkyard is a litter of broken parts: A glass panel is "broken out"; upholstery is "spilling," "ripped," and "burst[ing]"; wheels are missing; and every surface shows rust. The "parking lot of the dead" serves as a *memento mori*, a reminder that death and decay are ubiquitous.

Yet Doris collects working parts from this graveyard, "Carrying off headlights,/ Sparkplugs, bumpers." More important, out of the wreckage young love finds expression. If the snake-filled setting represents a version of the corrupted Garden of Eden after the Fall, Dickey's poem offers an alternative vision of the genesis of sexuality. In Dickey's version, the sexual moment engenders life out of death rather than mortality out of ever-youthful paradise. In the decayed junkyard, death lingers: "Through dust where the blacksnake dies/ Of boredom, and the beetle knows/ The compost has no more life." These lines are filled with images of a wasted world. The explicit association of the snake with death and the reference to dust (symbolic of mortality) and the beetle (also traditionally associated with death) reveal that the compost, which should generate new life out of waste, "has no more life." It is this morbid landscape that the lovers' sexual passion spurs back into vitality, as the snake "curved back/ Into life" and "The beetles reclaimed their field."

The imagery of the final stanza conjures up the youthful pride of a boy experimenting with sex and, typically, projecting his enthusiasm onto his motorcycle, the powerful machine between his legs. Alliteration connects the key words of the closing lines: "Wringing the handlebar for speed,/ Wild to be wreckage forever." However, this closing paean to wildness has grim overtones. Does the boy's desire to be wreckage become a death wish on the highway? Perhaps that connection back to all the wrecks of the junkyard he is leaving behind is meant to remind the reader that the speaker's experience is an initiation into the fallen adult world, where the ultimate result of passion is wreckage. The speaker conveys the message, but his desire does not allow him to hear it. The reader captures the poem's bittersweet "forever," poised against the fleeting brevity of the remembered encounter.

Christopher Ames

THE CHICAGO *DEFENDER* SENDS A MAN
TO LITTLE ROCK

Author: Gwendolyn Brooks (1917-
Type of poem: Narrative
First published: 1960, in *The Bean Eaters*

The Poem

A number of Gwendolyn Brooks's poems, particularly those written in the years of the Civil Rights movement, highlight major events in the African American struggle for legal equality. The title of this poem clearly conveys its historical context: A reporter from Chicago's black newspaper, the *Defender*, travels in the fall of 1957 to Little Rock, Arkansas, during that city's battles over school desegregation. In the actual historical events, the first nine black students ever to be admitted to Central High School were forbidden to enter the school by the governor of Arkansas, who used the state's National Guard to block them from entering. Hostile mobs from the community cursed and spat at the children, and they attacked both black and white journalists covering the incident. Eventually President Dwight Eisenhower sent federal troops with orders to safeguard the children and allow them to attend the school. The landmark incident marked the first serious test of the Supreme Court's 1954 *Brown v. Board of Education* decision forbidding segregation in public schools.

Creatively linking these real events with a poetic (re)creation, Brooks's poem reflects a reporter's first-person account of life in this racially charged southern city. Instead of beginning with descriptions of violence and hatred, the narrator records the everyday lives of ordinary people who look for jobs, have babies, repair their homes, and water their plants. On Sunday in church they sing hymns; afterward they have tea and cookies. Like Americans from coast to coast, they celebrate Christmas and enjoy baseball and music. In the tenth stanza, however, the mood shifts as the reporter, scratching his head, makes a crucial observation: "there is a puzzle in this town." The citizens appear to be "like people everywhere." There is no observable sign of the hatred and evil contained in the human heart. After hurling insults and launching vicious attacks, community members return to their ordinary lives.

The narrator imagines how disappointed his Chicago editor would be to hear such a banal account of Little Rock citizens, when in fact he has witnessed them harassing, spitting, and hurling rocks. Yet he cannot forget the shocking reality of their dualistic nature. Brooks closes the poem with the reporter's thought of another mob of ordinary people—those at the crucifixion of Christ—thereby forcing readers to reconsider how they recognize evil and to look within for evidence of hatred or bigotry that might not be immediately apparent.

Forms and Devices

References to music and love permeate Brooks's poem. Readers who know her work will not be surprised, for such images appear often in her poetry about the black community. However, their use here in describing the white community is quite different. Ironically even in a time of racial conflict, when people are behaving in inhuman ways, they "sing/ Sunday hymns like anything" and attend musical events where the beauty of Beethoven, Bach, and Offenbach fill their ears, if not their hearts. These musical images at first seem paradoxical in a protest poem, but they have a definite function. As critic and poet Haki R. Madhubuti writes in his introduction to *Say That the River Turns: The Impact of Gwendolyn Brooks* (1987), "it is her vision—her ability to see truths rather than trends, to seek meaning and not fads, to question ideas rather than gossip—that endears her to us." In this poem the truth for Brooks is that music is not an antidote to hate. Avid listeners are not necessarily transformed by its beauty; they may still embody evil.

The seventh stanza examines another paradox: how the capacities for love and hate coexist in the same place and even in the same people. The narrator notes that there is love as well as music in Little Rock. Images of "soft women" giving and receiving pleasure point to the people's desire to dull the pain or, as Brooks writes, "To wash away old semi-discomfitures." Such physical expressions of love appear to clarify uncertainties, but they actually cover up, rather than confront, the most serious problems of society. Many images are suggestive, their meanings not completely spelled out, and Brooks links ideas ordinarily kept apart: love and music appear in frightening juxtaposition with bigotry and violence.

The inextricability of form and content is another important aspect of "The Chicago *Defender* Sends a Man to Little Rock," one of the most compelling poems in her collection *The Bean Eaters*. The apparent normalcy of Little Rock lives is emphasized by the conventional line lengths and prosaic language. Yet after four stanzas, when the narrator finally interrupts the smooth litany of their days and nights, the lines are short, clipped. The reporter speaks: "I forecast/ And I believe." One expects his revelation to expose the evil in the community. Instead he makes a prediction about the festive holiday season. Then the poem quickly resumes its original form. Mirroring reality, no change occurs, the usual flow of events continues, and for the next three stanzas Brooks re-creates the laughter and tinsel of Christmas, the baseball games, and the twilight concerts. Readers experience through the poem's structure the frustrating inability to recognize and destroy the enemy easily, for the enemy is well hidden in this city of ordinary people. What is perhaps most striking about a poem on such a harsh subject is its overall lack of shocking detail. Only near the end does Brooks show the violence that lurks beneath the calm exterior: "And true, they are hurling spittle, rock,/ Garbage and fruit in Little Rock./ And I saw coiling storm a-writhe/ On bright madonnas. And a scythe/ Of men harassing brownish girls."

The unusually wide spaces between the last three lines allow readers time to read between the lines, to imagine what lies beneath the surface of this apparently placid poem and community, and then to compare what they find with their own understanding of the history of persecution and oppression.

Themes and Meanings

"The Chicago *Defender* Sends a Man to Little Rock" contains themes found in much of Gwendolyn Brooks's poetry. Undeniably it is a thoughtful criticism of contemporary society. In an interview from her autobiography *Report From Part One* (1972), Brooks says that much of a writer's use of themes depends upon the climate of America at the time: "I think it is the task or job or responsibility or pleasure or pride of any writer to respond to his climate. You write about what is in the world." Examining the United States in the late 1950's and early 1960's, she could not escape the existing racism and violence. The point of the poem is that we often do fail to see its existence in our communities, our neighbors, and even ourselves.

For the most part the poems in *The Bean Eaters* are about commonplace people, and this poem is no exception. Brooks demonstrates the extraordinary effects that "ordinary" lives can have on the course of history. She also shows that violence is often perpetrated by people who present a benign exterior. The poem attempts to see behind the mask. Brooks strips away illusions about evil and immerses readers in its very real, very conventional nature.

The eighth stanza shows how Little Rock citizens feign politeness, answer the phone, and respond to questions about the problems in their community. Even as they converse with reporters they remain firmly in denial about their own complicity in the social and psychological oppression. The voice of the poet then becomes the conscience for the larger community of readers who must sort through this series of paradoxical events to separate truth from lies.

There are two particularly notable ways in which "The Chicago *Defender* Sends a Man to Little Rock" differs from other poems on the theme of racial injustice. First is its basis in an actual confrontation that shocked the world and underscored the anguish of a people searching for equality in a country that continued to deny it. The poem invites the reader to identify with a narrator who is appalled that these oppressors "are like people everywhere." The second important distinction is the skillful way Brooks compresses a history of oppression into the final two lines of the poem as if to imply that little has been resolved in the years since Jesus' death.

With a gift for seeing truth no matter where or how it is hidden, Gwendolyn Brooks throughout her career has questioned suppositions about equality and justice. As she writes in her autobiography, a writer "needs to live richly with eyes open, and heart, too."

Carol F. Bender

CHILDE-HOOD

Author: Henry Vaughan (1622-1695)
Type of poem: Lyric
First published: 1655, in *Silex Scintillans*, second edition

The Poem

This religious poem by metaphysical poet Henry Vaughan idealizes childhood as a time of purity and superior insight, contrasted to the sin and misleading predilections of adulthood. The narrator wishes to recapture this innocence and piety, but he is able to see it only "as through a glass darkly," tainted by years in the corrupting adult world. Thus the poem is both hopeful and sadly nostalgic, since it describes a state of holiness that exists in this world but is unreachable to the speaker. The only hope, offered at the end through a biblical quotation, is to emulate the state when he finds it—as in the play of children or in the scriptures of the church.

The first stanza, beginning "I cannot reach it," both describes the ideal state of childhood and expresses the impossibility of an adult even fully understanding it. If the speaker could recapture that view, he states, he would surely go to heaven, as easily as children play games—in fact, through playing, instead of through suffering. "With their content too in my power" is a play on words: the content (substance) of the childlike thoughts would make him content (satisfied) on his path to heaven.

However, the next stanza makes clear how debased, even dangerous, the adult state is. The questions beginning the stanza do not ask whether adult men are corrupt, but why. Humankind's perverse nature (as expressed in Romans 7:19 and John 3:19) leads him to prefer the wolf to the lamb and dove, "hell-fire and brimstone streams" to "bright stars, and God's own beams." The more the speaker examines worldly existence, the more he values untainted childhood: "Since all that age doth teach, is ill/ Why should I not love childe-hood still?" Unlike the earlier questions, this one has an implied answer. The lessons of age are wrong, and so are the reasons they suggest for giving up childhood's spiritual state: "Those observations are but foul/ Which makes me wise to lose my soul."

However, the final stanzas not only celebrate childhood but also pine over its unreachability. It is "a short, swift span" that passes quickly; in one image, virtue is depicted as driven away, weeping like a rejected lover. The only answer, allowing one to understand this "age of mysteries," is to "live twice": to be born again in Christ, to become as a little child to enter the kingdom of heaven (John 3:3, Matthew 18:3, Luke 18:17). When the speaker states that he studies "Thee, more than ere I studyed man," "thee" can mean "God's face," childhood's virtue, and perhaps the scriptures, all at once. This life is "the *narrow way*," difficult and disapproved of by the world, but one's only chance for salvation (Matthew 7:13-14, Luke 13:24).

Forms and Devices

"Childe-hood" is composed in rhymed couplets, grouped in stanzas of varying lengths. The first stanza establishes the desired goal: recapturing the innocent piety and spiritual insight of childhood. Next, a longer stanza depicts the many barriers to this goal that are created by adult nature as well as the lessons taught by the fallen world. Finally, four shorter stanzas in more traditional lengths—three quatrains and a sextet—try to balance these two and find some solution.

Metaphysical poetry such as Vaughan's is known for its intellectual complexity conveyed through striking (sometimes incongruous) imagery; in "Childe-hood," this is seen in the references to, and often the reversal of, biblical imagery. In the second stanza, men embrace thorns, not in altruistic suffering as Christ did, but because of the "ill" lessons that this world has taught them. That stanza concludes by comparing the lure of these lessons with the temptation of Christ, when Satan told Jesus to jump off a cliff so the angels could hold him up. Unlike Christ, people too often give in, their dedication to "the world" leading them to "gravely cast themselves away."

Vaughan uses imagery of light for childhood and darkness for the adult state. In the first stanza childhood is described as a bright light, "white designs" that "dazzle" the adult eye, no longer accustomed to such spiritual brilliance. In the final stanza the speaker studies "through a long night" wishing for the reward of being able to see God as clearly as the bright light of "mid-day."

More subtly, the poet reinforces the unreachable nature of childhood's spiritual state by describing it in negative terms: It is "harmless," "love without lust" and "without self-ends" (that is, unselfish). Even the light is so bright as to make description impossible. Moreover, in the final stanza, all that the speaker can see and study is "Thy edges, and thy bordering light," while yearning to see "thy Center." The buried imagery is one of a book, of which the speaker can only perceive the white margins, unable to read the text in the center of the page. The speaker, despite his disdain of the world, is already too far gone to be able to understand or describe what he glimpses, unless he is reborn through Christ.

The poem also demonstrates metaphysical wordplay, such as that on "content" in the first stanza. Similarly, "gravely cast themselves away," in the third stanza, refers both to the perils of the (misguided) seriousness of adulthood and the literal grave to which the eternal life with Christ is the only alternative. In that same stanza, "Business and weighty action all/ Checking the poor child for his play" refers to serious adults criticizing children (who are actually their spiritual betters); it also implies a metaphor of literal weight, a burden to children that inhibits their play and a contrast to the guardian flight of angels in the next stanza.

Themes and Meanings

The religious significance of the poem should be clear. After a less distinguished career in secular poetry influenced by the school of Ben Jonson (1572-1637), Vaughan experienced a religious conversion in the late 1640's and began writing poetry drawing on many sources, including the Bible and the works of religious poet George Herbert (1593-1633). Many critics see Vaughan's works as traditional theology expressed in unconventional images. Yet Vaughan was also influenced by neo-

Platonic and occult ideas, perhaps learned from his twin brother Thomas, an alchemist and mystical philosopher. The idea that children maintain some memories of eternity, lost as they settle into the material world, can be found in the Hermetic texts and the works of Jakob Boehme (1575-1624), Cornelius Agrippa (1486-1535), Plotinus (A.D. 205-270), and even Plato (c. 428-c. 348 B.C.).

The biblical influences are central, however, as is the influence of Herbert's poem "The Collar," about the pursuit of the soul by God. Its last two lines are: "Methought I heard one calling, *Child!/* And I reply'd, *My Lord.*" The state desired by the speaker of Vaughan's poem is both that of actual childhood and the pre-Fall innocence of Adam in Paradise. As Vaughan's contemporary, Jeremy Taylor, wrote, "In Baptism we are born again," free of Adam's sin.

Much of Vaughan's religious poetry is concerned with the relationship of the individual soul to God and, as in "Childe-hood," sadly notes the difficulty of knowing God's presence in the fallen world humans inhabit. Because of this, some critics have called Vaughan a poet of frustration or even failure, especially when his work is compared with the greater assurance—and reassurance—of religious verse such as Herbert's.

Some critics find a political dimension to Vaughan's nostalgia and rejection of the world he saw around him. In his prose, such as *The Mount of Olives* (1652), Vaughan bemoans the harsh measures of the Puritans and their effect on the church. Certainly, the effects of the Civil War in England were far-reaching, and Vaughan's unhappiness with it may have provided further motive for a wish to retreat to childhood. Still, despite the condemnation of T. S. Eliot in a 1927 review of a study of Vaughan's poetry, one cannot dismiss it as mere immature failure to face the present.

Vaughan's view of childhood, which he shared with fellow metaphysical poet Thomas Traherne, would not be explored by a major artist until it became a primary concern of the poet William Blake, especially seen in his *Songs of Innocence* (1789). Many critics believe that Vaughan influenced the Romantic view of childhood, especially in the poems of William Wordsworth.

Bernadette Lynn Bosky

CHILDHOOD

Author: Rainer Maria Rilke (1875-1926)

Type of poem: Lyric

First published: 1906, as "Kindheit," in *Das Buch der Bilder* (expanded edition); English translation collected in *Translations from the Poetry of Rainer Maria Rilke*, 1938

The Poem

"Childhood" is a poem of thirty-three lines divided into four stanzas. The title would generally lead the reader to expect a poem describing a time of innocence and joy, and while "Childhood" does this to some extent, it also describes a contrasting sad side to childhood. The poem is written in the third person, which often serves to distance the poet from the speakers or perspectives in the poem. However, in "Childhood" the unnamed, pale child and his feelings of loneliness, isolation, and sadness resemble Rilke's remembrance of his own childhood quite closely.

"Childhood" begins with a short description of school; it is shown in an entirely negative light. The atmosphere is stuffy, the hours spent there are long and boring, and the feelings the child experiences are of anxiety and loneliness. The relief and joy of dismissal contrasts sharply with the "heavy lumpish time" in school. The streets ring out with children's voices, the town squares are full of bubbling fountains, and the outdoor world has endless space and possibilities. At the end of the first stanza a small child is introduced as different from all the others. Though he shares in the exultant feeling of release from school, he walks a different path, alone and lonely.

The second stanza shows the wider world from the child's perspective, one both distanced and perceptive. He watches men and women, children in brightly colored clothes, houses, here and there a dog. This description of the physical world suddenly changes to intense emotions underlying the seemingly simple neighborhood scene; feelings of silent terror alternate with trust. The stanza ends, as they all do, with a few words or phrases expressing the child's and poet's emotional perspective of the scene or event described. After observing the peaceful setting and sensing the conflicting emotions of fear and trust, there is a feeling of senseless sadness, dreams, and horror.

The third and fourth stanzas narrow their focus to the child's more immediate environment and playtime. As daylight begins to fade, the small, pale child plays with balls, hoops, and bats, rushes around blindly playing tag, and bumps into some grownups in the process. Evening quietly arrives; playtime is over as the child is led home firmly by the hand. Sometimes the child plays for hours at the pond with his sailboat, trying to forget the others whose boats are prettier. The poem ends with the boy contemplating his reflection in the water, "looking up as it sank down," wondering where childhood is taking him, where it all will lead.

Forms and Devices

"Childhood" was published in *Das Buch der Bilder* (the book of pictures), a collection of poetry that reveals a transition between Rilke's earlier phase emphasizing emotion and his more mature phase aiming for more precision in imagery and style. "Childhood" demonstrates both these phases of firm structure and impressionistic emotion. Though it appears to have an irregular form, divided into uneven stanzas (ten, seven, eight, and eight lines), there is a regular meter (iambic pentameter) and rhyme scheme. With the exception of the last verse, which introduces a third rhyme in the last line of the poem, there are two rhymes in each stanza, though the pattern varies. No rhymes are carried over to the next stanza.

"Childhood" makes its strongest impact on the reader through the use of juxtapositions of sounds and images. Rilke employs both alliteration and assonance to bring his descriptions to the reader's attention. The repeating of sounds, whether consonant or vowel, makes the phrase stand out and emphasizes the image. Rilke employs alliteration more frequently, and "Childhood" is full of consonantal pairs, for example: "dumpfen Dingen" (musty things), "Welt so weit" (world so wide), "großen grauen" (great gray), "Haschens Hast." Repetitious use of vowel sounds is also used effectively, but to truly notice these, the reader must read the poem aloud: "o Traum, o Grauen" (o dream, o horror), "kleinen steifen" (small stiff), "o entgleichende Vergleiche" (elusive comparisons).

Even more than sound, the juxtaposition of contrasting images and emotions alerts the reader to the child's perception of differences in the world he sees and the sense of otherness in himself. The anxiety, depression, and ennui of the school experience is sharply contrasted with the streets, squares, and gardens coming alive with children and movement. The wonderful time of release is diminished, however, by the continued loneliness of the child. The peaceful image of men, women, and children, and their houses and dogs is diminished by the silent terror alternating with trust, and again with a sadness and horror. A joyful game of tag closes with feelings of anxiety and worry. The final stanza begins with the idyllic image of children floating their sailboats on the pond but ends with a sad call to childhood, asking what the meaning of it all is.

Themes and Meanings

"Childhood" is a picture or evocation of childhood from Rilke's collection *Das Buch der Bilder*, which he intended to resemble a picture gallery full of paintings. The interest in pictures came early to Rilke, beginning in his childhood with a love of the visual arts. He later studied art history (among other subjects) at the university, and as a young man he lived in the artists' colony at Worpswede. There he became involved with several artists, befriending the painter Paula Modersohn-Becker and marrying the sculptor Clara Westhoff. Later in Paris he also worked for the sculptor Auguste Rodin. Rilke wrote monographs on Worpswede and Rodin, and his interest in and exposure to the visual arts played a significant role in his vision of poetry. He cultivated an artist's eye, and his obsession with *Schauen* (observing), a word that appears in this and another childhood poem ("From Childhood") in this collection, dominated his vision of what a poem should convey to its reader.

The child in "Childhood" is an observer of the outer world of school and play and the inner world of his reactions and emotions. The poem contains abundant visual images. Streets of children sparkle with "lights and colors," the children's sailboats are colorful "at a grayish pond," the day's "light fades away" slowly into evening, and a child's panoramic view can "see into it all from far away." Indeed, the poem's last image is a child staring at his own reflection as he ponders the meaning of childhood. As painters employ chiaroscuro, an arrangement of light and dark elements, so does Rilke juxtapose light and dark images and emotions to produce a dramatic effect. The bubbling fountains, colorful children, and lively streets contrast sharply with the heaviness and stuffiness of school. The ecstasy of freedom is followed by loneliness, silent terror "all at once replaced by total trust," the game of tag with anxiety. Rilke's picture of childhood is not one dimensional; it presents multiple shades of experience and feeling.

A recurring image of "Childhood" and other poems is that of *Einsamkeit*, which can be translated as both aloneness and loneliness. In other poems in this collection, Rilke writes of a "child still and alone" ("From Childhood") and of being "so entirely alone" ("Vorgefühl" [foreboding]). He titled two of the poems "Einsamkeit" and "Der Einsame" (the solitary one or lonely one). In "Childhood" the feeling of otherness, aloneness, or loneliness is repeated throughout. Although literature is not necessarily biography or autobiography, in Rilke's case much of his work reflects his personal experience. Some background to Rilke's childhood can provide insight into the emphasis on the child's feeling of isolation. Rilke was the only child of a mother who had wanted a daughter. He was dressed as a girl and treated as a daughter during the early years of his life. His father tried to counterbalance the influence of his mother by sending the boy to military school. The harsh discipline and other boys' hostility toward him made a lasting impression. The atmosphere of the school was alien to his character, and he felt his lack of inclusion keenly. It was this and the loneliness he faced because of the boys' shunning that turned him to writing. Rilke mentioned several times his feeling that he had been deprived of a happy childhood, and in his poetry he tried to redeem some image of a happier childhood for himself. "Childhood" does indeed contain some idyllic scenes of a carefree childhood, but the lurking shadows of sadness, anxiety, and otherness continually peer through the lighter images of play.

Shoshanah Dietz

CHILDREN IN EXILE

Author: James Fenton (1949-
Type of poem: Narrative
First published: 1982, in *The Memory of War: Poems, 1968-1982*

The Poem

"Children in Exile" is written in forty-nine stanzas of four lines each, an extra line space being inserted in the last stanza. The poem begins with a direct quote from a child in exile, who states one of the keynotes of the poem, that what we are is less important than what we do. Readers then are made aware of the general subject of the poem—that it involves children from Cambodia in exile in a strange country (readers later learn that this is Italy) in roughly the late 1970's. Though still children, the exiles "have learnt much." Far from being innocents, they have experienced ordeals that most of the adults who take care of them cannot even begin to imagine. They have escaped from the mass killings perpetrated by the Cambodian regime of Pol Pot, in power from 1975 to 1979, which was preceded by a civil war (in which the United States intervened) in which many were also killed and wounded. The children have physically escaped from their ordeal, but psychologically they are still wounded, and their dreams are troubled.

The "I" of the poem, a friendly Western adult observer, sees that the children are still in pain from their experiences. He muses on the tragic situation; these children were punished not for their own actions but because they happened to be children of people who were political opponents of the regime or who were otherwise persecuted. The children also, in a way, symbolize the entire Cambodian nation, which was so rent by civil conflict and government-sponsored killings that its own survival seemed in doubt. The children in exile are now free, but they do not realize their own freedom. The fear from their old experiences still troubles them, even in safe, touristy locales such as the Leaning Tower of Pisa, where a child becomes afraid even though there only friends around who want him to have fun. Yet amid the Italian spring the children's suffering begins to heal, and they evince curiosity about the landscape and people that surround them. Duschko the dog and the doves in the hayloft are part of the harmony of the landscape, which welcomes and accommodates the children.

Surrounded by love instead of fear, the children hurry to catch up on the education they have missed in their native land and to assimilate the culture of the West. One of the children has a twin sister who had escaped to America and has given birth to a baby. The children see America as the promised land; the narrator, on the other hand, deems the United States to be partially guilty of Cambodia's ruin. Regardless of whether they find the happiness they associate with America in America itself or in Europe, the children will flourish in the future. The narrator wishes them well and wishes them the freedom to dream of whatever future they want. Though the children are in exile from their homeland, they have found freedom and safety at last.

Forms and Devices

The most striking aspect of "Children In Exile" is that it is at once a serious political poem and an old-style, melodic ballad. Its stanzas are quatrains (four lines each), of which the second and fourth line rhyme. This form allows tremendous clarity, but it also allows breeziness and wit. Most of all, it connotes the poet's desire to tell a story. Given the subject of the poem, this is by no means an inevitable choice: The poem could be an elegy for the dead in Cambodia, for example, or a lament for the psychological trauma sustained by the children. However, the ballad form structures the poem as the story of the children's recovery in exile. It provides a kind of reassurance to readers, shielding them from the horrors of war much as the lush Italian landscape begins to shelter the children in the poem.

Fenton often plays havoc with the reader's expectations, as with the long digression about Duschko the dog and the doves in the hayloft, which not only provides a lighthearted, almost nonsense element that alleviates the poem's seriousness but also lulls the reader into accepting the children's safety and happiness, rather than their suffering, as a given. There is an exuberance about the poem that gives it an air of celebration despite its stern witness at the horrors of the Cambodian killings that have forced the children so far from home.

There is also a mock-epic aspect to the poem, as when Duschko the dog goes "mad" and eats "all those chickens," mimicking in a far more minor key the killings in Cambodia. Of course, the chickens are animals, not people, and in this mini-play a kind of restitution unfolds that is not admitted in the outer world. The dog, first suspicious of the children, comes to share his home with them and to love them. Within the fictive world of the poem, the brutal laws of external reality are softened and inverted.

Fenton's style is urbane and sophisticated, yet the poem is understandable to an educated reader after reading it once or twice. The poem's occasional nonsensical tinge may distract those who are looking for a traditional sort of political poem that seeks to rally people to a cause. For instance, the last line, with the children dreaming "Of Jesus, America, maths, Lego, music and dance," seems curiously anticlimactic; it is not a peroration that will whip a crowd into a frenzy. Its very modesty, the way it looks into the hearts of the children and sees what is there rather than imposing a grandiose adult agenda, is at the heart of the poem's winning combination of modesty and eloquence.

Themes and Meanings

When *The Memory of War* (1982), the volume including "Children in Exile," first appeared in Britain, many readers were immediately reminded of the 1930's political poetry of W. H. Auden. (Fenton makes this debt clear in "Children in Exile" by citing Auden's 1962 prose book *The Dyer's Hand* in the latter portion of the poem). Fenton, like Auden in the 1930's, was a young poet writing about conflicts in distant countries and making them immediate for the British reader, but there are certainly differences between them. Auden often implied that he was essentially an apolitical poet whom the onslaught of Fascism in the Spanish Civil War and after had forced into a partisan position. Fenton, on the other hand, had gone to Vietnam and Cambodia as a working journalist, freelancing for several newspapers and magazines. Among other things, he was a witness to the fall of Saigon to the Communist North Vietnamese in 1975. This event came only days after the Communist takeover in Cambodia that occasioned the suffering from which the Cambodian children in the poem are fleeing.

Although Fenton displays political sympathies of a center-left sort in the poem (as evinced by his giving the United States partial blame for the problems of Cambodia after 1975, a position with which some on the right would disagree), the poem is not a politically committed poem in the manner of Auden's "Spain" (1937). The poem's most explicit sympathies are noncontroversial; they are for civilization and common human decency. These values are made newly cogent by the suffering from which the children have escaped.

The poem should be read at least twice, once to comprehend its surface meaning and again to appreciate the considerable feeling that Fenton puts into the poem, as well as the way he uses whimsy and slight-of-hand to make the children's experience both special to them and also somehow representative. The setting of the Italian landscape, for instance, might be bypassed on the first reading in order to focus on the agony and redemption of the children themselves, yet Fenton's laid-back evocation of this landscape is a crucial prerequisite for the poem's sense of earned affirmation.

The poet, insofar as he projects himself in the poem, is successful at empathizing with the children yet distancing himself from them. One recognizes that he sees the children's dreams of Jesus and America as naïve, yet he does not mock these ideals or the childlike innocence, marred by untold suffering yet still resilient, that inspires them.

Despite his clear aspirations to emulate Auden, Fenton's techniques are also reminiscent of those used by his contemporaries, particularly Craig Raine, who in *A Martian Sends a Postcard Home* (1979) applied a metaphorical perspective to ordinary phenomena, and Andrew Motion, who in *Secret Narratives* (1983) related skewed verse-tales similar to Fenton's. Fenton's imaginativeness helps ballast his poem's political wisdom. The directly committed Auden was compelled to repudiate "Spain" within five years once his views had changed, but the humanity and compassion of Fenton's poem persist decades after the events they describe.

Nicholas Birns

THE CHILDREN OF THE NIGHT

Author: Edwin Arlington Robinson (1869-1935)
Type of work: Book of poems
First published: 1897

The Poems

At its publication in 1897, Edwin Arlington Robinson's *The Children of the Night* consisted of eighty-seven poems, forty-four of which had appeared in *The Torrent and the Night Before*, a pamphlet printed at the author's own expense the previous year. In addition, the new volume contained another forty-three poems. When the author incorporated *The Children of the Night* into later collections of his poetry he made some alterations, a situation that can be very confusing for readers. For example, some poems were eliminated altogether, and because of deletions the "Octaves" in the collections do not bear the same numbers that they did in the 1897 book. Nevertheless, while scholars find both the originals and revisions of interest, most students will find the later versions of *The Children of the Night* as useful for study as the original.

Robinson believed that he would be remembered primarily for his thirteen long narrative poems, beginning with *Merlin* (1917) and including *Tristram* (1927), which not only won for him a Pulitzer Prize but also was his only commercial success. Ironically, however, it is his short poems, many of them contained in *The Children of the Night*, on which Robinson's literary reputation now depends.

The poems in this collection fall into several different categories. Some of them are addressed to people who actually lived. For example, "Zola" pays tribute to the French novelist Émile Zola for his dedication to truth, while "Verlaine" is a defense of the French poet Paul Verlaine, who is believed to have influenced some of Robinson's works, notably "Luke Havergal." Other poems are about fictional characters from "Tilbury Town," which represents Gardiner, Maine, where Robinson spent most of his early years. Although all of them are relatively short, crisp in style, and ironic in tone, the Tilbury Town poems vary in subject matter and in pattern.

"John Evereldown," for instance, is written as a dialogue. In the first stanza an unnamed person asks John Evereldown where he is going so late at night. In the second Evereldown replies that he is on his way to Tilbury Town but is taking an indirect route through the woods so that no one can see him. Now even more puzzled, the interrogator urges Evereldown to come in and warm himself by the fire rather than continuing on his journey. In the fourth and final stanza Evereldown admits that he is drawn into the cold, dark night because in Tilbury Town he may find a woman to satisfy his obsessive lust.

"Luke Havergal" is one of the most obscure poems in the collection. The single speaker is not identified, except as a voice from the grave or perhaps from Havergal's own subconscious. This spirit speaks of the "hell" through which Havergal is passing as somehow related to a lost "paradise." It is evident that death has taken the woman Havergal loved, but since she is referred to in the third person, obviously it is not she who is addressing him. When the spirit urges him to "Go to the western gate," it is not clear whether Havergal is to transcend his grief and move on, trusting that he will meet his lost love in the next world, or whether he is being urged to pass through the gate of death immediately—to commit suicide.

While some Tilbury Town poems, such as these, are essentially static descriptions of emotional states, others are like short stories, moving toward a dramatic conclusion. The first twelve lines of "Richard Cory" could well be just another character sketch. Speaking in a single voice, the ordinary people of Tilbury Town describe the wealthy and elegant Cory, whom they admit they envied, noting his unfailing courtesy to those below him. The fourth stanza begins with the townspeople summing up their dull and desperate lives, but in the last two lines Richard Cory once again becomes the focal point of the poem. Robinson now sets the stage ("one calm summer night") and bluntly describes Cory's suicide. It is now clear why the townspeople were speaking of Cory in the past tense. It is also evident that, in the light of this ending, what they said must be reinterpreted. Moreover, the earlier part of the poem, which seemed static, was in fact preparing for the final dramatic action.

The Children of the Night also contains a number of poems in which, instead of voicing his opinions obliquely, the writer addresses his readers directly. In "Ballade by the Fire," Robinson is sitting by the fire, smoking, while his imagination creates ghostly figures from the past. In the second stanza, he wonders what the future may be. In the third stanza, however, the mood changes. Suddenly recognizing that death could well be close at hand, he urges himself into action. The envoy reflects this new resolution. Since we all know that life "is the game that must be played," we should "live and laugh" rather than be depressed by the "phantoms" with which everyone lives.

Forms and Devices

In *Children of the Night* Robinson demonstrates his knowledge of his craft and his poetic skill by utilizing a number of traditional forms. "Three Quatrains," "Two Quatrains," and "Richard Cory," for example, consist of Sicilian quatrains; the tetrameter poem "Two Men" is written in long measure, or long hymnal measure; and for "Boston" Robinson uses two Italian quatrains, shaped into an envelope stanza. The collection also includes an ode, "The Chorus of Old Men in 'Aegeus,'" and though "John Evereldown" does not have the most common ballad format, its question-answer pattern and its incremental repetition recall such well-known ballads as "Lord Randal" and "The Three Ravens."

Robinson is also adept in the most exacting French forms. "Ballade by the Fire" and "Ballade of Broken Flutes" meet the strict requirements of the *ballade*, including the refrain at the end of each stanza, the envoy, the limitation on the number of rhymes, and the rhyme pattern itself. Another difficult French form that Robinson handles superbly is the *villanelle*, as seen in "Villanelle of Change" and "The House on the Hill."

The poetic patterns that appear most frequently in *The Children of the Night*, however, are the Petrarchan sonnet and the blank verse octave. The poet uses the sonnet for a wide variety of poems. It is highly effective in the philosophical "Credo," in which the statement of despair in the octave is answered in the sestet by the proclamation that, despite the darkness all around him, the speaker can "feel the coming glory of the Light." Just as impressive are the Petrarchan sonnets that describe the people of Tilbury Town, often (as in "Cliff Klingenhagen") narrating a story to do so. In the octave of that poem, the speaker sets up a mystery. After their dinner together one evening, Cliff, the host, downs a glass of wormwood, while offering his guest the usual wine. In the sestet, Cliff smilingly refuses to explain, and all the speaker can say is that Cliff seems to be amazingly happy. It is left to the reader to guess the significance of Cliff's action and of the speaker's comment. Still another poem that illustrates Robinson's skill with the Petrarchan sonnet is "Fleming Helphenstine." Here, though it begins with a suggestion of distrust, the octave proceeds to establish Fleming as an open sort of man, who talks as easily as if he has known the narrator for a long time and, in fact, is an intimate of his. In the sestet, there is a dramatic reversal. The two men look closely at each other, and something happens that makes both of them "cringe and wince." Then the stranger apologizes and exits, both from the scene and from the narrator's life. Again in this poem, Robinson has used the Petrarchan sonnet with its two-part structure for high dramatic effect.

The octaves in the collection are not Robinson's most memorable poems, though they do provide some insight into his thinking at the time they were written. In the octave that starts "We thrill too strangely at the master's touch," for instance, the poet accuses human beings of backing off from the unhappy events which are part of life, forgetting that God has his own plans for human beings. The octave beginning "Tumultuously void of a clean scheme" is not quite as abstract at the previous one and, indeed, is built on an interesting image—humanity as a great "crazy" legion, controlled only by instinct and "Ignorance" and led "by drunk trumpeters." However, again, it is not quite effective. For some reason, Robinson's octaves lack the force of his other poems, even of those which, like the sonnets "Dear Friends" and "Credo," have the same sort of abstract subject matter. It may be that when he used traditional forms such as the sonnet, in which the octave establishing the topic or the situation is followed by a sestet with some kind of reversal or at least a resolution, Robinson was prevented from rambling toward an inconclusive conclusion, as he so often does in these octaves. At any rate, the poet evidently sensed that the blank verse octave was not effective. After *The Children of the Night*, Robinson wrote no more poems in that form.

It is unfortunate that so fine a craftsman as Robinson began publishing his work just when the fashions in poetry were changing. Through no fault of his own, Robinson was largely eclipsed by writers who were considered more modern, such as the Imagists. However, Robinson never abandoned traditional forms. While everyone else seemed to be writing free verse, he worked on perfecting blank verse in his long narrative poems. Ironically, those later works, which Robinson believed were his highest achievement, are now read far less often than his short poems, especially those that tell of Tilbury Town and its residents. At least, in one way, the changing styles have worked to his benefit, for now that the free verse flurry is over and some writers have turned once again to traditional forms, Robinson's skill can be fully appreciated.

Themes and Meanings

It is particularly ironic that so many critics and scholars classified Robinson as an old-fashioned writer because he clung to traditional forms, when in subject matter he was as unconventional as any of his contemporaries. There is not a trace of nineteenth century sentimentalism in Robinson's poetry. He does not believe that in this world God makes everything right. However, though they are pitiable, human beings are so blind, so intent on rejecting divine direction, that one can hardly blame God for permitting them to suffer. Nevertheless, Robinson believes that beyond the darkness there is light, and once they pass beyond their suffering, human beings can perceive God's plan.

Many of the poems in *The Children of the Night* deal with misery, failure, and death. Admittedly, some of Robinson's characters, such as the materialists in the octave beginning "To me the groaning of world-worshippers," do not realize that their lives are empty. The miser Aaron Stark, who represents the very worst in human nature, is actually pleased with his reputation for heartlessness; the pity of a tender-hearted soul, who recognizes his friendlessness, merely provides Stark with an excuse for laughter. However, not all of the prosperous are so blind as to be contented with their condition in life. Some, like the glittering Richard Cory, find that wealth and social status are not enough to bring happiness.

A nineteenth century sentimentalist might have had his characters find fulfillment in romantic love. However, Robinson is a twentieth century realist. Often, he knows, what others call love is merely a sexual obsession, like that which drives John Evereldown. In fact, love is so often both obsessive and possessive that it seems to make disaster inevitable. The husband in "The Story of the Ashes and the Flame," even though his wife has first been unfaithful and then deserted him, loves her so much that he retreats from life in order to dream of her return. Similarly, when the beloved one dies, as in "Luke Havergal," "Amaryllis," and "Reuben Bright," the person left behind is so grief-stricken that his own life virtually ends. One might take refuge in friendship, but Robinson shows it, too, as imperfect. In "An Old Story," the speaker recognizes in himself the human depravity which blights all relationships. Perversely, the more his friend demonstrated his loyalty, thereby earning the praise of others, the more violently the speaker disliked him. Now that the friend is dead, however, he realizes how much he has lost. The sad fact is that none of Robinson's characters really know one another. Thus in the poem "On the Night of a Friend's Wedding," the poet is surrounded by "Good friends" but is well aware that what they praise in him is a "mirage" that may "crumble out of sight" at any moment.

Nevertheless, Robinson's view of life is not unrelievedly pessimistic. Though the house described in "The House on the Hill" reeks of "ruin and decay" and Tilbury Town is filled with repressed people and broken dreams (like those of "The Clerks") one does not have to stay there. In "Boston," Robinson speaks of a town that has both "something new and fierce" and a "charmed antiquity." Such places are filled with the true aristocrats, who are dedicated to the search for truth and may, like Zola, in discovering it find also "the divine heart of man." In "Dear Friends," Robinson makes it clear that he holds his pursuit of art far more glorious than others' pursuit of wealth.

Robinson does not pin all his hopes for humanity either on reason or on creativity. His sympathy for even the most desperate souls in Tilbury Town, such as John Evereldown, lost in lust, and Reuben Bright, sunk in grief and despair, is intensified by his faith in God. The poet seems to believe that a dark night of the soul may be essential to a human being's development. In the octave "We thrill too strangely at the master's touch," he suggests that by enduring misery, by accepting "the splendid shame of uncreated failure," one may rise to a new level of life and bask in the light of eternity. This is the point of "The Torrent." In this poem Robinson describes a natural paradise, which will be destroyed by "hard men" with "screaming saws." However, the poem does not end there. Moments of "gladness" culminate in true joy; finally the speaker welcomes the destructive saws, because he knows that loss can clear the way for something better, failures can be "steps to the great place where trees and torrents go." In such passages Robinson makes it clear that, while a realist and a modernist, he is no pessimist but a man strongly influenced by the Transcendentalism of Ralph Waldo Emerson. It is significant that in "L'Envoi," the final poem in *The Children of the Light*, Robinson speaks of "transcendent music," which comes from no human source but directly from the hand of God. Thus the collection ends on a hopeful note, which is the more persuasive because the poet has not ignored either the pervasiveness of human unhappiness or the inevitability of death.

Rosemary M. Canfield Reisman

THE CHIMES OF NEVERWHERE

Author: Les A. Murray (1938-   )
Type of poem: Meditation
First published: 1987, in *The Daylight Moon*

The Poem

While Les Murray is much admired for his realistic descriptions of life in his native Australia, his poetry also reflects the broader literary heritage common to all English-speaking peoples. It may not be far-fetched to wonder whether "The Chimes of Neverwhere" was inspired by the famous poem by the English writer Thomas Gray, "Elegy Written in a Country Church-yard" (1751), in which Gray wonders how history would have been different if those buried around him had lived somewhere other than in their obscure, isolated village. "The Chimes of Neverwhere," too, deals with what did not happen, but in a very different manner.

Murray's poem is composed of eight four-line stanzas. In the first, italicized stanza, Murray asks, *"How many times did the Church prevent war?"* He then answers himself by pointing out that one cannot count events which did not occur. These nonhistorical wars, he then suggests, live in a place called "Neverwhere," where they are *"Treasures of the Devil."* In the second stanza, the poet explains that Neverwhere contains everything that did not happen or has been lost.

In the five stanzas that follow, Murray lists examples. In Neverwhere are the lost buildings, those destroyed after the German leader Adolf Hitler started World War II. There are also events that never happened. There was never a second chance for the Manchu dynasty in China or a written language for the Picts. Cigars were not imported into England early enough for either James I or James II to smoke one of them. The history of Armenia has long been a sad story of oppression, starvation, and misery. As for Peter and Heloise Abelard, they had only one child, for her parents had Peter castrated, and the lovers spent the rest of their days apart.

Murray continues with his odd assortment. There is an anonymous girl with whom the reader might have had an affair but did not, along with poems never written, inventions never finished. The Australians never gave anybody a title, nor did they have to fight in a Third World War.

In the sixth and seventh stanzas, Murray moves to the subject of religion. Neverwhere, he says, contains "half the works of sainthood," for divine grace has saved many of those threatened with martyrdom. Because of Christ's sacrifice, the poet adds, much evil that would otherwise have found its way to the earth will remain in Neverwhere.

The final stanza is again italicized, and it starts with a variation of the poem's opening question. This time, however, instead of answering the question, Murray indicates that a reply is unnecessary. It is enough to know that the Church, the earthly manifestation of God's grace, is always attempting to act for the benefit of humanity on this earth. Sometimes it does not succeed, and therefore in Neverwhere there is peace that never came to be, but then, Murray muses, such goodness is needed where there are also so many unborn children, a place which, by and large, is the home of the Devil.

Forms and Devices

"The Chimes of Neverwhere" is unlike many of Murray's poems in that it is more theoretical than realistic. However, while it lacks the detailed descriptions of the Australian landscape and the stories of rural life for which Murray is so much admired, it is consistent with Murray's poetic theory and with his other works in that it is clearly directed not toward an elite audience but to the average reader. Murray's poetical populism is evident even in his choice of words. Words of one and two syllables dominate the poem; in fact, several lines have no multisyllable words at all—for example, "is hard to place as near or far" and "in which I and boys my age were killed." Even the longer words are familiar: "happiness," "waterbed," "pointlessly," "enslavements," "sacrifice."

In his effort to be reader-friendly, Murray devotes his second stanza to explaining just what he means by Neverwhere. Moreover, even his allusions are either common knowledge or easy to trace. The girl with the come-hither look, for example, needs no annotation, nor do poems, inventions, soldiers, saints, or Christian concepts such as divine grace. Admittedly, outsiders might not know that the "Third AIF" was meant to remind one of the Second Australian Imperial Force that fought in World War II or that, unlike the mother country, Australia has no hereditary hierarchy. However, other than those rather localized references, there are only six allusions, all in the third stanza, that might require a glance into an encyclopedia.

Despite the fact that "The Chimes of Neverwhere" often alludes either to the possibility or to the reality of human suffering, the tone is generally good-natured, even lighthearted, in part because of the whimsical nature of the underlying idea, in part because of the poet's skillful use of meter and rhyme. In lines such as "and the mornings you might have woke to her" and "in which I and boys my age were killed," anapests speed up the tempo; if in the second instance a rollicking rhythm seems inappropriate, one must remember that the poet is celebrating the prevention of war.

The poem also jingles with a profusion of rhymes. Sometimes they are exact, placed at the end of a line, as "Neverwhere"/"there"/"despair"; "far"/"cigar"/"are"; and "took"/"look"/"book." They can also occur at the ends of alternate lines. More often, though, either conventional rhymes or near-rhymes are sprinkled into the poem just often enough to keep the sound alive. Thus, as in a musical composition, one can hear not only "her" and "were" but also slight variations, such as "war"/"occur"/"Neverwhere"/"near"/"far"/"there." These sounds are found just in the first two stanzas of the poem. As a result of this intricate patterning of meter and sound effects, "The Chimes of Neverwhere" has a lilting quality that is perfectly in tune with the poet's thematic intentions.

Themes and Meanings

Although Murray writes in a simple and direct fashion, hoping thus to express his ideas to a wider audience, he never descends to sentimentality or suggests that there are simple solutions to life's problems. In "The Chimes of Neverwhere," the poet does not ignore either the fact of suffering or the existence of evil. Individuals suffer from the cruelty of others, as Abelard did; nations are oppressed, as Armenia was; and one tyrant like Hitler can bring about a terrible, destructive war. There is always the possibility of evil; not once, but twice, the poet places the Devil in the country of what could have happened, but did not.

If one is to rejoice that such evils did not come to pass, one must lament the good that remains in Neverwhere, unrealized. Like Gray, who wondered if a poet who could have been as great as John Milton lay in that quiet churchyard, his epic of sin and salvation never written for the illumination of humankind, Murray believes that unfulfilled potentialities are to be lamented. They may even be considered a passive evil. No one's life was made easier by poems that were not "quite" finished or by inventions that were blocked from reaching the market. Similarly, though one cannot know that the love affair suggested in the fourth stanza would have turned out well or that the birth of children would make someone's life better, the fact that these possibilities are marooned means that good never had a chance. More specifically, divine grace did not have a chance to operate.

That the grace of God is the real subject of "The Chimes of Neverwhere" becomes clear in the last three stanzas of the poem. Because of Christ's sacrifice for the sins of the whole world, saints have been saved from martyrdom, and "billions" of human beings from agonizing death. The poet concludes by suggesting a new dimension to the question he posed at the beginning of the poem. At that point, one might assume that by "Church" Murray meant Roman Catholicism and that he was about to examine the peacemaking efforts of that body. At the end of "The Chimes of Neverwhere," however, it is evident that the world has a very different meaning. The Church, or Christianity, has brought peace not by its temporal efforts but by merely existing, thus enabling individuals to avail themselves of the grace bought by Christ's sacrifice. Finally, Murray returns to his whimsical construct. If there are failures of the Church in Neverwhere, at least those attempts at good can perhaps shield the children, unborn because of human evil, who are doomed to spend eternity in the presence of the Devil.

Rosemary M. Canfield Reisman

CHURCHILL'S FUNERAL

Author: Geoffrey Hill (1932-
Type of poem: Elegy
First published: 1994, in *New & Collected Poems, 1952-1992*

The Poem

"Churchill's Funeral" is a poem in five sections. The poem begins by flashing back to London during World War II. The stained-glass windows of the great churches of London have been damaged by German bombing. The people inside the churches, or those who are seeking to rescue the victims, have been wounded, maimed, or killed. There is a curious nobility about their deaths, however, a grandeur equal to the devastated beauty of the churches. This nobility is brought to mind, years later, by the state funeral of former British prime minister Winston Churchill at St. Paul's Cathedral in January, 1965.

The second section begins to explore the poem's theme in depth. The innocent soul—that exempt from politics or worldly damage—has a guilty twin, involved in both giving the laws and violating them. In the third stanza of the second section, "res publica" means "public thing" in Latin (it provides the origin for the English word "republic"). "Res publica" is usually spoken of as something positive, but the poem sees it as responsible for both war and those who seek to restore peace. Toward the end of the section, the benevolent aspects of the res publica are emphasized, "fierce tea-making/ in time of war" signifying a kind of healthy respect for custom and triviality in the midst of crisis, then, even more directly, praise of the "courage and kindness" that, for no other reason than a simple dedication to what is right, kept the faith in the midst of the Nazi attacks. These virtues are seen as those of ordinary people, beyond the grasp of the "maestros of the world" who dominate political affairs.

The third section begins with an epigraph from eighteenth century poet William Blake. "Lambeth," a London ecclesiastical building that is home to the archbishop of Canterbury, the head of the Church of England, is "the house of the lamb" if one considers both Hebrew and English etymologies (not its literal etymology, but one coined by the poet). Yet lambs symbolize peace, and if Lambeth is bombed in wartime, then it can be no more the house of the lamb. A catafalque is a hearse for use in carrying the dead at a funeral; the droning Heinkels (German bombers) render the scene a kind of ghastly performance in which Fame, personified as a woman, renders the meek victims of the past morally victorious even as they die; their reputation will long survive their deaths, as, inferentially, will that of the more visibly famous Churchill.

The fourth section commemorates three specific London churches damaged in the wartime bombings. All the churches are dedicated to St. Mary the Virgin, and symbolism of Mary (as the "Pietà" or mourning mother) is juxtaposed with the survival of ragwort and other lowly weeds after the blast to show that both grand and simple things help sustain the human spirit in a time of crisis.

The final section shows the city after wartime, recovering from the destruction. The hour of the valorous poor who were victims of the blast is over; in peacetime, ordinary hierarchies return. "The last salvo of poppies" at the end of the poem refers to the red flowers placed on wartime graves. The image is a tribute to the spirit of sacrifice that saved democracy during the two world wars. Yet it is also a questioning of the cost, the innocent human life that was sacrificed. Even after Churchill's funeral and all that it signifies, will the victims of the war ever be fully recompensed in spirit?

Forms and Devices

The poem is written in stanzas of four lines each; the poem's five individual sections have as few as four of these stanzas or as many as seven. There is little direct rhyme in the poem, though Hill, a master prosodist, often uses assonance or verbal echo to give his words a certain ring or to create undertones. In the last stanza, the presence of "bones" and "poppies" at the end of the second and fourth lines respectively produces a kinship of sound, in the repetition of the "-es," that juxtaposes the bones and poppies in a way that makes the final image meaningful to the reader. The beauty of the poppies attempts to cover the horror and symbolic poverty of the bare bones, but in a sense the poppies are no more than the bones' external manifestation. Were it not for the dead bones, there would be no need for poppies as a symbol of mourning. Hill's verbal juxtapositions make the reader think about the underlying issues of the poem.

The poet never makes an explicit declaration of his theme, allowing the reader to piece together the poem's overall thrust from hints and images. This being so, each image, even each word, gains more importance and seems chosen by the poet with exquisite, almost excruciating, care. Hill sometimes uses very common words, but he also includes very obscure words in his diction—words such as "lourd," which is not in most standard English dictionaries, being the French word for "heavy." More characteristic are words such as "catafalque," a rather formal and obscure English word. Hill's verse is dense with meaning, each small stanza packed with resonance and reverberation.

Another device that calls attention to each individual word is Hill's use of space on the page. Despite the erudition and density of Hill's verse, it is actually very spare, not taking up much of a page. There is therefore a great deal of "negative space," of whiteness on the paper, which serves to concentrate the reader's attention on the bare words themselves.

The poem is not a direct narrative; indeed, in the tradition of elegy, it is far more meditation than narration. Each section of the poem is like a scene in a play or, more apposite to the poem, one of a series of stained-glass windows on a linked theme. At times, as in the second section, the focus is broad and public. At others, as in the fourth section, the one devoted to Mary, the poet contracts his focus and looks at a particular section of the entire tableau. It is notable that Churchill himself never makes a direct appearance in the poem, even though it is ostensibly concerned with his funeral. This is typical of Hill's oblique and indirect approach to his material.

Themes and Meanings

The reader of "Churchill's Funeral" must first determine the poem's stance toward Churchill and his funeral. Churchill almost single-handedly rallied the British people to resist the aggression of Nazi Germany. His funeral is therefore the end of an era as well as a recapitulatory celebration of the victory over fascism. Hill's sketching of the damaged churches, however, implies that healing from the war will not be as total as it might seem to those who conveniently forget history in their pursuit of the pleasures of the present. Churchill's funeral also calls to mind the end of the British Empire, which had crumbled rapidly as many of Britain's colonies were given independence after the war. In earlier poems such as "An Apology for the Revival of Christian Architecture in England" (1978), which has a subsection entitled "A Short History of the British in India," Hill has very subtly and ambiguously considered the theme of British imperialism, so the end of empire could certainly be an aspect of Hill's interest in Churchill. In this light, the "last salvo of poppies" could refer not only to mourning but also to the last manifestation of traditional British valor as seen in Churchill's attitude toward empire and war.

Hill's interest here, though, lies less with Churchill himself than in how Churchill's funeral provides a point of closure for the many deaths suffered in the bombing of London. Churchill's funeral takes place in a great old London church, which recalls the many churches devastated in the war Churchill fought. In the epigraphs surrounding the poem's sections, Hill quotes such earlier British poets as William Blake and John Milton, both associated with a Protestant democratic optimism. Hill implies that this vision is what saw Britain through the war but also that the carnage of war to some degree mocks and satirizes the utopian aspects of the earlier poets' thought. For the ordinary Londoner killed in the bombing, no amount of utopian rhetoric can provide compensation, despite the nobility of the ideals associated with Britain during the war and throughout Britain's history.

Ultimately Hill's stance toward Churchill is unclear. It seems generally admiring, but he is at pains to focus on the ordinary victims of the bombings who did not have Churchill's fame or position of privilege. This focus may be partly attributable to the fact that Hill was a young boy during World War II. To a certain extent he is pleading that the immediate impact of wartime death not be swept under the rug in a search for reconciliation or transcendence.

Nicholas Birns

CIRCULATIONS OF THE SONG

Author: Robert Duncan (1919-1988)
Type of poem: Ode
First published: 1977; collected in *Ground Work: Before the War*, 1984

The Poem

"Circulations of the Song" is a long poem divided into twenty-two stanzas of various lengths. There are 306 lines in this highly developed irregular ode. The title suggests circular as well as cyclic patterns among the stanzas, while the subtitle ("After Jalal al-Din Rumi") indicates the model that Robert Duncan is using, that of thirteenth century Persian poet Jalal al-Din Rumi. Rumi, as he has been known for centuries, was one of the founders of a sect of the Sufi religion called the Dancing Mevlevi Dervishes; he was also one of the supreme poets of Persia. He had been a sober and strict theologian and preacher of the Sufi religion until he fell in love with a young man named Shams al-Din, who became Rumi's "beloved." After that transforming experience, Rumi began composing ecstatic odes, which were accompanied by dancing and music from the reed pipe and drum.

The subject of Duncan's poem is his longtime companion, artist Jess Collins. Duncan used the term "beloved" in many of his poems, but it is in this poem in which he most clearly identifies Jess as the beloved, though he does not use his name. The mood of the poem is ecstatic declamation, as Duncan seeks to find images and metaphors that can adequately express his devotion to Jess. Each major section is built around metaphors and image clusters that Duncan used throughout his poetic career, such as the tree and leaves, the stars, water wells, speech itself, sexual orgasm, the mythic fall, and the power of Hermes in his role as alchemist and gnostic guide. The poem concludes with the metaphor of the House, not only as a Jungian symbol of the psyche but also as the domestic household that he and Jess created in a world hostile to homosexual unions.

Many motifs surface as the poem moves along, some coming from Duncan's other major collections of poems, such as the fields and meadows of his early collection *The Opening of the Field* (1960) as well as trees, roots, leaves, and branches from his second collection, *Roots and Branches* (1964). Stanza 19 (none of the stanzas are numbered in the poem) features the bow of Eros, a principal motif in Duncan's third major collection, *Bending the Bow* (1968). All these motifs come together and flower in his final collection, *Ground Work: Before the War* (1984), in which "Circulations of the Song" was first collected. In this volume the earth is a collective metaphor for all of Duncan's work.

Forms and Devices

The formal requirements of the ode determine the structure of this long, complex poem, but the ecstatic, declamatory tone is taken from Rumi's odes in honor of his young lover, Shams al-Din. Duncan could not find a poetic tradition in Western literature that could serve as an adequate model for the ecstatic, visionary utterances of love that combine both human and divine aspects, a condition he saw as an expression of the "sublime." The search for the "divine beloved" does appear in highly sensual images in "The Song of Songs," but that work stands out from the other, more somber books of the Old Testament. Duncan's poem opens with the assertion that the beloved can never be found and attained in reason or intellectual pursuits. Duncan, like his great model, William Blake, believed that reason, without imagination, was essentially destructive: "If I do not know where He is/ He is in the very place of my not knowing." Only when the seeker abandons all rational pursuits does he have a chance of attaining union with the object of his love. Yet what leads him to love is passion guided by the imagination.

Each stanza entertains possible avenues to the beloved and displays Duncan's ingenious use of parables—sometimes quite similar to Rumi's—to articulate what is basically impossible to express: the depth of his devotion to Jess, who embodies the divine beloved. "The Mind is that fathomless darkness" which leads to nothing but the enemy of love: the self. Duncan gives direct credit to the odes of Rumi in stanza 7 when he states: "The rest is an Artesian well, an underground fountain// . . . Rising thru me/ the circuit Jalāl al-Dīn Rūmī/ in which at last! I come to read you, you/ come to be read by me."

Stanzas 14 through 17 trace the process of Duncan "falling" in love with Jess, a happy fall that saves him from his dangerous lean toward solipsism: "I am falling into an emptiness of Me," an emptiness that ensures that he will never "return into my Self." One of the requirements that Rumi records throughout his ecstatic love poetry is the necessity of abandoning the self and using the alchemy of divine love to attain union with the beloved. Yet only by becoming a servant of both human and divine love can he find true satisfaction. The fire of that love comes from the heart of the lover, and Duncan expresses its effect in unmistakably alchemical terms: "Molten informations of gold/ flood into my heart, arteries and veins,/ my blood, racing thruout with this news,/ pulses in a thousand chemical/ new centers of this learning." He directly quotes Rumi on the beloved—"He has climbed over the horizon like the sun"—and refers to Rumi's text as the agent of this love: "a wave of my own seeing you/ in the rapture of this reading."

In the final stanzas, Duncan identifies Jess as Eros, who wounds him with his arrow of love, an allusion to *Bending the Bow*'s use of the myth of Eros and Psyche as an example of the mystery of love. Duncan invokes Hermes and his "gnostic revelations" as the hidden source of both divine and sensuous love. Duncan's attainment of the beloved is demonstrated in serpentine images from the Garden of Eden, images that proclaim the mythic Fall as a victory, rather than a defeat, for the initiates of Dionysus, who celebrate in "the honeyd glow of the woodwind dance/ singing." The dance, a favorite metaphor of Duncan's, proclaims the full integration of the divine and the human in natural process and change. The final stanza commemorates the establishment of the House; that is, the household—one of Duncan's favorite words—of the love between Jess Collins and himself. Their household becomes "the Grand

Assemblage of Lives,/ the Great Assembly-House/ this Identity, this Ever-Presence, arranged// . . . now in the constant exchange/ renderd true." Jess as the divine beloved has enabled Duncan to establish an actual place in the world of process and change, anchored always in the "sweet constancy" of their shared lives.

Themes and Meanings

"Circulations of the Song" is a poem about love and about the frustrations of expressing the depth of that love fully. However, Duncan also wants to explore the connections between human and divine love. Throughout his writing life, he used the word "beloved" to embody the range and intensity of the love he held for Jess Collins. Duncan finally found an adequate model in the ecstatic utterances of Jalal al-Din Rumi, the founder of the Whirling Dervishes. Rumi was forced to create these modes of ecstatic expression so that he could articulate the sensuous and spiritual intensity of his devotion for his lover. The use of the ode and the dithyrambic verse form allowed Duncan to imitate and, at the same time, pay homage to one of his great poetic idols, Rumi, a fellow homosexual and practitioner of ecstatic passion. Duncan also revered the Greek god of the dance and sensuality, Dionysus, who combined human and divine rapture.

A devoted and proud romantic all his life, Duncan found Rumi's poetic models a perfect vehicle for expressing his own anti-rationalistic position and for celebrating feeling as the key to unlocking the power of the imagination to transform the fallen world into a bower of bliss. Only by "falling in love," or surrendering the self to the fires of passional love, can human beings attain higher knowledge and experience the profundity of love. Duncan's poem participates in the identical process that Rumi delineated in his odes. He called his poem "Circulations of the Song" because the quest for the beloved circulates throughout the history of poetry and has circulated from ancient Greece down to the present day. The heart was one of Duncan's principal poetic figures, and he used it both metaphorically and literally; the circulation system exchanges oxygen and carbon dioxide to sustain life itself. Duncan frequently used objects which serve on both literal and metaphoric levels.

Patrick Meanor

THE CIRCUMSTANCE

Author: Hart Crane (1899-1932)
Type of poem: Lyric
First published: 1933, in *The Collected Poems of Hart Crane*

The Poem

"The Circumstance" exists in draft versions that Hart Crane composed before his death in 1932. It was not published in Crane's lifetime and might best be regarded as a complete draft rather than as a poem the poet considered finished. Dedicated to Xochipilli, the Aztec flower god referred to in the poem, its twenty-four lines are divided into three stanzas of uneven length.

The poem is the speaker's effort to find, in pre-Columbian America, a better way of responding to time than he has found in his own culture. The first stanza describes the ruined site of a ritual sacrifice. The remains of a throne and a stone basin where sacrifices were performed remind the speaker of the bloody history of the Aztecs, including their fatal conflicts with the exploring Spaniards. The stanza may be interpreted as a description of the clash of the Aztecs with the Spaniards, each of whom saw the other as "a bloody foreign clown." On one hand, the Aztecs, who had not seen horses before, "dismounted" the Spaniards from their horses in battle. On the other hand, the Spaniards "dismounted" the Aztec rulers. It might be the blood and bones of either group floating in the stone basins. The history of conquest is bloody, no matter who wins, but Crane's sympathy seems to lie with the Aztecs.

The second stanza proposes ways to absorb, or at least take intellectual possession of, history, "more and more of Time," as the Aztec god has. Buying stones and displaying bones, as in a museum, represent a desire to stop time. Xochipilli, often portrayed with flowers and butterflies, might be said to "drink the sun" as flowers do—another way of dealing with time, by living in the moment. The Aztec flower god, by celebrating the cycle of nature and by existing as a stone statue, may have it both ways.

The phrase "stumbling bones" refers directly to the remains of those sacrificed by the Aztecs (or—less likely—those killed by the Spaniards). "You" may be taken as a way of addressing the reader, but it may also be taken to mean that the speaker is addressing himself as "you" as he tries to enter imaginatively into the past. The stanza struggles somehow to see love as triumphant over time, but the diction is halting, the link to Xochipilli is tenuous, and the victory is, at best, tentative. The glittering crown at the beginning is paralleled by the winds possessed "in halo full" at the end. Xochipilli's crown of gold or golden flowers parallels a Christian halo. Yet these parallels are not fully explored as variant answers to the questions that human mortality raises about time.

The third stanza gives the poem its central concluding statement, "You could stop time." Xochipilli participated in the history of his time, but he also stood beyond it as a god. Xochipilli's answer to the vastness of time is to be memorialized with

monuments and statues that have endured "as they did—and have done." But Xochipilli stands more prominently for the cycle of nature, the living and dying by which
life continues on earth.

Forms and Devices

Repetition and rhyme create parallelism and contribute to the hammering rhythm
and insistent tone of the poem. These devices also take the place of consistent meter,
though iambic pentameter is still the basis for the poem. The opening line is metrically
regular, as are other lines in the poem, including line 18, which begins the last stanza.
Iambic trimeter lines, such as lines 6 and 7, as well as more unusual lines, such as the
single trochee "Shins, sus-," contribute to the poem's tonal variety while not violating
the regular underlying rhythm.

The poem is rich in rhyme. The rhyme "crown/clown" in lines 1 and 3 in the first
stanza leads to an off-rhyme with "bone" at the end of the fourth line. "Bone" also
concludes the first stanza's sequence of internal rhyme, "stone/throne." The rhyme
and repetition resume in the second stanza with "stones/bones." The phrases "stumbling bones" and "unsuspecting shins" evoke an image of a person being led to a
sacrifice, where one-third of the syllables in "sustaining" will be lopped off like a
head. Difficult though the poem is, its rhythms are insistent. In the second stanza, the
series of present participles, "urging," "unsuspecting," and "sustaining," creates a
rhythm and a parallelism enhanced by the rhymes and consonant rhymes on "nothing," "shins," and "in." As the speaker struggles to find meaning in the figure of the
flower god, the word "answer" is repeated three times in the concluding stanza.

The second stanza is a long sequence of phrases comprising two dependent clauses:
"If you could buy the stones" and "If you/ Could drink the sun." Crane does not
resolve these conditional clauses with an independent clause until the final stanza,
where he concludes the "if" sequence on the independent clause, "You could stop
time." In fact, syntactical resolution is played with, suspended, or delayed until that
single independent clause around which the whole poem turns. The lines "as did and
does/ Xochipilli,—as they who've/ Gone have done, as they/ Who've done" in stanza
2 prepare the reader for "As they did–and have done" at the very end. This repetition
may be taken to represent the cycle of nature, words and phrases returning in slightly
different contexts, as flowers return each spring.

Some passages resist paraphrase but carry clear sensuous and emotive force.
"Desperate sweet eyepit-basins" manages to sound gory and tender at the same time.
"If you could die, then starve, who live/ Thereafter" may seem confusing at first
because it places death before starvation, but it clearly describes the fertility cycle.
Seeds die, then "starve" all winter before being nourished by spring rain and warmth.
Crane never exactly states who "Mercurially might add," but the phrase refers to time,
which defies logic by adding to our lives at the same time that it subtracts from them
and concentrates them.

Themes and Meanings

While in Mexico in September, 1931, Crane went with an archaeologist on a five-day trip to an Aztec village called Tepoztlan. By accident, Crane and the archaeologist arrived during the yearly festival honoring Tepozteco, the Aztec god of pulque, a native alcoholic beverage. Crane drank with village leaders and was encouraged to participate in the festival, including being invited to beat an ancient drum in a ceremony at dawn. In his letters, Crane expressed pleasure at joining uninhibitedly in the festival and winning the goodwill of the villagers. It was apparently after this experience that he wrote "The Circumstance."

Xochipilli was associated with pleasure—feasting, dancing, games, and frivolity—as well as with love. His mate was Xochiquetzalli, goddess of domestic labor and the harvest. It is easy to see why Crane, who led a short and reckless life, would find this Native American Dionysus appealing among the grim gods of the Aztec pantheon. Compared to the human sacrifices in other Aztec rituals, sacrifices to Xochipilli were relatively humane: The Aztecs used obsidian knives to draw blood from earlobes. The blood was then touched to plants to ensure their continuing fertility. Xochipilli, however, appears not to have been completely benign. Small doves were also sacrificed. He is frequently portrayed carrying a staff on which a human heart is impaled. Both the joyous and the bloody aspects of Xochipilli seem to have suited Crane's mood. Crane refers to "A god of flowers in statued/ Stone," but in a parallel phrase also describes Xochipilli as "death . . . in flowering stone."

"The Circumstance" is a difficult poem made more difficult by the knowledge that it may be incomplete. Critics have seen the poem as an echo, even a repetition, of "the Dance" from *The Bridge* (1930). "The Dance" is also a poem in which the poet tries to imagine himself into a primeval Native American world, violent but in harmony with the life and death that are inevitable in nature. Similarly, the central effort of "The Circumstance" is to respond to the dilemma of the brevity of human life in the vastness of time, but its imagery, though vivid and disturbing, is sometimes obscure. Art and religion, as represented by the ruins of Aztec culture, seem to both participate in and endure beyond (if not triumph over) the bloody events of history. The focus of the poem is more on the poet's subjective desire to overcome time, to live imaginatively in the past while recognizing the brevity of life and the inevitability of death.

By "the circumstance" Crane seems to mean the opposition between cultures, such as the Aztec and the Spanish, and, in a larger sense, between the cycle of nature and time, in which mortality finds itself. "The Circumstance" expresses both empathy for the Aztecs and envy that the poet cannot actually enter the pre-Columbian world. Crane seems to see Xochipilli, intimate with the blood and beauty of life, as a "more enduring answer" than rationalism (and perhaps than Christianity) to the problem of the hugeness of time and the smallness and brevity of life.

Thomas Lisk

CITY WITHOUT A NAME

Author: Czesław Miłosz (1911-
Type of poem: Lyric
First published: 1969, as "Miasto bez imienia," in *Miasto bez imienia*; English
translation collected in *The Collected Poems 1931-1987*, 1988

The Poem

"City Without a Name" is a long, biographical poem in free verse divided into
twelve sections. The speaker, the poet Czesław Miłosz, is physically traveling through
Death Valley, California, but the landscape of memory and the people who inhabit his
own personal city of remembrance, his "city without a name," are emotionally and
spiritually more real to him than the heat, sand, and salt of the desert. The first sections
of the poem set up this juxtaposition between past and present in which, paradoxically,
it is the present that seems motionless and almost lifeless; the only other person within
three hundred miles of the poet is an "Indian . . . walking a bicycle uphill." The past,
however, changes constantly in a kaleidoscope of time and images of his native
Lithuania.

The greater part of the poem's beginning is made up of long, three-line stanzas, but,
in the fifth section, the lines suddenly become short, curt, almost flippant as the poet
tries to put the past behind him. "Who cares?" and "Rest in peace" he says, but this
almost sarcastic mood soon changes back to the dominant meditative tone of the poem
and its correspondingly longer lines when, in the seventh section, the poet considers
his own personal situation as a man carried "By fate, or by what happens" far away
from his homeland and his physical past. "Time," he cries, "cuts me in two." An
emphatic "I" (distinct from "them") governs this section but, as the perspective shifts
again and the images or dreams return, the poet places himself within this movement
of time as he realizes that he is a being whose own present time may be drawing to a
close. He will then become part of the past as the people he remembers have become
part of the past of their ancestors and country.

What is his country? Does the poet now belong in the past or the present? He asks
himself why all these precise, generally trivial memories keep coming back to him
and why they are more real than reality. Why, in the desert, does he think of, smell,
and hear "the lands of birch and pine" and "the hounds' barking echoes"? Why is the
past "offering" itself to him? This questioning continues throughout the middle
sections of the poem until, as if overwhelmed by the accumulation of images, the
poetic line lengthens almost into prose and the poet sees himself living in the visions
of the past. The last lines dwell on the poet's seeming inability to reconcile this
paradox. Even in his poetry, he cannot reconcile his two worlds or find the "desired"
word so that the "bygone crying" of the past "can be transformed, at last, into
harmony." However, the poem does not end on a note of defeat. A final paradox or
perhaps a moment of intuitive understanding is revealed as the poet asserts that
perhaps he is "glad not/ to find the desired word."

Forms and Devices

"City Without a Name" is very representative of the poetry Miłosz has written in the United States. He has relaxed the structural formality of his earlier poetry by lengthening and shortening the lines at will (the last section is almost prose), and little effort is made to rhyme. In the English translation (by Miłosz himself), the fifth section does contain short bursts of rhyme: "lashes/Masses," "night/light," and "pity/highly"; the same device is also used in the more pensive but still short lines of section 7: "weepily/stupidity," "snow/know," and "new/two." However, this is not typical of Miłosz's later poetry or of the structure of "City Without a Name." In fact, its presence is meant to highlight thematic mood rather than poetic form.

The absence of metaphor, simile, and symbolism is very typical of Miłosz's later poetry. Nothing is a symbol of anything, and nothing resembles anything else; everything is concrete and is exactly what it is. Miłosz has said that "the accidents of life are definitely more important than the ideal object." He perceives no difference between the language of poetry and the language of the "real" world and wants no poetic finery or linguistic gymnastics that, in his opinion, separate rather than reconcile. In "City Without a Name," the dialectic between past and present is accomplished not through symbols or allusion but through the naming of concrete objects and people. Anna and Dora Drużyno, for instance, are real people rather than memories because they are named.

One poetic device that is dominant is the juxtaposition of a succession of dualities. The starting point for "City Without a Name" is the contrast between the sterility of Death Valley and the fecundity of the landscape of memory in the poet's mind or, more generally, between inner and outer reality. While camping in the desert in spring, the sound of bees unleashes the floodgates of memory as, in an almost cinematographic technique, the waterless silence of Death Valley, marked by the absence even of birds, dissolves into the shores of a river; the sound of flutes and drums is heard, and swallows fly over a pair of lovers. Something in Death Valley, perhaps a reaction to its aridity, has triggered the poet's own valley of the dead. Together with this cameralike fade-in/fade-out of sensory images, the poet lengthens and shortens his lines to represent the contrast between the past and the present and to underline the changing moods of the poem. A long line indicates remembrance and corresponds to more reflective passages, while shorter lines identify the present and the poet's reactions, often ironic and biting, to this involuntary time traveling. For example, the fifth section, with the shortest lines, is almost staccato in its sarcasm—"Doctors and lawyers,/ Well-turned-out majors/ Six feet of earth"—while the likewise short lines of section 7 mirror the poet's sardonic contemplation of his present situation: "So what else is new?/ I am not my own friend."

Themes and Meanings

The dominant theme of "City Without a Name" is self-definition. This questioning of identity, which has been paramount in all of Miłosz's work since his relocation to the West, is strongly linked to the inward musings of a man in the twilight of his years.

However, "City Without a Name" is not an egocentric poem. In fact, if the poet can affirm anything, it is that individuality is, paradoxically, communal. One must be defined by the past and, above all, by the people who share that past. In his book *Radzinna Europa* (1958; *Native Realm: A Search for Self-Definition*, 1968), Miłosz speaks of a "world defined by memory" in which "each experience branches into a series of associations, demands to be given permanency, to be linked up with the whole."

Nevertheless, the admission of such a perspective does not automatically bring acceptance. At times the poet gratefully relives the past or grudgingly perceives its importance, but, in other, blacker moments, he rails against the fact that he may only be the medium through which other experiences are filtered. He is afraid that the past may overwhelm the present, and, when past images begin to dominate, when he loses the present and only gains the past, he strikes out with anger and sarcasm. He cannot reconcile what is with what was. This striving for reconciliation is the corollary to the main theme of self-definition as the poem charts the poet's struggle to find the meaning of his life, to find his own place and time amid the multitude of voices and times that assail him. He has run through his life just as he is now running though the images of memory looking for the "last door," the one that will open on to knowledge and reconciliation, joining everything as one. At times he despairs of ever finding an answer: "And the gift was useless, if, later on, in the flarings of distant nights, there was not less bitterness but more." However, soon after this sad statement, the poem finishes with an entirely different perspective. Many critics have spoken of the epiphanies present in Miłosz's poems, the sudden moments of intuitive clarity in which his "last door" starts to open. "City Without a Name" ends with such a moment as the poet, who has striven to define his life and bring into harmony past and present, suddenly stands mute before images of a peaceful death and the sound of music. He does not want to speak; he does not want to define. Perhaps the experience, the feeling, is the harmony.

Charlene E. Suscavage

CLEARANCES

Author: Seamus Heaney (1939-
Type of poem: Sonnet sequence
First published: 1987, in *The Haw Lantern*

The Poem

An elegiac sequence of eight sonnets on the death of Seamus Heaney's mother, "Clearances" is a reworking and revisiting of many of his early domestic and agrarian poems. At the same time it represents an attempt to confront the importance of his mother in his life and work. As the eldest child, Heaney occupied a somewhat privileged place in the family, and his mother figured in many of his earlier works. The sequence emphasizes the private moments—folding sheets, peeling potatoes together, even the oedipal struggle he calls "our *Sons and Lovers* phase"—the two of them shared.

Even the entry point of the poem involves a private legacy, as he meditates on a cobble thrown at his maternal grandmother by an outraged fellow Protestant when she married a local Catholic man. The cobble is both an emblem of his attachment to his mother's side of the family and a literal keepsake, given to him by her. The intimate nature of that bequest represents the intensely private nature of the entire sequence. Similarly familiar—and familial—the second poem veers between memories of his grandparents' house and a vision of them welcoming their newly deceased daughter to their heavenly home, which, significantly, bears the same address as their earthly home.

Having placed his mother's death, Heaney is prepared to deal with his memories of their relationship. This he achieves in a series of four sonnets in which mother and son are isolated together. In number 3, the two of them sit at home peeling potatoes while the rest of the family attends Mass. In number 4 his education separates them, as she typically declines to pronounce words that are "beyond her," deferring to his greater acumen. For his part, he finds himself reverting to a grammar of home rather than of his schooling, although even that stratagem, consciously undertaken, pushes them apart. In the remarkable number 5, the shared act of folding sheets becomes an intricate dance that paradoxically requires them to pull away from each other as it brings them closer together. In number 6 he recalls the shared rituals of church attendance during Holy Week.

The seventh sonnet shows the family attending to his mother's death, with his normally taciturn father showing a surprising aptitude for the right words. Both numbers 7 and 8 play with the notions of presence and absence. When his mother dies, the family members all know that the space they surround, the space she has heretofore occupied, has "been emptied/ into us to keep." Similarly, in the final sonnet, Heaney imagines walking around a space that is "utterly empty," a beautifully realized metaphor for this elegiac sequence, in which Heaney circles around the space in his life which has been emptied by the death of his mother.

Forms and Devices

While the sequence consists of sonnets, no particular type of sonnet predominates. Heaney adheres rigorously to the fourteen-line sonnet form, yet as with his use of all forms, he bends it to his own ends. There are Shakespearean sonnets (as number 6 is), blank forms (number 7), and others that can only be described as Heaneyesque. He bends rhyme schemes to his own uses, varying patterns from poem to poem, thwarting the reader's expectations, so that the standard Petrarchan sonnet form, for instance, fails to materialize, and the rhyme scheme sends the poem in unexpected directions.

At times Heaney employs very regular rhymes, while at others (as in number 7) he rhymes "soul" with "oil," "breathed on" with "incensation," and "pride" with "bread." In the first two lines of the sestet (a sestet consists of the final six lines of a sonnet) in number 5, he rhymes "happened" with itself, thereby upsetting any expectations of formal regularity, yet the rhyme works beautifully, because he causes the stresses of the line to fall in slightly different ways. Heaney is typically mischievous in the matter of rhyme, partly because of his awareness of the irregularities of pronunciation in his native Northern Irish Catholic dialect: He has written elsewhere that in his native speech, "hushed" and "lulled" are exact rhymes for "pushed" and "pulled." That personal linguistic history, together with the early influence of the work of William Butler Yeats and Robert Frost, leads Heaney to maintain a tension between the formal regularity of the sonnet (and of the rhymed poem generally) and the rhythms of everyday speech. The use of slant rhymes, run-on lines, and rhymes on unexpected words allows Heaney to maintain the conversational mode within a highly regulated form.

As with rhyme schemes, the traditional split between a sonnet's octave (its first eight lines) and sestet stands open to reinterpretation. The meaning in several of the sonnets in "Clearances" follows the traditional split, with the opening octave acting as a single unit of meaning and the concluding sestet comprising a second unit. In other poems, however, Heaney introduces the directional break after line 7 (number 5), line 9 (number 8), or line 10 (number 7). What is consistent is that the poems contain two distinct movements, often striking out in quite different directions. The second sonnet, for instance, moves from a memory of childhood visits to his maternal grandparents' house in the octave to his mother's foreseen reunion with her parents in the afterlife. Similarly, in number 3, the octave concerns itself with the memory of the shared privacy of mother and son peeling potatoes on a Sunday morning. That glowing moment takes on different coloring in the sestet, where the speaker recalls it during the priest's deathbed work. At that moment, while others are crying or engrossed in their own thoughts, he recalls that that morning, with their breaths mingling, was the closest they would ever be. Throughout the sequence, the sonnets offer similar shifts and changes; they must be read as single units, to be sure, but as single units made up of two distinct segments.

Themes and Meanings

As one would expect in an elegiac sequence, "Clearances" is about mortality.

Rather than understand mortality narrowly as "death," however, one does well to consider mortality as pertaining broadly to life and death. His mother's death occasions in Heaney a meditation on his relationship with her, on the effects of death upon a family, on his own aging, and on both life and the afterlife.

Most immediately, the poems concern themselves with loss: to lose one's mother is inevitably to discover a hole in the world. Heaney's image, in the final poem, of walking around an empty space is a remarkably apt description of that condition of loss. Throughout the poem he has considered his relationship with his mother in its various nuances, from the initial closeness to the inevitable separation and distancing brought on by his education and career. Yet during his whole life the one constant of his relationship with his mother has been her presence. Now he finds that her absence will color both his future and, in a sense, all that has gone before.

The occasion of this particular death also takes on a universal quality. At her deathbed scene in number 7, Heaney declines to name any of the participants. His father is simply "he," the assembled family "we" or "the others." They are both recognizable as themselves and generic: This is any family standing around the deathbed of a parent as well as the very specific family to which he belongs. Such a strategy invites readers to identify with the scene, to see their own losses in his.

Certainly the confrontation with his mother's death leads him to consider his own. In number 8, the empty space in the world is both that which his mother occupied and the space formerly occupied by his birth tree, planted by his aunt and now cut down by subsequent owners of the family farm. That tree, "my coeval," becomes a "bright nowhere," a brilliant image of what it means for a being to go out of the world. The prospect of leaving the world has led to a consideration throughout the sequence of being in it, both in terms of his mother and in terms of his own career. The sonnets contain echoes and traces of his earlier work. The poem about folding sheets is a return to, and in a sense a critique of, his earlier "Churning Day." That poem was about textures—dense, close, even clotted. Sonnet number 5 here is about lines of force, about connecting and pulling away simultaneously, and about, as he himself has said, clarifying and simplifying the excess of words in "Churning Day." Similarly, the great closing image of the empty space is borrowed from the third poem in Heaney's "Station Island" sequence, here turned to a new and more poignant use. Throughout the sequence he works at coming to terms with his agrarian past, which received such strong treatment in his first three books, then was laid aside beginning in *North* (1975).

For Heaney, death is inextricably linked to life, and just as many of his earlier elegies celebrate the life of the deceased—a cousin, a friend, an old fisherman, the poet Robert Lowell—so here the elegy for his mother stands as both a meditation on her death and a celebration of her life and of his life with her.

Thomas C. Foster

THE CLOUD

Author: Percy Bysshe Shelley (1792-1822)
Type of poem: Lyric
First published: 1820, in *Prometheus Unbound: A Lyrical Drama in Four Acts with Other Poems*

The Poem

In six stanzas of between twelve and eighteen lines each, the first-person narrator of "The Cloud," who is the cloud itself, describes its various forms and functions throughout its life cycle. The first stanza captures the range of the cloud's moods. Gentle, it brings rain to nourish the earth's flowers and shade for the leaves of trees. The cloud can also be ferocious, however, bringing hail that whitens the ground, followed by thunderstorms.

Peaceful again in stanza 2, the cloud describes how it shrouds the snow on mountain peaks and sleeps during the storm. Then the cloud explains how it is controlled by atmospheric electricity (a belief that was common in Shelley's time but has since been disproved). The poet pictures the cloud as possessing a positive electrical charge that interacts with earth's negative charge to produce rain, either a fierce thunderstorm or more gentle showers. The attraction between the two kinds of electricity is depicted as love.

Stanza 3 describes a sunrise and a sunset from the cloud's perspective. At daybreak, just as Venus (the "morning star") becomes invisible, the sun's rays leap onto the mass of clouds driven by the wind; at sunset the cloud rests, with "wings folded," like a "brooding dove." In stanza 4 the moon, "that orbed maiden," rises at dusk and "Glides glimmering" over the cloud's "fleece-like floor." The type of cloud suggested here is altocumulus, a "thin roof" that sometimes breaks to reveal the stars. To the cloud the stars are like a "swarm of golden bees." When the breeze blows stronger the cloud breaks up, and through it the sky appears, "Like strips . . . fallen through me on high," until the reflection of the moon and stars can be seen in rivers, lakes, and seas.

In stanza 5 the cloud has become cirrostratus, a high cloud that produces a halo, "a burning zone," around the sun and a "garland of pearl" around the moon when they shine behind it. Then the cloud changes yet again and becomes stratocumulus, a low gray cloud that hangs "like a roof" and is "Sunbeam-proof." The second half of the stanza describes a cumulonimbus rain cloud that marches through the "triumphal arch" of the rainbow as it delivers its contents onto the "moist Earth."

The final stanza is a summation. The cloud explains its relationship to the elements in intimate terms: It is the "daughter of Earth and Water" and is nursed by the sky. In the life cycle of the cloud its endlessly circulating particles pass through the "pores of the ocean and shores" (the latter are the rivers). The cloud constantly changes its form, and yet it does not die. After rain has come and the sky is once more clear, the cloud laughs at its own "cenotaph," which is a monument erected in honor of someone who is buried elsewhere, and like a child emerging from the womb it arises and once more "unbuilds" the "blue dome of air."

Forms and Devices

Each stanza is composed of several quatrains that rhyme like a ballad stanza, *abcb*. There is also an internal rhyme in each stanza ("I bring fresh showers for the thirsting flowers," for example) in line 1 and in each subsequent uneven line number (line 3, line 5, and so on). The effect of this consistent rhyme scheme is to give the poem a sense of order and cohesion, since the meter, although it consists basically of iambic and anapestic feet, is constantly varied.

The imagery Shelley employs has the effect of humanizing nature. For example, flowers "thirst," and leaves, lazy in the noon sun, "dream." Buds "waken" after they have been at rest in the earth, like a child, "on their mother's breast." The earth does not merely rotate around the sun, it "dances"; the trees "groan" in the wind; thunder "struggles"; the sunrise has "meteor eyes"; it "leaps on the back" of the clouds; sunset "breathes"; the movement of the moon is the "beat of unseen feet"; stars "peep" and "peer"; heaven has a "blue smile," and the earth is depicted as "laughing" after a storm. The effect created is of a universe alive with feeling and divine influences, reminiscent of some of William Blake's *Songs of Innocence*.

Crowning all these images is the metaphor of the cloud itself as a laughing, winged child-god. The word "laugh" occurs three times in this context. In stanza 1 the cloud laughs in the midst of the thunderstorm; in stanza 4 it laughs again at the sight of the stars as they "whirl and flee," and in the final stanza the cloud silently laughs at the presence of the clear blue sky, which appears to be a memorial to the cloud's own demise. The cloud laughs because it knows this is an illusion. This image occurs elsewhere in Shelley's work. In *Prometheus Unbound* (1820), for example, published in the same volume as "The Cloud," the spirit of the earth is a winged child and, like the cloud in stanza 2, sleeping in the storm, is shown asleep, its lips moving, "amid the changing light of their own smiles," a close parallel to the laughing cloud.

The other notable quality of the images is that they make poetry from scientific processes. Shelley took a close interest in scientific matters, and his descriptions of the various forms and changes in this protean cloud are scientifically accurate. This accuracy applies also to other observations in the poem, such as the image of "sunbeams with their convex gleams." This phrase refers to the phenomenon of atmospheric refraction, in which the earth's atmosphere bends sunlight around the earth in a convex arc, as seen from the cloud's point of view (the same phenomenon would be concave if viewed from the earth).

Themes and Meanings

In an earlier poem entitled "Mutability," Shelley used clouds as a symbol of impermanence and likened them to human life, which is never the same from one day to the next. In *Prometheus Unbound* the cloud takes on a different meaning as a symbol of the material human form, which is illuminated by the transcendent light that shines from within it. "The Cloud" builds on both these meanings and adds a third. Certainly the cloud is transient, but impermanence is not the last word; everything in the poem goes through a cycle of dissolution and rebirth; nothing is forever lost. This is why the cloud is depicted as laughing: It knows this truth, and its laughter suggests that the essential reality of life, underlying all temporal phenomena, even its apparently dark or distressing elements, is bliss and joy. This bliss is propelled through the material world through the power of love—another belief that Shelley expressed frequently, especially in *Prometheus Unbound*.

The image of the cloud at sunset, resting with wings folded, "as still as a brooding dove," is also significant. It is a clear allusion to Book I of *Paradise Lost*, by John Milton, in which the Holy Spirit is described at the creation as sitting "Dove-like . . . brooding on the vast Abyss." The image suggests that the cloud is also a metaphor for the creative energy, which elsewhere in his writings Shelley saw embodied in an absolute One that effortlessly manifests its power through the material world. This power is usually hidden, as, for example, in "Hymn to Intellectual Beauty," but it is indestructible—the eternal dimension of existence which persists unchanged through all the cycles the material world undergoes. In this sense the cloud resembles the skylark in "To a Skylark," a poem Shelley wrote at about the same time that he wrote "The Cloud." The skylark sings in joy; its song comes not from itself but from an unmanifest creative source that merely uses the bird as its instrument. So it is with the cloud. All these meanings combine to suggest a world in which truth is effortlessly manifested and joyously perceived, an unpolluted paradise free of the ugliness that ignorant humans, who mistake illusion for reality, appear (but only appear) to impose upon it.

Bryan Aubrey

CONCORD HYMN

Author: Ralph Waldo Emerson (1803-1882)
Type of poem: Lyric
First published: 1837, as "Original Hymn"; collected as "Hymn, Sung at the Completion of the Concord Monument," in *Poems,* 1847

The Poem

This poem was first distributed as a leaflet on the occasion of the dedication of a monument (July 4, 1837) commemorating the battle of Lexington and Concord. However, since the cornerstone of the monument was laid late in 1836 and the monument carries the date 1836, some printed versions of the poem give that date. The poem was not printed again until it was included in Ralph Waldo Emerson's *Poems* (1847). The poem's original title was replaced in subsequent years by the now commonly accepted title "Concord Hymn." This short poem is composed of four stanzas of quatrains written in iambic tetrameter rhythm. The alternating lines rhyme in a pattern of *abab.*

In the first stanza Emerson briefly reenacts the early American Revolution battle that took place at Concord bridge on April 19, 1775. The first line describes the location as being by an arched, rustic ("rude") bridge crossing a stream. Patriotic dedication is expressed in the subsequent line, "Their flag to April's breeze unfurled." The release of the flag to the wind symbolizes the fact that there is no going back to the conditions preceding this battle. The third line emphasizes the location by repeating the word "Here." The phrase "the embattled farmers" reminds the reader that the Americans were soldier-farmers fighting a professional British army. The most famous line of the poem, "And fired the shot heard round the world," expresses another anomaly: These farmers changed not only their own lives but also the lives of people living in far distant countries. The United States' successful fight for independence from England inspired the oppressed people of other nations also to protest tyrannical conditions.

As the first stanza emphasizes the location of the battle, the second stanza emphasizes time—the period that has elapsed between the battle and the monument being erected to commemorate the battle. In the first line the identification of the enemy as "The foe" is softened by the concept that "the foe" has now been asleep (or perhaps dead) for many years. The second line semantically balances the "foe" (the English soldier) of the first line with his opponent, "the conqueror" (the American farmer), and then unites them in the same action of sleeping in silence. The third line explicitly identifies "Time," the great equalizer that has "swept" the "ruined bridge" away from that spot and into the stream that moves slowly ("creeps") toward the sea. Through time, nature removes political differences: "foe" and "conqueror" are united in time's dissolution.

The third stanza describes the immediate location ("On this green bank, by this soft stream"), the immediate action of dedicating a monument ("We set to-day a votive stone"), and the purpose of the monument ("That memory may their deed redeem"). The last line projects the poem into the future, at the same time alluding to the action of the past. Like "the sires" of the group gathered at the dedication, their "sons" will certainly recall the deed of the "embattled farmers."

The fourth and last stanza expresses an address to a "Spirit." This apostrophe or prayer unites the heroes who "dare/ To die" with their children who are "free" and requests that the Spirit "Bid Time and Nature" spare "The shaft" (the monument raised to the dead "embattled farmers." The poet is praying that the monument will not meet the fate of the ruined bridge.

Forms and Devices

Emerson believed that all of life consists of organic wholeness, and he wanted the form of his poetry—its rhyme, rhythm, symbolism, diction—to embody this view. His philosophic purpose did not always produce felicitous verse; indeed, critics of his first volume (*Poems*, 1847), which contained "Concord Hymn," highly criticized his use of poetic elements, finding philosophy and poetry at odds. However, they applauded "Concord Hymn" as an exception to this criticism.

Because of his belief in poetic liberty, Emerson himself wrote that he wanted "not tinkling rhyme, but grand Pindaric strokes" and "such rhymes as shall not suggest a restraint, but contrariwise the wildest freedom." Certainly, the drumbeat rhythm of "Concord Hymn" mimics its martial content; the line "the shot heard round the world" almost seems an echo of the actual fact. On the other hand, the rhythmic beat points to the original occasion of its publication; this poem was intended to provide lyrics for a hymn, both a song of patriotism and a prayer to the Spirit. In addition, the frequent masculine rhyme, both simple and effective, underscores the effectiveness of the historical action being commemorated by dedicating a memorial stone, that is also a "votive stone"; the poet intends the audience to remember the action of the past, the dedication of the present, and the people living in the future, all bound by the "Spirit" invoked in the final stanza.

The simple diction—most words are monosyllabic—also indicates strength, the strength of the farmers who fought and the simple stone that honors them. Action words in the first stanza ("arched," "unfurled," "embattled," "fired," "shot") relate to the farmers. Action words in the fourth stanza ("dared to die," "leave," "spare," "raise") relate to the Spirit. The use of these action words connects the farmers' actions with the Spirit's action, thus expressing Emerson's and the other American Transcendentalists' organic view of life.

Probably Emerson's most important contribution to American poetry was his use of the symbol. For him, Nature was itself a symbol of the Spirit. In "Concord Hymn," Nature, Time, and Spirit are capitalized; these abstract words provide a backdrop for the other actions. The poem uses natural actions ("slept" and "swept," "sleeps" and "creeps") to suggest that natural life pervades historic actions and political determination.

Diction used in the poem is filled with natural images ("the dark stream," "this green bank," "this soft stream"). Through the use of natural visual images of location, the poet indicates that nature and humankind share experiences when the individuals ("the embattled farmers") are true to the Spirit that Nature has placed within them.

Emerson's central symbol is the use of the bridge to represent a man-made object which has disappeared since the battle that took place on it. Likewise the monument (the North Bridge Battle Monument) represents a man-made object that will, like "the rude bridge," disappear and become part of the sea unless the Spirit bids "Time and Nature [to] gently spare/ The shaft." Although the "votive stone" represents a stronger man-made symbol, it will avoid the destruction of Nature only if humankind and the Spirit work together.

Themes and Meanings

Emerson's first collection, *Poems*, indicates an introspective thinker whose idiom was highly intellectualized. Yet a few poems toward the end of the volume, such as "Concord Hymn," deal more concretely with Emerson's life in Concord. In fact, Emerson's personal life and the lives of his family were tied very closely with the erection of the monument. The famous fight with the British redcoats had taken place near the Manse, the Emerson family home. Emerson's grandfather, Samuel Ripley, gave the town of Concord a piece of land on the condition that a monument commemorating the battle of April 19, 1775, would be erected there. On the occasion of the dedication of the monument, Ripley recited the original hymn, written by a "citizen of Concord" (Emerson), which was then sung by a choir to the tune of "Old Hundred." Thirty-eight years later, Emerson was part of the committee that hired Daniel Chester French to sculpt a statue of the "Minute Man"; the first stanza of "Concord Hymn" was engraved on its base. These circumstances connect the poet closely with the historical event, the Concord location, and his audience.

In addition to his personal connection with the circumstances celebrated in "Concord Hymn," Ralph Waldo Emerson saw himself as a prophet to the American people. In turn, many of the American people saw Emerson as a person who embodied the rugged individualism of the American pioneers and the minutemen who opposed the British Empire. In "Concord Hymn" Emerson expressed the "Self-Reliance" he described (in his famous essay of the same name) as essential to the individual's personal development. Against all odds, the "embattled farmers" faced death in order to acquire the liberty to express their own beliefs.

Emerson believed the power of this self-reliance arose because each individual is a microcosm of the Oversoul, the "Spirit" the narrator addresses in the fourth stanza. Since Nature and Time reflect the power of this Oversoul, the narrator appeals to the Spirit to "bid" them spare the shaft (the monument).

The conflict between Nature (exemplified in the destructiveness of Time) and the Spirit (expressed in the heroic patriotism of the minutemen) is a central theme of "Concord Hymn." This conflict somewhat qualifies the nationalistic spirit of the poem by pointing to the transience of human works (the bridge and possibly the monument). In the past, Time swept the ruined bridge "Down the dark stream." The persona prays to avert the changing of a "soft stream" to a "dark stream." However, while his exhortation to the Spirit provides a feeling of aesthetic conclusion, its tentative nature does not inspire any great religious confidence.

Agnes A. Shields

CONVERSATION OVERHEARD

Author: Quincy Troupe (1943-
Type of poem: Satire
First published: 1975; collected in *Snake-back Solos: Selected Poems, 1969-1977*, 1978

The Poem

Quincy Troupe's "Conversation Overheard" is an extended free-verse diatribe using indentation rather than spacing to mark the breaks between sections of the single, continuous stanza. The speaker observes the repetition and stagnation of routinized American life, characterized as a "treadmill" that does not allow forward progress. Images from popular culture, especially television ("idiot tube") images and advertisements, are used as symbols of meaningless, unprogressive experience. The speaker of the poem is asked by his "love" to consider the absurdity of commercialization and misinformation on television, exemplified by the political situation of the day: the corrupt activities of U.S. president Richard Nixon's administration, particularly of Vice President Spiro Agnew, who is mocked and accused of being a liar and who manipulates public opinion through television. Agnew's disingenuousness is compared to the false television commercials that glorify the success of sports figures—tennis champions and golfers—through the use of such products as suntan lotion.

The speaker continues with an extended critique of football star O. J. Simpson and his portrayal by advertisers. The mockery of Simpson is achieved through brief descriptions of commercials he made for Chevrolet automobiles. The image of Simpson running with a football and attempting to outpace a Chevrolet Corvette is juxtaposed with Simpson's early intention to be a social worker. Simpson's name is manipulated—"overjoyedsimpson"—and the football is described as "tucked under [his] brain" rather than under his arm. The poem is prophetic in that it foresees Simpson's future as a film star but also warns that race may be a factor in the kinds of roles he will receive—preference will be given to Joe Namath, "broadway joe," another highly talented football player who, as a white star, is more likely to be cast in romantic roles.

The repeated metaphor of the treadmill moves the poem toward a comparison of the wealthy and the "starving" masses. The images of wealth focus on excess of material possessions and vapid intellectual pursuits—"spacious/ bookshelves with no books on those shelves." Other Hollywood figures are ridiculed and questions of judicial correctness are raised. The plight of well-known white figures is contrasted to the dilemmas of black political prisoners, especially the Black Panthers and Angela Davis. The media is also indicted by the poet, who sees an obvious injustice in the treatment of black groups such as the Black Panthers as compared to the treatment of white racist organizations such as the Ku Klux Klan, the Minutemen, and the John Birch Society. These injustices are symbolized by police actions during the 1967

Detroit riots and the infamous 1960 incident in Sharpsville, South Africa, in which black protesters were killed by white police officers. The poem concludes with an unanswered question concerning the continuation of the treadmill as well as the inefficacy of the "truth seeking poet," implying that the author, whose recourse is the "street corner" and lovemaking with his "woman," escapes from his ability to act and therefore contribute to changing the inequities addressed in the poem.

Forms and Devices

The poem is written in a free-verse form that is conversational in tone and structure. The poet is situated in relation to his "love" who, like the poet, questions the truths presented on television, which some assume to be a "bible," a metaphor that refers to the alleged veracity of television statements. Certain metaphors and devices of language give structure to the poem, which uses satire to ridicule various personalities from popular culture and politics. The treadmill metaphor suggests the meaningless routine of American life, and expressions found in commercials are modified to achieve a mockery of the jargon of absurd television messages (for example, "no money down all we want is your life!").

In the conversation between the poet and his "love," the questions challenge the way the general public reacts to the hypocrisy of Nixon ("tricky dick nixon"), a symbol of deceit. The poet manipulates language to create patterns fashioned from the joining of words and the alteration of spelling: "ohjaysimpson," "orangejuicesimpson," and "overjoyedsimpson," each based on the use of the letters o and j. In addition to the satirical symbolism of Simpson, the poem also uses Joe Namath to discuss racism in typecasting.

The treadmill metaphor is also used to refer to those wealthier members of American society who, like the common folk, are also caught up in a relentless pursuit. The images of excess expressed through hyperbole—"five cadillacs," "25 diamond rings," "1000 silk suits," and "2000 pairs of alligator shoes"—imply that striving for material success, especially in the context of Hollywood, is an exaggeration of reality. Figures from Hollywood are used as symbols of emptiness and superficiality. Hopalong Cassidy, the cowboy character from popular Western films of the 1930's and television of the 1950's, is joined to descriptions of overabundance and fakery. The pretense of Hollywood creations is equated with the political falsehood represented by developments in the "test tube in washington," a metonymy that echoes the earlier references to Nixon and Agnew. Additional Hollywood personalities such as Zsa Zsa Gabor and Elizabeth Taylor are satirized, but Troupe also introduces Linda Kasabian, the coconspirator of Charles Manson, who induced a number of men and women to commit acts of murder; Kasabian became a film personality in a production about the Manson murders.

The treadmill metaphor is used to conclude the poem, as is the questioning device. The poet's frustration is represented in the use of both exclamation marks and question marks to emphasize the principal trope: "why are these people dancing and singing on this/ treadmill!!??" The suggestion of social stagnation and the lack of progressive political or cultural development is linked to images of celebration, implying that those who are "dancing and singing" are oblivious to the underlying reality of "the chess game," a metaphor indicating control of world economies and political activities by a select few.

Themes and Meanings

The overall theme of the poem concerns the complacency of Americans, corruption within national politics, the inanity of television, and blatant injustices of the criminal justice system, especially relating to racial issues and African American activists. The poet also questions his inability to be an agent of social transformation. Although the principal satire is directed toward certain figures of popular culture and politics, the poet concludes with an ironic note concerning his own reaction to the unresolved dilemmas of popular culture and social justice. The mockery is based on the satirical treatment of personalities from the political arena, television, and the commercial world of Hollywood. Satire is achieved through exaggeration and ridicule.

The indictment of American culture of the late 1960's includes the mockery of Nixon and Agnew; the White House is a symbol of deception and trickery. However, political corruption is not the only form of deception: Corruption in the form of false advertising can be found in the marketing devices of television commercials, as in the image "selling suntan lotion with foul breath." The central absurdities of television are found in the methods of selling products. The satire of popular culture mocks not only white images but also the pretensions of black personalities such as O. J. Simpson. The critique of Simpson directs the poem toward racial themes such as the upward mobility of black athletes and their manipulation by the Hollywood system. Simpson is portrayed as a black sellout who is unaware of the racial implications of Hollywood typecasting and who lacks intellectual depth. Beyond Simpson's role in deceptive advertising lies the larger dilemma: the huge profits garnered by certain people involved in the television and film industry while "millions of people are starving." The social conscience of the poet is implicitly anticapitalist, and he condemns profligacy and the accumulation of status symbols (as opposed to intellectual development). Acquisition of numerous material possessions affects the "soggy brains" of the wealthy. Images of beauty symbolized by Hollywood women of public renown are presented as grotesque and constructed.

"Conversation Overheard" also protests inequities in the criminal justice system, particularly the differing treatment of black and white groups and individuals. The falsification of truth through television coverage is linked to images drawn from controversial and politically oriented coverage of Charles Manson, Angela Davis, and the Black Panthers. The focus on racial bias in the criminal justice system is part of the overall criticism of American culture. The poem also attempts to explain the social upheavals of the 1960's as complicated by a racist social order. Especially important are the white organizations known for their hatred of African Americans—"the minutemen/ the white citizen's committee, the birch society"—groups that have not been subject to police action. The interrelated themes of corruption, deception, economic inequities, and injustice point to the imbalance of a world order sustained by a minority of the powerful. The poet ultimately blames the international power structure and suggests a worldwide conspiracy of manipulation.

Joseph McLaren

COOLE PARK, 1929

Author: William Butler Yeats (1865-1939)
Type of poem: Lyric
First published: 1931, in Lady Augusta Gregory's *Coole*; collected in *The Winding Stair and Other Poems*, 1933

The Poem

"Coole Park, 1929" is a thirty-two-line poem composed of four stanzas. William Butler Yeats wrote the poem to honor Lady Augusta Gregory (1852-1932). Lady Gregory was an important playwright and cofounder of Dublin's Abbey Theatre; she also received many Irish writers as extended guests at her elegant estate, Coole Park, in western Ireland. There they were surrounded by great natural beauty and were free to spend uninterrupted days writing their poems and plays. Coole Park represented an oasis of calm and beauty that contrasted sharply with the poverty that existed in Ireland during the first three decades of the twentieth century.

The poem is written in the first person. Yeats meditates upon the many visits he and other writers had made to Coole Park, where the aged Lady Gregory is now dying from cancer. At first reading, "Coole Park, 1929" can be interpreted simply as an extended compliment to Lady Gregory, but at a more profound level it is also a lyrical meditation on death and dying. The inclusion of the poem in Lady Gregory's 1931 memoir *Coole* was especially appropriate because in this work, which dealt largely with the architecture and gardens of Coole Park, she wrote eloquently about the intense grief she had experienced after the deaths of so many family members and friends who used to visit the estate.

In the first stanza Yeats speaks of the flight of a swallow. A swallow is a migratory bird that does not stay for lengthy periods of time in a single region. This image of a swallow reminds one of the transitory nature of human life. Yeats then speaks of Lady Gregory as "an aged woman" whose stay in this life would not be very long. He recalls not the exquisite beauty of the formal gardens at Coole Park but rather his recollections of a beautiful sycamore and the beautiful blue sky of western Ireland. He contrasts these impressions of the constant changes in life and in nature itself with the permanent nature of the literary works created at Coole Park.

In the second stanza Yeats refers to five people who had experienced the beauty of Coole Park, three of them deceased and two still living. Those deceased were Lady Gregory's beloved nephews John Shawe-Taylor, a well-known Dublin painter, and Hugh Lane, a collector of French paintings who was killed when German torpedoes sank the *Lusitania* off the coast of Ireland, and the Irish dramatist John Millington Synge, whose *Playboy of the Western World* (1907) had sparked a lively controversy because it portrayed Irish people in a realistic but not always favorable light. Those still living were Yeats himself and the Irish folklorist Douglas Hyde, who would later serve as president of the Republic of Ireland.

In the third stanza, Yeats compares those people whom Lady Gregory had befriended to swallows, but he adds that her "powerful character" persuaded her guests to use properly the precious time they spent at Coole Park and on this earth. In the final stanza, Yeats suggests to his reader that even though the gardens and mansion at Coole might not be preserved for future generations, readers should never forget the importance of Lady Gregory's contributions to the cultural life of Ireland. In Greek mythology, laurel wreaths were placed on the foreheads of heroes and heroines. In the final verse of "Coole Park, 1929," Yeats compares Lady Gregory to a Greek heroine worthy of admiration when he asks his readers to pay homage to the "laurelled head" of Lady Gregory.

Forms and Devices

For modern readers it is almost impossible to separate this poem about Coole Park from Yeats's very famous 1917 poem "The Wild Swans at Coole," in which he describes both the exquisite beauty of fall at Coole and the grief he felt because so many people whom he had met at Coole were now dead. The second poem in the book entitled *The Wild Swans at Coole* (1919) was an elegy for Lady Gregory's only child Robert, who was killed in action in World War I. Lady Gregory never really recovered from her grief. In "Coole Park, 1929," Yeats refers to five swallows who came to and then left Coole, but in the third stanza he writes that there were "half a dozen in formation there." The sixth and unnamed swallow is clearly her beloved Robert.

"Coole Park, 1929" effectively contrasts the continuing presence of an aged woman with the repeated departures and returns of swallows. Yeats's very choice of swallows may seem paradoxical because few people associate swallows with beauty. Swallows, however, mysteriously return to the same places for brief periods of time each year. The writers and artists who came to Coole found the inspiration and moral support which enabled them to reach their full creative potential. Yeats had the pleasure of returning to Coole several times between his first visit in 1896 and Lady Gregory's death thirty-six years later. He realized that she had helped him to develop from a writer with a "timid heart" into a richly complex poet. The artists who created works of lasting beauty at Coole had differing personalities. Yeats refers to Synge as a "meditative man" who found inspiration in the solitude of the Aran Islands. Lady Gregory's nephews Hugh Lane and John Shawe-Taylor were "impetuous" men convinced of their own importance, but their aunt persuaded them to use their wealth and interest in painting to improve the cultural life of Ireland by developing the talents of younger and poorer Irish painters.

Each time Yeats refers to swallows in this poem, the meaning is different. In the first stanza Yeats refers to a real flight of swallows, and readers can interpret this as the evocation of a pleasant memory of a visit to Coole. In the third stanza, however, the flights of swallows remind one that several of these "swallows" have completed their final flights and are now dead. Real swallows can fly, but the swallows whom Lady Gregory guided at Coole were free to dream and to create works that continue to bring pleasure to others long after their deaths.

Themes and Meanings

"Coole Park, 1929" evokes the complex nature of artistic creation. For writers such as Yeats and Synge, who lived through traumatic periods in Irish history, the tranquillity at Coole and the firm but gentle guidance that they received from Lady Gregory enabled them to produce poems and plays that continue to fascinate readers long after their deaths (Synge in 1909 and Yeats in 1939). Certain "swallows," such as Yeats, were privileged to return to Coole many times because these lives were long. Others, such as Synge and Hugh Lane, died at relatively young ages. Their artistic and literary creations, however, survived them.

In the final stanza of the poem, Yeats calls his reader "traveller, scholar, poet." All three are richly evocative terms that lead one to appreciate the complex nature of the creative and aesthetic experiences. People travel from one place to another, but they also undertake voyages of personal discovery. (Yeats does not need to add that everyone also travels toward death.) All thoughtful people are scholars in the sense that they reflect on the meaning of the past in their lives and strive to communicate their insights to others. The word "poet" derives from the Greek word "to create," and all people are thus poets because they attempt to create meaning in their lives.

Coole Park itself was demolished in 1941, nine years after Lady Gregory's death. Even the formal gardens no longer exist; the new owners decided to sell the land so that many modest houses could be built there. The beautiful architecture and natural beauty of Coole Park can, however, still be appreciated by readers of Yeats's poetry and Lady Gregory's memoir *Coole.* "Coole Park, 1929" continues to touch readers because it explores the importance of memory and friendship. When he wrote this poem in 1928, Yeats was sixty-three years old and had already survived many of his closest friends. Lady Gregory had been diagnosed with breast cancer in 1923, and her two operations had not been successful. It was obvious to her close friends that she was dying. The poem remains an eloquent meditation on the meanings of creativity, memory, and friendships.

Edmund J. Campion

THE COUNTRY OF MARRIAGE

Author: Wendell Berry (1934-
Type of poem: Lyric
First published: 1971; collected in *The Country of Marriage*, 1973

The Poem

"The Country of Marriage" is a pastoral lyric in free verse with seventy-eight lines and seven irregular stanzas. The title suggests the poem's dual celebration of country life and marriage. Both farming and marriage are valued as complementary expressions of love, fidelity, trust, and commitment. The poem is written in the first person, using the Berry persona of the "Mad Farmer," who reflects Berry's agrarian perspective. It is implicitly addressed to Berry's wife, Tanya, as a love poem, though she is not named directly but addressed throughout the poem in the second person.

As a poem about courtship, marriage, and the married life, "The Country of Marriage" echoes the form and sentiments of Edmund Spenser's "Epithalamion" (epithalamion means "wedding song or poem"). Berry, however, forsakes Spenser's classical allusions in favor of pastoral images drawn directly from the Berrys' marriage and life together on their Kentucky farm.

Stanza 1 opens with a dream: The speaker envisions his wife "walking at night along the streams/ of the country of my birth," merged with the forces of nature, "holding in your body the dark seed of my/ sleep." This discreetly eroticized dream of love and procreation sets their conjugal love within the context of the wider reproductive powers of nature.

Stanza 2 contrasts the security of their union with the prior loneliness and isolation of the speaker, who depicts himself as "a man lost in the woods in the dark," a wanderer who has lost his way and seeks "the solace of his native land." Berry's persona finds reassurance in his wife's words in a dream that he did not know he had dreamed, "like the earth's empowering brew rising/ in root and branch." Their life together reminds the speaker of a clearing in the forest, revealing a well-tended farm, with orchard, garden, and bright flowers. The pastoral images in stanza 3 reinforce the connection between country and marriage. Images of light and dark also dominate in this stanza, the light in the clearing accentuated by the darkness of the surrounding forest.

Stanza 4 reveals a pattern of the speaker launching out and returning to the emotional comfort of their relationship, filled with joy, surrendering and trusting to their love like a man venturing into "the forest unarmed." Images of descent, arrival, and rest suggest the pleasures of their love. In stanza 5 the poet affirms that the bond of their love surpasses a mere economic exchange: It is rich and limitless in its possibilities for their mutual growth and development. Again, his wife serves as a guide and source of support. The speaker stresses his unworthiness and affirms the blessedness of their union as an unearned gift, to be accepted as the plants accept "the bounty of the/ light."

What their love has taught him, the poet affirms in stanza 6, is the freedom of surrender to its bounty, as conveyed by the simile of their drinking the waters of a deep stream whose richness surpasses their thirst. Berry's water images imply the freedom, surrender, and trust essential to love. The last stanza unifies the images of light and darkness, water and rain, and flowers, orchards, and abundance in the promise of the marriage that they have "planted in this ground." The poet closes by praising his wife as a type of "all beautiful and honest women that you gather to/ yourself."

Forms and Devices

"The Country of Marriage" is the title poem of Berry's fourth poetry volume, which was dedicated to his wife Tanya. Each of the seven stanzas is organized around a series of metaphoric assertions of the poet's love for his wife. Berry, like Denise Levertov, is committed to the use of organic form, in which the content of a poem shapes its form. Berry's use of the confessional form also allows him to celebrate their conjugal love in a personal but discreet manner.

Each stanza opens with a poetic assertion or question which is then expanded through the use of a dominant metaphor, linking their love with nature. The delicacy and intimacy of the lines create a sense of rhetorical privacy, as in a love letter or courtship poem. The basic movement of each stanza is from separation and isolation to union, from dream and desire to surrender and union. The organic metaphors express a series of oppositions that convey the richness of their love: limited/limitless, known/unknown, possessed/unpossessed, worthy/unworthy, light/darkness, life/ death.

Another dominant trope for their love is expressed through the words trust, approach, surrender, descent, union, rest, and peace, which echo the Elizabethan conceit of "dying" into each other's love, often found in courtly love poetry. The energy of the poem seems to alternate between separation and union, losing and finding each other, suggesting the task of finding and defining oneself through love. There is a sense of indirect erotic tension and energy diffused throughout the poem, conveyed through the organic metaphors, which parallels the fecundity of nature.

The speaker celebrates the joy, happiness, and fulfillment of their marriage, always from the speaker's own point of view. His wife is addressed but never replies. The poem also conveys a tacit religious sensibility, reminiscent of St. Paul's celebration of love in I Corinthians 13, in that the qualities of conjugal love—its paradoxical, mysterious, generous, unpredictable, unbounded, and transcendent nature—suggest a parallel with divine love. A husband's and wife's love for each other mirrors God's love for humanity. These religious overtones are implied through Berry's consistent use of light and dark imagery throughout the poem.

Themes and Meanings

"The Country of Marriage" is a subtle, delicate celebration of married love. Through the intimacy of the confessional form, the poet reaffirms the ardency of his courtship and his fidelity to his marriage vows. Each stanza offers a subtle variation on the theme of the bonds of love and fidelity, mutual trust and affection, giving and receiving. The pastoral setting and organic form provide an appropriate context for the celebration of marital love.

Stanza 2 echoes the opening stanzas of Dante Alighieri's *The Divine Comedy*. Like Dante the pilgrim, Berry's speaker envisions himself lost in a dark wood in which the vision of the beloved appears to him as a spiritual guide as Beatrice did for Dante. Berry, like Dante, imagines himself a wanderer in his native land, spiritually lost, seeking the level ground to avoid the abyss. The metaphoric implications of Berry's persona as a pilgrim who has lost his way and seeks a guide suggests the belief in the transforming power of love shared by both poets. A crucial difference is that while Beatrice served as both muse and idealization of love, Berry's persona celebrates the fully realized marital relationship. He finds his way to a kind of "salvation" in the present life through the pleasures of marriage.

A central theme in the poem is the rejection of mere economic or utilitarian calculations of love. The poet asserts that "our bond is no little economy based on the exchange/ of my love and work for yours." Instead, their love is unbounded, immeasurable, a mystery, a blessing to be accepted "as a plant accepts from all the bounty of the/ light/ enough to live, and then accepts the dark." Their mutual love and surrender is an exercise in freedom and a way of accepting their mortality and the mysterious gift of life. Their relationship provides a continuous education and self-liberation in which "what I am learning to give you is my death/ to set you free of me, and me from myself/ into the dark and the new light." As husband and wife, they constantly renew themselves and each other through their marriage.

Their love is a mystery, an unbounded, constantly renewable gift, a mutual surprise and delight, as figured in the pastoral images of the last stanza: "a night of rain," "a clump of orange-blooming weeds beside the road," "the young orchard waiting in the snow." The last stanza ends with the poet's rededication of his love for his wife.

Berry's use of the pastoral form and the images of farming and husbandry to celebrate conjugal love places his poem within a long tradition of pastoral poetry that stretches through English poetry to the Greek and Roman classics of Theocritus, Vergil, and Horace. Most of all, perhaps, he resembles the Elizabethan and Metaphysical poets—Edmund Spenser, Andrew Marvell, and John Donne—who reinvigorated the English pastoral form. The subtle mastery of "The Country of Marriage" demonstrates why Berry is widely considered the foremost contemporary American pastoral poet.

Andrew J. Angyal

CRAFTSMANSHIP AND EMPTINESS

Author: Jalal al-Din Rumi (1207-1273)
Type of poem: Meditation
First published: Early thirteenth century, as part of *Masnavi-ye Ma'navi*; English
   translation collected in *One-Handed Basket Weaving*, 1991

The Poem
   "Craftsmanship and Emptiness" consists of a relatively few lines (lines 1369-1420
of book 5) from Jalal al-Din Rumi's enormous work *Mathnawi*. The Persian title
Mathnawi refers to the verse form used (rhyming couplets) and came to mean an
extensive didactic work that could include a variety of tales and other material. Rumi's
Mathnawi, left unfinished at his death, includes stories from the Qur'an (Koran) and
Islamic tradition, folk stories, and anecdotes. Even though its intent is serious, his
Mathnawi is funny and even bawdy at times. Written mostly in Persian, the book also
includes passages in Arabic, Turkish, and even Greek. Traditionally, it is referred to
as the "Qur'an in Persian," an indication of its high status. The title "Craftsmanship
and Emptiness" is not Rumi's, but was added by the translators. This translation makes
no effort to reproduce the rhyming couplet form of the original but instead is rendered
in free verse.
   Rumi is speaking to the reader in this poem; the relation is one of a spiritual teacher
instructing a disciple. The poem moves associatively from one topic to another closely
related topic. Its several sections illustrate the value of emptiness. Rumi begins by
reminding his audience of a topic he has spoken of before—emptiness as an opportunity for the craftsman to practice his craft. He lists examples that would be part of the
original audience's everyday experience. In the third stanza, Rumi addresses the
reader directly, admonishing the reader that it is foolish to fear death and emptiness,
which are a "beautiful expanse," while being deceived by the destructive things of the
world ("a scorpion pit").
   Having admonished the reader, Rumi turns to a story from an earlier Persian poet,
Attar, to expand and clarify what he has said. The story tells of a Hindu boy, captured
by a Muslim ruler and shown favor. The boy's parents have taught him to fear King
Mahmud; raised to a high standing (the king's vice-regent), the boy weeps in delight
and wishes that his parents could be there to see that their fears were all wrong.
   Rumi interprets the story's details by applying them to his audience. The parents,
whose fears previously governed the boy's feelings, are seen as human attachments.
These attachments keep one blind to the "beautiful expanse" of one's real situation
and keep one imprisoned in the "scorpion pit" of fears and selfish desires. Rumi
promises readers that one day they will experience the boy's tears of joy.
   The theme of attachment suggests the body, to which Rumi next turns. Rather than
advocating an extreme ascetic attitude toward the body, Rumi suggests that the body
is useful as well as frustrating and that one's best attitude toward it is patience. The
next few lines take up the theme of patience, using both natural images (the rose and

the camel) and human images (the prophets and the embroidered shirt) to show the reader how patience is part of life. Rumi concludes with three stanzas advising the reader to "live in" God—the Eternal—or be burned out like an abandoned campfire.

Forms and Devices

The comments in this section refer to Coleman Barks's translation (as collected in *Rumi: One-Handed Basket Weaving, Poems on the Theme of Work*, 1991, and *The Essential Rumi*, 1995). Other translators of Rumi have used very different styles. For example, Reynold A. Nicholson, who edited, translated, and commented on the entire *Mathnawi* (1925-1940), translated each couplet into a prose line, as in these lines: "Even such is the seeker at the court of God: when God comes, the seeker is naughted/ Although union with God is life on life, yet at first that life consists in dying to self" (*Tales of Mystic Meaning*, 1931, reprint 1995).

Barks used free verse divided into twenty-five verse paragraphs of varying length. Free verse allows Barks to focus on the meaning of Rumi's verses and to use line breaks to provide emphasis and rhythm. Barks has translated many of Rumi's poems in this style, including material from Rumi's quatrains and ghazals (a Persian poetic form) as well as the *Mathnawi*. Overall, Barks's translations have the effect of direct and colloquial speech. This effect, combined with Rumi's pungent stories and metaphors, accounts for the popularity of Barks's renderings.

The style Barks uses does not call attention to itself—there is no rhyme, no noticeable alliteration, and no strong rhythms. The sentences are worded directly and vigorously, with no unusual word choices. Sentence structures are varied, thus avoiding such devices as parallelism. The line endings are the major indication of rhythm. As a result, the language is lively, concise, direct, and transparent.

The lack of poetic ornament makes these thirteenth century poems seem very contemporary. Lack of ornamentation may also be particularly appropriate, since Rumi discounted the value of poetry and wrote the *Mathnawi* only at the urging of a close associate. In *Fīhi mā fīhi* (*Signs of the Unseen*, 1994), Rumi says that he is "vexed by poetry" and only composes it as a way to communicate with people who respond to poetry. Consistent with this attitude, the poems in the *Mathnawi* are intended to teach by entertaining the reader with entrancing stories.

Rumi uses metaphor, simile, allegory, and symbolic images to express his meaning in a vivid and appealing way. In the first few lines, he uses simple descriptive images—the builder, the water carrier, and the carpenter. He endows these images with symbolic meaning by pointing out the value of emptiness to each of these craftsmen. "Emptiness" then refers to the mode in which Rumi encourages the reader to experience God, but the word does not remain an abstraction. Instead, it is an "ocean" in which the reader is presumed to fish and a "beautiful expanse" in contrast to the "scorpion pit" where the reader has chosen to live.

After retelling Attar's story of King Mahmud and the young man, Rumi gives an allegorical interpretation, using details of the story to encourage the reader to abandon attachment to the fleeting things of the world and to not be afraid of the "emptiness" of God. Then, in comparing the body to a shirt of chain mail, Rumi uses a simile that would be more familiar to his original audience than to a modern one, but nonetheless is clear and forceful. Finally, in describing the individual mixing with God as being like honey mixing with milk, Rumi uses another simile that not only makes Rumi's point but also uses traditional Muslim imagery associated with paradise to reinforce the appeal of his advice.

Themes and Meanings

"Craftsmanship and Emptiness" is about surrender to the Divine. Rumi was a spiritual leader and teacher in Sufism, the mystical tradition in Islam. He founded the Mevlevi order, the group popularly known as whirling dervishes. As spiritual teacher, Rumi focused on the transforming experience of God that a human might have. "Craftsmanship and Emptiness" shows "misapprehension"—fearful clinging to the passing and unsatisfactory things of this world—as the thing that hinders one's experience of the divine emptiness.

Rumi's teaching about emptiness involves a paradox related to existence. The world that people ordinarily experience, which Rumi often calls "this world," seems to exist but really does not. The spiritual world, which Rumi often calls "that world," seems not to exist but is really the emptiness that is necessary for existence, and so is more real than this apparently real world. Thus, what seems most real to the ordinary human is not real at all, and what seems unreal and empty is the only reality.

In a favorite image, Rumi refers to "this world" as the foam on the ocean of reality ("that world"). The paradox of emptiness goes a step further. Humans as such are as void of reality as is this world. In "Emptiness," another selection from the *Mathnawi* translated by Barks, Rumi writes, "We are/ emptiness." For Rumi, emptiness is not discouraging; rather, human emptiness is necessary for humans to come to know God. Paradoxically, what seems negative is actually positive.

The story of King Mahmud and the Hindu boy presents this paradox in vivid narrative terms. Rumi tells us that "Mahmud" represents the spirit's emptiness—that is, the state which is spiritually desirable. Yet the boy's parents have taught him to fear Mahmud (emptiness) and cling to "beliefs," "bloodties," "desires," and "comforting habits," those seemingly real aspects of life which are void of reality. Unlike some other spiritual teachers, however, Rumi does not say that this world has no value at all. He knows that the body can be bothersome, but he also acknowledges that it can be helpful in teaching one patience.

The craftsmen at the poem's beginning are aware of the paradoxically greater reality of emptiness since they must find emptiness in order to practice their crafts. In this, they are like God, who brought forth the world out of emptiness. Rather than discouraging readers, Rumi's insistence on the value of emptiness is intended to leave them aware of the creative potential of the "invisible ocean" and to encourage them to enter it.

Gene Doty

CREDENCES OF SUMMER

Author: Wallace Stevens (1879-1955)
Type of poem: Meditation
First published: 1947, in *Transport to Summer*

The Poem

"Credences of Summer" is a blank-verse poem divided into ten sections, or cantos, of three five-line stanzas each. The title suggests a set of "truths" or declarations about this season; to Stevens summer was the epitome of the year's natural fullness, and it is often associated in his poetry with the creative process. This process, as described in canto VII of the poem, is a three-stage or "thrice concentred" activity. "Credences of Summer" is arranged accordingly, with cantos I through III devoted to the moment of experience that the individual artist or writer wishes to express in art or poetry. Cantos IV through VI describe the ordering of that moment in the artist's consciousness; cantos VII through IX are devoted to the finished articulation or rendering in art of that experience. Canto X, like the final sections in many of Stevens's longer meditative poems, serves as a coda that reiterates the imaginative process which the poem as a whole defines and exemplifies.

Canto I sets the poem's tone of contemplation with the pun on the word "broods" and with the declaration that at midsummer "the mind lays by its trouble," repeated with the addition of "and considers" in the next line. This moment of contemplation begins the poetic act—what Stevens called elsewhere the "act of the mind." Full of sensation, this moment will be accorded the mind's full attention, without "evasion" (canto II). The poet must look at a subject directly, not relying on the words or prescriptions of others, nor even on the poet's own previous perceptions: "Look at it in its essential barrenness/ And say this, this is the centre that I seek." Once the experience itself has been identified, it assumes an essential importance, becoming a "tower more precious than the view beyond" (canto III). For the duration of the moment, the creative intelligence satisfies itself with the directness and immediacy of sensory experience.

Canto IV illustrates the difficulty of ordering or understanding such experience, here represented by the harvested hay fields of Oley (Pennsylvania). The poet admits that reality tends to resist attempts to order it—for example, language's attempts to render in rational discourse one's most visceral experiences. Therefore he calls for a language that will be more than mere "secondary sounds" describing experience. In canto V he aims at a poetry that "contains" reality "without souvenir." That is, he would dispense with the devices and systems of the past in his own apprehension of the moment, hoping to compose a poetry that enriches rather than merely embellishes or decorates: "stripped of remembrance, it displays its strength."

The third and final phase of the poetic act, in cantos VII through IX, involves the satisfactory articulation of experience. Each canto in this phase presents a kind of "poet figure" who will "proclaim/ The meaning of the capture, this hard prize" called understanding. Then and only then, the poet argues, will one have arrived at a fully experienced reality. In canto VII the singers fill this role. In canto VIII the "trumpet of morning" sounds its "resounding cry," and in canto IX the "[s]oft, civil bird" of morning heralds "the spirit of the arranged"—the power of the poet's art to express experience in a way meaningful to others.

The final canto of "Credences of Summer" recapitulates the three-part process that has been in evidence throughout the poem, but here it is the "inhuman author" of summer itself that meditates like the "mind" of canto I, and that finds an "appropriate habit" or ordering principle as in canto V, and that then "completes" reality rather than succeeding merely in decorating it.

Forms and Devices

Stevens employs a highly formal structure and an elevated diction throughout "Credences of Summer," lending the poem's language a pronouncement-like gravity. His use of literary allusion and symbolism strengthens the tone of seemingly incontrovertible rhetoric in the poem.

First, the division of the poem into numbered cantos suggests an orderly argument as opposed to an impassioned lyrical poem such as an ode or sonnet. The blank verse (unrhymed iambic pentameter) allows Stevens a rhythmic flexibility that approaches prose discourse at times, furthering the reader's sense of being in the presence of an eminently reasonable, thoughtful persona speculating on the mind's ability to comprehend the phenomena of human experience. The diction heightens this effect; highly wrought terms abound: "infuriations," "inhalations," "apogee," "ancientness," and "clairvoyance." Elsewhere Stevens resorts to foreignisms: *douceurs, tristesses*. The long compound and complex sentences reinforce the formality. (No fewer than half a dozen sentences here extend to a five-line stanza or more, with the poem's final sentence stretching across three stanzas in all.)

In a poem that urges the mind to dispense with received metaphors and accepted systems of perceiving the world, it is ironic that Stevens should make such use of literary allusion. With his opening line—"Now in midsummer come and all fools slaughtered"—Stevens invokes the famous opening lines of Richard of Gloucester in Shakespeare's *Richard III*: "Now is the winter of our discontent/ Made glorious summer by this son of York." A few lines later it is Hamlet's "there is nothing either good or bad but thinking makes it so" as well as the gloomy Dane's divided self that one can hear echoed: "There is nothing more inscribed nor thought nor felt/ And this must comfort the heart's core against/ Its false disasters." Indeed, in the poem's insistence on seizing the moment of experience many critics have pointed out that "Credences of Summer" bears out Edgar's advice in King Lear that "ripeness is all."

Another influence is Walt Whitman, whose poems of ecstatic merging with natural phenomena are recalled repeatedly in "Credences of Summer." In this "folk-land [of] mostly marriage-hymns," Stevens places a hearty Whitmanesque character "[w]ho reads no book" and whose "ruddy ancientness/ Absorbs the ruddy summer" (canto III).

Masterplots II

Symbol is another of Stevens's main devices. The Whitmanesque old man, the "bristling soldier," the hermit, the king and his princes, the characters garbed in summer's motley—these are, to varying degrees, representative of human perspectives or ways of ordering reality. Against these traditional figures, Stevens seems to prefer poet-figures of a more rudimentary sort: the unidentified singers in the wood, the trumpet of morning, the brown-breasted robin. Opposite these, Stevens symbolizes physical reality as whatever is ultimately irreducible: "The rock [that] cannot be broken. It is the truth" (canto VI).

Themes and Meanings

Like much of the poetry of Wallace Stevens, "Credences of Summer" is deeply philosophical, concerned with the processes by which the human mind perceives and comes to understand the external "reality" it is at once separable from and itself a part of. Critics have cited several themes extending from this concern.

First, the poem can be read as a kind of prologue to Stevens's more famous "Notes Toward a Supreme Fiction," in which the poet proposes that the creation of literary art should have a force equal to nature's creative powers. "Credences of Summer" thus concerns the effects of a poet's creation upon the individual consciousness. Because people tend to perceive the world through the images, metaphors, and symbols ("fictions," as Stevens conceives them) with which artists, philosophers, and theologians have supplied them, the poet's task is to examine how such fictions or constructs of the mind are employed, eventually providing new fictions with which people can apprehend the world around them.

Other critics have pointed to the sense of crisis in the poem, suggesting that "Credences of Summer" expresses the poet's own doubts about his creative powers as he entered the latter stages of his literary career. Images of slaughter and of catastrophe begin the poem, which proceeds to invoke other terms of finality that may be read as spiritual or intellectual fatigue: the final mountain, last choirs, last sounds, and so on.

Steering between the extremes of a "supreme fiction" and a barren imagination, one might see the poem as a successful treatment of the problem that confronts any writer, that of expressing in a fulfilling way the experience of "being." Stevens once claimed that the chief difference between philosophers and poets was that philosophers sought to *prove* they existed while poets *enjoyed* their own existence. If so, then the sensory richness and rhetorical force with which "Credences of Summer" captures such a moment of accord between mind and matter, language and experience, can be cited as sufficient evidence of Stevens's credo. As Thomas Hines puts it in *The Later Poetry of Wallace Stevens*, "[f]ew poems in modern literature so thoroughly meditate the meaning of fulfillment, ripeness, and completed desire. . . . [It] shows the full value of the continuity of the creative process and how the projected fulfillment comes true in the completed vision of summer."

James Scruton

CUMBERLAND STATION

Author: Dave Smith (1942-
Type of poem: Elegy
First published: 1975; collected in *Cumberland Station*, 1976

The Poem

"Cumberland Station" is a free-verse elegy with nine stanzas that vary in length. The station in the poem's title is in Cumberland, Maryland, a town at the end of the Potomac River that was once considered the "Gateway to the West." While the station at one time served as a gateway, the poem explores how a station can change from a gateway to a "godforsaken/ wayside." Throughout the poem, the station reflects the speaker's moods. Like much of Dave Smith's work, the poem is autobiographical, exploring the effect of place and history on individuals who struggle against changing times and struggle to maintain their sense of self.

In the first stanza, the speaker mentions objects that he sees as he enters the Cumberland train station: "gray brick, ash, hand-bent railings, steps so big/ it takes hours to mount them, polished oak/ pews." These objects are fragments of a grand old station, a place of giants where "Big Daddy" once collected children for thunderous rides on steam engines, where crowds of people had food and purpose, where children rode free. The speaker identifies himself as a child who once ". . . walked uphill/ through flowers of soot to zing/ scared to death into the world." In the first two stanzas the images and bits of narrative create a nostalgic mood—even the soot and ash are beautiful, flowerlike.

Cumberland Station is no longer a place of giants, however; it is now a deserted and damaged hall. It presents a scene that disturbs the speaker: "I come here alone, shaken." In stanza 3, the changes in the speaker and the station are corroborated by the fallen state of Cumberland, a town where jobless, penniless families "cruise" the city with no purpose, a town of "shaken" people. To help the reader understand why Cumberland declined and why the town incites both fear and repulsion in the speaker, he recounts not only Big Daddy's death but also the death of a child who was "diced on a cowcatcher" and the deaths of two male relatives, an uncle who "coughed his youth/ into a gutter" and an alcoholic cousin who "slid on the ice."

After the speaker chronicles Cumberland's fall, in the center of the poem he asks a rhetorical question that stops the narrative: "Grandfather, you ask why I don't visit you/ now you have escaped the ticket-seller's cage." The question and the answer return the reader to themes introduced early in the poem—Cumberland is a fallen place, a place to which no one would wish to return. Yet the grandfather's question forces the speaker to contemplate the guilt and ambivalence that the return causes him. The speaker's intentions are good—he promises often that he will return, that he will free the grandfather, his only surviving relative, that they will escape "like brothers." When in Cumberland, however, the speaker is no longer himself—he is like "a demented cousin" who steals an abandoned newspaper. While he fears Cumberland

and the memories that the place evokes, he also longs for the past. He even wishes his grandfather were there to punish him, to tell him what is right and wrong.

Forms and Devices

Since the speaker in "Cumberland Station" tells a story, the poem could be labeled a narrative. Since the poet uses the narrative to express the speaker's psychological state (a state that the speaker only half understands), the poem could also be called a lyric. Finally, since the poem explores the transience of life, is reflective, and laments the loss of a time and place, it is also elegiac. The narrative style, the serious subject matter, and the elegiac form reveal the extent to which Smith draws on a poetic tradition that dates to the Anglo-Saxon period. In anonymous Old English poems, such as "The Seafarer" and "The Wanderer," isolated speakers journey, lamenting the loss of their lords or their families. Like the speakers in those poems, Smith's speaker also journeys, lamenting the loss of heroes and heroic times.

Since the lines vary in length and lack end rhyme, "Cumberland Station" could be called a free-verse poem. The line length is not completely irregular, however. Like "The Wanderer" and "The Seafarer," "Cumberland Station" has long lines, averaging ten syllables. Like Old English poems, there are also at least eight syllables in most lines, and the poet relies on accent and alliteration, rather than on a precise number of syllables or a precise meter, to create rhythm. Long lines usually indicate a serious subject, which is true in Old English poetry and in "Cumberland Station," so the form and the content reinforce each other. In addition, the poem, like Old English elegies, has a two-part structure: The first half of the poem is descriptive, with bits of narrative and concrete imagery; the second half is contemplative, with ruminations on morality, guilt, and responsibility.

While the elegiac form and the long line length draw on a tradition, Smith breaks with tradition by using enjambment throughout the poem, as is evident in the final three lines: "I wish I had the guts/ to tell you this is a place I hope/ I never have to go through again." By breaking these and most lines in mid-thought, by not ending lines with natural pauses where punctuation marks would usually appear, the poet denies a sense of closure, forcing the reader onward from one line to the next. In addition, the enjambment allows one to read a line in several ways. In the above passage, the "I hope" at the end of the second line is first read as modifying the place, but this "hope" is shifted to the speaker in the final line. The avoidance of closure at the ends of lines reinforces the speaker's inability to find closure in his life. Although there are periods at the ends of stanzas, and although the poem comes to a dramatic finish, the closure is only partial. The speaker is left wishing he had the "guts" to escape Cumberland station but not knowing whether he does. By using enjambment, the poet reinforces the speaker's psychological confusion, a confusion that is prototypically modern.

Themes and Meanings

"Cumberland Station" was first collected in a volume entitled *Cumberland Station*, which is divided into three parts. In part 1 the speaker is near the Atlantic coast, near

Tidewater, Virginia, but by the end of the first section, he has traveled to Cumberland, Maryland, a journey inland that continues through part 2, a movement to a fallen world that lacks vitality. In part 3 the speaker returns to the water (Tidewater), where there is a sense of renewal. In a poem from part 3, "Sailing the Back River," the speaker is a waterman who fishes for something other than fish; he sits in "the toy wheelhouse of fathers." He fishes the past, but he fishes to save his own life, not to rescue dead relatives, and he throws "out love/ like an anchor." While the speaker of this poem does not escape the past and does not live in a carefree land of plenty, he is optimistic, unlike the speaker in "Cumberland Station."

Images of fish, fishing, and water appear most frequently in part 3 of the collection, but they surface throughout the book, even in "Cumberland Station." In the center of the poem, the grandfather asks the speaker why he does not return to fish. On a literal level, the speaker does not fish because "soot owns even the fish" and the Potomac River is "sored," but on a symbolic level, he does not return because the town is a wasteland that he associates with too many tragedies. Fishing will not return the clean river, the healthy fish, or the dead (his nephew, his uncle, Big Daddy, or the "ash-haired kids"). In Cumberland one will only catch "bad/ news."

The mood of "Cumberland Station" is tragic. The city once offered pioneers a gateway through the mountains to the West and offered industrialists access to rich coal fields. Now, however, it is a fallen place that never fulfilled its promise. Like the Old English poets, Smith laments the loss of heroes and heroic times, the loss of what might have been—he mourns the loss of men such as Big Daddy and others who might have guided him. He also laments the modern industrial age that has fouled the Potomac to the point that one cannot fish. In addition, he laments the modern condition that allows generations to drift without moral guidance, without mentors to teach right from wrong, and without a sense of purpose or past.

Roark Mulligan

A CUT FLOWER

Author: Karl Shapiro (1913-
Type of poem: Lyric
First published: 1942, in *The Place of Love*; collected in *Person, Place and Thing*, 1942

The Poem

"A Cut Flower" is a poem of twenty-seven lines divided into three nine-line stanzas with no apparent rhyme scheme. Most of the lines fall into regular iambic pentameter, which means that each line has ten syllables, with five stresses, or accents, and the stress is on the second syllable in each metrical unit of two syllables. This meter is considered to mirror the natural rhythms of English speech most closely, and it contributes to the illusion that the poem is spoken testimony. Several of the lines deviate from this strict meter, which prevents the pattern from becoming monotonous and obtrusive.

From the first word, "I," it is clear that the poem is written in the first person, and by the second line it is apparent that it is not the poet speaking, but the flower itself. At the beginning of the poem the flower is growing in the ground. The first four lines speak of the freshness and beauty of the flower, qualities that attract bees who "sack my throat for kisses and suck love." The remainder of the first stanza hints that all is not well. The wind causes the flower to bend, because it is sick from lack of water and longs for rain.

The second stanza begins with a description of the creature who takes care of the flower, posed in the form of a question. The reader knows that it is a woman, and she seems to inspire love and awe with her tender acts of loosening the soil and touching the flower. The flower speculates on the origins of this creature and wonders if she is "Sent by the sun perhaps to help us grow." The remaining lines of this stanza introduce a darker theme with the opening of the seventh line, "I have seen Death," and the stanza concludes with a description of another flower, which apparently died a natural death. After opening on a positive note, the last stanza builds quickly to its conclusion. By the third line it is clear that something horrible is occurring from the speaker's point of view. The flower does not really understand what is happening, but it describes the experience of having been cut by "The thing sharper than frost" and its own subsequent sufferings in a vase of water. The stanza builds in intensity to the anguished cry of the last line: "Must I die now? Is this a part of life?"

The poem was written in 1942, when Shapiro had been in the U.S. Army for a year and was stationed in Australia. "A Cut Flower" appeared first in a privately printed collection that is not available because one of Shapiro's senior officers bought out almost the entire printing. It appeared subsequently in *Person, Place, and Thing* (1942), his first American collection, and was reprinted in *Selected Poems*, 1968.

Forms and Devices

"A Cut Flower" is a conceit, a type of intricate metaphor in which the spiritual qualities of the described subject are presented in a vehicle that shares no physical features with the subject. The vehicle in this case is the flower that wonders, questions, and tries to make sense of what he sees happening around and to him. In the first stanza, when the flower speaks of its own physical attributes, the reader accepts the idea of a talking flower, an example of the poetic device, personification. Yet by the second stanza, when the flower questions the identity of his caretaker and wonders where she comes from and where she goes, the reader understands that the poem is not about a flower. The subject is really a person who describes what is happening to him through the vehicle of the flower.

This realization that the poem is not about a flower is part of the irony used to heighten the effect of the poem. The title suggests a poem about a flower, yet a surprise occurs when it becomes apparent that the cut flower is not the true subject. Other ironies unfold. The flower wonders what kind of an animal the creature who tends him is, whereas the reader knows immediately that she is a woman tending her flower bed. The "thing sharper than frost" is recognized as scissors or garden shears, and the reader understands what is happening although the flower does not. Another irony is that the flower longs for angry rain that "bites like cold and hurts" in the first stanza, but in the last stanza the flower is "waist deep in rain," and dying. An important irony that provides tension in the poem is the difference between the flower's point of view and the woman's point of view, although the poem never describes what the woman is thinking. The reader understands that tending, cutting, and displaying the flower give the woman pleasure. Poetic compression allows the poet to suggest a great deal in a limited space.

Eight recurrent images have been identified in Shapiro's poetry. The second most common one is glass, often used to symbolize human barriers or painful confinements that must somehow be shattered to achieve release. The glass objects are typically items common in everyday life. This early poem foreshadows the prominence of Shapiro's glass imagery with the vase that will eventually be the flower's passageway to death. "My beauty leaks into the glass like rain," the flower says. The word "rain" occurs four times in the poem, twice in the first stanza and twice in the third. Rain has some of the same qualities as glass; it is transparent and, when it collects, can reflect objects.

Another use of a recurring image in Shapiro's work is the flower's confinement. Images of confinement, containment, encasement, and imprisonment abound in his poems, often in obvious ways. In "A Cut Flower," imprisonment in the vase where the flower finds itself trapped, awaiting death, is a logical outcome of the action. "Conscription Camp," "Troop Train," "Terminal," and "Garden in Chicago" are other examples of Shapiro poems that use images of confinement. In "Garden in Chicago" he finds himself confined by "elegant spears of iron fence." In another poem, "Surrounded," the poet suddenly sees his suburb confined by churches, "hemmed in by love, like Sunday." The churches themselves are surrounded by a ring of missiles with atomic warheads. Both positive and negative images can suggest confinement, and sometimes the image is both—as is the vase-enclosed flower, a lovely image that is nonetheless horrible to the flower itself.

Themes and Meanings

"A Cut Flower" is about life and death in an indifferent universe. It holds a mirror to the human condition: The flower tries to make sense of what is going on in its small world just as generation after generation of human beings have tried to make sense of theirs. At first the flower sees the world as beneficial; even when it bends from lack of rain, the woman tends it and brings it water. The flower believes that the woman is somehow a servant of the sun, sent to help it grow. The flower has mistaken the woman's purpose, however, and is horrified at what happens to it—just as human beings are sometimes shocked when their apparently benign world seems to turn on them with earthquakes, tornadoes, accidents, wars, or other disasters.

One can interpret the poem as a statement about religion without forcing the metaphor. The flower sees the sun as a divine, life-giving force and speculates that the sun may have sent the woman to tend it, yet the woman kills the flower. In the same way, human beings try to make sense of the universe and interpret as benign certain forces that in fact are indifferent; they are merely working out their own processes. Although many people have seen others die, they remain shocked at and even deny the idea of their own death. The flower understands that it is fading and tries to make sense of approaching death. The conclusion to the poem, "Is this a part of life?" is poignant and ironic, for the reader knows the answer.

Karl Shapiro is a loner whose poetry is related to, but does not completely belong to, several movements in modern poetry. Shapiro, Robert Lowell, and Randall Jarrell are the three major poets to have been influenced by the Fugitive school, a movement that flourished in the 1920's and was centered at Vanderbilt University in Nashville. The Fugitives' poetry was inclined toward irony, wit, satire, death, subtle cruelties, and indifference to suffering, many of which can be seen in "A Cut Flower." The Fugitives were a southern, regional movement, and Shapiro wrote a great many poems about the South and his place in it as a Jew. Later Shapiro was associated with the Beat generation of Allen Ginsberg, Gary Snyder, Gregory Corso, and Jack Kerouac, yet he maintained his individuality and distance.

Sheila Golburgh Johnson

DANCE SCRIPT WITH ELECTRIC BALLERINA

Author: Alice Fulton (1952-
Type of poem: Lyric
First published: 1983, in *Dance Script with Electric Ballerina*

The Poem

"Dance Script with Electric Ballerina," at eighty-four lines, is one of Alice Fulton's longer poems; it is an important one because it provides insight into Fulton's artistic objectives. Written in four stanzas of varying length, the free-verse poem presents the persona of a ballerina dancing and discussing her theory of dance. At times the ballerina seems to be addressing the ballet's audience, but at other times she seems to be speaking to a sympathetic co-conspirator, perhaps a fellow ballerina.

The poem begins with the ballerina "limbering up" before going on stage while explaining that she will not be performing the familiar, conventional ballet the audience might be anticipating; she warns, "If you expected sleeping/ beauty sprouting from a rococo/ doughnut of tulle, a figurine/ fit to top a music box, you might want/ your money back." As opposed to these visions of stylized female beauty, Fulton's ballerina wants to be "electric," with a "getup/ functional as light:/ feet bright and precise as eggbeaters,/ fingers quick as switch-/ blades and a miner's lamp for my tiara." In this way, the "electric ballerina" suggests the goals behind her rather unorthodox "dance script"—not grace, beauty, and lightness but power, daring, and illumination.

Fulton's ballerina is aware that her unusual aesthetic choices might not be well received. She notes that although ballet audiences like to discuss "brio" (vigor) and "ballon" (the lightness of a jump that seems to make the ballerina float in the air longer than possible), "spectators prefer/ gestures that don't endanger/ body and soul." In contrast, Fulton's ballerina seems to value what endangers, because the spectators' fear or surprise might shock them from passivity and cause them to reevaluate beauty. An excerpt from Fulton's journal, published in *The Poet's Notebook* (1995), sheds some light on this poem. Fulton discusses the Scottish dancer/choreographer Michael Clark. Clark has his dancers "gasp for breath above the music" in order to make an audience "aware of the effort." Clark sees "the hint of disequilibrium as a gain," and so does Fulton's ballerina, who is not interested in presenting a smooth, seamless ballet. Instead, she wants her "leaps angular and brief" to have the same disjointed and startling quality that Clark's choreography has.

As the poem progresses, the ballerina begins dancing. Predictably, the dance critics who watch the ballet do not understand what she is striving to accomplish. The second stanza ends with an italicized section which presents the criticisms that they will, presumably, publish in their reviews. The critics mistake her deliberate attempt to present the "strain" which is "a reminder/ of the pain that leads to grace" as ineptitude. They fault the ballerina for being "*ragged barbaric hysterical*" and say that she lacks "*authority fluency restraint*," among other things.

As the ballerina nears the end of her dance, she "can sense the movement/ notators' strobe vision/ picking the bones of flux into/ positions." Like a strobe light, the critics have only flashes of illumination, and their dependence on naming recognized positions shows how they are trapped by the conventions of time and space, absolutes which she battles to overcome as she dances. Instead of passively watching and labeling, the ballerina wants them to enjoy the gaps, to "see the gulf/ between gestures as a chance/ to find clairvoyance." Ultimately, however, the critics are too limited by their own conventions to understand her particular brand of iconoclasm. The ballerina wishes for a metaphor or model with which she could make the critics understand her; she seems to feel that such an understanding may one day be possible, but "till then" she is at a "stand-/ still" as she strikes her final position. She notes that "my chest heaves,/ joints shift, eyes dart—" rather defiantly reminding the reader that even then, despite appearances, she is still dancing.

Forms and Devices

In this poem Fulton does not heavily rely on some of the traditional poetic devices available to a poet, such as rhyme and meter, but other devices she uses with great skill. Fulton's choice of line breaks makes an interesting study, for example. On the page, "Dance Script with Electric Ballerina" looks somewhat ragged because the lines are of varying lengths and are not cordoned off into even-length stanzas. Here form reflects theme, because the ballerina is arguing in favor of ragged edges and "disequilibrium." In addition, Fulton uses her line breaks to create a rhythm that can pull the rug out from under the reader's feet. After strongly end-stopped lines, she might break a hyphenated word in half; this sudden enjambment leads to a halting music. Often Fulton, like the poet Marianne Moore before her, uses line breaks to underscore wit or puns. When Fulton cautions that the audience might want a refund if they expected "sleeping/ beauty," her line break reveals what audiences are really after when they choose such sugary, harmless concoctions—a type of reassuring stupor in which no one is changed because no one is challenged.

Another way that the poem seeks to disrupt equilibrium is by presenting sudden and shifting metaphors and rapidly juxtaposed images. The dancer asks, "You've seen kids on Independence Day, waving/ sparklers to sketch their initials on the night?" She continues, "Just so, I'd like to leave a residue/ of slash and glide, a trace-/ form on the riled air." The ballerina's language does "slash and glide" through the poem, shifting from one metaphor to another; moreover, the metaphors are all located in different worlds. Fulton follows her "strobe" metaphor with one from the world of geography, "fissures," followed by a "footage" metaphor from the film industry, in turn followed by mention of an "electrocardiograph," from the world of medicine. In this way the poet reproduces for the readers the unsettling effects of the ballet, hoping that the readers now have enough insight into her methods to rise above the critics' shortsightedness. Instead of requiring familiar "positions," the readers should enjoy the "flux" and leap the gulfs with the ballerina. As Fulton noted in an interview (*TriQuarterly*, 1995), gaps and gulfs are important to her concept of poetry; she questions "continuity and unity. . . . My notion of poetry itself suggests quick cuts—those moves that used to be called poetic leaps. They allow the readers to fill in the gaps and participate by recreating the poem's meaning in their own minds." Fulton, in relying on what is not on the page as well as what is written there, is influenced by Emily Dickinson; Fulton's admiration for Dickinson continues to deepen in her books that come after *Dance Script with Electric Ballerina*, such as *Sensual Math* (1995).

Themes and Meanings

On one level, "Dance Script with Electric Ballerina" is very clearly about a ballerina discussing her moves and delineating her beliefs about the correct aim for dance. Another layer of meaning is present, however: Fulton is presenting her own poetic credo; she hopes to do on the page what her ballerina does in performance.

Many images and metaphors in the poem can be read as pertaining to both dance and poetry. Early in the poem the dancer describes her "script" by saying, "I've dispensed with some conventions// I'm out to disprove the limited orbit of fingers." While one might first interpret this line to mean that the dancer wants to use her material—parts of her body, such as her hands—in new ways, Fulton also tries use her material to push beyond the "limited orbit of fingers"—the expected output from a writer's hand. Within the italicized section of critics' comments, many statements could have come from literary, not dance, reviewers. For example, the only positive critic in the section states, *"I'm mildly impressed/ by her good line,"* a comment which could easily refer to a poet.

In addition to using metaphors that can be read in two ways, Fulton uses metaphors that directly apply to writing. The ballerina wants to be like sparkler-waving children who "sketch their initials on the night." She talks of the "air patterns/ where I distill the scribbling moves" and wishes that her dance moves left a physical trace in the air that could be read like a language. She dreams of a perfect understanding when the critics overcome their lack of imagination but knows that until such communication can take place, she is only "signing space," and her signature so far is unintelligible to the critics.

If Fulton had tried to write a poem that only discussed her poetic credo, the poem might have failed because of self-consciousness. By creating her ballerina, Fulton wisely does two things at once: She presents a character who provides insight into the world of dance, and she articulates her unconventional views of what a poem should do. "Dance Script with Electric Ballerina" might serve as an introduction to the rest of Fulton's work. After seeing the dance critics fail because of their faulty expectations, her readers have enough information to judge her work more fairly. They should not expect a sugar-coated, soothing kind of poetry for a passive reader but a poetry that needs a fellow dancer to complete the electrical current she has begun.

Beth Ann Fennelly

DANNY DEEVER

Author: Rudyard Kipling (1865-1936)
Type of poem: Narrative
First published: 1890, in *Departmental Ditties, Barrack-Room Ballads, and Other Verses*, 1907

The Poem

"Danny Deever" is a description of a military execution: the hanging of a British soldier in India for the murder of another soldier in his own regiment. In a combination of responsorial verse reminiscent of a ballad or a hymn, and the observations of a third party, the structure of the four-stanza poem uses the common speech and points of view of representative members of the nineteenth century British army to express one of the most harsh demands of military life.

Danny Deever is the guilty soldier, but the reader learns of this only after an introductory question-and-answer half-stanza. The opening question, "What are the bugles blowin' for?" is asked by Files-on-Parade, a single voice that represents all the soldiers being "turned out" (called to formation); they are the files of "rank and file." Files asks his questions of the Colour-Sergeant, who would have been, in Kipling's time, a noncommissioned officer promoted for distinguished service, a soldier of significantly more experience than his juniors. The elder's face is white, and he is afraid of what he must watch. Why, when he has seen more of war than his subordinates? The observer makes the moment clear: Danny is to be hanged. The regiment is formed ("in 'ollow square"), and the prisoner is ritualistically stripped of the signs of his profession: the buttons on his uniform and the insignia of his rank.

Files then asks for explanations of his observance of behaviors that are not soldierly. In a formal military ceremony, some men are falling out of ranks breathing hard when the rapt stillness of attention is required. The Colour-Sergeant appears to make excuses—the sun, or the cold, has caused these things—but these accountings are as curt as the replies in the first stanza. They are the answers of a man with his own thoughts. The observer notes that Danny is paraded in front of his comrades and walked by his own coffin, and then he clearly indicates that Deever is "a sneakin', shootin' hound-."

Files then exclaims, with perhaps a tone of incredulity, that he has shared, as all soldiers do, the closeness and friendship of barracks life with the doomed man. Danny's cot was close to his, and Danny treated him to a drink many times. The observer sternly states that such things may be true, but those are not the soldiers' concerns now. Danny committed the unspeakable act of killing a comrade in his sleep, so the members of the regiment must face him even as they attend to his execution.

Finally, Files asks about indications that Danny's passing is one of darkness and struggle, and the Colour-Sergeant essentially concurs, although he does not explain why. From the view of the observer, the reader see the regiment march away. The observer gets the last word: The younger soldiers are severely shaken, "an' they'll want their beer to-day."

Forms and Devices

Rudyard Kipling, born in India, raised during the height of the British Empire, the first English writer to win the Nobel Prize, was immensely popular, and he served for some time as a "national voice." He told stories to common countrymen of the travails and hardships of soldiers and sailors far away from home, and he used the accented speech of the lower classes to tell them. "Danny Deever" combines that colloquial context with a question-and-answer conversation that brings with it the tradition of old English ballads. The rhythm, particularly the alliteration of the opening line and the repetition of the response, is militaristic and suggests a march from the outset.

The construction of the first half of each stanza is revealing. In the first, the Colour-Sergeant's repetitious response to Files's questions are dismissive; Files mocks him with his next question, and the Colour-Sergeant is suddenly serious and revealing. In the second stanza, the Colour-Sergeant is again brusque and so quick to answer Files's pestering questions that only the reader sees the contradictions in his answers. After all, the weather cannot be both hot and cold, so there must be another explanation for the soldiers' behavior.

By the third stanza, Files is disturbed and confused at the circumstances in which he finds himself, and he probably does not understand the Colour-Sergeant's answers. The latter expresses Files's observations as one would describe a soldier in the field, away from post ("sleepin' out an' far") and away from his mates, "drinkin' beer alone." The Colour-Sergeant is saddened at these circumstances, while Files is unnerved. In the last stanza, the rhythm of each of the two speakers is the same, as the experienced and the neophyte soldier watch the same event, Danny's death, at the same time.

The observer is situated in an interesting, and interested, fashion. He can overhear the conversation between Files and the Colour-Sergeant. His comments illuminate the give-and-take of the two speakers and slowly reveal the context in which the two soldiers discuss what is happening. He knows what is about to happen before Files does. He knows that Danny is the worst kind of criminal. He essentially tells Files and the Colour-Sergeant, at the end of the third stanza, that they must both "look 'im in the face" and admit to the horrible fact that they must participate in killing one of their own for killing one of their own.

Finally, in the fourth stanza, the reader sees that the observer is himself a soldier: "The regiment's in column, and they're marching us away." "Us" is the important word. He has overheard the conversation because he is in the ranks. In addition, his position allows him to note with certainty, but without condescension, and even with sympathy, that the forty-four "young recruits are shakin', an' they'll want their beer to-day." He is more experienced than either of the other men, and his position is intellectual. He has seen these things before, more often than has the Colour-Sergeant, and he knows what this ceremony means.

Themes and Meanings

"Danny Deever" captures the irony, comradeship, and demands of military life in a single ceremony. Those who serve in the military are expected to endure hardship, face death, obey orders, and do all these things willingly even though they may not have the experience to understand what is being asked of them.

Danny is the focus of the poem, but the stories Kipling tells are of the three other characters. In civilian society, the state carries out the trials, sentencing, and punishment of those who do wrong. In the military, all those functions are performed by the same organization of which the accused is a member. In Kipling's time, life in a regiment in India was arduous, but for many soldiers the army was the closest thing to a family they had ever known. The unit was hierarchical, to be sure, even castelike, but the business of fighting and protecting the empire was for many an adventure. Men relied upon one another, and on their shared experience, to enjoy the few things they could and to survive in battle.

Imagine then, the shock of finding a murderer in the midst of the regiment—and then realizing the irony that those who have put others to death must now do the same thing to a soldier who was once a friend. Hanging Danny is just as much a requirement, a mission, as fighting in battle, and it must be carried out in the same professional manner. From the inexperience, fear, and insecurity of Files, to the experienced and wiser Colour-Sergeant, to the observer, the chain of thematic effect is built. The conversationalists are the foundation, but the house of the army is built by those who know what the observer knows.

He knows that the ceremony begins with the Dead March, that all who commit crimes of the magnitude of murder will, eventually, see their own coffin. Yet he also knows that the man who made himself "nine 'undred of 'is county an' the Regiment's disgrace" must still somehow be considered a comrade and that the others must appreciate his fight for life and recognize the passing of his soul. Knowing all that, the observer thinks only that the soldiers will want beer to calm them, not sympathy or an explanation of the ways of the world and the army. They must learn those things for themselves. The final irony is certainly that of Files-on-Parade, for he, the youngest, the one who is too young to have seen battle, sees his first death not on the field but in his own camp.

David P. Smith

DARK HARBOR

Author: Mark Strand (1934-
Type of poem: Poetic sequence
First published: 1993

The Poem

Dark Harbor is a book-length poem in unrhymed verse, divided into forty-five sections that are identified sequentially by roman numerals. There is also an introduction in verse entitled "Proem." Each section, including "Proem," is written in tercets, but six of the sections end with stanzas of only one or two lines.

The title resonates with echoes of some of Strand's earlier books: *Sleeping with One Eye Open*, his first book of poems; *Reasons for Moving*, probably fueled by his life as the son of a salesman who moved his family too often for them to form long-term relationships with other people; and *Darker*, perhaps the first of Strand's books to convince the critics that his apparent preoccupation with the darker aspects of life was actually a vehicle for explorations of the human ability to find the light hidden in the darkness. Beyond these first three books, all of Strand's books of poetry (and even his children's books) push and pull readers through the dark harbors of the human journey.

Although *Dark Harbor* is not a narrative poem in the classic sense of a work that has a definable beginning, middle, and end, it has a combined sense of form and unity that gives it the sort of through-line of thought that one normally expects from a narrative. The narrator of the poem is a poet on a journey, an odyssey that takes him through a return to his places (both physical and spiritual) of origin and eventually brings him to a place of closure.

Each of the forty-five numbered sections is written from the first-person perspective of the narrator, but "Proem" is written from the perspective of an omniscient narrator. This narrator serves as a sort of Greek chorus who introduces the narrator of all that is to follow, the poet/narrator: "'This is my Main Street,' he said as he started off/ That morning, leaving the town to the others." These opening lines set the stage for the poet/narrator to take the reader on a journey. Halfway through "Proem" comes the first hard evidence that the narrator who is being introduced is indeed a poet, almost certainly Strand himself or an image of himself that he wants to project for the reader: "he would move his arms/ And begin to mark, almost as a painter would,/ The passages of greater and lesser worth, the silken/ Tropes and calls to this or that, coarsely conceived."

In section I the narrator describes the place of departure for the journey to come. He is in a dark place lighted by streetlamps, but he is wearing a white suit that outshines the moon. "In the night without end," others await his arrival at "the station" before they begin their journey somewhere beyond those still on Earth. In section II he describes the village or hamlet as a place where the reader has never been, a place where there are no trains or places for planes to land. (One might wonder from what sort of station they departed.) It is somewhere in the West that has considerable wind and snow. It is a place where people are not up on fashion and sleep well at night, an indication that those who dwell here have cleaner consciences than people elsewhere.

In section III the place begins to sound more like a small town. Midway through this section the narrator provides a bit of information that appears to contradict what he had said earlier about the reader having never been to this place: "And you pass by unsure if this coming back is a failure/ Or a sign of success, a sign that the time has come/ To embrace your origins as you would yourself." It is possible to interpret this "you" as the travelers that were waiting for him at the beginning of the journey or as someone to whom the reader has not been introduced. Throughout this poem it is often difficult to discern the identity of the narrator's "you." The final tercet of this section might even suggest that the narrator is referring to himself in the second person: "life looked to be simpler back in the town/ You started from look, there in the kitchen are Mom and Dad,/ He's reading the paper, she's killing a fly." It is possible that there is no single "you" consistent throughout the poem. Each usage could be relative to its particular section, leaving the reader to discern identity from the context.

Overall, the narrator paints a picture of returning home to the small town that he left long ago to live in a large city. Most of the sections are vignettes of the narrator's rediscovery or new evaluation of this small town, his place of origin. However, some of the sections are so abstract that they add little, if anything, to the geography of the poem. They appear more as commentaries on life in general. A few others make such sudden turns into sarcasm that they come across as comic, but the comedy, in perfect keeping with the title and the general mood of the poem, is always dark.

The final section, XLV, rounds out the collection by echoing elements of the first two sections: the cottages, unidentified people grouped together, angels singing, images of life after death. It gives both a feeling of completion and a sense of the cyclical nature of everything. This is the dark harbor of souls.

Forms and Devices

The first easily recognized device the poet uses in *Dark Harbor* is the introductory poem, "Proem." This is not a proem in the sense that some critics now use the term, a portmanteau created by combining the words "prose" and "poem." It is a proem in the classical sense—an introductory passage to a longer work that provides clues to the nature and origin of the work that is to follow.

Ironically, *Dark Harbor* reads very much like a prose poem. The rhythms are dictated more by syntax than by lineation. Strand uses a combination of three physical devices to give the poem a structured, poemlike appearance. First, he breaks the poem into lines; there are usually between ten and fifteen syllables to each line, but this is by no means a strict rule. Sometimes the lines end on weak or unstressed words, but the breaks usually wrap logically into the next line. Second, he begins each line with an uppercase letter. This accomplishes two things: It emphasizes the line breaks, and it adds a touch of formality, a punctuating element that helps define each line as a component that exists both within and outside of syntax. Third, he breaks each section into tercets. This gives a consistent appearance to all forty-five sections of the poem as well as "Proem," and it serves as a framing device, using white space to sometimes enhance, sometimes override the ostensible logic of the syntax. It also adds another element of formality that complements the high level of diction and wide variety of sentence structures employed throughout the poem.

Form is essential in all of Strand's poetry. In his essay "Notes on the Craft of Poetry," published in *Claims for Poetry* (Donald Hall, ed., 1982) Strand writes:

> [A]ll poetry is formal in that it exists within limits, limits that are either inherited by tradition or limits that language itself imposes. . . . [F]orm has to do with the structure or outward appearance of something but it also has to do with its essence. . . . [S]tructure and essence seem to come together, as do the disposition of words and their meanings.

For Strand, poetry is a marriage of form and function, and, for better or worse, without both elements there is no marriage, therefore, no poetry.

The most common and interesting images in *Dark Harbor* are those one sees upon looking up: stars, clouds, the sky, moon, sun, falling snow, even angels. These images do not, as might be expected, serve as counterpoints to the dark images of the earth and earthbound things, implying a good-versus-evil dialogue. Rather, they are symbolic of those elusive qualities that define the human spirit as distinctly different from anything else in nature. The dark is not a place of evil; it is simply a point of departure, a place from which we start our quests and inquiries. The light is what we seek, and Strand is critical of anyone who belittles that. "O you can make fun of the splendors of moonlight,/ But what would the human heart be if it wanted/ Only the dark, wanted nothing on earth/ But the sea's ink or the rock's black shade?"

There are no intentional end rhymes in this poem, but alliterations are not uncommon. Section XXVII makes good use of anaphora, the first six of the seven tercets beginning with the same word, and of alliterations and assonance. Together these tropes add a rich musical quality and an air of nobility to this particular section.

The overall tone of the poem is elegiac, but there are a few sections that provide comic relief, sometimes bordering on zaniness (as in section XIX, the shortest section) and sometimes slipping into a sarcastic mode that adds a different kind of bite to a work that already has a formidable set of teeth. Surrealism is the order of the day. From the very first scene, in which the unnamed group of travelers bands together to begin the journey from darkness, to the final scene, in which there are rumors of dead poets wandering, wishing "to be alive again," everything seems to happen somewhere between dream and reality. Strand's choices of forms and poetic devices give each section of this poem an individual character that allows each to stand on its own. Overall, the same choices give *Dark Harbor* the power of one uniform work that drives all of its component parts in a single direction.

Themes and Meanings

In her 1994 review of *Dark Harbor* for *Antioch Review*, Judith Hall said that the theme of the poem "is the poet's counterlife in art, from his initial departure from the enclosure of family and home, to his journey through a place of darkness and uncertainty, to his final sense of safe harbor within the community of other poets." At least in part, this could have been said about any of Strand's books. Strand has often been criticized for solipsism, an extreme form of concern for self, but these accusations have not deterred him from his search for self nor from his conviction that poetry is his means of discovery.

This is not to say that Strand sees only himself; nothing could be further from the truth. He, like all poets, is constantly examining, evaluating, and speculating about life. By unrelentingly seeking a clearer picture of himself within life and creating poems as windows through which to view his explorations, he makes it possible for those of us who lack his particular vision to become part of his quest.

More than any of his previous books, *Dark Harbor* exhibits Strand's concern with the community of poets, both living and dead, that has helped shape him as a poet and that continues to influence his poetry. No artist creates in a vacuum, and no poet seems more aware of this than Strand. He has often mentioned a handful of poets that have greatly influenced his work, and a few poets seem to drop in and out of this group. One who is always there, however, whether Strand is talking about himself or whether a critic is talking about him, is Elizabeth Bishop. Although their styles are very different, both wrote often about the relationships of art to life and life to art. The angels that appear and disappear in *Dark Harbor* are poets that have died, and it is not unreasonable to think that the last angel in the book, "one of the good ones, about to sing," is Bishop.

As might well be expected, darkness is one of the major themes of *Dark Harbor*. This darkness is not a Joseph Conrad type of darkness, an impending doom or a void into which one falls and from which one never returns. Strand's darkness creates more an air of nostalgia. It is a world of dreams in which the darkness is usually earthbound with at least some touch of heaven within reach. Sometimes, however, Strand's heaven is within the darkness or, as in section VIII, darkness, death, and heaven are inseparably bound to one another:

> . . . Oh my partner, my beautiful death,
> My black paradise, my fusty intoxicant,
> My symbolist muse, give me your breast
> Or your hand or your tongue that sleeps all day
> Behind its wall of reddish gums.
> Lay yourself down on the restaurant floor
> And recite all that's been kept from my happiness.
> Tell me I have not lived in vain, that the stars
> Will not die, that things will stay as they are,
> That what I have seen will last, that I was not born
> Into change, that what I have said has not been said for me.

This passage expresses one of the greatest fears of poets and other artists, the fear that their ideas and creations are either ephemeral or simply add nothing new. It also expresses a fear held by many people, artists and nonartists, that the world will change so much that nothing currently considered sacred will endure.

In several places in this poem "dark" refers to the future—not in a negative sense, but in the sense that we are not privy to what it holds. In these places Strand leads readers to believe that the dark that is the human inability to see the future is also the playground of imagination. We prefer to stare "Into the dark and imagine a fullness in which/ We are the stars, matching the emptiness/ Of the beginning, giving birth to ourselves/ Again and again." This is an old theme, dating back to Ecclesiastes and probably before. Everything is cyclical. We have been here before; we will be here again.

Edmund August

THE DARKLING THRUSH

Author: Thomas Hardy (1840-1928)
Type of poem: Lyric
First published: 1901, in *Poems of the Past and Present*

The Poem

"The Darkling Thrush" is a thirty-two-line lyric poem in four stanzas of eight lines each. The first two stanzas provide the setting of the poem. Hardy's poetic persona is standing at the edge of a "coppice," a thicket of bushes or small trees. He surveys a desolate scene at the end of a winter day. He is alone in that "haunted night"; all the rest of humankind "had sought their household fires." The second stanza continues the description and provides two important pieces of information. One concerns the time when the poem was written, December of 1900, which is always included in the printing of the poem. The words "the Century's corpse" and "the ancient pulse of germ and birth" refer to the turn of the century. The other important information is about the poet's state of mind. He is deeply depressed, stating that the dismal scene is "fervorless as I."

These first two stanzas comprise line after line of lyrical description. Details pertaining to death (the bine-stems "like strings from broken lyres," the "crypt," the "death-lament," the "ancient pulse" that is "shrunken hard and dry") add up to a depressing total. The scene of icy, clear death images and the harsh, austere feeling are firmly set in the reader's mind.

Now that the reader's mood has been captured by the frosty, deathly winter scene, surrounded by images of the land's and the century's death, the third stanza opens with a sudden, sharp contrast. A song bursts forth, a "full-hearted evensong/ Of joy illimited." Then another contrast unfolds as the source of the song is revealed: "an aged thrush, frail, gaunt and small." A weak, bedraggled, drab bird somehow has managed to overcome the cold, gloom, and death of winter and sing with its whole heart.

Does the bird sing because it knows some greater joy of which the poet is unaware? In the fourth stanza the poet reveals his agnostic lack of faith. There is "So little cause for carolings," he asserts. The bird's "ecstatic sound" is not founded in reason or faith. For a moment perhaps there is a note of hope, but the poet reveals his feelings in his verb tense. He "could think" there was some hope for the frosty world, but he cannot sustain his belief. In the end, the persona of the poet has no hope; he only observes with a touch of irony that the thrush seems to have hope.

The entire poem sustains an image of desolation. Even the song of "joy illimited" does not relieve the poet's depression. There is no transformation from the mood of death into human optimism, so the contrast of the thrush's song serves to heighten the poet's despair. The corpse of the old century never gives way to the birth of the new.

Forms and Devices

Thomas Hardy is a transitional poet, a bridge between the nineteenth and the twentieth centuries, and between Romantic Victorian and modern thought. "The Darkling Thrush" is particularly apt as a transitional poem, since it was written on and for the turn of the century. There is a strong contrast between form and meaning in the poem, just as there is a contrast between the bleak despair of the scene and the unreasonable joy of the thrush's song.

The form of the poem is traditional, of the nineteenth century, though the meaning is modern, of the twentieth. Hardy was sixty years old in 1900 and was technically competent in the meter and rhyme schemes that were already rooted in the past. The meter never varies from the da-dum da-dum of the basic English iambic tetrameter; the rhyme scheme is a perfect *ababcdcd*. While Hardy is sometimes criticized for lack of originality in this form, the effect of this controlled meter and rhyme scheme is remarkable in a poem about modern despair. The poet cannot control the chaos and decay around him, but he can control the form of the poem. The formal strictness of the verse is a bulwark against disorder.

At times the poet's language seems to be dictated by the unvarying ballad-like form of the poem even more than by his search for meaning. Hardy coins "nonce words," words invented for a single occasion, to fit the meter. "Blast-beruffled" is an example of a nonce word that is effective in description and musicality of language. On the other hand, the nonce word "outleant," coined to rhyme with "death-lament," is difficult to visualize and breaks the flow of the rhythm as the reader puzzles about the meaning.

Again, the meter of the poem demands that the poet write "strings from broken lyres" (line 6) instead of the more apt death image of "broken strings of lyres." Yet, through his mastery of his form, Hardy manages a broader emotional tone and complexity of imagination and irony than is normally found within a strict folk ballad or hymn meter.

The controlled, traditional form of "The Darkling Thrush" addresses Hardy's response to the lack of control he feels in the historical context of the event he is describing. The entire poem is a metaphor for the turn of the century. The death and desolation of the first two stanzas parallel the dying of the old century. The frost and winter and haunted night of the first stanza are the setting for the crypt in which the "Century's corpse" lies lamented by the wind. Hardy reveals his modern temperament when he breaks with the traditional rhythm of death and rebirth. This old century is not about to give way to new, vigorous life. "The ancient pulse of germ and birth/ Was shrunken hard and dry." The poet's persona is not the only depressed spirit; rather, "every spirit upon earth" is "fervorless as I."

Hardy departs from the traditional again in the effect of the bird's song. In the expected pattern of folklore or mythology, the joyful song of the thrush should herald the hope for the future that the new century must represent. In Hardy's metaphor, however, the thrush is aged, not a symbol of rebirth at all but a caroler without cause. His thrush is not singing a morning song of rejuvenation, but an evensong, a good-night air. Even in the new century, hope is fleeting. The metaphor seems at first to promise rebirth, but the poet has lost faith. He cannot believe.

Themes and Meanings

The primary theme of "The Darkling Thrush" is the despair of the modern temperament. Hardy describes in lyrical, descriptive detail the dying of the old world, but he cannot positively replace the dying with the new. Something is over, all is changed, civilization has decayed, and he does not know what will replace it. In "The Darkling Thrush," Hardy poses one of the central questions of the modern age and reveals himself as a significant voice of the early twentieth century.

Hardy the modern poet is an isolated man. He has lost his connection with those nineteenth century people who are inside by their household fires. They are connected with one another, and with the natural cycle of death and rebirth, but Hardy, the twentieth century persona, is alone in the cold, surrounded by images of death. He may yearn for that simpler, truer world, and he may seek to recapture something that is lost by using the form of folk themes, but that old century is dead, and the outlook for the new century is bleak indeed.

Hardy saw traditional agricultural society decaying, the earth destroyed by industrialization, and in "The Darkling Thrush" he clearly reveals that he cannot believe in a note of hope. He finds "so little cause for carolings" that he cannot picture the new century or describe it for the reader. Hardy is "unaware" of any hope for the future.

With his tale of the "darkling thrush," a thrush of evening rather than morning, Hardy rejects the Romantic themes of the nineteenth century. While the song of the thrush is the force that crystallizes his fervorless spirit, Hardy's thrush is aged, "frail, gaunt and small," not symbolizing new life but belonging to that dying old century. Even after hearing the thrush's "full-hearted evensong/ Of joy illimited," Hardy's depression is lifted only as far as a state of puzzlement. He comes into the new century unable to believe that even the thrush, that representative of nature, can have a reason to hope.

Susan Butterworth

THE DAY ZIMMER LOST RELIGION

Author: Paul Zimmer (1934-
Type of poem: Meditation
First published: 1976, in *The Zimmer Poems*

The Poem

"The Day Zimmer Lost Religion" is composed of three seven-line stanzas of blank verse (unrhymed iambic pentameter). The poem's tone is strongly colloquial as the adult speaker, or persona, recounts the events of a particular day in his childhood when he tested God by missing Mass "on purpose." The phrase "on purpose" focuses the poem on the idea of the test. The child Zimmer assumes that God will punish such behavior immediately, and when no such thing happens, the child concludes that God has evidently recognized that Zimmer is too mature to be frightened by his threats. That day becomes the day named in the title: "The Day Zimmer Lost Religion." Like many poems by Paul Zimmer, the persona of this poem shares the author's name, but it would be a mistake to assume that the two are exactly the same. The Zimmer of this poem, like that of the many other Zimmer poems, is a character created to relate and react to this set of events.

In the first of the stanzas, the persona looks into his past to remember how he expected God to punish him for missing Mass. His fantasies focus on some painful experiences of childhood. He first expects that Christ will show up like a flyweight boxer to pummel him for his failure to attend Mass. The boxing scene is extended as he remembers imagining the devil "roaring" in the stands to cheer his painful humiliation. The second stanza looks back further ("a long cold way") into the speaker's early life to the time when he served as an altar boy, wore a cassock and surplice (a black gown worn under a loose, white, knee-length robe), and assisted the priest during Mass by giving the appropriate Latin responses. In those days he evidently attended a Catholic school; his experience there was permeated by his sense of God's presence so that he imagined the eye of God overlooking all the activities of the school yard, ready to accuse any wrongdoing. The third stanza restates Zimmer's expectations of punishment; this time he imagines Christ as the "playground bully" who might arrive to beat him up for his betrayal of his faith. God's failure to deliver any of Zimmer's imagined punishments seems to confirm for him that God has met his match and is giving up, perhaps because Zimmer is now too old for religion. That, at least, is the young Zimmer's conclusion, although the adult Zimmer who narrates this poem implies something more.

Forms and Devices

The world of this poem is the world of the Catholic schoolboy, and the imagery of the poem grows out of the details of the boy's life in that world. It is a world of grubby little boys who admire boxers and who sometimes do their own share of unofficial fighting in the school yard (particularly if they must defend themselves against the school bully) regardless of what the priests may say to warn them against bad behavior. The boxing and the reference to the "dirty wind that blew/ The soot . . . across the school yard" suggests that it is an urban school.

Boxing establishes the first set of images for the poem as the child Zimmer waits for Christ to "climb down " from the crucifix on which the child usually sees him and to appear as a "wiry flyweight" boxer. Zimmer expects Christ to "club" him in his "blasphemous gut" and his "irreverent teeth" as if they had been sent into the boxing ring together. This imaginary fight even has a spectator: the devil himself. Like a spectator at a boxing match, he sits in reserved seats, roaring with delight at the rebellious Zimmer's punishment. The fighting imagery is extended in the last stanza in which Christ is no longer pictured as a boxer but as the playground bully who will appear in order to "pound" Zimmer until his "irreligious tongue" hangs out.

The language of religion also informs the poem, since the child Zimmer's offense is against God (as well as against his religious instructors who have warned him about the consequences of missing Mass). That is why the poem is furnished with details from the child Zimmer's religious life. The flyweight Jesus will drop him, he says, like a "red hot thurible" (an incense container that is swung from a chain, which an altar boy such as the young Zimmer might carry in a religious procession in church while wearing the cassock and surplice). Another example of the poem's religious diction is the use of "venial" to describe the soot that blows across the school yard. When used to describe sins, venial refers to relatively less important sins, unlike the more serious mortal sins that, the boy's teachers would have told him, could deprive him of God's grace. Like venial sins, the soot smudges everything in this tarnished world. Another component of the poem's diction is its colloquial language. The angry Christ will "wade into [Zimmer's] blasphemous gut," the devil roars until he develops hiccups, and Zimmer uses the slang term "mice" to refer to the bruises on the face of the crucified Christ.

One last image in the poem deserves discussion—the reference to God reigning as a "One-eyed triangle" as he glares down at the playground. That image of God comes from the picture on the great seal of the United States, represented on a one-dollar bill, in which a pyramid is crowned by a huge eye from which light radiates. The child has evidently tied the idea of the pyramid to his teachers' explanation of the concept of the Trinity—God as Father, Son, and Holy Spirit—which is sometimes represented as a triangle. Tellingly, the child sees the image as threatening.

Themes and Meanings

"The Day Zimmer Lost Religion" looks back, half humorously, at a time when the persona decided to test God by missing Mass. His teachers have surely told him that he is obligated to attend Mass, and the fact that he is missing it intentionally may even raise this to the level of a mortal sin, one that is committed with one's full knowledge and volition. The child's teachers may also have warned him against testing God since the desire to control God by forcing Him to take a particular action is also usually considered sinful. Significantly, the child tests God with the expectation that God will immediately punish his wrongdoing, probably in the same very personal way that his teachers might give him corporal punishment. He imagines God first as a boxer and then as a playground bully, the result of his vision of God as the omnipresent threat looming over the playground. In fact, his understanding of God seems confined to a picture of Him as judge. Even his memories of his days as an altar boy seem negative. His role in the service was to "mumble" the Latin responses, and he describes the bell he rang (the bell that marks the holiest point in the Mass, the point when Christ is actually present in the bread and wine) as "obscure."

The poem has an additional level, however, that establishes the irony at its heart. When the threatening God fails to deliver Zimmer's punishment, the child assumes that God feels that he has met his match: "of course He never came, knowing that/ I was grown up and ready for Him now." That final line leads the reader to the poem's point. Instead of the child's assumption that being "ready" for God means that one is ready to win a conflict with him, the reader is invited to see this readiness in another sense: When the child is truly grown up, he will be ready for another understanding of a god who is more interested in love than punishment. An ironic point of view in poetry, as in fiction, often arises from the disparity between what the speaker understands and the deeper understanding that is offered to the reader. That disparity is intrinsic in adults' views of what they understood in childhood. In "The Day Zimmer Lost Religion," it invites the reader to gently laugh with the adult Zimmer, who looks back at his juvenile testing of God and his childish fantasy about the punishments God might inflict on him while hinting at a grown-up understanding of what being ready for God might mean.

Ann D. Garbett

THE DAY'S CHORES: A LIST

Author: Patricia Hampl (1946-
Type of poem: Meditation
First published: 1978, in *Woman Before an Aquarium*, 1978

The Poem

"The Day's Chores: A List" is in twelve numbered sections. In section 1 (one stanza of eight lines), the speaker sleepily encounters a cup of tea, noting the cup's color and contemplating its ingredients. She opens one eye at a time, perhaps reluctant to come fully awake. Section 2 identifies the first actual chore and issues the first command: Water the plants. The plants are seen as a substitute for a pet; they will at least respond ("purr with pleasure") to being tended. Section 3, the briefest section with only two lines, issues the second command: Observe the sun. This will be remembered in the final stanza, where it will have become a metaphor for living fully awake.

Section 4 expresses the importance of having work to do. Although work is seen as a stand-in for something more dramatic or romantic ("The back of my dreams has been broken"), the speaker announces that since she now understands the importance of her work, it is like a lover to her. Section 5 includes more advice about being awake and attentive, in this case just sitting and listening to the chair creaking and to the person who sat in it before her. This is clearly a spiritual cue to be open to all manner of awareness: Someone who was much older, spoke another language, and was not even present can still offer spiritual company. Section 6 speaks of listening to people now present or to other writers, as long as these writers are truthful about their inner selves.

Section 7, the longest so far with twenty lines, finds the speaker of the poem riding the city bus, "once in daylight/ and again at night." There, she is confided in by an old woman, and again she listens attentively. This section stresses the need for getting out, mingling, and connecting with others. In section 8, she goes to the grocery store and attends to the quality of the food she eats and the nutrients her body needs. She pretends each item is written on one of her fingertips, again stressing the conscious physical involvement in life that she demands of herself. Section 9 involves house-work—cleaning, laundering, responding to the mail, all before dark. In this section and in section 8, there are new mentions of the world of sleep and shadow and a sense that the speaker is aware of the dangers of not keeping her eyes wide open to life.

In section 10, the speaker yields to temptation and allows herself a brief nap, justifying it as a way to have a "second morning" or new energy for the balance of the day. Section 11 lets the day begin to die—a late dinner with someone she loves, candlelight, taking inventory in a diary. The speaker celebrates a sense of having met the day's demands and takes pride in the thought that the list of chores is not "tattered" and has no "crossed-off" items; she has attended to the chores single-mindedly and efficiently, leaving virtually nothing undone and having adhered to an original plan.

Section 12, the last and longest section (two stanzas and twenty-nine lines) steps back, reconsiders and reaffirms the speaker's definition of what her chores or tasks have encompassed with a "list within the list," and again celebrates her success in having lived the day as fully awake as possible. She has been careful to observe the sun (section 3) as a hero worthy of honor and now has a sense of "his heart." The reader images that her sleep will be both peaceful and deep.

Forms and Devices

The poem has 123 lines and twelve sections that vary in length from two to twenty-nine lines. There is no observable meter or rhyme scheme; pattern and stress are inherent in line length and line break. Stress is sometimes pounded out by several successive spondees: "the night not one star sang out." The twelve stanzas are numbered in a manner similar to some of William Blake's work, and they constitute, very ostensibly, a list to be checked off as the day progresses. Yet not all of them are like items taken from a "to-do" memo pad: Some do not involve an imperative at all and clearly have nothing to do with any work or physical action. Often, an object is merely named, and the implication is that this object deserves attention and contemplation: "A pale blue cup/ with tea in it." Only three give a directive (water plants, shop, keep house); the rest are habits to be cultivated and have to do with being, listening, mingling, seeing, and reflecting.

The first stanza sets up the "list" or sets the precedent for its nature: a simple object, a precise image, and a sharp contrast between night and day:

> A pale blue cup
> with tea in it,
> melted-down flowers
> first thing in the morning
> after one brown eye opens,
> and then the other,
> shining
> like the night they came from.

Sharp as the images are, Hampl requires little in the way of simile and metaphor. Eyes shine "like the night they came from"; she has redefined her life's direction, claiming that "The back of my dreams has been broken"; grocery items are "decisions"; there is a "slump in the afternoon"; waking from a nap is "a second morning"; her diary is either "fat" or "slivered," depending on the rigor of the day's demands; and the day's chores, when completed, make up "a set of filed cards." More important is the painting created by the poem and the delicate colors that wash over and through its lines: pale blue, purple, orange, brown, and white, the colors of a cottage still life.

Themes and Meanings

Though written in 1978, this poem could easily be claimed by the proponents of the "voluntary simplicity" movement of the late 1990's as their creed. The speaker of the poem has learned to see through the busy surface of life down to its rock-bottom essentials, and what she identifies as her life-shaping force is work. The numbered stanzas are not the only similarity between Hampl and William Blake: Hampl's poetry is also comparable to Blake's in its use of imperatives, either direct or implied. One of Blake's imperatives is a perfect gloss for Hampl's theme: "The most sublime act is to set another before you." The speaker in Hampl's poem has learned that her "duty" is her work, and she meets it willingly: "Now that I understand/ who it is, I try not/ to keep a lover waiting." She lives with the conviction that "The first task is always before me." Its identity changes as the day progresses, and she must merely acknowledge its claim on her attention: "I call it/ groceries, laundry,/ poem, paint kitchen table." She keeps inventory: "a precise diary," "a set of filed cards." She claims with pride that "The list is not tattered,/ no crossed-off thoughts." Since she knows what her work is, she has rarely had to revise the list, and it seems to be a new list every morning ("the list is not tattered") by having had its chores carried over to another day.

The sun and "a wizened orange" are important to this assurance. She tosses the orange up, exercising complete control, holds it in her hand, and says she thereby has "a sense of the sun,/ his heart" as though she has sucked this day's orange dry, every chore, every piece of wakeful living noted and accomplished.

Her list contains both private and public chores; it allows her to remain a whole, integrated person. Evidently, her chores occasionally feel like mere chores to her. She is slow in waking and longs for the short nap, maybe even "the reentry of shadows," but she remains proudly committed to her covenant with life: "the sun has been observed/ personally by me today." Her index cards have no index; she attends to the day's demands as they present themselves to her, not bound by any proscribed idea of order. Like the orange, the chores have been "perfectly held/ wedge by wedge."

Carla Graham

DEAD SOLDIERS

Author: James Fenton (1949-
Type of poem: Narrative
First published: 1981; collected in *The Memory of War: Poems, 1968-1982*, 1982

The Poem

"Dead Soldiers" is James Fenton's narrative of his memory of a luncheon engagement in 1973 on the edge of a jungle battlefield with a member of the Cambodian royal family—Prince Norodom Chantaraingsey—during that country's long-running civil war. The poem's ten stanzas contain varying numbers of lines of free verse that are deliberately conversational, straightforward, and nonpoetic in the traditional sense. This is poetry as news report, a deceptively simple account that gains power from the total impact of the poem rather than from the individual lines or words.

In the first five stanzas, the poem simply recounts the events of the lunch: It was hot and the poet was "glad of [his] white suit for the first time that day." The meal was an elaborate one: Dishes of frogs' legs, pregnant turtles and their eggs, marsh irises in fish sauce, and banana salad were served on the "dazzling tablecloth" and were accompanied by crates of brandy and soda, which were brought in by bicycles. During the lunch, armored personnel carriers (APCs—military vehicles similar to tanks) were spread out along the roadside to fire into the jungle at the unseen and perhaps absent enemy. Despite the elaborate menu, the meal was largely a liquid one during which many bottles of Napoleon brandy were steadily consumed. These empty bottles, known in slang as "dead soldiers," give the poem its title. While drinking and dining, the poet talked with the prince. Now, years later, the poet wishes instead he had spoken with the prince's drunken aide, a man who was the brother of Saloth Sar, better known as Pol Pot, leader of the violently revolutionary Khmer Rouge faction against whom the prince was fighting.

In the second five stanzas of the poem, the poet recalls that he did speak later with the prince's aide, who was nicknamed "the Jockey Cap," and that he was convinced that when the ruling elite was ousted from power, both the prince and the Jockey Cap would end up in comfortable exile in the south of France far from any war. In that setting, the only conflicts they would face would be "cafe warfare," and, if they had to be "reduced in circumstances" (a tellingly ironic phrase), they would continue to enjoy the good life that they had managed to import even into the midst of jungle fighting. Now, however, the poet realizes he was wrong because the conflict was a family quarrel as much as a revolution or a civil war: The prince was fighting his nephew Prince Norodom Sihanouk while the Jockey Cap was pitted against his brother Pol Pot. In such a struggle, the conflict is so vicious that the combatants are less concerned about victory for themselves than in simply keeping their relatives from tasting even the faintest fruits of victory. The poem concludes with the observations that while the two princes and Pol Pot are still fighting, the Jockey Cap probably has not "survived his good/ connections."

Forms and Devices

In form and presentation, "Dead Soldiers" is often closer to a prose news story than a traditional poem. Fenton has chosen to use irregular free verse without rhyme or other familiar devices, most likely because these obvious devices might come between his story and the reader. The purpose seems clear: to present the incidents of the poem and their meaning without any interpretation (except that of irony). The major poetic devices Fenton employs in "Dead Soldiers" are deceptively straightforward narrative coupled with a devastatingly dry use of irony. The narrative allows him to load the poem with a number of details that, innocent enough in themselves, coalesce to present the image of a murderous civil war waged with the incongruous juxtaposition of brutal savagery and elaborate luxury. The irony permits Fenton to comment upon people and events without overtly taking a moral position, a most useful device when writing about a situation so stained with confusion and ambiguity. Perhaps only deadpan narrative such as that employed in "Dead Soldiers" could successfully present the surreal scene of the poem: an elaborate luncheon, held on the edge of a jungle battlefield, complete with ice, brandy, soda, and almost decadent dishes. While the diners ate frogs' legs and the eggs of pregnant turtles ("boiled in the carapace"), troops and military vehicles advanced around them, firing into the sugar palms.

The narrative of the poem dissolves into irony. The site was not a true battlefield at all. The APCs fired into the jungle but "met no resistance." This supposedly military event was actually nothing but a drunken picnic, and the only "dead soldiers" it brought were the empty bottles of Napoleon brandy that piled up at the feet of the diners. Fenton inserts another sharp and typically understated irony when he notes that "On every bottle, Napoleon Bonaparte/ Pleaded for the authenticity of the spirit." On the surface, the narrative is blandly truthful: The image of the French emperor without validates the spirit within; in other words, a picture of Napoleon on the label means there is indeed brandy ("spirits" in the literal but also metaphorical sense) inside the bottle. Fenton's underlying meaning is much more corrosive: Napoleon, perhaps the most famous military genius of all time, was summoned up to validate this futile alcoholic exercise in the tropics as a real battle, something to equal the epic events of Napoleon's greatest victories and defeats at Austerlitz and Waterloo respectively. Few comparisons could be more ironic or more devastating.

This devastating irony is underscored by the poem's next shift, which is a forecast of the prince and the Jockey Cap in the future, living in France "after the game was up," as if the civil war in Cambodia, perhaps all Indochina, was only a contest from which the lucky few could escape into comfortable exile. That setting replicates, in ironic reversal, the scene of the poem. In the future, the elegant life of dining and drinking will indeed be the only real thing; actual battle will be reduced to nothing but "cafe warfare" and matchboxes will easily substitute for APCs—perhaps because back in Cambodia, real APCs were as useless as matchboxes. In a sense, the phony yet deadly war that the prince played with real lives in Cambodia is reduced to its essence of make-believe: Nothing is real now, and nothing will be real then, except for the death and suffering of the "dead soldiers" (not the bottles, but human beings) who are invoked but never mentioned throughout the poem.

In "Dead Soldiers," Fenton switches constantly, almost casually, between these two levels of pretense and reality. On one hand, there is the battlefield that is actually the setting for an alcoholic revelry, but on the other hand, somewhere in the jungle, men and women are really suffering and dying. In one sense, there are figures who posture as leaders of countries and revolutions, but, in another sense, they are actually locked in an intense family conflict that involves only themselves, no matter how many thousands it kills, maims, and destroys. These contradictions are made stronger by the poem's indirect, matter-of-fact presentation of them.

Themes and Meanings

During his career, Fenton was a freelance reporter in Indochina, and a number of his poems deal with the violent revolutionary and civil wars in that region that he witnessed firsthand. The central theme of "Dead Soldiers" focuses on two primary aspects of those conflicts: first, the manner in which the brutality of war can coexist with a superficial "cultured" life; and second, the tendency for interfamily conflicts to be the most vicious and unforgiving of all. The first theme is announced boldly in the second line of the poem when Fenton notes that the prince had "Invited [him] to lunch on the battlefield," an invitation that would make sense perhaps only in such a surreal atmosphere as that of the Cambodian civil war. Yet the invitation is consistent with the situation because, as the poem notes with characteristic irony, "They lived well, the mad Norodoms, they had style." While this luncheon was unfolding, troops and armored personnel carriers were pushing into the jungle, seeking rebel soldiers to fight and kill, but none were there. However, just because there were no casualties on this particular battlefield does not mean there were none elsewhere or that the war was without victims. Those casualties and that violence were real and the luxurious lunch only underscored their true horror. The second theme, that of internecine family conflict, is more casually introduced and embroidered upon. In the fifth stanza, the poem casually notes that the prince's drunken aide, the Jockey Cap, was Saloth Sar's brother and reveals, a few lines later, that "Saloth Sar, for instance,/ Was Pol Pot's real name." In such a casual fashion is the identity of one of the twentieth century's most infamous mass murderers uncovered and linked to this seemingly minor incident in a distant jungle.

"Dead Soldiers" is a deceptively simple poem, a story that seems to have no meaning beyond the events it relates. However, once its narrative is opened to reveal its ironies and deeper references, it is clear that Fenton is writing a modern variant of Joseph Conrad's *Heart of Darkness* (1902), where the slim veneer of "civilization" is all too ready to crack, and the dead soldiers of his title are not only so many empty bottles but also too many fallen bodies.

Michael Witkoski

DEAR AUNT CHOFI

Author: Daisy Zamora (1950-

Type of poem: Epistle/letter in verse

First published: 1988, as "Querida tía Chofi," in *En limpio se escribe la vida*, 1988; English translation collected in *Clean Slate*, 1993

The Poem

"Dear Aunt Chofi" is a long poem in free verse with thirteen stanzas containing more than ninety-five lines in the English version. The title clearly suggests a letter from a niece to her aunt and serves to underscore the monologic nature of the poem, which is a one-sided conversation between the niece and her deceased Aunt Sofía. The narrator, "I," addresses herself to "you," the aunt, thus making the reader an outside observer, an eavesdropper on a conversation in print. Chofi is a fond nickname for Sofía, which means "wisdom." As she eulogizes her aunt, the narrator reviews the aunt's life.

The first stanza takes Aunt Chofi from birth to widowhood. She was "A rebel from birth" who insisted on marrying the man she loved despite her family's disapproval. The family's judgment was better than Sofía's, but that "purgatory" chapter of her life ended when her husband broke his neck in a drunken fall. "And I listened to you tell it," says the narrator, who heard Aunt Chofi's stories while witnessing her activities, described in the second stanza, as a baker, a creator of popular and religious images for ritualistic consumption at weddings and baptisms.

The third and fourth stanzas reveal that Chofi was an artist who smoked incessantly and painted vigorously, ignoring, or perhaps requiring, the chaos around her. As she painted, she was "Always talking, conversing" while her room became an ashtray for innumerable cigarette butts.

In the fifth, sixth, and seventh stanzas, the reader learns that Chofi was a sort of *curandera*, or folk healer, who served as "midwife, nurse" and who "laid out corpses, attended drunks,/ defended all lost causes// . . . even fought with the Guard/ and ended up exiled in Mexico." "The Guard" refers to the National Guard of Nicaragua, an American-trained army that supported the Somoza family dictatorship of thirty years that led to the Sandinista revolution in the late 1970's.

The eighth and ninth stanzas portray an older Aunt Chofi with "graying hair." A mother herself, Aunt Chofi "slaved" so her daughter could study in Mexico and the United States, but the daughter distanced herself ever further from her mother. Indeed, Aunt Chofi dies without her only daughter present. Though the daughter received the news of her mother's death in distant Buenos Aires, Argentina, the niece was with her aunt, as the tenth stanza indicates: "The morning before your death/ you were the same as ever,/ vociferous and loud-mouthed/ only complaining of great pain."

The last three stanzas bring Aunt Chofi full circle, from her birth as a rebel to her posthumous condition, where she will "answer only to bones," not to parents, husbands, daughters, or societal expectations. Aunt Chofi believed she had had many lives, many incarnations: in one "a little girl who died/ at birth, in another an adventurous male." The poet implies that "Dear Aunt Chofi" is another reincarnation of her beloved Sofía: "Now that you no longer exist, exist no longer/ perhaps you recognize yourself/ in this mirror." If the eyes are the mirror of the soul, this poem is surely the mirror of a life as well as a celebration of it.

Forms and Devices

The most obvious and most important device in this poem is the form itself. As the title indicates, the poem is a letter to Aunt Chofi. Unlike most letters, however, this one anticipates no reply, for it asks no questions, and it engages in no dialogue. The poet mentions herself only twice, and then only as Chofi's audience, demonstrating the importance of storytelling and the oral tradition: "I listened to you tell it" and "You, who told me about your perils." The remainder of the poem is addressed directly to Aunt Chofi, using the familiar *tú* form in the Spanish to indicate the intimacy of the relationship between the niece and her aunt. The poem recounts the aunt's life in a past tense that suggests repeated or ongoing activity rather than completed, finalized activity. Unfortunately, the use of the imperfect in Spanish, like the use of the *tú* form, is difficult to capture in translation to English.

The poem depends primarily on the list technique to build an image of Aunt Chofi by accretion of detail and to suggest the rich chaos that was her life: "Your habitat filled with brushes,/ oil paints, plaster molds, easels,/ canvases, canvas stretchers, statues of saints." The poet uses several metaphors as well. Aunt Chofi was an "Admirable Amazon in [her] fantastic feats." She was a "Witch doctor" who mixed medicines and potions to cure and prevent disease. Her life with her drunken husband was "a purgatory, a living hell."

Such metaphors create a vivid image of Chofi's personality, but perhaps the most important symbol in the poem is the mirror. Aunt Chofi has told her niece about her "perils in the mirror"—perhaps a reference to aging—and the niece has responded with "this mirror," the poem itself, which is meant to mirror the sheer energy and vivacity of Aunt Chofi's life. As Chofi, the "artisan" of paint brush and cake decorating, rendered her saints and Cinderellas, so too has the poet rendered a likeness of her aunt.

Themes and Meanings

"Dear Aunt Chofi" is about the life of a particular woman, but it is also about the artist as woman and rebel and about a woman's life in Nicaragua during a particular historical period. Doubly an artist (both painter and baker), Chofi's art was in her cakes, which she baked and decorated with such popular images as Snow White and the Seven Dwarfs and Cinderella for such conventional occasions as baptisms, first communions, adolescent coming out parties, and weddings. Yet Chofi was a woman who resisted societal expectations. She married against her family's wishes, she smoked when women were not allowed to smoke, and she ignored her housekeeping responsibilities, leaving her bed unmade while she painted canvases. Drawn to the mysterious, she "fell in love/ with the first legitimate guru from India/ to pass through Managua" and invented drinks to prevent "all possible diseases." Unlike most women, she never settled down but was "Always in transit," living in various rented rooms. Yet she was a beautiful young woman and later a dedicated mother to her only daughter.

Daisy Zamora grew up in a Nicaragua under the dictatorship of the Somoza family. When she was only four years old, her father was one of a group of insurgents imprisoned for attempting to overthrow the tyrannical government of Anastasio Somoza García, the father of the Anastasio Somoza Debayle who was overthrown by Zamora and her fellow revolutionaries in 1979. The Somoza dictatorship's power was maintained by the U.S.-trained and backed National Guard. As the poem informs the reader, Aunt Chofi's resistance to the Guard forced her into exile in Mexico. In fact, many Nicaraguans lived in exile during the Somoza dictatorship.

This poem, like many of her others in *Clean Slate*, focuses on a woman who manages to break through the limitations that her family and society try to impose. Though the consequences of self-motivation and striving to achieve her dreams may be as serious as the "living hell" of her marriage to Guillermo, the resultant freedom portrayed here seems well worth the difficulties. Another of Zamora's themes, motherhood, also arises in "Dear Aunt Chofi." Sadly, despite Chofi's dedication to her daughter, her daughter travels farther and farther away in an apparent attempt to create a physical distance to replicate the personal distance that she desires.

"Dear Aunt Chofi" is a "web of intimate sensibilities, founded in the concrete and even the mundane," as Barbara Paschke points out in her introduction to Zamora's *Riverbed of Memory* (1992). In "Dear Aunt Chofi," Daisy Zamora chronicles her aunt's life while witnessing to the time, place, and conditions for women evoked in the poem.

Linda Ledford-Miller

DEATH & CO.

Author: Sylvia Plath (1932-1963)
Type of poem: Meditation
First published: 1963; collected in *Ariel*, 1965

The Poem

"Death & Co." is a short poem in free verse, its thirty-one lines divided into seven stanzas. The title suggests the name of a business or corporation; its function is to establish the mood of the poem, which is ironic and mocking. Death is often viewed with ambivalence, something that not only takes away life but also (sometimes mistakenly) offers comfort to those who are in pain or who believe in an afterlife; death can seem cold and officious, but also, perhaps, ironic in the form it finally takes. The poem is written in the first person in the form of a confession monologue in which the speaker mockingly describes a terrifying—and coldly businesslike—scene unfolding before her eyes. While it is often the case that poets use a persona to distinguish themselves from the poem's speaker, no such distinction is implied in this poem. The poet Sylvia Plath, like the speaker, conceives a monologue wherein one person speaks alone. Although Plath is considered by many to be a "confessional" poet, this poem seems less like a confession to someone, explicitly or implicitly, and more like a monologue to the self.

"Death & Co." begins with the idea of a duality, a form common to many of the subjects in Plath's poetry. In this case, the speaker, while being visited by two mordant and menacing figures, becomes aware that death is not singular but has two faces. It is a realization that does not surprise her ("It seems perfectly natural now"), but it terrifies her nonetheless. She graphically describes first the one face and then the other, beginning with "the one who never looks up." He is cold and distant, and his eyes are lidded to avoid contact with the speaker. He reminds her of a marble statue, a death mask "like Blake's." In the second stanza, the poet continues the litany of characteristics that distinguish the first face of death. He publicly exhibits the trademark signs of the *memento mori*, reminding the speaker how accomplished he is by the appearance of his many birthmarks. By the end of this stanza, the poet realizes that she is his next victim. Her statement "I am red meat" mocks the serious nature of her realization while revealing her inevitable fear of the moment. She steps aside as he tries to grab her: "I am not his yet." Still overtly threatening, he begins to play a psychological game with her by undermining those things in her physical world she feels are safe: her physical attractiveness and her children. The speaker of the poem notes his overarching self-confidence.

While he is a perfectionist, a kind of artist bragging about his accomplishments, his partner is oily, sociable, and fawning. The first wants to be respected and admired, the second "wants to be loved." Yet they operate together: "The frost makes a flower,/ The dew makes a star." Hoping to be noticed by neither figure, the speaker retreats into stasis. However, the lure and inevitability of the business the two contradictory figures have come for is pronounced, in the speaker's mind, by the inevitable ringing of the bells. By the last line of the poem she knows her time is up, but her sarcasm remains: "Somebody's done for."

Forms and Devices

Early criticism of Plath's poetry tended to see it as confessional in nature, an autobiography of the poet's personal neuroses. Following that line of thinking, readers who examine the imagery closely will time and again be referred back to the poet's own desperate life, which was filled with shame and psychic fragility. The early critics viewed her work as successful not because it was strictly confessional but because the self placed at the center of the poem makes "vulnerability and shame" representative of a wider civilization. The private events are universalized through the speaking voice. However, later literary critics began to focus more on her developing poetic and the achievement of her voice and tone, while admitting that much of her content was in fact drawn from her own life. Perhaps the strongest reason to believe that Plath's clever crafting of her poetry places her outside the strictly confessional school of poetry (a school that includes the poets John Berryman, Theodore Roethke, and Anne Sexton) is that she avoids sounding confessional; she lacks self-pity and an overreaction to what might seem appropriately terrifying. In other words, she constructs in her later poems dramatically staged performances that pose a tension through the face-off between life, movement, and energy on one hand and death, inertia, and passivity on the other.

This juxtaposition between life force and death force may be said to be at the heart of "Death & Co.," which reads like a bizarre juxtaposition of things public and private. Characteristic of this poem as well as several other of Plath's later poems are the self-reflexive quality of her experience, a rhythmic energy, clearly ambiguous images, and the colloquialisms of the speaking voice. All of this suggests that the poem is staged as a process of change and discovery narrated by a speaker who is both mocking and vengeful. For instance, "Death & Co." opens with a juxtaposition of the two figures of death that appear before the speaker. As the poet's discovery of their business unfolds, she carefully controls her response to their visit with a form of self-parody that helps keep in mind the exchange between the audience's reception and her own feelings. She imposes limits of rhyme and rhythm so she can measure changes within her personal situation. The rhythmical energy of the speaking voice, in fact, is a reminder of how sporting, playful, vengeful, or mocking she can be. The first two stanzas, for example, include the repetition of numbers ("Two, of course there are two"), colors ("nude/ Verdigris" and "red meat"), alliteration ("balled, like Blake's"), and slant rhyme ("birthmarks that are his trademark"). Sentence patterns are repeated again and again with interesting developments: "He tells me how badly I photograph./ He tells me how sweet." The rhymes are widely separated ("sweet" in the third stanza rhymes with "feet" in the fourth stanza). However, the self-conscious, performing, and poetic self of the speaker puts her in touch with moment-to-moment changes and forces the audience to sit rapt, to accept the form as expression and artifact. It is characteristic of Plath to end her poetry with the same ironic awareness held by the speaker throughout the poem. In the final stanza and last line of "Death & Co.," her ear for music and vernacular is right on the mark. She is still recording her speaker's shifting sensibility even to the point that the speaker, feeling personally diminished, still maintains her voice of manic buffoonery.

Themes and Meanings

"Death & Co." is a poem about life and death. How does a woman with a troubled relationship to both life and death envision the moment when death comes to visit her? How does her poetic vision of this complicated scene get articulated? References to death abound in Plath's poems (she attempted suicide three times, the last successfully), yet her differing figures of death reveal a fascination more with how the living view death itself than with what they imagine death to be like after life. One may wonder if this is a kind of madness. In her many poems that address the theme of death (especially her last poems, collected in *Ariel*), the images are frightening and surreal. Still, the poetry out of which "Death & Co." comes is not without a kind of history. Emily Dickinson wrote harrowing poems on madness and dying, while Theodore Roethke, Anne Sexton, Robert Lowell, and Hayden Carruth all have explored similar subject matter.

The common theme among Plath's "death poems" is, interestingly, the ambivalent attitude toward death they reveal. In "Death & Co.," the ambivalence takes the form of a speaker who seems part of a dramatically staged performance of being in wait for death while revealing an assertiveness, wit, ingenuity, and sheer life force in attempting to outwit death. She performs even though she is faced with the suffering and pain of personal failure (how badly she photographs and her dead babies) as well as inherited cultural myths. The speaker avoids confessional or self-pitying overreactions. In fact, the performing self suggests underlying feelings of comedy.

"Death & Co." is also about poetry as a process of discovery and reaction. As the poet reveals the speaker's fantasy (or her madness) about death as a slowly savored, dramatic show of loss, pain, and personal diminishment, readers see that the shifting sensibility offers a close-up scrutiny of just how one is shaped by and impelled to shape her material. In her occasional narrative asides ("I am red meat," "I am not his yet," "I do not stir") it is not clear whether she speaks to an audience or to herself. What is important is not to whom she addresses her monologue but that she experiences this performance as an emotionally charged process of discovery and reaction. The self-conscious performance, then, becomes a substitute for a fixed identity, suggesting that for Plath any attempted literary shaping or definition of self is inadequate and unfinished.

Holli G. Levitsky

DEPRESSION DAYS

Author: Pat Mora (1942-
Type of poem: Lyric
First published: 1995, in *Agua Santa/Holy Water*

The Poem

"Depression Days" is a short poem in free verse, consisting of thirty-five lines divided into seven stanzas. The title suggests not only a mood but also a specific historical period, 1929-1939. The Depression evokes a time of hardship and suffering because of a shortage of provisions and work. The poem, dedicated to Eduardo Delgado, focuses on the challenges presented to the main character by economic misery and racial discrimination. Pat Mora refers to him in the third person and does not specifically identify him by name until the fifth stanza, when she calls him her "uncle."

The historical context is important to an understanding of "Depression Days." The poem emphasizes the economic impact of the Great Depression and the involvement of Mora's uncle with the Civilian Conservation Corps (CCC), mentioned in line eight. The CCC, one of the most popular relief agencies of the New Deal, provided outdoor employment for numerous young men from 1933 to 1942. Many of the jobs were in conservation, usually in the nation's parks and forests. The enrollees lived in camp-sites set up in different states participating in the relief program. One of those work camps is the specific setting for the poem.

The poem begins by projecting the character into darkness as he spends "his last fifteen cents" to purchase a movie ticket. With the last coins in his pocket, he buys a ticket to forget the harsh realities of his personal life. Literally and figuratively, "He buys the dark." He escapes the light and reality by hiding in the darkness of a theater. As the film begins, he joins its seafaring men on the deck of the ship as their voices sing out, "Red Sails in the Sunset," a popular English song of the mid 1930's. Once on board the ship, the character embarks on a metaphoric voyage of self-discovery.

The next five stanzas begin exactly the same, with "He tries not to think," and then catalog life's harsh realities, which the man tries to obliterate from his mind as he adventures in the films. His first memory focuses on the previous night, presumably in the campsite, as he lay on his cot. This frame begins another movie, starring himself in the private role of "border kid playing CCC lumberjack." The dark continues in the second stanza, but here it is a darkness left by the death of his father. The death has obligated the young man to work with the CCC, a work program established by President Franklin D. Roosevelt to provide financial assistance to needy families.

The poem then describes the natural elements with which the workers must contend. The character tries not to think of the other Mexican workers who joined him in the truck in the cold morning as they rode to work. The only Spanish line in the poem is their own comment to each other regarding the weather: "¡Caramba, qué frío!" The workers' growling stomachs, which sound like the grinding gears in a truck, reveal their need to earn paychecks to buy food. Later, the "desert wind" makes its way into "the barracks" where the young workers reside, "herding" them like animals to gather near the warm stove. Delgado jokingly questions the reality of his own life as he asks, "Am I alive, doc?"

The fifth stanza introduces a disturbing conflict involving the sergeant. Because the Army directed the CCC work camps, a sergeant supervises this group. The young man, now identified as Delgado, tries to forget the sergeant's voice "spitting" out his name and his own voice confirming that he indeed is Delgado. The stern frown and twitch of lips describe the sergeant's attitude. The sixth stanza continues with Delgado trying to forget the sergeant's words: "You don't look Mexican, Delgado. Just change your name . . ./ . . . and you've got a job." Having the power to select those who get jobs, the sergeant offers Delgado an opportunity and a solution if only the latter will abandon his name and identity.

The seventh stanza concludes the poem by repeating the opening line: Delgado "buys the dark/ with his last fifteen cents" and returns to the darkness, where he began. The stanza indirectly reveals Delgado's rejection of the sergeant's proposition and recalls those affected by his decision.

Forms and Devices

Cinematic images structure "Depression Days." Mora effectively contrasts the fantasy of films with the reality of Delgado's life. They provide a means to escape and a chance to assume romanticized roles in several different films. The poem begins with the character watching "Reel after reel," but the second stanza intrudes with a very personal projection of scenes that Delgado "tries not to think of." The following five stanzas list experiences that he would prefer to forget but cannot. Those scenes are private, but they also apply to many others who found themselves in the same predicament during the Great Depression. The darkness of the theater functions as a framing device for the poem. Within the frame, Mora unravels a very disturbing experience.

The imagery of money and hunger in the poem is particularly relevant to the Great Depression. In both the first and last stanzas Delgado "buys the dark" with fifteen cents." References to "hungry for paychecks," the offer of a job, "the bare icebox," and "the price of eggs and names and skin" remind readers of Delgado's hunger and desperate need for a job. The young men's extreme hunger becomes more evident through their growling stomachs, "screechy as gears." Their hunger is further emphasized by references to "bare flesh" and the question involving being alive. In the last line Mora juxtaposes "the price of eggs" with the price of the last two items, "names and skin"—the price to be paid for having a Mexican name or dark-complected skin.

Mora uses repetition as a technique to remind the readers of the reason Delgado seeks the darkness. The first two lines in stanza 1 are repeated in stanza 7: "He buys the dark/ with his last fifteen cents." Enclosed within these two stanzas, the other five stanzas begin by repeating the refrain: "He tries not to think," followed by those scenes Delgado wishes to forget. The repetition reinforces the fact that he does think about them.

Themes and Meanings

Two closely related themes appear in "Depression Days," a powerful political poem about a significant historical decade and its effect on Mexican Americans. One of the themes is the horror of racial discrimination. Delgado, victimized because of his Mexican name, vividly exemplifies the object of racial discrimination. Discrimination threatens to deprive the "border kid" of a job. Although he is of Mexican ancestry, Delgado does not appear to be Mexican and could easily pass for Anglo, so he faces a terrible dilemma: Forsaking his cultural heritage and his identity would assure him of a job and thus end his economic misery.

The issue of identity is another prevalent theme in this poem, as it is in several of Mora's other works. The sergeant's order to Delgado to change his name so that he can get a job is a very tempting offer, given the time period and the economic crisis. Delgado remembers at this decisive point "his father who never understood/ this country." His family name, which comes from his father, provides him with a sense of who he is. Delgado has to consider whether changing his name would solve his problems and would allow him to fit in any better. An image of his mother comes to mind as he considers what his decision will mean. If Delgado changes his name he will gain a job, but he will also lose his identity. Names provide a sense of cultural heritage, of where one comes from. They identify people as individuals. In the poem "Legal Alien," Mora writes about the feeling of discomfort caused by living in two cultures, "sliding back and forth/ between the fringes of both worlds." Frequently, people who are bilingual and bicultural have no definite place in either world and can claim membership in neither. Mora does not provide a solution to the problems of discrimination and identity, nor does she philosophize. Instead, she poses a challenge for readers to consider what they would do in Delgado's situation.

Gloria Duarte-Valverde

A DESCRIPTION OF A CITY SHOWER

Author: Jonathan Swift (1667-1745)
Type of poem: Mock pastoral
First published: 1710; collected in *Miscellanies in Prose and Verse*, 1711

The Poem

Jonathan Swift's "A Description of a City Shower" is a sixty-three-line poem written in thirty-one of the end-rhymed iambic pentameter couplets still known as "heroic couplets," with the final line of iambic hexameter creating a closing triplet. (The heroic couplet was the most popular verse form of Swift's day and takes its name from its frequent use in English translations of classical epic—or, as it was then termed, "heroic"—poetry.) Swift's title is somewhat ironically misleading: Although he certainly provides a vivid enough description of a turbulent rain shower rolling through the streets of early eighteenth century London, the poem's central concern is with the city's inhabitants who are caught by Swift in a series of comic vignettes as they scurry to avoid the impending "flood."

At the time of the poem's initial publication, London was the center of English commerce and culture as well as Europe's leading trade center—a bustling, rapidly expanding metropolis that progressive Englishmen could regard with great pride. ("When a man is tired of London," wrote Samuel Johnson, a leading eighteenth century man of letters, "he is tired of life; for there is in London all that life can afford.") The Great Fire of 1666 had destroyed huge stretches of the city, and much of the newly rebuilt London, including the Christopher Wren-designed St. Paul's Cathedral, struck resident Londoners and visitors alike as a dazzling achievement.

However, if the lofty prospect of Wren's cathedral could dazzle a viewer, only a slight shift in perspective—downward, to eye or ground level—was likely to elicit an entirely different set of responses. Swift's London, like any great city, was a place of dramatic contrasts. Much of the landscape was admittedly new, but parts of the old city remained, replete with dark, claustrophobic streets and badly overcrowded tenements in which poverty and disease were the rule. Plumbing was primitive if not nonexistent, making waste disposal an enormous and constant problem. (The poem's final three lines, which might strike a modern reader as purposefully disgusting, are exaggerated only in a technical sense; many a Londoner no doubt witnessed worse.) Even in London's better areas, open drains ("Kennels") ran down the sides of dirt streets; in the early morning, when the contents of morning chamber pots were routinely tossed out of second-floor windows, pedestrians were well-advised to keep to the inside of the sidewalks. This London—the London seen by the "needy Poet" caught in the "Dust and Rain" of the street—is the London of Swift's poem. It is a city packed with perfectly ordinary people, all of them—like Susan taking down her clothes from the clothesline and the foppish young law student (the "Templer spruce") waiting for a break in the rain—doing perfectly ordinary things. Yet the poem's language—ornate, elevated, and rich with classical allusions—suggests that this seemingly everyday event is anything but ordinary.

Forms and Devices

The time during which Swift lived and wrote has often been termed the neoclassical age because the period witnessed a sweeping revival of classical literature. The works of Greek and Roman writers were studied, praised, and frequently imitated, and most educated English readers of Swift's day would have been familiar with the poetic genres of the ancient world. One very popular and often imitated classical genre was pastoral poetry (from *pastor*, the Latin word for shepherd), which celebrated rural life and often contrasted the (supposedly) simple, unspoiled life of herdsmen and farmers with the hectic, corrupt, and overly civilized life of city dwellers.

While Swift had no objections to the pastoral poems of such classical writers as the great Roman poet Vergil, he had little patience with the shallowness and artificiality of much eighteenth century pastoral poetry, which used highly ornate language to describe the lives of its rural subjects in lavish, unrealistic detail. For Swift, this not only made for bad poetry but also made for poetry that was aesthetically dishonest and morally irresponsible. (The primary purpose of art, according to neoclassical literary theory, was to provide moral instruction, and moral instruction could hardly proceed from what was essentially a lie.) To demonstrate how empty pastoral poetry had become as a form in the hands of most eighteenth century imitators, Swift and several of his contemporaries wrote a number of poems such as "A Description of a City Shower" that employ the elevated language and classical allusions of pastoral poetry to describe seemingly ordinary scenes of urban life. This form (of which John Gay's 1714 *The Shepherd's Week* is an outstanding example) lies somewhere between satire and parody and is known as "mock pastoral." The results of such compoundings of realism with romance vary in complexity, but the most obvious common effect is an ironic—and intentionally comic, if dark—sense of incongruity created by the discrepancy between the poem's "high" language and its "low" subject matter.

In "A Description of a City Shower," the incongruity first arises from the degree of seriousness assigned to an event as commonplace as a rain shower. In addition to the grandiose language found in the poem's first twelve lines, the scene seems charged with a nearly epic sense of anticipation. Prophecies and oracles often play important roles in both classical epics and tragedies, and here Swift provides a bevy of signs and omens ("Prognosticks")—from the behavior of the "pensive Cat" to various physical aches and pains—that seem to portend something much grander and more ominous than a simple shower. It is in the poem's second verse paragraph, however, that Swift's design becomes strikingly clear. Word choice, allusion, and imagery combine to create the comic incongruity characteristic of the mock pastoral form. The personified south wind rises in the sky ("the Welkin") on "dabbled [dirty] Wings" and brings with it a dark cloud heavy with rain. While Swift's comparison of the rain cloud to a "Drunkard" that, having "swill'd more Liquor than it could contain," is preparing to give "it up again" may strike modern readers as rather crude, it would hardly have offended the eighteenth century sensibility, which would have delighted in Swift's clever spin on the extended simile so typical of epic poetry.

As the rain begins in earnest, the language of the third and fourth verse paragraphs continues to stress the ironic gap between classical literature and everyday behavior, even going so far as to suggest that the coming "deluge" will rival the biblical flood of Noah. As Londoners dart about in search of shelter, old enmities are forgotten. "Triumphant Tories, and desponding Whigs" (members of opposing political parties) put aside their differences "and join to save their Wigs." In the poem's most elaborate "epic" simile, a "Beau" (a young man-about-town) who is nervously waiting out the rain within a sedan chair is compared to the Greeks hiding within the Trojan Horse, bringing to mind Aeneas's account of the fall of Troy in book 2 of Vergil's *Aeneid* (c. 29-19 B.C.; English translation, 1553). The final image of the "huge Confluent" coursing uncontrollably through London seems nearly apocalyptic, threatening to engulf the entire city—until one realizes that the distance between Smithfield market and Holborn bridge is little more than a stone's throw.

Themes and Meanings

Swift remains the premier satirist in the English language. (His 1726 prose satire *Gulliver's Travels* is arguably the finest satire in any language.) Besides a powerful intelligence and an essential dissatisfaction with the human condition, the satirist must possess an eye keen enough to discern the follies that so often arise from confusing appearance and reality—which is precisely what eighteenth century pastoral poetry routinely did. The facts of eighteenth century rural life were cold and hard. Farmers and rural workers lived lives at the other end of the spectrum from the hazily romantic imaginings of pastoral poetry. Like their lower-class counterparts in the city, they worked long, back-breaking hours, usually for little more than a subsistence wage. No amount of flowery language or elaborate, classical imagery could improve their lot or effectively substitute fantasy for reality.

It would be wrong, however, to imagine a savagely indignant Swift behind "A Description of a City Shower." The tone, in fact, is much more one of wry amusement than anger, and even the poem's array of frankly repellent images—from the poet's filthy coat to the "Drowned Puppies," decaying fish, and "Dead Cats" of the concluding lines—in the end seem more comically grotesque than offensive.

Michael Stuprich

A DESCRIPTION OF THE MORNING

Author: Jonathan Swift (1667-1745)
Type of poem: Satire
First published: 1709; collected in *Miscellanies in Prose and Verse*, 1711

The Poem

Jonathan Swift was much involved in the launching of his friend Sir Richard Steele's new literary enterprise, a thrice-weekly paper of familiar essays and news called *The Tatler*. One of Swift's contributions was the eighteen-line poem called "A Description of the Morning," which appeared in the ninth paper on April 30, 1709, only two weeks after the publication debuted. The poem gives a series of photographic impressions of London life, specifically, as Steele remarked, of life in the West End of London.

The poem opens at daybreak, with only a few coaches yet on the scene to carry about their passengers. The first scene is of Betty, a stock name for a female servant, leaving her master's bed. In an effort to cover up her deed, she goes to her room and ruffles the covers of her own unused bed. Next, three cleaners take the stage for their brief appearances. An apprentice cleans with a half-hearted effort, while Moll skillfully whirls her mop as a prelude to scrubbing the entry stairs. A youth sweeps the "kennel," or gutter, with a stubby broom (in search of used nails, as a note by Swift explains).

Two workers next demand the reader's attention, one selling coal—then widely used domestically for cooking and warmth or for cottage industries requiring fire—the other announcing his availability to sweep chimneys. The "shriller notes" of the sweep imply the grim reality that children were forced into this dangerous and debilitating job, often working from dawn to dusk. While bill collectors ("duns") gather before an aristocrat's house, another loud voice intrudes. It belongs to another "Moll": This one may be selling brick dust, used as a scouring powder, or (since Swift calls her "Brickdust Moll") Swift may have in mind her working-class complexion, scorched by the sun. The name "Moll" has seedy associations. Cutpurse Moll was the name of an infamous seventeenth century pickpocket, and the name in Swift's day was associated with prostitution.

While the above are all starting their day, another group has just finished their night's work. Thieves are welcomed back to jail by the "turnkey," or jail keeper, who has let them out to steal—for his sizable cut of the take. Next, ironically, "watchful bailiffs" assume their posts. The poems closes with schoolboys reluctantly finding their way to school.

Forms and Devices

The poem, satiric in manner, has models in the classical satires of Horace and Juvenal and contains echoes of William Shakespeare's *As You Like It*. Swift's satires tend to be Juvenalian, or biting, but here he tends more to the Horatian, or urbane and gentle, mode. As with all true satires, the poem points to human failings with an eye to correction. The poem was also one of the first English examples of what is variously called the town eclogue, urban pastoral, or ironic pastoral—all designating a poem about the city. In "A Description of the Morning" and its companion piece, "A Description of a City Shower," which also appeared in *The Tatler*, Swift introduced something quite out of the norm for Augustan poetry. Steele avowed that Swift "has run into a Way perfectly New" of presenting "the Incidents just as they really appear." This puts Swift toward the head of a long line of realistic writers.

The poem takes the simple form of a list or series of snapshots. Several deftly drawn characters make cameo appearances, and each actively engages in work which defines both their individual lives and, collectively, the life of the city as seen from the working-class perspective. The upper classes would not even be awake yet in eighteenth century England. C. N. Manlove has noticed that the series of scenes has a general movement from the inside to the outside: from the master's bedroom to the entry way to the street and finally to the lord's front gate. Similarly, as the morning broadens into day, the verbs move from the past tense to the present.

Themes and Meanings

"A Description of the Morning" has much in common with Swift's other work in both prose and poetry. Swift loves detail, especially detail that exposes human weakness and gives no quarter to vanity, as in his descriptions of the human body and bodily functions in *Gulliver's Travels*. No direct commentary is needed; the facts are made to speak for themselves. Similarly, Swift here makes no explicit comment on the morality or quality of working-class London. Yet taken together, the scenes give the impression of a city that is a noisy, dirty place. It is populated by people who at best are reluctant to work or learn and at worst are deceptive, manipulative, and immoral.

Swift, the dean of St. Patrick's Cathedral in Dublin, is ever fulfilling the preacher's role in pointing up the weakness in human nature and the resultant failings in human behavior. Master and servant alike are involved in sexual sin, which they take pains to keep hidden, while further immorality is suggested by the twice-used stock name for a prostitute, Moll. The moral and social order is shown to be in an advanced state of decay, as those charged with maintaining law and order use their power to rob the very people they are charged with protecting—all for personal gain.

Lesser lapses fill in the gaps. The young apprentice scrimps by with the mere appearance of cleanliness, and schoolboys dawdle, reluctant to take advantage of their educational privilege. Even more subtle is the suggestion of class distinction and the gap between rich and poor. The conveyances out at daybreak are "hackney" coaches, which means they are for hire or rent. The rich would have their own. The bill collectors gathering before the gate are dependent on "his Lordship," and men and women ignominiously bawl through the streets in search of customers. Such detail as the "broomy stumps," suggesting worn-out equipment, points to the Spartan condition of the youth's life as he looks for recyclable nails.

Swift does not force this kind of judgment from his readers; the narrative voice never obtrudes. He also makes no effort to tie the descriptions together by a narrative thread or any other device. The images bump against one another with all the randomness typical of the street. Yet, with all its apparent indirection, the poem gives a subtle critique of human nature. With its realism so concretely realized, the pettiness, nastiness, and seaminess of urban London become undeniable. The satiric touch is lighter than usual for Swift, who often pushes the filth under readers' noses. For example, he spares them images of the chamber pot, routinely dumped into the street in his day. Such understatement allows the reader to draw conclusions personally, but they are made nearly inevitable: Such pervasive shortcomings must point to elemental flaws in human character, which, as Swift is always suggesting, need radical moral solutions.

Wayne Martindale

THE DESERT MUSIC

Author: William Carlos Williams (1883-1963)
Type of poem: Lyric
First published: 1951; collected in *The Desert Music and Other Poems*, 1954

The Poem

"The Desert Music" is a relatively lengthy open-form poem. The title refers to the topic of the poem, a desert journey, as well as to the musical imagery present throughout the work. The poem is written primarily in the first person and appears to be drawn from the personal experiences of the author. The poet functions as a speaker of the poem as well as an observer within the poem. In describing his purpose, the speaker states that his goal is, when describing his desert journey, "—to tell/ what subsequently I saw and what heard." When functioning as an observer, the speaker identifies himself by name (William Carlos Williams). He also mentions that the group with which he is traveling includes a total of seven members, and he specifically describes an incident involving one of his friends in particular (identified by the initial H.). In addition, as speaker, Williams refers to the actions of his wife, giving her name as Floss.

The journey described in the poem is likened to a dance that begins and ends with the speaker's observation of a figure located on the international bridge between the United States and Mexico:

> —the dance begins: to end about
> a form propped motionless—on the bridge
> between Juarez and El Paso—unrecognizable
> in the semi-dark.

Here the speaker establishes a specific setting for the events outlined in the poem. He describes a journey, taken with several friends, from California, through El Paso, Texas, to Juarez, Mexico.

The events in the poem are generally presented chronologically as the speaker travels from one location to the next. There are numerous references to the characteristics of the people that the speaker encounters while in each specific location. First he describes the figure on the bridge, then he describes the attributes of the Texans he meets throughout his travels. He asks, "What makes Texans so tall?" Later he describes the children who beg for pennies (expressing annoyance at their grasping fingers), the Indians at the market booths (who seem to be asleep but are actually alert), and a woman he observes while at a nightclub. Williams expresses his admiration for this woman, a striptease dancer, because she does not let her worn-out form prevent her from practicing the art of dancing. In general, the speaker's descriptions are brief but vivid, and they focus on what is observable to the human eye. However, the speaker interjects his concerns as a poet regarding the best way to create a poem that will reflect the experiences of his journey without copying nature.

The closing of the poem is similar to its opening in that the speaker again refers to the figure by the side of the bridge. The events presented seem to have taken place over a period of several days, with much of the description focusing on incidents occurring during the evening hours. The return to a description of the unknown figure near the international boundary seems to mark, for the speaker, the beginning and end of his journey.

Forms and Devices

Although a number of poetic devices, such as repetition and imagery, are present within the poem, in general, one of the interesting features associated with "The Desert Music" (as well as with many of Williams's other poems) is the absence of conventional form and content. As previously noted, the poem is open in its form and therefore does not include the use of a specific rhyming pattern or a specific metrical construction. To establish a coherence and a cadence, Williams uses punctuation such as dashes, commas, and end marks to signify the ways in which the lines should be read. Williams was often recognized as a poet who experimented with various forms and techniques in his effort to imitate the sounds and scenes of life.

Williams is also noted for using language that is direct and succinct rather than language that ornaments or embellishes. "The Desert Music" uses the common vernacular, and Williams presents images in an economical fashion. As a result, some of the scenes depicted have almost a photographic quality. The market scene is particularly vivid in its presentation. Williams identifies the items sold in the market booths in a way that renders the "baked red-clay utensils, daubed/ with blue, silver-ware,/ dried peppers, onions, print goods, children's/ clothing" visible and concrete.

While "The Desert Music" presents many vivid images and is somewhat reminiscent of Williams's earlier poems that have been closely associated with the Imagist movement, this poem illustrates his move toward Objectivism. In this latter approach to poetry, the poem becomes an object, and in "The Desert Music" the poet struggles with the question, "How shall we get said what must be said?" To answer this question within the framework of "The Desert Music," Williams repeatedly refers to music and dance.

The speaker first mentions music when he describes the figure on the bridge. In referring to the music of the desert in relationship to the figure, the speaker says, "A music/ supersedes his composure, hallooing to us/ across a great distance" Later, the speaker notes the presence of music as he and his friends drive through the desert. He describes the music as being the "music of survival, subdued, distant, half/ heard." When describing the erotic dancer, he notes that "She fits/ the music," suggesting that as a result she is able to transcend her audience and become virtuous through her art.

In addition to repeatedly referring to music and dance, the speaker repeats his concerns about producing a poem that does not copy nature but rather imitates it in a unique way. He also questions the purpose of writing poetry. In an implied conversation, the speaker responds to the question, "Why/ does one want to write a poem?" His response is direct and simple: "Because it is there to be written." This question-

and-response pattern is evident throughout the poem in a way that resembles a refrain in a musical composition, and Williams's thoughts are interspersed with the descriptions of the desert journey.

Themes and Meanings

"The Desert Music" is a poem about imitating life through the creation of poetry. The speaker continually raises questions relating to the nature and significance of poetry. He responds to the questions in the form of an open dialogue and defines himself as a poet in an insistent and repetitive manner. The form of the poem serves as a challenge to the conventions of the Romantics and the Georgians, who Williams felt were restricted in their approach to poetry by their use of traditional patterns of organization. The poem also expresses a resistance to the use of elevated language and traditional subject matter. The poem is seen as an enduring object connected to the reality of human experience through the use of precise and rhythmic language.

"The Desert Music" is also a poem about a journey taken as a way of finding "relief from that changeless, endless/ inescapable and insistent music." During the journey from California to Mexico, Williams appears to be searching for companionship and for experiences that will help him make connections with the people he meets. The photographic images he presents seem to reflect his interest in the particular, rather than the general, aspects of life. The cyclical nature ("Egg-shaped!") of the journey isolates the events described in the poem within a specific time frame and presents the journey as being complete.

The common subject matter of the poem links the everyday experiences of the individual to the poetic structure, and even though the speaker continually interrupts the description of the journey, it is possible to trace the travels of Williams and his companions. The figure on the bridge is present at both the beginning and the ending of the poem, and his location at the international boundary is significant because it is there that he will not be disturbed.

"The Desert Music" incorporates within its structure the theme of the significance of poetry as well as the theme of the importance of shared experiences and objects. While these themes are often addressed in modern poetry, the uniqueness of Williams's method of presentation sets this poem apart. The absence of a prescribed form as well as the absence of ornamental language lend a somewhat raw quality to the work that many readers have found refreshing and provocative. In addition, the presence of the two themes in juxtaposition to each other creates a tension between the experience of the poet and the experience of the reader.

Julie Sherrick

DESIGN

Author: Robert Frost (1874-1963)
Type of poem: Sonnet
First published: 1922; collected in *A Further Range*, 1936

The Poem

"Design" is an atypical Petrarchan (or Italian) sonnet, because though its octave (the first eight lines) sets forth a situation, and the sestet (the final six lines) reacts to it, Robert Frost's theme is not love, and his sestet concludes with a couplet—more common to the Shakespearean (Elizabethan) sonnet. Further, though the octave rhyme scheme is the Petrarchan *abbaabba*, the sestet is a rare *acaacc*, a three-rhyme pattern that is unusually restrictive for a poem in English, which is a difficult rhyming language. Since the structure of the poem departs from tradition, the reader may wonder about the appropriateness of "Design" as its title; perhaps Frost is mocking, or at least questioning, the very notion of order.

The literal content of the sonnet seems straightforward. While wandering about the countryside, the first-person narrator, apparently Frost himself, is on a hill and happens to see a flower—a "heal-all"—on which a spider sits with a dead moth. The spider is fat (probably from having consumed a previous victim), dimpled, and white. The flower, also white, is "like a froth," and the moth is said to be similar to "a white piece of rigid satin cloth." The three objects presumably are dead, like "the ingredients of a witches' broth." The lilting rhythm of the opening five words and the description of the spider as dimpled are deceptive, for the lightness of touch they convey is quickly overtaken by the subsequent details and their pervasive focus upon death. The octave, therefore, does not merely develop the sonnet's substantive base; by toying with the reader, it also establishes a mood of uncertainty, even foreboding, and raises questions about what is to come in the second part.

The reader of a sonnet normally can expect commentary, perhaps even resolution, in a sestet. Such is not the case in the last six lines of Frost's poem, which consist of three questions and a closing speculative statement. In the first four lines, a perplexed narrator articulates the same matters that bother the reader, whose surrogate he is. He wonders, for instance, about the incongruous scene, asking how its components— flower, spider, moth—happened to come together at that particular place and time. What "steered" them there, he asks—and for what purpose or "design"? In the closing couplet, the speaker reiterates his concern: Did chance bring about the meeting, or did some power orchestrate the event? Indeed, would a supreme being even bother with such insignificant matters?

By raising unanswered questions in the sestet, Frost leaves the reader with a sense of unease, incompleteness. The incongruity between the confident clarity of the title and subsequent descriptions and questions is heightened by Frost's emphatic use of the word "design" twice in the last two lines. So whereas the title initially exudes a forthright assertiveness suggestive of order, once one reads through the poem, the title

"Design" takes on ironic, maybe even skeptical overtones. Like so much else in the Frost canon, this is a linguistically simple poem—75 percent of the words are monosyllabic—that plumbs the depths of the human condition.

Forms and Devices

Frost begins "Design" deceptively in that he describes the dead spider as dimpled, for the term more often is used about a baby and usually has pleasant connotations. A dimple, though, is simply an indentation, so Frost may be literal in his description of a fat, shriveled creature whose color has faded.

The heal-all, more commonly known as self-heal, is a violet-blue flower reputed to have medicinal powers, but here it is white, similarly drained of its color in death. The third object in the poem is a moth, also white, like the rigid satin cloth that typically lines a coffin. Further, to emphasize death, Frost surely chose the adjective "rigid" to suggest rigor mortis. The narrator also links the three things with blight, a condition of destructive decay. In the light of all this, how can the objects be said to be ready to begin the morning "right," or correctly? Maybe Frost is punning, leading the reader astray, as he does at the start of the sonnet. (Perhaps he intends "rite," as in a ritual.) The next line, with its allusion to a witches' broth, an essential component of an unholy ceremony, suggests this possibility.

The octave concludes with a variation on its opening, a list of the three objects, now joined as ingredients of an unsavory stew. Frost first calls attention to the spider's whiteness by describing it as a snow drop, an early-blooming flower. The next part of the series—"a flower like a froth"—could provide a link either to the snow-drop or to the white heal-all, but why does Frost say "froth"? Simply because the white flowers resemble foam? His choice of language may be more purposeful, with "froth" referring to a salivary foam indicative of disease. Similarly evoking various interpretations is the comparison of the dead moth's wings to a paper kite. In addition to denoting a toy that wafts in a breeze, the word "kite" refers to a bird of prey, and white kites are used in Asian funeral rites. In sum, Frost's octave incrementally develops an unmistakable image pattern of death, destruction, disease, and decay.

In the first few lines of the sestet, there is a temporary shift in style and tone, attributable to such words as "wayside," "innocent," and "kindred," all of which have positive connotations. Having moved toward serenity with his first two questions, Frost attempts his answer by raising a third one: "What but design of darkness to appall?" In a poem dominated by an albino death scene, the word "darkness" is jarring and signals an abrupt shift in tone. This shift is reinforced by the last word, which is the most heavily accented of the seven words in the line. "Appall" means to dismay or to fill with consternation, either of which sense fits the context, and it derives from Latin and Middle English words which refer to growing pale or faint, both of which meanings are relevant. They suggest that the startled narrator and reader might become as white as the dead trio. Immediately upon raising the dreadful possibility of some malevolent force having been responsible for the albino tableau, Frost ends the poem inconclusively. "If," the first word of his last line, warrants the most emphasis.

Themes and Meanings

Since he alludes to the New Testament book of Matthew elsewhere in his poetry, Frost certainly had read Matthew 10:29: "Are not two sparrows sold for a farthing? And one of them shall not fall on the ground without your Father." He was familiar, therefore, with the tradition of an omniscient and omnipotent God. He surely had read Job's impassioned questioning of God's purpose. In addition, Frost taught the philosophy of William James to students at Plymouth Normal School in New Hampshire, and in James's *Pragmatism* is the statement: "Let me pass to a very cognate philosophic problem, the question of design in nature." This text may or may not have served as Frost's source for the poem. In any event, Frost, like poets that preceded and followed him, was skeptical about the extent to which the Creator was benign, and he wondered about the degree of his involvement with his creations.

For example, William Blake in "The Tyger" (1794) wonders whether the same God could create both the fierce and the gentle; he asks the tiger, "Did he who made the lamb make thee?" In Thomas Hardy's "An August Midnight" (1899), a spider symbolizes evil in God's design. In Robert Lowell's "Mr. Edwards and the Spider" (1946), the black widow represents the damned soul. On the other hand, in Walt Whitman's "A Noiseless Patient Spider" (1891), the creature is benign.

Frost is expressing a sense of bewilderment felt by many religious people at one time or another: How does one reconcile death and evil with a benevolent deity? Fundamental to this problem is the extent to which God assumes a monitoring role—whether God watches over the details of the world or is concerned only with the grand design. Does Frost's bleak scene of death in "Design" call Matthew into question? Moreover, Genesis 1:31 says, "God saw everything that he had made, and, behold, it was very good." Does Frost intend the sonnet "Design," a meditation upon a dark reality, to refute this judgment? More likely, given the prevalence of questions in the sestet and the "If" at the start of the last line, he is unready to reach definitive conclusions. The questions alone are unsettling enough.

"Design" is one of Robert Frost's greatest poems, a structural and substantive masterpiece. His deliberate departures from sonnet traditions, his richly allusive language, and the sly ironic touches complement one another, and they demonstrate that an artist sometimes attains a degree of perfection that is lacking in nature.

Gerald H. Strauss

DIEN CAI DAU

Author: Yusef Komunyakaa (1947-
Type of poetry: Poetic sequence
First published: 1988

The Poems

The forty-three poems of *Dien Cai Dau* focus powerfully on familiar Vietnam War-era images, nightmares, and moral dilemmas that the United States at large still mulls over. Yusef Komunyakaa's subtle lyrical poems also provoke larger questions: When is killing right or wrong in wartime? How does one define a moral act in such chaos? How do "loving" relations (between men and women, between comrades in arms, between combatants) mutate in such conditions? What is the lasting effect on the survivors, the culture, and the land?

Komunyakaa, as a former combatant, chooses not to moralize. Though haunted by his Vietnam experience, he is not brutalized or desensitized. The poems (many of which reappear in the Pulitzer Prize-winning *Neon Vernacular*, 1993) show the poet remembering past battle scenes and grappling with unresolved moral questions that filter the present with ghostlike intensity. The phrase *dien cai dau* (loosely translatable as "crazy head") refers to the dizzying effects of war on all participants. Komunyakaa shows soldiers as "crazy heads" reacting "logically" to the illogical chaos of war. The war between cultures (black and white, Asian and American, men and women) is mediated by the observing poet, himself one of those struggling to make sense of the strangely beautiful but horrifying events of a very peculiar war.

Komunyakaa avoids abstractions. Poem after poem provides the voice of the simple soldier, fearful yet fascinated amid killing and destruction. "You and I Are Disappearing" presents a recurring memory of a girl burning to death in a linked series of metaphorical images: "She burns like a cattail torch/ dipped in gasoline./ She glows like the fat tip/ of a banker's cigar,/ silent as quicksilver./ A tiger under a rainbow/ at nightfall." The end of the poem carries Komunyakaa's emotional response: "She burns like a burning bush/ driven by a godawful wind." The "godawful wind" is the war itself, fueled by ill-defined, largely out-of-control forces.

The poems illustrate the ironies of this confused war. As soldiers view a Bob Hope United Service Organizations (USO) show in "Communiqué," inflamed lust contrasts with the horrifying "show" of war the soldiers cannot forget. "[W]e want the Gold Diggers,/ want a flash of legs/ through the hemorrhage of vermilion, giving us/ something to kill for." When the show ends and the music of desire has dissipated, the sitting soldiers hold their helmets "like rain-polished skulls."

Despite the carnage and destruction, all is not despair—for there are survivors. Those fated to live, even for the moment, cultivate a mystical, eclectic religiosity that borders on superstition. Belief in ghosts and higher beings helps to explain the shocking present. In "Thanks," the soldier wonders about this ill-defined presence, possibly a god, that has kept him alive: "What made me spot the monarch/ writhing on a single thread/ tied to a farmer's gate,/ holding the day together/ like an unfingered guitar string,/ is beyond me." Though he refuses to codify the force into a recognizable theology, he believes fully that "something" protects him while allowing others to die. Intuitively connecting the seen with the unseen is a means of staying alive, of "living right." When all rules are suspended, new connections freely combine in patterns of thought that do not necessarily disappear when veterans return home. In "Report from the Skull's Diorama," the soldier, now at home, relives a battle scene when he sees a photograph used by the enemy as propaganda (*"VC didn't kill/ Dr. Martin Luther King"*). He sees again the chopper leaving the battle zone, strewn with bodies and propaganda "leaflets/ clinging to the men & stumps,/ waving to me across the years." The meaning of the scene and the rightness and wrongness of actions are still somehow superfluous, overwhelmed in the present, at home, by haunting images.

Many poems in *Dien Cai Dau* depict the hyperalert fear emanating from life-threatening experiences. With lives on the line, the soldiers are open, their pores aware. "Red Pagoda" illustrates how the seemingly indefensible brutality of war can become inherently sane when placed in context. When the soldiers, fresh from a firefight, find they are unscathed, they destroy a pagoda in a real and symbolic frenzy in order to kill the fear and sense of frustration imposed by the war: "in our joy, we kick/ & smash the pagoda/ till it's dried blood/ covering the ground."

To stay alive, the soldier must be aware of the environment and all that lives there. Amid snakes, monkeys, and exotic plants live the Vietcong, who are there to kill Americans. In this natural world, insights are needed that cannot be found on linear military maps. In "A Greenness Taller Than Gods," Komunyakaa asks, "When will we learn/ to move like trees move?" Each plant, each shadow is ominous and fascinating. Even the grass they walk on aims "for the family jewels." A soldier cries over the death of a boy: "He won't stay dead, dammit!" Because this intense world produces memories that "won't stay down," all of life, both past and present, remains alive.

Forms and Devices

Komunyakaa, a master of the free verse form and the editor of several volumes of jazz poetry, follows the internal rhythm of the line, "hearing" the power of the image and tailoring the meaning for effect, in terms of both style and tone. In "Please," a poem from *Toys in a Field* (1986), he displays the sense of the dance as he describes a fellow soldier running to his death: "You were a greenhorn, so fearless,/ even foolish, & when I said *go*, Henry,/ you went dancing on a red string/ of bullets from that tree line/ as it moved from a low cloud."

In *Dien Cai Dau*, Komunyakaa focuses on narratives composed of imagery-rich scenes filled with color and sensory detail. He is not afraid to intersperse action with matter-of-fact dialogue. In "Fragging," as five men "pull straws/ under a tree on a hillside," one says, "Hell,/ the truth is the truth." The statement is specific to the moment at hand, yet it provokes larger questions that linger through the poem. What is the truth in war? Who counts and who does not? What acts are justifiable? When the fifth soldier "a finger/ into a metal ring, he's married/ to his devil." That juxtaposition of "married" to the "devil" is Komunyakaa's comment on the scene. When the grenade explodes, "Everything/ breaks for green cover,/ like a hundred red birds/ released from a wooden box." The colorful freshness of the metaphor contrasts with the messiness of the moral dilemmas. The metaphorical phrases function as action photographs, the moment frozen at its most significant stage. The color and beauty mesmerize, the very transparency of the language making the horror of the actions, as well as its peculiar logic, all too clear.

The metaphorical language captures the surreal immediacy of action while also suggesting that larger themes are at work. When Komunyakaa tells the reader, in "Ambush," that "A tiger circles us, in his broken cage/ between sky & what's human," he describes a real creature stalking soldiers in the jungle. On another level, the broken cage functions as a metaphor for the jungled chaos itself, and the tiger stands in as the looming violence the soldiers fight against, both within themselves and without. When Komunyakaa remembers "the cough of a mortar tube," the weapon is specific and real, and yet it is also a metaphor for the technological horror that threatens to obliterate all semblance of humanity.

Like a jazz composer, Komunyakaa routinely juxtaposes the seemingly incongruous. This coming together of unusual images (of beauty and horror, of nature's serenity and war's destruction) forces the reader to make surprising connections and gives the poems a surreal immediacy that reverberates. In "2527th Birthday of the Buddha," a monk leaps from a motorcycle, very much alive. Within moments, "he burned like a bundle of black joss sticks." The final line, "Waves of saffron robes bowed to the gasoline can," links the modern motorcycle and the gasoline can with the "ancient" Buddhist robes, showing, without explication, the crash of cultures as the crass modern world bangs against ancient dignity in an absurd struggle. The strange beauty of the saffron robes combines with a horror beyond words.

Succinct detail shows the soldier's intimacy with the natural world and past actions. In "Camouflaging the Chimera," the dreamy peace between actions is illustrated with quiet, fluid pacing. "We hugged bamboo & and leaned/ against a breeze off the river,/ slow-dragging with ghosts." The originality of the figurative language and the stacking of image upon image carries the meaning of the poem.

The brevity of the lines also conveys movement. Because few lines contain more than five words, imagery is highlighted and never strays far from the moment or strains for effect. Imagery is exact to the moment and yet reveals more beyond the immediate moment, such the scene of rape in "Re-creating the Scene": "They hold her down/ with their eyes,/ taking turns, piling stones/ on her father's grave." The pacing is immediate, phrased in active verbs and everyday language yet conveying the sacrilege, the desecration of more than simple flesh. Verb acting upon verb produces the compounding image symbolizing the larger rape the war is committing on the soldiers, the Vietnamese people, and the land itself.

Isolating a single scene with photographic clarity reveals the contradictions soldiers faced daily. In "A Break from the Bush," the linked, dancing fragments of meaning build and confuse even while they demonstrate the irony of a soldier's fate: "CI, who in three days will trip/ a fragmentation mine, runs after the ball/ into the whitecaps,/ laughing." Komunyakaa mixes a memory that captures the laughter and the beauty of the ocean waves with the ominous reality of death and war.

A sense of the fantastic pervades the imagery. In "Prisoners," the captured Vietcong look "like/ marionettes hooked to strings of light." Those puppets, propped up by an unreal light, at first merely fascinate. Further reflection reveals their real significance, for all the soldiers are mere puppets fighting for autonomy against larger forces. The rhythm of movement at the end of "Jungle Surrender" links a series of images from the story of the moment that ache for later reflection: "Moving toward what waits behind the trees./ the prisoner goes deeper into himself, away/ from how a man's heart divides him, deeper/ into the jungle's indigo mystery & beauty." This later reflection is the reason for the writing of these poems.

Themes and Meanings

For the American soldier fighting to survive in an alien jungle, even the familiar could be turned on its head. In "Hanoi Hannah," even Ray Charles's voice echoing in the darkness becomes a tool of propaganda for the Vietcong, reminding the soldier that nothing exists in isolation. Even in remote Southeast Asia, the realities of American racial and cultural history intervene. When the death of Martin Luther King, Jr., is also used as a propaganda weapon, it is directly linked for the black soldier with the deaths of comrades in arms.

Komunyakaa portrays the absurd sense of chaos in a world that nothing can be pinned to, a world where those in control remake the rules daily for their own good, where even the leaders are adrift in currents they cannot understand, where the results of actions can only be seen in retrospect. In "Re-creating the Scene," when a Vietnamese woman is raped by three soldiers, "she floats on their rage/ like a torn water flower,/ defining night inside a machine/ where men are gods." When authorities intervene, the woman is killed, the story is confused by counterstories, and nothing is settled; as for the baby that survives, its future is as uncertain as the men, the country, and the war itself.

When chaos dispenses with civilized "rules," when fear overwhelms love, present desires take precedence over longterm goals. In "One More Loss to Count," an American soldier and a Vietnamese woman, each with lovers elsewhere, slide into the arms of the moment. Even as he acts, the soldier recognizes that a line has been crossed and that there is no pretending that anything of worth can be preserved. Vietnam itself, the poems suggest, has crossed the line, both for soldiers and for those left at home, and thus has tainted the delicate balance of "civilized" morality for some time to come.

Even when the soldiers are "safe" at home they struggle to digest the past and understand what was lost and gained. Haunted by ghosts, the soldier knows, in "Missing in Action," that "we can't make one man/ walk the earth again." Something irretrievable has been lost, Komunyakaa suggests, and the men, the culture, and the earth itself must remake themselves in new forms.

Classifications of race, nationality, and gender are also changed when normal contexts are destroyed. In "Tu Do Street," the familiar segregated worlds the black soldier knew in America lose their boundaries as black and white soldiers sleep with the same women—whose brothers fight them in the bush. All of them are more interconnected than any can realize: "these rooms/ run into each other like tunnels/ leading to the underworld." Above all, they are connected by a heightened knowledge of death. In "Donut Dollies," when battle-weary soldiers with "the names of dead men/ caught in their throats" fail to notice the perky "dollies" who greet them, both the numb infantrymen and the women must learn new roles.

Those experiencing the extremes are linked to those who have shared similar moments, all holders of "insider knowledge." Komunyakaa seeks understanding, even kinship, with those he fought against. "Prisoners" describes his fascination with Vietcong prisoners of war who fail to crack under interrogation: "I remember how one day/ I almost bowed to such figures." In "Sappers," a soldier marvels at the enemy's determination, even as they push forward to kill him: "Opium, horse, nothing/ sends anybody through concertina/ this way." As the Vietcong "try to fling themselves/ into our arms," he marvels at the intimacy he feels for those who share similar visions of death, passion, and hate.

Haunted by ghosts, Komunyakaa vividly describes the soldier reliving scenes that he still milks for meaning. For those who have lived intensely, memories are the haunting heartbeat of the present. In a literal sense, the soldier, well trained to avoid danger, has trouble adjusting to a world of "safety." In "Losses," the soldier, back home, "scouts the edge of town,/ always with one ear/ cocked & ready to retreat." In a metaphorical sense, he replays endless scenes, working to find meaning for past moments he had no time to ponder in the heat of battle. The lessons learned—the intimacy of man with nature, the link between killing and lust, the new definitions of race and culture, the raw excitement of extreme behavior and its accompanying emotional explosiveness—must be linked with those irretrievable moments before the present can proceed. Until these ghosts are exorcised, more "crazy heads" will rule the day.

Mark Vogel

DIFFICULT TIMES

Author: Bertolt Brecht (1898-1956)
Type of poem: Meditation
First published: 1964, as "Schwierige Zeiten," in *Gedichte, vol. 7: 1948-1956*; English
   translation collected in *Bertolt Brecht: Poems, 1913-1956*, 1976

The Poem

"Difficult Times" is a short (nine lines), unrhymed poem, written in free verse with
an irregular rhythmic pattern. Using the first person, Brecht makes it clear that it is he
who is speaking directly to the reader.

The first image is of the speaker standing at his desk and looking out the window,
presumably ruminating during a lull in his work. There is a hint of restlessness implied
in this action. As he looks into the garden, he vaguely discerns an elderberry bush
("elder tree"). He sees red and black shapes that remind him of such a bush that existed
in his childhood home in Augsburg. The poem's last four lines concern indecision and
the fact that he would need to put on his glasses in order to see the tree clearly. He
"quite seriously" debates with himself whether to go from the desk to the table to get
his spectacles, thus enabling him to see "Those black berries again." The poem ends
without stating whether he decides to get his glasses, but the fact that it does not say
that he does implies inaction.

The reason or reasons why the speaker is living in "Difficult Times" are not
explicitly stated in the poem. However, the poem was written very late in Brecht's life,
and the indecision, inability to see well, and perhaps even the physical difficulty of
going from one part of the room to another obviously reflect the difficulties of
advancing age. (In another late poem, "Things Change," Brecht refers to himself as
both a young man and "an old man forgetting his name.") In addition, Brecht may be
implying that both personal regrets and the political situation in Europe have made
the times difficult. As an exile from his native land, Brecht had moved from place to
place, changing countries of residence, as he once put it, "more often than I changed
shirts." He had had several wives and numerous mistresses (sometimes simultaneously), so that difficult memories and personal regrets would seem inevitable.

Forms and Devices

In his many essays about the style and function of poetry, Brecht spoke of writing
in "Basic German" and of using what he calls the *gestich* form. In Brecht's *Selected
Poems* (1947), edited by R. H. Hays, this is explained as "slightly formalized speech
rhythms with certain forced pauses produced by arbitrary line divisions to preserve a
calculated emphasis." The *gestich* form is evident here. This form includes the notion
that the poem when read aloud should follow the "gesture" of the reader—as an actor
would deliver lines of dialogue in a play. Brecht also cited his desire to avoid
traditional poetic forms with many layers of hidden meanings which would make
them less intelligible to the "folk" for whom he is writing. As Hays notes, Brecht's

work, including this poem, "lacks sensuous decoration and uses images with economy in the service of the idea."

Despite Brecht's stated intentions not to employ layers of hidden meanings, traditional poetic devices, and symbols in his poetry, the very nature of the genre makes such a course difficult. Poetry is a form in which "shorthand" language is used to express ideas and meanings which would require in prose more length, more detail, and more explication. Brecht uses symbolism in "Difficult Times." The desk indicates the work of writing, and the eyeglasses a potential aid in seeing one's situation and life more clearly. The elderberry bush (also known as the tamarind) also has symbolic biblical and folkloric connotations. In *The Magic Garden* (1976), by Anthony S. Mercante, two entries are notable, and both are tragic. First, it is said that the wood from the elder was used to construct the cross on which Christ was crucified. Second, as the legend goes, Judas Iscariot, although he had been forgiven by Jesus, was so distraught over his act of betrayal that "he saw a tamarind tree, tall and beautiful. Then the Devil entered his mind and he took a rope, made a noose, and hanged himself from the tree, which became short and twisted."

These negative images connect in an ironic way to the poet's childhood memory of the elder tree. As a child, Brecht was presumably innocent, trusting, and relatively happy. Then, as a young man, by his own account, his experience as a medical corpsman in the German army reinforced what he had decided in 1916 about patriotism and armed service: "[T]he statement that it is sweet and an honor to die for the Fatherland can only be rated as propaganda." By the end of World War I he had joined the many young men of his generation in their disillusionment, distrust of government, and hatred of armed conflict. Now, forty years later, the world had endured an even bloodier war; still the prospect of permanent peace was as distant as ever.

Themes and Meanings

The poem's primary level of meaning concerns the difficulties of growing older—the physical difficulties (failing senses), the mental difficulties (failing concentration and difficulties in making decisions), and the fact that one remembers one's youth, when one was healthier and happier. Beyond these meanings, however, if one looks at Brecht's life, one can also theorize that he may be brooding over particular memories, regrets, and dissatisfactions. As most people do, Brecht probably had regrets about the life he had led, goals he had not reached, and people he had hurt.

It is conceivable, for example, that Brecht suffered some remorse over his use of "collaborators" to compose the plays which brought him acclaim. Bruce Cook, in *Brecht in Exile* (1982), explains that Brecht rationalized this practice by stating that "the work profits if many take part in it." (Brecht did credit those who worked with him, although credit was given in very small type on the reverse side of the title page, tucked into the copyright material.) John Fuegi, in *Brecht & Company* (1994), argues that great as he had been as a theatrical innovator and director, Brecht had not in fact been the playwright he had pretended to be. Those who had actually created the works never received the money nor the acclaim they deserved.

Perhaps more than personal concerns, Political and social concerns could also have made Brecht's last years "Difficult Times." In all Brecht's work the most consistently recognizable element is social content. All the plays (the genre for which he is best known) were meant to "teach" audiences, to make them aware of universal problems, particularly the absence of peace and the horrors of war. Now, back in his homeland in the 1950's, after living many years abroad, he was undoubtedly disturbed by the fact of the Cold War.

After the rise of Adolf Hitler in the 1930's, Brecht had become active in the fight against fascism, which in Europe at the time widely meant favoring communism. He fled Hitler's Germany to live in various Scandinavian countries, including Finland (until that government formed an alliance with the Third Reich), finally settling in Santa Monica, California, in 1941. He left there in October, 1947, and ultimately accepted the invitation of the East German government to head a theater—the Berlin Ensemble—in the communist sector of Berlin. However, between the time of his leaving Europe and his return, a number of disquieting events had taken place.

Although before World War II Brecht has publicly affirmed that the Soviet Union represented the "most progressive social system of our age," he had to admit after the purges under Soviet dictator Josef Stalin and the subsequent revelations about life in the Soviet Union that there was not too much difference between various types of totalitarian regimes. Neither fascism nor communism had provided much benefit for the "folk," and now the former allies against Hitler seemed determined to avoid permanent peace. All was not well in a world divided, a city divided, and people in conflict.

In his introduction to Klaus Volker's book *Brecht Chronicle* (1975), Carl Weber writes that "the refugee and persecuted are becoming the archetypes of the century," and assuredly Brecht fits this profile, notwithstanding the fact that much of that characterization was carefully created by the man himself. Although at the time this poem was written Brecht was no longer a persecuted refugee, the times remained difficult for him, probably largely because of his reflections. An aura of discontent permeates the poem. It suggests regret about the past and uneasiness about the present with no suggestion of future improvement, as after old age comes death.

Edythe M. McGovern

THE DISAPPOINTMENT

Author: Aphra Behn (1640-1689)
Type of poem: Narrative
First published: 1684, in *Poems upon Several Occasions, with a Voyage to the Island of Love*

The Poem

"The Disappointment" is a narrative poem in lyric form. It consists of fourteen numbered stanzas of ten lines each, and it tells the story of a single romantic tryst. It is written from the woman's point of view, explaining her frustration or disappointment when her young "Swain" is unable to make good on his promise.

Sexual dysfunction was a subject of ridicule in erotic poetry long before it became a subject of concern in advice columns. There is a classical precedent for "The Disappointment" in the last book of Ovid's *Amores* (*Loves*, 2 B.C.); however, the immediate source is an anonymous French poem, "Sur une Impuissance" (on an impotence, 1661), which Aphra Behn freely translates. Her poem is frankly erotic, and the author would have been called a "libertine" even in the relatively carefree days of King Charles II, affectionately known as the Merry Monarch. Behn was called much worse in the eighteenth and nineteenth centuries, but in the twentieth century was hailed as the first English woman to earn a living as a writer. Today "The Disappointment" tends to amuse readers rather than to shock or to titillate. Behn appeals to feminists as a woman who was comfortable with her sexuality.

The lovers in the poem have Greek names; he is "the Amorous *Lysander*," and she is "fair *Cloris*." They are said to be a shepherd and a shepherdess who meet toward dusk in "a lone Thicket made for Love." Their embraces become a kind of sexual warfare in which he prepares to take the victor's "Spoils." The story is straightforward. Lysander comes upon Cloris by surprise. He uses a degree of "force," but she "permits" his advances. She does all the talking, saying no in a way that he takes, correctly, to mean yes (stanza 3):

> *My Dearer Honour ev'n to You*
> *I cannot, must not give—Retire,*
> *Or take this Life, whose chiefest part*
> *I gave you with the Conquest of my Heart.*

They kiss and touch until she is "half dead and breathless," indeed "Defenceless." She offers her virginity, but he is "Unable to perform the Sacrifice." He tries to rouse himself but fails miserably. She offers to help, but she finds that it is no use and runs away. He is left alone, cursing (stanza 9):

> He curs'd his Birth, his Fate, his Stars;
> But more the *Shepherdess*'s Charms,
> Whose soft betwitching Influence
> Had Damn'd him to the *Hell* of Impotence.

Forms and Devices

The verse stanzas divide the story into a series of moments. Each stanza is composed of two quatrains and a couplet, rhyming *abbacddcee* or occasionally *abbacdcdee*. The rhymes are sometimes partial, as with "guess" and "exprest" in stanza 12, but these half rhymes only add to the comic effect. The last line of each stanza is a stately iambic pentameter, whereas the other lines are in iambic tetrameter; the longer line stops the movement and lets the reader savor the situation. For example, when Lysander approaches the "Altar" of love, Behn calls it "That Fountain where Delight still flows,/ And gives the Universal World Repose."

The poem is thus more like a sequence of songs than a short story, more like a set of snapshots than a film. In photojournalism the trick is to capture interesting poses at the right intervals. Behn's timing is just right—and certainly better than poor Lysander's. The first seven of the fourteen stanzas are devoted to his approach, the last seven to his unhappy retreat. The first stanza stops with her eyes, the second with her speechless response to Lysander, the third with her acquiescence to his approaches, and so forth. Similarly, the last stanza ends with his curse, the penultimate with her disappearance, the third from last with her hasty departure. The poem's central line reveals that Lysander is "Unable to perform." The last line, indeed the last word, gives the diagnosis: "Impotence."

Behn uses poetic paraphrase to give the poem a comic seriousness. She says that Lysander spots Cloris as the sun is setting, or rather as "That Gilded Planet of the Day/ . . . Was now descending to the Sea." She uses poetic exaggeration, or hyperbole, to make the story seem serious but not too serious. The only light available is the light from Cloris' eyes, which are brighter than the sun. She also employs mythological references to make the characters seem important, even while the reader realizes that they are mere flesh and blood. The chariot is that of Helios of Greek myth. When Cloris is still sufficiently in the dark to think that a "Potent God" awaits her, in stanza 11, Lysander's organ is called *"Priapas"*—that is, Priapus, the god of male fertility. Yet Lysander's Priapas turns out to be "Fabulous" (in the sense of being a fable, "as Poets feign," not in the modern sense of being especially good). Cloris runs away as Daphne ran away from Apollo when Apollo accosted her, or as Venus ran from the sight of her "slain" lover, Adonis. Classical elements such as these give the poem a mock-heroic quality. Aphra Behn wrote poems under the pen name Astrea, a mythological reference to the Roman goddess of justice who was said to have lived on earth in the Golden Age.

Themes and Meanings

"The Disappointment" is a poem on the sensitive and sometimes taboo subject of male impotence. Other English poets wrote on such topics before the twentieth century, none more infamously than Behn's friend John Wilmot, the second earl of Rochester, whose poem "Imperfect Enjoyment" was based on the same French original as Behn's poem and first appeared in the same volume of poetry. Rochester was thought to have written both poems until scholars established Behn's authorship from manuscript evidence. Whereas "Imperfect Enjoyment" sympathizes with the impotent man, who ends up cursing the temptress, "The Disappointment" sympathizes with the woman. In the last stanza, the narrative turns from the third person to the first as the narrator says, "The *Nymph* is Resentments none but I/ Can well Imagine or Condole." "Resentments" here is closer to the French *rensentement*, a feeling of injury, than to the modern sense of personal grievance. The female narrator can imagine the female lover's position better than a male narrator possibly could, and so can offer condolence. The feeling of disappointment is mutual, of course, and like other versions, Behn's narrative ends with the man's lament. When Behn's shepherd curses the shepherdess and her "Influence," he also curses the stars, and with just as much reason. "Influence" was a technical term in astrology, describing the way a heavenly body can affect humans through rays that flow into them, and Behn used the word in the old sense as well as the modern one. The man could as well blame the stars or planets as blame the equally unfortunate woman.

Behn reveals herself as a good psychologist, realizing that the real "Strife" is not so much between two lovers as between desire and fulfillment. She introduces Lysander as a man with "an impatient Passion," which bodes ill. Before he can "perform," he is "o'er-Ravished"—that is, overstimulated (stanza 7). He is "too transported," or moved, by what he sees. His pleasure becomes pain, Behn explains in stanza 8, because "too much Love destroys" the pleasure. At this point no technique or "Art" can help him. His overzealous "Rage" for sex has "debauch'd his Love." When Cloris tries to arouse him, she finds "a snake." More specifically, she finds that he is "Disarm'd of all his Awful Fires./ And Cold as Flow'rs bath'd in the Morning-Dew." The imagery suggests (but does not confirm) that he has ejaculated prematurely.

It took real spunk for a woman to write a poem like "The Disappointment" in the seventeenth century, and Aphra Behn certainly had it. She wrote plays for the stage at a time when humor was often bawdy, and she was notable for her love intrigues. The satirist Alexander Pope remarked of her stage presence that she "loosely does . . . tread [the stage]/ Who safely puts all characters to bed." She did not cater to men's fantasies; she told it as she saw it. Women who read "The Disappointment" can understand why feminists from Virginia Woolf to Germaine Greer have embraced Aphra Behn as a true predecessor.

Thomas Willard

A DISPLAY OF MACKEREL

Author: Mark Doty (1953-
Type of poem: Meditation
First published: 1995, in *Atlantis*

The Poem

Mark Doty's "A Display of Mackerel" is a meditation on beauty and on beauty's ability to triumph over death. This free-verse poem comprises seventeen three-line stanzas and describes the poet's encounter with a display of fish. Doty skillfully explores the rich implications of this encounter. As the living poet admires the dead fish, the human soul encounters the extraordinary beauty of the display and finds within this beauty a possible antidote for the fear of death. With gradually expanding complexity, Doty infuses this encounter with associations and intimations that transcend the mere fact of mackerel on ice. Through a systematic appraisal of paradoxes, the poet leads his reader along the pathways of the poetic imagination, dismantling humanity's anxieties about life, death, and the eternity of the soul.

"A Display of Mackerel" opens with a straightforward description of the fish lying on ice in rows. Having established a foundation of mundane description, Doty quickly departs from factuality and starts to explore the associations the mackerel inspire in him. Shortly after the first stanza, the first images of the extraordinary, the beautiful, and the precious begin to intrude upon the everyday: Not only are the fish dark and cold, but also "each [is] a foot of luminosity." By the third stanza, the fish have become a lens through which Doty will consider important issues of existence: "radiant sections/ like seams of lead/ in a Tiffany window." Despite the fact that they are dead, cold, and nonhuman, the mackerel represent a precious, shimmering realm of existence far removed from unpleasant and unsettling conceptions of death.

In the next few stanzas, Doty extends his meditations on life and death and draws the reader into this process by way of direct address. The poet instructs the readers to expand their consideration of the fish: "think abalone" and "think sun on gasoline." In the tradition of Romantic poets such as William Wordsworth—who viewed nature as a primary source of the highest poetic and spiritual revelation—Doty perceives divine significance in the universe of beauty and selflessness the mackerel inhabit: "Splendor, and splendor,/ and not a one in any way/ distinguished from the other."

Midway through the poem, the poetic transformation of the mackerel into exemplars of life, death, and the unity of existence is complete. As the momentum of poetic imagery and paradox increases, "A Display of Mackerel" accumulates terms and phrases that suggest spiritual and existential complexity: "they're *all* exact expressions/ of the one soul,/ each a perfect fulfillment/ of heaven's template." Once the connection between the mackerel and spirituality has been consummated, Doty consolidates the poem's personification of and identification with the fish by considering an existential trade. Would humanity exchange its troubled, individualistic ideas of life for the serenity and beauty of a mackerel's existence?

> Suppose we could iridesce,
>
> like these, and lose ourselves
> entirely in the universe
> of shimmer—would you want
>
> to be yourself only,
> unduplicatable, doomed
> to be lost?

Having extracted beauty and this question from his encounter with the display of mackerel, Doty completes the arc of the poem by returning to the fish. While they were an objective "they" in the poem's opening description, the fish are personified by Doty at the end of the poem; they are no longer alien but intimate. He knows that they prefer to be as they are, "flashing" and "multitudinous." He knows that they do not care that they are dead. He can imagine their happiness "even on ice, to be together, selfless,/ which is the price of gleaming."

Forms and Devices

"A Display of Mackerel" and the collection to which it belongs, *Atlantis*, mark an important transition in Doty's work. While *My Alexandria* (1993) is praised for its explorations of the theme of loss, the poems in that collection articulate a conflicted and skeptical attitude about poetry's transcendent powers. In contrast, "A Display of Mackerel" insists upon hope in the face of loss and revels in the ability of poetry to redeem and transform reality. In this poem and throughout *Atlantis*, Doty constructs numerous paradoxical linkages between the natural and the human-made ("sun on gasoline"), between the dead and the living ("bolting forward, heedless of stasis"), and between individuality and collectivity ("the rainbowed school// in which no verb is singular,/ or every one is"). These paradoxical juxtapositions produce an atmosphere in which impossibilities become possible, connections between disparate elements flourish, and the poetic imagination transforms everyday reality.

The poem mixes several levels of poetic language to create this magical, transformative effect. The language of precise description ("parallel rows") combines with spiritual terms ("each a perfect fulfillment/ of heaven's template"), blends with language relating to natural beauty ("luminosity," "radiant," "shimmer," "gleaming"), and mixes with worldly value ("Tiffany window," and "this enameling the jeweler's/ made"). This combination of linguistic levels produces a fluid, multiple context in which Doty reveals his meditations on life and death. When taken as a whole, this mixture of levels of beauty and value suggests one of the important meanings of the poem: There is spiritual awakening in the most ordinary moments, and there is significance in the most accidental encounters. By combining this multiplicity of types of language into one poem, Doty replicates the spiritual oneness the poem proposes.

The juxtaposition of paradoxical ideas and this mixture of levels of language support a third poetic technique contributing to the poem's meditative atmosphere: Imagery, that very basic element of poetic expression, is amplified in "A Display of Mackerel." Doty's quickly shifting use of poetic imagery feeds the paradoxical and combinative logic of the poem. In the course of the poem, the fish are related to images of light, windows, rainbows, soapbubbles, jewelry, and a classroom. The speed at which Doty introduces and then alters these images contributes to the wonder and magic that lies behind the poem's expression. In general, Doty's imagery falls into two categories that, taken together, point to the two realms of existence the poem's meditations are bridging. On one hand, the poem is filled with images of external beauty; on the other hand, there are many images of internal spirituality and intellect. Together, the two categories form an equation between beauty and spirit that Doty extends to all of creation. Living or dead, fish or human, individual or collective, life is beautiful; the end of life need not be tragic.

Themes and Meanings

"A Display of Mackerel" is an excellent example of poetry's ability to link complex realizations about self and existence to that which is generally considered mundane and even unpleasant. In Doty's hands, a display of dead fish becomes a window into the nature of the soul and a measure of human anxiety about death. In the course of the poem he asks and alludes to several important questions: What are the boundaries of life and death? Is death final and annihilating? Or may death be eclipsed by something else? By applying imagination to the observed world, Doty harmonizes levels of expression and orders of existence. The "price of gleaming" indicated in the poem's final line is a happiness, a selflessness, and a togetherness that confounds even death. Persisting beyond the boundaries of individual existence and physiological function, this greater form of existence, predicated on total investment in the gleaming accident of the spirit, is a refuge for the poet and an antidote to the tragedy of death. It is not a solution to death per se but rather an awareness of beauty's relentlessness that is at least partially realized by the poem itself.

Yet in these meditations on life and death, the reader can sense a tragedy behind the poem. The collection to which this poem belongs is dedicated to Wally Roberts, Doty's lover who died a year before the publication of *Atlantis* of complications due to acquired immunodeficiency syndrome (AIDS). In the light of this death—which is chronicled in Doty's memoir *Heaven's Coast* (1996)—one may read this poem and a large part of Doty's work as engaged in a dialogue with loss and the redemption of love in spite of death. By considering how love and death influence the meaning of "A Display of Mackerel," one may read Doty's poetry as an important late twentieth century expression of themes that run throughout the history of Western literature (the elegy, Romanticism, modernism). The intimation that in the end life triumphs over death—that there is a possible antidote to the losses of death—is crucial to reading this poem as an antielegy, a celebration of the beauty of the spirit in spite of death.

Finally, "A Display of Mackerel" is firmly grounded in an impressive poetic tradition. Echoing the spiritual luminosity of Wordsworth, the poem also invites comparisons with the transcendental poetry of Emily Dickinson and the meditations of Wallace Stevens. "A Display of Mackerel" is an excellent example of the vitality of the poetic imagination in American literature. It is a meditation on the power poetry holds to strip reality of its familiarity and to address the complexities of the soul.

Daniel M. Scott III

THE DISTANCES

Author: Charles Olson (1910-1970)
Type of poem: Meditation
First published: 1960, in *The Distances*

The Poem

"The Distances" is a meditation on love and human alienation, but the poem does not present its argument or define its terms in a straightforward way. The poem begins, "So the distances are Galatea," with the conjunction "so" suggesting that the reader has walked into the middle of a conversation. Something has been left out, and this is typical of Olson's poetry—he often juxtaposes fragments so that the reader must draw the connections or attempt to fill in the blanks. The reader may wonder what kind of "distances" the speaker has in mind and how such distances are connected to the mythological Galatea. The poem is a sometimes cryptic, sometimes disturbing, but finally profoundly moving meditation on the "distances" that human beings put between themselves and others, and the powerful force that "knows no distance," love. The philosophical discussion is illustrated by references to a Greek myth, a newspaper story from Florida, Olson's book *Call Me Ishmael*, the Greek god Zeus, and the Roman leaders Julius Caesar and his adopted son, Caesar Augustus.

The poem opens and closes with references to the myth of Pygmalion and Galatea. In the myth, Pygmalion, the King of Cyprus, falls in love with the unattainable Aphrodite, goddess of love. He sculpts an ivory image of her, places it in his bed, and then prays to Aphrodite for compassion. The goddess brings the statue to life as Galatea, an actual woman who becomes Pygmalion's wife. Following these brief references to the Pygmalion myth are references to "a German inventor in Key West/ who had a Cuban girl, and kept her, after her death/ in his bed." These lines allude to an incident reported in the Key West newspapers in 1952, in which police arrested an eighty-three-year-old man, Karl Tanzler, who had fallen in love with an ill Cuban girl, removed her body from its grave, preserved it, and kept it for eight years in his house. The police found the corpse dressed for bed, with fresh flowers in its hair.

From this bizarre modern version of the Pygmalion story, the poem moves to its most obscure section, in which "sons" go "down La Cluny's steps to the old man sitting/ a god throned on torsoes" in search of "a secret" that can perhaps "undo distance." "La Cluny" may refer to the Musée de Cluny in Paris or to the Abbaye de Cluny in Mâcon, France, but the geographical referent is less important than the psychological theme. In *Call Me Ishmael*, Olson traces the theme of the rebellious or exiled son, separated from the father, through various ancient myths and connects this theme with the idea that the "deeper part" of the human self is obscure and buried. To discover this deeper self one needs to "go down" into the depths of the psyche, where one will find, "throned on torsos," the father, "your own grim sire, who did beget ye, exiled sons." The separation of father from son, suggests Olson, is psychologically entangled with the distance between the superficial self and the deep self.

Threaded throughout the poem are repeated references to "old Zeus" and "young Augustus," and just before the poem's end the speaker imagines "[Julius] Caesar" stroking the cheek of his adopted son, "young Augustus [Octavian]." At this point all of the stories are conflated: "old Zeus" hides "young/ Galatea"; "the girl who makes you weep" is both Galatea and "the corpse [kept] alive by all/ your arts"; and Julius strokes the "stone face" of "young Augustus." The poem ends with a kind of prayer that love will "yield/ to this man/ that the impossible distance/ be healed." The prayer is answered with Aphrodite's words: "I wake you,/ stone. Love this man."

Forms and Devices

Although "The Distances" is rich in imagery and allusion, most of the forms and devices of traditional poetry are absent. Olson uses no rhyme, no meter, and no stanza breaks, and he violates conventions of syntax, spelling ("torsoes" instead of "torsos"), capitalization, and punctuation. His lines are unpredictable in length, in spacing, and in their left margins, which may begin at any of four different tab settings. In some ways the poem has the look of the American poet William Carlos Williams's well-known "triadic stanza," in which the left margin of each line is indented farther than the previous line's, so that each three-line stanza looks like a descending set of steps. Olson, however, is not as regular as Williams in his use of the pattern; his margins move in an entirely unpredictable manner. The lines are heavily enjambed, and punctuation is sparse. In fact, no periods appear until the poem's final line. In addition, none of the stories is fully told. Instead readers are given bits and pieces of narrative. All of this forces the reader to read slowly and to re-read. The unpredictable line breaks and irregular spacings suggest a hesitating, uncertain voice groping toward meaning. This uncertainty is further stressed when, at two points, sentences with the syntax of statements conclude with question marks.

The jagged, broken quality of the poem's form is offset, however, by several patterns of repetition and contrast. The most obvious of these is the pair of names "old Zeus" and "young Augustus," which are repeated together or singly six times in the poem. The paired names stress the "distance" between both old-young and human-divine, but they also personify the kinds of desire—for "mastery" and "control"—that people mistake or substitute for love and that end up creating "the distances." The different stories referred to in the poem repeat a similar theme, which Olson stresses by blending details of the Pygmalion, the Key West, and the La Cluny stories into one another.

Pygmalion and the German inventor believe that they can create an object for their love, while the "sons" in La Cluny learn nothing and "go away" disappointed because they expected to find, and hence to possess or control, the "secret" that can "undo distance." One final structural contrast in the poem is the juxtaposition of abstract, metaphysical language, as in "Death is a loving matter, then, a horror/ we cannot bide," with vivid, concrete images, such as the German inventor with the dead Cuban girl in his bed. Olson's is an erudite, intellectually demanding poetry.

Themes and Meanings

The poem's title states its topic: the "distances" that human beings create that isolate them from one another and from the world in which they live. Distances separate men from women, fathers from sons, the old from the young, the divine from the human, and the superficial self from the deep self. The poem suggests that such distances arise because people misunderstand the nature of love; instead of recognizing love as a universal force of nature that "places all where each is, as they are, for every moment," they understand love to mean their own "mastery" or "control" over whatever persons or objects they find most precious. Love then becomes perverted into little more than a form of greed. Like the German inventor, people convince themselves that they can turn death into life, or they search for the "secret" that will "undo distance" and give them the mastery they desire.

The poem suggests that human beings, having created these "distances" by seeing human relationships in terms of "mastery" or "control," cannot hope to "undo distance" by means of mastery or control. Instead they must yield to the power of love, a divine force of nature personified by Aphrodite, which alone can heal "the impossible distance" between man and woman, father and son, the old and the young, the divine and the human, the superficial self and the deep self.

Pygmalion is mistaken when he believes that he can somehow compel or possess Aphrodite's love by producing a stone image of her and setting it in his bed—that is precisely the kind of misunderstanding of love that creates "the distances." However, unlike the German inventor, Pygmalion corrects his mistake when, instead of seeking to control the goddess, he yields to her power and adopts a reverent attitude of prayer. It is this new attitude, this change of heart, that leads the goddess to bring the stone to life—not as Aphrodite, which was Pygmalion's original greedy desire, but as Galatea, an actual woman who is capable of giving to Pygmalion what each human, according to this poem, needs most vitally: love.

Gary Grieve-Carlson

DO NOT WEEP, MAIDEN, FOR WAR IS KIND

Author: Stephen Crane (1871-1900)
Type of poem: Meditation
First published: 1899, in *War Is Kind*

The Poem

"Do not weep, maiden, for war is kind" is Stephen Crane's poem about war and its aftermath. In twenty-six lines, the persona of the poem addresses the loved ones of the soldiers who died on the battlefield amid mayhem and chaos. Crane's use of blank verse is well suited for the subject of war because it lacks the harmonious patterns of rhyme and meter. The poem is composed of five stanzas, and the indented beginning of the second and fourth stanzas characterize a change in setting. While the first, third, and fifth stanzas focus on the survivors of dead soldiers, the indented stanzas graphically depict scenes of the battlefield. The refrain gives a structural unity to the entire poem as it consistently appears before and after each stanza: "Do not weep./ War is kind." This chorus of two lines helps to connect the emotional experience with the actual experience of war.

The poem begins with the pain of separation between a maiden and her lover who died on the battlefield. To heighten the tragic effect, the persona describes the last moment of the dying lover who "threw wild hands toward the sky" in a frantic state as he fell from his horse while "the affrighted steed ran on alone." A perceptive reader will note the ambivalent tone of the persona: On one hand, there is sympathy for the maiden's unfulfilled love; on the other hand, there is sympathy for the soldier's agony whose death marks a moment of escape from the painful state of psychological terror and physical injury.

In the third stanza, after the refrain, the poet presents another scene of tragic separation with the regiment's drums in the backdrop to cue the reader about a battle scene. Intensifying the emotional effect of the tragic separation, the speaker addresses the fatherless "babe." Again, the graphic description of the dying soldier as he tumbles "in the yellow trenches" suggests an ambivalent attitude on the part of the speaker. His fall in death makes a mockery of the glorious display of the regiment's flag with its eagle and flashing colors of red and gold. Marching behind this flag, the dying soldiers cannot rise to heroic heights because they are like wounded animals who are guided by instincts of rage and fear. Furthermore, the persona ridicules "the virtue of slaughter" that is exalted by the regiment as it trains soldiers to "drill and die." The ambivalence between tragic separation and a sense of relief amid a setting of death and destruction is also evoked through the contrasting images of the sunshine in the "yellow trench" of the fallen soldier's grave site and "slaughter" on the battlefield that creates a field "where a thousand corpses lie."

In the last stanza, the speaker addresses the mother of a dead soldier who is being honored as a hero by his regiment. Unlike stanzas 1 and 3, this stanza is not followed by a graphic depiction of her son's dying moment. In this instance, the refrain echoes a reminder to the reader that the last moment of this soldier must have been marked with the same tragic moment of pain and panic that is the lot of the regiment's men "who drill and die." The "splendid shroud" of the regiment evokes the contrast between the brutality of the battlefield and the relief that comes to the embattled and wounded soldiers in the form of death.

Forms and Devices

The title of the poem resonates with irony as it juxtaposes tears with kindness and invites the reader to connect the brutal image of war to a kind reality despite the brutal setting of a battlefield. Although the poet does not address the readers directly, he allows them to witness scenes of tragic separation between the maiden and her lover, between the child and the father, and between the mother and her son to enhance the ironic effect. The irony of the poem contrasts the expected reaction of the mourners who suffer the pangs of separation with the unexpected outcome for the fallen soldiers who are freed from their emotional and physical trauma by death. The pervasive sense of loss for a loved one makes the title sound like an understatement, thus announcing the ironic intent of the author. At the same time, the psychological and physical condition of the falling soldiers ridicules the notion of romantic heroism that disregards the realism of the battlefield where the presence of death can promise relief.

In addition to the contrasting images, which contribute to the ironic effect, Crane makes powerful use of symbol and simile to enhance the realism of the tragic outcome of war. Images such as the "wild hands" of the soldier mounted on "the affrighted steed" and "booming drums" symbolize the emotional state of men who are in a state of panic, anger, and fear. In the last stanza, the mourning mother's "heart hung humble as a button" is a simile reiterating the sorrow and helpless condition of a woman whose son has been snatched from her. The juxtaposition of the mourning mother's pain with the heroic farewell and "the splendid shroud" of her son frames the question of the "unexplained glory" claimed by the military's regiment. The contrast between romantic glory and the reality of war is also reinforced by a sarcastic tone as the poet personifies the great "Battle-God" with his "Kingdom" that consists of corpses.

The ambivalent attitude of the persona toward the tragic theme of separation confirms Crane's naturalist trend in portraying the changing phases and faces of natural forces. However, for Crane the natural cycle of events encompasses both benign and malignant forces that contribute to the complexity of the human condition. Because Crane incorporates nature's role in an ambivalent manner, it is difficult to blame nature as the source of tragedy in human life. In fact, the alternating shift from dialogue to description in the poem allows the poet to emphasize the ambivalence of the persona's attitude toward war. Ultimately, death appears as a tragic experience for the bereaved, yet it marks a moment of relief from pain.

Themes and Meanings

"Do not weep, maiden, for war is kind" is a poem in Crane's collection of poems titled *War Is Kind*. In this poem, Crane attempts to depict the theme of war in the emerging tradition of realism that questions the honor and glory of war heroes. Crane is a naturalist as well as a realist who repudiates the heroic tradition of Romanticism without compromising the complexity of human reality. The poem portrays the pain of separation caused by the brutality of war; therefore, Crane's criticism is directed toward warmongers and not strictly toward the overpowering forces of nature. Furthermore, most naturalists at this time depicted natural forces in biological terms, but Crane does not discount the psychological forces that connect human reality to one's physical surroundings and environment. Both the mourners and the dead soldiers must succumb to the supremacy of natural forces, yet the horror of the soldiers and the sorrow of the mourners are two different conditions resulting from war. In this short poem, Crane links sensory images and psychological realism to capture both the mental pain of the bereaved and the physical pain of the falling soldiers. The irony implicit in the title also illustrates the ironies latent in human reality. In this case, the irony exposes the hypocrisy of the mythic glory attributed to warring soldiers as well as the nonheroic demeanor of soldiers on the battlefield.

Although Crane uses the setting of war in many of his works, including his famous Civil War novel *The Red Badge of Courage* (1895), it was only a year before the publication of this poem that he personally observed war scenes. He was so strongly drawn to the setting of war that he attempted to join the United States Navy for active service in the Spanish-American War, but he was rejected. Consequently, in 1898 he became a war correspondent. In his war memoirs Crane writes, "It is because war is neither magnificent nor squalid; it is simply life, and an expression of life can always evade us. We can never tell life, one to another, although sometimes we think we can." In this poem, Crane attempts to capture the complexity of human life as he illustrates that in the face of adversity and pain neither the magnificent flag nor the squalid dust of the trenches can eliminate the tragic pain of separation experienced by those who have lost their loved ones on the battlefield. Crane acknowledges the controlling presence of natural forces, but, as a realist, his descriptions are not restricted to external objects and sensory images; instead, he strives to include human relationships and attitudes as an integral part of human reality.

Mabel Khawaja

THE DOVER BITCH: A CRITICISM OF LIFE

Author: Anthony Hecht (1923-
Type of poem: Satire
First published: 1960; collected in *The Hard Hours*, 1967

The Poem

In "Dover Beach" (1867), one of the most frequently anthologized texts in all of English literature, Matthew Arnold created a monument to Victorian angst over cosmic instability and the erosion of faith. Standing by the shore at the southern edge of England, the poet, bemoaning post-Darwinian doubt, turns to the woman beside him and proclaims that the only consolation and certainty remaining in a violent, desolate universe is their love for each other.

In "The Dover Bitch: A Criticism of Life," Anthony Hecht offers an irreverent but resonant sequel to the familiar Arnold poem. The unnamed narrator of Hecht's revision presents himself as a straight-talking acquaintance of the bombastic Arnold. Offering a dramatically different reading of the situation in "Dover Beach," he suggests that the beloved woman on whom the poet counts as the last bastion of constancy is in truth vulgar and unfaithful. He even admits to occasional casual sexual trysts with her.

In appropriating Arnold's high-minded poem to the sensibilities of a smart aleck, Hecht is offering a comic lesson in narrative perspective, a reminder that, however authoritative the proclamations in "Dover Beach" appear, there are alternatives to the way its speaker sees the world. The woman addressed in Arnold's poem is treated as part of the theatrical scenery, not as a sovereign consciousness with thoughts and feelings of her own. Hecht's speaker, however, is most intent on trying to represent her point of view. Reducing Arnold to a literary prop, he attempts to characterize her reactions to the Victorian poet's ardent rhetoric during their night at Dover Beach. Hecht's speaker claims that, far from being enamored of Arnold or inspired by his grandiose speech, she had more mundane matters on her mind, like what his whiskers might feel like against her skin. "The Dover Bitch" explains that she became angry at Arnold for ignoring her as a living, sensual woman and for using her as a mere pretext for his florid oratory.

"Dover Beach" is a monument to the "high seriousness" that, in an 1880 book called *The Study of Poetry*, Arnold extolled as a criterion for great poetry. Hecht's revision is an exercise in drollery. In contrast to the studied formality of "Dover Beach," written in four stanzas of carefully organized blank verse, "The Dover Bitch" is composed in a single twenty-nine-line stanza of free verse that simulates the nonchalance of vernacular speech. Like a casual conversation, the run-on lines seem to ramble, and instead of concluding the poem merely halts.

Forms and Devices

"So there stood Matthew Arnold and this girl," begins the anonymous speaker of

"The Dover Bitch," a cheeky man who does not himself pretend to "poetry" but addresses the reader bluntly in the unadorned English of the streets, a language ostensibly so frank that it does not shy away from the tactless word "bitch." The speaker's consistent preference for colloquial over fancy language reinforces his claim to be a candid alternative to Arnold's specious magniloquence. Filled with casual utterances such as the expletives "so" and "well now" and the contractions "I'll," "it's," and "mustn't," Hecht's speaker offers the illusion of verbal spontaneity—and thus sincerity—in contrast to the evasiveness of Arnold's meticulously contrived clauses.

The speaker's apparent ability to summarize all of Arnold's elegant words in barely three lines is an implicit attack on the older poet's verbosity: "Try to be true to me,/ And I'll do the same for you, for things are bad/ All over, etc., etc." is presumably what Arnold would have said had he shared this speaker's honesty and his knack for getting directly to the point. The "etc., etc." is devastating ridicule of "Dover Beach" for being redundant, as if one need not pay much attention to exactly what Arnold is saying beyond his banal affirmation of faithful love in a treacherous world.

The subsequent account of the woman's reactions to Arnold remains colloquial and sassy, suggesting that she shares the speaker's impatience with Arnold's decorous, evasive oratory. Repetition of the sloppy, slangy intensifier "really" ("really felt sad," "really angry," "really tough") distances her further from Arnold the fastidious stylist. The line that informs readers of her resentment at being addressed "As sort of a mournful cosmic last resort"—another comic reduction of Arnold's elegant poetry—is abruptly and comically followed by the judgment that this "Is really tough on a girl, and she was pretty"—an assertion in very simple English of very simple truths that Arnold's exquisite proclamations seem to ignore. The woman deploys a vocabulary including "one or two unprintable things," obscenities that are inconceivable within Arnold's chaste and earnest poem. The speaker seems, again, to suggest that there is a greater honesty in plain, even profane English.

"She's really all right" is the speaker's final, unpretentious, and tolerant judgment. In a loose, hedonistic society where encounters are casual and occasional, he is not ashamed to admit that, neither presuming nor desiring any exclusive claim to her attention, he meets her about once a year. Arnold lamented his inability to rely on anything in this bleak universe except the woman standing beside him, and although Hecht's speaker exposes even that faith in personal love as deluded, he characterizes her as "dependable as they come." It is faint praise, since "they" evidently do not come very dependable at all, but the speaker seems willing, all in all, to settle for much less—the merely human—than Arnold is.

The final line of "The Dover Bitch" is a nonchalant non sequitur, a further affront to the tradition of the well-made poem. "And sometimes I bring her a bottle of *Nuit d'Amour*," says the speaker, in an afterthought that reinforces the image of an ordinary man speaking without premeditation. *Nuit d'Amour*, the name of what is evidently either perfume or wine, answers the woman's longing for "all the wine and enormous beds/ And blandishments in French and the perfumes," a physical longing that

Arnold's metaphysical abstractions leave unsatisfied. By contrast, Hecht's speaker gives her *Nuit d'Amour*, which means "night of love" and provides an alternative, carnal version of love in answer to Arnold's abstract meditations.

Themes and Meanings

For all its mockery of Arnold, Hecht's dramatic monologue is a tribute to the power that its predecessor continues to exert. Moreover, for all its irreverence, "The Dover Bitch" is nevertheless a love poem, though it is a poem about love without illusions—as if that were not a contradiction in terms, as if love were not irreducibly itself an illusion. As an alternative to the elevated but perhaps empty sentiments that the speaker in "Dover Beach" proffers his companion, Hecht's speaker offers a kind of love that is candid and carnal, and all the more ardent for his acceptance of his beloved's imperfections. While Arnold can love the woman standing beside him on the coast at Dover evidently only by elevating her into a disembodied philosophical principle, Hecht's speaker embraces concrete love by embracing a woman who is alive in an imperfect body, one "running to fat."

In *The Study of Poetry* Arnold called poetry "a criticism of life," by which he meant not an attack on, but a disinterested examination of, the subject as it is in itself. Hecht echoes the phrase in the subtitle he attaches to "The Dover Bitch," as though the poem that follows is, in contrast to Victorian obfuscations, going to allow readers to examine life for what it is in itself. Hecht's appropriation of the phrase "a criticism of life" is perhaps also a coy play on the contemporary sense of criticism as deprecation, as though the shabby world of materialism and lust celebrated by the speaker is a sorry disappointment.

The speaker may be somewhat self-deluding when he presents himself as a clear-eyed modern man impatient with Victorian sublimation. Hecht published "The Dover Bitch" in 1960, just before a wave of feminism swept over American culture. The poem at first seems more sexually enlightened than its nineteenth century predecessor, not only in its recognition of the claims of the libido but also in its refusal to treat a woman as mere appendage to her male companion. However, just as in "Dover Beach," the woman on the strand remains unnamed and voiceless. Hecht's poem imagines what is going on in the woman's mind while she listens to Arnold on the beach, but it refuses direct access to that mind, filtering it instead through the words of the male speaker, who persistently reduces her to "this girl." Though he poses as a champion of liberation, he controls her thoughts and feelings. Hecht suggests that, though the speaker prides himself on seeing through Victorian delusions to the tangible realities of the here and now, materialism and cynicism are simply another set of illusions to which people cling as a stay against cosmic erosion.

Steven G. Kellman

A DREAM OF A BROTHER

Author: Robert Bly (1926-
Type of poem: Meditation
First published: 1986, in *Selected Poems*

The Poem

"A Dream of a Brother" consists of twenty lines divided into five unrhymed quatrains written on an iambic pentameter base. That this is a dream poem, or a dreamed meditation, is made immediately clear both by the title and in the first line: "I fall asleep, and dream. . . ." This fact is important structurally and thematically. Bly has said that he began the original version of what finally became this poem by imagining his own childhood as having been made up of two individual personalities, "one of whom had betrayed the other." It is, therefore, not surprising that the poem begins with another instance of betrayal by alluding to the Old Testament story of Joseph and his brothers. In the first stanza the speaker dreams that he shows his father a "coat stained with goat's blood," a clear reference to the biblical story. In the second stanza, he says, "I sent my brother away." Having banished his brother, as Joseph's brothers did him, the speaker enfolds the biblical allusions into a quintessentially American context: "I heard he was . . . taken in by traveling Sioux."

There is a strong break after the third stanza. This is not surprising, since the two rather distinct sections of this poem come from two totally different sections in an earlier, much longer, poem entitled "The Shadow Goes Away," published in *Sleepers Joining Hands* (1973). Although in the two final stanzas Bly merges the times and places he has alluded to in the opening stanzas, these stanzas are much more personal and immediate, much more literal and specific than the first three.

The fourth stanza begins by referring to a rural high school (like the one Bly himself attended) and ends, apparently years later, in a large city (Bly lived in New York for a time). The betrayed and abandoned "brother," described as having been taken "to the other side of the river," is not missed until readers are suddenly told, "I noticed he was gone." Since the dream imagery is still in place at the end of the poem, one wonders whether this "brother" is exclusively the literal brother he seemed to be earlier or if he may now be primarily a substitute brother. He may be a "double," or an imaginary brother, buried within the speaker's own psyche and rediscovered only later in life.

In the fifth and final stanza the speaker, depressed, thinking of death, sits on the ground and weeps. "Impulses to die shoot up in the dark" near him. These impulses, like rays of light in the dark room of a dream, seem to suggest something positive, even if it is still somewhat vague or dreamlike. The poem ends with a single-line sentence that attempts to catapult the reader—as it apparently has the speaker—into a moment of insight or illumination: "In the dark the marmoset opens his eyes."

Forms and Devices

"A Dream of a Brother" had a complicated composition and publication history. In an introductory note in his *Selected Poems* (1986), Bly reports that he rewrote the poems from *Sleepers Joining Hands*, "some in minor detail, others in a larger way." "A Dream of a Brother" is one of these largely rewritten poems. Indeed, it has been culled from two separate, rather disparate, parts of the much longer and thematically quite different poem, "The Shadow Goes Away"—which itself was only the first section of a very long free-verse poem, "Sleepers Joining Hands," the title poem in Bly's book of the same name.

In addition to the fact that "A Dream of a Brother" is only one fourth as long as "The Shadow Goes Away," it is also a much more formal poem, although Bly eschews the use of a strict metrical pattern and other more formal poetic devices, perhaps for the obvious reason that such devices would seem to be inappropriate in a dream poem. Instead of such devices Bly relies on the more informal devices of juxtaposition, allusion, and imagery to organize and control his poem. The poem is also organized through the use of comparisons and contrasts. Some of these, such as the comparison between Joseph and his brothers and the speaker and his brother, are explicit, while others, such as the comparison between a literal brother and an imaginary one, are merely implied.

The poem is further built around three dominant dichotomies, each of which makes use of its own set of allusions, even though the imagery overlaps from one allusion to the next and from one stanza to another. These comparisons and contrasts, dichotomies, doubled-up allusions, and complex images bind the poem together structurally; they also come together thematically in the vivid and somewhat enigmatic reference in the final line of the poem. Allusion, startling juxtaposition, and "deep images" (Bly's own term) are devices that Bly uses in many of his poems. The deep image—which sometimes occurs as a non sequitur, at the end of a poem, or even as a kind of afterthought to the rest of the poem—is intended to connect the physical world with the spiritual world. Bly uses it to shock the reader into recognition or illumination. In the case of "A Dream of a Brother" the introduction of the marmoset (a small monkey) at the very end of the poem is important to Bly's theme; it also binds the other elements of the poem together.

Themes and Meanings

Since "A Dream of a Brother" is a dream meditation, it need not conform to the logical conventions of waking reality, and Bly exploits this possibility to the fullest by juxtaposing and drawing together disparate images and allusions. The parallel between the biblical story of Joseph and his brothers is particularly significant for the theme of the poem because Joseph was a dreamer and an interpreter of dreams. In his first stanza Bly alludes both to Joseph's "coat stained with goat's blood" and to one of his dreams, in which bundles of his brother's sheaves bow down to him. Bly counts on his readers being familiar with this biblical story and remembering that, at the end of the story, Joseph is reunited with his father and reconciled with his brothers.

To explore his subject in depth Bly draws heavily on the work of Sigmund Freud, the founder of psychoanalysis, and on Freud's student, Carl Jung, another analytical psychologist. Bly draws especially on their detailed studies of dreams and of the ways dreams affect waking life. Jung is perhaps best known for describing what he called the "collective unconscious," a substratum of the psyche in which universal, timeless, and cross-cultural elements meet and merge. Such a collective deep state of mind (itself a kind of "deep image") is most clearly evidenced in dreams or dreamlike reveries. Bly's account of his relationship with his brother—or, in terms of the Jungian trappings in the poem, his "relationship" with a separate side of his own consciousness, a "double" whom he sees as a "brother"—is therefore significant both literally and psychologically in the poem.

By drawing parallels among Jungian theory, the biblical story, early American history, and his own life, Bly stresses the universality of his theme. Further, at the end of his poem, he seems to suggest a resolution similar to that found in the biblical story. Bly's poem resolves itself with the curious and surprising reference to the marmoset ("In the dark the marmoset opens his eyes") in the final line of the poem. The suggestion seems to be that, at the end of the poem, the marmoset, although still asleep, has come to some kind of understanding. He "opens his eyes" and is awakened without literally awakening. This action is in keeping with Bly's larger theme, since he has seemed to suggest throughout the poem that people can understand things, can "see" them—even things they might not know or understand when they are awake—during sleep. In this sense "A Dream of a Brother" is both a dream journey and a dream journal describing that journey.

William V. Davis

A DREAM OF GOVERNORS

Author: Louis Simpson (1923-
Type of poem: Lyric
First published: 1957; collected in *A Dream of Governors*, 1959

The Poem

"A Dream of Governors" is the title poem of a five-part collection of twenty-nine poems. This lyric poem is divided into five stanzas, each composed of eight lines. An epigraph borrowed from poet Mark Van Doren provides the source for the poem's title: "The deepest dream is of mad governors." The repetitive use of "dream" in the title and the epigraph suggests a common human experience and a basic framework for the poem. Thus the events occur in a dreamworld in which deeply hidden and subjective thoughts, experiences, wishes, and inner truths surface briefly into consciousness before returning to oblivion. The poem is written in the third person from the standpoint of an objective observer who sees, hears, and feels everything the sleeper does in the dream episode. "A Dream of Governors" also uses the familiar childhood memory of reading or listening to fairy tales. Thus, the first stanza introduces characters and plot suggestive of a typical fantasy. The cast includes a knight and his lady, a dragon, a witch, and a chorus. In this scenario, the knight relives stereotypical plot actions. As a young knight, he travels from far away and accepts the supreme task of combating the city's local enemy, a dragon. After slaying the monster and routing the witch, the brave hero returns and receives his rewards. Crowned king, he marries the lady and plans to live happily ever after.

The second stanza presents emphatic contradictions. All is not well in this imaginary world. Joy has vanished. Physically, decades of idleness have transformed the vigorous hero into an aged monarch whose arduous exploits are ridiculed and recounted poetically as ancient history. The stanza's last two lines stress the ruler's self-doubts and questions. The third stanza reinforces these disturbing thoughts. The first declamatory lines recall the tedious choral platitudes in Greek tragedies. Ironically, the king apparently disregards these allusions to human folly and its ruinous consequences. His reflections parallel Jocasta's generalizations in Sophocles' *Oidipous Tyrannos* (c. 428 B.C.; *Oedipus Tyrannus*) that dreams should not be taken seriously. Yet the king's actions in the fourth stanza reverse Jocasta's advice as the monarch responds to the choral wisdom. In his solitary night journey, the king returns to the earlier scene of his heroism and appeals to the witch to restore "evil" and provide him with a goal. The fifth stanza completes the dream odyssey yet leaves the future open. When the queen hears the king's returning footsteps, she closes the storybook, for her husband's request has ended their make-believe, fantasy existence. Together, the royal couple watches the reality and the uncertain fate of their new world begin to unfold.

Forms and Devices

As in his other early poems, Louis Simpson follows the formal rules for regular stanzas, meters, and rhyme in "A Dream of Governors." However, he combines these conventional elements with imaginative images, metaphors, and symbols. Simpson's often-repeated poetic objective, stated in the final chapter of his book *Ships Going into the Blue: Essays and Notes on Poetry* (1994), is drawn from Joseph Conrad's preface to his novel *The Nigger of the "Narcissus"* (1897): "My task which I am trying to achieve is . . . to make you hear, to make you feel—it is, before all, to make you *see*." Simpson uses traditional rhymed stanzas (*ababcdcd*) and iambic meters (an unaccented syllable followed by an accented syllable representing an emphatic rhythm of sound). Such a tightly controlled, conventional form provides a practical, objective base for launching imaginative, subjective, and emotional imagery or metaphors. Any unusual metaphoric or symbolic content in such a synthesis becomes much more believable and acceptable when wrapped in commonplace formulas.

The central metaphor suggests the implicit analogy between two ostensibly different things: dreams and fairy tales. In his article "Dead Horses and Live Issues" (*A Company of Poets*, 1981), Simpson, describing poetic creation, states, "The images are connected in a dream; and the deeper the dream, the stronger, the more logical, are the connections." Both dreams and fairy tales share this feature: sequences of logically related images or actions. Another parallel points to the term "governors," common to both title and epigraph, which refers to controls or restraints. However, the epigraph's qualifier, "mad," also underlines unconscious dream sensations, emotions, ideas, or even frenetic activities that lack controls or restraints. Key images that stress hearing, feeling, and seeing, combined with imaginative, associational images (mental or literary connections or relations between thoughts, feelings, or sensations arising from previous experiences), dominate the literal details supporting the basic metaphor. Visual images, along with feelings of pity, depict a frustrated and troubled sovereign who is the object of ridicule and who is absorbed with doubts about his worth. Antiphonal declamations of a Greek chorus and of Jocasta's voice echo throughout the third stanza. Moonlight visually illuminates the witch scene in stanza 4. All three imagery patterns flow together in the conclusion. The queen listens to her husband's approaching footsteps; fearful feelings of uncertainty dominate the couple's "silence," for they, recalling Metaphysical poet John Donne's lovers in "The Canonization," watch the significant event in their new world, the birth and rising flight of the winged serpent, rise in "each other's eyes."

One universal conflict, familiar throughout world legends, underscores two symbols. References to the mythic dragon signify humanity's ancient struggle against evil, while the knight represents the universal "Everyman" who battles the foe. His combat is the supreme test of power and control over this primal devil figure who symbolizes the unrestrained instincts that may surface in the deepest dream. One poem, "The Silent Generation," in the fourth section of Simpson's collection *A Dream of Governors*, provides additional thoughts on Adolf Hitler, a contemporary symbol of evil: "It was my generation/ That put the Devil down/ With great enthusiasm./ But now our occupation/ Is gone. Our education/ Is wasted on the town." The last lines also repeat the king's motive for restoring evil to the kingdom.

Themes and Meanings

"A Dream of Governors" is a poem about the human condition, about the governors, the rational and irrational desires and ideas that control human actions. In another sense, it is also about poetic vision, about Simpson's early efforts to demonstrate his way of seeing, feeling, understanding, and transmitting the meaning that he sees in the actions and experiences in people's lives. By juxtaposing the literal details and interrelationships of ordinary people in unusual patterns (dreams and fairy tales), Simpson shows the outer event as well as the inner truth of the experiences, the hidden reality behind the experiences.

One of the basic desires controlling human actions is the conscious need for feelings of worth, honor, and self-validation gained from societal approval or rewards for deeds accomplished. The young knight who wants to become a hero by slaying the evil dragon, receiving a king's crown, and marrying his lady exemplifies this basic desire, the wish fulfillment promised in a dream or fairy tale. Likewise, contemporary people also have the same ambition to overcome their personal, competitive dragons and become successful heroes. They, too, dream that their endeavors will merit constant rewards, honor, and praise. Analogously, both fairy-tale heroes and modern people suffer frustration, rejection, and self-doubt when their valiant efforts are only a distant memory and not a constant presence in society's mind, and both suffer when either of these instincts for self-worth or self-doubt become an obsession that destroys the balance between rational and irrational thought and actions.

The basic need for keeping balances is another significant controlling force in both the king's life and in a modern person's life. In "Dead Horses and Live Issues," Simpson states that "poetry represents . . . the total mind, including both reason and unreason." He exposes the fairy-tale king to the traditional echoing maxims about the ruinous folly of letting extreme behavior or attitudes govern his actions. Simpson presents opposing views and does not sermonize; he lets the character decide what his resultant actions will be. Ultimately, this objectivity is what leads the king back to the battleground. The youthful hero has killed the dragon, but his instinctual fear of it is buried deep within his mind. His mature self-conquest and his control of his irrational instincts and fears allow him to balance the extremes between his rational and irrational thoughts. Therefore, both king and humanity are able to request the restoration of "evil" to balance their lives. Contemporary humans may read the poem and think it is only about the fairy-tale king. Some will see the analogy with human conditions. More likely, readers will see additional levels of meaning. In an interview with Alberta Turner in *Fifty Contemporary Poets: The Creative Process* (1977), Simpson states, "If a poet were sure of the exact meaning of his poem it would be a poem with a limited meaning. But I want my poetry to open on the unknown."

Betsy P. Harfst

THE DREAM OF THE UNIFIED FIELD

Author: Jorie Graham (1951-
Type of poem: Lyric
First published: 1993, in *Materialism*

The Poem

"The Dream of the Unified Field" is a relatively long poem in free verse subdivided into seven sections that are further divided into twelve stanzas. It challenges conventional notions of organizational patterns of poetry while confronting the fallacy behind humankind's desire to unify experience. This fallacy is implied in its title, a reference to Albert Einstein's unsuccessful attempts to prove the theory of the unified field. The speaker (apparently Graham herself) attempts to yoke walking through a snowstorm to take a black leotard to her young daughter together with her own childhood experiences with ballet master Madame Sakaroff and finally with the initial contact of Christopher Columbus with the New World. As she weaves through the poem, she connects the immediate and personal with the distant and impersonal in ways that work naturally as well as in ways that she must force to work, thus reinforcing the impact of the title.

In the first section of the poem, as the speaker treks through the snow to carry the leotard to her daughter, she becomes caught in the "motion" of the snow—the patterns it creates in falling, the "arabesques" that it, like her daughter, performs. The transience of the snowflakes, "Gone as they hit the earth," also strikes her as she moves through their motion, finding in their symbols a clue to her own meaning, her own existence.

Upon completion of her task, she is taken by the sight and sound of a "huge flock of starlings" coursing through the snow and finally alighting in ever-shifting patterns on a bare-limbed oak tree. "Foliage of the tree of the world's waiting" she calls them, and they return her to the vision of her daughter through the window as she performs her pirouettes: "I watch the head explode, then recollect, explode, recollect."

Drawn by the screech of a single crow in the midst of the flock of starlings, the speaker feels the emptiness in her pocket which once held the balled-up leotard, and, "terrified" at that emptiness, returns to watch the unknowing child through the window. The crow draws her attention more closely, and she minutely separates the colors that make up his "blackness" as he suddenly lifts and ascends in one "blunt clean stroke" only to land to disappear again.

Crowlike, the vision of Madame Sakaroff in her studio in Stalingrad intrudes upon her consciousness. Uniting "The dream of Europe" with the New World, black crow with black dress, bird with "bird-headed knob," the vision of Madame Sakaroff brings in more explicitly the need to connect with or reject old patterns of belief. "*No one must believe in God again,*" the speaker hears as, entranced, she watches Madame Sakaroff encounter herself ("her eyes eyed themselves") in the "silver film" of the mirror. That vision, however, ultimately proves unsuccessful; the speaker finds in it "no signal" and "no information" as she turns helplessly to the window of her present, seeking "what" she "should know to save" her child.

Unable to "know," she centers herself within the snowstorm, taking possession of it as well as the blizzard of her own experiences, and, through them, the "Age behind the clouds, The Great Heights." Her own desire to possess, to seek, to know becomes connected with an explorer, the "Admiral" Christopher Columbus as he, also in the midst of a snowstorm (a fiction manufactured to force the unity that may not really exist), takes harbor in Puerto de San Nicolas and places the cross signalling possession "on a conspicuous height." As the speaker had clothed her daughter in the black leotard, he clothes the young "very black Indian" woman captured by his men and returns her (apparently against her will) to her people. The final vision of the poem is the glint of gold on her nose "which was a sign there was/ gold/ on that land."

Forms and Devices

Appropriately for a poem first appearing in a collection entitled *Materialism*, "The Dream of the Unified Field" contains startlingly vivid images that seek to re-create actual experience. Not technically metaphors, the images nonetheless interconnect and react on each other, reinforcing the impact as they amass. The blackness of the leotard, the blackness of the birds, the blackness of Madame Sakaroff, even the blackness of the Indian girl all contribute to the "dream" of unity that informs the poem. Similarly, the patterning and repatterning of the dance ("I watch the head explode then recollect, explode, recollect"), the birds on the tree ("scatter, blow away, scatter, recollect"), the swirling snow ("the arabesques and runnels, gathering and loosening"), and experience ("they stick, accrue,/ grip up, connect") unite the patterning and repatterning of history, thought, and meaning both in the individual and the species. This movement reflects the building of imagery in the poem from the personal experience in the opening to the quintessential experience of burgeoning civilization at the end. Connecting these experiences is the long road, the footfall, the "white sleeping geography" often obscured by blinding snow and often directionless. It is briefly lit only by the flash of the silver mirror, the glint of the gold on the girl's nose.

The ever-changing imagery of the poem provides the perfect vehicle for the cinematic techniques that critic Helen Vendler, in *The Given and the Made* (1995), see as pervasive in Graham's poetry: "close and far focus, panning, jump-cutting, emphasis on point of view and looking." In this poem Graham employs each of these techniques, from the close-up of the crow to the panorama as it streaks into the air and lands again, from the jumps from bird to child, from child to woman, and from woman to admiral. These techniques are reinforced by the cinematic frames provided by the window that forms a frame through which she watches her daughter dance and the mirror that doubles the image of Madame Sakaroff.

The interlaced imagery in the poem also gives rise to organic patterns of lineation. Vendler notes that the use of long lines and long sentences is a distinguishing characteristic of Graham's work. In an interview with Thomas Gardner in *Denver Quarterly* 26 (Spring, 1992), Graham attributes these long lines to her need to write in lines that contain more than the typical five stresses, because they cannot be spoken or even understood "in one breath unit for the most part (and since our desire *is* to grasp them in one breath unit) [it] causes us to read the line very quickly."

Reading quickly leads, she feels, to a "rush in the line" that creates "a very different relationship with the silence: one that makes it aggressive—or at least oceanic—something that won't stay at bay. You have *fear* in the rush that can perhaps cause you to hear the *fearful* in what is rushed against." This "rush" is evident throughout "The Dream of the Unified Field" in the dashes that link images and concepts ("the century—minutes, houses going by—The Great/ Heights—") as it is in the long lines that attempt to capture and hold the essence and music of experience. An example is Madame Sakaroff's encounter with herself ("I . . ./ saw the light rippling almost shuddering where her body finally/ touched/ the image, the silver film between them like something that would have/ shed itself in nature now"). In *The Breaking of Style: Hopkins, Heaney, Graham* (1995), Vendler finds a metaphor of "Earthly desire itself" in Graham's lineation, "desire always prolonging itself further and further over a gap it nonetheless does not wish to close. In this search by desire, mind will always outrun body."

Themes and Meanings

Finding meaning in existence, finding patterns in experience, connecting in a world that has, for the most part, lost its religious and philosophical underpinning lies at the core of "The Dream of the Unified Field." Graham brings together the New World and the Old, America and Europe, innocence and experience, nature and civilization. She does so in a way that makes sense, but in a way that also seems deliberately to challenge readers to accept the connections, urges them to doubt the logic. As Graham moves from image to image, the reader must make a leap of faith, holding each in mind until, finally, at the end they coalesce into one image of desire, of longing—to possess, to protect, to comprehend, to save. Even the end is not the end, however. It is actually the beginning, with the gleam of gold luring the reader even as it lured Columbus and his followers to ever-present possibility, to the potential that is being alive. That the poem does not circle back on itself, that it does not return to the sight of the child in the black leotard but ends instead with the "very black Indian" girl with the "little piece of/ gold on her nose" brings the poem back to the title instead, to the "dream" that the unified field exists.

Jaquelyn W. Walsh

DREAMING IN DAYLIGHT

Author: Robert Penn Warren (1905-1989)
Type of poem: Meditation
First published: 1979; collected in *Being Here: Poetry, 1977-1980*, 1980

The Poem

"Dreaming in Daylight" is a poem in free verse; its forty-one lines are divided into twenty unrhymed couplets plus one final, single-line phrase. The title suggests the contradictory images of darkness and light and of nighttime dreaming (in which intuition and emotion have full play) and daydreaming (which connotes rational meditation). Written from the second-person singular point of view, the poem's only implied persona is poet Robert Penn Warren, who is also the speaker of the poem. Addressing himself as "you," he recounts to the reader personal experiences grounded in a familiar activity: a mountain climb.

In the first two stanzas, the climber energetically clambers up rocks, through thickets, and over brooks. Stopping for breath, he quotes some verse and then perceives—in the next three stanzas—that "Small eyes, or larger, with glitter in darkness, are watching" from stone crevices, leaf shadows, and hollow logs. To the climber, the eyes of nature are "like conscience . . ./ Like remorse" judging him as an outsider who does not belong. The speaker's interpretation of a watchful nature prepares the reader for the next fourteen lines. Falling into meditation about self, he complains of feeling a mysterious, internal, and physical unease that sparks a concern about his own identity: "Do you/ Know your own name?" Questioning himself as he questions the reader, the poet describes the sea below as a "heaving ocean of pastness" from which he is trying to escape. However, his flight causes him regret: "Oh, try/ To think of something your life has meant." As he seeks to contemplate his life's meaning, he admits he is more a stranger to himself than to nature.

After the twelfth couplet, there is a shift from internal to external action as the climber energetically resumes the ascent, moving higher—"For the past creeps behind you, like foam"—until he reaches the isolated peak. Now at the peak, the climber again becomes reflective and urgently admonishes himself to remember the few people he has truly loved. In the poem's last seven lines, the climber returns to his bed and wakes from his recurrent dream of being spied upon by peering, "dark-glistening" eyes. The speaker, in the last line, repeats his failure of self-discovery. The dream of the daylight has become one with the dream of night. The poet's vision is triggered by precise observation of details in nature that become metaphors for unfulfilled quests or unanswered questions. The poem concludes with the recurrent image of the alienating eyes of nature that mysteriously instill a feeling of guilt or regret in the poet for remaining a stranger to himself.

Forms and Devices

References to nature abound in Warren's poems, providing him with much of his inspiration and imagery, and "Dreaming in Daylight" is no exception. The mountain landscape seen by the climber at first presents friendly, explicit images: rocks, thickets, brooks, birches, crevices, and leaves. Yet these become implicit images of isolation and estrangement such as the "stern rock, majestic and snagged" that is a "sky-bare" peak where frost has destroyed any vegetation. They also become images of alienation: glittering, reproachful eyes peering from a "rotted-out log, from earth-aperture," metaphors for conscience or remorse that imply that the climber does not belong on the mountain. Below the mountain is a "beach of/ History" and a sea of the past from which the climber is seeking to escape by moving higher. Both serve as metaphors for the poet's concern with related issues of self-identity. Such imagery clarifies Warren's less-than-sanguine attitude toward nature. In his introduction to Joseph Conrad's novel *Nostromo* (1904), Warren observes that "man is precariously balanced in his humanity between the black inward abyss of himself and the black outward abyss of nature." Similar examples of a threatening nature can be found in Warren's later poems.

The syntax offers a variety of long and short sentences, with many phrases or sentences interrupted at the end of one stanza and completed in the next: "This/ Is the end." This structure lends a sense of ebb and flow, of activity and thought stopping and starting. The athletic and expended energy of the mountain ascent is suggested by action verbs and active images: "clamber," "crash," "leap," "past birches," "up bluffside." However, when the climber stops and meditates the verbs become more passive and imply internal activity: "feel," "try to think," "know," "wake," and forms of the verb "to be." Sometimes action and nonaction verbs are juxtaposed to suggest that the physical activity of the climb is interrupted by periodic contemplation: "Move higher!/ For the past creeps behind you" and "You clamber up the few mossed shards that frost has ripped off./ Then stop." The poem's last five lines, as the speaker wakes from a dream, employ verbs such as "wake" and "peer" and reinforce the recurrent images of the eyes of nature "dark-glistening, like/ Conscience." The images reactivate thought of one's alienation and ignorance of self.

The continual use of the second-person singular, even though the speaker is clearly the protagonist, is significant. The poet disguises himself behind "you" and in so doing pulls the readers into his experience, compelling them to consider the same issues of identity and life's meaning that he does. At the poem's conclusion, after twenty stanzas of recurrent image patterns and self-accusatory questions, Warren characteristically concludes the work by reiterating the persona's realization that he is less a stranger to nature than to himself.

Themes and Meanings

Written when Warren was in his seventies, "Dreaming in Daylight" appears in the collection *Being Here: Poetry, 1977-1980*. In an afterword, Warren discloses that the poems are placed in thematic order "played against, or with, a shadowy narrative, a shadowy autobiography." Within the five divisions of poems moving from childhood to youth to old age, the poem at hand is listed in part 2, which finds the poet (the protagonist of all the poems) in young manhood after initially wrestling as a boy in part 1 with childhood memories and issues of life and death. Like other works in its division, the poem treats one of Warren's major themes: man's ageless drive toward self-discovery and self-determination.

Victor H. Standberg, in *The Poetic Vision of Robert Penn Warren* (1977), suggests that for Warren, individuals encounter a sense of alienation as they search for their identity in a perplexing, often corrupt or indifferent world. To overcome estrangement and pursue their intended purpose, they must undergo a period of intense self-examination that ideally can lead to further knowledge about self and the world. Although the search may not always end in success, Warren does not counsel giving up. In this piece, the poet searches for his identity within nature, a typical Warren landscape. Yet in spite of his initial joy in seeking unity with nature, the poet finds in nature no oneness but rather rejection embodied by hidden animal eyes telling him he does not belong there. The author seems to posit that the natural world is indifferent to human affairs and is neither helpful nor sympathetic as a guide in interpreting human life and in answering questions of life and death. Consequently, the climber experiences the pain of isolation and estrangement in his attempted communication with the forces of nature. He feels with dread that some mysterious internal activity "like gastritis or migraine" is going on inside himself (which may be reminiscent of the cancer or stroke that felled his parents in earlier poems). With nightmarish energy, the climber ascends ever higher to flee from the pursuing foam of the waters of the past and from history below, whose contemplation is essential to identity.

In *Knowledge and the Image of Man* (1975), Warren explains that "man's process of self-definition means that he distinguishes himself from the world and from other men. He . . . discovers separateness . . . and the pain of self-criticism and the pain of isolation." The poem's protagonist has distanced himself from the past and from history to find himself ousted by nature, abandoned by the companionship of memory, and reduced to trying desperately to recall the few people he has ever loved. Finally, the poet, waking from a nightmare ("a dream of eyes"), realizes that he has not yet achieved self-discovery. The seeker of the self has not been successful in the search. The poem may be seen as the emergence of the poet's artistic purpose or perhaps even as the final-phase efforts of a poet nearing his life's end. Yet clearly the work represents major Warren themes and demonstrates his marked accessibility to readers.

Christian H. Moe

EACH AND ALL

Author: Ralph Waldo Emerson (1803-1882)
Type of poem: Lyric
First published: 1839; collected in *Poems*, 1847

The Poem

"Each and All" is usually treated as one of Ralph Waldo Emerson's best nature poems. It seems to have developed from a journal passage Emerson recorded in 1834 about recalling seeing seashells on the shore when he was a boy. He picked some up and took them home. When he got them there and looked at them, they appeared "dry and ugly." From that episode, he said in the journal passage, he learned that what he called "Composition"—things in arrangement with other things—was more important than the beauty of anything alone in terms of its effect on the viewer.

The poem recounts the process through which the first-person narrator, who seems to be a version of Emerson himself, becomes aware of "the perfect whole." It begins with the observation that "yon red-cloaked clown," apparently a man standing in a field, does not think about the observer looking at him, nor does the heifer think of the person who hears her lowing. It then refers to a sexton ringing his church bell without thinking of Napoleon listening. Emerson is alluding to Napoleon Bonaparte, emperor of France from 1804 to 1815, about whom Emerson wrote an essay in his book *Representative Men* (1850). Emerson had read that Napoleon paused whenever he heard the bell of a parish church because, Napoleon himself said, the sound reminded him of a period from his youth when he was happy. In "Each and All," the narrator speaks of Napoleon stopping his horse while his armies march through the Alps. Napoleon listens to the church bells ringing even though the sexton who rings them is unaware that he is there. From these episodes, the narrator concludes that one cannot know how one's life influences other people's lives and beliefs. In fact, the narrator says that each one is needed by every other one: "Nothing is fair or good alone."

The narrator then recounts a series of episodes in which he learns the truth of this conclusion. First, he tells of hearing a sparrow sing magnificently and bringing the bird home. There, the bird sings the same song it sang when it was free, but it no longer "cheers" the narrator, for, he says, he did not bring home the river and sky where the bird first sang. These parts of the bird's natural setting, he says, sang to his eye, while the bird in captivity sings only to his ear. The narrator next recounts an episode similar to the one Emerson recounts in his journal involving the seashells. The narrator brings home beautiful shells, which, when taken from the shore, become "poor, unsightly, noisome things." Their beauty remains, he feels, on the shore "With the sun and the sand and the wild uproar."

The next episode the narrator recounts involves a lover who "watched his graceful maid," knowing that "her beauty's best attire/ Was woven still by the snow-white choir." Just as the narrator puts the bird in a cage, so the lover marries the maid and takes her to his "hermitage"—his home. There he notices that even though she becomes "a gentle wife," she no longer seems to be a fairylike creature. Her ability to enchant the lover resulted, the narrator believes, largely from her being among her friends. When she was separated from her friends, the "enchantment was undone."

As a result of these episodes, in each of which something loses beauty when separated from its setting, the narrator decides that beauty is a "cheat." Consequently, the narrator decides that he covets nothing but truth. He declares that he will leave beauty behind just as he left behind his youthful games. Yet even as he makes this declaration, he finds himself in the midst of a beautiful natural scene that he describes in detail. He sees the ground-pine curling in a wreathlike shape as it runs "over the club-moss burrs"; he inhales the aroma of the violet; he sees oaks and firs, and the pine cones and acorns from which new trees will grow. The sky soars above him; he sees and hears "the rolling river" and "the morning bird." He concludes the poem, "Beauty through my senses stole;/ I yielded myself to the perfect whole."

Forms and Devices

"Each and All" consists primarily of four-stress couplets. The poem's fairly regular rhythm and rhymes, some people feel, are supposed to imitate the patterns Emerson claims to find in nature. According to this theory, the fact that the poem contains some lines that are written in an *abab* pattern, one line (ending with "shore") that rhymes only with lines separated from it by a number of lines, and one line (ending with "ground") that rhymes with no other line—as well as the poem's having an odd number of lines—indicate that the symmetry Emerson finds in nature is not exact.

Most readers of the poem see it as being divided into three parts. The first consists of four images or episodes followed by a conclusion about all things needing other things (lines 1-12). The second consists of three more images or episodes (lines 13-36). In the final part, the poet arrives at a conclusion about the earlier material, only to discover that his conclusion is incorrect (lines 37-51).

Critics often accuse Emerson of being more interested in nature as idea than in nature itself. Thus, critics say, his writing about nature tends to be rather vague. Although "Each and All" contains several images drawn from human interaction with other humans, such as the episodes involving the "clown," Napoleon, and the wife, the poem is for the most part dependent on imagery drawn from nature. Emerson deals with several specific parts of nature and specific ideas about nature. The images he uses—the seashells, the birds, the trees—place the reader in a familiar world of experience, a world in which the reader can participate through the vividness of the images.

The poem itself takes the form of a mental journey of discovery. One critic writes of its "dramatic" structure, a term that implies that the parts of the poem interact with one another, just as the parts of nature that Emerson treats within the poem interact with one another. The narrator begins his journey with generalizations about relationships between things. Then he observes the results of separation of things. He then draws the logical but wrong conclusion that beauty is a "cheat," a childhood thing to be outgrown, and that he, now that he is mature, will no longer be concerned with beauty. However, nature leads him, in spite of himself, to an appreciation of beauty again, which, as in most of Emerson's writing, cannot be separated from truth. In his first book, *Nature* (1836), Emerson says that beauty and truth "are but different faces of the same All." The narrator of "Each and All" reaches this truth not through logical processes but through a moment of insight in which he recognizes that nature forms a "perfect whole."

Themes and Meanings

"Each and All" echoes the idea—which Emerson voices in many places—that things by themselves are unaffecting and even ugly but that when placed in context, usually their natural context, they become beautiful. Even putrefaction, Emerson writes, is beautiful when seen as the source of new life.

Central to the poem is the speaker's interaction with the parts of nature. At the poem's end, in spite of himself, the speaker interacts with the natural world—he sees the parts of nature around him, inhales the violet's odor, and sees and hears "the rolling river, the morning bird." Consequently, he once again becomes aware of beauty and recognizes that he is a part of "the perfect whole." Emerson seems to be saying here that reason alone is not a sufficient guide for understanding the world of nature and humankind's relationship to that world. The poem is also about human interaction with other humans. At least in part it deals with the idea that the interactions are so extensive that people affect other people of whose lives they are not even aware.

Central to the poem is Emerson's idea that truth often cannot be attained through logical means or even through experience and reflection on experience. In fact, for Emerson, experience is decidedly not the best teacher. Instead, as Emerson writes in work after work, insight or intuition is often a better guide to truth than experience is. Thus, logical processes based on experience lead the narrator of "Each and All" astray. A moment of intuition communicates to him the truth; namely, that beauty and truth are inseparable parts of the unity of nature.

Richard Tuerk

EASTER 1984

Author: Les A. Murray (1938-
Type of poem: Lyric
First published: 1987, in *The Daylight Moon*

The Poem

"Easter 1984" is a short lyric on the subject of the role of Jesus Christ and Christianity in human history. The first section of the poem evokes the crucifixion of Christ. Christ is referred to in the first couplet as "human dignity," the humanity of the Savior healing people "in the middle of the day"—not only referring to the time of day but also meaning in the open rather than in secret.

The second couplet relates humankind's hostile, uncomprehending response to Jesus's generosity: "we moved in on him slowly," too used to old systems of law, vengeance, and the strange mixture of anarchy and retribution that is at the root of purely human systems of justice: "If this was God, we would get even." The Crucifixion, it is implied, was an act of fear, of humans fearing their own potential, fearing the opportunities that Christ's healing would have brought them. Christ's dual divine-human nature redeems humankind, yet humankind fears being redeemed, wanting instead to continue the normal state of affairs. "We'd send it to be abstract again," the poem says, suggesting that by crucifying Jesus humankind had made divinity once again abstract, loosed it from being incarnated in humanity. Therefore, a hesitant and uncomprehending humankind falsely feels liberated.

However, as the second section of the poem suggests, this was not the end of the story. The killing of Christ did not extinguish the qualities he brought to the world. "It would not stop being human"; in other words, the divinity did not totally fade from humankind. Christ's gifts were now a permanent part of the human character. Eventually, this process of evolution will result in humankind's total redemption and the fading of the need ever to torture or kill anyone again.

The third stanza is the most difficult of the poem. "The day when life increased" is Easter—the first Easter, the day of Christ's resurrection. On Easter, human life attained an unprecedented dignity, became "haloed in poignancy." For once, the guards, who usually arrest people, were themselves arrested, and human liberty and potential were at last released. The lines "Four have been this human/ night and day, steadily" refer to the four canonical Gospels of Matthew. Mark, Luke, and John, through which the message of Christ has been communicated. "Three fell, two went on" refers to the historical fortunes of the religion Christ founded. As the Christian church grew, five principal patriarchates, where the main leaders of the church lived, were established. These were located in Antioch, Alexandria, Jerusalem, Constantinople, and Rome. Three of these cities fell to Islam in the seventh century, but two, Constantinople and Rome, "went on," yielding today's Eastern Orthodox Church and Roman Catholic Church, respectively. The poet then refers to the Shroud of Turin, once thought to be an actual relic of the Crucifixion but found unauthentic through a scientific laser probe. The implication is that if the shroud had been real, the laser would have revealed what Christians know already: that Christ made human dignity no longer something to be futilely strived for but an essential part of human identity.

Forms and Devices

The poem is written in three sections of seven couplets each. Les Murray's choice of a couplet form is unusual, because in English this mode of versification is usually associated with satire. Perhaps Murray was influenced by the ghazal, an Urdu poetic form whose couplets have a generally spiritual and lofty tone. Also, unlike the traditional English couplet, the lines of "Easter 1984" do not rhyme directly; at most they are linked by a sort of off-rhyme that does not intrude upon the reader. Off-rhymes such as "dignity" and "day" at the beginning of the first section, "again" and "risen" in the last couplet of the first section, or "human" and "on" in the fourth couplet of the third section are very close in sound even though they do not completely rhyme. Alternately, there are some true rhymes such as "him" and "limb" in the fifth couplet of the first section, as well as one instance (increased/poignancy/ecstasy/released) at the beginning of the third section where there is an *abba* rhyme scheme stretched across two couplets. Sometimes these almost-rhymes have definite undertones of meaning, as in "forgotten" and "human" in the last couplet of the poem, where the first word represents a deprivation that is healed by the second.

It is not symbol-hunting in a Christian poem to hypothesize that the three sections of the poem allude to the Holy Trinity. (Equally, the couplet form could be expressing the dual divine-human nature of Christ.) The "O" placed at the beginning of each of the last two sections is also worthy of note. "O" traditionally begins an invocation or prayer in Christian worship. It is a call, whether it be a call to God, to Christ, or to the speaker's fellow worshippers. It is not only the meaning but also the verbal shape of the "O" that matters. "O" connotes roundness, a kind of perfection, much as God is perfect and is as inaccessible to human reasons as a circle is to purely rectilinear geometry. In this way, the poem can suggest the fullness of God even though, as an imperfect verbal artifact, it cannot completely convey it. Murray thus joins much earlier Christian poets in English such as George Herbert in using the shape of a poem to aid him in fashioning his sacral verse.

The diction of the poem is an interesting mixture of traditional religious language and colloquial speech. Murray is not afraid to make allusions that puzzle the reader, as with the different numbers (four, then the seemingly incompatible three and two) in the third section, or to be unabashedly sentimental. "Human," drastically overexposed as an adjective, gains new force from the way Murray explores the willingness of many humans to disallow any sense of divinity in their ideas of humanity.

Themes and Meanings

"Easter 1984" is at once a traditional devotional poem and a departure from the mainstream of religious poetry as it was written for much of the twentieth century. Most of this poetry, as typified by the work of T. S. Eliot or W. H. Auden, starts from a position of alienation or despair and then reaches a position suggesting wholeness or redemption. Murray, on the other hand, starts from the position that Christ's victory has already been won and that the task of humanity is to understand the nature and terms of this victory.

The Easter theme is explicitly elaborated in the poem, but why is it titled "Easter 1984"? Murray may simply have written the poem in 1984, but there seem to be larger reverberations. To most "literary" readers, "1984" is most likely to suggest George Orwell's novel of that name (published in 1949), which depicts a Soviet-style totalitarian system in which Christianity, or any religion, has no place. Murray, writing from the vantage point of the "real" 1984, does not have so pessimistic a vision. Christianity, though hardly triumphant, has persisted and endured. This is the thrust of the mysterious "Three fell, two went on" line, which expands the poem from a consideration of the Crucifixion as such to include the course of Christian history. By going into the historic fate of humanity's belief in Christ, Murray includes both the defeats and victories of Christianity on the worldly level.

Murray is a convert to Roman Catholicism, but this poem seems less an extension or application of religious dogma—which characteristically the zeal of the convert poet might produce—than an expression of religious feeling. Murray wishes to bear witness to the beauty and majesty of Christ's resurrection, not to castigate those who are indifferent to it. His treatment of the theme of "humanity" is crucial. Human nature—human "meanness," for lack of a better word—is what makes people refuse the challenge of the redemption Christ offers them. At the end Christ's love becomes "the baseline of the human" instead of being completely above the here-and-now. Christianity is a higher humanism, so it can still have relevance to humankind, just as Murray's references have made clear that Christianity is a force in human history as well as spirituality.

Murray's Australian nationality may contribute to his unusually forceful exposition of the Christian theme. Unlike America, so long ideologically anchored by the Puritan vision of the "New Jerusalem," Australia has had no founding or sustaining religious myth. Against this background, the function of religious poetry is somewhat different. Although Murray is very much his own person as a poet and should not be considered a part of a general Australian trend, his preference for testifying to Christ's glory rather than proclaiming the authority of his dogma may well reflect his nationality.

Nicholas Birns

EFFORT AT SPEECH BETWEEN TWO PEOPLE

Author: Muriel Rukeyser (1913-1980)
Type of poem: Lyric
First published: 1935, in *Theory of Flight*

The Poem

"Effort at Speech Between Two People" appeared in Muriel Rukeyser's first book of poetry, *Theory of Flight*, which was awarded the prestigious Yale Younger Poets Prize when Rukeyser was twenty-one years old. The poem is a lyric meditation on the difficulty of communication. Its thirty-six lines are divided into seven unrhymed stanzas; four stanzas of six lines each alternate with three stanzas of four lines each. The colons that appear at the beginning of each stanza give an illusion of alternating speakers, but the content of the stanzas does not seem to follow this interpretation. The fact that the poet does not make it clear that more than one person is speaking suggests instead an internal monologue with one person sorrowfully considering the impossibility of truly knowing someone else and of being known in return. The opening words show that the speaker is eager, even desperate, to learn and to know: "Speak to me." That taut, imperative sentence is repeated twice in the poem. The speaker also repeats the promise "I will be open," implying a willingness to tell the deepest truths and to listen to others and truly hear what they have to say.

The gender of the speaker is not given, but the lyric poem traditionally reflects the voice of the author. The illustrative memories of childhood also suggest a female speaker. She reveals chronological stages of her life in tiny vignettes: She remembers her third birthday when she was read a sad story about a pink rabbit who died, burned her finger on the flame of a birthday candle, and was told to be happy. She recalls, at nine years old, crying at the sad beauty of Frédéric Chopin's music that her widowed aunt played on a piano. At the age of fourteen, she says, she had thoughts of suicide and was saved only by the beauty of a sunset.

Another problematic issue emerges as she reviews who she is now. She lost someone she loved, and, thinking about their past together, she concludes, "I think he never loved me." The object of her love is unspecified. It could be a friend, a lover, or her father. He liked to sail, and the thought of waves and seagulls reminds her of him and his love for the sea. Though he told her blithely that he loved her, he is no longer there (he is presumably dead, for she speculates on "what a tragedy his life was, really"). The true tragedy, however, seems to be that he was unable to be emotionally close to her. Throughout the poem, the speaker calls out to be known. It could be a cry to other people to take the time and to have the openness to share themselves with her, or, just as relevant, it could be herself whom she addresses and whom she wants to know. Without self-understanding and acceptance, she cannot be open enough to give herself to knowing another. However, even if she is open enough, the chances of finding another person equally self-aware and willing to share personal truths are not high. It takes effort and trust, and those qualities seem limited in an alienated society where, even in a crowded street, people do not speak to each another.

Forms and Devices

Rukeyser uses several rhetorical devices to slow the pace of the poem and to suggest pauses, as though the speaker is thinking carefully about what is being said. These devices include colons that are combined with spaces within a line, spaces between sentences, and ellipses in two lines of the final stanza. These spaces and punctuation marks provide visuals breaks that slow the reading and imply that speaking openly to another person about one's feelings is difficult and that the words of self-revelation do not flow easily and casually.

The poem is written in free verse without rhyme or a definite metrical pattern. It relies instead on imagery, the repetition of key words and phrases, and the juxtaposition of those images and phrases. The speaker states that she is "not happy," and she reinforces that sentiment throughout the poem with the words "unhappy," "lonely," and a second use of "not happy." There are many images of sadness in her life—being read the story of a rabbit that died, burning finger, weeping, thinking of leaping out a window, and being deserted by someone she loved. However, she also has memories of moments of sheer joy and beauty—the "white sails against a sky like music," the piano music composed by Chopin, and the sunset with light that "melted clouds and plains to beauty."

Just as short sentences and phrases are repeated, though in no predictable pattern, so too are specific words and concepts repeated. Some of these are state-of-being adjectives ("open," "happy," and "close"), while others are action verbs ("speak," "tell," "link," "love," "take my hand," and "grow to know"). These all function as possibilities of action and conditions of existence. They also function as metaphors for the giving of life, for ideals of what human beings could be and what changes there would be in social interaction if individuals could learn to break through to genuine communication with themselves and others. The juxtaposition of these phrases and images is vital in creating the tone and meaning of the poem. The speaker not only thinks of her aunt playing the piano but also remembers that her aunt is a widow; the music thus stirs the speaker both to sadness and to a rather pleasing melancholy and self-awareness ("I was fruitily sentimental,/ fluid"). The sea that carries haunting memories of a lost love also brings the beautiful image of "little lips of foam/ that ride small waves." Even in the crowded street where no one speaks to each other, "the morning shone."

Themes and Meanings

The basic theme of the poem is asserted in the title: an effort at speech as opposed to clear and meaningful speech that is heard and understood. The poem expresses the need to share and communicate, and it implies the difficulty of achieving this with others or even with oneself. Critic Louise Kertesz, in *The Poetic Vision of Muriel Rukeyser* (1980), refers to "Effort at Speech Between Two People" as a classic dialogue, but whether the poem is seen as a dialogue or a monologue, the message is the same: It is difficult to know oneself and to know others, and it is difficult to reveal oneself in a world where people move in crowds and do not speak. The world is a lonely place where strangers ache with the need for intimacy. This theme is made explicit in the rhythmic refrains "Grow to know me" and "Speak to me," which express the human need to communicate and the difficulty of achieving true communication.

This need to know people applies to knowing oneself, as shown by the speaker's memories of earlier eras of her life and her attempts to understand what she is now. It also refers to the basic human longing to be understood (as in the phrase "First my mind in your hand"), which, for the speaker, should precede touch and make possible the linking of the minutes of the day with each other or make "separate entities" come together like pieces of a puzzle. Further, this need to know refers to knowing other people. To know other people is to learn what humans share in common and thus reduce the sense of individual isolation. To know and learn about others is to create a sense of human community to which people can feel they belong. "Speak to me," repeats the speaker, reassuring the other person (or another part of herself) that she will be open and receptive rather than judgmental and separate. In a larger sense, the poem speaks clearly not only to the need for a change in consciousness and openness in the individual or between two individuals but also to the imperative need for increased communication and openness among all people, groups, and nations.

"Breathe-in experience, breathe-out poetry" is the opening line of the first poem in Rukeyser's first volume of verse ("Poem Out of Childhood," in *Theory of Flight*). Rukeyser thus announced her desire to communicate and share with others. She believed that poetry was a way "to share something of our experience by turning it into something and giving it to somebody." Poetry itself, then, is an effort at speech between two people, between writer and receptive reader. Rukeyser wrote repeatedly on behalf of liberal political causes, speaking out for freedom and justice at all levels. All her poetry, including "Effort at Speech Between Two People," reaches out to touch, to teach, and to communicate, always with the central theme that human beings could and must share themselves with others. That emotional intimacy has the power to transform society.

Lois A. Marchino

ELEGY FOR JANE

Author: Theodore Roethke (1908-1963)
Type of poem: Elegy
First published: 1953, in *The Waking: Poems 1933-1953*

The Poem

"Elegy for Jane," subtitled "My Student, Thrown by a Horse," is a poem in free verse whose twenty-two lines are divided into four stanzas. The poem follows the elegiac tradition insofar as it mourns the death of a loved one. The first nine lines follow the custom of honoring the deceased by describing Jane's delicacy and youthful exuberance. Roethke describes Jane as a light, quick animal, the epitome of the lovely in nature. Her neck curls are damp as plant tendrils, trailing, winding, and new. Quick and nervous in her movements, Jane's smile was nonetheless wide as a fish's ("pickerel"). Jane was also shy, for she had to be startled into talking. Once she started talking, however, she showed that she delighted in her thoughts. These lines may be alluding to Roethke's calling on her in class and her corresponding pleasure in answering.

When she was happy, Jane was like a bird with its tail in the wind; her song was so energetic that small branches trembled. The courage and adventurousness that causes a tail to be immersed in wind implies a daring that might have resulted in Jane's being thrown to her death by a horse. Jane's vitality was so inspiring that all nature rejoiced in her exuberance, even such gloomy natural items as shade and mold. Jane's happiness was so beneficent that the leaves turned to kissing.

The following stanza states that when Jane was sad, she plunged from a joy that even shade and mold reflected into an abyss of sadness so deep that "even a father could not find her" (line 11). The soaring bird suddenly fell to the rough earth and stirred its fundamental element, water. Jane, usually a joyous wren flying into the wind, sometimes dove into such unhappiness that her cheek scraped dried grass and stirred water.

The third stanza continues the bird metaphor, only this time Jane is a sparrow who is forever gone. The speaker also identifies himself with nature, not as a soaring or plunging bird but as a passive plant that can only wait, rooted in the earth. He is a fern whose thin leaves make thin shadows, implying that the speaker is grief-stricken to the point of being skeletal himself. The speaker's grief parallels Jane's deep sadness, for now that Jane is gone the speaker is no longer consoled by nature's beauties, its wet stones and moss lit by twilight.

The last stanza again refers to Jane's active but shy personality in birdlike terms; she moves from being described as a joyful wren to a lost sparrow to a skittery pigeon. Roethke longs to bring Jane back from death, but in addition to his powerlessness in the face of death, Roethke feels impotent in that his feelings are not legitimized because, being only her teacher and not a father or lover, he has no socially sanctioned right to grieve her loss publicly. Roethke mourns not only for the loss of Jane to himself and to all nature but also for his sense that no one will recognize his loss or console him.

Forms and Devices

Roethke is famous for inventing a new form, a long poem in parts, which seems borrowed from drama. In the relatively short poem "Elegy for Jane," as in his other works, the parts are "fluid," allowing him to swing back and forth through time. The first two stanzas are nostalgic, the third brings the speaker into the sorrowful present of Jane's death, while the last combines a wish for Jane's resurrection with the grim realizations that Jane is gone forever and that Roethke's own grief has no socially approved existence.

Roethke interlaces his dramatic stanzas with long, leisurely lines followed by energetic short lines that punctuate his lengthy descriptions with cogent, staccatoed points (as line 7, "The shade sang with her," and line 22, "Neither father nor lover"). "Elegy for Jane" uses Roethke's typical juxtaposition of opposing elements. The metaphor of Jane as a bird joyfully darting into the sky, then thudding sadly to earth in sadness and in death, also symbolizes a soul's ascent and descent. Images of energy and life contrast with those of stasis and death. Jane darts, skitters, startles, casts herself down, even scrapes her cheek when she is sad, all active images that contrast powerfully with those of immobility: "waiting like a fern," "sleep," and "damp grave."

Another juxtaposition of opposites is the contrast between water images and those of land and sky. Water also symbolizes flux, perhaps beyond or undergirding life and death. Jane's smile is like a pickerel, presumably swimming in water, and her grave is damp. Water is the element in which Jane swims and lives, and it is the element in which she is buried. Dampness itself is not ominous, and the speaker implies that ordinarily he would be consoled by "wetness on stones." The use of water as the ground of both life and death evokes Walt Whitman's "Out of the Cradle, Endlessly Rocking," in which the sea is the "old mother." Roethke's images of stasis—waiting, stones, moss, sleep—are not portrayed as undesirable but as a backdrop for movement, vitality, and light. Roethke suggests that were it not for Jane's death, even the light fleeting on moss would delight him. Her death has not only robbed him of herself and all pleasure but also turned him into a shadow, not a being of light. Light in this and other Roethke poems symbolizes life. Jane's syllables were light, her thoughts were delightful to her, and her pickerel smile evokes a fish whose scales glimmer in water.

Roethke uses iambic, trochaic, anapestic, and sprung rhythms in "Elegy for Jane." He mixes these varied metrics with lists of varied images, marked by three elements. Stanza 1 is marked by images of rapid movement, and stanza 2 by images of stasis. The concluding stanza is shaped by the vitality of fantasy juxtaposed with a moribund actuality—vital fantasy and deathly reality are balanced. The long lines and repetition of water and movement images control the poem's pacing, giving it the deliberateness of a dirge. The short, terrible last line is as final in its loneliness as the lowering of a casket into a grave.

Themes and Meanings

Although Roethke can usually find transcendent happiness even in melancholy images, such as mold or stones or moss in the last light of day, Jane's death has silenced the speaker's joy in any of nature's light or dark aspects. That society does not sanction his right to grieve in front of others forces him to mourn only to the elements over Jane's "damp grave." His sense of abandonment and loneliness finally diminishes him into a shadow. Both Jane's physical death and society's prohibition against his open expression of grief leave the speaker alienated from nature and humans. Although "Elegy for Jane" gives the impression of being a classical elegy, it is not. The standard celebration of the vegetative god, Adonis, contains regeneration. "Elegy for Jane" contains no regeneration, unless it is in a mysterious diffusion of Jane's darting energy into the windy, scattered movements of nature.

"Elegy for Jane" can be seen as Roethke's comment on the finality of nature's cycle. Jane is presented as one of life's small, treasured creatures whose death is a violation of the natural order in that she died before flowering. Although Roethke's lengthy, cadenced lines with his layered images are reminiscent of Whitman's long lines, they are different. Whitman simply cataloged images of all kinds. Roethke's detailed, meticulously described small things imply value—the tiny things of this world are at least as significant as the large. That Roethke acknowledged death as part of nature's cycle is seen in his juxtaposition of damp neck hair that sprawls like young plants with the "damp grave." This interruption of the natural cycle by the demise of a girl who made the leaves kiss violates the cosmic order of birth, growth, aging, and death. Jane's death is also terrible on a personal level. It has disrupted the speaker's connection with a creation that he found exhilarating in all its aspects, in its mold as well as in its birds, in its stones as well as in its trees. Jane's ups and downs reflected the light and shadows of nature in which the speaker once reveled. Her premature death and the lack of social ritual available to the speaker result not only in grief but also in a hopeless acceptance of a devastated outer and inner landscape.

Mary Hanford Bruce

ELEGY FOR JOHN DONNE

Author: Joseph Brodsky (1940-1996)
Type of poem: Elegy
First published: 1965, as "Bolshaya Elegiya Dzhonu Donnu," in *Stikhotvoreniya i poemy*; English translation collected in *Selected Poems*, 1973

The Poem

As the title "Elegy for John Donne" indicates, the poem is an elegy, a formal and sustained lament in verse form mourning the death of a particular person—in this case, the death of John Donne, the seventeenth century Metaphysical poet. The Russian title includes the word *bolshaya* ("big"), which connotes the importance and depth of this tribute to Donne. This adjective is omitted in the translation by George L. Kline used here. In the original and in translation, the poem is written in pentameter (ten syllables per poetic line), the metrical line used in Donne's Holy Sonnets. The Russian version uses a precise rhyme scheme (*ababcdcd*); this English version does not.

The poem can be divided into four parts. In part 1 (lines 1-95), the absolute silence that Donne's death has caused is felt throughout the world. Likening death to sleep—a celebrated Donnean metaphor—Joseph Brodsky gives the reader a catalog remarkable for its inclusiveness. Images of simple, everyday household items (beds, walls, carpets, pots, pans, doors) sleep next to a greater sleeping cosmos: St. Paul's Cathedral, London, the sea, "this Island," angels, even God.

In the second part (lines 96-127), this silence is broken by the sound of weeping: "But hark! Do you not hear in the chill night/ a sound of sobs, the whispered voice of fear?" There is a change in perspective. The speaker in this section addresses several questions, trying to discover who is crying, asking in succession his angel, the cherubim, Saint Paul, God, and Gabriel. Only silence answers back.

In the third section (lines 128-184), Donne's soul identifies itself as the one grieving and credits Donne with the power of soaring above the "dark sins and passions" of which his poetry speaks so eloquently. Again, the reader is given a catalog of some of the varied subjects of Donne's poetic voice: Hell, Heaven, love, life, lust, the Last Judgment. This section ends with the soul claiming that it is Donne himself who weeps: "It is not I who sob. 'Tis thou, John Donne:/ thou liest alone."

By the last section (lines 129-213), dawn, the image of regeneration and rebirth, starts to break. Brodsky likens Donne to a wild bird who will wake at dawn so that he can finish his final lines, uniting body and soul. Throughout the poem, the images of sleep and silence are intensified by the snow falling and swirling in, on, and between the poetic lines.

Forms and Devices

The power of "Elegy for John Donne" is characterized by Brodsky's use of images, metaphors, and specific allusions to Donne's work. The strongest image is that of the silence that pervades the entire poem, a silence so deep that the reader can hear his or her own breath. The snow gently falling and blanketing all things sleeping adds to the intensity of silence and darkness. The images range from the smallest, most insignificant items to the cosmic order of the universe: "Dark Hell-fires sleep, and glorious Paradise." Brodsky's lists are reminiscent of the staccato lists in Donne's poems. In lines 7 and 8, Brodsky strings together sleeping images: "fresh linen, nightlamp, chests of drawers, a clock,/ a mirror, stairways, doors." Donne, in Holy Sonnet 7, enumerates the causes of sleep/death: "War, dearth, age, agues, tyrannies,/ Despair, law, chance."

The poem, as a whole, turns on the metaphor of death as sleep. Donne, too, employs this metaphor in several of his poems. Brodsky's sleep image permeates the poem, especially in the first part where, because Donne is dead, "All these things have sunk in sleep./ Yes, all things." This is strongly reminiscent of the dead world that Donne experienced after the early death of his wife: "The world's whole sap is sunk . . . Life is shrunk,/ Dead and interred" ("A Nocturnal upon St. Lucy's Day, Being the Shortest Day"). In Holy Sonnet 6, Donne writes, "And gluttonous death will instantly unjoint/ My body and soul, and I shall sleep a space." "Elegy for John Donne" moves from deep night toward a physical waking from sleep as dawn breaks at the end of the poem and toward a spiritual waking from death: "But see, there from the clouds will shine/ that star which made thy world endure till now." This echoes Donne's own conviction that "One short sleep past, we wake eternally" (Holy Sonnet 10).

Specific allusions to Donne's poetry, prose, and life abound and give the poem added depth and significance. Some knowledge of Donne's poetic voice enriches the reader's experience and enhances the power of Brodsky's poem. The juxtaposition of anxiety and sin in line 73 evokes many of Donne's Holy Sonnets. In line 42 ("This Island sleeps, embraced by lonely dreams"), the key words "Island" and "lonely" echo and deny Donne's assertion that "No man is an island, entire of itself; every man is a piece of the continent, a part of the main" ("Meditation XVII" from *Devotions upon Emergent Occasions*, 1624). Both the sound of weeping and the image of tears permeate Donne's poetry. Other images shared by both poets include shadows, mirrors, the crucifix, windows, and the sea.

A crucial echoing image is Brodsky's tolling bell, now silent: "No din of baying hound/ or tolling bell disturbs the silent air," resounding in its silence Donne's bell that called him toward death when he was seriously ill: "never send to know for whom the bells toll; it tolls for thee" ("Meditation XVII"). Donne implies that, when a member of the community dies, those involved in that community participate in that death, just as Brodsky implies that Donne's death has diminished the world and its inhabitants.

Themes and Meanings

"Elegy for John Donne" embodies several important themes. Brodsky posits that, when a poet dies, the world he or she has created also dies, as Donne testifies in "The Will": "I'll undo/ The world by dying." Brodsky intensifies the totality of this dead world by including the world as he knows it in the sleep that settles upon the universe. Simultaneously, however, Brodsky asserts the immortality of the world created by the genius of the poet. Donne's England comes vibrantly alive because of Brodsky's power of evocation.

Another crucial theme is the affinity between Brodsky and Donne. They share a strong spiritual bond: Both of them are Metaphysical poets deeply concerned with realities, beyond the merely physical, of love, death, solitude, sin, salvation, and regeneration; both are poets that are lone islands isolated from the greater sea of humanity, Donne because of his thwarted political ambitions and his self-imposed exile from a world that did not understand him and Brodsky because of political powers that accused him of scorning useful work that would contribute to the good of Communism. Eventually, Brodsky was tried for "social parasitism" and exiled to five years of forced labor at a state farm in Arkhangel'sk; he left his homeland for good in 1972 when he emigrated to the United States. This shared loneliness resounds throughout "Elegy for John Donne."

Brodsky's poem moves toward regeneration, especially near the end of the poem, where images of falling rain and wet earth signal rebirth. The star, mentioned twice in the latter part, illuminates the final moment of spiritual awakening. At first, the star is hidden, yet felt, as Brodsky imagines Donne "himself entrusting to that steady star/ which now is closed in clouds." This star soars into full view at the close of the poem, where it clearly evokes the stars with which Dante Alighieri (another exiled poet) ends each of the three parts to his *La divina commedia* (c.1320; *The Divine Comedy*, 1472), especially at the end of *Inferno*, when Dante physically and spiritually has conquered death: "we emerged to see—once more—the stars." Using the image of the star pointing to a transcendent reality of a possible reunion with the Creator, Brodsky ends his poem, "But see, there from the clouds will shine/ that star which made thy world endure till now."

The poem, as a whole, is held together by Brodsky's brilliant intertwining metaphor of weaving, using such ephemeral material as snowflake needles to thread together the web of images and allusions, healing the torn body and stitching together body to soul, night to dawn, and earth to heaven. Early in the poem, the needle is threadless as the soul of Donne is shown as "needle-thin,/ yet without thread." By the end of the poem, the snow closes the gap between Donne's body and soul, "its needles flying back and forth, back, forth!" This metaphor is complimented by the conventional metaphor of the body as a garment for the soul. In death, it is torn, full of holes, and in shreds. The metaphors combine in the symbolic and transcendent image of the star "bringing the healing needle home."

Koos Daley

ELEVEN ADDRESSES TO THE LORD

Author: John Berryman (1914-1972)
Type of poem: Poetic sequence
First published: 1970, in *Love & Fame*

The Poem

The title of "Eleven Addresses to the Lord" suggests its basic structure and intent. Eleven short poems, each capable of standing alone but enhanced by association with the others, compose the whole. Each poem is written in quatrains of varying line length; rhyme is often, though not consistently, used.

In the first address, Berryman (there is no perceivable distance between the persona-narrator and the author) praises God as the "Master of beauty" and the fashioner of things exquisitely small and lovely (the snowflake) and grandly inspiring (the earth). These are common ways of looking at God, of course, but soon Berryman's focus becomes more personal: God has come to his rescue "again and again" over the years. Had he not, the implication is quite clear, the narrator would have destroyed himself as so many of his friends have done. Both the praise of God's creation and gratitude for his sustaining blessing are traditional poetic gestures with a heritage at least as old as Christian poetry. What is less traditional, however, is the open doubt expressed by the poet: "I have no idea whether we live again."

The first address sets the pattern that the succeeding ten will follow in whole or in part: praise of God and his creation, gratitude for his assistance, and a strain of doubt that is sometimes subtle but elsewhere blatant enough to border on cynicism or sarcasm. Address 2 finds Berryman once again praising God the creator and especially for his "certain goodness to me." By the end of number two, however, doubt once more encroaches: "I say 'Thy kingdom come,' it means nothing to me."

Addresses 3 and 4 are closely related. Three is perhaps the most conventional of the eleven poems. Here, Berryman prays that God protect him from his sinful nature, which in the past, it is obvious from the allusions, has caused the author to hurt others as well as himself. Having called for God's aid in the third address, in the fourth Berryman wonders whether God is there to hear his request and prays for strength and faith.

The fifth address narrows the focus to one specific question: What follows life? Probably the damned will suffer no pains of hell; the faithful will likely receive no heavenly reward, either. "Rest may be your ultimate gift," Berryman surmises. The sixth address locates the source of Berryman's conflicts with God and his fellow man. Until he was twelve, he served at Mass six days a week; then his father committed suicide, and thereafter, "Confusions & afflictions/ followed my days."

The seventh address advises a desolate young woman to look to Justin Martyr's words of wisdom. The eighth ("A Prayer for the Self"), ninth, and tenth addresses find Berryman asking for God's blessing, as God blessed him before. In the eleventh address, Berryman cites martyrs who died for their faith and ends this moving poetic sequence by praying for the strength to bear up under whatever "Thou wilt award."

Forms and Devices

Berryman has long been considered one of the twentieth century's great innovators, a master manipulator of poetic conventions. These manipulations are most fully developed in *The Dream Songs* (1969) and are, to a degree at least, more muted in "Eleven Addresses to the Lord." Nevertheless, Berryman provocatively utilizes many poetic devices to enhance the sequence's complex interplay of sincerity and irony. Indeed, just as the poem thematically wavers between faith and doubt, its form varies from the almost anachronistically traditional to innovations that, especially in a context of conventional devices, are deliberately jarring.

At first glance the conventional elements seem to predominate. The title predisposes the reader to expect something traditional, "Eleven Addresses to the Lord" being as appropriate for the twelfth century as the twentieth. Moreover, the individual poems seem very close to Horation odes—that is, discourses on a single subject employing an unvarying stanzaic pattern. As with this centuries-old form, the language, initially at least, seems appropriately lofty and dignified.

Even if the reader did not recognize the Horatian ode form, however, one glance at the page would seem to promise poetic conventionality: All sections are written in apparently standard quatrains. This promise seems confirmed at the beginning of the poem, where God is described as "Master of beauty, craftsman of the snowflake"— imagery so traditional as to border on the trite. Proceeding through the poem, the reader encounters rhyme both internal and end, placing this sequence once more, apparently, in the conventional category.

Save for the quatrain, however, which is maintained throughout, these early impressions of stylistic conventionality are soon shattered. Line lengths vary with no apparent pattern. Predictably, the meter also varies, from as many as seven accented syllables per line to as few as two. This at first glance "old-fashioned" poem is, therefore, written in free verse. Similarly, although Berryman writes beautifully and rhythmically, the rhythm is less than conventional. Indeed, there is hardly a single line in the entire sequence that has a consistent rhythm (that is, entirely iambic or entirely trochaic).

When the reader turns to other apparently conventional features of the poem, a similar undermining of tradition is found. Berryman uses rhyme, for instance, but in no discernible pattern. Some of the addresses have no rhymes, others one or two or several. Moreover, the rhymes are rarely strong rhymes but are almost invariably slant rhymes ("begins" and "eloquence"; "done" and "come") or combinations that barely hint of rhyme and can hardly be classified even as slant rhymes ("Paul" and "chair"; "man" and "doom").

The diction and imagery are also deliberately inconsistent in tone and effect. "Through" is anachronistically and unnecessarily spelled "thro'," while "and" is sometimes written using the modern stenographer's ampersand ("&"). The syntax is sometimes so determinedly poetic as to be stilted ("cross am I sometimes"), while elsewhere Berryman throws in a slangy colloquialism: "Uh-huh." And Berryman's God may be "craftsman of the snowflake"—an image poets centuries ago would have been very comfortable with—but what medieval poet would dare describe part of God's creation as the "boring Moon"? All of these deliberate inconsistencies serve to jar the reader out of complacency and underscore a thematic development that is equally ambiguous.

Themes and Meanings

"Eleven Addresses to the Lord" was originally collected as part 4 of *Love & Fame* (1970), a volume that explores with often shocking frankness John Berryman's relationship with women and his public life. In "Eleven Addresses to the Lord," however, Berryman's public life for the most part disappears as a subject, and love becomes his love for God.

Critical reaction to the collection as a whole and to "Eleven Addresses to the Lord" specifically has been mixed, with a number of critics taking at face value Berryman's self-congratulatory bombast in the earlier sections of the collection and concluding that his expressions of faith in "Eleven Addresses to the Lord" are uniformly sincere. Examination of the poem's forms and devices, however, should warn the reader against assuming that anything in the poem is free from ambiguity and irony.

Berryman's ambivalence toward God is evident from the very beginning of the sequence. In the first quatrain of the first address, God is praised in conventional terms as "craftsman of the snowflake," but that craftsman also created "the boring Moon." This ambiguity leads directly to that quatrain's final line, in which the author thanks God for "such as it is my gift." Is his gift analogous to the "Earth so gorgeous" or the "boring Moon"? If the latter, should such a gift truly elicit gratitude to God? Two stanzas later Berryman praises God in apparently unequivocal terms for repeatedly rescuing him. This, however, is immediately followed by "You have allowed my brilliant friends to destroy themselves," the "allowed" being troubling in reference to a supposedly merciful, loving God.

Is God truly loving or indifferent? The next quatrain concludes that there is no clear answer. Rather, God is "unknowable, as I am unknowable to my guinea pigs." This doubt is stated in the clearest possible terms in the next stanza in reference to the possibility of an afterlife: "I have no idea whether we live again." Still, Berryman insists that he believes in Christ's resurrection as firmly as he believes he sits "in this blue chair." The reader might well wonder what color chair Berryman was sitting in when he penned that line.

The first address ends in an apparently unequivocal expression of faith, but given what has gone before, readers cannot with confidence know whether this ending is sincere or ironic bordering on the sarcastic. The following ten sections of the sequence address varying specific aspects of the question of faith. Everywhere apparently sincere avowals are undercut with at least subtle irony and often open doubt. Berryman clearly defines the problem: in questions of religious faith, he states in the last line of address 6, "I identify with everybody, even the heresiarchs."

Dennis Vannatta

EMMETT TILL

Author: Wanda Coleman (1946-
Type of poem: Elegy
First published: 1986; collected in *African Sleeping Sickness: Poems & Stories*, 1990

The Poem

"Emmett Till" is an elegy in four parts that shows American racism at its ugliest in the pre-civil rights era. Wanda Coleman's title is the name of a fourteen-year-old black boy who was murdered and has since become a popular historical figure in fiction and poetry. The facts surrounding his death have been recorded by journalists and historians: Till was visiting a great-uncle in Money, Mississippi, in 1955. According to testimony, he whistled at the wife of a local store owner. She was white. One of the biggest taboos in the pre-civil rights South was a black male showing interest in a white female. The fact that Till was a boy did not matter; this kind of behavior required that white men teach "a lesson" to the youthful offender. This lesson evokes several stereotypes that were the crux of considerable racial tension. One was that black people were always thinking about sex; the other was that white women, who were more virtuous than anyone else, had to be protected at any cost. Hearing about the incident secondhand, the white woman's husband and brother-in-law took Till away from his great-uncle's residence. Three days later, a local fisherman saw feet sticking up from the Tallahatchie River. Those feet were attached to the mutilated body of Till. His murder and the subsequent trial were widely publicized, and some historians have credited his murder with inducing the birth struggles of the Civil Rights movement. Because of the brutality of his death, especially for such a minor offense, African American writers tell and retell Till's story as a symbol for the tragic stories of many nameless African American males.

In the first of the four parts, the third-person narrator provides the setting and atmosphere that permeated the "hate-inspired" Jim Crow South. The narrator also describes the natural movement of the river and its part in Till's transcendence. Because of its role, the waters of the river are "sanctified" for the final journey as the bloated body of the dead child is carried home. The narrator charges the water with a sacred duty even as it erodes stone and Till's flesh, a testament to its dual nature as nurturer and destroyer. The second part of the poem relates Till's transgression: the whistle at the store owner's wife. The narrator even speculates about his motivation: She was desirable, and, as any red-blooded, all-American boy would, Till reacted. This "rape by eye" was enough to make two white men angry enough to kill, while the black community, impotent with rage and ineffective slogans, watched. Part 3 gives the details of the men taking Emmett away from his great-uncle's home and to the water. The narrator does not describe the murder but refers to it as "the deed." In part 4, a black preacher eulogizes Till by recapping the time, place, and events of his murder. "Weighted down" but "too light," Till's body rises, Christlike, on the third day.

The refrains in parts 1 through 3, alphabetical lists of rivers in the United States, exemplify the pastoral elegy's use of nature. The absence of a river refrain in part 4 makes the narrator's mention of "the tallahatchie," the river that held Till's body in its "mulky arm," even more emphatic. This part focuses on "murder" and Till's resurrection to a higher existence.

Forms and Devices

Coleman's masterful use of imagery creates the powerful effect of this poem. The most visible images involve water and religion. The poem begins with the "river jordan," which functioned in the Bible as, among other things, a safe passageway for the Israelites to get to the Promised Land; many African Americans also saw such a spiritual crossing as better than their material existence. This is followed by the haunting refrains of the rivers in alphabetical order, beginning with "*the alabama*" and ending with "*the yellowstone*." The river's destruction of Till's flesh is attributed to the men who dragged him from home and are thus responsible for "blood river born." As nurturer, the river "come[s] forth to carry the dead child home." The narrator invests the river with maternal instincts: "river mother carries him" and "from the mulky arm of the tallahatchie." Even mythology is utilized as Till's body becomes "waftage" in "that grotesque swim up the styx." Finally, just as the Israelites were carried by the Jordan, Till "was carried forth to that promised land" by the river. Though the overwhelming use of water is positive in its ability to cleanse, nourish, and nurture, two references evoke negative images. These occur in part 2, as the narrator relates that Till's offense makes a white man "pass water mad/ make a whole tributary of intolerance."

Coleman's religious imagery is also powerful. In addition to the narrator's reference to the Jordan, Till's mother, a modern-day Mary, is "the black madonna/ bereft of babe." Like Christ, Till was also "crucified" and "crown[ed]" before he "crossed over into campground." Finally, Till is "baptized" and "*on that third day/ he rose*" to complete the Christian cycle of sin, redemption, and resurrection. Thus, another martyr is created from the "nidus" (breeding ground) of racism.

Claiming not to see herself in "terms of a tradition," Coleman admits, in a 1990 interview in *Black American Literature Forum* (*BALF*), that she draws from the black tradition and the culture of the black church. In part 4, for example, the voice of the black community emerges in the traditional verbal pattern of "call-response," which is most often found between a preacher and the congregation. All of the preacher's statements (calls) are punctuated by the congregation's responses: "lord!" or "lord! lord!" Also, Coleman acknowledges the African American church as the race's strongest institution, which often nurtured its members in times of racial conflict.

Also worth noting is Coleman's use of multiple voices. The primary narrator is objective, describing the scenes from a distance, but the poem also contains the voice of a bulletin/commentator that reveals the impact of the murder: "killing of 14-year-old/ stirs nation. there will be a public wake." Moreover, consistent with conventions of the pastoral elegy, the rage of the black community comes through in the language of the people: "but she be a white woman. but he be/ a black boy," and "cuz she was white woman virtue and he/ be a black boy lust." The second quotation differs from the first in that individuals are no longer involved; they have become symbols of racial conflict.

Themes and Meanings

"As a writer I feel I best serve my readership when I rehumanize the dehumanized, when I illuminate what is in darkness, when I give blood and bone to statistics that are too easily dismissed," says Coleman in *BALF*. The world's final view of Till was his grotesquely disfigured face and bloated body, so the narrator reminds us that "(once it was human)" as she tells Till's story and illuminates racism "from the deep dank murk of consciousness." According to Stephen Henderson in *Understanding the New Black Poetry* (1973), much black poetry deals with the theme of liberation from either physical or political bondage. This poem is a variation on a historically popular theme: the preference for death over slavery. Here, set free by death, Till is "sovereign at last." Thus, Coleman's theme emphasizes the liberated spirit and the enduring legacy of Till, which can be seen in her dominant images.

Coleman's irreverent parodies of "America, the Beautiful" and "The Star-Spangled Banner" reveal the brutality of a Jim Crow system in a democratic society and the hypocrisy of America, which fostered this hostile climate for African Americans. Coleman juxtaposes the ideal with the reality. For example, the beauty of America is revealed by the "purple mountains" majesty and the "amber" waves of grain, but the ugliness is revealed by the narrator's insistent questioning of what people can see: "oh say do you see the men off/ the bank dredging in that/ strange jetsam," and "oh say Emmett Till can you see Emmett Till/ crossed over into campground." This ugliness, this dehumanization "in a supposedly great nation like this one" is what Coleman, in the *BALF* interview, refers to as "gangrenous," as "cancer" in need of excising.

First, however, someone must "talk seriously" about American racism, "the only major untouched area" in literature, Coleman concludes. Thus, "spirit uplifted," Till represents the collective spirit of African Americans in this country. His rising symbolizes the race's refusal to stay down. The Tallahatchie, for example, could be any river, as evidenced by the alphabetical listing of American rivers, and Emmett Till could be any black person who has died violently at the hands of whites for some perceived offense and without due process. In this poem, his death becomes a symbol of the lack of both democracy and Christianity in a supposedly democratic and Christian society.

Loretta McBride

ETHICS

Author: Linda Pastan (1932-
Type of poem: Lyric
First published: 1979; collected in *Waiting for My Life,* 1981

The Poem

"Ethics" raises a number of significant philosophical issues, and it does so in language that is clear and direct and in a voice that immediately elicits an emotional and intellectual response from readers. The poem's title, like its subject, is rather abstract, but Pastan immediately and consistently grounds the poem in her unique narrative voice.

As a student in a philosophy course years ago, the speaker says in the poem's opening lines, she was given one of those difficult questions that ethics teachers like to pose—what are often called "values clarification" questions—and asked to choose between saving a great work of art (a Rembrandt painting) or an old woman from a fire in a museum. There is never a "correct" answer to such questions, of course; rather, the process of thinking the question through often exposes the student's own value system in clearer outline. The first part of the poem makes the students' values clear and reveals that the question is hardly relevant to them: "Restless," "caring little for pictures or old age," the students can only answer "half-heartedly."

This classroom exercise in the first part of the poem is interrupted, at least in the speaker's own mind, when she recalls that sometimes the woman in the ethics question "borrowed my grandmother's face." The abstract philosophical question, in other words, has been personalized, made human by the speaker's own real-life experiences, by the memory of her grandmother. This recollection is a hint of what is to come in the poem's closing lines.

In the last section of what is essentially the longer first half of the poem, the speaker—still imagining herself as the student in that philosophy class—tells readers about the year when she answered her teacher's question with one of her own: "why not let the woman decide herself?" She gave, in short, a clever response, and one that offered autonomy to the imaginary character in this ethics exercise. The point is important, because Pastan the poet is in a sense doing the same thing in her own poem—she is personalizing an abstract ethics issue, giving it human dimensions. The teacher, using the academic jargon of the profession, notes that Linda "eschews" (avoids or shuns) "the burdens of responsibility." The teacher, in short, like all good teachers, tries to bring the discussion back to the subject and to the classroom exercise.

Although there is no stanza break at this point, the poem clearly shifts focus after line 16. The first two-thirds of the poem recall a school experience; in the last third, the poem shifts to the immediate present ("This fall"). Past tense becomes present tense, and the ethical conundrum of the first part of the poem is tentatively answered. The speaker is now standing in a "real museum" looking at an actual painting; the abstract example of the academic exercise has become "a real Rembrandt," and the speaker herself an "old woman,/ or nearly so, myself."

With this new perspective, which only time could give her, the speaker now is able to look closely at both choices in the ethical problem. The colors of the painting—Pastan is describing what Rembrandt does in his most famous works—are "darker than autumn,/ darker even than winter—the browns of earth." She recognizes how Rembrandt has captured something natural, even mystical, in his paintings, for she observes further the ways in which "earth's most radiant elements burn/ through the canvas."

Her conclusion from this intimate knowledge of both subjects? She still cannot answer the ethical challenge. Rather, she goes beyond the question—as she first did in lines 13-14 with her clever answer—to the realization "that woman/ and painting and season are almost one/ and all beyond saving by children." She overthrows the very terms of the ethical choice of the first part of the poem, in other words. The ethics problem implied that human life can be reduced to categories; now, as an older woman, she knows truths which transcend any such limitations.

What started as an ethics exercise, then, has become something much more important: the recognition of the power of art, an understanding of the seasons of human life, and the realization of how she herself, the speaker, shares so much with both the last seasonal stages of autumn and winter and the Rembrandt painting, where one can also sense something beyond those seasons ("darker than autumn,/ darker even than winter"). The speaker thus comes to see how Rembrandt has captured nature and yet has also rendered something mystically beyond, that "burns through the canvas."

Finally, the speaker knows, in a poignant recognition, that "woman/ and painting and season"—are "beyond saving by children." The restless students in the ethics class at the start of the poem can know nothing about old age, or about art, or even about natural life cycles—and they certainly cannot save one or the other from the death or destruction that awaits them all.

Forms and Devices

For a poem that deals with some rather abstract philosophical issues, "Ethics" is remarkably accessible. Pastan accomplishes this feat by using language that is clear and direct and metaphors that tie the experiences of the poem together for the reader. The language in the poem is almost monosyllabic: fire, chairs, life. The most difficult vocabulary (eschews, responsibility) appears mainly in the philosophy teacher's language. Likewise, the experiences of the poem are rendered as physical images: restless students on hard chairs, the speaker's grandmother in her kitchen and then wandering in a museum, the speaker herself as an older woman standing in "a real museum." The abstract nature of the poem's subject, in short, is softened somewhat in the concrete ways that Pastan renders it. Only the last few lines, when the speaker describes an essentially mystical experience, cause any difficulty in understanding.

The language is also made approachable through alliteration and assonance—

through poetic devices, in other words, that lead readers to move from word to word more easily: "real Rembrandt" (line 18), for example, or "autumn," "brown," "burn," (lines 20-22). The devices Pastan employs help to bring the complex ideas in the poem down to earth.

The central metaphor of the poem is the poem's very subject and idea. The old woman and the Rembrandt painting, which are posed as ethical opposites in the first lines of the poem, have become, by the end of the poem, the same thing, and they are joined by the seasons as well. One element comes to stand—as in any metaphorical comparison—for the other. Old age, the seasons, and the dark colors and "radiant elements" in Rembrandt's paintings have so much in common: fullness, value, and beauty.

Themes and Meanings

For such a short poem, Pastan has packed into "Ethics" a great deal of meaning. Some commentators see the poem as containing a *carpe diem*, or, "seize the day," theme, as in a number of famous older poems (such as Robert Herrick's "To the Virgins, to Make Much of Time" and A. E. Housman's "Loveliest of Trees, the Cherry Now"), but the focus in Pastan's poem is quite different from the typical *carpe diem* theme. The poem seems both more accepting and more critical. Restless young people sitting on hard chairs, the speaker contends, cannot appreciate the fullness of life or its complex cycles. They cannot see the significance of the ethics question, nor are they capable of understanding either the full force of old age, with its proximity to death, or the true beauty of great art.

Rather than being depressed by her own approaching death, the speaker seems to be accepting it. In fact, the comparison with the Rembrandt painting carries an affirmation of life. Only as an old woman ("or nearly so") has the speaker been able to appreciate the power of the painting and the mystical ways in which human life, art, and nature are linked. The poem seems to be chiding youth for its shallowness; better not waste great paintings, or old age, on them, the speaker implies, since they cannot appreciate either. By the end of the poem, readers have been led to see that the academic exercise poses a false choice and that the real opposition is between spring and fall, between the shallowness of youth and the depth of old age, when one can finally experience life's more powerful truths.

David Peck

THE EXEQUY

Author: Henry King (1592-1669)
Type of poem: Elegy
First published: 1657, in *Poems, Elegies, Paradoxes, and Sonnets*

The Poem

"The Exequy" is an elegy of 120 lines of iambic tetrameter couplets, a verse form popular in a wide variety of early seventeenth century English lyrics. The second line fittingly designates the poem a "complaint" (or lament), and it appropriately sustains a tone of grief over a personal loss throughout. Henry King wrote the elegy on the death of his wife Anne, who died seven years after they were married, having borne him five children. Although first-person speakers are never identical with the authors, the speaker of "The Exequy" reflects, with reasonable accuracy, King's personal grief over the loss of his wife. He originally gave his elegy the subtitle "To His Matchlesse Never To Be Forgotten Freind."

The text is divided into eleven verse paragraphs of varying lengths, ranging from two to eighteen lines. Essentially, the speaker expresses his grief, develops a meditation on time, and looks to the future. In the opening paragraph, the poet establishes an elegiac tone through an address to the burial site, the "Shrine," offering poetry instead of flowers as a fitting adornment for his "Dear Loss." In the second paragraph, the address turns to the dead wife as the object of the speaker's meditation and emotion. She has become his book or library, and his only business, which he peruses though blinded by tears. Paragraph 3 introduces images and metaphors related to the cosmos. Grief reminds him that she died before reaching the normal midpoint of life, and the effect on the speaker has been that of an eclipse, as earth has interposed between himself and his beloved, metaphorically depicted as his sun. The poem's metaphors in this section become increasingly complex, as if to suggest that meditation allays the speaker's grief.

In the fourth paragraph, the speaker expresses an especially poignant, yet normal, reaction to bereavement, an effort to strike a bargain with fate. He could willingly give her up for a period, a year or even ten years, if he knew she would return. However, the subsequent paragraph brings the realization that he cannot hope to see her again until Judgment Day, when all the resurrected are assembled. Whatever consolation the speaker can wring from this event derives from the hope of a reunion in the remote future.

In a long paragraph continuing the section on grief, the poet invokes the earth to keep what he can no longer possess but to restore its charge fully on Judgment Day. The section concludes with a single, two-line paragraph, as if the grave were being closed: "So close the ground, and 'bout her shade/ Black curtains draw, my *Bride* is laid." In the remaining paragraphs, the speaker turns to his own future and looks forward to death, when his body will join hers in the earth. The images and figures of speech emphasize both the transience of life and the inevitable march of time. The speaker views himself as moving inexorably toward death, as a ship on a long voyage or an army unit ready to join a battle already underway. By viewing his own existence as tending toward her and rejoining her in death, he finds some consolation for his loss and a kind of subdued acceptance of the future. The poem concludes on a note of personal reconciliation and hope for reunion: "I am content to live/ Divided, with but half a heart,/ Till we shall meet and never part."

Forms and Devices

The elegy's most prominent figure of speech is apostrophe, an address to an inanimate object or abstraction as if it were alive or to a person absent or dead as if present or alive. In its application, apostrophe is thus related to personification. It establishes a dignified, somewhat elevated tone and is often hortative and ecstatic. However, King's apostrophes are restrained, decorous, and appropriately subdued in tone. Initially, the apostrophe is to the grave, metaphorically the "Shrine of my dead Saint." Imperceptibly, however, the dead Saint becomes the object of the speaker's address as he develops the theme of mourning. Shifting the subject of the apostrophe usually marks a transition in the tone or movement of the poem. The change from his wife to earth signals the speaker's intent to close the section on grieving. He admonishes earth to hold her body but to yield it in its entirety on Doomsday. The poem's final apostrophe, beginning "Sleep on my *Love* in thy cold bed/ Never to be disquieted," once more treats the dead person as if alive; it establishes a meditative tone, allowing the speaker to make a transition to his own journey toward death. The apostrophes do more than establish a serious tone; they also focus attention on the dead wife and her resting place. They have the effect of increasing the immediacy of the speaker's expressed emotions of loss and grief.

"The Exequy" is often included in anthologies of Metaphysical poetry, the poetic tradition founded by English poet John Donne. The primary reasons for its place in the Donne tradition are its meditative content, its reasoned analysis, and its striking and complex metaphors and similes. The dead wife becomes a "book," then, hyperbolically, the speaker's "library," which occupies all of his attention. Her dying has been like the setting sun that will not rise again. First, she is his day, then a falling star, and finally her death becomes a never-ending eclipse as earth is placed between her and the speaker. While some figures are brief and striking, others are more ingenious, intricate, and complex. The remote comparison of her burial to an eclipse, a never-ending one at that, represents a bold metaphysical conceit.

In the section looking forward to his own death, the speaker employs more conventional figures. He metaphorically equates his own journey toward death with that of a ship sailing inexorably toward its destination. In a further comparison, he portrays himself as a military unit joining a battle that has already consumed his love. The passage introduces a memorable simile: "My pulse like a soft Drum/ Beats my approch, tells *Thee* I come." The figures that indicate his own passage of time are designed to convey a sense of steady, constant movement, whereas those applied to her suggest more rapid and overwhelming movement.

Themes and Meanings

In its thematic development, "The Exequy" follows the overall pattern of an elegy. The poem begins with a statement of mourning and loss (lines 1-80), followed by passages of acceptance and reconciliation in which the speaker comes to terms with his grief (lines 81-114). The concluding section (lines 115-120) looks to the future in the spirit of hope and acceptance, although the hopeful tone in King's poem is remarkably moderate. Unlike many elegies written about subjects whom the poet scarcely knew or perhaps had never met, King's poem includes a genuine sense of personal loss and grief. The speaker refers to the youth of his bride, suggesting that death overtook her before she had reached the halfway point of life. In another passage, the speaker refers to himself as older and, therefore, reasonably expects that he would be first to die. While it does not give the specific cause of her death, the poem suggests that she died of a fever. Although the tone remains restrained and dignified, the speaker goes beyond the conventional, formulaic expressions often found in elegies. The resolution to look toward the future is achieved only through the poignant theme stressing that the speaker will join his wife in death.

At a deeper level, the poem develops a meditation on time. The first and more distant form is the time of Judgment Day, when the speaker asserts that his wife will be resurrected entirely. Until then, she sleeps in the earth, which the poem invokes to fully render her back. The vision of Judgment Day is consistent with the literal belief in bodily resurrection, a belief widely held in the seventeenth century. This idea was often accompanied by another somewhat contradictory one: that the soul of the deceased had gone to heaven and would rejoin the body at a later time. King expresses a simpler version, making no reference to a separate existence of the soul. Rather, the speaker derives comfort from the hope of a final and permanent reunion in the distant future.

More vividly expressed is the speaker's contemplation of his death, when he will join her in the grave. Picturing the inexorable movement of his own allotted time, he designates each passing minute and hour as moving him measurably toward his goal. Even a night's sleep brings him eight hours closer to his destination, a westward journey toward death. Each pulse beat marks his movement toward the end of life, the final battlefield. The prospect of his own death becomes not a subject for grief but a welcome assurance and a means of reconciling the speaker to his wife.

Stanley Archer

EXILE

Author: Julia Alvarez (1950-
Type of poem: Narrative
First published: 1995, in *The Other Side/El Otro Lado*

The Poem

Julia Alvarez's "Exile" consists of seventeen four-line stanzas that convey a sense of shared recollection between the poem's persona and her father. As she reflects upon the family's abrupt departure from their Dominican homeland and their subsequent cultural adjustment to New York City, she reveals that, as the poem's title suggests, this uprooting creates a sense of exile: a lamentation for those places and things left behind and a confused uncertainty about the new. The chronological sequencing of events gives the poem an autobiographical tone, but, placed as it is in a chapter in *The Other Side/El Otro Lado* entitled "Making up the Past," one must acknowledge that this exile narrative encompasses the universal experiences of many immigrants, powerfully demonstrated via the memories of the poem's persona.

Because the poem relies on an innocent, almost childlike, voice, memories of the family's departure and arrival are shrouded in a child's observations and interpretation of the adult intrigue necessary for a clandestine flight from their homeland. Alvarez alludes to Papi's "worried whispers," uncle's "phony chuckles," and Mami's consoling promise that "there was a better surprise" in store for the children at the end of their journey. The persona reveals that she was "young" at the time of the family's flight and thus "didn't think adult things could go wrong"; this sense of expectation versus reality haunts the entire poem.

The first glimpse of the disappointment that awaits the family occurs in the pivotal middle stanza, which opens with a quick reversal of Mami's promise through the persona's revelation that she (the persona) has "already swum ahead." Her childish instincts have seen through the parental subterfuge surrounding their exodus to the inevitable loss and danger inherent in their situation. These elements of complication and conflict are more fully developed in the stanzas that follow: the persona's "fitful sleep" at the "dark, deserted airport" and her intuitive knowledge that Papi's final glance at the horizon signals a severing of the familiar moorings that have held the family fast. This notion of being "set adrift" permeates the remainder of the poem as the persona continues to recall, in this one-sided conversation with Papi, her initial experiences in the family's "new city."

Alvarez provides a catalog of big-city images and the persona's father's explanations of these strange, new phenomena: "escalators/ as moving belts; elevators: pulleys and ropes;/ blond hair and blue eyes: a genetic code." It is not, however, the technological wonders that dominate the poem's final stanzas but rather the image of a "summery display" in Macy's store window. Here, the American ideal, the handsome mannequin father, "slim and sure of himself," is dramatically contrasted to the persona's father, with his "thick mustache," too-formal three-piece suit, fedora hat, and telling accent. The persona recalls how she and her father stood in front of the window marveling at the implements of ease and leisure displayed there: "beach pails, the shovels, the sandcastles/ no wave would ever topple, the red and blue boats" or the storybook girl who "waded in colored plastic."

As the persona and her father back away, almost recoiling from the unreal specter of the store display, their own reflections, superimposed upon the glass, reveal a stark contrast. They stand apart as "visitors to this country," exiles whose uncertain future in a land of plastic and ease haunts their "big-eyed" faces, like those of the island swimmers in the home they have left behind, whose faces, "right before plunging in," are "eager, afraid."

Forms and Devices

The poem's italicized epigram consists of two place names, Ciudad Trujillo (now known as Santo Domingo, a port city in the Dominican Republic) and New York City, along with the date 1960. This important information sets the stage for the exile experience in terms of time and place. It becomes apparent, then, that the poem will consist of adult recollections of childhood memories, and the use of direct address to the persona's father, who never speaks, reveals the close relationship that the two share. His name, Papi, is repeated six times in the poem, reinforcing his importance in the persona's life as well as his preeminence in the family, thus evoking a great sense of loss as the poem develops to reveal his metamorphosis into an uncertain outsider in his chosen land of exile.

Dramatic contrasts such as the images of the family's homeland compared to New York City, the father's fall from knowledge to uncertainty, and the expectation of the vacation at the beach that is promised compared to the false beach scene that awaits the persona and her father in the reality of New York all demonstrate the conflicting nature of culture shock and its unnerving effects on newly arrived immigrants. The inner conflicts faced by those in exile from their homelands are further developed by the repeated use of water imagery to reinforce the struggle of the immigrants to resist submersion in their new culture. They must adapt and learn to navigate the deep, unknown, treacherous waters like the persona's imagined vision of the struggling swimmer whom Papi "frantically" tries to wave back to safety. The act of exile, by its very nature, is a risky plunge into an uncharted pool, leaving behind the safe harbor of that which is known for the unfamiliar surroundings that frequently reject those who are somehow different.

This sense of being the outsider, full of wonder and fear, is heightened by the language Alvarez employs. Her simple, everyday vocabulary convincingly conveys a tone of childish recollection filtered through adult experience and draws the reader into a sympathetic identification with the persona. Her misty memories of the family's journey, arrival, and reaction to New York depict a scene universal and familiar; the reader, too, experiences the rushed departure from a curfew-bound place, the disappointing artificiality of the new culture, and the loss of personal dignity inherent in the exile experience. The use of direct address, the constant use of "you" in reference to Papi, also has the effect of pulling readers into the story, making them participants who are also reflected, in one side or the other, of the glass of Macy's store window.

Themes and Meanings

"Exile," rich with watery images of beaches and divers, is about learning how to swim; simultaneously, and more important, the poem threads the liquid images throughout the narrative of the persona's immigration memories to create a natural comparison of the immigrant experience to that of swimmers learning to brave the deep pools of their new environment. Swimming is the perfect metaphor for the hastily departed immigrants who dive into an idealized America to discover, with some surprise, their own vulnerability and a keen sense of loss.

This juxtaposition of dramatically different expectation and reality heightens the poem's sense of unease. The beachwear-clad family in the department store window marks a sharp line between the privileged, successful upper-class American (who can afford to shop at Macy's) and the almost mirror inversion of the out-of-place persona and her Papi. (They are never named; they represent universal immigrant experiences of exile.) We sense that they are swimming against the current, but the persona has been told by her uncles "*What a good time she'll have learning to swim!*" This prediction, and her own admission that she "had already swum ahead," seems to foreshadow the rapid assimilation of the persona, like most children, into a new culture; but the portrayal of the artificial pursuits of the window people leads to the conclusion that her old culture offered a more tranquil, a more natural immersion. The exile experience of the persona, as for many immigrant children, thus represents a tremendous loss of culture.

This idea of loss is reinforced by the final images of the poem, which convey an implicit juxtaposition of the persona and her father to the "two swimmers looking down" into the quiet waters surrounding their homeland, ready to plunge, "eager, afraid." This current of longing, plus the comment that the swimmers' faces reveal that they are "not yet sure of the outcome," reflects the tenacious position that the persona and her father, and many immigrants before and since, have faced.

Julia Alvarez's poem "Exile" leaves one feeling submerged, like the newly arrived family, through the many water images she employs. Stanza 5's almost baptismal description of the persona's dreamy descent into the "deep waters," arms out "like Jesus' on His cross," also contains the mysterious, supernatural realism of magical levitation that occurs on "that night," the night of the family's departure. The poem provides a powerful picture of an inevitable clash of cultures, from the sustaining values of the old ways to the shallow capitalistic pursuits of the new, and the reader may come away feeling plunged into this uncertain pool of adjustment.

Kathleen M. Bartlett

THE EXPLOSION

Author: Philip Larkin (1922-1985)
Type of poem: Pastoral
First published: 1974, in *High Windows*

The Poem

"The Explosion" is a short poem of twenty-five lines made up of eight unrhymed tercets and a final, isolated one-line stanza. It is written in trochaic tetrameter with a number of metrical variations and substitutions. The speaker of the poem is an observer and commentator on the crucial event of the poem, an explosion at a mine. The language is clearly that of a speaker who is more highly educated than the working-class people that the poem represents. He is not involved in their lives but attempts to render their nature and experience as fully and truthfully as possible. The title of the poem announces the event and suggests its significance: It is "the" explosion rather than "an" explosion. The poem also begins with a description of the world surrounding the event. In the first tercet, the speaker describes how "On the day of the explosion/ Shadows pointed towards the pithead." These "shadows" are an omen of the terrible event that is to follow, but they are balanced, to some degree, by the sun in which "the slagheap slept." Both the sun and sleeping suggest the continuation of a peaceful world.

The next three tercets deal with the mine workers. They are defined as a group rather than singled out as individuals. Their "oath-edged talk and pipe-smoke" define them as men of the working class at ease with one another. One of them is more adventurous and active as he hunts some rabbits. The rabbits escape, but he finds a nest with a lark's eggs in it. He does not destroy or harm this nest but shows it to the others and returns them to their place in the grass. The fourth tercet sums the miners up as types: "So they passed in beards and moleskins,/ Fathers, brothers, nicknames, laughter." Significantly, they pass through the "tall gates standing open." The scene is normal and benign; they pass to their usual work and all is "open" and apparent.

It is significant that poet Philip Larkin does not described the actual explosion but rather its effects on the outer world. With the tremor, cows stop chewing and the sun is "dimmed." Readers do not see its effect on the miners who are dying under the earth. That horror and suffering is hidden from view; clearly, it is not what Larkin is interested in about the event. The sixth tercet is in italics and announces a change in speaker and language. It is now the language of church, formal and stately and attempting to provide consolation: "*The dead go on before us, they/ Are sitting in God's house in comfort,/ We shall see them face to face.*" The next two tercets return to the ordinary language of the speaker and that of the miners' wives; it also alters the comforting religious view of the church speaker. The wives of the dead miners see their men in a new way, "Larger than in life they managed." After this transformation, the final line of the poem recalls the miners as they were and as they are: "One showing the eggs unbroken." Their lives and their deaths were a harmonious, unbroken whole.

Forms and Devices

"The Explosion" is written in trochaic tetrameter without rhyme, both of which are very unusual in the poetry of Larkin, who used the iambic meter, usually pentameter and hexameter, and brilliant rhyme. There must have been something in the event and his treatment of it that insisted on this meter. Perhaps it was the transformation of very ordinary workers into people on a higher plane that demanded he abandon his usual metrical practice. Trochaic tetrameter does have a parallel in American literature: It is the meter that Henry Wadsworth Longfellow used in *The Song of Hiawatha* (1855). Larkin does not fall into the monotone chant that Longfellow did, but the meter does have a propulsive effect as it moves from the announcement of the event to its occurrence and consequences. Larkin does use the traditional sound patterns such as alliteration: "In the sun the slagheap slept." The miners are also portrayed predominately through the use of verbs: "One chased after rabbits; lost them;/ Came back with a nest of lark's eggs;/ Showed them; lodged them in the grasses."

There is also some significant imagery in the poem. For example, the first tercet contrasts the shadows that "pointed" to the pithead with the sun that "slept" on the slagheap. The slagheap is also an indicator of the world with which the poem deals: a mining community with its own special landscape. The workers are also defined with a few class-specific images: They wear "pitboots," their talk is "oath-edged," and they cough "pipe-smoke." The men, unaccustomed to talk, are described as "Shouldering off the freshened silence." It is a gesture that says more than words about the type of people these workers are. They speak with their bodies to relieve the silence.

There is an interesting shift in diction, tense, and speaker in the sixth tercet, which is presented in the formal and resounding language of the preacher in a church or, more likely, a chapel. The preacher uses the future tense while the wives use a past tense that reunites them with their men. This formal language is also contrasted to the simpler words ascribed to the wives of the dead men, and the passage uses a significant metaphor. The dead miners are "Gold as on a coin, or walking/ Somehow from the sun" toward their wives. The metaphor defines the transformation of the miners from ordinary working men to men of value and even greatness as the figure on a gold coin suggests. Furthermore, the sun image also returns at this point of the poem. The sun is no longer sleeping at the slagheap; rather, it is behind the men as they are walking to their spouses.

The description of one of the workers finding a lark's eggs is an image that develops into a metaphor and, finally, a symbol. The worker does not destroy these eggs or displace them; he shows them to his fellow workers and then returns them to the grass. In the last, isolated line in the poem, the worker is evoked once more. He is "showing the eggs unbroken." The unbroken eggs are a symbol of the world and lives of the miners. Even in death, their world remains as it was, or perhaps it is even enhanced; it is unbroken.

Themes and Meanings

"The Explosion" is about the lives of British working-class people. Larkin portrays them in all of their ordinariness in the first part of the poem. He describes their walk to work, their dress, and, above all, their interaction with one another. A few words and significant gestures define the closeness of the men to each other and to their world of work. The origins of the poem can be found in a British Broadcasting Corporation (BBC) television program that Larkin saw in 1969; the natural lives of these people gave him a subject on which he had not often written.

The theme of the poem is made clear by the symbol of the unbroken eggs. The lives and deaths of the miners form an unbroken whole, a harmonious and organic life that seems almost to come from another century. A possible influence for Larkin's theme is the early novels and stories of D. H. Lawrence, who portrayed the lives of miners as harsh but in touch with the primal earth. Larkin softens the romanticism of Lawrence, but his attitude is similar in many ways. Another important theme is that of transformation. After the miners' deaths, the survivors are given the usual comfort of the church. They are told that their men are not suffering but "*sitting in God's house in comfort*" and that they will one day see them "*face to face.*" However, Larkin then offers a very different and more convincing transformation and consolation by having these wives see their men as larger than they were in life but still rooted to that organic world they inhabited. They are "walking/ Somehow from the sun" toward their wives and now exist on a different plane, "Gold as on a coin." They are not in a Christian heaven but remain closely connected to the living.

"The Explosion" is the last poem in *High Windows* (1974), even though it was written earlier than a number of other poems in the collection. The poem gives a very different view of death than nearly all of the poems in the book. Larkin's view of his inevitable death was filled with terror and horror. The union of the dead and the living seen in the conclusion of "The Explosion" gives a more hopeful and human perspective. There have been relatively few poems written about the working class, since poetry seems to be written and supported by people of a more educated class. However, Larkin provides both an insight into that world and a sympathetic and realistic view of its wholeness.

James Sullivan

EXPOSURE

Author: Wilfred Owen (1893-1918)
Type of poem: Meditation
First published: 1920, in *Poems by Wilfred Owen*

The Poem

"Exposure" examines the sensations of soldiers slowly freezing to death in the trenches of World War I in a poem of forty lines divided into eight stanzas. The persona of the poem adopts the identity of all the soldiers as they huddle against the wind and snow on the war front waiting for something to happen. As the cold sets in, sentries and ordinary soldiers watch confusing flares in the frontline fortification from which they have withdrawn for the night. Gusts of wind moan on the barbed wire of no-man's-land like dying men, while guns rumble in the distance, apocalyptic portents of other possible wars. The numb soldiers ask, "What are we doing here?" but nothing happens.

Dawn itself, traditionally a symbol of hope, is ominous as "clouds sag stormy," the men grow colder and wetter, and the new day marshals its cloudy troops to usher in a new day of fighting for the soldiers. Suddenly, bullets fly but are tossed about by the wind, which appears to be a more powerful instrument of death than the artillery.

In the fifth stanza, the snow and cold send the soldiers into a numbed reverie about home. The bemused soldiers ask of their freezing selves, "Is it that we are dying?" In stanza 6, their disembodied ghosts visit the banked early-morning fires of home and observe crickets on the hearth and mice playing while the household sleeps; however, the ghosts feel shut out of this domestic scene and must turn back to their own slow deaths on the front. Faith in the comforts and certainties of home clashes with the conviction that God intended for these men to die in cold misery. The love of God itself is remote and seems to be dying.

The last stanza observes that God's frost will freeze the mud in which the soldiers find themselves, and it will freeze their hands, foreheads, and, finally, their eyes in their final act of dying. The next morning, burial parties with "shovels in their shaking grasp" will half recognize their comrades, who died of exposure while nothing in particular was happening in the war. They were felled by wind, snow, mud, and the seeming indifference of God rather than by wounds caused by bullets and bayonets.

Forms and Devices

"Exposure" exemplifies one of Wilfred Owen's most noted techniques: the use of slant rhymes such as wire/war, grow/gray, and us/ice. Emily Dickinson and Gerard Manley Hopkins also used this type of rhyme, as does Welsh poetry, but Owen seems not to have been familiar with any of these traditions. Slant rhyme and assonance bring out the jarring sensations of war and move "Exposure" and Owen's other poems away from more refined poetic forms of earlier centuries.

Owen also eschews elegant language, preferring to record more stark images such as "mad gusts," "twitching agonies," and "flickering gunnery." The only images that are nurturing and warm are the ones that depict the fires of home in stanzas 6 and 7, and they stand in ironic contrast to the freezing soldiers. Indeed, the warmth of home seems to mock the realities of war, since civilians "believe not otherwise can kind fires burn;/ Nor ever suns smile true on child, or field, or fruit." This clash of home-front experience and battlefield reality is also echoed in Owen's poem "Futility" in its vain hope that "the kind old sun" of childhood will know how to rouse a dead comrade.

The stillness of slowly freezing to death becomes a counterpoint to the progressive verbs in the poem: "watching," "twitching," "massing," "shivering," "wandering," "fingering," "shrivelling," "puckering," and, finally, "dying." As in other Owen poems such as "Greater Love" and "Arms and the Boy," the occasional attractive word such as "nonchalance" is used ironically to depict the carelessness of the wind as it tosses snowflakes around and "knives" the soldiers.

The heroic "war music" of Homer's *Iliad* (c. 800 B.C.; English translation, 1616), Vergil's *Aeneid* (c. 29-19 B.C.; English translation, 1553), or William Shakespeare's *Henry IV* (c. 1597-1598) and *Henry V* (c. 1598-1599) is absent from Owen's war poems. Instead, an eerie keening of wind on wire in "Exposure" and "the shrill demented choirs of wailing shells" in "Anthem for Doomed Youth" are in evidence, a cacophony of dissonance and loss. The English composer Benjamin Britten recognized these musical possibilities in Owen's poetry in his choral masterpiece *War Requiem*, an elegy to the dead of both world wars first performed in 1962.

"Exposure" depicts a gray landscape broken only by the dull brown of dawn and the white snowflakes and ice. The "pale flakes" are personified as they "with fingering stealth come feeling for our faces," as blind as the "snow-dazed" soldiers and the dead with their eyes frozen. This bleak landscape is highlighted by the streaks of unnaturally colored phosphorescent flares. Again, the warm colors of home are contrasted with the moonscape of no-man's-land. At home, fires are "glozed/ With crusted dark-red jewels" and a kind sun shines on all. The soldier is only permitted a glimpse of home and must soon turn back to his task of dying in a strange landscape bereft of family and the love of God.

Themes and Meanings

To understand the meaning of "Exposure," and indeed of all of Owen's poetry, it is necessary to turn to his own words: "Above all I am not concerned with Poetry. My subject is War, and the pity of War. The Poetry is the pity." Owen's desire to convey the pity of war led him to the antipoetic devices that make his work so powerful. The particular pity conveyed in "Exposure" is the irony of dying of exposure to the elements rather than "the monstrous anger of the guns." Thoughtful students of World War I may realize that many died of cold and disease, but Owen is correct in supposing that these mundane, though no less tragic, ways to die are lost in the heroic jingoism of most wars. Bullets are hot and searing, while cold is dehumanizing. The aching brains of the dying cannot understand why nothing is happening, why they are where they are, and why God seems present only in "His frost," not his love; the befuddled questioning of the fifth lines of each stanza mirrors the confusion of a brain slowly freezing to death.

Unlike English poets Sir Philip Sidney or Percy Bysshe Shelley, Owen does not see poets as teachers or "unacknowledged legislators." He says, "all a poet can do today is warn; that is why the True Poets must be truthful." Owen strives for the aching cold of truthfulness in "Exposure" as the poem exposes the reader to the cold indifference of nature and nature's God.

Stanzas 7 and 8 deal specifically with Owen's view of God's role in death by exposure. Owen came to mistrust the dogmas of national churches, finding solace only in the role of Christ, a passive emblem of love who gives his life for his friends just as soldiers often die for their comrades. Owen's poem "At a Calvary near the Ancre" explores the role of Christ in the war, but "Exposure" appears loveless and Christless. Owen's poetic mentor, Siegfried Sassoon, also reflects skepticism toward the warlike nature of the church's God and his indifference to the plight of the soldier. Sassoon encouraged Owen to tell the truth of the pitiless nature of the nationalistic God in poetry such as "Exposure," which frankly blasphemes conventional pieties.

"Exposure" is not one of Owen's best-known poems, but it is surely one of his bleakest. The unrelieved cold and misery of the freezing soldiers are contrasted to the warmth of the home front, a home front that cannot imagine and chooses not to see their pain, offering instead a platitudinous God for comfort; the soldiers' real God "will fasten on this mud and [them],/ Shrivelling . . . puckering," and ultimately killing with no pity. The pity of "Exposure" is the pity of indifference: the indifference of nature, of the home front, of God, and of the soldiers themselves, who are "not loath" to freeze into the icy destiny to which they were born. At the end of the poem, the staring eyes of the dead convey the icy indifference of men for whom the world knew no pity. In "Exposure," Wilfred Owen's dead-eyed soldiers lie frozen as a warning to an indifferent world of the pity of war.

Isabel B. Stanley

THE FACE IN THE MIRROR

Author: Robert Graves (1895-1985)
Type of poem: Lyric
First published: 1957; collected in *5 Pens in Hand*, 1958

The Poem

"The Face in the Mirror," an autobiographical lyric poem, presents a definitive image of the poet's aging face. Simultaneously, it includes reflections upon central moments and concepts in his life, which carved that face so graphically. Weaving physical description with allusions to significant memories, Robert Graves creates poetic tension in stanzas 1 and 2 and resolves it in stanza 3.

The tension in stanza 1 develops as the poet describes his eyes and brows. The eyes are "Grey" and "haunted." The softened spelling of "gray," juxtaposed with two hard syllables in "haunted," achieves poetic tension, while the many-syllabled, hyphenated adverb "absent-mindedly" softens the sense of "glaring," the verb it modifies, to such a degree that it seems to modify "eyes." Readers, then, see haunted, hollow eyes staring vacantly from the mirror. This image heightens tension and holds readers hostage, although they may wish, desperately, to look away. With readers' eyes pinned to grotesquely mirrored eyes, Graves makes the first autobiographical allusion of the poem: a reference to the most grotesque event of his life, World War I.

Grotesquerie continues in stanza 2. The poet expands the mirrored image to include an array of broken and lined facial features, from crown ("coarse . . . hair, flying frenetic") to "Jowls." Again juxtaposing marred, bigger-than-life features, he makes them more grotesque against the image of few teeth between full, glowingly red lips, drawn together in judgmental fashion. In this stanza, however, the poet's allusion to significant memories is woven throughout the lines ("low tackling" in line 1; "pugilistic" in line 4), while in stanza 1 he reserved it for the end. These allusions emphasize, physically, Graves's participation in sports, which he reveals also left him marked and ugly.

The final stanza, less prosaic and more lyrical for all its pathos, has a lighter air than do the other stanzas. Graves's ending resolves tension, allowing readers to experience an epiphany, akin to his own, when he confronts the mirrored reality of his aging face behind which he continually forgets that he is no longer young. Here, the poem confirms an old Hebrew notion that people look in a mirror and walk away, promptly forgetting their own images. In lines 3-5, Graves indicates that such looking and forgetting is not a new experience for him when he "once more" asks "the mirrored man" why "He still stands ready, with a boy's presumption,/ To court the queen in her high silk pavilion." This "moment of truth" reminds him of his two selves—one external and aging, visible to himself only in a mirror, the other internal and perpetually young, the perceived self. Graves manages to catch both selves in the pause of an uplifted hand with "razor poised." As readers grasp the poem's truth, theirs becomes the face in the mirror.

Forms and Devices

Graves, a noted lyric poet, uses an array of poetic devices to achieve his ends. He uses the poem, an extended metaphor, to explore distinctions between his "face in the mirror" and his inner face. As an extended metaphor, the work becomes a metaphysical conceit. Indeed, Graves's canon is filled with metaphysical leanings, for he considered all true poetry a thing of inspiration. He called it "muse poetry."

Within the poem, Graves uses poetic tension and sprung rhythm. Poetic tension relies on juxtaposition of sounds and of sensory images and meanings, devices that Graves uses repeatedly in this work. Sprung rhythm, however, breaks the familiar patterns of rhyme, displacing melodious sounds often expected from lyric poetry. Here, Graves uses unnecessary functional words ("Somewhat," "Because of"), prosaic syntax, and prolific semicolons to distort rhythm and melody; however, the third line of each stanza rhymes, and lines 1, 2, 4, and 5 have the same ending sounds within each separate stanza.

By definition, lyrics are brief, subjective poems marked by the individual and personal emotion of the poet; their rhythms vary, they can be unrhymed, and, ideally, they are pensive and melancholy enlargements of the poem's theme. "The Face in the Mirror" fulfills these requirements in the use of poetic devices and in terms of melancholic theme. It is Graves's use of assonance and alliteration that brings the sounds of melody to the poem's prosaic lines: the *a*, *i*, and *o* sounds; the alliterative *d*'s, *t*'s, *f*'s, and *p*'s; and the vowel alliteration in lines such as "I pause with razor poised, scowling derision." Arguably, Graves breaks the textbook definition of assonance and alliteration, but the sounds of assonance and alliteration cohere throughout this poem, providing a reader's ear with the sense of rhyme and melody associated with lyric forms.

Themes and Meanings

"The Face in the Mirror" is autobiographical. It presents a definitive image of the poet's face, and its allusions to "old-world fighting" (World War I), "low tackling" and pugilism (fighting through life), and "a boy's presumption,/ To court the queen in her high silk pavilion" (the muse) reference influencing factors in the poet's life. Stanza 1 presents the poet's literal face. Shrapnel, embedded since the war forty years before, makes the face look grotesque ("one brow drooping/ . . . over the eye"), but the allusion indicates that the primary grotesquerie was World War I itself, which marked the man with internal aberrations. In that war, bright young poets, friends of the teenage Graves, died. Worse, soldiers died from "friendly fire" due to disorganization among commanders. Once, Graves, mangled by enemy fire, was left for dead in the field. These aberrations appear as sprung rhythms in the poem, causing it, like his life, to fall short of melody. Yet as Graves's long, renowned, prolific life as a poet was dotted with accolades, the poem is dotted with assonance and alliteration. That neither his life nor his poetry represent the song he meant to sing is clear when Graves explains, in the foreword to his 1958 *Collected Works*, that only the first poem in the collection (written before he entered the war) represented the poetry he might have written had he not been "caught up" in the war, which, he said, "permanently changed my outlook on life."

Stanza 2 juxtaposes nonmelodic phrases and broken, etched images descriptive of the poet's photographed face. Again, grotesquerie marks the mirrored image but, on a deeper level, refers to his serious participation in sports and possibly to verbal "fights" with critics, publishers, and fellow poets over what defines poetry as poetry. Most of these fights concerned Graves's contention that only "muse poetry" was true poetry. Those who disagreed, Graves said, wrote "Apollonian poetry"—poetry of the intellect that, he argued, fell short of presenting pure truth.

Stanza 3 also uses grotesquerie, but the tone of it becomes bemused self-perception. Graves mocks himself with old familiarity: He has been in this posture before. Nevertheless, the emotional impact on readers, looking over his shoulder into the mirror, remains arresting. The autobiographical allusion is to the poet's overweening interest in the muse, "the queen in her high silk pavilion," a reference to Graves's belief that all true poetry is inspired by the muse. In time, he believed in the "White Goddess" (the muse of truth) and the "Black Goddess" (the wisdom of darkness or pain). Graves believed that the dual nature of the goddess brought both poetry and pain to humankind, and that, as poets, humankind inevitably embraced both. Nevertheless, Graves also argued that a poem always says what it means. Ultimately, disputes over these beliefs in his professional life marked him as greatly as did World War I.

Graves expands the grotesquerie of images in the poem to the grotesquerie of life itself. He puzzles over universal questions, pausing in his shaving ritual to ask the ugly face in the mirror why he, who had no pleasing physical feature, who had become ugly because of marks life placed upon him, who had learned that muses have little mercy upon man, still dreamed that dream of idealistic youth: His queen would deign to be courted by him. In that moment of the poet's mocking awareness of the ridiculous, the poem achieves its greatest power: It is an awareness that, no matter what marks life etches upon people's faces, something within them keeps its biggest dream. In that "pause," readers enter the poet's truth.

Published in 1957, during a time that many literary theorists identify as the cusp between the end of modernism and the advent of postmodernism, "The Face in the Mirror" has marks of postmodern texts: It is self-reflexive—Graves peers at his face in a mirror, reading it as a text written upon by events he could no more control than a blank sheet of paper controls a poet's pen; it reflects the belief of both postmodernists and Graves that pure poetry lives in blank sheets, visible only to the muse who, in her time, reveals it to poets as truth; and it poses unanswered questions, leaving readers to find answers, since truth comes from the muse within the poem rather than from the poet, and her answer is always universal truth. This poem asks: How can it be that, within an old, battered man, a youth survives, expectant dreams intact? Universally, readers know that such a youth lives in them, but they cannot say why.

Jo Culbertson Davis

THE FARMER'S BRIDE

Author: Charlotte Mew (1869-1928)
Type of poem: Dramatic monologue
First published: 1912; collected in *The Farmer's Bride*, 1916

The Poem

"The Farmer's Bride" is a description of a wife, narrated by her husband. The first two stanzas of the poem are written in the past tense, and the last four shift to the present tense to describe the present situation. He first states that he married her three years ago, when she was very young. The proposal and subsequent marriage were rushed; he decided in the summer and married her soon after without spending much time with her, because he was busy with the fall harvest.

As soon as they were married, she became unhappy and afraid of him. The implication is that she was afraid of his sexual advances; he matter-of-factly characterizes her as being afraid of "love and me and all things human." Since he associates womanliness with sexuality and welcoming smiles, she became more like a "fay," or fairy, to him, something spiritual and intangible rather than physically present.

Her fear of him and repugnance at her life reached an apex when she fled from home soon after their marriage; they were married "at harvest-time," and she ran away in the fall. The other farmers presumed that she was merely tending the sheep, though it was night and she should have been in bed. When they found her gone, she led them on a long chase. She was swift as a hare, but they captured her and locked her in her house.

Now, three years later, she makes a place for herself at the farm, doing her housework adequately and communing with small animals. The only thing that brings out her original fear is the presence of men. Her fear is evident in her eyes; she does not voice it, but the husband knows that she does not want him near. The woman remains uncommunicative, except to call the animals, who are very responsive to her. The farmer hears this from the other women on the farm, who see her with the animals but do not seem to speak with her themselves.

The fourth stanza changes tone. Rather than continue his objective description, the speaker begins to characterize his wife sympathetically as shy and slight, sweet and wild. He regrets that these qualities are not available to him and are reserved for herself. There is another turn in the fifth stanza, as the speaker wistfully notes the passing of fall into winter. Looking to Christmas, he laments that this is a family time and they have no children: "What's Christmas-time without there be/ Some other in the house than we!"

The final stanza brings the buried emotion and repressed sexuality to the fore. He begins with a description of her sleeping alone, a stairway above him, again implying that they are not sexually intimate. All of his love and longing for her surface in the final four lines as he imaginatively grasps at her soft, youthful image.

Forms and Devices

"The Farmer's Bride" is a skillful rendering of the dramatic monologue. The farmer, who describes his wife's actions, reveals more and more of his own feelings and failings until readers know his character and understand the reason for his wife's behavior. The poem is as understated and evocative as its speaker, a fact that makes his revelations of love and strong sexual feelings, which are unrequited and unconsummated, truly poignant.

The unfolding revelation of the man and woman's relationship during the monologue complicates what could be seen as a straightforward story of male oppression. Throughout, the husband reveals his inability to recognize his wife's reaction to his patriarchal power, seen in his choice of her, his capturing and locking her in his house, and his defining her in terms of his own needs ("But what to me?") and projecting his feelings onto her ("poor maid").

However, his perceptive understanding of her fears and his refusal to force himself on her, together with his outburst of emotion at the end, make him sympathetic. The tensions in the poem between his obtuse conventionality and his unexpected tender patience and respect for her person create a multilayered, sympathetic character. Much of the power of the poem stems from his feelings of anger and frustration at being denied his wife's affection and his realization of his part in it.

Imagery and similes are used as part of the dramatic irony. The farmer describes his wife in natural similes: "like a hare," "like a mouse," "as a leveret," "as a young larch tree," "as the first wild violets." These similes idealize, diminish, and feminize the wife rather than individualize and humanize her. He never speaks her name. The similes show the reader that the farmer sees human beings and their emotions as part of the natural world. He sees love and sexuality as "natural" rather than as socially constructed, so it does not occur to him to cultivate these feelings in his wife.

Further irony is seen in the wife's escape into nature in order to eschew social expectations. By communing only with animals, she is shunning "all things human." The statement "*I've* hardly heard her speak at all" emphasizes the farmer's bitterness at her decision not to communicate with him. She is asserting her own right to choose by positioning herself in nature in order to flee the society of men, and she is strong in this environment. She has authority with the animals; they look to her as children look to adults for assurance and care.

The overall seasonal structure of the poem also shows the speaker's view of essential human nature. The events are ordered by seasonal chronology: He chooses her in summer and marries her at harvest time. She runs away in the fall, and the distance between them grows as winter passes and they are alone in the house together. In the world in which he lives, it is as "natural" that women submit to being wives as it is that autumn brings the harvest and winter brings Christmas joy for children.

The melodic lines and beautiful natural images belie the uneducated diction and expected roughness of the taciturn, working-class, male farmer. They humanize and underscore the fears and frustrations and unhappiness he relates.

Themes and Meanings

"The Farmer's Bride" is about innocence and ignorance. The bride is too young to marry and to have sex with a man she hardly knows. The imagery of the first stanza is of a smiling, attractive, competent girl whom the farmer has chosen because she will make a good farm wife. Unfortunately, her youthful innocence is matched by the farmer's insensitivity toward the young, sexually naïve, frightened girl and his ignorance of a woman's needs and humanity. He chooses her as he would his cattle, seeing no need to woo her. Having no concern for her feelings, he expects her simply to step into the role of his wife.

To him, as a farmer, human nature is not much more complicated than animal nature. The pairing of two people is not guided by more than the natural urge to procreate, the social roles of man and wife, and the man's need for someone to keep house for him.

Mew also indicates that the man is not cruel, only conventional, in her description of the townspeople's (probably the men) chasing her and locking her up. They seem to think the same way the farmer does: A wife, even a young, frightened wife, belongs at home with her husband. Even the women make little attempt to help her; they are perhaps busy with their chores or have forgotten their own transition into married life.

Their expectations and actions are based on what "should properly" be done. Although they run after her and bring her home forcibly, they are acting, in their minds, according to what is socially, and even naturally, prescribed. What the poem depicts as a somewhat frightening scene—the townspeople chasing a young woman as hounds chase a hare—most likely seems protective to them, since she is cold and afraid and "belongs" home in her bed.

By the end of his monologue, the speaker has revealed his love and his bewilderment that it is not returned. By the last two stanzas, when readers see his desire for children and his longing for his wife, their sympathy is with the farmer's unrequited love. We fully understand what he dimly understands: His wife has again fled from him (this time emotionally), and he has been complicit in alienating her.

Critics have found this poem unrealistic, saying that a farmer would have forced himself on his new bride without qualms. Yet the brilliance of the poem comes from the characterization of a man, a common hardworking farmer, with a sensuous appreciation of the life around him and with respect and gentleness toward his wife. Thus, what could have been a clichéd poem about an oppressive brute or a failed marriage becomes instead an insightful study of human misunderstanding that explores problems of class and gender without making them seem stereotypical.

Sandra J. Holstein

THE FEELINGS

Author: Sharon Olds (1942-
Type of poem: Elegy
First published: 1991; collected in *The Father*, 1992

The Poem

"The Feelings" is a forty-one-line poem in free verse, artistically recounting the poet's feelings immediately following her father's death. It is highly personal and familial, as are many of Sharon Olds's poems. Written in the first person and past tense, the experience seems fixed, inevitable, available to retrospective analysis. The poem begins in a hospital room, the poet watching as an intern "listened" to her father's stopped heart, and concludes with the poet contemplating the meaning of life the following morning as her husband lies atop her. The "feelings" include physical sensations—such as her father's "faintly moist" face and hair "like a wolf's"—and emotional and philosophical reactions to the father's death.

Inasmuch as it recounts her reaction to her father's death and moves her beyond that death, "The Feelings" may be considered an elegy. However, unlike traditional elegies such as John Milton's "Lycidas," Percy Bysshe Shelley's "Adonais," or Matthew Arnold's "Rugby Chapel," there is no recounting of the wonderful qualities of the deceased or sorrow at the loss of this positive force in the world. Olds's father apparently deserved no such praise (a conclusion bolstered by references to him in other Olds poems). Nor was he a figure to arouse intense hatred, as is found, for instance, in Sylvia Plath's "Daddy." He was more of a nonentity, whose claim to attention is that he was the poet's father.

The poem moves through a series of relationships. In the first six lines, Olds's intimate relationship to her father contrasts with the alien presence of the intern. The poet, realizing her father is dead, stares at the intern "as if he or I/ were wild, were from some other world." The loss of her father seems to threaten the poet's identity and makes her unnaturally wary of others. The alienation of poet and intern broadens in lines 7 to 17 to include "everyone else in the room," presumably other hospital personnel, who mistakenly—according to the poem—believe in the Christian God and who believe that the body on the bed is only a "shell" from which the spirit has departed; the poet alone knows her father is "entirely gone."

In lines 18 to 21, Olds imagines herself, in the Eskimo tradition, letting her father float away in the "death canoe"; in lines 29 to 34, she imagines herself accompanying him to the crematorium and touching his ashes to her tongue, but in reality she walks out of the hospital room and does not attend him. Lines 34 to 41 add an interesting postscript, in which Olds returns to a living relationship. The poet is under her husband's body the next morning, which crushes her "sweetly," holding her "hard to this world." This sensual image is likened to a fruit, with tears coming out "like juice and sugar." This image is then tied back to the death of her father as the fruit's "skin thins and breaks and rips." The last two lines suggest recognition, if not acceptance, of this immutable mortal destiny: "there are/ laws on this earth and we live by them."

Forms and Devices

In a strong juxtaposition of contrasts, this poem is at once sensual and philosophical, concrete and abstract. The father's silent heart, the poet's wet face, their dry lips, and the weight of the husband's body all locate the poem firmly in the physical world. The dissonance between the poet's atheism and the Christian beliefs of other people in the "death chamber," as well as the conclusion—"there are/ laws on this earth and we live by them"—make this poem a philosophical disquisition.

Another forceful contrast is the relationship between death, with her father, and life, with her husband (the latter also associated with procreation). The paradox of juxtaposed life and death appears succinctly in the image of the fruit, which is crushed "sweetly," where tears are like juice and sugar, and where they come out to be tasted only as "the skin thins and breaks and rips." In some ways, this "contrarieties of life" paradox is similar to the paradox in John Keats's "Ode on Melancholy," where "in the very temple of Delight/ Veil'd Melancholy has her sovran shrine."

In another contrasting juxtaposition, Olds shares a physical intimacy with both dead father and living husband. She "held hard" to her father's foot, "felt the dryness of his lips under/ [her] lips," and "felt his hair rush through [her] fingers." She imagines herself at the crematorium, touching "his ashes in their warmth" and bringing her "finger to [her] tongue." This intimacy with the dead father provides continuity and contrast with the image of her "husband's body on [her]/ crushing [her] sweetly." Ironically, the live husband does not demonstrate any more life than the dead father: In this poem, he is just a sweet, crushing weight. However, these two bodies are not the focus of the poem; as springboards for the poet's ruminations, they serve their purpose silently.

All these paradoxes enhance the sense of mystery about death and its meaning, which in turn illustrates the paradox of life itself: It is a sweet fruit and a fragile container that, at some moment, will inevitably burst into death ("tears" and "sugar"). The extensive use of paradox appropriately conveys the wide, even irreconcilable, range of the feelings expressed in the poem.

Themes and Meanings

The many faces of Olds's relationship to her father are represented in over fifty poems in *The Father* and in many other poems by Olds published before and after. One of her fortes is poetry about relationships—she has written numerous poems about, for instance, her son, her daughter, her husband, and her elder sister. Curiously, although Olds's mother is occasionally mentioned in her poetry, her father seems to be, by far, her most animating subject. This must be due, in part, to Olds's implied model of conception, in which personhood originates in a single sperm (with the father) while the mother presumably serves as a sort of incubator. Thus, Olds the author/poet is authored by her father, making her connection to him uniquely significant.

Putting dozens of poems in a nutshell, Olds appears to be entranced with the idea of "the father" but rather disappointed with the actual model allotted her. The moments of tenderness between them primarily take place without mutual conscious intention—as in the many poems in which Olds treats her dying and unconscious father with tenderness. He is matter, revered for having cast her into the world, connected by the mystery of biology, and valued as such despite failing by the usual measures of fatherhood: According to other poems, for instance, he was an alcoholic, thrown out of the house by Olds's mother to a chorus of cheers from the children. Olds's treatment of her father as more matter than person achieves succinct expression in "The Dead Body," where she refers to him as "this man who had so little consciousness, who was/ 90% his body."

In "The Feelings," the idealized concept of "the father" supersedes the actual relationship to the dead man in the room. That he has stopped breathing seems to make it easier for Olds to treat him as more of a concept than a person of mostly unpleasant traits. Furthermore, the father's absence of personhood as defined by an interesting set of conscious characteristics—"personality"—makes him interesting in only two ways: as a piece of matter and as Olds's father. In that sense, Olds is similar to Gerard Manley Hopkins's character Margaret ("Spring and Fall"), who, while lamenting "goldengrove unleaving" (the leaves falling in autumn), is unconsciously lamenting her own mortality. Olds does not describe a person worth caring for because of positive attributes; therefore, her father is worth caring about only in the way that any death is significant or in the sense that this death strikes home as a reminder of Olds's own mortality—the death of her "author" foreshadows her own death.

The poem ends on a note of heroic stoicism. The author has stared death in the face—her father's and, vicariously, her own—has admitted the laws of this earth, and continues on. At first, "The Feelings" seems to be about a unique and intimate relationship between Olds and her father. Their closeness contrasts with the alien presence of the hospital personnel. Since Olds's father lacks a necessary personhood to qualify as "other," however, this poem takes on a more solipsistic note. In the end, it is Olds alone who faces the bittersweet world. Her only intimate connection to the rest of humanity is that everyone lives under the same law of mortality.

Scott Moncrieff

FLESH AND BLOOD

Author: C. K. Williams (1936-
Type of work: Book of poems
First published: 1987

The Poems

One hundred thirty poems make up *Flesh and Blood*, C. K. Williams's fifth book of poetry and winner of the National Book Critics Circle Award. There are three parts to the book; it would not be far from the mark to say that the first ninety-six poems represent chaos, the next thirty-three order, and the final long poem harmony. The long first part contains individually titled stanzas, and except for a few pairs (back-to-back "Alzheimer," "Snow," and "Drought" poems), little at first suggests an arranged sequence. Instead, the themes are disparate and the poems stand alone.

The thirty-three poems of part 2 are also titled stanzas, but thematic keys are given as well. The first half of each title gives one of five themes: "Reading," "Suicide," "Love," "Good Mother," and "Vehicle." The second part of the title, following a colon, renders the poem more specific, as in "Reading: The Gym" or "Suicide: Anne." Of the five thematic groupings, there are six poems in the first, three in the second, ten in the third, and seven each in the fourth and fifth. With these themes in mind, the reader can identify poems in part 1 that correspond to themes in part 2. "Girl Meets Boy" and "Experience" are "Love" poems, while "Easter" extends the Good Mother theme to include a father. The "Vehicle" poems are speculative, and many poems in part 1 are also of this type. In "Herakles" and "Cowboys," for example, Williams speculates on the nature of heroism in myth and movie. In part 2 "Suicide: Anne" explores the psychological ground of poet Anne Sexton.

Part 3 is a single poem of 144 lines, "La Petit Salvié" (the small redemption). It is an elegy to scholar and poet Paul Zweig, Williams's friend who lived in France as a semi-exile, dead at age forty-eight. These final stanzas, less than a seventh of the book, rise to a high pitch both as a speculative instrument and as a "flesh and blood" record. (*Flesh and Blood* is dedicated to another Paul—Paul B. Williams, the poet's father.)

One of the two most notable formal aspects of the poems is the fact that each poem in the book is eight lines long. *Flesh and Blood* therefore consists of 147 stanzas that appear very similar to one another and are usually presented 2 to a page. The other is Williams's use of a very long poetic line—so long that it virtually always wraps around onto the next line on the page. Without a flexible line of great length, 147 eight-line stanzas could easily induce ennui, sinking the project. Williams, whose lines vary from 18 to 30 syllables and whose stanzas vary from 174 to 215 syllables (as an analysis of 15 stanzas shows), uses diverse kinds of language, varied themes, and a plethora of tones and moods to strike the emotional and intellectual quality of his verse. A typical stanza from *Flesh and Blood* (190 syllables) is one-third longer that a typical sonnet, and the extra room often gives the stanza-poems a wider and deeper reach.

The materials for the poems come via the poet's eye as an observer of the human species. The best poems are the nonspeculative ones that show humans in situations with well-defined character motivation in postmodern settings. Linda Gregerson, writing in *Poetry*, sees the poems as "an impassioned essay on the moral life of urban humanity." This characterization certainly holds true regarding the Good Mother series in part 2. Williams is able to show, with use of fine detail, the treatment children receive from unwitting parents. "Good Mother: The Plane" is an example; a mother is waiting for a flight, hours late, with a child in tow, and she "finally loses patience."

Forms and Devices

Just before Williams' first book (*Lies*, 1969) came out, Anne Sexton was asked to write something for the cover. Her words on the inside front flap describe the writer as "a demon" and a "master of metaphor." One of Williams's masterful metaphors is in "Suicide: Anne," in which he uses the phrase "a badly started nail" to stand for Sexton's emotionally aberrant life. This ingenious metaphor contains two braided truths as well as an impersonal exactness. An unstraight nail is incorrigible, an obdurate life unyielding. In "Regret," the metaphor "in its cold coils" works at a similar level.

A metaphor sometimes waits awhile before it is completed in *Flesh and Blood*. The first poem, "Elms," for example, becomes a metaphor for the last. The trees of the avenue are chain-sawed down until "naked facing buildings stare." One at a time "the winds of time" destroy all living things. Zweig's death, like the loss of the elms, exposes Williams to his unprotected thoughts. In stanza 15 of "La Petit Salvié," he writes about "Clearing clumps of shrubs" from Zweig's small, crumbling estate in the Dordogne at a time when Zweig is weak with fever. He tells of "sawing down a storm-split plum" and of "malevolently armoured maguey:/ their roots are as frail as flesh," "The winds of time" become in stanza 2 "a perfect breeze" that washes across Zweig's bed.

In "Sixteen: Tuscany" Williams likens young men drawn to his teenage daughter to bees. There are, among others, "two vacationing Sicilian bees." The last line, "The air is filled with promises of pollen," translates as possible romance, sexuality, and fecundity. Williams often prefaces a metaphor with the two-word device "the way . . . ," as in "Hooks." Here bus riders look at a pretty girl's artificial hand "[t]he way someone would glance at [an] unruly, apparently ferocious but really quite friendly dog."

Flesh and Blood is the third of Williams's books to use the long line, which has developed a characteristic quality and has become his trademark. With his third book conversational and his fourth book narrational, his long line came to display a language that challenges the traditional view that poetry is concise, tight-knit, and economical. Particularly interesting is the use Williams makes of polysyllabic abstract words and long adjectival clusters. The result is a prosody heavy with unstressed syllables, capable of cadence and incantation, not far from natural speech (although natural speakers never show such lexical wealth), charged semantically to a degree usually found only in compressed verse forms.

In "Guatemala: 1964" phrases such as "implacable, picturesque aloofness" and "disconcertingly beyond suspicion" conjure more than they define. Williams seems to enjoy sewing strings of conjecture into sentence fabrics. In "Herakles" he wonders if the hero's "feats and deeds be not exemplary but cautionary." A prose writer might find the assonance unsuitable, whereas a traditional lyricist might complain of prosy, abstract diction. Williams is plainly exploring the limits and challenging norms.

"First Desires" contains such turns of phrase as "ardent arpeggios" and "chromatic dissonance." An indigent person who traces texts in a public library, in "The Critic," has "blood-rimmed eyes as rapt as David's doing psalms." The words "inconceivable capitulation," in "Repression," beg more questions than they pin down. "Reading: The Cop" describes an armed guard's weapon as "a large-caliber, dull-black stockless machine gun," and "Souls" says that carnival teddy bears are "unrelentingly filthy, matted with the sticky, sickly, ghastly, dark gray sheen/ you see on bums."

Besides adjectival phrases and abstract diction, the poems include foreign words and phrases (usually French), European place names, musical terms (as in "Junior High School Concert: Salle Rosini"), and mythological names. The effect is that Williams takes his poetry in directions that seem to defy such traditional descriptions as narrative and lyric. Gregerson probably misses as many descriptive terms as she includes in her list of Williams's genres: "didactic fables, documentaries, confessions, indictments, portraits, billet doux." The poems' speculation, satire, sketches, and situations contain a broad spectrum of humanity: lover, child, parent, cleric, professional, laborer, aged person, invalid, criminal, politician, cultural leader, artist, and hero.

Themes and Meanings

Williams is notable for his psychological insights and character studies as well as for his strong, expressive manner. Bruce Bauer, writing about *Tar* (1983) in *Poetry*, noted that "one has the feeling, unusual when reading today's poets, that [Williams] is truly interested in the lives around him." If anything, his interest in humanity is more pronounced in *Flesh and Blood*.

Williams adopts five different stances in the poems: He observes others; he participates in events; he seeks to explicate psychological states; given a situation, he imagines a scenario; and, least frequently, he is a watcher of nature.

Williams acts something like a sociological psychologist in many of his poems, presenting vignettes charged with human energy. He explains in "American Native" why the Henry Wadsworth Longfellow poetry his father once read to him will no longer serve: "A teacher attempted to make us understand that our vision of exotics and minorities was so contaminated/ that we not only had corrupted ideas of history but didn't know what went on under our noses." Williams's poems represent his personal struggle to find out. In "Crime" a robber is shot by police, and neighborhood children rush in to grab the dropped change; in "Pregnant" an unwed teen pushes the fetus in with her hands; in "Men" a garbage man viciously mocks a fellow worker who is in pain.

The meaning of Williams's work is seldom in question. None of the difficulty that supposedly makes poems avant-garde is here, yet he never talks down. His art is concerned with revealed clarity. As an observer he is keen of eye and discerning of detail, discriminatingly weighing without seeming to do so. In "Love: Loss" he portrays an exact motivation in terms of the Orpheus-Eurydice tale. The "pretty post-teen princess gone to the grim gutter" approaches "the half-respectful wino" in pretense of wanting a smoke, but when "their solitudes emerge" her heart fails, and she turns, leaves, and "picks herself back to the silver path . . . to the boiling whispers."

Sometimes Williams as participant compares himself to mythological figures, as in "Medusa." While in a Rotterdam "hookers' bar" at the age of twenty, he watches a prostitute flaunt her wares, beg him, and, when he refuses, maul herself "My virginity,/ that dread I fought so hard to lose," he says, "stone by stone was rising back inside me." In "Peace," another poem in which Williams is a participant, the opposite effect occurs. His wife and he go to bed, angry. Their bodies during the long, cold night are back to back, not touching. Then "toward dawn, . . . though justice won't I know be served, I pull her to me."

Some poems are about the aged. "Love: The Dance" describes a septuagenarian couple performing "old-time ballroom swirls, deft romantic dips." The poet sees them in archetypal terms, dancing "the waltz of life, the waltz of death," and concludes, "and still the heart-work left undone." It is children, parents, and lovers, however, that dominate the poems. For example, "Good Mother: The Street" shows the theme of a mother's commitment and a child's helplessness in terms both gentle and horrible. "Vehicle: Absence" and "Vehicle: Violence" use Williams's "the way . . . " device discussed earlier to compare carnal love with the loss of a loved one and violence with the "anger, pride, the primal passion to prevail" of boxers.

In "Bishop Tutu's Visit to the White House: 1984" Williams imagines something he cannot see. Because of the bishop's humanity and the president's indifference, he presumes that the man of God "will be wounded . . . humiliated . . . mortified." Another cultural exchange poem, "USOCA" (United States out of Central America), sounds a similar key. "Andean musicians . . . embarrassed" by so few rally attendees, show "smiles . . . like precious doves of hope" when their music meets with mild applause.

"The Mistress," "The Lover," and "Twins" are about adultery. In the first, the public telephone upon which a man depends for a liaison has "been savaged"—the receiver "wires thrust back up the coin slot." Desire and disappointment leave him "breathing like a bloody beast." In the second, a wife is surprised to learn that her affair with her husband's employee is common knowledge. While in a lady's room stall she overhears the two men called "the blind pig" and "that sanctimonious, lying bastard," and herself called "the horny bitch." In "Twins," unknown to everyone, a woman is carrying two fetuses. When the second is born she lets it die, believing that one is the husband's, the other her lover's. This poem and "Normality" appear in quotation marks, as though they are in the words of speakers other than the poet.

The strongest poem in *Flesh and Blood* is the final poem, "La Petit Salvié." This poem should be read in whole stanzas so that the speculative argument that Williams presents regarding time and mortality can be apprised. Parts of stanza 14 show the bonding of artist to artist. Williams and Zweig read poems to each other, "out behind the house in canvas chairs . . . in your apartment, a park in Paris—anywhere: sidewalk, restaurant, museum." Envy ("you are unimaginably insecure") and creative commerce ensue. Most important, kinship develops between them, with "envy sublimated into warmth and brothership." Stanza 10, referring to Zweig after his death, ends in italics, quotes, and monosyllables: " '*and I have a ghost I love and who loves me.*' "

John Young

THE FLYING CHANGE

Author: Henry Taylor (1942-
Type of poem: Lyric
First published: 1974; collected in *The Flying Change*, 1985

The Poem

"The Flying Change" is a short poem; in its two distinct parts the speaker establishes a metaphor comparing a maneuver that is taught to a cantering horse to a stance
the speaker has adopted for his own life. The poem's two parts are numbered, as if to
underscore their distinctive characters, and they look quite different on the page and
exhibit very different voices.

Part 1 is a prose poem, set out on the page like a standard paragraph. It sounds rather
like a textbook on horsemanship in its explanation of the flying change maneuver. It
describes the nature of a horse's canter, a gait in which the animal's "leading foreleg
is the last to touch the ground before the moment of suspension" as the horse moves
forward. The horse can canter by leading with either the right or left foreleg, but as it
rounds a curve, it usually leads with the inside foreleg. If the horse must change leads
to put the inside foreleg first (the "flying change), it can do so easily when it is running
free. If the horse is being ridden, however, the rider's added weight makes the shift
more difficult, and the rider must teach the horse to compensate in order to carry out
the change. Part 1 of the poem explains these matters in a matter-of-fact, third-person
voice and without editorial comment except for the last sentence: "The aim of
teaching a horse to move beneath you is to remind him how he moved when he was
free."

In part 2 Taylor changes form and voice to create a short (three five-line stanzas)
series of statements in which a first-person speaker indirectly compares himself to the
horse that must learn to do what once it did naturally. The images of this part recall
the diagonal motion of the flying change made by the horse; they also suggest the idea
of suspended motion (the moment of the change) and the idea of the tensions between
one's innate abilities and what one learns to do. Thus the first image is of a leaf turned
"sideways in the wind," which somehow moves the speaker "like a whipcrack" into
a past where, rather like a horse in training, he once studied moves on a "barbered
stretch of ground." Later, he says, he taught himself to move away from those past
skills, skills which he still possesses but "must outlive," as if they are no longer useful
to him. The act of cupping water in his hands reminds him of how age must affect him,
making his hands "a sieve" instead of a cup. Time can never stand still, but—like the
horse shifting its leading hoof and thus suspended for a moment in air—the speaker
briefly feels "sustained in time."

Forms and Devices

The division of this short poem into two parts strongly suggests its two voices, the
"textbook" voice which explains the riding maneuver and the personal voice of one

who finds himself also making a "flying change" and cherishing the brief moment of suspension above the earth. In the second part, Taylor uses five-line stanzas in iambic pentameter for the development of his speaker's understanding of how the flying change applies to him. In each stanza, the first and fourth lines demonstrate slant rhyme, as do the second and fifth. The slant rhyme mutes the poem's rhyme to such a degree that the reader may not notice the rhyme at first reading, but the *nd* sound of "wind" in the first line of part 2 echoes the *nd* of "ground" at the end of the fourth line, while "day" and "away" in lines 2 and 5 create true rhyme. Similar effects apply to the rhyme in the other stanzas.

The poem's lines are also heavily enjambed so that their sense runs on from one line to the next. That effect is particularly noticeable between the three stanzas of part 2. In each case, Taylor withholds an important element of a sentence's grammar until the first line of the following stanza. The effect is to make the reader see two layers of meaning in the lines. At the end of the first stanza, the speaker suggests that he taught himself to "drift away"; only in the first line of the following stanza does the reader understand that he drifted away not from the world in general but from something specific—skills which he still has.

The poem's central metaphor lies in the description of the flying change itself, and in part 1 Taylor concentrates specifically two elements of that change. One is the moment of suspension as the horse shifts its lead foot; the other is the commentary included in the last sentence of that part. The whole point of teaching a horse to carry a rider is to teach it to maintain some of its natural movement under the "unnatural" burden of its rider, "to remind him how he moved when he was free." In the second part, that metaphor is expanded to apply to the speaker, who also finds himself executing a flying change.

The poem's form can now be seen to echo its content in that the second part, with its careful stanza organization, its rhyme and iambic pentameter, seems to suggest the schooling of both horses and humans to make artful things seem natural, things such as running while carrying a rider or writing a line of iambics. Indeed, the suspension of a line to balance its meaning between two stanzas seems to suggest the horse's task of balancing the rider while shifting its weight in the canter.

In the thirteenth line of part 2, Taylor refers to "works and days," an allusion to the Greek poet Hesiod (eighth century B.C.), who wrote a poem called "Works and Days" about the proper conduct of agricultural life—another instance of Taylor's submerging elements of art in a poem which is partly about art and nature. In fact, much of the *Flying Change* collection deals with agricultural life.

Themes and Meanings

"The art which conceals art" is a phrase that has often been used to indicate the artist's task. Ideally, a poet (or any other artist) wants the created work to seem natural and inevitable rather than artificial and labored. On one level, that is the concern of "The Flying Change." The horse's art is its running, and, as the impersonal voice of part 1 points out, when it successfully carries a rider, it moves as if it were unburdened.

(It is notable that in the course of concealing his art, Taylor has created the bookish tone of that discussion, just as he created the three metered stanzas which follow it.) Like the horse that must appear free while performing a task, so the poet's task is to manage carefully ordered steps without appearing to carry a burden. The speaker of part 2 suggests that this feat is possible and that it may even allow the artist moments when he seems completely free of earth-bound concerns, however illusory that freedom, like the horse's freedom, may be.

On another level, the poem seems to address the more general tension between the speaker's desire for freedom and the constraints of time and age and obligation. Like the horse, the speaker has taught himself to cease the practice of skills he still has, skills he says he must outlive, as if age has brought him to the necessity of moving beyond the skills of his earlier years. This is a recognition that many people come to—that growth (which suggests maturity and adulthood) may require one to abandon some of the colt's pleasures in freedom. Yet the poem suggests that, like a well-schooled horse, one can somehow retain the memory of what free movement was like.

Because it is time which brings one to these contradictions, time is a significant issue in the second section. The act of cupping water in his hands reminds the speaker that advancing age will make his hands no better than a sieve for holding water in this very natural way. In fact, the whole world seems to be moving in a "mindless plunge" as it races through time. There is no stopping this process—except, the poem suggests, that the art of the flying change, the moment in which time seems to be held in suspension, may allow one to experience for a moment the brilliant sensation being free of the pull of earth and time, an illusion created by the flying change.

Ann D. Garbett

FORMAL ELEGY

Author: John Berryman (1914-1972)
Type of poem: Elegy
First published: 1964, in *Of Poetry and Power: Poems Occasioned by the Presidency and by the Death of John F. Kennedy*; collected in *Collected Poems, 1937-1971*, 1991

The Poem

"Formal Elegy" is written in what one would generally call free verse. It incorporates occasional rhymes but does not follow any strict form. Its ten stanzas range in length from two to twenty lines. The title suggests a closure to the confusion surrounding President John F. Kennedy's assassination; yet, characteristic of John Berryman's work, the poem indicates an inability to settle upon any conclusion. Written primarily in the first person, the poem occasionally lapses into third person and first person plural. It consists of scattered images of Kennedy; accused assassin Lee Harvey Oswald and his murderer, Jack Ruby; Dallas, Texas; Arlington Cemetery; and the poet himself. Almost all images are offered in relation to television, which the poet considers another player in the tragedy. This poem is a traditional elegy only in that it attempts to encompass all of the poet's thoughts upon the subject. It does not specifically elegize Kennedy but seems to elegize the entire sequence of events related to his presidency and assassination.

In the first stanza, "Formal Elegy" presents the reader with several images that establish the poem's tone and scope: Americans as survivors, the shocked poet, and the killers and the killed. The beginning of the second stanza—"Yes, it looks like a wilderness"—attempts to summarize this confusion, and the third stanza relates the confusion to television, which has presented these scattered images to the public. In the fourth stanza, the speaker likens himself to a car, another machine, which represents the mechanical perceptions people have acquired through television by recalling images of cars as they appeared throughout the televised drama in question. The following two stanzas relate television to people: their paralysis in front of their television sets, their perceptions of Dallas, and their perceptions of Kennedy himself, who now moves and acts only on television. The next three stanzas relate the events to the poet, a one-time Texan and an indirect participant (through television), who takes some of the shame upon himself.

The poems ends with its longest stanza, which, as any good elegy should, points the reader toward the future; yet, this future is less secure. Kennedy's youth is mourned but then dismissed in a half-hearted attempt to face facts. The end suggests that the nation should "continue," that it will, as it always has, though "stunned, survive." Yet due to television's persistence in numbing people to horrors, this ability to survive is no longer admirable but is an "insolence," a symbol that the nation is unable to move (or be moved) either physically, away from its black-and-white screens, or emotionally, toward a more natural grief.

Forms and Devices

Berryman's fragmented style represents the nation's confusion. The poem's images are many and disjointed, their only commonality existing in their having been first seen in televised reports concerning Kennedy. However, the poem's language acquires continuity through these images as it assumes the reader's familiarity with the events surrounding Kennedy's assassination. Thus, the speaker relies upon his audience's knowledge, through television, of these references. Television, therefore, is the subject of the poem; the human actors are merely the objects.

"Nobody goes anywhere," the poem asserts, "lengthened (days) into TV." From now on, but especially in this crisis, Americans are lost to the images reflected on a television screen. "Some in their places are constrained to weep," the speaker tells us, portraying the messages of television as "Black foam. A weaving snake. An invulnerable sleep." Though what has happened is real, what people see is somewhat unreal. Televised images actually become reality as "Images of Mr Kennedy blue the air,/ who is little now, with no chance to grow great."

The poem resembles a montage of Kennedy's television images, and the speaker calls the reader's specific attention to the images themselves: Kennedy's hair "kept not wholly real"; the car in the motorcade, where "Onto him climbed/ a-many and went his way"; Ruby's "mad claim/ he shot to spare the Lady's testifying"; Kennedy's casket, which "I sidled in & past"; "schoolgirls in Dallas"; and "black & white together, stunned." The language of the commentary also refers to images, to what people see rather than (necessarily) to reality: "it looks like a wilderness"; "Fat Dallas, a fit set"; "He seemed good:/ brainy in riot, daring, cool"; "We compose our faces." The speaker comments upon televised images by speaking in their own terms, leaving the reader with the postmodern sense that reality is different for each person rather than a truth known to all. Yet since national television has homogenized these images, they have become the only truth.

The poem's montage, then, creates its own reality, displaying for the reader, as it did for the viewer, a confusing sequence of events, repetitious, nonchronological, and without conclusion. The elegy must, therefore, be disjointed as well. Viewers could not draw a conclusion and neither can the elegy; it must tell the truth as it knows it: without certainty.

Therefore, Berryman's fragmented presentation and his alternately reverent and irreverent tones further emphasize the scattered nature of the poem's images. In this sense, the poem is not really an elegy at all. It offers no conclusion, no satisfaction, and no understanding. It merely reflects on a relatively new American condition—the age of television—while it literally reflects a situation that promises to become a classic example of this condition. Images are key; their meanings and order are not. People learn from their memories. As a culture, Americans remember what they see, and what they see is now fuzzy and unreliable.

Themes and Meanings

"Formal Elegy," as an elegy, attempts to point the reader toward the future following the death of someone important. Traditionally, elegies offer hope; this one offers little. In the final stanza, the speaker echoes what we now recognize as the sentiments of a generation that watched these details unfold on television screens across the nation; yet there is much less reverence here: "Everybody should/ have his sweet boneyards. Yet let the young not go,/ our apprentice King! Alas,/ muffled, he must." There is sorrow for the youth of the president who was "ours." Yet the reference to Kennedy as king recalls the press's image of Camelot, and, in this poem, images created by the press are not necessarily to be trusted. The speaker had claimed earlier that "I would not perhaps have voted for him next time," and so the term "apprentice King" implies that this young president had much to learn and was not (yet) a hero. The tragedy is his youth; all that is known is that he "seemed good."

The next step, the speaker tells Americans, is to "abandon the scene of disorder. Drop/ them shattered bodies into tranquil places,/ where moulder as you will. We compose our faces/ . . . ready again." From the tone of the poem thus far, the reader can understand this as a shameful method of dealing with grief, yet it is the way Americans always survive. The problem now is the emphasis on image, on the effect of a disjointed televised history upon people in need of continuity. People will "abandon" this reality since their memories, constructed by others, are not real. The irreverent tone concerning the burial reflects the speaker's expectations of the American public to "moulder as you will." In understanding history only through the television, American reverence for those once considered "excellent" will steadily decay.

The speaker refers to American people as "black & white," possibly referring also to the medium through which Americans understand themselves: "All black & white together, stunned, survive/ the final insolence to the head of you;/ bow./ Over-whelmed-un, live." People of all races in America will not only "survive" this crisis, but also will survive it "All black & white together," themselves a mass of jumbled images. No longer separate entities, human and individual, they will become one audience to a mass-media show, acting, thinking, and remembering only images. Ultimately, they are not overwhelmed but merely waylaid. The poem's final suggestion then becomes a twist on the traditional elegy's hopeful tone: "The man of a wise face opened it to speak:/ Let us continue." Americans always continue, but, from now on, they will be colder and harder.

Earlier, the speaker expressed his personal wish that future "bullets swim astray/ sent to the President, and that all around/ help, and his heart keep sound." The final images draw sharp contrast between this wish and the nation's probable progress toward recovery. This poem's primary images are of images themselves, and their message asserts that empty images are now standard. In the future, people will "compose [their] faces/ . . . ready again" for more of the same, reacting each time with colder and more composed faces.

Judith Collins

FOUR GOOD THINGS

Author: James McMichael (1939-
Type of poem: Narrative
First published: 1980

The Poem

Four Good Things is a book-length narrative poem by California poet James McMichael. The poem is autobiographical, and McMichael makes no distinctions between himself and the speaker of the poem. The speaker describes, comments upon, and observes his world without being judgmental. By the poem's end, he has reconciled himself to the role of the past in the present.

The poem begins in the late 1940's and covers a period into the late 1960's or early 1970's. While the speaker states his age in the poem once, he eschews traditional chronology for a more loosely constructed sense of time. Each of *Four Good Things*'s sixteen stanzas describes an episode in the speaker's life from childhood through early adulthood. The first ten stanzas depict the speaker's boyhood and college years. He writes about his care provider, Florence, his father's career as a real estate agent in Pasadena, California, his mother's cancer, and ultimately, his father's death. He also describes his father's second marriage to Lucille and his adolescence living with her and her family.

The eleventh stanza begins the second section of the poem, which describes how private lives in the nineteenth century were affected by industrialization. This section is set in rural England in the 1850's and later. Stanza 12 is the turning point in the poem's narrative. Here McMichael connects the American capitalism he knew as a boy with the industrial period in England. His intent in this stanza is to draw together his personal past with the historical events he thinks shaped it.

Stanza 13 presents McMichael and his companion, Linda, on their way to Manchester, England, the heart of the British industrial movement. Once there, he hopes to establish how the world became so commercial and so interested in defining self-worth by possessions. Restless and plagued by his inability to sleep, the speaker meditates on the issues of desire, need, forgiveness, and time. He is apparently distressed that his life is directionless and disturbed over the confusion he feels in wanting to explain everything about the relationship of the past to the present at once.

The third section of the poem, stanza 15, has McMichael encountering a mentally disturbed young man named Antony. Antony is institutionalized and cared for by his mother, who visits him and takes him out for drives. The speaker contemplates how he and Antony live lives that are quite different although they are parallel in time. Once he and Linda part from Antony, they drive into Manchester, where McMichael encounters the people of that city. He observes their possessions and their living habits and is again intrigued and disturbed by the people living lives parallel to his. He comments on how materialism has replaced thinking and interaction among families: "They steady us, these things we've made."

Back at home in California in the last stanza of the poem, McMichael considers how he has and has not changed because of his experiences. He recalls how easily he has fit back into his American life, and he tries to draw parallels between the lives of the English and his own life. The poem ends with Linda telling him a story about a ski trip she took in Europe, where she saw farmers working in the winter. The point of the story would seem to be that "life goes on" and people do what they must to survive. Those tactics are different for everyone.

Forms and Devices

Four Good Things is a free-verse poem of sixty-nine pages. While its meter alludes at times to blank verse, blank verse is employed inconsistently. Sections are not numbered, but the sixteen stanzas are separated by white space. Reviewers in the early 1980's found McMichael's use of language appropriately "inelegant" for a poem about commerce and materialism. There are "unpoetical" phrasings, some vulgarity, and some obscenities. The poem's phrasing is similar to prose, leading critic Robert van Hallberg to praise McMichael for "reclaim[ing] for poetry some of the prerogatives ceded to prose, fictional and expository" writing.

The predominant imagery in the poetry involves mapping. Secondary images are created by references to home building and driving. The poem is set in neighborhoods in Pasadena and Manchester, which are deliberately depicted as being not too different. Mapping is the metaphor that unifies the poem, and *Four Good Things* is itself a map of its speaker's experiences. Mental maps created by memory, futuristic mappings of the past in the present, street maps of Pasadena, and road maps around Manchester are all described in the poem.

The first five lines of the opening stanza depict how Florence walked to the bus stop to get a ride to the grocery store and how she walked by the houses, not the addresses, of the neighbors. McMichael's father is also connected to maps. He designed a subdivision, the Pasadena Tracts, which failed to attract buyers; he "would be somewhere within his maps at any time," says the speaker. The use of "within" indicates that his father used his maps to dream or to plan his future. In the fifth stanza, a teacher walking along an English river with her students instructs them to map the plants growing there. In the sixth stanza, the speaker takes a mental walk through old neighborhoods that are now abandoned.

The seventh stanza switches tone to describe Pasadena in the way that a group of real estate agents viewing a new development site would view it. The changes in the rugged landscape, forged over time, are quickly altered when schools, hotels, and shops replace trees, open spaces, and water sources diverted for subdivisions. With the eye of a documentary filmmaker, the speaker comments, "The balance of trade was not in Pasadena's favor." To see how this has transpired, he looks into the city's suburban past and finds that "[t]he wealth of the invisible elite went into their homes." He particularly addresses the role of the Greene brothers, whose bungalows made Pasadena famous. Charles Sumner Greene and Henry Mather Greene were the premiere architects of the California Arts and Crafts movement of the late nineteenth and early twentieth centuries. Their integration of homes into the local landscape and use of local building materials are mentioned by the speaker with appreciation. He particularly likes their houses because their mapping was evident: "Everything showed you how it went together." Many such houses were razed for the very kind of anonymous development his father was promoting.

The sereneness of urban Pasadena is troublesome to the speaker. He sees the people comfortable in their houses, trading up to buy something more prestigious, and he wonders: "What did people do all day?" As a boy, he collected stamps that, when glued into his albums, provided a map of the world for his youthful imagination. As he surveys the people around him, he finds that their preoccupations are like his but different. He maps his worry about his mother's death from cancer in the hopes of coming to terms with his instinctual impulse to worry about why he does not understand the world better. The topical, regional allusions combined with information about his father's death and stepmother's dispersal of the estate, are somewhat like push-pins stuck into an urban planner's map of suburbia.

When the tenth stanza moves the poem to England in the 1850's, mapping is used to discuss how the enclosure acts changed the landscape of agricultural Britain. Enclosure, which was initiated during the reign of King Henry VII in 1489, allowed landlords to fence and redistribute farmland. It also allowed the landlords to force their tenants to farm the land according to its owners' needs. In the eighteenth century, enclosures reduced the amount of available land for tenants to farm, and when new property boundaries were drawn many people lost their homes. Abandoned farms and towns and increased poverty were caused by rapacious enclosure. A second major wave of enclosing occurred in the nineteenth century, and the consequences were as devastating to the poor as they had been a hundred years earlier. The poet is particularly interested in how the displaced poor became the factory workers in industrial cities such as Manchester. Enclosure remapped Britain and paved the way for the need for factories in the later years of the British Empire. McMichael's descriptions of enclosures are historically accurate, and his depiction of the factories' squalor is consonant with the socialist studies done by Friedrich Engels for his book *The Conditions of the Working Class in England* (1859).

From the old maps, the poet takes the reader back to California, to the Pasadena area suburbs where the landscapers' trees provide the boundaries between one house and another. Roads built by developer Henry Huntington are linked to the highways that remapped Southern California and brought in new people to buy new homes. Relentless urban sprawl eliminated the Greene and Greene houses in large numbers, and the populations of the neighborhoods the speaker knew as a child changed terrifically.

The trip to Manchester calls for both real road maps and symbolic maps. The jet-lag-induced insomnia of stanza 13 causes McMichael to move about in his memory to try to understand why he is the way he is. He speaks of his desire to know himself better in terms of driving to get somewhere. His difficulty in such an endeavor is that he has no map and no one to direct him on his journey but his own flawed self.

Stanza 16 begins with McMichael describing himself as a tenant with a lawn he has the ability to let go to waste (a term used in enclosure documents to describe uncultivated land). He parallels himself at this point in his life with the tenants who worked for their lives in England in the past. He drives through neighborhoods he has known to construct a map connecting his past to the present. Then he remembers how he and Linda had driven around England with a map as tourists; they had the freedom to see only what they wanted to see. When he drives in Pasadena, he is mainly confronted with things he does not want to see. Shifting between past and present, between what he wants and what is inevitable, he maps out a sense of closure. He decides that he is putting too much pressure on himself to try to account for his own history in the history of the world. In the end, he seems to be on the verge of balancing the functions of history, personal responsibility, chance, and change within his life. He has mapped his world; he knows where he is and seems willing to begin to map a future.

Themes and Meanings

Published in 1980, *Four Good Things* raised questions about American life that had not been routinely considered in poetry. The poem reveals the emptiness of a life based on goods, services, and the acquisition of possessions. McMichael offers a vision in this poem of the historical conditions that produced himself, the modern person living in suburban Southern California.

Through the use of images of mapping, driving, and building homes, roads, and bridges, McMichael shows how the past determines the present. His argument in the poem is that industrialization, with its emphasis on acquisition and its definition of power as military or commercial might, forever changed the landscape of Britain and America. The purpose of the poem is to depict someone who has stopped taking a life of materialism for granted and has paused to ask himself if the things he has are really "good."

Four Good Things is a personal narrative in which the poet-speaker speculates on the type of life he is living and what the quality of such an existence is. It is not primarily a philosophical interpretation that he develops, but a practical one that will allow him to get on with his life. At the end of the poem, he understands how the past is carried into the present and how everyone's lives are, to a certain degree, determined by circumstances. He accepts these things as part of himself; he neither despises himself for who he is nor blames the world for being what it is.

While some evidence of an epic structure is evident in the poem, it is wrong to think of *Four Good Things* as an epic poem. The speaker does go on a quest for self-realization, descending metaphorically into the underworld of insomnia and meeting a man who, like the blind prophet Tiresias, seems to know more about the world than his physical circumstances would allow. However, *Four Good Things* lacks adventure, epic language and devices, and other perspectives within the poem to extend its range beyond the viewpoint of the speaker. That the speaker has thought of the epic similarities is suggested by his saying he has read *Madame Bovary* (1857),

Gustav Flaubert's great novel of a woman's quest for knowledge of herself and *Roughing It* (1872), Mark Twain's travel narrative that takes him to Nevada and California in the nineteenth century.

Beverly Schneller